INTERNATIONAL HANDBOOK ON INTERNAL MIGRATION

INTERNATIONAL HANDBOOK ON INTERNAL MIGRATION

EDITED BY

Charles B. Nam, William J. Serow, and David F. Sly

GREENWOOD PRESS
New York • Westport, Connecticut • London

Library of Congress Cataloging-in-Publication Data

International handbook on internal migration / edited by Charles B.
Nam, William J. Serow, and David F. Sly.

    p. cm.

  Bibliography: p.

  Includes index.

  ISBN: 0–313–25858–9 (lib. bdg. : alk. paper)

    1. Migration, Internal. I. Nam, Charles B. II. Serow, William
J. III. Sly, David F.

  HB1952.I55 1990

  304.8—dc20   89–7487

British Library Cataloguing in Publication Data is available.

Library of Congress Catalog Card Number: 89–7487
ISBN: 0–313–25858–9

First published in 1990

Greenwood Press, Inc.
88 Post Road West, Westport, Connecticut 06881

Printed in the United States of America

The paper used in this book complies with the
Permanent Paper Standard issued by the National
Information Standards Organization (Z39.48–1984).

10 9 8 7 6 5 4 3 2 1

CONTENTS

FIGURES

viii   FIGURES

TABLES

INTERNATIONAL
HANDBOOK ON
INTERNAL
MIGRATION

INTRODUCTION

Demographers have acknowledged the importance of internal migration as a component of localized population change and as the major component influencing population redistribution within countries for some time. However, the profession's preoccupation with growth at the nation-state level and its obvious impact on development relegated the study of migration to a relatively less significant role than the study of fertility and mortality (Bogue, 1969; Kirk, 1960). While there can be no doubt that the problems of population growth and fluctuating levels of fertility were and still are significant enough to command a great deal of attention, there can also be no doubt that during the 1970s and 1980s we have increasingly come to realize that if we are to develop a more complete understanding of the reciprocal relationships between population and social and economic change, an understanding of migration and its causes and consequences is no less significant, and perhaps even more complex.

A number of factors and events—some specifically centered around less developed country issues, some more developed country issues, and some both—helped to make more manifest the place and role of migration. Among these was the position adopted by many governments at the first World Population Conference that clearly stated that they regarded population distribution issues and problems as no less and in many instances more important for their national development than growth issues per se. Similarly, during the 1970s there was a new consciousness of the growth of large cities around the world and of the problems and challenges that these places posed for development on the one hand and the quality of life on the other.

Also during the 1970s there were several reversals of long-established migration trends in some countries and the debunking of myths about trends in others. The 1970 round of population censuses saw an unprecedented number of countries include questions on migration, more detailed tabulations from these, and the creation of micro-data files. These innovations facilitated more detailed analyses than had been possible in the past, and we began to realize clearly that, despite the growth being experienced by many large cities in less developed countries and the many migrants taking up residence in these, in most less developed countries the volume of rural-to-rural migration exceeded the volume of rural-to-urban migration. In others, new evidence suggested that patterns of circulation were perhaps more important for the number of people in cities than was the simpler process of rural-to-urban permanent migration.

In many more developed countries the large cities of large urban agglomerations showed signs of attracting new migrants and retaining current residents, reversing long-standing tendencies of avoiding city residence and moving from cities. Along with this was a totally unexpected paradox: In many countries the nonmetropolitan population that had been declining in relative terms for decades as the metropolitan population grew also had a new attractiveness for migrants, and in some countries the number of migrants from metropolitan to non-metropolitan areas actually exceeded the number from nonmetropolitan to metro-politan areas. Similarly, there were unprecedented numbers of elderly migrants emerging in many countries where larger cohorts of persons were entering the older ages better off socially and economically than were the smaller cohorts of the past.

Events and phenomena such as those listed above challenged many earlier assumptions and previous explanations and sparked a new interest in migration theory and approaches to the study of migration. Whereas only a few years ago migration analysis was largely of interest to demographers and sociologists, efforts to explain these types of new discoveries attracted economists, geog-raphers, urban planners, and psychologists. Micro-, macro-, and household theo-ries of migration are now available to help explain a large number of different types of migration.

The development of interest in migration in terms of both its causes and consequences at the individual, household, and aggregate levels since the mid-1970s has spawned a number of valuable publications. Some of these review data and measurement problems (Goldstein and Sly, 1975a, 1975b; Willekens and Rogers, 1978). Others focus on methodological and theoretical issues (Bilsborrow et al., 1984; De Jong and Gardner, 1981). Still others focus on specific types of migration or the role of migration in relation to some specific issue or area of the world (Costello et al., 1987; Fawcett et al., 1984; Pryor, 1979; Stinner et al., 1982; United Nations, 1981, 1984; Zachariah and Conde, 1981).

While all of these types of works are extremely useful, none of them provides a broad review of the state of migration knowledge and research in particular countries. They do not, for example, review the specific types of data available within countries on a country-by-country basis. Similarly, none of them provides a general review of specific migration trends and patterns in a large number of countries across regions of the world, just as none of them examines the specific causes and consequences of various types of mobility on a country-by-country basis.

The present volume represents an effort to fill this void. In short, it contains twenty-one migration country case studies. Each of the individual case studies is an original piece authored specifically for this volume by an expert in the field. In the vast majority of instances authors are also residents of the country. Where they are not, they are internationally recognized experts on migration research in the country they are writing about. Although the major objective of the volume has been to make available comprehensive overviews of migration emphasizing the particular aspects unique to a large number of individual countries, the editors also felt that a vital service could be performed if the individual country case studies were organized in such a way that the reader wishing to compare one country with another or one group of countries with another could do so.

With this in mind a common outline was developed, and each author was asked to adhere as closely as possible to it. This request was made with the full realization that data availability would limit and in some cases even preclude addressing all issues in some countries. Likewise, space limitations prohibited many authors from fully exploiting the data available for their country. Similarly, authors were not instructed to give emphasis to any particular section of the outline, but rather to attempt to reflect as best possible the past and current trends in migration and the current research emphasis on the causes and consequences of migration as reflected in the topics included. The outline that was provided to the authors is reproduced below.

1. Data on Migration

   A. Definitions of Migration
      (1). The spatial dimension: what units of political geography define migration
      (2). The temporal dimension: what is the time period over which migration is measured

   B. Sources of Data
      (1). Census
      (2). Population registers
      (3). Regular surveys
      (4). Special surveys

   C. Quality of Data

2. Principal Population Movements

   A. The National Level
      (1). The volume of movement over time
      (2). The age and sex structure of movement over time

   B. Interregional Migration
      (1). The volume of movement over time
      (2). The age and sex structure of movement over time

   C. Migration in the Metropolitan-Nonmetropolitan or Urban-Rural Context
      (1). Migration between metro/urban areas
      (2). Migration between metro/urban and nonmetro/rural areas
      (3). Migration between nonmetro/rural areas

3. Who Moves
   A. Characteristics of Movers
      (1). Interregional
           —demographic
           —socioeconomic
           —other
      (2). Metro/nonmetro or Urban/rural
           —demographic
           —socioeconomic
           —other
      (3). Repeat, return, and chronic movers

4. Consequences of Migration: The Aggregate Level
   A. Demographic: Population Redistribution
      (1). Age
      (2). Sex
      (3). Race/ethnicity
   B. Social
      (1). Centralization
      (2). Concentration
      (3). Segregation
      (4). Journey to work
      (5). Communications
   C. Environmental
      (1). Physical
      (2). Social
   D. Economic
      (1). Labor market differentials
           —employment levels and rates
           —structure of employment opportunities
           —wage and income differentials
      (2). Specialization and trade
   E. Political

5. Why People Move
   A. Economic Reasons
      (1). Employment and educational opportunities
      (2). Wages and income
   B. Social and Environmental Reasons
      (1). Family
      (2). Retirement
      (3). Involuntary moves

6. Consequences of Migration: The Individual Level

   The remainder of this chapter presents a brief review of the outline's major
sections. Although these reviews are based on the individual country chapters

that follow, we have not attempted to develop a comprehensive country-by-country comparison. Alternatively, the review that follows tends to emphasize the range of observations that can be made from the country case studies, giving particular attention to the similarities and differences that exist across countries. By doing so we hope to provide the reader with a broad overview that will help the person wanting to read about a particular country appreciate some of its uniqueness as well as similarities with other countries. At the same time we hope to afford the reader who wants to examine countries in greater detail some perspective on the types of comparisons and contrasts that are possible.

DATA ON MIGRATION

In discussing migration, it is important to distinguish analytically between migration (the act of moving) and the migrant (the unit or individual who engages in the act). It is particularly important to bear this distinction in mind when talking about definitions of migration and their formal operationalization in statistical data collection systems. This results from the fact that in the vast majority of countries of the world it is migrants and not migrations that are counted statistically. That is, in most countries of the world migrants are enumerated, and from these data inferences are made about the volume and pattern of migration that exist in that country. The problems resulting from this paradox are more salient in countries that must rely on censuses for their migration data, but the importance of the issue is also influenced by the spatial and temporal parameters employed to define migration.

Three types of questions are included in censuses to gather information on migration. The first of these asks individuals for their place of birth. This information can then be compared with a person's place of residence at the time of the census; all persons not living in their place of birth are classified as migrants and those in their place of birth as nonmigrants. The use of this type of question relies on persons knowing their place of birth, but it is also limited by a number of other considerations. For example, some "places" that may have existed at an earlier period (the time of a person's birth) may not longer exist, or their names or borders may have changed.

In addition to these types of problems, it is important to realize that this type of question represents a limited effort to identify migrants independent of many of the migrations they may have made. For example, it does not provide a true count of the number of migrants in a population because those who moved to another residence and then returned to their place of birth prior to the census are not counted as migrants. Similarly, it does not provide a count of migrations because any migrants who may have made multiple migrations over their lifetime produce only one migration: that from their place of birth to their place of current residence. In short, with this type of data the temporal dimension varies from individual to individual, and the spatial dimension assumes that all persons resided at the place of their birth and made only one move after this.

A second type of question routinely employed in censuses asks persons for their place of previous residence or their place of residence at some earlier date (usually from one to five years prior to the census). Although these types of questions provide information on more current migrants and by inference on more current trends and patterns of migration, in reality they suffer to a lesser degree from the same problems as discussed above. The third type of census question employed to obtain migration data asks for the year that a person moved into his or her current residence. This type of question is particularly useful for identifying migrants over specific time intervals, but unless it is combined with a question on place of last residence it does not yield any information that allows the researcher to identify place-to-place patterns of migration.

These types of questions are also the ones most commonly used in surveys. The advantage of surveys over censuses generally is that surveys can be used to ask questions about reasons for moving and probing can be done to obtain information on the characteristics of migrants (and nonmigrants) prior to their move. Surveys can also be used to improve migration data in a number of different ways, some of which are discussed in individual country case studies. The reality of the situation, however, is that only a few countries make limited use of innovative techniques, and no country uses them for official estimates of migration.

Although many countries rely on information from censuses and surveys to identify migrants and migrations, a number of countries make use of population registers and/or administrative records. The principal advantage of these types of sources is that they can be used directly to obtain information on migrations as well as migrants. In the case of population registers, it is at least theoretically possible to obtain both current information and a record of every move ever made by any individual. These types of sources, however, rely on the individual to report changes in residence. In some instances this may not happen at all, whereas in others it may occur after the lapse of a considerable amount of time.

No matter what data system is used to obtain migration information, all definitions of migration are derived from data demarcating changes of residence. The areal reference of residence varies markedly from one country to the next, and it is not unusual to find an equal amount of variation within countries which have multiple sources of data to draw from. The range here can run from a change of dwelling unit to a change involving crossing the borders of minor civil divisions on up to a change involving crossing the border of some major (state, province, or region) political or socioeconomic area. In this sense it is important to realize that, although within any country heavy reliance is placed on official sources for migration data, many different "official" definitions of a migrant or a migration may exist depending on the legal or administrative issues involved.

Comparisons of migration data within countries must always be made with full knowledge (1) of how legal definitions of residence have changed over time and (2) of the stability of borders used to define residential changes. Comparisons of data across countries must similarly be made with the full realization that legal definitions of residence vary and that the sizes and systems for defining and demarcating areal units, be they political or socioeconomic, vary widely.

Among the countries included in this volume one can find the full range of possible data sources useful for the study of migration. Significant points with respect to this, however, are that no country relies entirely on a single source of data for official purposes and no country has a data collection system that was designed solely or even primarily for the purpose of gathering the full range of data necessary to chart the patterns and trends in migration and the causes and consequences of migration. This results in part from the complexity of the issues involved. Migration patterns and trends can, for example, be conceptualized in individual, household, or aggregate terms. No matter which of these conceptualizations is adopted, important policy, program and planning, and theoretical questions emerge which require an extremely broad range of data when the causes and consequences of migration are to be considered. Thus, in considering the data situation in any individual country, it is more important to be cognizant of the combination of data sources available and the consistency of defining parameters between sources and over time.

In each of the more developed countries examined, the basic data on migration consist of a combination of (1) a census, a registration system, and surveys, (2) a census and registration system, (3) a registration system and surveys, (4) a census, surveys, and administrative records, or (5) a census and administrative records. Thus, among these countries the most common source of data on migration is the census. It should be noted that, even in those countries where a census is not part of the federal routine data collection system, census data on migration exist for earlier periods. The only country that has discontinued censuses (the Netherlands) does have population registers.

In all of the more developed countries extensive use of survey data is now common. However, not all countries (e.g., Canada) use survey data for official federal estimates of migration. Nevertheless, in these countries survey data are employed for many legal and administrative purposes at and below the federal level of political organization. Where survey data are employed for broad official estimates of migration, these are most commonly derived from a survey done in conjunction with a census or a labor force or housing survey. The most common administrative records employed are those maintained in conjunction with national tax, health, or family welfare systems.

Sources of migration data in the less developed countries included here are considerably more restricted, particularly when it comes to the goal of obtaining a consistent definition of a migrant or a migration. All of the less developed countries included in this volume with the exception of China rely primarily on data collected in their population census for information on migration. In all of these countries some survey data exist, but nearly all of them are plagued by problems relating to small sample sizes, geographic coverage, coordination with other data collection systems, and/or lack of historical sequence. Indeed, the lack of historical sequence even exists in many of the countries with respect to census data. Some countries such as China, Egypt, and Indonesia have registration systems, but only China relies heavily on them; even here inconsistencies in the reporting system and compliance problems make comparisons of local data from one place to another difficult. None of these countries makes official use of administrative records.

Despite the more restricted sources for migration data in less developed countries, it is important to note that tremendous strides have been made in recent years to reduce the data problems in these countries. For example, some countries such as Indonesia have introduced regular intercensal population surveys, and others such as Botswana have conducted national migration surveys, while still others such as Thailand have included migration questions in national longitudinal surveys. The apparently simple fact that all of the countries included here conducted a census in or around 1980 and that all of these censuses contained questions on migration represents a significant achievement which will be of even greater value if this can be repeated in the 1990 round of censuses. Finally, the increased availability of survey data in all countries even when limited in geographic coverage, sample size, or by definitional incompatibilities with other data sources presents a much broader base for knowledge about migration (albeit limited) than existed just a few years ago.

Many of the factors influencing the quality of migration data have already been mentioned above and are related to the type of statistical data collection system from which it is derived. In addition, the authors of the country case studies seem to agree that the quality of data has improved over time and that some data systems within their country provide more valid information than others.

PRINCIPAL POPULATION MOVEMENTS

The variety and volume of principal population movements described in the individual country reports clearly highlight the constraints placed on migration analysis by data availability and the geopolitical and temporal parameters used to define migration. For example, volumes of migration in some countries such as Thailand and Indonesia are described as low, but this in part reflects the fact that migration in these countries is measured principally at the regional level. Even when comparisons can be made over what appear to be similar major regional boundaries, the size of the areas must be taken into consideration. Provinces in the Netherlands are on the average much smaller than are provinces in Thailand or Indonesia. Similarly, comparisons are difficult when principal population movements must be described in different countries or within one country across time in terms of different temporal parameters.

Nevertheless, some general observations can be made with caution about both the levels and trends of migration at the national level. Examination of the levels and trends of migration in less developed countries at major levels (regions, provinces, and states) of geopolitical demarcation using lifetime migration data suggests that rates of migration in these countries have been relatively low. By contrast, when data are available for much lower level areas of demarcation, the data suggest quite high levels of migration. For example, in India the percentages of the total population which were interstate migrants in 1961, 1971, and 1981 were only 3.3, 3.4, and 3.6, respectively, but the percentages of persons who were living in a place other than where they were born was much greater at each census (33.0, 30.4, and 30.7, respectively). Similarly, lifetime interstate migrants in Brazil totaled 13.1, 14.3, and 15.6 percent, respectively, of the population in 1960, 1970, and 1980, whereas lifetime intermunicipal migrants were 31.1, 32.5, and 38.9 percent of the population at each of these points in time.

These same data can be used to illustrate some other apparent generalizations. For example, the country reports suggest a wide variation within countries in the trend of migration. In some countries such as Brazil and Indonesia there appears to have been a steady increase in the number of lifetime migrants at each succeeding census, whereas in other countries such as Guatemala and Egypt migration appears to have peaked at some point after 1950 and declined in more recent years. In still other countries such as India and Thailand, the data suggest that the most outstanding feature of lifetime migration trends is stability during the 1960s and 1970s. The reader needs to bear in mind, however, that in nearly all countries the number of migrants has increased dramatically over time even when rates have remained stable or declined.

In many less developed countries examined here, rural/urban migration is discussed as one of the most significant forms of migration. Yet in nearly all countries the role and significance of rural/urban migration can be fully appreciated only when viewed in the context of other origin–destination forms of migration and how these have changed over time. In Botswana, for example, rural/urban migration abated for some time as a result of migration from rural areas of the country to urban and rural areas in South Africa (emigration). In more recent years, however, the role of emigration has decreased, while that of migration within the rural sector has increased. In other countries such as Ecuador and Brazil the dominant flows of migration have been different in different parts of the country and/or changed over time. Urban-to-urban migration flows have dominated in some provinces of Ecuador, whereas in others rural-to-urban flows make up the vast majority of all migration.

Among more developed countries the availability of data over longer periods of time, at lower levels of geographic detail and frequently for shorter intervals of time, makes the description of migration trends more complex and detailed. Nevertheless, a number of generalizations can be drawn from the data and discussions related to these nations. First, although there are some marked differences in definitions of migration, there is a substantial amount of variation in the rates of migration among developed countries. In some countries such as Canada and the United States rates of migration are quite high, whereas in other countries such as the United Kingdom they are intermediate and in still other countries such as Italy and the Netherlands they are clearly rather low. Moreover, this type of variation tends to maintain itself whether we are talking about moves from one house to another, from one place to another, or from one region to another, even though there are marked differences in the size of the migration-defining units and the units of temporal observation.

Second, among many more developed countries, migration appears to have peaked sometime during the 1960s or 1970s and to have declined since then. The evidence presented for a number of countries suggests that the declining rates of total migration have resulted more from sharper decreases in long-distance migration than from short-distance migration, and that the declines in migration have been associated with changes in the origin/destination patterns of migration. The most recent data for some countries, however, suggest that rates of migration may have increased during the late 1980s.

Third, in nearly all developed countries migration has played a key role in the metropolitanization process, and various dimensions of this process have had a strong influence on the pattern and timing of migration. For example, in nearly all countries the growth of large cities was enhanced by rural-to-urban migration, just as the growth of suburban and commuting communities surrounding these large cores was strongly affected by both rural-to-urban and core-to-suburban migration as well as urban-to-urban migration, even though the significance of these origin–destination types of migration appears to have begun and ended at different times in the various countries. In this sense it may well be that some metropolitan development parameters are more important than the chronological differences that can be observed.

Similarly, in many of the countries discussed below some sort of a shift has taken place which is described in somewhat different national terms, but which generally suggests a migration pattern reversing the long-term trend of migration toward metropolitan areas or large cities and their suburban communities. In nearly all instances, this pattern is described as occurring after the development of large cities and their suburban communities reached some undefined developmental level. Although the precise factors responsible for this pattern are not clearly specified in any one country, and although the range of possible factors mentioned across countries is very diverse, the fact that this phenomenon did occur in countries as different from one another in terms of size as Canada and the Netherlands, in terms of postwar reconstruction as the Federal Republic of Germany and the United States, and in terms of historical patterns of migration as France, Israel, Italy, and the United Kingdom should be a challenge to theorists.

Finally, a central question concerning this "reversal" centers around its duration. In at least two countries (Canada and the United States) recent evidence suggests that it was short-lived and had actually reversed again during the 1980s. In most other countries where the pattern has existed, such evidence is not available, but in most of these countries direct data for the most recent periods of time are not available.

Although these similarities and differences in the levels and patterns of migration can be noted across countries, it can only be done in the most general sense because differences in the defining parameters of migration differ across countries. This problem is further compounded because the definitions of geographical units such as regions, metropolitan areas, municipalities, and other minor civil divisions differ, as do definitions of urban and rural. Thus, although such broad observations can be gleaned from the chapters in this book, the reader should study each in some detail to take account of this kind of difference as well as others that many of the authors bring out concerning the demographic, economic, historical, political, and social contexts within which migration has occurred in each individual country.

THE DETERMINANTS OF MIGRATION

Within the various country case studies presented below, the determinants of migration are analyzed in terms of three broad approaches. In some of the country case studies primary attention is placed on identifying the characteristics of migrants and nonmigrants and making inferences about the determinants of migration from these. This approach is particularly salient among those countries that must rely primarily on census data for the analysis of the determinants of migration. For this reason it leads researchers to consider a relatively narrow range of factors that influence migration. Chief among these factors are age, sex, education, labor force status, occupation, income, and marital status. While inferences about the causes and determinants of migration are frequently made from these types of analyses, it is important to bear in mind that the characteristics of migrants in this context are measured (at the time of the census) after the migration has occurred and may very well have changed from an earlier point in time or before the migration occurred.

A second approach used to identify the determinants of migration is also based on characteristics, but in this instance the characteristics of interest belong to areas, not individuals. This approach is generally based on census data and involves relating the characteristics of areas to their migration experience. The underlying idea is that one can identify the characteristics of areas that attract or repel migrants in varying degrees. The characteristics that generally receive attention within this approach are those that can be considered to be dimensions of the organization or environment of the area, including government policies or programs intended to alter the organization. Specific examples of types of factors associated with this approach include economic dimensions as reflected in such things as the unemployment rate, industrial structure, or average income; infrastructure amenities as reflected in the availability of schools, medical facilities, or housing; and environmental dimensions such as the availability and quality of land or climate.

The third approach involves employing direct data from migrants and nonmigrants about their reasons and motives for migrating or not migrating. Data of this type must be collected in surveys. When they are so gathered, the surveys are frequently limited in geographic coverage and/or type of migration studied. Moreover, such surveys are usually conducted after (and frequently quite some time after) migration has occurred, making it difficult for some people to accurately report all the reasons they may have had for moving or accurately prioritizing the reasons in terms of major and minor ones.

With these general approaches and their limitations in mind, we can observe certain generalized patterns in the factors associated with migration and in the reasons for migration across countries. In less developed countries migration appears to be concentrated in certain age groups, usually showing peaks in the early years and among those 20 to 24 and 25 to 29. The relatively large numbers in the earliest ages can be viewed as a function of the later peaks, which are also the peak childbearing ages. However, some authors have suggested that the peak may also represent, quite apart from this, an attempt by parents to locate in places (primarily urban) where children can secure an education. In most less developed countries the age patterns of migration are different for males and females, with peaks being reached for females at earlier ages. It is usually assumed that these differences are related to differences in patterns of education, work, and marriage.

With rural-to-urban migration playing such a dominant role in most of the less developed countries, it is not surprising that most authors have emphasized the contrasting physical, social, and economic environments of such areas in their efforts to explain migration. The generalized scenario that emerges in this sense is one of increasing population pressure in rural areas resulting from high population growth rates on fixed or slowly expanding agricultural land, coupled with a lack of employment opportunities outside of agriculture and the lack of amenities such as education in particular as generating or ''push'' factors behind much of the migration originating in rural areas. One of the values of the individual chapters is to observe how the importance of these factors is emphasized differently and combined with other factors such as natural disasters, environmental deterioration, family systems and rites of passage, and government policies to influence the uniqueness of the individual countries.

While the objective conditions have been emphasized as responsible for migration from rural areas, most authors attribute the attractiveness of urban areas to a combination of objective and subjective conditions. That is, though without doubt there are both more employment opportunities and more varied opportunities for employment in urban than in rural areas in less developed countries, unemployment and underemployment rates are so high in urban centers that the chances of migrants securing employment are generally much lower than they are perceived to be. Similarly, social amenities are present in such areas, but the rapid growth of urban centers coupled with the relatively low socioeconomic status of most migrants puts them in a competitively weak position to gain access to most such amenities which are in relatively short supply.

Where migration between rural areas forms a significant part of the overall national migration pattern in less developed countries, it too seems to be grounded in economic terms. Government programs to open up new agricultural territory tend to attract both urban and rural migrants to rural areas, and various tenure systems that require agricultural laborers to work on large landholdings attract both permanent and seasonal workers depending on the situation. In many countries, however, a significant amount of migration within the rural sector appears to be related to marriage. Again, however, it must be emphasized that factors unique to each country are examined in this book, and that the weight of such factors varies in terms of their role in explaining migration in each country. Moreover, in all countries there are alternative urban centers varying in size and distance from rural areas which also vary markedly, as do the individuals and households within them. Indeed, only when these factors are examined in the real-world context of individual countries can the full complexity of the migration process be realized.

Within the more developed countries examined here, the reasons and causes for migration appear to be even more complex if for no other reason than that data are available in more detail. There is considerable variation in the age and sex structure of migration across countries, but in all countries migration reaches a peak in the young adult ages for most types of migration and in a number of countries sharp increases are reported at or near retirement ages. Migration between large urban agglomerations appears to be closely tied to employment changes, but a few authors have noted that the precise role of employment changes in migration is becoming increasingly complex to understand and evaluate as the number of two-worker families has increased. Similarly, it appears that some people (households) are less willing to move today than they were a few years ago when household employment opportunities were different and when economic cycles had less impact on the cost and value of housing.

Within the more developed countries the movement from the centers of large urban agglomerations appears to have been influenced substantially by non-economic factors such as a desire to live in less densely settled areas and areas offering more varied housing and environmental opportunities. The extent to which this could be done and when it was done was surely influenced by transportation technology, the availability of housing including its financing, and the decentralization and accessibility of urban services. Surely in a number of European countries postwar reconstruction played a vital role in this process.

The recent trend of movement out of or away from large urban agglomerations altogether has sparked a new debate about the reasons for migration in many of these countries. On the one hand, some researchers are suggesting that this phenomenon is influenced strongly by demographic factors such as the aging of the population and the increased mobility of the older population. Others observe that in some countries the decentralization of light industry and manufacturing is playing a key role in the movement from metropolitan areas, as is an increasing preference for nonurban lifestyles. Yet in many countries there is evidence that it is an extension of the broader agglomeration process. As the older suburbs are taking on many of the characteristics and functions of central cores, persons are now merely able to move further from them and still remain within the commuting range of the suburbs, which now function for them as the cores did in the past for people living in the suburbs. To some extent all of these forces are probably operating in most of the countries experiencing this phenomenon, and the extent to which one dominates over the others is extremely difficult to determine.

THE CONSEQUENCES OF MIGRATION

In less developed countries the consequences of migration center around the redistribution of population between rural and urban areas. Population densities would be considerably higher in rural areas, and the problems of population pressure would be far more serious than what they are in the absence of rural-urban migration. Migration has therefore had a positive effect. At the same time migration is contributing to the rapid growth, unemployment, strained infrastructures, and growing slums that can be found in and around many urban centers in the less developed countries of the world. Similarly, several authors note that migration may be presenting opportunities for education and employment to many rural-urban migrants who could not receive these benefits in the rural sector. However, they also note that the prospects for development in rural areas are diminished, as it is the most productive and industrious who leave the rural for the urban sector.

Several authors have also noted that in particular rural areas of some countries where rural-urban migration is concentrated in the very young age groups and where it is highly male in sex structure strains on rural agricultural productivity have arisen, as have problems resulting from the breakup of families. When older persons and females are left behind, there is also evidence to suggest that the young suffer by being forced to perform tasks that keep them out of school and deprive them of an education. Again, however, there is contrary evidence to suggest that in many instances rural-urban migration produces the income necessary to pay the school fees of young children and to produce remittances that circulate wealth back into the rural economies.

In short, the evidence on the consequences of migration in less developed countries is mixed at best. To a substantial degree, as suggested by several authors, this has resulted from the fact that much more attention has been given to the causes than the consequences of migration. In this sense it is important to realize that it is considerably easier to study the causes than the effects since it is extremely difficult to analytically separate the contribution of migration from that of all other things that may have changed over time. Nevertheless, examination of the individual studies in this volume will provide the reader with a broad perspective of the importance of internal migration as an agent of social and economic change in less developed countries.

Among the more developed countries examined here migration has had the long-term effect of significantly increasing population concentration and of leading to population decentralization around the major points of population concentration. In recent years as the net exchange of population between metropolitan and nonmetropolitan areas has reversed or approached zero, the long-term redistributional impact of migration may have slowed down appreciably in many countries. However, there is little, if any, evidence to suggest that the process of population decentralization has been altered. A number of the other consequences of migration in more developed countries appear to be closely tied and interrelated to migration's effects on concentration and decentralization. Yet it is difficult to assess precisely the extent to which these are consequences of migration or the products of broader changes in urban structure, which may themselves lead to migration.

Although all such "consequences" cannot be mentioned here, the example of reduced travel time serves to illustrate the problem. Some authors have mentioned that migration has led to reduced travel time by allowing persons to live closer to places of work and other places that must be traveled to on a daily or routine basis. While it may be true that migration has accomplished this, it is also true that people select new places of residence, in part, with the goal of reducing travel time. Similarly, it is possible that travel time has been reduced not merely because people are moving closer to places they travel to, but also because the places they travel to are decentralizing, and that this, in turn, has affected the decentralization of population. In short, migration is a process that is occurring simultaneously with a number of other processes. Therefore, it is probably better to view many "consequences of migration" as concomitants of migration until we better understand the interrelationships between these processes.

Nevertheless, a number of other consequences that can be more directly traced to migration have been occurring in more developed countries. Many of these are related to patterns of segregation and result from the selective character of migration. For instance, in a number of countries where migration is selective by age we find that increasing age segregation is occurring as the younger segments of the population move from some areas, reducing the reproductive potential of these areas and leaving the middle-aged and older population there to age in place. Also contributing to the process of age segregation in some countries has been the increase in elderly migration and the fact that in many countries this migration has tended to be directed toward relatively few places. As a result, the concentration of older persons in them has increased, and that in other places has decreased. Other dimensions of segregation mentioned by the authors of the country case studies include racial, ethnic, and social differentiation.

Migration has also had an important effect on the distribution of political power in a number of countries. In countries where political representation is allocated on the basis of proportions of national population, shifts in population distribution between units of apportionment will result in corresponding shifts in political power. Thus, in a number of countries where major shifts in population distribution have occurred quite dramatic shifts have taken place in the locus of political power, and much of this has been a product of migration.

REFERENCES

Bilsborrow, Richard E. et al. (eds.). 1984. *Migration Surveys in Low Income Countries.* London: Croom Helm.

Boque, Donald J. 1969. *Principles of Demography.* New York: John Wiley and Sons, Inc.

Costello, Michael A. et al. 1987. *Mobility and Employment in Urban Southeast Asia.* Boulder, Colo.: Westview Press.

De Jong, Gordon, and Gardner, Richard (eds.). 1981. *Migration Decision Making.* New York: Pergamon Press.

Fawcett, James T. et al. (eds.). 1984. *Women in the Cities of Asia: Migration and Urban Adaptation.* Boulder, Colo.: Westview Replica Editions.

Goldstein, Sidney, and Sly, David F. (eds.). 1975a. *Basic Data Needed for the Study of Urbanization.* Liege, Belgium: Ordina Editions.

————. 1975b. *The Measurement of Urbanization and Projection of Urbanization.* Liege, Belgium: Ordina Editions.

Kirk, Dudley. 1960. "Some Reflections in American Demography in the Nineteen Sixties." *Population Index* 26: 305–10.

Pryor, Robin J. (ed.). 1979. *Migration and Development in South-East Asia.* Kuala Lumpur: Oxford University Press.

Stinner, William F. et al. (eds.). 1982. *Return Migration and Remittances: Developing a Caribbean Perspective.* Washington, D.C.: Smithsonian Institution.

United Nations. 1981. *Population Distribution Policies in Development Planning.* New York: United Nations Publication E.81.XIII.5.

————. 1984. *Population Distribution, Migration and Development.* New York: United Nations Publication ST/ESA/SER.A/89.

Willekens, Frans, and Rogers, Andrei. 1978. *Spatial Population Analysis.* Laxenburg, Austria: International Institute for Applied Systems Analysis.

Zachariah, K.C., and Conde, Julien. 1981. *Migration in West Africa.* New York: Oxford University Press.

1

BOTSWANA

James Cobbe

Botswana (formerly the Bechuanaland Protectorate) is a large country of about 582,000 square kilometers in the southern African plateau. Its mean elevation above sea level is 1,000 meters. The population of about 1 million is concentrated along the rail line in the east of the country, with only about one-fifth of the total living in the arid and desert regions of the west and the Okavango Delta area of the northwest. Prior to independence, most of the population subsisted from dry land agriculture (maize and sorghum) and cattle, supplemented by remittances from male migrants primarily to South Africa. There was very little modern economic activity in the country, and less than 4 percent of the population lived in towns, although some traditional villages are very large. Since independence, migration has contributed to urbanization and impacted rural settlement patterns, but a large (though quantitatively uncertain) proportion of the migration has been of a temporary or circulatory nature.

DATA ON MIGRATION

Definitions

Administratively and politically, Botswana is divided into six towns and eleven districts. Three towns (Gaborone, Francistown, and Lobatse) have existed in some form for most of this century; the others owe their existence to mining operations that started after independence (1966). These towns and districts are the geographic units most often used to determine migration; however, in some instances they have been aggregated, and in others they have been split. For example, the 1981 census split Ngamiland into three census districts, Kgalagadi into two, and Central District into six. Population densities vary markedly within the country, and one aggregation used for some purposes is "remote areas"—

very low population density regions that are nevertheless essentially politically defined (including most of the remaining Khoi-San Bushman population).

With respect to the time period over which a move is considered migration, there is no consistency of practice in Botswana. The 1981 census defines a mover as someone who was living elsewhere a year earlier; data collected for the 1984–85 Labour Force Survey, on the other hand, were based on questions as to whether the respondent had *ever* moved. In contrast, the National Migration Study (NMS) carried out in the late seventies permitted respondents to self-define their status by classifying as migrants those who had been absent from what they regarded as their permanent homes for more than one year.

It follows that discussion of migration in Botswana, and summary statements on its extent and effects, must be interpreted with great caution because they can vary enormously depending on the data source. For example, the National Migration Study concluded that, in 1979, 15 percent of the de facto population were internal migrants (Botswana, 1982, 24), whereas the Labour Force Survey reports 59.1 percent of the population aged 12 or more as lifetime migrants (Botswana, n.d., 29).

Source of Data

There are two major data sources on migration in Botswana, the census and occasional surveys. The 1981 census was the first reasonably satisfactory census to include data on migration in any detail. The first six censuses, taken at irregular intervals between 1904 and 1956, were not based on enumeration areas, and their accuracy is very much doubted. The 1964 census did use a house-to-house canvas, but the enumeration basis was defined in terms of village of allegiance. The 1971 census was the first to use enumeration areas and to be conducted on a de facto basis, but its coverage has been seriously questioned and it does not contain useful information on internal migration.

The 1981 census is potentially a valuable source of data on internal migration. The questionnaire included a column for each individual enumerated which asked where that individual lived "this time last year." Possible responses included not born, in this dwelling, elsewhere in this locality, elsewhere in Botswana (to be identified by a code number for locality), and other country (similarly identified by code number). The census appears to have been well designed and planned and carefully carried out (although there were some problems with data processing).

Migration from Botswana to the Republic of South Africa, largely for employment in that country's gold mines, has been an important feature of Botswana's economy and society since the late nineteenth century. Lack of reliable data on these migration flows, and lack of knowledge concerning their consequences and effects, were two of the motivations for a large research effort known as the National Migration Study. This study took place over a period of five years (1977 to 1982), although data were collected mainly in 1978 and 1979.

As it turned out, the study focused more on internal than external migration. In addition to its three-volume report (Botswana, 1982), several academic publications (e.g., Brown, 1983; Izzard, 1982, 1985; Kerven, 1979, 1984; Lucas, 1985; Lucas and Stark, 1985) as well as statistical data were produced. The study is perhaps most notable for the contributions it made to understanding and clarification of such concepts as "household" in Botswana and to the social processes involved in migration.

In recent years, with mining developments, the establishment and growth of modern government and education, the unusually rapid growth of the country's economy, and the rapid growth of towns in a country which in the 1950s could be argued to have had no modern towns at all, there has been a heightened interest in internal migration. Accordingly, there is now the tendency to incorporate migration questions in many surveys designed for other primary purposes (e.g., the 1984–85 Labour Force Survey).

PRINCIPAL POPULATION MOVEMENTS

Botswana has been undergoing rapid economic, social, and political change over the last thirty years. For over a century, migration from Botswana to other parts of southern Africa, mostly to South African mines, has been a crucial feature of rural life (see, e.g., Schapera, 1947). Since independence, a new pattern of migration from rural areas to towns has emerged and become quantitatively more important. In 1964, the three existing towns (Gaborone, Lobatse, and Francistown) were reported in the census to have a combined population of 20,845. By the 1981 census, the total population in the six recognized urban areas had grown to 150,021, about 16 percent of the total population (941,027). Thus, the bulk of the adult urban population was not urban-born, and many people retain some links with rural areas. The intensity of these links, and the probability of permanent urban residence, vary considerably across individuals, but many urban residents retain rights to land and cattle in rural areas. The data in Table 1.1 shows that about one urban person in five migrated out of the urban areas in 1980–81, although overall there was a net urban in-migration rate of about 5.8 percent per annum.

In addition to rural-urban migration, there are two types of movement within the rural sector which are significant. One is seasonal movement in connection with the agricultural cycle (both movement from large traditional villages— Serowe, for example, has a population approaching 10,000—to croplands, and movement with cattle between grazing areas), which will not be dealt with here. The other is more permanent migration between rural areas, particularly between regions with different forms of land tenure and different agricultural bases. This type of migration can be further subdivided into three distinct types of flow. By far the largest flow is to permanent settlements on arable land and to cattle posts, away from established villages. Discussing this movement, the National Migration Study (NMS) commented:

Table 1.1
Interdistrict Migration Rates, Botswana, 1980–81

Census District	In-migration Rate (%)	Out-migration Rate (%)	Net Migration Rate (%)	1981 Population
Urban:				
Gaborone	21.01%	17.51%	3.50%	59,657
Francistown	27.17%	19.55%	7.62%	31,065
Lobatse	18.44%	21.61%	-3.17%	19,034
Selebi-Phikve	24.98%	21.67%	3.31%	29,467
Orapa	33.55%	18.02%	15.53%	5,229
Jwaneng	64.94%	20.82%	44.12%	5,567
Rural:				
Ngwaketse	4.90%	6.06%	-1.16%	104,182
Barolong	8.25%	7.28%	.97%	15,471
South East	7.23%	6.84%	.39%	30,648
Kweneng	3.62%	3.76%	-.14%	117,127
Kgatleng	6.00%	7.65%	-1.65%	44,461
Central:				
Serowe	6.04%	9.02%	-2.98%	92,227
Mahalapye/Tuli	6.90%	6.25%	.65%	82,982
Bobonong	7.10%	8.70%	-1.60%	46,436
Boteti	6.92%	8.13%	-1.21%	26,406
Tutume	5.96%	9.00%	-3.04%	75,277
North East	8.15%	8.62%	-.47%	36,636
Ngamiland	2.34%	3.16%	-.82%	68,063
Chobe	10.33%	6.43%	3.90%	7,934
Ghanzi	4.51%	3.80%	.71%	19,096
Kgalagadi	7.18%	4.89%	2.29%	24,059

Sources: Botswana (1985), 10 and Botswana (1983), Part 3, Table 1

Many of these non-village settlers maintain a village dwelling, and migrate back to the established villages on a short-term basis. . . . The characteristics of the permanent lands dwellers vary from those of the villagers. Fewer female-headed dwellings have migrated permanently to the lands, and the heads of dwellings tend to be older and less educated than their village counterparts. The permanent lands areas are markedly deficient in dwelling unit heads in the young adult age range, indicating the extent to which this age group migrates to centres of employment and away from agricultural zones. (Botswana, 1982, 27).

In a secondary flow, some 4,000 Batswana are employed on the 400 freehold farms owned and operated on a commercial basis mostly by persons of white South African origin and situated along certain portions of the country's borders. Virtually all these employees are migrants, three-quarters of them men, and most come from small- or medium-size villages fairly close to the farms. A third flow involves the "remote area dwellers," the groups of rural people who for reasons of ethnic, social, or geographic distance from the dominant society are so labelled by the government. Anthropologists tend to argue that, although there is much movement among these people (some of whom can reasonably be termed nomadic), they include few true migrants since most of their movements are circular from one temporary dwelling to another (e.g., Wilmsen, 1982).

Table 1.1 shows that, although the net migration rates for rural districts are mostly quite small, the gross in- and out-migration rates are large despite the fact that the areas are geographically large. Only seven out of thirty of these rates are below 5 percent per annum, and eight are above 8 percent per annum. Table 1.2 illustrates a perhaps more significant feature of rural-rural migration in Botswana, namely, that the great bulk of it is intraregional movement, either to the large central villages that are a feature of Botswana society or to permanent lands.

Before we examine data on the demographic characteristics of migrants, we first need to understand some peculiarities of the overall de facto population. Since the early 1960s, it has been illegal under South African law for black female Batswana to enter South Africa for purposes of employment or residence. However, men continued to be recruited for work on South African mines, farms, and elsewhere. The 1981 census, which very likely underenumerated absentees, identified 29,322 men but only 6,333 women absent in South Africa; the effects of South African discrimination against female migrants are made clear by this and by the fact that absentees elsewhere in southern Africa included 2,479 men and 2,761 women. The result is that Botswana had an unusually low sex ratio (89.0 in 1981).

Because of the international migration pattern, the sex ratio in Botswana, which in 1981 was 100.0 for the 0 to 4 age group, is lowest (71.4) for the 20 to 24 age group and climbs back to 98.1 for the 60 to 64 age group.

This explains some of the apparent contradictions of the age-sex data of

Table 1.2
Source and Destination of Movements for Citizen Population Aged 12 Years or More Who Have Ever Moved, Based on Interviews in the Twelve Months Ending April 30, 1985

| | From Urban | | From Rural | | | From Abroad |
	Gaborone	Other	Southeast	East	Other	
Destination						
Urban:						
Gaborone	608	2,375	24,713	13,956	1,532	1,564
Other	2,164	3,563	12,371	34,723	2,636	3,317
Total to Urban	2,772	5,938	37,084	48,679	4,168	4,881
Rural:						
Southeast	5,166	3,273	55,971	1,834	1,030	12,720
East	4,861	10,113	2,134	81,321	3,028	6,131
Other	283	842	1,205	2,213	39,324	3,502
Total to Rural	10,310	14,228	59,310	85,368	43,382	22,353

Note: Southeast consists of Kweneng, Kgatleng, South-East, Barolong, and Ngwaketse districts; East: North-East, Tutume, Boteti, Serowe, Bobonong, and Mahalapye; and Other: Chobe, Nagmiland, Ghanzi and Kgalagadi.

Source: Botswana, n.d., 92.

Table 1.3
Age and Sex Distribution of Internal Movers, 1980–81

Age	Male Movers		Female Movers		Total	
	Number	% of age group	Number	% of age group	Number	% of age group
0-9	18,238	11.4%	19,363	12.0%	37,601	11.7%
10-19	22,197	21.8%	26,253	23.8%	48,450	22.8%
20-29	18,406	31.1%	18,597	22.7%	37,003	26.3%
30-39	9,714	26.1%	7,539	16.2%	17,253	20.6%
40-49	6,033	20.7%	4,829	14.3%	10,862	17.3%
50-59	3,710	17.2%	3,345	13.6%	7,055	15.3%
60+	4,152	14.0%	4,276	12.1%	8,428	13.0%
Not stated	975	22.3%	798	16.9%	1,773	19.5%
Total	83,425		85,000		168,425	
Average		18.8%		17.1%		17.9%
Total Population:	443,104		497,923		941,027	

Sources: Botswana (1985), 12, 14; Botswana (1983) and author's calculations

internal migrants. Tables 1.3 and 1.4 show that there have been more female than male migrants whether we look at a one-year period or lifetime movements. At the same time, men are more likely to be migrants than women, the percentages being 18.8 versus 17.1 on a one-year basis and 63.1 versus 56.1 on a lifetime one. Looking at age-specific patterns, we can see that men in their 20s, 30s, and 40 and over are much more likely than similarly aged women to have

Table 1.4
Age and Sex Distribution of the Ever-Moved Population Aged 12+, Based on Interviews in the Twelve Months Ending April 30, 1985

Age	Male Movers		Female Movers		Total	
	Number	% of age group	Number	% of age group	Number	% of age group
12-14	13,267	36.8%	12,234	33.5%	25,501	35.1%
15-19	19,771	47.9%	24,587	51.3%	44,358	49.7%
20-24	20,942	67.9%	30,583	61.8%	51,525	64.1%
25-34	32,517	76.5%	42,862	63.6%	75,379	68.5%
35-44	22,698	76.5%	27,518	60.6%	50,216	66.8%
45-54	18,859	71.5%	21,663	60.1%	40,522	64.9%
55-64	12,440	71.0%	13,727	54.5%	26,167	61.2%
65+	14,933	67.7%	15,739	55.5%	30,672	60.8%
Not stated	34	52.3%	17	34.0%	51	35.2%
Total/	155,461		188,930		344,391	
Average		63.1%		56.1%		59.1%

Note: Small numbers of persons who did not state whether they had moved are included in totals; this explains the apparent discrepancy in the "not stated" age group -- most not stateds for migration also did not state age.

Sources: author's calculations from data in Botswana, n.d., 92.

moved in the last year. This is not true of the under 20 age group, among whom females are more likely to have moved than males. At the same time, on a lifetime basis, 15- to 19-year-old females are more likely to have moved than males, although the probabilities are higher for males in every other age group. This pattern reflects a recent tendency for young women, unable to migrate to South Africa like their male brothers, to move independently into towns within Botswana.

CHARACTERISTICS OF MOVERS

With allowance for the peculiarities introduced by the presence of international migration by men only and the tendency for females to outnumber males in the education system below the university level, the information on internal migrants in Botswana is consistent with that in many developing countries. The education enrollment by sex pattern is caused by the traditional practice of males taking responsibility for livestock at early ages, reducing their participation in formal education in rural areas.

According to the 1981 census, persons who had moved in the year before the census were more likely to have done so the more educated they were. Table 1.5 shows that more than one-third of those with at least a primary education had moved. In all education categories, men were slightly more likely to move than women, but the differential is substantially smaller at the highest level. For both men and women, those with no education or only an incomplete primary education were less likely than average to have moved, whereas those with completed primary education or more than primary education were more likely than average to have moved.

Table 1.5
Migrants in 1980–81 Aged 12+, by Sex and Education

	Male Movers		Female Movers		Total	
	Number	%	Number	%	Number	%
No school/unknown	24,198	19.7%	18,836	15.1%	43,034	17.4%
Some primary	17,752	22.3%	22,091	19.4%	39,843	20.0%
Completed primary	10,590	30.7%	12,842	26.6%	23,432	28.3%
More than primary	7,884	37.2%	6,793	35.2%	14,677	36.2%
Total	60,424	23.4%	60,562	18.5%	120,986	21.2%

Note: The "%" column shows migrants as a percentage of migrants and non-migrants for each row category.

Sources: Botswana (1983), Table 31 and author's calculations

Census data also show that fertility was noticeably lower for women migrants than for women who had not moved, and the difference appears too large to be explained by the differential in education alone. For example, in the 15- to 29-year-old age group, 48.5 percent of migrant females had no children, as opposed to only 38.5 percent of nonmigrants. At the other end of the scale, 2.9 percent of the nonmigrants already had five children, whereas only 1.7 percent of the migrants did (Botswana, 1983, Table 32). Drawing conclusions from the published tables, which are very aggregated, is difficult. For example, an important cause of migration in the younger portion of this age category is continuation of education. Young women who become pregnant are usually immediately expelled from school, so this may explain part of the difference in proportions of those with no children.

Table 1.6 shows data from the 1981 census on the economic activity status of migrants. As one might expect in a country with most wage employees in towns, and towns growing rapidly by in-migration, employees and those actively seeking work are overrepresented among both male and female migrants. For men, the economically nonactive are overrepresented among migrants. This at first seems strange, but it is probably explained by the rapid expansion of secondary and postsecondary education and the fact that in order to attend school at this level most students must migrate to towns or large villages. Those females whose status was classified as "periodic piece jobs" (i.e., casually employed) were also overrepresented among migrants. The explanation here is probably the tendency mentioned earlier for young women to migrate independently to towns, and the necessity for some of them, unable to find jobs or sufficient support from relatives or lovers, to resort to activities so classified to survive. The self-

Table 1.6
Migrants in 1980–81 Aged 12+, by Sex and Economic Activity Status

	Male Movers		Female Movers		Total	
	Number	%	Number	%	Number	%
Employee	25,421	29.7%	10,231	27.0%	35,652	28.9%
Self-employed	1,079	18.4%	583	16.1%	1,662	17.5%
Periodic piece work	917	20.9%	468	21.6%	1,385	21.1%
Family agriculture	11,946	15.4%	10,745	16.3%	22,691	15.8%
Actively seeking work	4,052	27.4%	4,101	23.5%	8,153	25.3%
Economically inactive	16,948	24.5%	34,411	18.7%	51,359	20.3%
Total	60,363	23.5%	60,539	19.4%	120,902	21.3%

Note: The "%" column shows migrants as a percentage of migrants and non-migrants for each row category.

Sources: Botswana (1983), Table 30 and author's calculations

employed and those engaged in family agriculture are underrepresented among migrants, as one would expect; the surprising data are the high proportions of people in these categories who had moved in the last year. Among men, those dependent on periodic piece jobs, and among women, the economically nonactive, are also underrepresented in the migrant group, though not by very much.

MOTIVATIONS FOR MIGRATION

Employment

Employment is a major reason for migration. The three new towns (Selebi-Phikwe, Orapa, and Jwaneng) all owe their existence to new mines—copper and nickel in the first case, diamonds in the last two. Essentially everyone in those towns is a migrant, and those who have jobs migrated to get them. Access to the diamond mining towns, which are remote, is deliberately restricted, but Selebi-Phikwe has attracted a large population that is not directly employed in the mines. Table 1.7 throws some more light on employment as a motivation for migration movement. Fewer than 30 percent of the employed have never moved, but both the unemployed and those not in the labor force are more likely never to have moved than the general population. The survey asked those who had moved to classify themselves into one of three groups on the basis of their situation just before their last move: had they arranged a job before they moved, did they

Table 1.7

Percentage Distribution of Population Aged 12 Years or More, by Migrant Status and Current Economic Activity, Based on Interviews in the Twelve Months Ending April 30, 1985

Migrant Status	Current Economic Activity Status			
	Employed	Unemployed	Not in Labor Force	Total
Never moved	29.4%	42.9%	54.8%	40.9%
Ever moved	70.6%	57.1%	45.2%	59.1%
Of whom: work arranged before move	30.7%	2.6%	2.7%	18.4%
work expected	19.8%	28.2%	6.2%	17.3%
work not expected	49.4%	69.2%	91.2%	64.3%
Subtotal	99.9%	100.0%	100.1%	100.0%
Total persons	274,782	93,096	215,041	582,919

Note: "Employed" includes self-employed and unpaid family workers. "Not stated" (8 in number) and "not known if moved" (236) omitted from calculations.

Source: Botswana, n.d., 92. (author's calculations)

expect to find work after the move, or did they not expect to find work even though they were moving? Almost half of those employed, and almost 70 percent of the unemployed, did not expect to find work as a result of their move. Clearly, therefore, seeking work is not the only motivation for migration.

Education and Amenities

Among the young, as already mentioned, continuation of education is a frequent reason for migration. All postsecondary and most secondary schools are still in towns or large villages. As late as 1983, there were only twenty junior secondary schools in the entire country, but by 1985 there were forty-two. Over 99 percent of the secondary school students are 13 years of age or older, and by 1985 they numbered over 32,000. Thus, attendance at secondary school contributes a significant amount to migration.

While some pupils move alone to attend school, in other instances whole families migrate in order to give their children a better chance at education. In a country the size of Texas with a total population of only a million, access to the amenities of modernity (e.g., health facilities, modern entertainment, shopping) is also a motivation for migration to towns or large villages. This is particularly so because until recently these amenities were almost totally absent in Botswana and even now are largely confined to the towns and large villages. Yet, familiarity with them is widespread among the rural population because of the tradition of temporary migration to work in South Africa or Zimbabwe (formerly Rhodesia) and, in recent years, Botswana's own towns.

Social and Environmental Reasons

Family reunification is almost certainly one of the reasons for migration. Although the practice of maintaining two residences is very widespread (more than half of the village residents maintain a second dwelling on their arable lands; see Botswana, 1982, 27), a proportion of male migrants to towns are eventually joined by their wives and children, or at least some of them. Available data do not permit an estimate of their numbers.

It is still very unusual for urban dwellers in Botswana to have broken all ties with rural areas. In most of the country, agricultural land tenure is still based on customary law, so most males have some rights to arable land maintained through relatives. Cattle remain a very important vehicle for holding wealth, and many of the wage employed own cattle and travel regularly to their cattle posts on weekends. It is not unusual for those who cease to be employed in towns to return to their rural base.

CONSEQUENCES OF MIGRATION

Migration has helped to transform the structure of Botswana over the last twenty to thirty years. The capital, Gaborone, has gone from a small government post and rail stop to a city of over 50,000 people. What was formerly the main town in the south of the country, Lobatse, has gone into decline as its economic attractions have diminished relative to those of Gaborone. Three entirely new towns, based on mining, have risen from bare land. Francistown, close to the Zimbabwe border, has grown rapidly and added some manufacturing (mostly textiles and apparel) to what was formerly a commercial center and railhead for the neighboring freehold farms.

At the same time, the rural settlement pattern has been changing (Silitshena, 1982). The old pattern was based on a network of villages, fitting into a hierarchy from quite small to surprisingly large. However, the smaller villages have lost population while the larger ones have gained, and a rising proportion of the rural population is living permanently where agricultural activities take place, or in new, small hamlets not yet recognized by government.

The data suggest a population that can be divided into three groups. About 40 percent, if the Labour Force Survey can be believed, have never moved. The vast majority of these live in rural areas. Of the 60 percent who have moved, a small proportion is presumably permanently settled in their new locations, typically either "permanent lands" or, among the more securely and better paid employed, in towns. But the 1981 census found that close to one in five of the population had moved in the previous year. Some of these are classic circular migrants moving between jobs (often in towns) and rural bases. Others are moving temporarily in connection with education or perceived better economic or social conditions. An econometric analysis of the NMS data convinced R.E.B. Lucas (1985) that, under Botswana conditions, the creation of an extra urban job induced more than one adult migrant to move to town, adding to the nonemployed adults in town. However, the Labour Force Survey finding that so many migrants did not expect employment may mean that his specifications omitted important noneconomic motivations for migration.

Some population movements are connected with political developments outside the country's borders. During the Zimbabwean war of independence, substantial numbers of refugees entered Botswana. Insecurity along the border with what was then Rhodesia induced some persons to migrate away from the border areas; they later moved back. Similarly, refugees from South Africa frequently enter Botswana, and although most proceed further north, there is some insecurity along the South African border, and there have been armed raids into Botswana by South African forces. Again, this situation may have induced some movements of persons in the affected areas. An obvious complication is that, in both cases, the borders do not delineate settlement patterns of ethnic groups, so that there are individuals for whom citizenship is ambiguous and residence histories may include periods on both sides of the border.

At the individual and household level, considerable concern has been expressed about the effects of migration patterns. Much of this has been in the context of unaccompanied male migration to South Africa, which, predictably, has deleterious effects at times on wives and children left behind, despite massive remittance flows from the bulk of such migrants. The NMS data on both internal and South African remittances have been analyzed in detail by Lucas and Stark (1985). Of course, unaccompanied male migration has similar effects whether the destination is domestic or foreign, as has been documented by W. Izzard (1982, 1985) and B. Brown (1983), among others. Concern has also been raised about the effects of migration on agricultural production (e.g., Kerven, 1982). Yet another concern centers on the social impact of migration to towns of young unaccompanied females, and the plight in particular of unmarried mothers and their children. Independent women are not a traditional category in Botswana society, but, in recent years in a highly mobile society undergoing rapid transformation, large numbers who fit this description have appeared. Many have very insecure sources of economic support, raising questions about their own welfare and that of their children.

REFERENCES

Bell, M. 1982. "Education, Mobility, and Employment." In Botswana, 1982, 442–97.
Botswana. Central Statistics Office, Ministry of Finance and Development Planning, Republic of Botswana. 1982. In C. Kerven (ed.), *Migration in Botswana, Patterns, Causes and Consequences*. Final Report, National Migration Study, 3 volumes. Gaborone.
———. 1983. *Census Administrative/Technical Report and National Statistical Tables*. Gaborone.
———. 1985. *Country Profile, 1985, Botswana*. Gaborone.
———. *Labour Force Survey, 1984–85*. Gaborone.
Brown, B. 1983. "The Impact of Male Labour Migration on Women in Botswana." *African Affairs* 82:367–88.
Bryant, C., B. Stephens, and S. Macliver. 1978. "Rural to Urban Migration: Some Data from Botswana." *African Studies Review* 21:85–99.
Colclough, C., and S. McCarthy. 1980. *The Political Economy of Botswana: A Study of Growth and Distribution*. London: Oxford University Press.
Cooper, D. 1982. "Socio-economic and Regional Factors of Wage Migration and Employment." In Botswana, 1982, 297–336.
International Bank for Reconstruction and Development. 1986. *Financing Adjustment with Growth in Sub-Saharan Africa, 1986–90*. Washington, D.C.
Izzard, W. 1982. "Rural-Urban Migration in a Developing Country: The Case of Women Migrants in Botswana." Ph.D. thesis. Oxford University.
———. 1985. "Migrants and Mothers: Case-studies from Botswana." *Journal of Southern African Studies* 11:258–80.
Kerven, C. (ed.). 1979. *Workshop on Migration Research*. Gaborone: National Migration Study.
———. 1982. "The Effects of Migration on Agricultural Production." In Botswana 1982, 526–626.
———. 1984. "Academics, Practitioners and All Kinds of Women in Development: A Reply to Peters." *Journal of Southern African Studies* 10:259–68.
Lipton, M. 1978. *Employment and Labour Use in Botswana*. Gaborone: Ministry of Finance and Development Planning.

Lucas, R.E.B. 1985. "Migration Amongst the Batswana." *Economic Journal* 95:358–82.

———, and O. Stark. 1985. "Motivations to Remit—Evidence from Botswana." *Journal of Political Economy* 93:901–18.

Peters, P. 1983. "Gender, Developmental Cycles and Historical Process: A Critique of Recent Research on Women in Botswana." *Journal of Southern African Studies* 10:83–105.

Schapera, I. 1947. *Migrant Labour and Tribal Life: A Study of Conditions in the Bechuanaland Protectorate*. London: Oxford University Press.

Silitshena, R. 1982. "Rural Settlement Patterns." In Botswana 1982, 149–97.

Taylor, J. 1986. "Measuring Circulation in Botswana." *Area* 18:203–8.

Wilmsen, E. 1982. "Migration Patterns of Remote Area Dwellers." In Botswana 1982, 337–76.

2

BRAZIL

George Martine

Throughout its history and well into the twentieth century, most of Brazil's population was located in scattered rural communities. In consonance with its export-oriented, primary economy, the few isolated cities on the coastline served as points for exploration of the hinterland and as commercial entrepôts for the shipment of produce and minerals back to the metropolis. With the redivision of internal labor prompted by the Great Depression, internal migration was stimulated, both in the direction of the cities (where import-substituting industries were beginning to flourish) as well as toward successive frontier regions in Brazil's vast interior. These bipolar currents persisted throughout the postwar period. Only in the late sixties have movements toward the frontier abated. In more recent years, a rural exodus, prompted by agricultural modernization and rapid population growth, has contributed to increasing concentration of population in larger urban centers.

DATA ON MIGRATION

By comparison to most developing countries, Brazilian census data on internal migration seem reasonably complete and accurate.[1] Data of increasing diversity and depth are available from five consecutive decennial censuses. The first concrete information on internal migration (place of birth) was presented in the 1940 demographic census. This census permitted a description of lifetime migration flows between the various states. With the same questions in the 1950 census intercensal migration, it was possible to apply indirect techniques to estimate intercensal migration.

The 1960 census added three new dimensions: (1) the spatial element in the definition of "migrant" was broadened to include the *municipio* as well as the state; (2) a third time-space element in the migration history of the respondent (state of previous residence) was added; and (3) all intermunicipal migrants were queried as to duration of residence in their present municipality and state of residence.

The 1970 census repeated the 1960 items and added a question on the rural-urban residence on intermunicipal migrants in their previous domicile. The census volumes published a wide array of tables referring to migration, crosstabulated with duration of residence, age and sex, rural-urban residence (previous and present), as well as state of birth and state of previous residence. Moreover, for the first time, researchers were given access to special tabulations designed according to their own specifications.

The 1980 census included, first, a question on intramunicipal (i.e., rural-urban or vice versa) moves, by individuals who otherwise would not have been counted as migrants, as well as by intermunicipal migrants after their change of residence across a municipal or state boundary. Second, a question was inserted concerning the municipality of previous residence, making it possible to identify the origin of migration streams at a more localized level than the state. Third, previous place (state) of residence and duration of residence were asked of all respondents, thus making it possible to quantify return migration. Finally, the categories for tabulation of duration-of-residence data were altered from 0–10 to 0–9 in order to effectively cover a decennial period (instead of eleven years as in the 1960 and 1970 tabulations).

In short, the quality, coverage, and relevance of migration data from the demographic census have improved progressively from 1940 to the present. Not all of the modifications introduced in recent censuses have been adequately evaluated, leaving many doubts as to their quality and utility (Carvalho, 1985; Martine and Camargo, 1984b). Perhaps the main difficulty encountered in the utilization of census data for studying migration comes from the inadequacy of space and time referents in the definition of migration. In a continental-sized country such as Brazil, which is marked by severe climatic, cultural, and socioeconomic differences, and which has undergone rapid but unequal social change, such limitations are greatly enlarged.

Other direct or indirect sources of information on migration are very limited by comparison. Brazil has never had any sort of population register, and the coverage of its vital statistics system is still uneven. Only in some of the more advanced states, such as Sao Paulo and Rio Grande do Sul, can vital statistics information be used confidently. Household surveys have been done on at least a yearly basis since 1968. On two occasions, migration questions have been inserted, but results have not been up to expectations. Despite large samples, they have been insufficient to permit generalization for any meaningfully differentiated spatial unit, social group, or migration stream.

Another innovative data source was the Migration Information System (SIMI) implemented in 1978. This instrument aimed at providing detailed information on the fluctuations in movements and characteristics of migrants who passed through the various migration-assistance centers, which had been set up all over Brazil in the mid- and late 1970s (Minter, 1980). Doubts over the representativeness of data and the completeness of coverage led to the virtual abandonment of the system in the mid-1980s. The more interesting data which it has provided were collected in centers connected with large-scale public works and/or colonization projects where coverage was somewhat more complete over a given period of time.

PRINCIPAL POPULATION MOVEMENTS

The absolute and relative number of persons defined as migrants by census data increased significantly over the 1940–1980 period. According to Table 2.1, the number of persons who resided in a state other than that of their birth in 1940 was 3.5 million. This number increased progressively until it reached 18.3 million in 1980. This corresponds to an increase from 8.9 percent to 15.6 percent of the total native population. The same trend appears at the municipal level where the number of persons who resided in a municipality other than that of their birth increased from 21.8 million in 1960 to 46.3 million in 1980. This represents a move from 31.1 percent to 38.9 percent of the total population. Finally, intramunicipal movements, measured for the first time in 1980, show that an additional 7.6 million persons changed their place of residence from a rural to urban area (or vice versa) within their municipality of birth. Thus, at least 45 percent of the total population had made some relevant change of residence by 1980. Overall, interstate mobility showed a greater increase in the 1950s while intermunicipal movements grew faster in the 1970s.

The increasing geographic mobility has to be viewed against a backdrop of profound historical transformation. In 1930, most of the 36 million people lived

Table 2.1
Indicators of Internal Migration, Brazil, 1940–80

Year	Lifetime inter-state Migrants (in 000s) (1)	Lifetime inter-municipal Migrants (in 000s) (2)	Intermunicipal Migrants w/less than 10 yrs. of residence (in 000s) (3)	(1) as % of Total Native Population (4)	(2) as % of Total Pop. (5)	(3) as % of Total Pop. (6)
1940	3,527	–	–	8.9	–	–
1950	5,264	–	–	10.4	–	–
1960	9,039	21,804	3,215*	13.1	31.1	18.6*
1970	13,185	30,270	4,203*	14.3	32.5	17.6*
1980	18,347	46,342	6,051	15.6	38.9	20.2

Source – Calculated from IBGE, Demographic Censuses, various years.

* – Census figures adjusted to intercensal period.

in rural areas relatively near the coast of the Southeast and Northeast regions. From the 1930s until the 1970s, two main tendencies marked population movements: one stream was directed toward the growing number of ever-larger cities, and the other, toward successive loci of frontier expansion. Each of these is examined below, followed by an overview of how these separate trends affected interstate and interregional migration.[2]

Urbanization in Brazil

The 1929 stock market crash had profound effects on the future of economic development. Agricultural prices declined drastically, freeing much of the rural workforce. Part of the population movements originating at this time went to the cities where their initial absorption was chaotic. Incipient industrialization gradually helped create employment and eventually stimulated further urbanward migrations. Brazil's balance-of-payments problems at this point prompted entrepreneurs to initiate industrialization as a means of substituting imports. The internal market for industrial products, originally concentrated in the Rio de Janeiro–Sao Paulo region, rapidly expanded to cover most of the country.

Once the industrialization process was initiated, it provoked reflex actions over the entire territory. A national market was constituted, and the various regions were integrated to the benefit of the hegemonic industrial region around the Sao Paulo–Rio axis. The need to integrate the various regional markets stimulated land transport facilities. Concomitantly, migration potential was increased as communications improved and travel between regions became more viable.

The rural-urban movements initiated in the 1930s were reinforced in the 1940s, as a result of the Second World War. The demand for various industrial products increased, and, given the limited capacity of Brazilian industry, the solution was to double work shifts. Wages rose rapidly and thereby attracted further migratory movements. With immigration curtailed during the war, additional personnel came from rural areas. Simultaneously, the government was making a serious attempt to improve the social conditions of urban workers in the areas of health, sanitation, housing, and education. At this time, mortality rates began to decline with improved sanitation and the importation of technologies to control contagious diseases.

All of these factors coalesced to promote rapid urban growth. While precise data are lacking, it is probable that a net total of some 3 million migrants left rural areas for urban areas between 1940 and 1950. This is equivalent to some 10 percent of the total 1940 rural population. The number of cities rose from fifty-one to eighty, while the rural percentage declined from 69 to 64 percent (see Table 2.2).

The postwar period witnessed the reinforcement of the urbanization–industrialization trend. The population increased rapidly (3.0 percent a year) during the 1950s. The agrarian structure was marked by a strong concentration at both

Table 2.2
Evolution of Population Distribution in Brazil, 1940–80 (in percentages)

Place of Residence	1940	1950	1960	1970	1980
Rural Areas	68. 8	63. 8	55. 2	44. 1	32. 4
Localities under 10,000	12. 6	12. 2	12. 1	9. 6	10. 0
" 10 to 20,000	2. 6	2. 9	3. 4	5. 3	4. 0
" 20 to 50,000	2. 2	3. 2	4. 5	5. 4	6. 5
" 50 to 100,000	2. 0	2. 5	2. 7	3. 5	4. 6
" 100 to 500,000	4. 1	4. 3	5. 4	6. 1	11. 0
" 500,000 +	7. 7	11. 1	16. 2	26. 1	31. 5
Total	100%	100%	100%	100%	100%

SOURCE: Cf.   Table 2. 1

extremes of the land tenure scale, in *latifundios* and *minifundios,* both of which are generally conducive to out-migration. In a few states, notably Sao Paulo and Rio Grande do Sul, the mechanization of agriculture also contributed to rural out-migration. Meanwhile, rural-urban differentials in wages and lifestyles, and the enactment of social policies that largely benefitted urban workers, coupled with improved transport and communication, served as forces of attraction. All told, it can be estimated that some 7 million people migrated from rural to urban areas during the 1950s. This is about 21 percent of the rural population at the beginning of the decade. The number of cities rose from 85 to 155, and the percent rural declined to 55.

The 1960s were marked by several social transformations, chief of which was the 1964 military takeover and the imposition of a conservative-modernization model. Its aim was the rapid technical upgrading of industrial and agricultural production without changing the highly stratified social structure. The introduction of the Green Revolution technological package provoked an intensification of the rural exodus, which persisted throughout the 1970s. The logic and the scale of agricultural production were altered, pushing out small farmers of all types. Even in areas not directly affected by modernization, speculation in land had basically the same impact as the prospects and promises of modernization pushed up land values and expelled squatters, sharecroppers, tenants, and small owners.

The basic infrastructure in all of the country was being greatly improved. Spectacular changes occurred in transport and communications as locally produced buses, trucks, and cars multiplied traffic in all directions, and the communications sector saw dramatic improvements. Undoubtedly, the "bright lights" of rapidly expanding cities served to attract migrants in this changing context.

This combination of push and pull factors accelerated the rural exodus. Rural-urban migration grew to 12.8 million people between 1960 and 1970 (equivalent to 33 percent of the population residing in rural areas in 1960) and to 15.6 million in the 1970s. This latter flow, similar in size to the total population of Australia or Czechoslovakia, equaled some 38 percent of the 1970 rural population. Despite the significant increase in rural-urban migration, it was only in the 1970s (when the natural increase had started to decline) that the rural population decreased from 41 million in 1970 to 38.6 million in 1980. By this time, the annual pace of out-migration (1.5 million migrants) was about one-third faster than the absolute natural increase (approximately 1 million persons per annum) of rural areas.

The number of cities increased to 257 in 1970 and 419 in 1980. Cities of 100,000 or more included some 43 percent of the total population in 1980 while rural areas accounted for only 32 percent of the total population. Although city growth rates do not show the systematic advantages of one or the other size class over the four decades, the most significant growth was occurring in the largest cities and metropolitan areas. Of the country's total increase of 25.9 million persons during the 1970s, 43.9 percent accrued to ten cities. The metropolitan area of Sao Paulo alone accounted for 17.2 percent of the country's total growth.

Migrations to the Agricultural Frontier

The same factors that stimulated rural-urban migration also promoted interiorization and occupation of new agricultural frontiers.[3] In the early 1930s, the rural labor force, freed by the bankruptcy of the coffee economy, spread in the direction of Parana. As agricultural prices recuperated in the late 1930s and 1940s, a large strip of fertile land in Parana, Santa Catarina, Sao Paulo, and Mato Grosso was invaded. Close to 400,000 migrants moved to rural areas of Parana alone during the 1940s (equal to some 13 percent of the country's rural-urban movements during this decade). During the 1950s, Parana absorbed some 800,000 rural migrants (12 percent of all rural-urban movements in that decade).

Migration to the Central Zone frontier (basically the states of Mato Grosso, Goias, and Maranhao) had begun slowly in the 1940s and grew rapidly in the 1950s. Unlike the Parana frontier, this movement was initiated spontaneously by subsistence farmers from the arid Northeast and overpopulated agricultural areas in the Southeast with little capital or technology. Several government enterprises, such as the construction of a new state capital city, stimulated the transfer of capitalist interests to this region and the concentration of land. The construction of a new nation's capital in Brasilia stimulated road-building between the Center-West and the Southeast as well as between Brasilia and Belem in the North. Regional development helped stimulate some 400,000 migrants to head toward rural areas in the Central Zone during the 1950s.

During the 1960s, these frontier movements quickly receded. The 1970s brought the largest government effort for the promotion and organization of frontier movements. The chosen area for large-scale colonization was the Amazon region. Plans proposing to relocate 1 million families were soon shelved, however, and the total number of persons who moved to rural areas in the vast Amazon region was probably less than 400,000. When compared to the 16 million persons who left the country's rural areas during the 1970s, this does not represent a relevant alternative to urban concentration. Moreover, it can be observed that a large number of the colonists who did settle in colonization projects or in other rural areas of the Amazon region tended to move on rather quickly. Even in the Amazon, cities now tend to grow much faster than rural areas. Thus, in the first two frontier phases, population growth was largely a rural phenomenon; by contrast, some 64 percent of Amazonian growth during the 1970s occurred in urban areas. Overall, frontier growth has practically played itself out as an alternative to urban concentration. The number of migrants attracted to frontier regions is progressively less meaningful in terms of population absorption. City growth is occurring at an increasing rate even within recent frontier areas. In short, the apparently contradictory trends that marked population redistribution within the last half-century are now converging toward urban concentration.

Interstate and Interregional Migration

To understand the implications of the two main redistribution trends discussed above, it is useful to classify states into (1) Older Areas of Settlement, (2) Stagnated Frontier Areas, (3) Current Frontier Areas, and (4) the Industrial Axis (Martine and Camargo, 1984a). Although this scheme is somewhat arbitrary (and leaves out the recently created Federal District), it provides a useful tool for understanding migration processes.

The Older Areas of Settlement are those areas occupied for extractive and agricultural reasons between the seventeenth and nineteenth century. With the exception of the land-bound state of Minas Gerais, all have populations concentrated near the coast. Although the urban areas have received large flows of in-migration, their net interchange of migrants with other states and regions has produced substantial deficits during recent decades. The two largest and most permanent providers of net out-migration to the rest of the country since 1940 are the states of Minas Gerais and those in the Northeast region. Both had a relatively large population in 1940 (Minas Gerais accounted for 16.4 percent, and the nine northeastern states for 32 percent of the nation's total population), but by 1980 these shares had dropped (to 11.2 percent and 25.6 percent, respectively). Other relatively prosperous states, such as Rio Grande do Sul, and Santa Catarina, have also suffered permanent net losses of out-migration, although on a smaller scale. Finally, the small state of Espirito Santo has also experienced permanent net losses (see Table 2.3).

The states in the Stagnated Frontier Areas category had large-scale frontier-oriented migrations from the 1940s until the late 1960s, mostly to rural areas.

Table 2.3
Net Interstate Migration Flows by Type of Region, 1940–80 (thousands of persons)

Type of Regions & States	1940-50	1950-60	1960-70	1970-80
Early Settlement Areas	- 944. 9	-2, 396. 6	-2, 759. 6	-2, 562. 5
Northeast Region	- 305. 8	-1, 543. 6	-1, 128. 3	-1, 872. 1
Minas Gerais	- 455. 0	- 550. 0	-1, 226. 5	- 520. 5
Espirito Santo	- 102. 0	- 45. 2	- 66. 6	- 24. 2
Santa Catarina	- 13. 5	- 77. 5	- 85. 2	- 29. 9
Rio Grande do Sul	- 68. 4	- 180. 2	- 252. 9	- 115. 8
Stagnated Frontier	558. 0	1, 489. 6	847. 5	-1, 511. 1
Parana	438. 6	964. 9	576. 6	-1, 326. 8
Mato Grosso do Sul	- 12. 2	111. 0	260. 2	112. 4[a]
Goias	124. 6	190. 0	136. 3	- 89. 0
Maranhao	7. 1	222. 7	- 125. 5	- 207. 7
Current Frontier	- 2. 2	9. 2	16. 0	763. 8
Northern Region	- 2. 2	9. 2	16. 0	587. 4
Mato Grosso	-	-	-	176. 4[a]
Industrial Axis	388. 9	767. 2	1, 626. 0	2, 980. 3
Sao Paulo	61. 9	309. 7	1, 050. 2	2, 637. 5
Rio de Janeiro	327. 1	457. 5	575. 8	342. 8
Federal District	-	130. 6	270. 2	329. 6

Note: Data refer to the sum of net interstate migration of the
states which make up the group.

a - Author's estimates

Source: IBGE, Censos Demograficos and Tabulacoes IBGE, Diretoria
Tecnica (DESPO), Rio de Janeiro, 1984.

These include Parana, as well as those in the Central Frontier Zone—Mato
Grosso do Sul, Goias, and Maranhao. Although migrations to agricultural areas
dwindled during the 1960s, these states experienced rapid growth in their towns
and cities. Thus, the net migration flow remained high except in Maranhao,
which was already experiencing an overall loss.

Perhaps the most striking feature of the data presented in Table 2.3 is the
reversal in migration patterns of the states in this group between the 1960s and
1970s. Despite rapid urban growth between 1970 and 1980, the net migration
flow of these previously flourishing frontier areas is now negative. For instance,
Parana state (whose capital, Curitiba, grew at an annual rate of 5.8%) went from
a positive net migration of 577,000 in the 1960s to a negative one of 1.3 million
in the 1970s. The reasons for this surprising and abrupt reversal are to be found

in the previously described modernization process, which was felt in all regions but had its greatest impact on the rich lands of Parana. But even in less densely settled areas such as Goias, Mato Grosso do Sul and Maranhao, the frontier has come to an abrupt end.

The Current Frontier Area is composed of states in the Amazon region. Government colonization projects designed in 1970 to drain off excess rural workers from other regions were soon shelved. Nevertheless, a combination of government propaganda and the aspirations of the land-hungry landless masses provoked sizeable migration flows to the Amazon region. It is estimated that the states in this area acquired close to 800,000 net migrants in the 1970s. Unlike earlier frontier regions, however, the majority of the migrants ended up in the towns and cities. There are already signs that the frontier cycle is closing rapidly in this area and that this region will soon become a net provider of out-migrants.

Finally, for the last fifty years, the states in the Industrial Axis have been siphoning off a large and growing number of migrants from the rest of the country. Moreover, the Rio-Sao Paulo axis has benefitted most from government efforts to promote industrial modernization since the 1950s. Within this axis, all indicators point to a growing polarization around the Sao Paulo nucleus. This is reflected in met migration data which show that Sao Paulo received 88.5 percent of the total net migration to this region in the 1970s, as compared to 15.9 percent in the 1940s. Growth of the Sao Paulo metropolitan region is particularly significant, as is the rapid growth of cities within a 200 km radius of this metropolis. A megalopolis is definitely in the offing.

THE "DETERMINANTS" OF MIGRATION

At the aggregate level, several studies carried out during the 1960s and 1970s attempted to relate regional and sectoral wage differentials and internal migration. Gian Sahota (1968), using an econometric model, measured the responsiveness of migration to differentials in earnings and other variables. In the same vein, Douglas Graham and Sergio Buarque (1971) estimated net migration for each state from 1872 to 1970 and found a significant association between relative state income and rates of migration. However, migration only began to reduce the differential growth between higher and lower income states after the 1950s. Lorene Yap (1973) used a macroeconomic model and demonstrated that rural-to-urban migration, despite its intensity, has had a positive effect on the growth and distribution of national product.

Several other studies based on aggregate data deal more specifically with the relationship between internal population distribution and urban growth. For instance, Milton Da Mata (1973) analyzed the association between transfers of population from rural-to-urban areas and differences in per capita income levels and different rates of growth of employment opportunities. Hamilton Tolosa (1973) considered the impact of internal migration on interregional and personal income distribution. He found that intraregional migrants tended to settle in small and medium-sized urban centers, whereas interregional movers went to larger cities and metropolitan areas.

Paradoxically, the historical-structuralist school also points out the functionality of the migration process but stresses the fact that it permits the maintenance of an abundant reserve of personnel for the urban-industrial society. The size and distribution of the population over space are held to reflect the evolution of economic organization. Hence, the structural changes that provoke the sectoral and spatial reallocation of economic activities are the principal determinants of the direction, intensity, and characteristics of internal migration (Balan, 1973; Lopes and Patarra, 1973). The marginalization of the migrant population is dependent on the need to maintain the availability of a large stock of workers. The appearance of huge slums on the urban periphery is the result of structural changes in places of origin and, more importantly, of the need to maintain a large supply of workers on call (Garcia Castro, 1979; Lopes, 1973; Singer, 1973).

Numerous research efforts have also attempted to analyze migration at the more local level. Space limitations allow only a partial listing of such studies. The first survey was that carried out by Bertram Hutchinson (1963). He examined the impact of varying historical contexts on the assimilation of migrants. Daniel Hogan and Manoel Berlinck (1973) took up this concern by looking at the differential migrant motivations by social status and the changing profile of job opportunities in the city of Sao Paulo. Jose Pastore's (1969) study showed that earlier arrivals to Brasilia generally enjoy a privileged situation by comparison to latecomers. A more recent study of intraurban mobility in Brasilia reveals the impact of government investments in housing and in the organization of urban space on the migrant's motivation (Paviani and Farret, 1987).

Janice Perlman's (1977) study of lower-class residents in Rio de Janeiro showed that a rather broad mixture of "push" and "pull" factors is necessary to explain the decision to migrate. A number of other microstudies (Brito and Merrick, 1974; Duarte, 1979; Silva, 1973) have examined other dimensions of migration at this level, and, in general, one can conclude that both aggregate and local surveys data show the predominance of economic motives of migration in Brazil. The end result of the various structural changes outlined in the previous section determines the specific forms in which they affect migration. It is generally impossible to determine the precise weight of each element in the chain of events leading to the actual decision to migrate, but their aggregate influence is unquestionable and verifiable in the varying mobility rates of different regions.

DEMOGRAPHIC AND SOCIOECONOMIC CHARACTERISTICS OF MIGRATION

Among the total lifetime intermunicipal migrants in 1980, the ratio of men to women was 0.968. This ratio was somewhat higher among migrants with ten or fewer years of residence (0.986) and much higher among lifetime migrants with a rural destination (1.119). Lifetime intramunicipal migrants to an urban destination had a sex ratio of 0.929. These ratios are in accordance with time-proven patterns according to which females find greater opportunities for employment in cities and men in frontier regions. Much the same patterns are found in the 1960 and 1970 census data.

Beyond being able to say that migrants generally tend to be older than non-migrants and that their dependency ratio tends to be much more favorable, generalizations about migration and age are more difficult to make. Migrations to metropolitan areas are concentrated in the 15 to 34 age groups and have a modal age of 20 to 24. Migrants to metropolitan areas in the North and Northeast tend to be younger than those in the Southeast (Minter, 1976). The southeastern metropoles attract migrants from all over the country, while local intrastate migrants predominate elsewhere. Thus, older migrants coming to Sao Paulo and Rio seem to reflect the selectivity of more experienced step migrants. At the other extreme, migrations to frontier regions are selective of male adults and family migrations. For instance, the 1980–86 SIMI data for Rondonia show that some 62 to 75 percent of all migrants were males. At the same time, the age distribution of the total migrant population is underrepresented at both extremes (0–14 and 50 and over) and bulges in the 20 to 39 age groups (Rondonia, 1980–86). Examination of the age-sex composition of migrants to Parana and Goias at the heyday of their frontier movements reveals similar patterns.

During the 1970s, the socioeconomic characteristics of migrants were the object of considerable study. The overwhelming thrust of this research, however, focuses on migrants *after* arrival. By comparing the characteristics of migrants to those of natives and appraising the changes in characteristics with duration of residence, these studies purport to show how well migrants fit into their new environments (Martine, 1979). Here we will focus only on migration to metropolitan areas since they represent some 36 percent of all lifetime migrants and one-third of all migrants who made at least one intramunicipal move during the last intercensal period. Their significance in the overall picture cannot be overestimated. Special tabulations from the 1970 census provide the basis for the following overview of such migrants.

It is commonly held that migrants are responsible for explosive urban growth and the accompanying social problems. By extension, such problems would be attributable to the inability of migrants to compete for productive employment. The data reveal a somewhat different picture. First, migrants constitute an inordinately high proportion of the economically active population (EAP) in metropolitan cities, making up 45 percent of the total population in the nine metropolitan areas (MAs) and 62 percent of their EAP. The proportion of active migrants is highest in the more dynamic industrial areas. Recent migrants, who supposedly contribute most to social problems, are surprisingly well represented in the EAP. Some 12 and 13 percent, respectively, of all working males and females in the nine MAs have been in the city for two or less years; the participation of this group is equivalent to one-third that of all natives (Martine and

Peliano, 1978, Chapter 1). These figures are influenced by the age composition of the migrant and nonmigrant populations. Migrants tend to have greater proportions in the 10 to 29 age categories and lower proportions attending school. One would expect that over time the lower schooling would lead to inferior occupational opportunities and income levels. The data show that this is not always true, however.

Educational achievement is systematically lower only among female migrants, with the more developed MAs in the Southeast region showing the greatest differences. Educational differences among women by migration status are indeed reflected in lower occupational and income levels. Migrant women begin working at much younger ages and are concentrated in domestic services. Migrants' participation in this category decreases rapidly with age but generally remains much higher than among natives. As will be seen below, this occupational specialization leads to lower income levels among female migrants.

The occupational structure of male migrants is not dominated by any such concentration. Nevertheless, a few significant patterns emerge, particularly when combined with duration of residence. The construction industry absorbs the greatest number of migrants in all MAs, and within it, unskilled construction workers dominate among recent migrants. Participation in this category recedes quickly with duration of residence. It seems that this physically strenuous, underpaid job is attractive to recent migrants because it is easiest to obtain. As soon as the recent migrants acquire further skills and contacts, they either move up to other occupations within the same industry or to other types of jobs. The services also attract a large number of migrants and help negate the commonly held view that the informal sector is more attractive to recent arrivals (Martine and Peliano, 1978, Chapter 2). As suggested above, a growing proportion of migrants are found in middle-level occupations as duration of residence increases. While this indicates that the occupational profile of male migrants improves considerably with duration of residence, whether it is attributable to upward mobility or selective remigration is less obvious.

Table 2.4 presents data on income by migration status for the economically active populations of Sao Paulo and Fortaleza, the richest and least developed areas, respectively, of MAs. Although the income level is clearly higher in Sao Paulo, it improves dramatically with duration of residence among both sexes for migrants. It is interesting to note, however, that in Fortaleza the reverse is true among male migrants while, among the female population, the situation of natives and total migrants is identical.

A review of migrant-native differentials for other areal units confirms the patterns noted above (Martine, 1979). More specifically, comparisons between natives and migrants were inconclusive, but migrants always improved drastically as length of residence increased. It has been suggested that "the significant improvement in the socioeconomic conditions of migrants by length of residence, observed in most Brazilian studies, is attributable in large part to the selective retention of the more privileged segments of the migrant population and

Table 2.4
Income Distribution of the Economically Active Population by Migration Status and Sex: Metropolitan Areas of Sao Paulo and Fortaleza, Brazil, 1970

(percent distribution)

I. Sao Paulo

Male cruzerio	Years Resident 0 to 2	3 to 5	6 to 10	11+	Total	Native
0 to 100	5	5	5	3	5	8
101 to 200	37	26	23	16	23	20
201 to 500	42	48	48	42	42	34
501 to 1000	9	13	15	26	19	23
1001 or more	7	8	9	13	11	15

Female

	0 to 2	3 to 5	6 to 10	11+	Total	Native
0 to 100	33	24	21	15	22	18
101 to 200	44	45	41	35	39	32
201 to 500	18	23	29	35	28	35
501 to 1000	4	6	7	11	8	12
1001 or more	1	2	2	4	3	3

II. Fortaleza

Male cruzerio	Years Resident 0 to 2	3 to 5	6 to 10	11+	Total	Native
0 to 100	35	24	21	17	21	40
101 to 200	42	46	44	40	41	35
201 to 500	14	21	24	26	24	16
501 to 1000	4	4	5	10	9	5
1001 or more	5	5	6	7	5	4

Female

	0 to 2	3 to 5	6 to 10	11+	Total	Native
0 to 100	81	68	58	50	61	62
101 to 200	15	24	27	30	27	26
201 to 500	3	5	11	13	9	9
501 to 1000	1	2	3	6	2	2
1001 or more	0	1	1	1	1	1

Source: Martine and Peliano, 1978

to expulsion of those less prepared to compete for the reduced number of employment opportunities in the urban labor market'' (Martine, 1979, 37).

With respect to the broader issues of repeat and return migration, duration-of-residence data show that migrants with two or fewer years of residence accounted for 28 percent of all intermunicipal migrants in 1960, 25 percent in 1970, and 23 percent in 1980. Migrants with up to one year of residence made up 13 percent, 12 percent, and 11 percent, respectively, of all migrants in each of these censuses. In short, recent migrants account for such a disproportionate amount of all migrants that their size can only be explained through high rates of repeat migration. One attempt to quantify this phenomenon concluded that "once the migratory process has been initiated, the probability that the migrant will move again is relatively high (58%), when compared to the equivalent probability among migrants who remain for more than a year in the municipality" (Gomes et al., n.d.). The prevalence of repeat migration has also been documented in a number of field surveys, whether in urban areas, modern agricultural regions, or frontier zones (Gonzales and Bastos, 1973; Mougeot, 1980; Silva, 1986).

Many researchers in Brazil have automatically associated repeat migration with return migration, but the two are clearly separate phenomena. The number and proportion of people who actually return to their place of birth is, according to aggregate evidence, relatively small. The 1980 census showed that only 7 percent of the migrant population were defined as return migrants, one-third of these having returned in the last two years. To what extent this is due to deficiencies in the data (since they only permit analysis of return migration at the level of the state of birth) or to the real difficulties of migrants in returning to their place of origin (either because of the distance factor or the scarcity of jobs) is difficult to determine.

In proportionate terms, the Northeast region had the greatest number of return migrants. A field study of five communities in the Northeast concluded that the majority were unsuccessful in their attempts to obtain better jobs; two-thirds had left home originally without a clear notion of the job market. Nevertheless, return migration is not linked to economic motives since the migrants are aware that the job market is even worse in the Northeast than elsewhere. The most common motives given for return migration were *saudades* (roughly "homesickness") and illness. In both cases this can be interpreted as a return to an established local network of relationships within which important problems have customarily been dealt with (Scott, 1986).

CONCLUDING REMARKS

We have focused on the broad historical changes that have occurred in Brazilian society over recent decades and on their impacts on the spatial mobility of population. In a country as diversified and dynamic as Brazil, the task of analyzing and summarizing such trends is not easy. Internal migration patterns, inasmuch as they constitute mainly a response to changes in the spatial distribution of economic opportunities, are at once the result and cause of development. Supposedly, migration leads to a more efficient economic and internal allocation of labor; however, cold figures on population redistribution belie considerable upheaval in the lives of millions of people. Moreover, the apparent rationality of the process is placed in doubt by the current convergence of the two traditional redistribution patterns into a marked tendency toward metropolitan and conurbation. These are some of the issues that public policy—whose role has only been indirectly mentioned here—will have to face with increasing vigor in coming years.

NOTES

1. The discussion of migration data is based on Carvalho (1985) and Martine and Camargo (1984b).

2. The following discussions are based largely on Martine and Camargo (1984a), Martine and Garcia (1987), Chapter 4 and Martine (1987). Supporting data and bibliography can be found in these studies.

3. This section on frontier expansion in Brazil summarizes a discussion found in Martine (1981, 1982, and 1987), which contains an extensive bibliography on this question.

REFERENCES

Balan, Jorge. 1973. "Urbanizacion, Migraciones Internas y Desarollo Regional." In CEDEPLAR—*Migracoes Internas e Desenvolvimento Regional,* Vol. 2. Belo Horizonte, Federal University of Minas Gerais.

Brito, Fausto, and Thomas Merrick. 1974. "Migrancao, Absorcao de Mao-de-Obra e Distribuciao da Renda." *Estudos Economicos* 4:75–122.

Carvalho, Jose Alberto. 1985. "Estimativas Indiretas e Dados sobre Migracoes: Uma Avaliacao Conceitual e Metodologica das Informacoes Censitarias Recentes." *Revista Brasileria de Estudos Populacionais* 2(1):31–74.

Da Mata, Milton. 1973. "Urbanizacao e Migracoes Internas." *Pesquisa e Planejamento Economico* 3(3):717–22.

Duarte, Renato. 1979. "Migration and Urban Poverty in Northeast Brazil." Ph.D. Thesis, University of Chicago.

Garcia Castro, Mary. 1979. "O Migrante na Cidade do Rio de Janeiro." M.A. Thesis, Federal University of Rio de Janeiro.

Gomes, L.C., N. do Valle, and A.C. Olinto. N.d. "Recupcracao de Informacao e Migracao." Mimeographed. Rio de Janeiro, FIBGE.

Gonzalez, Elbio, and Maria Inex Bastos. 1973. *Migracao para Brasilia.* Brasilia, University of Brasilia.

Graham, Douglas H., and Sergio Buarque de Holanda. 1971. *Migration, Regional and Urban Growth and Development in Brazil.* Sao Paulo: University of Sao Paulo, Instituto de Pesquisas Economicas (IPE).

Hogan, Daniel, and Manoel Berlinck. 1973. "Occupation, Access to Information and the Use of Urban Resources." Mimeographed. Liege: International Union for the Scientific Study of Population.

Hutchinson, Bertram. 1963. "Urban Social Mobility Rates in Brazil Related to Migration and Changing Occupational Structure." *America Latina* 6(3):47–61.

Lopes, Juarez Brandao. 1973. "Desenvolvimento e Migracoes: Uma Abordagem Historico-Estrutural." *Estudos CEBRAP,* Sao Paulo, October/December.

———, and Neide Patarra. 1974. "Redistribucao Regional e Rural-Urbana da Populacao Brasileira." *Cadernos CEBRAP,* no. 20.

Martine, George. 1979. "Migraciones Internas: Investigacion para que?" *Notas de Poblacion* 7(19):9–38.

———. 1987. "Migraco e Absorcao Populacional no Tropico Omindo." *Seminar on Technologies for Human Settlement in the Tropics.* Manaus, ECLA/IPEA.

———, and Liscio Camargo. 1984a. "Crescimento e Distribucao da Populacao Brasileira." *Revista Brasileira de Estudos Populacionais* (Sao Paulo) 1 (½):99–144.

————. 1984b. "Os Dados Censitarios sobre Migracoes Internas: Evolucao e Utilizacao." In ABEP, *Censos, Consensos e Contrasensos*. Ouro Preto, pp. 183–214.

————. 1986. "As Migracoes de Origem Rural numa Perspectiva Historica: Algumas Notas." *V Encontro da ABEP*, Aguas de Sao Pedro.

————, and Ronaldo Garcia. 1987. *Os Impactos Sociais da Modernizacao Agricola*. Sao Paulo: Editora Caetes/Hucitec.

————, and J.C. Peliano. 1978. *Migrants no Mercado de Trabalho Metropolitano*. Serie Estudos Para o Planejamento, no. 19.

————. 1981. "Recent Colonization Experiences in Brazil: Expectations Versus Reality." In Jorge Balan (ed.), *Why People Move*. Paris: UNESCO Press, pp. 270–92.

————. 1982. "Colonization in Rondonia: Continuities and Perspectives," In P. Peek and G. Standing (eds.), *State Policies and Migration*. London: Croom Helm, pp. 146–70.

Minter, M. 1976. *Mudancas na Composicao do Emprego e na Distribuicao da Renda: Efeitos Sobre as Migracoes Internas*. Ministry of the Interior, Brasilia.

————. 1980. *Sistema de Informacoes sobre Migracoes Internas*. Ministry of the Interior, Brasilia.

Mougeot, Luc. 1980. "City-ward Migration and Migration Retention During Frontier Development in Brazil's North Region." Ph.D. Dissertation, Michigan State University.

Pastore, Jose. 1969. *Brasilia, A Cidade e o Homen*. Sao Paulo: Companhia Editora Nacional.

Paviani, Aldo, and Ricardo Farret. 1987. *Mobilidade Residencial Intra-Urbana: O Caso de Brasilia*. Mimeographed. University of Brasilia.

Perlman, Janice. 1977. *O Mito da Marginalidade*. Rio de Janerio: Editora Paz e Terra.

Rondonia. *Boletim de Migracao*. 1980–86. Secretariate of Planning, Rondonia, Porto Velho.

Sahota, Gian. 1968. "An Economic Analysis of Internal Migration in Brazil." *Journal of Political Economy* 76:218–51.

Scott, R. Parry. 1986. "O Retorno ao Nordeste: Refugo, Familia e Reproducao." *Anais do V Encontro Nacional de Estudos Populacionais*, Vol. 2. Sao Paulo, pp. 665–723.

Silva, Lea Melo da. 1973. "Pesquisia de Fluxos Migratorios para Brasilia." In CEDEPLAR, *Migracoes Internas*, Vol. 1. Belo Horizonte, Federal University of Minas Gerais.

————. 1986. "Retencao e Selecao Migratorias em Rio Branco, Acre." In Luis Aragon and Luc Mougeot (eds.), *Migracoes Internas na Amazonia*, Cadernos NAEA, no. 8. Belem, pp. 182–219.

Singer, Paul. 1973. *Economia Politica da Urbanizacao*. Sao Paulo: Editora Brasiliense, Edicoes CEBRAP.

Tolosa, Hamilton. 1973. "Macroeconomia da Urbanizacao Brasileira." *Pesquisa e Planejamento Economico* 3(3):585–644.

Yap, Lorene. 1973. "Internal Migration and Economic Development in Brazil." Ph.D. Dissertation, Harvard University.

3

CANADA

Jacques Ledent

From the late seventeenth century to the early twentieth century, the growth and spatial distribution of the Canadian population were shaped by successive waves of European immigrants. For the last half century, however, internal migration has become more influential in determining spatial growth patterns.

According to preliminary estimates of the 1986 census, Canada had 25.3 million inhabitants. Virtually all of the population lives along the U.S. border, with larger concentrations in the two eastern provinces that were developed first historically—Quebec and Ontario. In 1986 these provinces contained 25.8 and 35.9 percent, respectively, of the national population. The westward movement of population, which began in the nineteenth century with the linkage of the Atlantic and Pacific by railway, continues today. By 1986 the two westernmost provinces (Alberta and British Columbia) had a combined share of 20.8 percent of national population.

DATA ON MIGRATION

The main source of information on internal migration in Canada is a question posed on the long census form about place (municipality) of residence five years before the census date.[1] The answers to this question enable the national statistical bureau, Statistics Canada, to tabulate—disaggregated by sex and age—how many people live in a spatial unit different from that inhabited five years earlier (with a possible breakdown by origin and/or destination). Such tabulations are routinely prepared—through proper spatial aggregation—in relation to (1) Canada's main political entities (municipalities, census divisions or counties, and provinces), and (2) some statistical units defined by Statistics Canada (metropolitan and nonmetropolitan areas). Additional tables are also established, using a special algorithm, with regard to an adequately defined urban-rural dimension.

Because it is taken only every fifth year, the census is of little help in assessing the cyclical evolution of internal migration. Fortunately, such an assessment can be made using annual migration data produced by Statistics Canada and based on two administrative files containing relevant geographical information.

Historically, the older of these two files is the family allowance file maintained by Health and Welfare Canada. Since 1956, this file has been used to compile changes of address reported by parents of children entitled to family allowances (all children ages 0 to 17). Recurring compilations allow Statistics Canada to produce yearly estimates of the number of interprovincial moves made by children and, using a system of ad hoc factors, of the corresponding numbers for adults.

The second administrative data file—which generates somewhat more comprehensive information on internal migration—is the income tax file maintained by Revenue Canada. Since 1976, Statistics Canada has used this file to compare the address reported in a given year by each tax filer to that reported in the previous year. This allows yearly estimates of intercounty movements (movements between census divisions) for tax filers and their dependents (about 90 percent of the population). Employing an indirect approach, these data are used to obtain sex- and age-specific (0–17, 18–24, 25–44, 45–64, and 65 and over) estimates.

The migration estimates from the family allowance file are in the count of moves that actually took place. By contrast, those from the income tax file and from the quinquennial census are in the form of transfers resulting from a comparison of addresses reported at two fixed points in time. The difference between such transfers and the underlying moves is, however, much less in the case of the income tax file than in the case of the census file, as the possibility of multiple moves is much less in a one-year interval than in a five-year interval.

Thus, the three data sources just described provide complementary insights into geographical mobility. Only in the case of interprovincial movements for the entire population can the two administrative data files be seen as competing. Because Statistics Canada (1987) recently concluded that the income tax estimates led to slightly smaller errors, Revenue Canada's taxation file has replaced the family allowance file as the source of official estimates of interprovincial movements. The family allowance estimates are still used, however, as preliminary estimates until the income tax estimates become available about twelve months later.

PRINCIPAL POPULATION MOVEMENTS

The National Level

Aggregate data drawn from the 1981 census[2] show that, out of 1,000 Canadian residents in 1981 who were also residents in 1976, 463 were *movers* (lived in a house in 1981 different from that inhabited in 1976), 207 were *migrants* (lived in a different municipality), and 53 were *interprovincial migrants* (lived in a different province). Comparison of these proportions with the corresponding ones drawn from three previous censuses—1961, 1971, and 1976—suggests (see Panel A of Table 3.1) that the historical increase in the proportion of movers and migrants stopped in the seventies. By contrast, the proportion of interprovincial migrants, which decreased somewhat between the late sixties and early seventies, increased substantially from the early to late seventies, to surpass its previous high of the late sixties and to bring the proportion of migrants who crossed provincial boundaries (or interprovincial migrant share) to slightly over one-fourth.

As suggested by Table 3.2A, the three migration proportions just considered display similar regularities over the age continuum. After an initial decrease, the curve depicting the age variations of each proportion drops to a minimum for the age group 15 to 19 and then increases sharply. It reaches a maximum for the age group 25 to 29, and then it levels off. This diagram does not present the actual values of the three proportions over the 1976–81 period but rather their standardized values.[3] Thus, in comparison to the total population, young adults (and their children) are more likely to change provinces than to change houses or municipalities, whereas the older population is more prone to change houses than municipalities or provinces.

The sex-specific figures displayed in Panels B–D of Table 3.1 suggest no sex differential, although males are perhaps slightly more prone than females to cross provincial boundaries. When the three sex-specific migration proportions are crossclassified by age (see Table 3.2B), substantial sex differentials appear. In particular, the proportion of movers and migrants is much higher for females than males among adolescents (15–19) and young adults (20–24).

Table 3.2C shows the age regularities of the proportion of migrants through time. Quite interestingly, for most age groups the levels are less in 1976–81 than in the 1971–76 and the 1966–71 periods. This observation can also be made in the case of the proportion of movers. Thus, it seems that the true propensity to become a mover or a migrant declined somewhat more significantly between the last two quinquennial periods than suggested by the small declines observed above. Although not shown here, the true propensity to change provinces increased in the late seventies to a level surpassing the previous high of the 1966–71 period.

Interregional Migration

Using data from the family allowance file,[4] Table 3.3A shows the annual changes registered over a twenty-five-year period (1961–62 to 1985–86)[5] in the interprovincial migration rate (ratio of all interprovincial moves to the population of the ten provinces). At first glance, the propensity to change provinces appears to have decreased over time. A simple linear regression of the logarithmic value of this rate against time confirms this (the t-ratio of the time variable has a -3.10 value), although the coefficient of determination is low (0.29). However, the

Table 3.1

Migration Proportions According to Type for the Two Sexes Separated and Aggregated: Various Quinquennial Periods

Period	Proportion of			
	Movers (1)	Migrants (2)	Interprovincial migrants (3)	Interprovincial migrant share (4)=(3)/(2)
A. Both Sexes				
1956-1961	0. 437	0. 177	0. 036	0. 203
1966-1971	0. 451	0. 206	0. 049	0. 235
1971-1976	0. 467	0. 224	0. 047	0. 208
1976-1981	0. 463	0. 207	0. 053	0. 253
B. Males				
1956-1961	0. 434	0. 175	0. 036	0. 206
1966-1971	0. 450	0. 205	0. 050	0. 243
1971-1976	0. 466	0. 225	0. 048	0. 213
1976-1981	0. 462	0. 209	0. 054	0. 261
C. Females				
1956-1961	0. 440	0. 179	0. 036	0. 200
1966-1971	0. 452	0. 208	0. 047	0. 228
1971-1976	0. 469	0. 224	0. 045	0. 202
1976-1981	0. 463	0. 207	0. 051	0. 244
D. Female to male ratio (C/B)				
1956-1961	0. 986	0. 978	1. 010	1. 033
1966-1971	1. 006	1. 013	0. 949	0. 936
1971-1976	1. 007	0. 998	0. 947	0. 949
1976-1981	1. 002	0. 988	0. 928	0. 938

Sources: 1956-1961: 1961 Census of Canada-Population sample – General characteristics of migrant and non-migrant population-Catalogue 98-509, Table I1

1966-1971: 1971 Census of Canada – Population-Internal migration – Catalogue 92-719 (Table 31).

1971-1976: 1976 Census of Canda-Population: Demographic characteristics-Catalogue 92-828 (Table 35).

1976-1981: 1981 Census of Canada-Population-Mobility status-Catalogue 92-907 (Table 1).

Table 3.2A
Standardized Migration Proportions by Age and Distance of Move, Canada, 1981

Age	Movers	Migrants	Interprovincial Migrants
5-14	.070	.071	.075
15-19	.055	.057	.063
20-24	.096	.108	.120
25-29	.119	.128	.139
30-34	.100	.106	.111
35-44	.069	.069	.073
45-54	.049	.047	.047
55-64	.042	.040	.032
65+	.041	.038	.026

Table 3.2B
Migration Proportions by Age, Gender, and Distance of Move, Canada, 1981

(female to male ratios)

Age	Movers	Migrants	Interprovincial Migrants
5-14	1.00	1.00	1.01
15-19	1.13	1.13	1.00
20-24	1.23	1.24	1.01
25-29	1.01	1.01	0.93
30-34	0.92	0.92	0.91
35-44	0.90	0.87	0.87
45-54	0.93	0.90	0.85
55-64	1.07	1.05	1.02
65+	1.10	0.98	1.03

Table 3.2C
Migration Proportions by Age, Canada, 1961, 1971, 1976, 1981

Age	1961	1971	1976	1981
5-14	.18	.20	.23	.21
15-19	.16	.18	.19	.17
20-24	.29	.35	.35	.32
25-29	.31	.38	.41	.37
30-34	.25	.31	.34	.32
35-44	.18	.20	.22	.21
45-64	.11	.12	.14	.11
65+	.10	.12	.13	.10

Sources: 1961, 1971, 1976 and 1981 Censuses of Canada

51

Table 3.3A

Interprovincial Migration Rate, Canada, 1961–62 to 1985–86 (rate per 1,000 persons)

1961–62	16. 0	1973–74	19. 2
1962–63	16. 6	1974–75	17. 9
1963–64	17. 1	1975–76	15. 8
1964–65	17. 4	1976–77	16. 5
1965–66	19. 0	1977–78	16. 7
1966–67	19. 8	1978–79	16. 1
1967–68	18. 3	1979–80	16. 9
1968–69	17. 0	1980–81	17. 9
1969–70	19. 2	1981–82	17. 8
1970–71	18. 4	1982–83	14. 6
1971–72	17. 8	1983–84	14. 9
1972–73	17. 1	1984–85	14. 6
		1985–86	14. 3

Table 3.3B

In-Migration Share of Selected Provinces, Canada, 1961–62 to 1985–86 (percent)

	Quebec	Ontario	Alberta	British Columbia
1961–62	15. 0	26. 0	15. 0	12. 5
1962–63	14. 0	27. 0	14. 0	13. 5
1963–64	13. 0	29. 0	13. 5	15. 0
1964–65	12. 5	29. 5	13. 0	16. 0
1965–66	12. 0	29. 0	12. 5	19. 0
1966–67	11. 5	29. 0	14. 0	19. 0
1967–68	11. 0	26. 5	14. 5	18. 0
1968–69	11. 0	27. 0	15. 0	18. 0
1969–70	9. 0	32. 5	15. 5	19. 0
1970–71	9. 0	32. 5	15. 0	18. 0
1971–72	10. 0	28. 0	15. 5	19. 0
1972–73	9. 5	25. 0	16. 0	20. 0
1973–74	9. 5	24. 0	16. 5	20. 0
1974–75	9. 5	21. 0	19. 0	19. 0
1975–76	9. 0	22. 0	20. 0	15. 0
1976–77	8. 5	24. 0	21. 0	15. 0
1977–78	6. 0	27. 0	22. 0	16. 0
1978–79	6. 5	24. 0	23. 0	17. 0
1979–80	6. 0	22. 0	25. 0	20. 0
1980–81	6. 0	20. 5	27. 0	19. 5
1981–82	6. 5	23. 0	28. 5	16. 0
1982–83	7. 0	27. 0	22. 0	15. 0
1983–04	8. 0	31. 0	16. 0	16. 5
1984–85	9. 0	30. 5	17. 0	16. 0
1985–86	9. 0	30. 0	19. 0	16. 0

Note: rounded to nearest one half of one percent

Source: Health and Welfare Canada, Family Allowance File

more impressive value (0.61) registered by the coefficient of determination obtained by substituting a quadratic for the linear expression function of time suggests that it is more likely that the interprovincial migration rate registered variations that followed an inverted U-shaped pattern. Because the highest rate appears to have occurred midway through the seventies, this is not contradictory to the pattern ascertained earlier from sparse census data. This pattern is consistent with W. Zelinsky's (1971) hypothesis that the historical increase in interregional migration does not continue indefinitely (Lee, 1966), but may stop owing to the substitution of information flows for migration and eventually leads to a reversal.

At a more disaggregated level (whether or not they have followed an inverted U-shaped pattern), the provincial out-migration rates have been oriented downward for some time (except for Alberta and British Columbia).[6] In addition, despite their somewhat different evolutions, they have registered ups and downs that correspond with the national business cycle. Thus, interprovincial migration seems to increase during periods of favorable economic conditions and decrease during periods of unfavorable conditions.

Although the destination choice patterns of interprovincial migrants should be analyzed separately for migration out of each province, some meaningful insights can be gained from examining the destination allocation of the entire "pool" of interprovincial migrants. Table 3.3B, which displays the annual variations in each province's in-migration share, shows:

1. The opportunities offered by the then booming exploitation of Alberta's natural resources rapidly increased this province's in-migration share from about 15 percent in the early seventies to 28.5 percent in 1981–82. This share dropped back rather quickly to its earlier level when Alberta's economic boom ran out of steam.

2. More or less stable during the first decade, the attraction which Ontario held for the other provinces declined steadily in the second decade before strengthening in the early eighties as Alberta's competitive position weakened.

3. British Columbia's in-migration share appears to have fluctuated more or less around a stationary level.

4. The attraction exerted by Quebec on all the other provinces decreased almost continuously over the sixties and seventies before reversing slightly in the early eighties.

Overall, the annual variations exhibited by the ten in-migration shares appear to reflect the differential evolution of economic opportunities. This is not always as clear as could be expected, however, as some in-migration shares, especially the one for British Columbia, show.

Migration Between Metropolitan and Nonmetropolitan Areas

According to the 1981 census, 797,460 persons who resided in a metropolitan area (CMA)[7] in 1976 lived in a nonmetropolitan area in 1981, whereas 736,915 persons who resided in a nonmetropolitan area in 1976 lived in a CMA in 1981. This resulted in a net loss of 60,545 persons for the existing set of 24 CMAs.

Any comparison of these transfers with those registered during the two previous quinquennial periods is hampered somewhat by the changing number of CMAs being considered. To circumvent this difficulty, Table 3.4 uses a constant

Table 3.4
CMA/Non-CMA Migration Flows and Propensities, 1966 to 1981, by Quinquennial Period

Period	Gross migration flows and propensities			CMA net inmigration flow
	Beginning-of-period residence	End-of-period residence		
		CMA	Non-CMA	
1966-1971	CMA[a]	501,080[c] (.0539)[b]	562,610 (.0606)	+121,340
	Non-CMA[a]	683,950 (.0846)	1,115,115 (.1379)	
1971-1976	CMA	529,115 (.0491)	780,310 (.0724)	-105,055
	Non-CMA	675,255 (.0777)	1,387,435 (.1596)	
1976-1981	CMA	656,370 (.0548)	803,495 (.0671)	- 68,795
	Non-CMA	734,700 (.0757)	1,350,825 (.1391)	

Sources: 1966-1971:   1971 Census of Canada - Population - Internal migration - Catalogue 92-719.
    1971-1976:   1976 Census of Canada - Population: Demographic characteristics - Mobility status - Catalogue 92-828.
    1976-1981:   1981 Census of Canada - Population - Mobility status - Catalogue 92-907.

Notes: a.   To facilitate comparison of periods, only the 22 CMAs in existence in 1971 (in their 1971, 1976, and 1981 limits, respectively) are considered here. (Oshawa and Trois-Rivieres which became CMAs in 1976 and 1981, respectively, are excluded).

    b.   The migration propensities in parentheses are defined as ratios of gross flows to corresponding beginning-of-period populations surviving to the end of the period in Canada. For the first two periods no adjustment is made to account for those people whose beginning-of-period municipality of residence is unknown.

    c.   CMA to CMA gross flows refer to transfers to another CMA (intra-CMA transfers are excluded).

set of 22 metropolitan areas in displaying the movements observed between metropolitan and nonmetropolitan areas during the last three intercensal periods.

Clearly, the redistribution of population owing to migration switched from a situation in which CMAs experienced a net gain of 121,340 persons in 1966–71 to one in which they registered a net loss of 105,055 persons in 1971–76. The latter trend continued from 1976 to 1981; however, the net loss was only 68,795 persons. Examination of the gross flows between the two types of areas suggests that the reversal in the net population exchange resulted from (1) an increase in the propensity of CMA residents to move to nonmetropolitan areas, and (2) a decrease in the proportion of nonmetropolitan residents who moved to CMAs. The reduction in the net loss to CMAs in the late seventies essentially resulted from a reduced attraction of nonmetropolitan areas to CMA residents.

WHO MOVES?

A number of different characteristics can be examined in an effort to determine who moves. We have already noted the importance of age in this sense, and it will be important for us to bear in mind that more or less significant mobility differentials observed for the whole population may conceal meaningful differentials of varying nature with age because (1) these cancel out at the aggregate level, or (2) the allocation of the population according to the alternative statuses varies somewhat substantially over the life cycle (especially in the case of marital status).

For each of the four characteristics considered here, possession of a given status is as of the census date—that is, after an eventual move has taken place. This must be kept in mind when trying to interpret the influence on mobility of personal factors that are prone to change over the life cycle (such as marital or activity status).

Marital Status

Divorced persons (regardless of sex and age) appear to be much more mobile than those who are single or widowed. Married people,[8] however, are even more mobile in the younger ages, whereas beyond age 30 they tend to have similar migration propensities as those who are single or widowed. This holds for all three migration types (see Table 3.5A for intermunicipal migration).

Mother Tongue

For this rather permanent characteristic—mother tongue[9]—migration differentials, while persisting across sex and age, vary somewhat according to migration type (see Table 3.6). In the case of a change of houses (see Table 3.6A), people in the three language groups have comparable migration propensities, even though people with English as their mother tongue are, in virtually all age

Table 3.5A
Proportion of Migrants by Age and Marital Status, Canada, 1981

Age	Single	Married	Widowed	Divorced
15-19	.15	.44	.13	.33
20-24	.24	.43	.29	.37
25-29	.30	.40	.31	.36
30-34	.26	.32	.30	.35
35-44	.18	.21	.20	.27
45-54	.12	.12	.12	.20
55-64	.11	.11	.12	.17
65+	.10	.10	.11	.15

Table 3.5B
Proportion of Migrants by Age and Education, Canada, 1981

Age	0-8 yrs	9-13 yrs	14+ yrs	University
15-19	.17	.16	.17	.17
20-24	.23	.29	.32	.32
25-29	.22	.30	.37	.48
30-34	.20	.26	.30	.39
35-44	.15	.19	.22	.26
45-54	.10	.13	.14	.17
55-64	.09	.12	.13	.15
65+	.09	.11	.12	.14

Table 3.5C
Proportion of Migrants by Age and Labor Force Status, Canada, 1981

Age	Employed	Unemployed	Not in Labor Force
15-19	.19	.18	.15
20-24	.32	.26	.30
25-29	.38	.36	.35
30-34	.31	.33	.29
35-44	.21	.24	.18
45-54	.12	.18	.12
55-64	.09	.16	.13
65+	.08	.14	.10

Source: 1981 Census of Canada

Table 3.6A
Proportion of Movers by Age and Mother Tongue, Canada, 1981

Age	English	French	Other
5-14	.50	.42	.44
15-19	.39	.33	.37
20-24	.66	.62	.56
25-29	.81	.78	.73
30-34	.68	.64	.65
35-44	.47	.46	.42
45-54	.32	.30	.30
55-64	.27	.27	.26
65+	.26	.28	.26

Table 3.6B
Proportion of Migrants by Age and Mother Tongue, Canada, 1981

Age	English	French	Other
5-14	.23	.18	.13
15-19	.18	.14	.12
20-24	.34	.28	.21
25-29	.39	.36	.28
30-34	.32	.29	.25
35-44	.22	.18	.17
45-54	.14	.10	.10
55-64	.12	.09	.09
65+	.10	.10	.08

Table 3.6C
Proportion of Interprovincial Migrants by Age and Mother Tongue, Canada, 1981

Age	English	French	Other
5-14	.07	.02	.03
15-19	.06	.02	.03
20-24	.11	.03	.05
25-29	.13	.04	.08
30-34	.10	.03	.07
35-44	.07	.02	.04
45-54	.04	.01	.03
55-64	.03	.01	.02
65+	.02	.01	.02

Source: 1981 Census of Canada

groups, slightly more mobile than those whose mother tongue is French or another language. In the case of a change of municipalities (see Table 3.6B), the differentials between the three language groups are more pronounced. The migration propensity of people with French as their mother tongue is intermediate between the higher propensity of those with English as their mother tongue and the lower propensity of those with neither English nor French. A similar picture emerges in the case of a change of provinces (see Table 3.6C), except that the relative positions of the two groups other than English are reversed. This results from the fact that the majority of French-speaking Canadians reside in just one province (Quebec) and are less inclined to leave it for the predominantly English-speaking rest of Canada.

Education Level

Mobility tends to increase with the number of years of schooling as illustrated by Table 3.5B. The magnitude of the differential separating the four educational statuses here varies greatly by type of migration. People who attended a university are about twice as likely to change houses, three times more likely to change municipalities, and about five times more likely to change provinces than those with eight years of schooling or less. Because of the more or less permanent nature of this characteristic (after normal education is completed), the above results tend to persist across age and sex.

Activity Status

For this characteristic, Canadians do not display strikingly different mobility behavior. Yet, as suggested by Table 3.5C, people in the older age groups who are unemployed have a comparatively higher propensity to change houses, municipalities, or provinces. Interestingly, a comparison of the two sexes suggests that the higher mobility of young female adults (especially in age group 20–24) results from a comparatively higher mobility propensity of females who are not in the labor force (as well as from the comparatively higher proportion of females as against males who are not in the labor force). But as is the case with marital status, the true influence of activity status on geographical mobility may be blurred by the likelihood that a movement is linked (as a cause or a consequence) to a change in activity status.

WHY PEOPLE MOVE

With no comprehensive migration survey knowledge of the reasons why Canadians move, information is gleaned almost exclusively from the numerous econometric studies that focus on interprovincial (intermetropolitan) migration. On the whole, these studies show that migration is responsive to economic incentives. In seeking to increase their well-being, people tend to move to other provinces to obtain (1) higher wages and employment opportunities (Courchene, 1970; Grant and Vanderkamp, 1976) and (2) higher unemployment benefits and lower taxes (Shaw, 1985; Winer and Gauthier, 1982).

They move, however, only when the potential payoffs they can secure in terms of private incomes and public (fiscal) benefits offset their relocation costs, including the psychic costs incurred in leaving behind family and friends. Thus, distance, a proxy for such relocation costs, appears to be, without exception, a significant deterrent of interprovincial migration. Perception of relocation costs, however, depends on an individual's personal characteristics and tastes, so that the responsiveness of migration to economic incentives depends on the composition (age, ethnic/cultural background, and province of birth) of the population at risk of migrating (Liaw and Ledent, 1987).

Clearly responsive to economic factors, interprovincial migration is also influenced by noneconomic factors. Canadians tend to move to provinces with a milder temperature (than their own), a similar ethnic composition, and a similar culture/language (Liaw and Ledent, 1987). There is a presumption that the role of such noneconomic factors may be increasing because, with rising real incomes, people can afford to pay more attention to quality-of-life factors in their decision to migrate (Ledent and Liaw, 1985). This supports P. Shaw (1985) who, in a study, found that the influence of traditional economic (employment-related) factors on migration is decreasing.

CONSEQUENCES OF MIGRATION

Economic Consequences

Migration has proceeded from declining to expanding regions.[10] Presumably, this process helps reallocate labor from regions of excess demand and reduce unemployment to regions of excess supply, while wages (and thus incomes) tend to become more equal. The evidence of the last four decades, however, shows fairly persistent income disparities between provinces, with considerable year-to-year fluctuations. Yet there has been a trend toward a narrowing of wage differentials and a widening of unemployment disparities.

Several migration-related factors may account for the persistence of such income and unemployment disparities:[11]

1. Migration is not exclusively economically determined. The migration of students, retirees, and civilian and military transferees can be influenced by noneconomic factors.

2. Migration has inevitable costs, and persons disenchanted with the payoffs of their move may move again, often back to their province of origin.

3. Migration may involve a lag process; potential migrants may react slowly to changes in economic conditions.

4. Migration may have destabilizing effects because of its selective character.[12]

Nevertheless, even if the role of migration in achieving regional balance is questionable, it has tended to equalize the wage and employment opportunities of individual labor market participants (Grant and Vanderkamp, 1987, 11).

Social and Political Consequences

Examination of the destination allocation of each province's out-migration flow suggests that Ontario is a watershed in the sense that Canadians rarely cross this province to go east or west.[13] Rather, they tend to move within the eastern or the western provinces but not between them. Ontario, however, bridges the country as its out-migrants are bound to the east and the west in similar proportions (although the western proportion is slightly higher). Thus, "population redistribution does not serve to allow the inhabitants of the various regions of Canada to get to know each other (but) Ontario acts as a kind of hinge in the nation's social exchanges" (Beaujot and McQuillan, 1982).

A significant political consequence of migration is reflected in the allocation of seats in the federal parliament, which is in theory related to the provinces' respective shares of the national population. Because internal migration has in the recent past been responsible for an increase in the combined share of the two westernmost provinces and a decrease in the Quebec share, it has undoubtedly contributed to the growing political strength of the west as opposed to the east and to the political unrest that was prevalent in Quebec during the seventies.

NOTES

1. One in five respondents filled out this form in the last three censuses.

2. The corresponding results from the census completed in 1986 were not available at the time this chapter was prepared.

3. These standardized values were obtained by dividing each actual value by a weighted sum of the relevant age-specific proportions, where the weights are the widths of the various age groups considered.

4. This subsection draws heavily on Part A of Ledent and Liaw (1985).

5. Each annual period $(t, t + 1)$ refers to a fiscal year beginning June 1, year t, and ending May 31, year $(t + 1)$.

6. An inverted U-shaped pattern was observed for five provinces (Newfoundland, Quebec, Ontario, Manitoba, and Saskatchewan) and a monotonic decline for three others (Prince-Edward Island, Nova Scotia, and New Brunswick).

7. A CMA is an area with an urbanized core of 100,000 inhabitants or more.

8. People who are engaged in consensual (not legalized) unions are considered by Statistics Canada as being married.

9. According to the 1981 census, the distribution of the Canadian population by mother tongue is: English (60.8 percent), French (25.6 percent), and other (13.6 percent).

10. This subsection draws heavily on Grant and Vanderkamp (1987).

11. Aside from such migration-related reasons, other reasons for the persistence of such differentials include: slow reaction of employers to excess supplies of labor, wage rigidities, and existence of public policies that tend to favor declining regions. (The

generosity of the unemployment benefits distributed by the federal government appears to retard migration out of the depressed areas in the eastern provinces.)

12. Because of the selectivity process of migration, regions that are net gainers (losers) through the migration exchange gain (lose) people who are younger, better educated, and earn higher incomes. In other words, migration brings about a favorable (unfavorable) change in the socioeconomic composition of the population in the advantaged (disadvantaged) regions. Thus, at first glance it can be seen as the basis for perpetuating regional disparities. But this conclusion is doubtful, as there exists rather sketchy evidence of a direct link between possession of propitious traits with higher productivity or greater entrepreneurship.

13. This subsection draws heavily on Beaujot and McQuillan (1982).

REFERENCES

Beaujot, R., and K. McQuillan. 1982. *Growth and Dualism—The Demographic Development of Canadian Society*. Toronto, Ontario: Gage Publishing Co.

Courchene, T.J. 1970. "Interprovincial Migration and Economic Adjustment." *Canadian Journal of Economics* 3:550–76.

Grant, E.K., and J. Vanderkamp. 1976. *The Economic Causes and Effects of Migration: Canada, 1965–1971*. Ottawa, Ontario: Information Canada (for the Economic Council of Canada).

———, and J. Vanderkamp. 1987. "The Role of Migration in Balancing Regional Supply and Demand Discrepancies." Discussion Paper on the Demographic Review. Ottawa, Ontario: Institute for Research on Public Policy.

Ledent, J., and K.L. Liaw. 1985. "Interprovincial Migration Outflows in Canada, 1961–1983: Characterization and Explanation." QSEP Research Report No. 141. Faculty of Sciences, McMaster University, Hamilton, Ontario.

Lee, E.S. 1966. "A Theory of Migration." *Demography* 3:47–57.

Liaw, K.L., and J. Ledent. 1987. "Nested Logit Model and Maximum Quasi-likelihood Method—A Flexible Methodology for Analyzing Interregional Patterns." *Regional Science and Urban Economics* 17:67–68.

Shaw, P. 1985. *Intermetropolitan Migration in Canada: Changing Determinants over Three Decades*. Toronto, Ontario: New Canada Press.

Statistics Canada. 1987. *Population Estimation Methods, Canada* Catalogue 91-528E. Ottawa, Ontario: Supply and Services Canada.

Winer, S.L., and D. Gauthier. 1982. *Internal Migration and Fiscal Structure: An Econometric Study of the Determinants of Interprovincial Migration in Canada*. Ottawa, Ontario: Supply and Services Canada (for the Economic Council of Canada).

Zelinsky, W. 1971. "The Hypothesis of the Mobility Transition." *Geographical Review* 61:219–49.

4

CHINA

Sidney Goldstein and Alice Goldstein

The Chinese government's modernization goals and its concerted efforts to control population growth through its one-child family policy have received worldwide attention. Less well known is the considerable attention given to problems related to the rural-urban distribution of population, to the relations between migration on the one hand and employment opportunities and rural-urban development on the other, to the rates of urban growth, and to the efforts by policy makers to control population distribution and migration as part of the broader efforts at central planning and development.

Few definitive national data sets on migration in China since the establishment of the People's Republic in 1949 have been available to the researcher. This situation derives in part from the decentralized nature of the statistical record-keeping system and in part from the sporadic way in which such records were kept. Especially during the Great Leap Forward (1958–60) and the Cultural Revolution (1966–76), considerable disruption occurred in the collection of statistics and their reporting to a central authority. In addition, because migration in China is specifically defined and controlled in terms of the household registration system (as will be detailed below), data collection efforts on migration beyond registration statistics were of little interest to policy makers and researchers until the early 1980s, for two reasons: (1) policy makers considered that since migration was being controlled, there was no need to study it and (2) it was assumed that the registration statistics could be used to provide whatever information on migration was desired, at least at the local level. For these reasons, too, the 1982 census did not ask any direct questions related to migration. As a result of this lack of data, no full agreement exists among experts on the volume and character of migration.

The researcher interested in such migration must therefore rely on relatively localized data and some limited information available from the census. This chapter will briefly review some of the evidence available from diverse sources—

the 1982 census, studies based on registry samples, surveys of migration in specific locations, and general surveys with a migration component. In order to fit the findings from these studies into a national framework, it is necessary, first, to review some of the general information trends since 1949 and to discuss the state's policies on migration as they had evolved by the 1980s and how they are carried out. Because the primary goal of China's migration policies is control of city growth, the primary focus of the following brief review will be on migration in relation to urbanization and industrialization.

DATA ON MIGRATION SINCE 1949

Much of traditional migration in China involved movement from the densely populated eastern coastal regions to the northeastern provinces, particularly Heilongjiang, and to the border regions, especially Inner Mongolia and Xinjiang. These streams continued after 1949, as peasants continued to move from over-crowded, limited lands to seek new areas for cultivation (Ma Xia, 1987). Both Heilongjiang and Inner Mongolia estimate that their populations were each increased by about 5 million persons through in-migration. Migrants to the northeast were predominantly young, single males; they evidently planned to establish themselves and obtain land before returning to their place of origin to find a bride and bring a family to their new homes. In Inner Mongolia, in-migrants participated in expanding cultivation to 40 to 50 million mu of land (1 mu $=$ $\frac{1}{15}$ hectare).

Rural-rural migration thus continues to play a role in affording opportunities for livelihood to peasants. The amount of cultivable land still unused is rapidly shrinking, however, and concerns regarding ecological damage are being voiced (*China Daily*, December 16, 1985). A much more important migration stream in China, from the point of view of modernization, is that going from rural to urban places.

In the years immediately following the communist accession to power in 1949, the government sought to stabilize the economy and stimulate industrialization. Rapid urbanization was seen as necessary, and city population grew rapidly. By 1953, China's urban population of 78 million was already one-third larger than it had been in 1949 (State Statistical Bureau, 1983, 103–4). Much of the growth was due to rural-to-urban migration as peasants heeded the call to assist in reconstruction and industrialization. Some of the rural-urban migrants were also cadres whose service in the army and whose communist allegiance qualified them to assume leadership roles in the cities (Liu, 1987, 47–48).

The First Five-Year Plan (1953–58), with its clear urban bias, coincided with the collectivization of agriculture and culminated in 1958 with establishment of the commune system. Together these caused massive rural dislocations (Orleans, 1982). Peasants flocked to the cities, despite a directive issued as early as April 1953 which tried to control rural outflow by establishing departments to centralize the hiring of peasants (Liu, 1987). In the next few years, other attempts were made to control rural-urban migration, including travel restrictions and grain rationing in cities (Chang, 1979). Still the rural outflow continued. By 1956, the pressures on cities caused by rural in-migrants were so great that millions were mobilized (especially youths) to move from cities to the countryside, and a series of laws were passed in an attempt to stem the flow into cities (Sit, 1985,11).

In 1958, with the initiation of the Great Leap Forward (1958–60), all controls were abandoned as the government attempted to accelerate industrialization. The rush to the cities was so great that the rural labor force was reduced by an estimated 23 million and crops were left unharvested (Xue, 1982). Some attempts were made to reduce cityward migration and send newly recruited workers back to the countryside. It was not until the collapse of the Great Leap Forward that urban growth was halted. By then the urban population had increased to 131 million, or 19.7 percent of the total population (almost double the 10.6 percent urban in 1949).

After 1960, millions of urban residents were relocated to villages, so that over a period of about four years, the urban population declined. With the onset of the Cultural Revolution (1966–76), school graduates and intellectuals were encouraged, sometimes forcibly, to settle in the countryside. In addition, thousands of youths roamed the nation in response to the doctrine that the more places visited, the more "revolutionary" the individual (Liu, 1987). With controls on migration abandoned, many undoubtedly were drawn to urban residence (cf., Sharping, 1987, 103–4).

In 1976, a change in leadership ended the Cultural Revolution and its attendant chaotic mobility. Gradually, rusticated youths and others returned to their cities of origin. Rural-urban migration as well as natural increase continued to contribute to a steady increase in the urban population. By 1980, 191.5 million persons lived in urban places.

Attempts to measure the extent of net rural-urban migration during 1949–81 and its relative contribution to urban growth (Sit, 1985) must be viewed as very crude, given the approximate character of both the basic population data and the estimates of natural increase, and the fact that the migration estimates represent residuals. The estimates suggest that from a high of 14 million net, accounting for 70 percent of the 20 million increase in urban population between 1949 and 1953, migration's role declined to a net of only 9 million during 1953–57, equivalent to only 42 percent of total growth in the four-year interval. The voluminous exodus of the 1957–63 period, approaching a net loss of 36 million according to these estimates, not only wiped out the natural increase of 18 million, but also reduced the urban population by another 18 million. A substantial part of this loss was, in turn, canceled by a net in-migration of some 16.5 million persons in the next two years, making migration four times more important than natural increase in urban growth.

Thereafter, instability continued to characterize urban growth. The effect of the Cultural Revolution is evidenced in a net loss through migration of almost 5 million, reducing the estimated 23 million urban natural increase of the period by about one-quarter (26.9 percent). The pendulum swing following the Cultural Revolution manifests itself in a return to the post-Great Leap Forward importance of migration in urban growth as population movement again accounted for over 80 percent of urban growth in the period 1978–81.

Overall, for the period 1949–81, Victor Sit reports that on balance, migration was responsible for only 20 percent of the urban population increase in China, but this net masks vastly larger streams of in- and out-migration, many of them representing responses to government policies outlined above. Since then, government policy has continued to affect urban growth rates, manifesting itself differentially by city size, as later analysis of registry data will illustrate.

MIGRATION AND URBANIZATION

As in other developing countries, cities exert considerable attraction for China's rural population. Substantial differences characterize the quality of life between urban and rural places, despite ostensible efforts to reduce them. Higher incomes, better housing, sanitation facilities, educational opportunities, more varied entertainment, and greater availability of consumer goods all have provided convincing stimuli for a shift from village to city. Furthermore, at least until the mid-1980s, the difference in ownership systems that characterizes urban and rural places (Davis-Friedmann, 1983, 18–19) had meant that urban job security has been more stable; a wide range of benefits have also been associated with urban employment in state-owned enterprises. Some of these conditions are changing as a result of economic liberalization in China, which allows greater freedom in organizing production and in management, and provides opportunities for higher income, especially in rural areas. Nonetheless, the attraction of urban places for peasants is likely to remain strong.

Of the 1 billion persons enumerated in China's 1982 census, 206 million were living in its 236 cities and 2,664 other urban places. Its 20 percent level of urbanization is thus somewhat lower than that of developing countries generally (30 percent in 1980). But the number of people living in China's urban places is greater than the total population of all but three countries in the world. Moreover, the situation is particularly challenging from a policy perspective because almost 800 million persons still live in rural areas and are largely engaged in agricultural activities. Because of the rapidity with which change is occurring and because of the vast size of the rural population, the Chinese recognize that efforts to modernize the country must sooner or later involve the absorption of several hundred million peasants into nonagricultural activities and possibly into urban places.

Policies on Urbanization

Given this situation, the government has become especially concerned that the too rapid growth of big cities could give rise to many problems affecting housing, employment, and services. Past policies failed to cope adequately with city development and urban population growth, and often had a clear urban bias (Kirkby, 1985). By 1982, the urban population was disproportionally concentrated in cities of 1 million or more, and the "super cities" like Shanghai and Beijing were experiencing acute infrastructure strains. (For a full discussion of China's urban structure as documented by the 1982 census, see Goldstein, 1985.)

Chinese policy makers maintain that the number of big cities and the size of their population need correction. Accordingly, they have developed a basic urban policy of (1) strictly limiting the size of big cities; (2) properly developing medium-size cities (those of 200,000 to 500,000); and (3) encouraging the growth of small cities and county towns. As part of this policy, since about 1982 the government has also fostered the growth of small marketing centers and other rural locations that are not classified as urban. Policy makers hope that these places will eventually form the nuclei of towns and small cities, providing alternative urban centers for the absorption of surplus rural population.

Controlling Permanent Migration

Paralleling the urban policy and closely tied to it is its migration policy. The government's position states that migration, especially to urban places, must be compatible with economic development (Yeh and Xu, 1984). Specific principles have been developed to meet these goals: (1) rural-to-urban migration must be strictly controlled, especially movement to China's three municipalities; (2) movement from towns to cities, from small to big cities, and from rural places to suburbs must be properly limited; (3) movement between places of similar size does not need control; (4) movement from larger to smaller cities or from urban to rural places should be encouraged. (A detailed discussion of migration policies is presented in Goldstein and Goldstein, 1985.)

The major mechanism used to regulate population movement is the household registration system. It both defines and attempts to control permanent population movement. Each individual has an official place of residence. To effect a permanent change in residence, permission must be granted by the appropriate authorities in the place of origin and/or destination. Movement within a given location is unrestricted.

Within the workings of this system, migrants are defined as those persons who have legally changed their registration from one place to another. Such legal change in domicile has been closely integrated with job placement, housing, and rationed foodstuffs, especially grains and edible oils. Until the 1980s, an individual could obtain grain only from the place of official registration. Even if a peasant moved to an urban location for a period of time, without an official change in registration, he or she had to obtain the grain supply from the commune of origin. With the introduction in 1979 of the economic responsibility system in rural areas and the encouragement of private enterprise, grain and other foods have become available through private outlets (although at somewhat higher prices). One of the major deterrents to migration is therefore being removed, and, as later discussion shows, migration outside the legally sanctioned registration system has increased considerably.

Responsibility for issuing permits to transfer household registration rests with a large number of work units and government bureaus. Some centralized control is exercised by the city Public Security Bureau, but only for checking the validity of credentials, not for restricting the number of migrants. Thus, the manner in which the control is exercised does not insure coordination among the varying agencies authorized to issue permits, nor does it allow for easy achievement of any specific goal.

The organization and operation of the registration system can be exemplified by the process in Weifang, a medium-sized city in Shandong Province (Interviews with city officials). In urban places, every household has a household registration book. In rural areas,[1] the individual cards of all village members are centrally held. Single workers or cadres (administrators and officials at all levels) who live in their work units use a collective household registrar. A household registrar is created when a new household is established or moves into the community. The household registrar includes records of births, deaths, in- and out-migration, and changes in marital status, occupation, and education.

Implementation of the registration system to control urban growth varies somewhat from one area to another, but the criteria established in Weifang are generally similar to criteria reported in other cities:

1. Persons may obtain urban registration if they are nonagricultural workers or cadres assigned to work in the city. The families of such workers may move with the transferees only if they already have urban registration.

2. University graduates automatically receive urban household registration and are usually assigned by the state to work in urban places.

3. Persons who have worked in other cities and are retired and who have family members living in Weifang may join their families.

4. Workers and cadres who have been assigned jobs in mountain or border areas for a specified time or who have jobs that require considerable moving about may move to Weifang once their assignments are completed if they already have relatives (spouse, parents, children, siblings, grandparents) living in the city.

5. Demobilized soldiers and criminals may return to Weifang if that is their city of origin.

Temporary Mobility

The household registration system was designed primarily to control permanent relocation. It works somewhat more erratically for temporary migrants. If an individual plans to stay in an urban place for three days or more, whether for business, family visit, entertainment, or education, temporary registration is required. A temporary registration is valid for only three months and must be renewed through reapplication.

The requirements are not always rigorously enforced, nor is careful attention given to the length of time that an individual remains at a destination, provided the individual does not become a burden on the community. A "temporary" stay may last a year or more. No central reporting of temporary migrants is required such as is collected monthly for permanent moves. Data may be obtained from hotels, work units, and neighborhoods. But not all units are covered, and data are seldom gathered regularly. Furthermore, the statistics from the various sources are not routinely collated. In order to fill this important data gap, city officials are increasingly conducting special surveys to allow them to estimate the number of temporary migrants in their jurisdiction.

Casual, spontaneous movement, involving sojourns from a few days to several years, has been a feature of Chinese life to varying degrees from long before the current regime (Skinner, 1987). While it was severely curtailed with the institution of the commune system in 1958 (Griffin, 1984), it has been increasing as a result of the new agricultural policy—the responsibility system—introduced in 1979. Because the new policy places a premium on individual initiative and more efficient production, a large number of peasants are no longer needed in the production of basic crops.

The system has therefore created a substantial increase in rural surplus labor, compounded by the entrance into the labor force of youths born during earlier periods of high fertility. The reforms have also diversified rural production, thus creatig a need for expanding markets, and have increased rural income, leading to greater consumer demand. At the same time, the number of free markets and the demand for services of all sorts (repair workers, tailors, barbers, nursemaids, housekeepers) have grown greatly in urban places, as has the need for construction and other unskilled workers. The cities have tried to upgrade the quality and quantity of their housing, to improve infrastructure, and to raise the quality and variety of their food supply. These developments have spurred the movement of thousands of people from rural to urban areas. Most come on a temporary basis (i.e., without changing their registration status), but their duration of residence in the city may vary from a few hours or days to several years. (For a fuller discussion of temporary mobility, see Goldstein and Goldstein, 1985.)

MOBILITY AS DOCUMENTED BY THE 1982 CENSUS

As discussed above, an individual is officially a permanent migrant only if a move involving a change in household registration is made. Persons living in cities who are not de jure residents are not counted in the city population in enumerations based on household registers. Since de facto residents of cities may be numerous and have different characteristics from de jure residents, their omission from urban registers distorts data on the size and composition of urban places and rural areas.

Given the controls that the registration system exercises, Chinese authorities saw no need to include a question on migration in the 1982 census. Yet, recognizing that the registration system could yield misleading results, China's 1982 census identified and counted as residents persons who had been living in a given locality for more than one year, even though they were registered elsewhere, as well as persons residing in the locality for less than one year. Persons who went from rural places to a city or another county temporarily for work or other activities and who came back frequently were enumerated in their place of household registration.

The census therefore classified each household member in one of five categories of residence: (1) residing and registered in the locality (individuals who had been away from their place of registration sporadically or for less than one year were included here); (2) residing in a locality for more than one year but registered elsewhere; (3) residing in a locality for less than one year but absent continuously from the place of registration for more than one year; (4) living in a locality at the time of the census but not having a settled registration status (this category includes such persons as demobilized soldiers waiting for job assignments, students, and ex-criminals, and may also include persons missed by the registration system entirely); and (5) originally having lived in a locality but abroad at the time of the census for work or study and therefore without registration. Unfortunately, to date, no tabulations have been made available on the characteristics of the populations included in these groups.

Of the 1.002 billion persons enumerated by the census (excluding military personnel and the populations of Taiwan, Hong Kong, Macao, and Tibet), 98.9 percent (990.7 million) were living in their place of registration (State Statistical Bureau, 1985, Appendix 4). Of the remainder, 6.4 million persons were residing in places where they had lived for more than one year without permanent registration and 4.8 million reported residence with registration still to be settled. Only a smaller number (210,000) were reported as residing in the particular location at which they were enumerated but absent continuously from their legal place of registration for more than one year. Still fewer (57,000) were reported as living overseas.

Thus, China has a substantial number of mobile persons, even though they constitute a small proportion (about 1 percent) of the total population. Many more were mobile: Some had officially changed their place of registration. Others, who had been away from their place of registration intermittently or for less than one year and who had not changed registration, were counted as living at place of origin and were not identified as migrants.

Census data on population mobility are very incomplete. Information on migration, either permanent or temporary, must therefore emanate from registry data for individual localities, statistics gathered in the relatively few surveys that have focused on migration, and impressions gained from interviews with officials and local authorities.

INSIGHTS FROM POPULATION REGISTERS

Household registration statistics on migration are often maintained at the city level by the Public Security Bureaus. Used to help monitor city growth, these statistics are often simple counts of the number of in- and out-migrants in any given year or aggregations over several years. While data on the characteristics of migrants are on the records, they are not generally included in available tabulations. In some instances, however, studies using samples drawn from the registration records have undertaken some analysis of migrant characteristics (Wei, 1984; Yang, 1986). They suggest that, despite the controls imposed, migration accounts for an important segment of growth in some cities, but that its importance tends to vary inversely with city size. Data from two cities, Beijing and Weifang, can illustrate the point.

Citywide Migration Levels

Since 1949, migration has played a variable role in the growth of Beijing (Wei, 1984). During the 1950s, migration was 50 percent more important than natural increase, partly reflecting policies during the Great Leap Forward favoring big city growth. This relation changed dramatically in the 1960s when out-migration far exceeded in-migration; both economic readjustments and the turmoil of the Cultural Revolution, with its emphasis on the rural sector, were factors in the turnaround. The reestablishment in the 1970s of less disruptive policies, and a focus on economic construction and on resumption of higher education in the capital, once again have led to net migration constituting a substantial part of total growth. Since 1970, net migration has accounted for between 40 and 44 percent of Beijing's population increase. These net rates mask considerable fluctuations in the gross numbers. During the first six months of 1983, for example, 102,000 persons migrated to the capital and 43,000 persons left. Given the municipality's population (9.3 million), this represented a net migration rate of 6.3 per 1,000.

A somewhat different picture emerges for Weifang, Shandong Province—a medium-sized city of almost 400,000 persons, where the available data cover a five-year period. Although the Public Security Bureau reportedly limited in-migration rigidly, migration accounted for an important segment of the city's growth. Of the 49,000 persons permanently added to the household registration, 17,500 were through natural increase and 31,700 through net migration (the result of 61,600 moving in and 29,900 moving out). Weifang's rate of migration gain therefore accounted for almost two-thirds of the total growth (Interview with city officials, 1983). A large part of the movement (in and out) was motivated by economic considerations (primarily job assignments and transfers) and educational factors. Some was also related to family reunification in connection with retirement or disability, marriage, and rectification of forced moves during earlier periods. The relatively heavy in-migration clearly accounts for some of the substantial growth of this medium-sized city over the five-year period compared to the lower rate of growth in the much larger city of Beijing. That the numbers involved are not greater in either city can be attributed to China's urban growth policy as it works through the registration system.

Provincial Migration Patterns

The household registration system can also be used to provide information on migration at the provincial level. To do so, the registers must be sampled in locations throughout the province, since generally detailed information on migrants is not centrally available. Such samples will, of course, provide insights into rural-to-rural movement as well as into migration involving urban places as origin and/or destination.

One study now underway, using a sample of registration records in Zhejiang Province, can serve as an illustration (Yang, 1986). Zhejiang is an east coast province that had a population of 38.8 million in 1982. In 1985, the registries of 20 urban and rural locations were sampled to identify persons who had officially changed residence in 1984 by moving across a township, town, or city boundary. Since the sampling ratios varied by urban-rural type of location, for analytic purposes the data on the 323,228 sampled persons have been weighted to reflect the distribution of population among cities, towns, and rural places. The weighted data are used in the text. The numbers are equivalent to about 5.5 percent of the total population in each residence category.

Indicative of the relatively high level of mobility despite the fairly stringent controls exercised (and recognizing that these data do not include any temporary movers), 2.1 percent of the weighted sample qualified as migrants, having either moved within, into, or out of the province during 1984. Distance played a key role in migration: only 11 percent of the in-migrants to urban places had come from another province; 89 percent of the moves involved migration within the province.

The population redistribution did, however, have an important differential impact on cities and towns. In the urban places in the sample 19,412 persons (based on those whose urban and rural origin is known) were classified as in-migrants and 8,761 were identified as out-migrants, most of them to other urban places in the province. In all, therefore, the sampled urban places gained 10,651 persons in 1984. However, whereas cities gained, on balance, at a rate of 18.1 per 1,000 in one year, the towns gained 23.2 per 1,000. Both of these comparatively high growth rates contrast sharply with the 5.7 per 1,000 loss experienced by the small number of rural townships sampled.

The considerable shift in rural-urban population in Zhejiang resulting from migration is also documented by comparison of the origins of the sampled migrants. The city samples lost 644 persons in their exchange with other cities and towns not included in the sampled locations. A considerable proportion of these were earlier migrants who had completed their education and were returning home or moving to take jobs. However, the sampled cities gained 7,321 persons from rural areas. Thus, all the migration gain experienced by cities was from rural in-migration. Similarly, migration to towns was heavily rural in origin. Of the 3,975 migrants netted by towns, most of which was for work-related reasons, 3,606 or 90.7 percent came from rural places.

These numbers mask the extent of the rural-urban shift. Only 231 persons were recorded as going from cities to rural areas, and only 662 went to rural places from towns. The urban-rural exchange was, therefore, virtually unidirectional from rural to urban, but more so in the case of the cities. In all, some 11,820 persons moved from rural-to-urban locations, but only 893 moved in the reverse direction, and about three-fourths of these left towns. Furthermore, the movement recorded in the sampled townships of the province indicated net losses about equally divided between other rural places and urban locations. On balance, therefore, a population shift occurred to urban places, accompanied by a small decline in the rural population.

SURVEYS AS SOURCES OF MIGRATION DATA

Official records do not provide the in-depth information needed for a thorough study of migration. Records do not identify those persons who have not officially changed their household registration—the temporary migrants—nor do they contain information on the broader spectrum of individual and household characteristics. Unfortunately, surveys on migration have been relatively rare. Once policy makers, planners, and scholars became sensitive in the mid-1980s to the key role of population redistribution in attempts to modernize, more surveys focusing on migration were initiated. In addition, general surveys, designed to focus on topics other than migration, have also yielded some insights on population mobility. This review will first turn to such general surveys.

The Guangzhou and Shanghai Surveys

Since 1985, a series of omnibus surveys designed to obtain information on consumer behavior in various Chinese cities have been undertaken by NSO/SRG International Research. For the 1986 Guangzhou and Shanghai surveys, arrangements were made to include three census-type questions on migration: (1) "In what province, municipality, or autonomous region were you born?" (2) "In what province, municipality, or autonomous region were you living 5 years ago, on May 1, 1981?" (3) "Was the place where you were living 5 years ago a city, a town, or a commune?" The information from these questions was analyzed in conjunction with data on basic characteristics of migrants and nonmigrants (Goldstein and Goldstein, 1986).

The samples of 1,000 individuals age 15 and over in each location were chosen on the basis of the household registration records and therefore include only de jure residents. Coverage included the inner city and the suburban counties, and the samples were weighted to approximate the age and sex distribution of the universe. In addition to collecting information on migration, the surveys also ascertained respondent's age, sex, education, labor force status, occupation, personal and family income, living arrangements, and role in household decision making.

The surveys reveal that very little migration had taken place to these two large cities between 1981 and 1986. Only 1.5 percent of Guangzhou's population and

2.8 percent of Shanghai's reported moving into the respective cities as registered residents. This is in sharp contrast to the levels of migration covering earlier periods as indicated by answers to the question on province of birth. Largely reflecting the heavy development of industry in Shanghai during the 1950s and 1960s, one-third of the municipality's 1986 population reported having been born elsewhere in China. By contrast, only about 5 percent of Guangzhou's population was born in another province. Most of its growth from migration must have come from within its own province of Guangdong. Since Shanghai is a municipality and does not have its own province, migration to it is, by definition, interprovincial. These data confirm the earlier observation that, on a de jure basis, China has been successful in recent years in controlling migration to its million-plus cities. If temporary residents had been included in the samples, the migration patterns would undoubtedly have been very different.

Lifetime migrants are differentially distributed by a number of variables, compared to nonmigrants. One-third of all men and women born in the province (nonmigrants) were between 15 and 24 years of age, compared to only 8 percent of the lifetime migrant men and 3 percent of the women. By contrast, 45 percent of all the male migrants and half of all the women migrants were 55 years and older, in comparison to only 11 and 13 percent, respectively, of the nonmigrants. Clearly, the major contribution by migration to the growth of Shanghai and Guangzhou was made decades ago. This is reinforced by the evidence on age differentials based on residence in another province five years earlier. For males and females, the percentage of migrants did not exceed 4 percent of the population in any age group. Moreover, in the ages 15 to 24, which tend to be the peak migration ages in most countries, the percentage was zero for males and only 0.5 for females.

Among recent migrants, males outnumber females by 38 percent, whereas among the nonmigrants the sex ratio is virtually balanced at 102.3. The favored position of males may reflect priorities given to labor force members with particular skills, as suggested by the particularly high sex ratios of migrants in the 25 to 44 age group, 216.1 (compared to 108.5 in the nonmigrant population). In part, the sex ratios may reflect the policy of allowing return migration at the time of retirement: The sex ratio of migrants 55 and over (postretirement for most) is 130.4, compared with only 85.1 among nonmigrants.

Clearly, therefore, these exploratory data suggest the value of questions on lifetime and recent migration and indicate that the patterns observed (despite the small number in some cells) are consistent with policies designed to control both urban growth and permanent migration. The value of these data argues for inclusion of similar or modified questions in other omnibus surveys and in the next Chinese census. Concurrently, larger samples to insure inclusion of a greater number of recent migrants are needed, as are questions on reasons for movement. Even more important is the need to include temporary migrants in the samples since temporary, rather than permanent, migration now seems to constitute the major mechanism through which movement to big cities occurs.

The Shanghai Survey of Temporary Migrants

In an attempt to assess the extent and character of temporary migration in Shanghai, researchers at Fudan University turned to a variety of data sources to identify such migrants (Zheng et al., 1985). For purposes of their study, they defined a temporary migrant as "someone who lives inside the inner city of Shanghai at the time of the survey, does not have a registration card for Shanghai residence, and is engaged in social and economic activities."

Four sources of data were used:

1. A sample household survey was undertaken, with August 11, 1984, as the reference point and all interviews completed within two days of that date. Every household in the forty-six sampled neighborhoods was interviewed. The survey indicated that 338,000 temporary migrants were residents in local households on August 11.

2. To augment the survey, a complete census of all hotels was undertaken, yielding an additional 125,700 temporary migrants. Sample counts were also taken of hotels outside the inner city of Shanghai to identify migrants who were staying at places in nearby towns but whose activities took place mostly inside the city. Most of these were peasants who came from other provinces to sell their agricultural and side-line products. About 20,000 were estimated to fall in this category.

3. Temporary migrants who were living on boats as crew or boat people were also included. An estimated 19,000 such temporary migrants were identified.

4. Finally, estimates were obtained on a residue group consisting of construction workers (66,000) who reside in temporary worksheds, peasant traders (2,500) who sleep in the free markets, and transients (1,200) who use the facilities at bus and train stations for shelter.

These temporary migrants were seen as benefitting both themselves, through their exposure to modern urban ideas and values, and Shanghai's population, by providing services and helping to increase the size of the city's consumer market. They may also be contributing to the transformation of the rural labor force from agricultural to nonagricultural workers; even if they return to their rural origins, they are unlikely to resume agricultural work. At the same time, however, the heavy influx of these persons into Shanghai (and other cities) was regarded as having negative consequences by adding to urban congestion, straining urban services, and increasing crime and accidents.

The fairly "loose" definition of temporary migrant allowed for inclusion of persons staying in Shanghai for a range of purposes and various durations. Of those residing in households, 33 percent were in the city five years or longer and 49 percent for a year or longer. Only 3 percent had been resident in Shanghai less than a week. Were it not for the fact that their temporary status depended on lack of Shanghai registration, a large percentage of these migrants would qualify as "permanent" residents under criteria employed by other countries.

Shanghai is not the only destination for temporary movement. Reports indicate that Beijing has to cope with an estimated 1 million transients (*China Daily,*

March 24, 1987) from all regions of the country. Of this number, some 60 percent come to engage in some form of economic activity. They work mostly in service and retail trades and in construction. The construction activity alone absorbs an estimated 200,000 temporary migrants. Another 50,000 are women who have come to the capital to serve as housekeepers. Among those who come to the city to work, more than half come from rural places (*China Daily*, July 19, 1986), and an equally large percentage expect to stay more than three months.

Although the nation's largest cities are clearly very attractive destinations for temporary migrants, cities of all sizes attract such persons. One Chinese researcher has estimated that the temporary population of some cities may equal 10 to 20 percent of the resident population (Banister, 1986, 10). The free markets have especially served to accelerate such mobility since most are served by peasants from the countryside. Although such vending may often entail daily commuting from nearby rural areas, in many instances vendors, especially those selling staple goods or rare items, may come over long distances and stay in the market for months at a time.

The Chinese Academy of Social Science (CASS) Migration Surveys

There is no doubt that China's "floating population" is increasing, raising the country's level of urbanization and creating important links between city and country. Under a policy that encourages "leaving the land but not the village," temporary migration is also helping to solve the problems of surplus rural labor. Chinese scholars and officials are coming to recognize that the data needed to evaluate the extent of such mobility and its impact have not been adequate. They have also become aware of the need for more in-depth evaluation of permanent migration, including the extent and nature of such migration to towns under the policy that is encouraging small-town growth. How permanent migration relates to both temporary mobility and economic development is a critical issue for research.

In response to the need for a better data base, in June 1984 the Population Research Center of the Chinese Academy of Social Science, with support from the United Nations' Fund for Population Activities (UNFPA), organized a workshop to explore ways to undertake surveys to assess the extent and patterns of migration, including temporary mobility. The workshop developed a series of test surveys in selected cities, towns, and villages to assess the extent of different forms of movement and the characteristics of movers. Evaluation of the pilot surveys and a series of planning sessions undertaken during September to December 1986 by thirteen participating provincial academies and three universities. In all, 29,900 households in seventy-two cities and towns in sixteen provinces were surveyed. Analyses of the data are currently underway.

The five component parts of the survey questionnaire indicate the population groups covered: (1) permanent residents; (2) in-migrants since 1949, with or without registration but living in a location more than one year; (3) earlier out-migrants who have returned after being absent more than one year; (4) temporary residents, that is, those not registered locally and living in a location less than one year; and (5) out-migrants since 1949 or since the household was established, who have not returned. The survey thereby provides the basis for identifying and assessing the migration status of all household members since 1949.

For each household member, standard information on sociodemographic characteristics was obtained, including relationship to head, age, sex, place of birth, urban-rural status, nationality, marital status, fertility, education, occupation, type of ownership (state collective or private), and income in 1978 and 1986. For in-migrants, information was ascertained on place of birth, type of origin, age at move, education and occupation at time of move, reasons for move, and comparative evaluation of conditions before and after the move. For return migrants, the information collected included frequency of moves since 1949 which involved an absence of one year or more, as well as absences during 1986 that extended over one or more days. The dates of last move (for long and short term), destinations, and reasons for move were ascertained. Temporary migrants were classified by duration of residence along with socioeconomic characteristics, origin, date of in-migration, and reasons for move. Finally, for out-migrants who had not returned, information was collected on socioeconomic characteristics at time of out-migration, destination and date of move, and reasons for move.

Although not constituting a representative national sample, the CASS study is the most comprehensive effort yet undertaken in China to assess migration in relation to urbanization. Coming during a period of major economic changes, the results of the survey should provide important insights into the success of efforts to control the growth of big cities and to foster the development of smaller ones and especially of towns. In this context, the emphasis given to both permanent and temporary migration should be particularly valuable in indicating the comparative reliance on these different forms of population mobility for coping with economic change, and the extent to which individuals with different socioeconomic characteristics are involved in one or the other. The fact that the surveys were conducted in 16 provinces should enhance the value of the study by allowing assessment of provincial and regional differences in patterns and the ways in which these relate to variations in development level, nature of the urban hierarchy, and composition of population.

Other Migration Studies

Individual researchers have undertaken studies with more localized coverage than CASS to gain some insights into various migration streams and types of movement. Because of space constraints, only two will be discussed.

In order to assess migrant and ethnic integration in minority regions of China, a survey was undertaken in rural Chifeng, Inner Mongolia, in 1985 (Ma, 1987).

Containing three types of economy—agriculture, mixed agriculture/animal husbandry, and animal husbandry—Chifeng is representative of many areas in the frontier minority regions which are potential areas of resettlement for persons from more densely populated areas. The Chifeng study evaluated four dimensions of adjustment: (1) satisfaction with present residence, (2) income improvement through migration, (3) friendship patterns, and (4) neighborhood patterns. The socioeconomic differentials between migrants and natives were examined, as were language use and intermarriage between Han migrants and Mongolian natives, the two major ethnic groups in Chifeng. School and residential segregation patterns were also examined.

The survey collected information from 2,089 households in the sample area. Of these, 43 percent had one or more migrant members. The results suggest the following: Pursuit of higher income has been the most important motivation for migration since 1949. Migrants and natives have similar patterns of education, occupation, and income. Migrants whose moves were arranged by the government earn less than their native neighbors because they live segregated from native villages, and income differentials among the residents resulted mainly from differences in economic activities and related price changes. Residential segregation between Han and Mongolians in Chifeng is not high within villages but relatively high between villages; more school than residential segregation exists because of language differentials. Intermarriages constitute 14 percent of the total marriages of interviewed household heads. The relative size of the ethnic group and ability to speak the other group's language are suggested as the most important factors affecting integration.

This study also suggests that rural-rural migration will remain at a low level, whereas rural-town migration may increase in the near future; government projects promoting rural-rural migration will not be feasible because of natural limitations (especially land quality and water supply) in the frontier areas. As the first survey on migrant and ethnic integration undertaken in Inner Mongolia, the study suggests that the relationship between Han and Mongolians is generally good, but some issues need to be resolved. A parallel study in Xinjiang Province is now being launched.

Marriage Migration in Sichuan

A different type of study has been undertaken in Dabao, a rural area in Sichuan Province, near the provincial capital of Chengdu (Wang, 1985). Designed to assess the extent and characteristics of "marriage migration" in the period 1980–82, this study relied on registration data for its information source. The underlying thesis of the research was that women use marriage as a way to achieve financial betterment. According to Chinese regulations, a woman can migrate only if marriage occurs first. Even within these constraints, not all marriages can result in migration since movement is also restricted from rural-to-urban places and from small to big cities. Therefore, most marriage migration that can occur must be rural-to-rural, urban-to-urban, or from large to medium or small cities or to rural places. Urban-to-rural migration rarely occurs. Since the Dabao study was undertaken in rural places, the observed marriage norms still played a key role in influencing marriage decisions.

Of 227 marriages in Dabao in 1980–82, 102, or 45 percent, involved migrant brides; by contrast, only 3 of the grooms were migrants. The heavy influx of brides is in large measure a function of the heavily unbalanced sex ratios in the area. During 1980–81, the sex ratio among single males age 20 and over hovered at about 180. The full reasons for this imbalance are not clear, but may include the out-migration of females for marriage and for work elsewhere. What the marriage migration data do suggest is that heavy reliance was placed on migration of females to mitigate the negative effects of the highly distorted sex ration.

Evidently, one side effect of this migration was, in turn, to create imbalances in areas of origin: The movement tended to follow a pattern of chain migration— with brides arranging for relatives and friends also to marry men in Dabao— which was an attractive proposition because of the better economic conditions in Dabao compared to origin. Indeed, the problem was sufficiently serious to lead the local governments to consider restricting such movement to avoid creating serious sex ratio imbalances at origin. To the extent that such marriage migration is widespread in rural China, the phenomenon would be similar to extensive female migration in other Asian countries (e.g., India) for purposes of marriage (Bose, 1980).

THE FUTURE OF MIGRATION RESEARCH IN CHINA

In sum, the Chinese situation with respect to migration statistics and the role of migration in population redistribution is clearly unique. The major role of government policy in controlling urban growth, and doing so through control of migration, greatly restricts the extent of legal migration that involves a permanent change in registration. Operating under the assumption that the controls had been effective and that the registration system provided whatever information was needed to ascertain the volume and characteristics of migrants, China did not include direct questions on migration in any of the three censuses undertaken since 1949.

Yet, throughout this period, and especially during the Great Leap Forward and the Cultural Revolution, massive movements of population occurred, although a considerable part of the redistribution was canceled by return migration in the "postcrisis" periods. Most recently, and beginning almost concurrent with the 1982 census, introduction of the responsibility system in rural China has led to sharp changes in occupational activities and has compounded the impact of population increase on the creation of rural surplus labor. This, in turn, has given rise to increased recognition of the possible role of population movement in achieving a more favorable equilibrium between population distribution and economic opportunities.

Interest in migration has skyrocketed as attention has focused on (1) the development of towns and small cities as "absorption centers" for rural surplus labor and (2) the growing reliance on temporary migration. Temporary migration is seen as a way of meeting both the labor force needs of bigger cities while controlling pressures on their infrastructure, and the desire of many rural residents to live in cities, often in order to make a livelihood through market and service activities. Concurrently, the unbalanced distribution of China's population between its eastern seaboard provinces and its border regions may argue for concerted efforts in the decades ahead to resettle millions of persons in the less developed and more heavily minority areas (Fei, 1984).

In response to these varied problems associated with surplus labor, urban and rural development, population density, and maintenance of good minority relations, the last five years have witnessed a striking increase in scholarly and official interest in migration statistics and a growing recognition of the possible need to reassess policies with respect to population movement.

Indeed, a recent news report (*China Daily*, May 15, 1987) indicates that the question of how better to use the surplus labor has become a major question. Recognizing that present city facilities and services are inadequate to meet all the demands of their residents, the symposium assessed alternative ways to cope with the surplus rural labor. All seemed to agree that one way was to build small towns or satellite cities and to develop rural industries. Others, however, maintained that, as long as the migration was congruent with economic needs, rural workers should also be allowed to come into the cities as a way of helping to eliminate "segregation" between cities and rural places and enhancing the economies of both. Still a third view holds that migration to the city was a self-regulating process in that, should overurbanization occur as a result of pressures on employment and infrastructure, many migrants would return voluntarily to their rural homes.

The increased consideration being given to alternative policies is a healthy development. The efforts to pursue research on the topics are encouraging for what they portend about the future volume and quality of data on population movement in all its forms. Indeed, if current lines of inquiry continue, China could ultimately have one of the more sophisticated sets of migration statistics, judged by the coverage of different forms of movement and the ability to relate them to the social and economic characteristics of movers and of their places of origin and destination.

Indicative of the increasing recognition of the importance of population redistribution to China's overall development efforts, the middecade census undertaken in China in 1987 (it was, in fact, to be a 1 percent survey) included a migration component. Questions on the rural-urban character of previous residence, duration of residence, and reasons for movement were asked. Mobility was based on de facto residence and not on registration status. The data collected in this survey thus provide a comprehensive picture of migration in China and allow for analysis of migration differentials at the national, regional, and provincial level. Inclusion of such questions at middecade augurs well for attention to migration in the 1990 census round. The nation will thereby obtain the information needed for local areas of all sizes and locations to be able fully to assess the relation of population redistribution to urban and rural development efforts, as well as to other demographic processes and to changes in socioeconomic and demographic composition.

Clearly, a decennial census will not be sufficient, because of the limited attention it can give to migration and because of the pace at which changes in patterns are likely to occur. The need for large surveys, such as that initiated on an exploratory basis by CASS, will therefore persist, parallel to or integrated with the large-scale fertility studies already completed and in process (China Population Information Centre, 1984; Coale, 1984). In any case, the current efforts to develop and test different research designs, definitions, and measures of population movement should greatly enhance China's ability to assess the relations between migration and development and lay a firm basis for future research on the topic. In so doing, China may well, in turn, make major contributions to the development of more sophisticated methods for measuring and assessing migration in other developing countries.

NOTE

Partial support for this research from the William and Flora Hewlett and American Express Foundations is acknowledged with deep appreciation.
1. In China, cities typically include some rural areas (counties) in their jurisdiction.

REFERENCES

Banister, Judith. 1986. *Urban-Rural Population Projections for China*. CIR Staff Paper No. 15. Washington, D.C.: Center for International Research, Bureau of the Census.

Bose, Ashish. 1980. *India's Urbanization: 1901–2001*. 2nd rev. ed. New Delhi: Tata McGraw-Hill.

Chang, Parris H. 1979. "Control of Urbanization: The Chinese Approach," *Asia Quarterly*, pp. 215–28.

China Daily
    May 15, 1987. "Labourer Influx Cited."
    March 24, 1987. "Transients Pack Populous Capital."
    July 19, 1986. "Outsiders Swarm into the Capital."
    December 16, 1985. "Migration to Northwest Has Limits."

China Population Information Centre. 1984. *Analysis on China's National One-per-Thousand-Population Fertility Sampling Survey*. Beijing: China Population Information Centre.

Coale, Ansley. 1984. *Rapid Population Change in China, 1952–1982*. Washington, D.C.: National Academy Press.

Davis-Friedmann, Deborah. 1983. *Long Lives: Chinese Elderly and the Communist Revolution*. Cambridge, Mass.: Harvard University.

Fei Xiaotong. 1984. "Frontier Development, Training, and Usage of Human Mental Resources." Unpublished paper, Beijing University, Beijing.

Goldstein, Sidney. 1985. *Urbanization in China: New Insights from the 1982 Census*. Paper No. 93. Honolulu: East-West Population Institute, East-West Center.

————, and Alice Goldstein. 1986. Unpublished tabulations, Brown University, Province, R.I.

————. 1985. *Population Mobility in the People's Republic of China*. Paper No. 95. Honolulu: East-West Population Institute, East-West Center.

Griffin, Keith (ed.). 1984. *Institutional Reform and Economic Development in the Chinese Countryside*. Armonk, N.Y.: M. E. Sharpe, Inc.

Kirkby, Richard J. R. 1985. *Urbanization in China: Town and Country in a Developing Economy, 1949–2000 A.D.* New York: Columbia University Press.

Liu Gang. 1987. "Labor Mobility in Greater Beijing: A New Pattern of Urbanization." Unpublished thesis, Department of Sociology, Brown University, Providence, R.I.

Ma Rong. 1987. "Migrant and Ethnic Integration in Rural Chifeng, Inner Mongolia Autonomous Region, China." Ph.D. dissertation, Department of Sociology, Brown University, Providence, R.I.

Ma Xia. 1987. "Internal Migration in China During the Past Three Decades." Unpublished paper, Population Research Center, Chinese Academy of Social Sciences, Beijing.

Orleans, Leo A. 1982. "China's Urban Population: Concepts, Conglomerations, and Concerns." In *China Under the Four Modernizations*, Part 1, Selected Papers submitted to the Joint Economic Committee, 97th Congress of the United States. Washington, D.C.: U.S. Government Printing Office, pp. 268–302.

Sharping, Thomas. 1987. "Urbanization in China Since 1949—Comment." *China Quarterly* 109:101–9.

Sit, Victor F.S. 1985. "Introduction: Urbanization and City Development in the People's Republic of China." In Victor F.S. Sit (ed.), *Chinese Cities: The Growth of the Metropolis Since 1949*. New York: Oxford University Press.

Skinner, G. Williams. 1987. "Mobility Strategies in Late Imperial China: A Regional Systems Analysis." In Carol A. Smith (ed.), *Regional Analysis*, Vol. 2, *Socio Systems*. New York: Academic Press, pp. 327–64.

State Statistical Bureau (SSB). 1985. *1982 Population Census of China*. Beijing: State Statistical Publishing House.

————. 1983. *Statistical Yearbook of China 1983*. Hong Kong: Economic Information and Agency.

Wang Xiaogao. 1985. "Marriage Migration in Dabao Rural Area, Peng County, Sichuan Province." Unpublished paper, Department of Sociology, Brown University, Providence, R.I.

Wei Jinsheng. 1984. "Internal Migration of Beijing, the Capital, Since the Founding of the People's Republic of China." Paper presented at International Symposium on Population and Development, Beijing, December.

Xue, Mu Qiao. 1982. *Current Economic Problems in China*. Boulder, Colo.: Westview Press.

Yang, Xui Shi. 1986. "Migration in Zhejiang Province." Unpublished paper, Brown University, Providence, R.I.

Yeh, A. G., and Xu Xueqiang. 1984. "Provincial Variation of Urbanization and Urban Primacy in China." *Annals of Regional Sciences* 18 (November):1–20.

Zheng Qizhen, Guo Shenyang, Zhang Yunfan, and Wang Jufen. 1985. "A Preliminary Inquiry into the Problem of Floating Population in Shanghai City Proper," *Population Research (Renkou Yanjui)* 3:2–7.

5

ECUADOR

Diego Palacios

Population redistribution in Ecuador since 1950 has largely been influenced by the transformation and modernization of agriculture, and the commercial cycles of the export economy. Population redistribution resulted in rapid urban growth and concentration in the two principal cities, Quito and Guayaquil, and in some secondary urban centers. Since the 1970s, the eastern provinces (the Oriente) have received a significant flow of migration with the rise of the petroleum industry and a vast colonization zone. Urban-to-urban migration has been the largest flow, followed by the rural-to-urban stream. Only in the Oriente region has rural-to-rural migration remained important.

DATA ON MIGRATION

Traditionally, the basic source of migration data has been the census. The first national enumeration was carried out in 1950, and data were aggregated at the provincial level. Age, sex, marital status, language, education, and place of birth data were recorded. The lifetime migration data referred to the province of birth and the province of residence at the time of the 1950 census. Migration data were published for only two provinces (Pichincha and Guayas) where Quito, the capital, and Guayaquil, the second city, are located.

The second census was taken in 1962 when, for the first time, migration data were tabulated for the province of previous residence and the province of residence in 1962. The census also presented the age and sex characteristics of the migrants and the duration of current residence.

The third census (1974) presented data on urban and rural residence, and included data on children ever born. Migration data were gathered using previous and 1974 provinces of residence, and these were classified by rural and urban residence. Place of birth and province of enumeration data were also published. In the 1982 census basically the same data on migration were collected, but this census did not present information on the duration of residence crosstabulated by urban and rural areas.

Another source of data on internal migration has been special surveys on population mobility and labor force composition. As of 1986, two specific surveys had been carried out by the Ecuadorian Census Office, though the geographical coverage of both surveys was limited.[1] The 1975 survey covered in-migration to Quito, Guayaquil, and the rest of the urban sector. The 1979 special survey only concentrated on in-migration to the urban areas of the Sierra, excluding all the other regions of the country.

POPULATION GROWTH AND URBANIZATION

A Basic Distinction: Ecuadorian Regions

The topographical configuration of Ecuador divides it into three major regions. The Sierra, located in the inter-Andean mountain basins, is the smallest but most populated. It contains almost all Indians and has the highest population density.[2] Economic activity has been concentrated on large quasi-feudal agricultural landholdings which produce for domestic consumption. However, subsistence agriculture on small farms is characteristic of a large proportion of the rural population.

The Costa region has been the most dynamic economic area during the last two centuries with an extensive colonization frontier. It has been integrated into the international market through the export of agricultural products. The Oriente region, the easternmost part of the country in the Amazon Basin, is sparsely populated by aboriginal tribes and colonists. The majority of the population migrated after the discovery of oil in the northern part of the Oriente. Aside from oil, the main economic activities have been the extraction of forest products, cattle raising, and agricultural production for household consumption. The major limitation on the economic expansion of the Oriente has been the lack of easy transportation.

Population Growth and Redistribution Since 1950

From 1950 to 1962 an agricultural boom occurred in the coastal area. The production and export of bananas in Esmeraldas, Manabi, El Oro, Los Rios, and Guayas were largely responsible for this prosperity. These provinces had a net flow of in-migrants, coming largely from the stagnant region of Sierra. The agricultural sector of Sierra, excluding Azuay which was exporting quinine, remained stagnant. This lack of economic growth in the rural sector brought urban growth in some centers in Sierra, especially Quito where in-migrants from the deprived smaller towns and rural areas settled. This trend continued through the 1980s so that, by the time of the last census, the proportion of the population in Sierra had declined significantly while that in Costa and Oriente had increased

(see Table 5.1). Indeed, by 1974 Costa had overtaken Sierra as the most populous region of the country, and this difference further increased by 1982. The
proportional increase in Oriente, especially after 1974, was a product of movement from the central and southern highlands to the eastern provinces as the oil
industry expanded.

The Sierra had increasing rates of urban growth throughout the period 1950–
82, while rural population growth fluctuated from very low to medium levels.
Only during the second intercensal period (1962–74) did the rural population
grow at relatively higher rates, possibly because of the land redistribution that
was initiated during this period inhibiting the rural population from migrating.
The coastal region showed higher rates of urban growth than the Sierra. However, these rates have declined since 1962, with the most important drop occurring in the last intercensal period.

Most of the provinces had high rates of urban population growth in the 1950–
82 period. In the Sierra, Pichincha, Loja, and Azuay had high rates of urban
growth caused by a steady intraprovincial rural-to-urban migration flow as well
as by natural increase. These provinces did not receive any important migration
flow from other provinces. In the coastal region, between 1950 and 1962, all
provinces experienced rapid urban growth, with the exception of Manabi.

Urban growth in the Sierra provinces has traditionally been concentrated in the
provincial capitals; however, a reversal occurred in the last intercensal period.
The coastal provinces showed impressive growth rates for their secondary cities
during the 1950–74 period, which coincides with the peak of the plantation
economy. In the last decade, however, there were signs of the concentration of
population growth in the provincial capitals. The Oriente, as a whole, showed a
tendency toward high rates of urban growth in the provincial capitals during the
last intercensal period.

Table 5.1
Distribution of the Population of Ecuador by Region, 1950–82 (percent)

Region	1950	1962	1974	1982
Sierra	57.97	50.75	48.25	47.17
Costa	40.54	47.53	48.75	48.96
Oriente	1.45	1.67	2.66	3.27
Galapagos	0.04	0.05	0.06	0.08
Unknown	–	–	0.28	0.52
Total	100.00	100.00	100.00	100.00

Sources: INEC: Population Censuses of Ecuador
1950, 1962, 1974, and 1982.

PRINCIPAL POPULATION MOVEMENTS

Internal Migration at the National Level

The Ecuadorian population has become increasingly mobile over time. Multiple factors could account for this phenomenon. Improvement in transportation facilitated migration, and the diffusion of communication technology played an important role in creating the "motives" for migrating. The modernization and commercialization of the rural sector since 1964 created the conditions to increase permanent out-migration of rural households and incentives for other types of population mobility such as temporary migration, circulation, and commuting. While data on these latter forms of mobility are sparse, by 1962 11.5 percent of the total native population had changed their residence and moved to another province. By 1974 the proportion of lifetime migrants[3] increased to 13.4 percent and by 1982 to 16 percent (see Table 5.2).

If intraprovincial migration is also considered (see Table 5.3), the migrant population is far greater. This indicates that intercantonal migration is almost as important as interprovincial mobility, suggesting the existence of step migration. According to 1974 census data, about one-fourth of the total native population migrated at least once across or within provinces. The overall mobility would be greater if intra- and interprovincial circulation and temporary migration could be considered.

Age, Sex, and Educational Characteristics of Migrants

Published materials from the 1974 and 1982 censuses do not contain the sex structure of the migrant population. The 1962 census recorded and published this information. These data indicate a slight predominance of males (see Table 5.4). Nevertheless, the sex distribution of the migrant population in Ecuador varies

Table 5.2
Interprovincial Lifetime Migration, Ecuador, 1962–82[1] (thousands of persons)

Census Year	(1) Native Population	(2) Interprov. Lifetime migr.	(2)/(1) Ratio
1962	4,451.1	511.7	11.5
1974	6,512.9	873.5	13.4
1982	8,035.3	1,288.0	16.0

[1]Excluding international migrants and non-responses

Source: INEC, Population Censuses of 1962, 1974, and 1982

Table 5.3
Intraprovincial Lifetime Migration, Ecuador, 1962–82[1] (thousands of persons)

Census Year	Intraprovincial Migration
1962	36. 8
1974	739. 6
1982	476. 2[2]

[1] Excluding non-responses and international migrants
[2] Only urban-to-rural and rural-to-urban movements, not considered intraurban and intrarural flows

Source: INEC, Population Censuses of 1962, 1974, and 1982.

depending on the distance involved, on the type of move—if permanent or temporary—and on the place of destination—if small town, frontier area, or large city. In a recent study, Brea (1986) shows that males predominated in circular migration and in frontier area moves. Meanwhile, women were equally migratory in permanent migration to industrial and other agricultural areas.

The age distribution of migrants (see Table 5.5) indicates a selectivity for migrants between 10 and 49 years of age. It seems important to indicate that the proportion of the younger migrants (0 to 9 years) was reduced from 14.2 in 1974 to 10.2 in 1982. This indicates the compound effect of a decline in fertility and probably the reduction of children's employment opportunities in places of destination.

Selectivity for more educated migrants (see Table 5.6) was stronger over time. However, it is important to keep in mind that the overall level of education was greatly improved over this period. In 1974, around 21 percent of the permanent migrants had at least a high school education, while for 1982 this figure was 29

Table 5.4
Interprovincial Lifetime Migration by Sex, Ecuador, 1962[1] (thousands of persons)

Census Year	Male		Female	
	Volume	%	Volume	%
1962	275. 6	53. 9	236. 1	46. 1

[1] Excluding non-responses and internationl migrants
Source: INEC, Population Census of 1962

Table 5.5
Interprovincial Lifetime Migration by Age, Ecuador, 1962–82 (thousands of persons)

Census Year		0-9	10-29	30-49	50-69	70+	Total
				Age groups			
1962	Vol	81.3	240.7	165.9	69.7	15.7	573.3
	%	14.2	42.0	28.9	12.2	2.7	100.0
1974	Vol	97.5	409.0	241.6	100.0	25.1	873.5[1]
	%	11.2	46.8	27.7	11.5	2.8	100.0
1982	Vol	130.1	592.5	361.1	146.6	38.9	1,299.1[2]
	%	10.2	46.7	28.4	11.6	3.1	100.0

[1]Includes intraprovincial migrants
[2]Excludes intraprovincial and international migrants

Source: INEC, Population Censuses of 1962, 1974, and 1982.

Table 5.6
Interprovincial Lifetime Migration by Educational Attainment, Ecuador, 1974 and 1982 (thousands of persons)

Educational Level[1]	1974		1982	
	Volume	%	Volume	%
None	148.7	17.9	143.8	11.9
Liter. Centers	2.6	0.3	23.8	1.1
Elementary	492.6	59.3	618.3	51.1
High school	142.6	17.2	266.1	22.0
University	31.5	3.8	83.4	6.0
Not estab.	12.3	1.5	82.9	6.9
Total	830.4	100.0	1,208.4	100.0

[1]Migrant population 6 years of age and over

Source: INEC, Population Censuses of 1974 and 1982

percent. The educational attainment of the in-migrants to Quito and Guayaquil in 1982 was even higher than that of the native populations in those two cities. While this may have resulted from selectivity, it is possible that migrants have a greater probability of being enrolled in school in Quito and Guayaquil, which increases their average levels of schooling (CEPAR, 1986).

Interregional Patterns of Migration

Intraregional migration has been the predominant type of internal mobility in Ecuador (see Table 5.7). This reflects the considerable physical barriers that tended to discourage migration across regions. During the last decade, these natural obstacles were surmounted through an extensive governmental program of road building. From 1962 to 1974 the importance of interregional migration— particularly from Sierra to Costa —increased slightly, but by 1982 there was a substantial drop in interregional moves, even though travel across regions was facilitated.

The decline of interregional migration seems to have resulted from three factors. First, the decay of the coastal export economy reduced the magnitude of in-migration from Sierra. Second, the industrialization strategy followed by the country since 1970 seems to have improved the relative situation of Quito and other cities in the highlands, and these places increasingly attracted migrants from their own regions. Finally, the trend toward centralization in Quito (which followed the export of oil) reduced the magnitude of interregional migration and increased the flow to the capital city.

Traditionally, there have been several well-defined patterns of interregional migration. Since the 1960s the highland provinces have received most of their migrants from within the region. Since 1962, in-migration to the coastal provinces has been largely an intraregional phenomenon. By 1962, Costa received

Table 5.7
Lifetime Intraregional and Interregional Migration as a Proportion of Total In-Migration, Ecuador, 1974 and 1982 (thousands of persons)

Census Year	Intraregional Migration		Interregional Migration		Total Internal Migration	
	Volume	%	Volume	%	Volume	%
1962	307. 1	60. 0	204. 5	40. 0	511. 7	100. 0
1974	517. 9	59. 3	355. 6	40. 7	873. 5	100. 0
1982	805. 7	62. 6	482. 3	37. 4	1, 288. 0	100. 0

Sources: INEC, Population Censuses of 1962, 1974, and 1982.

51.3 percent of its in-migrants from the same region. However, by the last intercensal period intraregional migration increased to 62.2 percent (see Table 5.8). In-migration to Oriente has largely come from Sierra and Costa, which contribute more than 90 percent of the Oriente's in-migration.

Considering out-migration, Sierra has been sending more of its population to other regions than has Costa. From 1962 to 1974, more than 48 percent of Sierra's out-migrants relocated to a different region. By contrast, only 24.8 percent of Costa's out-migrants relocated outside the region. During the period 1974–82, the Sierra retained more of its migratory population within the region, while Costa was sending a larger proportion of its migrants to other regions. Oriente's out-migration, on the other hand, has been almost entirely an inter-regional phenomenon. In short, Costa migrants were more likely to stay within their region, whereas Sierra and Oriente's migrants were more inclined to move to other regions. This pattern is consistent with the more dynamic economy in

Table 5.8
Lifetime Interregional In-Migration and Out-Migration as a Proportion of Total Migration, by Province, Ecuador, 1962–82[1]

PROVINCE	In-migration			Out-migration		
	1962	1974	1982	1962	1974	1982
SIERRA	74.9	70.1	71.9	51.5	52.8	56.8
Carchi	92.6	90.1	88.3	88.2	90.7	92.7
Bolivar	69.9	56.3	54.7	43.1	49.8	54.9
Chimbor.	77.3	66.5	71.9	50.1	55.8	58.7
Canar	50.7	56.9	50.5	47.8	46.3	48.7
Azuay	30.9	61.1	59.9	27.6	30.3	32.9
Loja	62.2	43.3	40.1	23.7	30.8	39.5
COSTA	51.3	56.9	62.2	75.2	69.1	67.9
Esmerald.	71.4	70.1	72.7	69.4	66.3	66.6
Manabi	65.4	70.4	72.7	86.4	81.9	78.5
Los Rios	65.1	63.2	65.8	86.5	74.6	78.8
Guayas	51.3	59.7	66.7	59.3	53.6	50.5
El Oro	27.2	27.6	27.3	62.6	52.5	46.3
ORIENTE	6.8	7.2	8.1	24.1	28.2	25.1
Napo	6.7	11.4	8.1	35.9	21.8	18.1
Pastaza	15.8	11.3	18.1	19.6	39.7	33.3
Morona S.	2.4	4.2	6.1	23.2	27.9	33.4
Zamora Ch.	1.9	2.8	3.5	10.9	14.2	14.1

[1]Excluding Galapagos Province

Source: INEC, Population Censuses of 1950, 1962, 1974, and 1982.

Costa than in the Sierra and Oriente. Yet these major patterns have shown some signs of change during the last intercensal period.

At the provincial level, migrants from the northern and central provinces of Sierra, except Pichincha, were more inclined to move within their own region than those from the southern provinces, who were more attracted by coastal and eastern destinations. In Costa, only Guayas and El Oro were more prone to send and receive migrants to and from other regions, while Manabi, Esmeraldas, and Los Rios had primarily intraregional flows. In the eastern provinces of Napo and Zamora Chinchipe, interregional in- and out-migration flows were surely influenced by their status as oil-producing and colonization areas, respectively. They have attracted population from the more deprived zones of the highlands and even from the coastal provinces.

Overall, two major systems of internal migration may be distinguished in Ecuador. The first is centered around Guayas and El Oro provinces which receive migrants from the central and southern provinces of Sierra (Chimborazo, Bolivar, Canar, Azuay, Loja) and from central Costa (Manabi and Los Rios). The second is focused on Pichincha which attracts migrants from the northern and central Sierra (Carchi, Imbabura, Cotopaxi, Tungurahua, Chimborazo) and from northern Oriente (Napo and Pastaza). In addition, several lesser migration systems can be delineated. The southern provinces of the Sierra have a significant interchange of population with Morona, Santiago, and Zamora Chinchipe in the Oriente. Tungurahua in the central highlands has sent and received migrants from the Oriente Province of Pastaza, whereas Pichincha has had some interchange with Esmeraldas.

Provincial Lifetime In-Migration and Out-Migration Trends

All Sierra provinces except Pichincha have experienced net lifetime out-migration for the last two intercensal periods (see Table 5.9). In some of the highland provinces (Carchi, Cotopaxi, and Tungurahua), the level of out-migration has increased since 1974, but in other provinces (e.g., Bolivar, Loja, and Chimborazo) the out-migration has become weaker. In others, out-migration has remained almost constant or has increased moderately. As a whole, the Sierra had net out-migration during the period 1962–82, though this tendency is weakening.

Costa, by way of contrast, had positive net migration rates during 1962–82. Guayas registered high net in-migration rates, probably because of employment opportunities in Guayaquil in the city and on the nearby agricultural farms. El Oro had important flows of in-migrants between 1962 and 1982 as a result of the economic boom induced by banana production and export. Esmeraldas, regarded as the new colonization zone in the coastal area, attracted some migrants, but after 1974 the in-migration rate declined substantially. Other provinces such as Manabi and Los Rios experienced significant out-migration. A strong drought affected Manabi during the 1950s and 1960s, and Los Rios has experienced high

Table 5.9

Lifetime Interprovincial In-Migration, Out-Migration, and Net Migration Rates, Ecuador, 1962–82[1]

REGION PROVINCE	In-migration Rate			Out-migraton Rate			Net Migration Rate		
	1962	1974	1982	1962	1974	1982	1962	1974	1982
SIERRA	15.1	12.1	9.3	18.7	15.8	14.9	-3.6	-3.7	-5.6
Carchi	6.5	7.2	5.6	35.5	23.8	21.6	-29.1	-16.6	-17.1
Imbabura	11.1	9.5	9.1	23.4	18.3	15.2	-12.3	-8.8	-6.2
Pichincha	28.2	24.8	21.1	6.9	6.6	6.8	21.3	18.2	14.3
Cotopaxi	7.9	6.5	4.7	24.3	20.2	21.5	-16.4	-13.7	-16.8
Tungurah.	2.6	7.7	7.9	19.1	17.1	22.2	-16.4	-9.4	-14.3
Bolivar	5.8	5.5	4.4	40.7	28.5	13.4	-34.9	-23.1	-9.1
Chimbor.	5.1	6.1	4.7	26.5	20.1	14.9	-21.4	-14.1	-10.2
Canar	9.2	7.6	7.4	19.6	16.5	15.7	-10.4	-8.9	-8.3
Azuay	7.8	5.4	4.4	18.9	18.9	17.7	-11.1	-13.5	-13.3
Loja	5.1	3.3	2.1	33.7	21.4	11.1	-28.7	-18.1	-8.9
COSTA	15.8	13.7	13.1	14.4	11.3	8.9	1.4	2.4	3.2
Esmerald.	17.6	17.2	10.1	19.6	13.1	8.8	2.1	4.2	1.2
Manabi	2.9	2.8	1.6	27.1	15.8	10.2	-24.2	-13.1	-8.6
Los Rios	15.8	15.8	16.9	25.3	19.7	16.9	-9.5	-3.8	0
Guayas	19.8	16.8	18.2	5.7	6.2	5.8	14.1	10.6	12.4
El Oro	23.9	23.6	24.1	16.7	13.1	10.9	7.2	10.5	13.1
ORIENTE	34.5	32.7	27.8	11	8.8	6.6	23.5	23.9	21.2
Napo	37.5	30.4	23.1	6.8	4.9	6.2	30.7	25.5	16.8
Pastaza	37.1	34.9	40.8	22.6	23.6	12.6	14.5	11.3	28.2
Morona S.	25.2	26.9	12.3	11.3	7.1	4.2	13.9	19.8	8.1
Zamora Ch.	41.2	47.4	46.1	13.7	8.9	5.8	27.5	38.5	30.2

[1]Excluding Galapagos Province

Sources: INEC, Population Censuses of 1962, 1974, and 1982.

levels of population pressure. In fact, its population density increased from 21.1 inhabitants per square kilometer in 1950 to 76.8 in 1982. It is now the second most densely populated province in the country.

All of the provinces of Oriente registered positive rates of net in-migration. The most important flows in the 1962–74 intercensal period were directed to the northern provinces (Napo and Pastaza) and to the southern province of Zamora Chinchipe. In the second intercensal period Zamora Chinchipe had the highest net migration rate in the Oriente.

The contribution of each province to lifetime migration and the distribution of lifetime migrants among provinces is shown in Table 5.10. Considering out-migration at a regional level, it can be argued that the contribution of the Sierra has been increasing over time, while that of the Costa has been decreasing. At the provincial level, the major contribution to total out-migration has come from

Table 5.10
**Provincial Contribution to Total Lifetime In-Migration and Out-Migration, Ec-
uador, 1962–82[1]**

REGION	1962		1974		1982	
PROVINCE	Inmig	Outmig	Inmig	Outmig	Inmig	Outmig
SIERRA	43.6	57.1	44.4	54.2	41.3	61.8
Carchi	1.1	3.3	0.6	3.5	1.1	4.1
Imbabura	2.4	4.5	2.1	4.4	3.1	5.2
Pichincha	28.1	7.4	30.2	7.3	24.2	7.8
Cotopaxi	1.7	5.5	1.7	5.1	1.4	6.5
Tungurah.	2.5	5.5	2.3	4.7	2.8	7.8
Bolivar	9.1	4.7	0.7	4.5	1.1	3.5
Chimbor.	2.1	7.1	1.5	6.4	2.5	8.1
Canar	1.3	2.8	1.2	2.6	1.6	3.5
Azuay	2.3	7.9	2.7	6.4	2.4	9.5
Loja	1.3	8.4	1.4	9.3	1.1	6.1
COSTA	49.8	41.1	48.3	43.4	54.4	37.1
Esmerald.	4.1	3.1	3.4	3.7	2.4	2.2
Manabi	2.6	14.8	1.9	17.9	2.1	12.3
Los Rios	6.9	8.6	5.6	8.7	7.7	8.3
Guayas	29.1	10.7	31.2	8.8	34.8	11.1
El Oro	7.1	3.9	6.2	4.2	7.5	3.4
ORIENTE	6.6	1.8	7.1	2.2	4.1	1.1
Napo	2.1	0.4	3.3	0.6	0.6	0.3
Pastaza	0.9	0.6	0.9	0.5	1.1	0.3
Morona S.	1.6	0.4	1.4	0.6	1.3	0.3
Zamora Ch.	1.8	0.4	1.5	0.5	0.9	0.1
Total	100	100	100	100	100	100

[1]Excluding Galapagos Province

Source: INEC, Population Censuses of 1950, 1962, 1974, and 1982.

Manabi and Loja. With regard to in-migration, Guayas and Pichincha had received almost two-thirds of the total lifetime migrants as of 1982. Also significant, though less important, has been the movement of migrants to El Oro,
Napo, and Los Rios.

Urban and Rural Context in Ecuadorian Internal Migration

When we consider in-migration flows as a proportion of total lifetime in-
migration by regions and provinces in 1982, we see clearly that in Sierra and
Costa urban-to-urban flows have predominated. Of the total lifetime in-migration

to the Sierra, 59 percent was urban-to-urban, while for Costa that figure was about 53 percent (see Table 5.11). Two other in-migration flows were relatively unimportant: the rural-to-rural and urban-to-rural streams, which range between 7 and 12 percent of total in-migration in both regions, respectively.

The case of the Oriente is peculiar. Almost one-third of the lifetime in-migration in 1982 came from urban areas to rural parts of the region, and over one-fourth was rural-to-rural in-migration. In other words, almost 57 percent of total in-migration to the Oriente relocated in a rural area, a fact that demonstrates the importance of this region as the major colonization zone of the country.

Between 1974 and 1982 rural-to-rural and urban-to-rural migration flows had a sharp decline. Lifetime rural in-migration, from both urban and rural areas, to the Sierra was about 32 percent of total in-migration to the region. In comparison, for the Costa that figure was 38 percent and for the Oriente it was 82 percent. Those proportions compare with 18, 21, and 56 percent in 1982.

By contrast, urban in-migration flows increased sharply between 1962 and 1982, and were directed to the provinces with large regional or provincial centers such as Quito in Pichincha, Guayaquil in Guayas, Cuenca in Azuay, Ambato in Tungurahua, and Machala in El Oro. Similarly, in the last decade in-migration to the Oriente provinces has had an increasing urban orientation.

Rural in-migration was important in Pichincha, Canar, Los Rios, El Oro, and the Oriental provinces of Napo and Zamora Chichipe. On the other hand, it appears that rural lifetime in-migration rates were, on the whole, higher in the

Table 5.11
Lifetime Interprovincial Migration by Type of Flow, Ecuador, 1974 (thousands of persons)

Flow Type		Sierra		Costa		Oriente		Galapagos		Total	
		In	Out	In	Out	In	Out	In	Out	In	Out
Rural–	N	42	73	60	59	24	4	.3	.1	126	136
Rural	%	7	10	10	10	26	14	9	6	10	10
Urban–	N	339	385	331	297	307	12	2	.7	699	695
Urban	%	59	54	53	52	29	44	63	45	54	53
Rural–	N	130	164	155	128	13	6	.3	.6	299	299
Urban	%	23	23	25	23	15	23	12	43	23	23
Urban–	N	61	87	75	84	28	5	.4	.1	165	177
Rural	%	11	12	12	15	31	20	15	7	13	14
Total	N	572	709	622	569	91	27	3	1	1,288	1,306

Source: INEC, Population Census of 1974.

Table 5.12
Lifetime Interprovincial Migration by Type of Flow, Ecuador, 1982

Flow Type		Sierra		Costa		Oriente		Galapagos		Total	
		In	Out	In	Out	In	Out	In	Out	In	Out
Rural-	N	55	92	76	60	23	3	.2	.1	155	155
Rural	%	15	18	18	17	40	22	13	8	18	18
Urban-	N	199	235	194	160	7	5	.8	.4	401	401
Urban	%	53	47	45	44	12	35	53	41	46	46
Rural-	N	59	80	74	53	3	3	.1	.4	136	136
Urban	%	16	16	17	15	5	19	7	41	16	16
Urban-	N	66	91	90	86	25	4	.4	.1	191	191
Rural	%	17	18	21	25	43	23	26	11	21	21
Total	N	379	498	435	359	58	16	2	1	873	873

Source: INEC, Population Census of 1982.

Costa region than in Sierra in both census years, which indicates that the coastal areas offered more and better opportunities to lifetime migrants.

Comparison of lifetime out-migration data from the 1982 and 1974 population censuses are also presented in Tables 5.11 and 5.12, respectively. The data highlight the increasing importance of intraurban flows and the decline of rural-to-rural out-migration in all the regions. Urban out-migration in the Sierra provinces of Bolivar, Cotopaxi, and Loja has been very significant. These areas have lost migrants in a magnitude comparable to their 1982 urban populations. This process has been more moderate in Costa, except for Manabi Province. In Oriente, sizeable urban out-migration rates have been registered for Pastaza, Zamora Chinchipe, and Napo. On the other hand, rural lifetime out-migration rates have been considerable in Bolivar, Manabi, and Pastaza.

CONSEQUENCES OF MIGRATION

Urbanization and Sectoral Change

Urbanization has been one of the major features of Ecuadorian social and economic change. In 1950, less than 29 percent of the population was living in urban places; by 1982, that figure had increased to almost 50 percent (CEPAR, 1985).

Urban concentration has also been significant. Quito and Guayaquil contained 25 percent of the total national population in 1982, whereas 30 years earlier they had accounted for only 14 percent of the population. This trend surely continued in the last decade because of the continuing flow of migrants to those centers.

The contributions of inter- and intraprovincial migration to the growth of provincial urban areas in 1982 and 1974 are shown in Table 5.13. (These figures ignore the effects of migrant fertility in their urban relocation.) In Sierra, urban areas of all provinces except Pichincha registered a net loss of population owing to heavy out-migration. Bolivar registered a net urban out-migration that slightly exceeded its 1982 urban population. Loja, Canar, Cotopaxi, and Carchi also experienced high net urban out-migration. By 1982, almost 27 percent of Pichincha's urban population was composed of migrants, most of whom had moved to Quito.

Table 5.13
Contribution of Net Migration to Size of the Urban Population, by Province, Ecuador, 1982[1] (thousands of persons)

REGION PROVINCE	(a) Urban Pop 1982	(b) Net Life Interprov Migration	(c) Net Life Intraprov Migration	(d=a-b-c) Urban Pop. w/o Migr	Ratio (d/a)
SIERRA	1,707	− 4	42	1,669	0.97
Carchi	48	− 21	1	68	1.41
Imbabura	92	− 21	6	108	1.17
Pichincha	973	263	− 1	711	0.73
Cotopaxi	43	− 32	1	74	1.72
Tungurah.	120	− 25	5	141	1.17
Bolivar	23	− 23	− .2	46	2.03
Chimbor.	89	− 40	10	120	1.34
Canar	28	− 13	.2	41	1.47
Azuay	169	− 24	10	184	1.09
Loja	121	− 68	10	178	1.48
COSTA	2,199	105	52	2,042	0.93
Esmerald.	119	− 10	10	119	1.01
Manabi	319	− 111	21	409	1.28
Los Rios	148	− 47	− 1	196	1.32
Guayas	1,400	254	15	1,131	0.81
El Oro	214	19	7	187	0.88
ORIENTE	58	22	− 3	38	0.66
Napo	17	13	− 3	6	0.35
Pastaza	20	1	.3	19	0.93
Morona S.	10	5	− .6	6	0.56
Zamora Ch.	11	3	.2	8	0.73

[1]Excluding Galapagos Province

Source: INEC, Population Census of 1982.   Ecuador

The case of Guayas in Costa is similar, with 19 percent of its 1982 urban population composed of migrants. El Oro also had an important migrant contribution on the order of 12 percent. In the Oriente the migrant contribution to urban growth has also been significant, particularly in Napo and Morona Santiago where 65 and 45 percent, respectively, of the actual urban population are migrants.

In brief, urban growth owing to migration has been important in Pichincha and Guayas provinces. The migration to these provinces has largely been directed to Quito and Guayaquil. The growth of those cities is attributable more to in-migration than to natural increase. Statistical evidence is presented in Table 5.14, which shows that 63 and 56 percent of the urban growth for Quito and Guayaquil, respectively, between 1974 and 1982 was due to in-migration. These figures would surely have been higher if the fertility of migrants had been considered.

As urbanization proceeded, the sectoral growth of employment also changed substantially. One of the most important features of the sectoral transformation has been the high rates of growth of the informal sector. This sector comprises people engaged in personal services such as maids, shoeshiners, deliverers, petty traders and street vendors, and miscellaneous workers in other temporary activities. The growth of the modern urban sector, in terms of employment creation, was almost negligible between 1950 and 1980, and in some specific activities employment actually decreased.

Apparently, most migrants to urban areas were employed in the informal sector. According to a survey of migration to the urban areas of Sierra, 65 percent of rural in-migrants 12 years of age and over with less than five years of residence in the urban areas were employed in the informal sector (INEC, 1977, Table 21). This fact gives strong support to the assertion that the informal sector constitutes the main employer of migrant labor in urban areas. However, engage-

Table 5.14

Contribution of Migration to Urban Growth in Quito and Guayaquil, 1974–82 (thousands of persons)

City	1974	1982	Absolute Increase	Net Migration 1974–1982	Contrib. of Migration
Quito	823. 2	1, 199. 3	376. 1	208. 8	55. 5
Guayaquil	599. 8	866. 4	266. 6	168. 0	63. 0

Not considering suburban areas outside city area. If those areas are considered the contribution increases to 63. 1 for Quito and 56. 9 for Guayaquil.

Sources: INEC, Population Censuses of 1974 and 1982.

ment in informal activities is particularly important for the rural-to-urban migrant since only 36 percent of the intraurban migrants were employed in that sector (INEC, 1977, Table 21.1). Obviously, the growth of the informal sector has been particularly significant in Quito and Guayaquil. Between 1974 and 1982, Guayas and Pichincha almost doubled the participation rates in the service sector where informal employment is included in census statistics (Ecuador, INEC, 1974 and 1982).

NOTES

1. The Special Surveys are: INEC, *Encuesta de Poblacion y Qcupacion. Area Urban-Quito- Guayaquil* (Quito: INEC, 1976) and INEC, *Encuesta de Migracion Urbana de la Sierra* (Quito: INEC, 1979).

2. The Sierra comprises ten provinces, one of which, Pichincha, contains the capital city of Quito.

3. Corresponds to lifetime interprovincial migration data obtained from the population censuses of Ecuador (1962, 1974, and 1982). According to the census definition, an individual is considered a migrant if he or she has changed the province and area of last previous residence at any given point in the past.

REFERENCES

Brea, J. 1986. "Effects of Structural Characteristics and Personal Attributes upon Labor Mobility in Ecuador." Ph.D. dissertation, Department of Geography, Ohio State University.

Bromley, R. 1972. "Agricultural Colonization in the Upper Amazon Basin, The Impact of Oil Discoveries." *Journal of Economic and Social Geography* 63, no. 4:275–94.

Burt, A.L. et al. 1960. "Santo Domingo de los Colorados: A New Pioneer Zone in Ecuador." *Economic Geography* 36:221–30.

Carron, J.M. 1980. "Dinamica de la poblacion del Ecuador en el period 1962–1974." In J. Barsky et al. *Ecuador: cambios en el agro serrano.* Quito: CEPLAES-FLACSO.

Centro de Estudios de Poblacion y Paternidad Responsable (CEPAR). 1984. *Perfil demografico del Ecuador.* Quito: San Pablo.

———. 1985a. *Poblacion y desarrollo socioeconomico en el Ecuador.* Quito: San Paulo.

———. 1985b. *Inmigracion a Quito y Guayaquil, un estudio de casos.* Quito: San Paulo.

———. 1986a. *Aspectos socioeconomicos en el proceso demografico.* Quito: San Paulo.

———. 1986b. *Migraciones internas en el Ecuador.* Quito: San Paulo.

Collin, A. 1980. "From Colonization to Agricultural Development: The Case of Coastal Ecuador." In D.A. Preston (ed.), *Environment, Society, and Rural Change in Latin America.* New York: John Wiley and Sons.

De la Tabla, J. 1982. "Obrajes y obrajeros del Quito colonial." *Anuario de Estudios Americanos* 39:341–65.

Economic Commission for Latin America (ECLA). 1984. *Statistical Yearbook for Latin America.* Santiago: ECLA.

Ecuador. "Direccion Nacional de Estadistica 1950." *I Censo Nacional de Poblacion.* Quito: La Nacion.

———. "Direccion Nacional de Estadistica 1962." *II Censo Nacional de Poblacion y I de Vivienda.* Quito: La Nacion.

———. 1976. Instituto Nacional de Estadisticas y Censos (INEC). *Encuesta de Poblacion y Ocupacion.* Quito: INEC.

———. 1977. Instituto Nacional de Estadisticas y Censos (INEC). *Encuesta de migracion al area urbana de la Sierra.* Quito: INEC.

Hiraoka, M., and S. Yamamoto. 1980. "Agricultural Development in the Upper Amazon of Ecuador." *Geographical Review* 70, no. 4:423–46.

Hurtado, O. 1982. *El poder politico en el Ecuador.* Quito: Planeta.

Luzuriage, C., and C. Zuvekas. 1980. "Income Distribution and Poverty in Rural Ecuador: A Survey of the Literature, 1950–1979." USAID Working Paper.

Ortiz, J. 1980. "La poblacion ecuatoriana en la epopca colonial: cuestionnes y calculos." *Anuario de Estudios Americanos* 37:235–77.

Peek, P. 1980. "Agrarian Change and Labor Migration in the Sierra of Ecuador." *International Labor Review:* 609–23.

Preston, D. 1965. "Changes in the Economic Geography of Banana Production in Ecuador." *Transactions of the Institute of British Geographers* 37:77–90.

———. 1980. "Rural Emigration and the Future of Agriculture in Ecuador." In D.A. Preston (ed.), *Environment, Society, and Rural Change in Latin America.* New York: John Wiley and Sons.

Preston, D.A., and G.A. Taveras. 1980. "Changes in Land Tenure Distribution as Result of Rural Inmigration in Highland Ecuador." *Journal of Economic and Social Geography* 71, no. 2:98–107.

Redclift, M.R. 1978. *Agrarian Reform and Peasant Organization on the Ecuadorian Coast.* London: Athlone Press.

———, and D.A. Preston. 1980. "Agrarian Reform and Rural Change in Ecuador." In D.A. Preston (ed.), *Environment, Society, and Rural Change in Latin America.* New York: John Wiley and Sons.

Velasco, J. de. 1981. *Historia del Reino de Quito en la America Meridional.* Caracas: Ayacucho.

Weil, E.T. et al. 1973. *Area Handbook for Ecuador.* Washington, D.C.: American University.

Wilkie, J.W., and A. Perkal. 1984. *Statistical Abstract for Latin America,* Vol. 24.

6

EGYPT

Mohamed El-Attar

The migration process has contributed substantially to population redistribution in Egypt over time. Migration has been affected by elements of social and economic development. In turn, the impact of population transfers, especially from rural areas to the nation's capital and other centers, has resulted in apparent overurbanization with its dysfunctional consequences of shortages of housing, transportation, employment, service, facilities, and amenities (Goldstein, 1987; Ibrahim, 1982).

DATA ON MIGRATION

Knowledge about migration in Egypt, as in most developing countries, has been limited primarily by available statistics (Yap, 1975, 2). Until 1976, census data on place of birth and place of residence at time of enumeration were the sole source of statistics on migration (El-Attar, 1987; El-Badry, 1965a, 1965b; Nassef, 1973; United Nations, 1970, 1976). Although spatial information recorded in the census relates to the smallest minor civil divisions, the tabulated data permit measurement of migration only on the governorate level. In Egypt, there are twenty-five governorates: four are frontier governorates (El-Wadi El-Gedid, Matrouh, Red Sea, and Sinai), and four are entirely urban governorates (Alexandria, Cairo, Port Said, and Suez). Cairo and Alexandria are the largest urban governorates. A lifetime migrant is a person whose governorate of birth differs from his or her governorate of enumeration (United Nations, 1970, 5). By this definition, Egyptians born abroad, foreigners, and persons with "unstated" birthplace are excluded as migrants.

An ancient Greek historian once stated that "Egypt is a gift of the Nile." To wit, seven of the nonfrontier governorates are located along the Nile Valley where there is a narrow strip of vegetation as the river streams northward through the desert environment. At Cairo, the river starts to form its delta and gives rise to intensive agriculture. It is here that population density exerts the utmost pressure on residential and agrarian lands.

The migration data presented come from Egypt's five most recent population censuses.[1] The 1976 census is the only one of these that provides migration data beyond the traditional lifetime migration. These data are limited in scope since they impair international comparability, provide inaccurate measurement of current migration, and elucidate neither the socioeconomic characteristics of migrants nor the reasons for migration (El-Badry, 1965a; United Nations, 1970). Unlike lifetime migration data based on a question on "place of birth" that was first collected in the 1927 census, the 1976 data should provide more enhanced analysis because of the direct data on internal migration first collected in that census (CAPMAS, 1978, 8).

With enactment of Law 260 in 1960, Civil Registration Offices were charged with requiring all adults (over 16 years of age) within the respective localities to carry an individual or family identification card. This ID was to include (1) date and place of birth, (2) education, (3) kind of employer, (4) occupation, (5) religion, and (6) number of children alive (Hassan and El-Dayem, 1973, 206). However, a number of limitations have rendered the system ineffective and unreliable, namely, (1) the law was not obligatory for females, and enforcement has been limited to big cities, (2) there is inaccurate accountability, since the practice does not reflect the migration of those who have been away from their birthplace but who have returned to it sometime after registration, and (3) the information in the Registration Offices has not been kept up to date, especially with regard to changes in socioeconomic and demographic characteristics. If these limitations could be overcome, this source would be cheaper but of greater value than census data in studies of internal migration, particularly with reference to the characteristics of moving population at place of origin (Hassan and El-Dayem, 1973, 208).

A question on previous place of residence was first included in the 1966 census, but the sample nature of that census limited its application. Because of such limitations, the 1976 census is the most valuable source of data on migration in Egypt, particularly with regard to last previous place of residence and reasons for migrating. The absence of time series data limits the examination of quantity, quality, and type of residence of migrants and reasons of migration, at least, until data from the 1986 census are processed. Thus, analysis of Egyptian intergovernorate migration over time, of necessity, will be based on lifetime migration information.

PRINCIPAL POPULATION MOVEMENTS

Intergovernorate Migration

Table 6.1 indicates that, with the exception of 1976, intergovernorate migration rates have generally been increasing from census to census since 1927.

Expressed in percentages, the rates on the national level are 7.0, 6.9, 9.0, 11.7, and 9.7 for 1927, 1937, 1947, 1960, and 1976, respectively. The decline in the rate for 1976 does not reflect a reduction in the number of migrants. While the rate decreased as noted, the number increased from 3.0 million to 3.6 million persons. Another factor not to be overlooked in the drop of the rate in 1976 was the emigration of Egyptians to the oil-producing Arab states. The number of Egyptians abroad in 1976 has been estimated at 1.4 million persons, or 3.7 percent (CAPMAS, 1987, 1). Net in-migration has been the characteristic of only the four urban governorates and the governorates of Ismailia and Red Sea. The contiguity of Cairo to the governorates of Giza in the south and Kalyubia in the north has been instrumental in their net in-migration since 1947 for Giza and 1976 for Kalyubia. Specifically, the urban expansion of Cairo has resulted in the creation of Greater Cairo through the encroachment of its advancing boundaries with those of the two contiguous governorates. In fact, this trio of governorates has become the most economically advanced area in Egypt. In-migration rose from 990,645 persons, or 43.4 percent of national in-migration in 1927, to 3,550,032 persons, or 60.2 percent in 1976. Their corresponding relative shares of out-migration were 17.2 percent and 17.6 percent for 1927 and 1976, respectively. Net in-migration rates for the trio were thus 10.4 percent and 16.9 percent for 1927 and 1976, respectively.

This analysis utilizes census data where migration was considered as a movement of persons away from place of birth. Therefore, comparison of migration from one census to another is not possible for governorates that did not exist in their present form in all censuses. For example, some have experienced changes in their boundaries, administrative status, and wars. The governorates of Damietta, El-Wadi El -Gedid, Ismailia, Kafr El-Sheikh, Matrouh, Port Said, Sinai, and Suez are examples.

The 1967 and 1973 wars caused the exodus of population from the governorates of the Canal Zone and delayed the resumption of normal life in these governorates at the time of the 1976 census. These factors restrict the usefulness of lifetime migration and require the utilization of other data to reach a meaningful conclusion about actual population movement over time in the affected governorates.

The 1976 census reports include data on migration in two forms: (1) place of enumeration and duration of residence and (2) place of enumeration and place of residence on June 5, 1967.

Table 6.2 summarizes these data in the form of percentage distributions for the governorates. The region most affected by hostilities includes the four governorates of Ismailia, Port Said, Sinai, and Suez. These four governorates lost population through lifetime out-migration at an average rate of 28.4 percent over the nine-year span in comparison with 9.3 percent for the twenty-one other governorates (CAPMAS, 1980, Table 13). Duration of residence for these four governorates differs significantly in magnitude from the others and among themselves. Ismailia's high level relates to its composition of urban and rural

Table 6.1
Lifetime In-, Out-, and Net Migration Rates by Governorates in Egypt, 1927 to 1976

Governorate	In-Migration					Out-Migration					Net Migration*				
	1927	1937	1947	1960	1976	1927	1937	1947	1960	1976	1927	1937	1947	1960	1976
Cairo	26.6	25.9	26.0	36.5	27.2	6.2	5.7	4.5	10.4	9.0	21.8	21.5	22.5	29.1	20.0
Alexandria	19.7	19.9	21.9	26.8	18.6	6.3	7.3	7.5	8.5	4.9	14.3	13.4	15.6	20.1	14.4
Port Said	29.6	26.8	29.0	30.5	25.9	5.9	5.9	9.2	16.7	24.0	25.2	22.2	21.9	16.6	2.4
Ismailia				39.0	24.4				14.4	17.1				28.8	8.9
Suez	30.5	30.6	38.3	45.5	45.6	8.2	8.5	12.2	15.5	42.0	24.3	24.2	29.8	35.5	6.3
Damietta	24.7	16.7	14.3	9.6	6.2	72.5^x	53.0^x	41.4^x	12.9	9.3	-173.8^x	-77.2^x	-46.4^x	-3.8	-3.5
Dakahlia	3.2	2.5	2.5	3.5	2.3	6.3	7.5	8.3	11.1	10.3	-3.2	-5.4	-6.4	-8.5	-8.9
Sharkia	4.3	3.9	9.3	3.8	2.9	5.0	5.2	6.8	9.7	8.7	-0.8	-1.3	2.7	-6.6	-6.4
Kalyubia	5.0	4.3	6.5	9.3	12.9	8.5	8.0	12.1	13.3	8.9	-3.9	-4.1	-6.6	-4.5	4.4
Kafr El-Sheikt				5.8	3.6				5.9	5.0				-0.1	-1.5
Gharbia	3.7	3.4	3.8	6.1	3.9	5.0	5.1	6.9	12.9	9.9	-1.3	-1.7	-3.4	-7.9	-6.7
Menoufia	1.7	1.4	1.7	2.6	1.5	9.6	11.7	22.1	22.5	19.0	-8.7	-11.6	-26.2	-25.7	-21.6
Behera	6.0	5.9	5.3	6.4	4.9	4.0	4.8	10.6	7.8	5.7	2.0	1.2	-5.9	-1.6	-0.8
Giza	7.1	6.5	10.0	21.2	23.4	10.3	7.7	8.0	8.2	5.3	-3.6	-1.4	2.3	14.2	19.1

106

Beni-Suef	4.4	3.8	3.2	3.6	2.1	4.9	4.3	10.7	8.5	8.5	-0.5	-0.6	-2.4	-5.3	-7.0
Fayoum	2.6	2.0	1.9	2.9	1.7	3.2	3.1	4.0	7.2	7.7	-0.7	-1.2	-2.2	-4.6	-6.5
Minya	3.6	3.0	2.6	3.0	1.5	3.4	3.0	3.5	5.0	5.1	0.0	0.0	-1.0	-2.1	-3.8
Assyut	1.7	1.6	1.5	2.7	2.1	9.5	8.1	9.5	12.7	11.7	-8.6	-7.0	-8.9	-11.4	-10.8
Souhag	0.9	0.1	0.9	2.2	1.1	10.3	9.0	11.9	15.0	14.2	-10.5	-8.8	-12.5	-15.1	-15.2
Kena	1.4	1.1	1.3	2.1	1.4	6.9	7.2	10.0	14.2	12.2	-5.9	-6.6	-9.7	-14.2	-12.2
Aswan	9.2	9.9	12.2	13.2	12.4	14.9	14.4	20.4	22.8	12.5	-6.6	-5.3	-10.3	-12.4	0.0
Red Sea	*(12.3)*	38.5	38.4	57.5	45.4	*(14.5)*	4.2	7.3	22.0	14.9	*(-2.5)*	35.9	33.5	45.6	35.8
Matrouh		7.9	7.2	7.9	14.4		15.9	12.4	24.1	4.4		-9.4	-5.9	-21.3	-10.4
El-Wadi El-Gedid		2.6	3.0	4.2	10.4		17.3	15.4	33.5	12.3		-17.7	-14.6	-44.1	-2.1
Sinai		23.4	19.2	29.6	31.2		12.1	11.3	32.9	365.4[x]		12.9	9.0	-4.9	-334.8[x]
Total	7.0	6.9	9.0	11.7	9.7	7.0	6.9	9.0	11.7	9.7					

The braced figures (12.3, 14.5, −2.5) are combined values for Red Sea, Matrouh, El-Wadi El-Gedid, and Sinai.

Source: Compiled and computed from 1976: Central Agency for Public Mobilization and Statistics (CAPMAS) (1980: table 13). 1960: CAPMAS (1963: table 14). 1947, 1937: Statistical and Census Department (1954: table 13). 1927: Statistical and Census Department (1942: table 13).

*Population living in each governorate is used as the base.

[x] These figures are doubtful.

Table 6.2
Percentage Distribution* of the Egyptian Population by Year of Residence in Governorate of Enumeration and Mobility Status on June 5, 1967, and on Census Date

Governorate of Enumeration, 1976	Residence Since:						Population With:			Population Base**	
	1936 and Before	1937–46	1947–56	1957–66	1967–76	1973–76	Change in Residence	No Change in Residence			
							1976	1976	6/5/67	1976	6/5/67
Cairo	12.5	9.4	17.9	29.1	31.1	13.1	28.1	71.9	92.0	5,010,074	3,871,761
Alexandria	15.4	10.3	18.5	27.3	28.5	11.7	19.3	80.7	93.8	2,300,302	1,776,674
Port Said	3.2	1.7	1.5	1.4	92.2	90.1	88.7	11.3	93.4	260,366	208,193
Suez	1.0	0.6	0.7	0.7	97.0	96.2	94.0	6.0	87.5	192,141	144,490
Damietta	16.0	9.3	14.6	27.3	32.7	14.0	12.7	87.3	96.6	575,381	419,803
Dakahlia	19.0	9.8	14.7	26.8	29.7	12.2	7.0	93.0	98.6	2,733,634	2,005,104
Sharkia	19.1	9.8	14.0	26.0	31.2	13.0	8.1	91.9	98.1	2,613,010	1,891,817
Kalyubia	16.8	8.5	13.4	25.1	36.2	16.5	16.5	83.5	91.9	1,677,241	1,205,595
Kafr El-Sheikh	17.5	10.5	14.3	26.1	31.7	12.6	8.8	91.2	98.1	1,405,478	1,015,380
Gharbia	19.7	10.2	15.7	26.6	27.8	11.6	8.0	92.0	98.5	2,290,235	1,713,390
Menoufia	23.4	9.6	13.8	25.0	28.1	11.9	3.4	96.6	98.9	1,709,374	1,258,873
Behera	17.1	10.0	14.6	26.5	31.8	12.4	9.7	90.3	97.9	2,460,666	1,761,300
Ismailia	6.3	4.1	6.1	10.6	72.9	65.1	65.5	34.5	89.8	352,895	255,768

Giza	13.4	7.9	12.9	25.1	40.6	18.7	27.8	72.2	87.7	2,393,167	1,727,062
Beni-Suef	23.2	11.1	13.6	22.2	30.0	12.4	5.0	95.0	98.8	1,108,977	798,186
Fayoum	21.2	10.4	13.0	23.7	31.8	13.5	5.0	95.0	99.2	1,140,657	798,613
Minya	23.5	11.5	13.9	21.4	29.8	12.5	4.5	95.5	99.1	2,051,606	1,478,322
Assyut	21.9	10.3	13.4	22.9	31.5	13.5	5.8	94.2	98.1	1,696,067	1,210,922
Souhag	23.2	10.7	13.3	23.4	29.3	11.8	3.7	96.3	99.3	1,922,420	1,388,171
Kena	23.7	10.8	13.4	22.5	29.6	11.9	3.8	96.2	98.8	1,707,086	1,233,186
Aswan	18.6	8.5	12.5	26.6	33.7	14.3	19.1	80.9	94.8	616,707	445,628
Red Sea	6.1	6.0	10.9	26.7	50.3	25.1	50.2	49.8	74.4	55,039	46,410
Matrouh	14.6	8.8	12.3	23.0	41.3	18.3	15.9	84.1	88.3	111,730	75,781
El-Wadi El-Gedid	15.9	8.4	11.3	26.1	38.2	16.9	14.5	85.4	94.4	85,017	58,083
Sinai	10.8	5.4	6.8	11.8	65.2	53.9	48.0	52.0	70.9	5,644	7,079
Total	18.1	9.7	14.5	25.2	32.5	14.7	14.1	85.9	96.0	36,478,914	26,789,591

Source: Compiled and computed from CAPMAS (1980: tables 15 and 16).

*Percentages of any governorate may not add to 100 due to rounding.

**Excluding population with unstated information numbering 31,935 and 3,855 for 1976 and 1967, respectively.

categories, while that of Sinai is due to its isolation east of the Suez Canal. Indices of duration of residence are very low for the period before 1967 and very high for the period after 1967. In fact, the period between 1973 and 1976 shows the highest percentage of residence for the four war-torn governorates in contrast to the others. This reflects the effect of the vast development and reconstruction activities after the 1973 war. The rate of in-migration to the four governorates reached 30 percent compared with 9.3 percent for all other governorates. The thinning of the population in Sinai related to the fact that it was not fully under Egyptian rule when the 1976 census was undertaken. The proportion of population residing in Sinai on June 5, 1967, and counted in other governorates in 1976 amounted to 84.3 percent of the governorate's population in 1967 (CAPMAS, 1980, Table 16).

The general pattern of duration of residence as revealed by Table 6.2 can be summarized as follows: (1) a relatively high level of migration for 1936 and before, reflecting the movement of long-time residents who may or may not be migrants; (2) a medium level of migration for the period between 1937 and 1946, denoting the impact of World War II, the incipient population pressure on farm land, and the rudimentary expansion in public works and civil service; (3) continued increases in migration during 1947–56, a period of rising expectations which resulted in political, social, and economic changes that culminated in the establishment of the Egyptian Republic, nationalization of the Suez Canal, and the 1956 war; and (4) increasing geographic mobility during the period 1967 to 1976.

Rural-Urban Migration

In considering rural-urban migration, a move must involve a transition between types of places of residence. The definition of urban-rural residence in Egypt neither covers all censuses or remains unchanged over time. Such factors hamper comparability of rural and urban populations, especially when definitions are based on administrative rather than geographic criteria as is the case in Egypt.[2]

Intergovernorate migration flow is dominated by the movement of population from rural areas to urban centers. In fact, the rural-urban differentials in population growth are basically a function of internal migration. The urban population of Egypt increased from roughly 26 percent in 1927 to 44 percent in 1986 (CAPMAS, 1987, 12) and is expected to reach 56 percent by the year 2000 (United Nations, 180). For the intercensal periods 1927–37, 1937–47, 1947–60, and 1960–76, the annual rates of urban population growth were 1.5, 3.4, 3.2, and 3.0 percent, respectively, compared with rural rates of 1.0, 1.0, 1.8, and 1.5 percent. In his analysis of lifetime migration between 1937 and 1960, El-Badry (1956b, 161) found that "most of the out-migration is directed towards the urban governorates." The indices he obtained for in-migrants to the urban governorates as a ratio of out-migrants of all other governorates were above fifty with few exceptions. In the 1966 census, H.A.A. Sayed and H.H.M. Zaky (1985, 174) found that lifetime migrants to urban areas accounted for roughly 91 percent of all migrants. It should be noted that administrative reclassification of rural-urban type of residence contributed to this percentage (Nassef, 1973).

The 1976 census data showed that the intergovernorate migration flux was still led by the transfer of the population from all parts of the nation to Greater Cairo (consisting of the city of Cairo proper, the city of Giza, and the southern parts of the governorate of Kalyubia), the other urban governorates, and urban areas in the rest of governorates. Of the 3.6 million lifetime migrants (CAPMAS, 1980, Table 13), 89.8 percent (3.2 million) went to urban residences and the rest (10.2 percent) to rural areas. The percentage going to Alexandria, Cairo, Giza, and Kalyubia were 12.0, 38.3, 14.5, and 5.5, respectively. In total, the four governorates received 70.3 percent (2.5 million) of all lifetime migrants, or 78.3 percent (3.2 million) (CAPMAS, 1980, Table 13). Analyzing lifetime migration streams for the intercensal decade 1966–76, Sayed and Zaky (1985, 174–77) found that "the share of the rural-urban stream was the minimum among all other streams," and expected, accordingly, a decrease in such stream and an increase in the "urban-rural migration" in the future. They relate this decrease to (1) the international emigration of Egyptians to the oil-producing Arab countries, (2) migration by stages, and (3) areas defined "administratively" as urban which actually maintain rural characteristics.

Rural-Urban Age-Sex Differentials

In 1976, there were 104 males for every 100 females. The sex ratios for migrants and nonmigrants in urban areas were 106 and 103, respectively. The corresponding sex ratios in rural areas were 116 and 103. That is, there were no differences in the sex ratios of the nonmigrant population in urban and rural areas, whereas there was an extra 10 males for every 100 females among rural migrants. Differences in the sex ratios of migrants and nonmigrants were still greater in large urban centers. The sex ratios of migrants to Cairo and Alexandria were 110 and 117, in comparison with 102 and 103 for nonmigrants. Rural-urban age differentials existed between migrants and nonmigrants. Median ages in years were 19.6 for total population, 31.8 for urban migrants, 35 for rural migrants, 17.5 for urban nonmigrants, and 18.8 for rural nonmigrants (CAPMAS, 1980, Table 12).

Table 6.3 depicts the age-sex structure of nonmigrants and lifetime migrants for urban and rural areas in 1976. The pyramids clearly reflect the selectivity of migrants with regard to age, sex, and fertility in urban and rural areas. Urban migrants consisted roughly of 15 percent under 15 years of age, 77 percent at ages 15 to 59, and 8 percent at ages 60 years old and over, compared with 44, 52, and 5, respectively, for the three age categories of urban nonmigrants. The computations showed a slight relative excess (0.2 percent) in urban nonmigrants under 5 years of age over their rural counterparts. This might be related to the

Table 6.3
Age-Sex Structure of Migrants and Nonmigrants, Urban and Rural, Egypt, 1976 (percent)

Migrants	Urban		Rural	
	Male	Female	Male	Female
0-4	1.8	1.8	1.6	1.6
5-9	2.5	2.5	2.0	2.0
10-14	3.8	3.8	2.6	2.6
15-19	4.8	4.4	3.8	3.6
20-24	5.2	6.2	4.8	5.6
25-29	5.3	6.0	5.6	5.8
30-34	5.2	5.4	5.6	5.0
35-39	5.4	4.4	6.0	4.6
40-44	4.8	4.0	5.8	4.4
45-49	4.0	3.2	4.8	3.4
50-54	3.8	3.0	4.0	3.2
55-59	2.5	1.8	2.8	1.8
60-64	2.0	2.0	2.4	2.0
65-69	1.6	1.0	1.8	1.2
70-74	1.0	0.8	1.0	1.0
75+	0.8	0.6	1.0	1.0

Nonmigrants	Urban		Rural	
	Male	Female	Male	Female
0-4	7.8	7.6	7.8	7.6
5-9	7.0	6.8	7.4	6.8
10-14	8.0	7.4	7.6	6.5
15-19	6.6	6.2	5.8	4.6
20-24	4.6	5.0	3.8	3.6
25-29	3.6	3.8	3.4	3.4
30-34	2.6	3.8	2.6	3.0
35-39	2.2	2.6	2.8	2.8
40-44	2.0	2.4	2.4	2.6
45-49	1.6	1.8	2.2	2.2
50-54	1.4	1.8	2.0	2.2
55-59	1.0	1.0	1.5	1.0
60-64	1.0	1.2	1.6	1.4
65-69	0.8	0.8	1.0	0.8
70-74	0.6	0.8	0.8	0.8
75+	0.4	0.6	0.6	0.6

Source: CAPMAS, 1980

delivery of some rural birth in urban localities; hence, the census considered them to be nonmigrants of the respective urban areas of their birthplace. With regard to sex-age differentials, Table 6.3 indicates that migration in Egypt was no longer selective of males for all age categories. In urban areas, migration was selective of females for ages 15 to 19, 20 to 24, and 25 to 29 for which the sex ratios were 98, 81, and 86, as compared with 108, 95, and 100 for nonmigrants in the three age groups, respectively. Among rural migrants the situation was slightly different: Females outnumbered males in ages 20 to 24 and 25 to 29. The sex ratios for these two age groups were 89 and 96 in comparison with 102 and 97 for nonmigrants. Migration was selective of males in the following ages (30 to 49) where the sex ratio is 115 and 124 for urban and rural migrants, respectively. The corresponding ratios for nonmigrants were 101 and 93, respectively. The selectivity for females in the younger age groups (sex ratio under 100) may have been related to patterns of education, marriage, and work. Migration was also selective for children and the elderly: fewer children and more elderly were found among migrants than among nonmigrants in urban and rural areas.

WHO MOVES

The Educational Status of Migrants

The literature of Western countries documents inconclusive statements about the educational selectivity of migrants (Hamilton, 1959; Thomas, 1938). Generally, it has been found that migrants were of higher educational status than nonmigrants in Egypt (El-Boraey, 1985).

Table 6.4 gives the percentage distribution of nonmigrants and intergovernorate migrants 10 years old and over by educational status and governorate of enumeration in 1976. The statistics indicate that nearly half of these migrants (46.4 percent) were classed as illiterates. The percentage of illiterate migrants ranged from 31.4 in Suez to 66.7 in Kafr El-Sheikh. The second highest educational category was "primary to below university first degree," which covered 25.4 percent of migrants, followed by the category "read and write" (21.6 percent). Some governorates had more of one category than the other while the reverse occurred for other governorates. For instance, Cairo and Giza had more migrants with university schooling and fewer in the "read and write" category, while Kalyubia had relatively the reverse magnitudes. Comparison of migrants and nonmigrants indicated that migrants were, on the whole, better educated than nonmigrants (see bottom of Table 6.4). The national percentage distribution of nonmigrants for the five educational categories (illiterate, read and write, below university first degree, university first degree, and above university first degree) were, respectively, 59.4, 20.8, 18.3, 1.5, and less than 0.5. It must be noted, however, that some governorates had relatively more migrants with less education than that of nonmigrants: Cairo, Alexandria, Port Said, Suez, Dametta, Dakahlia, Sharkia, Kafr El-Sheikh, Menougia, Assegut, Red Sea, and El-Wadi El-Gedid.

The presence of institutions of higher learning in a given governorate accounts for some concentration in the educational categories "university first degree" and "above university first degree." This is exemplified by the governorates of Alexandria, Assyut, Cairo, Dakahlia, Gharbia, Giza, Menoufia, and Sharkia, to mention just a few.

All in all, analysis of the data in this section revealed that the Egyptian intergovernorate migrants tended to have a better educational profile than nonmigrants. The high percentages of illiterates among migrants could be related to the engagement of these people in construction and other marginal activities in urban centers.

Table 6.4

Percentage Distribution* of Migrants 10 Years Old and Over by Education and Governorate, Egypt, 1976

Governorate of Enumeration	Illiterate	Read and Write	Below University First Degree	University First Degree	Above University First Degree	Number of Migrants[x]
Cairo	45.3	22.7	25.2	6.4	0.2	1,323,386
Alexandria	49.9	22.4	21.7	5.8	0.3	415,533
Port Said	36.3	24.7	36.3	2.7	0.1	192,047
Suez	31.4	20.0	19.4	1.1	**	138,162
Damietta	51.8	25.7	19.5	2.9	0.1	65,661
Dakahlia	46.2	20.8	27.8	5.0	0.2	177,234
Sharkia	53.4	17.6	24.9	4.0	0.1	193,424
Kalyubia	48.9	25.9	22.9	2.3	0.1	241,957
Kafr El-Sheikh	66.7	13.8	16.4	3.0	0.1	110,399
Gharbia	43.6	21.5	29.3	5.3	0.2	171,680
Menoufia	43.2	18.7	32.5	5.4	0.2	63,622
Behera	62.1	20.1	15.5	2.2	0.1	223,344
Ismailia	50.2	23.8	24.0	1.9	**	180,884
Giza	40.6	22.4	28.7	7.7	0.6	595,963
Beni-Suef	52.7	18.4	24.3	4.5	0.1	51,146
Fayoum	57.9	15.4	22.0	4.5	0.2	53,571
Minya	50.4	17.2	27.8	4.5	0.2	83,812
Assyut	39.4	13.7	41.0	5.4	0.5	91,322
Souhag	47.2	15.1	31.5	6.1	0.1	63,558
Kena	44.1	20.0	30.7	5.0	0.1	57,795
Aswan	47.8	24.6	24.5	3.0	0.1	95,526
Red Sea	48.6	25.6	22.3	3.4	0.1	24,829
Matrouh	47.5	22.2	24.4	5.7	0.1	15,251
El-Wadi El-Gedid	41.3	18.5	34.5	5.6	0.1	10,824
Sinai	56.5	21.5	18.9	3.1	0.1	3,868
Total Male	29.4	28.8	33.3	7.9	0.5	2,366,049
Total Female	64.8	14.9	18.0	2.2	0.1	2,308,747
Total Total	46.4	21.6	25.4	5.0	0.3	4,644,796

Source: Compiled and computed from CAPMAS (1980: table 19).

*Percentages of any governorate may not add to 100 due to rounding.

**Less than .05.

[x]Excluding the unstated category numbering: 23,250 males and 36,544 females.

Occupational Profile of Migrants

Internal migration has been hypothesized as a consequence of changes in the occupational structure (El-Attar and Tarver, 1972). Although occupation is related to education and income, it is very difficult to generalize about its composition among migrants in developing countries (Todaro, 1976, 27). Accordingly, the present analysis examines the occupational differentials of migrants and compares them with those of nonmigrants.

Table 6.5 gives the percentage distribution of intergovernorate migrants and that of nonmigrants 15 years old and over in Egypt by socio-occupational grouping in 1976. On the whole, the occupational composition of migrants consists roughly of 17 percent white-collar workers, 14 percent blue-collar workers, 7 percent service workers, 5 percent farm and kindred workers, and 57 percent not

Table 6.5
Percentage Distribution* of Migrants 15 Years Old and Over by Socio-Occupational Category and Governorate, Egypt, 1976

Governorate of Enumeration	White-Collar	Blue-Collar	Service Workers	Farmers and Others	Not Occupied	Number of Migrants[x]
Cairo	21.0	16.3	9.1	0.6	53.0	1,243,919
Alexandria	16.9	18.3	8.5	2.7	53.6	390,003
Port Said	17.9	13.8	4.8	3.2	60.3	153,534
Suez	12.8	21.5	5.6	4.3	55.9	110,376
Damietta	12.4	15.7	4.7	12.2	55.0	58,597
Dakahlia	16.0	7.5	4.0	11.1	61.4	159,383
Sharkia	14.1	6.6	3.4	12.5	63.4	172,960
Kalyubia	13.2	22.5	6.3	1.6	56.5	214,755
Kafr El-Sheikh	10.7	4.8	3.1	23.8	57.6	98,014
Gharbia	18.2	14.5	4.8	3.0	59.5	156,971
Menoufia	17.3	7.1	4.0	4.2	67.4	57,474
Behera	9.7	11.2	3.8	15.7	59.6	204,441
Ismailia	11.8	13.0	4.9	12.3	58.1	147,791
Giza	20.7	15.2	7.8	1.0	55.3	535,363
Beni-Suef	16.1	6.9	4.3	6.4	66.3	46,580
Fayoum	15.0	5.9	4.1	10.5	64.5	49,523
Minya	14.8	5.8	4.3	5.8	69.3	77,806
Assyut	14.9	4.5	4.1	4.7	71.7	84,843
Souhag	18.1	5.0	4.0	4.6	68.4	58,398
Kena	17.6	10.1	5.2	4.7	62.5	52,105
Aswan	14.8	14.9	7.1	7.5	55.7	83,100
Red Sea	13.4	30.0	7.5	2.3	46.7	22,839
Matrouh	21.2	18.7	8.1	4.9	47.1	13,786
El-Wadi El-Gedid	20.2	6.9	5.6	12.1	55.2	9,576
Sinai	13.4	46.7	12.5	6.9	20.5	9,900
Total — Male	29.2	28.3	12.2	9.0	21.3	2,081,847
Total — Female	5.8	0.5	1.4	0.3	91.9	2,123,619
Total — Total	17.4	14.3	6.7	4.6	57.0	4,205,466

Source: Compiled and computed from CAPMAS (1980: table 20).

*Percentage total of any governorate may not add to 100 due to rounding.

[x]Excluding migrants without occupations numbering: 76,108 males and 28,400 females.

occupied. The percentages corresponding to nonmigrants were 8, 8, 3, 22 and 58, respectively. Except for the "not occupied," the statistics show marked differences in the quality and quantity of the occupational composition of migrants and nonmigrants. Migrants constituted significantly more of white-collar, blue-collar, and service occupations and far less of farm and kindred workers. The category "not occupied" consists mainly of females (92 percent among migrants and 95 percent for nonmigrants) who are presumably housewives.

Differentials among governorates in their migrants' occupational composition are conspicuous. The data in Table 6.5 show that, with the exception of the frontier governorates, the governorate of Cairo had the highest percentage of white-collar and service workers and the lowest percentage of farm and kindred workers. In other governorates, construction and other related activities in urban areas attracted farm and unskilled workers from nearby rural areas, as was the case with Alexandria, Port Said, Suez, Damietta, and Kalyubia. Since there is a strong relationship between education and occupation, one expects high percentages of white-collar workers and, to a lesser degree, service workers in the urban governorates and in governorates having colleges and universities as in Giza, Gharbia, and Menoufia.

Industrial Profile of Migrants

Introduction of new industries requires new skills and services. The population 6 years old and over increased by almost 44 percent (from 21.1 million to 30.3 million) between 1960 and 1976 (CAPMAS, 1978, Table 3; Department of Statistics and Census, 1963, Table 4). In the meantime, agriculture increased by 10.8 percent, but its relative share decreased by 4.8 percentage points and that of manufacturing increased by 1.1 percentage points during the period 1960 to 1976. In fact, the change in manufacturing in that period was 92.0 percent (from 0.7 million to 1.4 million).

Table 6.6 gives the industrial pattern of migrants and nonmigrants 6 years old and over by governorate of enumeration in Egypt in 1976. On the whole, the industrial pattern of migrants was entirely different from that of nonmigrants. In quantitative terms, the factor accounting for the highest percentage among migrants was "public and personal services" (12.9 percent), as compared with 4.9 percent for nonmigrants. Agricultural and kindred activities accounted for the highest percentage (18.5) in the nonmigrant population. The second highest industrial sector among migrants was "manufacturing" (8.2 percent), followed by "commerce" (4.8 percent), "agriculture" (4.6 percent), and "transportation" (3.4 percent). A possible generalization about the industrial pattern of migrants by governorates is that there are pronounced differences in migration rates among industrial sectors. For example, while Fayoum's nonmigrants had 28.2 percent in agriculture, only 10.8 percent of migrants were so categorized. The percentage of the "inactive" was smaller among migrants (15.4 males and 46.3 females) than among nonmigrants (20.3 males and 47.2 females); both exhibited a predominance of males in economic activities. However, female migrants showed a slightly higher percentage of participation than nonmigrant females, especially in "public and personal services" (5.4 percent for migrants and 1.6 percent for nonmigrants). Another observation is that female migrants tend to participate less in agriculture and more in nonagricultural activities.

WHY PEOPLE MOVE

Table 6.7 gives the percentage distribution of migrants in Egypt by reasons for changing previous residence and governorates of enumeration in 1976. The table presents the data in eight categorical reasons as given in the census: work, education, marriage, divorce/widowing, return from compulsory migration, change of residence, accompanying, and other.

The leading reason was "accompanying," accounting for 2.4 million or roughly 48 percent of all migrants. Two-thirds of these were females (1.6 million). "Work" was the second most reported reason (almost 26 percent), followed by "marriage" (22 percent), and "return from compulsory migration" (5 percent). "Education" and "change of residence" had roughly equal shares (3.8 and 3.6). The "other" category formed 1.3 percent, while "divorce/widowing" constituted two-tenths of 1 percent. The indices for the governorates exhibit generally the same pattern for the entire nation with the exception of Sinai. Sex differentials were very conspicuous for all reasons, especially "marriage."

Journey to Work

One of the tables in the 1976 internal migration data crossclassifies workers by their governorate of residence and governorate of work (CAPMAS, 1978, Table 26). The data revealed that of the 10.2 million workers, 4 percent worked in a governorate different from their governorate of residence. The governorate with the highest percentage doing so was Giza (20.3), followed by Kalyubia (10.7) and Cairo (7.6). These governorates formed Greater Cairo. Of those working in a governorate different from that of their residence, 90.3 percent of those in Giza and 79.1 percent of those in Kalyubia worked in Cairo. The percentages of those working in Giza and Kalyubia were 32.2 and 47.1, respectively. The percentages of those in the other governorates ranged between 0.5 percent in Aswan and 3.1 percent in Menoufia.

CONSEQUENCES OF MIGRATION

In Egypt, migration has substantial consequences, especially with regard to the rapid population growth of major urban centers, social and economic conditions, the environment, and welfare of individuals.

A basic fact about Egypt is the impossibility of increasing its cultivable land in an amount necessary to absorb the annual growth in its population. Thus, while

Table 6.6
Industrial Pattern of Intergovernorate Migrants 6 Years Old and Over by Governorate of Enumeration, Egypt, 1976*

Governorate of Enumeration	Agriculture, Hunting, Fishing	Mining	Manufac-turing	Electric, Gas, and Water	Construc-tion	Commerce, Restaurants, Hotels	Transport, etc.	Finance, etc.	Public and Personal Service	Inactive	Number of Migrants[x]
Cairo	0.6	0.2	10.5	0.5	3.8	7.0	4.2	0.8	16.3	56.1	1,358,214
Alexandria	2.9	0.2	13.6	0.5	3.3	5.9	3.9	0.6	12.6	56.4	426,738
Port Said	2.7	0.1	3.6	0.3	2.5	4.7	5.7	0.3	10.0	70.3	210,336
Suez	3.3	0.5	6.1	0.5	5.8	4.1	4.6	0.2	6.6	68.3	157,038
Damietta	11.2	0.1	11.4	0.2	1.7	3.3	2.0	0.4	10.0	59.6	68,977
Dakahlia	10.8	**	4.0	0.6	1.1	3.6	2.1	0.5	12.3	65.0	184,089
Sharkia	12.8	0.1	2.9	0.3	1.1	2.5	2.2	0.5	11.3	66.5	202,504
Kalyubia	1.5	0.2	15.4	0.4	3.0	3.5	3.5	0.3	9.3	62.8	256,943
Kafr El-Sheikh	25.3	**	1.9	0.2	0.9	2.5	1.2	0.4	7.9	59.7	117,119
Gharbia	3.0	0.1	11.8	0.2	1.5	3.7	2.8	0.6	13.2	63.1	175,833
Menoufia	4.2	0.1	4.5	0.3	0.8	2.5	1.9	0.5	14.4	70.9	65,869
Behera	14.5	0.1	7.3	0.3	3.6	2.5	1.6	0.3	7.0	62.5	231,070
Ismailia	10.1	0.1	1.9	0.3	4.7	3.0	4.0	0.2	7.5	68.2	205,479
Giza	1.0	0.2	8.3	0.4	3.8	5.6	3.3	0.9	15.6	60.8	626,743
Beni-Suef	6.3	**	3.0	0.3	1.3	3.4	2.2	0.5	13.4	69.7	52,846

Fayoum	10.5	**	3.0	0.4	0.9	3.0	1.9	0.7	12.8	66.8	55,332
Minya	6.0	**	3.0	0.3	0.8	2.8	2.0	0.7	12.4	72.0	87,250
Assyut	4.8	**	2.2	0.4	0.9	2.7	1.8	0.5	12.7	73.9	93,972
Souhag	4.8	**	2.4	0.4	0.8	2.3	2.1	0.8	14.8	71.6	66,940
Kena	4.8	0.3	6.5	0.7	1.3	2.9	2.8	0.6	12.8	67.3	60,657
Aswan	6.7	0.9	5.2	1.4	2.1	4.2	3.4	0.3	11.5	64.3	104,329
Red Sea	2.3	21.9	1.6	0.1	3.6	2.5	3.2	1.1	10.0	53.6	26,043
Matrouh	3.9	0.8	3.5	0.4	10.3	5.6	4.4	0.5	16.1	54.4	16,367
El-Wadi El-Gedid	10.6	0.2	1.2	0.4	2.9	2.3	1.9	0.4	18.7	61.5	11,538
Sinai	5.9	11.1	0.9	0.3	33.7	3.5	3.4	1.8	9.9	29.4	4,049
Total Male	8.7	0.6	15.5	0.8	6.1	9.2	6.7	1.0	20.5	30.9	2,427,100
Total Female	0.4	**	0.8	0.1	0.1	0.5	0.2	0.2	5.4	92.3	2,439,175
Total	4.6	0.3	8.2	0.4	3.1	4.8	3.4	0.6	12.9	61.7	4,866,275

Source: Compiled and computed from CAPMAS (1980: table 18).

*Percentages of any governorate may not add to 100 due to rounding.

**Value less than .05.

xExcluding the unstated cases numbering 36,569 males and 6,732 females.

119

Table 6.7
Percentage Distribution* of Migrants by Reasons for Changing Previous Residence and Governorate, Egypt, 1976

Governorate of Enumeration	Work	Education	Marriage	Divorce/ Widowhood
Cairo	34.4%	3.6%	11.4%	0.2%
Alexandria	37.1	4.2	8.4	0.1
Port Said	2.6	0.5	0.3	**
Suez	6.6	0.1	0.2	**
Damietta	24.6	1.8	15.1	0.2
Dakahlia	24.6	7.4	17.3	0.2
Sharkia	22.3	4.3	20.6	0.2
Kalyubia	24.3	1.1	9.8	0.2
Kafr El-Sheikh	25.6	4.5	14.9	0.1
Gharbia	29.6	3.8	18.1	0.3
Menoufia	20.8	6.6	27.6	0.4
Behera	27.6	1.4	18.1	0.2
Ismailia	8.3	0.4	1.0	**
Giza	18.4	3.4	11.2	0.2
Beni-Suef	22.8	4.5	30.7	0.3
Fayoum	25.4	5.9	29.4	0.4
Minya	23.3	9.1	27.9	0.4
Assyut	19.8	22.9	20.3	0.2
Souhag	23.0	8.3	25.3	0.2
Kena	27.2	6.4	16.4	0.3
Aswan	28.5	3.7	4.6	0.2
Red Sea	41.2	1.4	2.0	**
Matrouh	40.5	1.7	8.8	0.1
El-Wadi El-Gedid	29.6	7.0	4.6	0.1
Sinai	54.5	0.1	0.1	**
Total: Male	46.7	5.5	2.1	**
Total: Female	4.2	2.0	22.1	0.3
Total	25.5	3.8	12.1	0.2

Source. Compiled and computed from CAPMAS (1980; table 21)
* - excludes unstated: 51,281 male and 49,569 female
** - less than 0.05

Return from Compulsory Migration	Change of Residence	Accom- panying	Other	Number of Migrants
1.7%	3.2%	44.4%	1.1%	1,378,898
1.5	1.9	45.9	0.9	427,605
31.2	**	65.1	0.2	227,541
19.8	**	73.2	**	178,563
3.2	4.6	48.8	1.7	70,758
3.7	2.2	42.7	2.0	185,900
5.8	2.2	43.2	1.5	203,802
1.7	6.8	54.0	2.1	270,587
1.2	1.6	51.0	1.0	119,962
2.4	1.7	42.4	1.7	179,332
4.4	2.3	35.2	2.6	66,470
2.6	1.3	46.7	1.2	235,272
19.4	0.6	69.2	1.0	226,490
1.1	12.1	52.2	1.3	651,797
2.9	1.4	33.9	3.4	53,244
1.6	1.4	34.3	1.5	56,090
1.9	1.3	34.0	2.1	88,931
1.7	0.6	30.9	3.5	94,120
2.7	1.5	36.4	2.6	68,459
4.2	1.0	42.6	1.9	61,603
15.6	1.4	45.8	0.3	112,126
0.8	0.3	52.6	1.7	27,236
0.8	1.0	45.5	1.6	17,124
2.1	2.4	52.1	2.1	11,710
15.4	1.0	28.6	0.4	4,585
6.7	5.3	32.0	1.5	2,519,800 [*]
3.5	1.8	65.0	1.1	2,498,405
5.1	3.6	48.5	1.3	5,018,205

the total area of Egypt is 386,000 square miles, about 96 percent (48,205,049) of Egypt's total population (50,455,049) in 1986 was packed into 3.6 percent (14,000 square miles) of the total area. The remainder of the area is desert. Rural inhabitants comprised 56 percent of the total population in 1986 (CAPMAS, 1987, Table 2). Rural population pressure, lack of employment opportunities, and bad environmental conditions (caused by deficient public amenities) impel the people to migrate to urban centers. Houses connected to a public network of purified water comprised 73 percent of the total houses in Egypt in 1986 (CAPMAS, 1987, 8). The specific percentages for major residential and geographical types are approximately as follows: urban, 92; rural, 56; urban governorates, 97; Lower Egypt, 73; Upper Egypt, 58; and frontier governorates, 66. The percentages for electricity are roughly: total, 87; urban, 96; and rural, 79.

The tapering off of the urban population growth rate between 1976 and 1986 cannot be considered to be the result of reduction in rural-urban migration since emigration to the Arab-Gulf states (1.4 and 2.2 million in 1976 and 1986, respectively) has been responsible for the decline. The population of Greater Cairo in 1986 reached 9.8 million persons. This type of growth puts strain on the limited development resources and polarizes rural-urban competition, which most often results in disbursing resources in favor of urban areas. Stopping rural-to-urban migration requires bringing about a balance between rural and urban areas in all aspects of life. This is an infeasible measure, and the consequences will be continued rural-to-urban migration, and consequent problems to policy makers of sheltering, feeding, transporting, employing, and providing health services to an expanded urban population. Although the government established several other universities in Lower and Upper Egypt, the number of students enrolled in schools in the vicinity of Cairo accounted for almost 51 percent of total enrollment of all universities (682,348) in 1984–85 (CAPMAS, 1986, 169). Rural-urban differentials in health facilities reflect some of the imbalance between them in this regard. The number of persons per bed in treatment units in 1985 was 3,008 in rural areas and 348 persons in urban areas (CAPMAS, 1986, 123; 1987, 12).

NOTES

I am grateful to the Central Agency for Public Mobilization and Statistics (CAPMAS), Cairo Demographic Center (CDC), and Institute of National Planning. Among the CAPMAS staff special thanks are due Dr. A.M. Haliouda (president) and Messrs. A.F. Sultan, A. El-Baz, Dr. F.S. Murad, I.R. Abdel-Khaleq and S.Z. Amin. Dr. M.A. El-Badry (Director, CDC) and his staff at the CDC have provided relevant publications. Thanks are also due Mr. A.M. El-Hakeem.

1. Egypt is one of the few developing countries with a long history of population censuses. The first census dates back to 3340 B.C. (CAPMAS, 1986). However, modern censuses in Egypt began in 1882, the eleventh of which was taken in 1986. The year and population (in millions) for each census are as follows (CAPMAS, 1986, 9): 1880—4.5, 1882—6.7; 1897—9.6; 1907—11.2; 1917—12.7; 1927—14.2; 1937—15.9; 1947—

19.0; 1960—26.0; 1966—30.1; 1976—36.6; and 1986—48. The 1986 census excludes 2.2 million persons living abroad (CAPMAS, 1987). These data indicate that the doubling time of Egypt's population is becoming shorter over time.

2. Although the undertaking of modern censuses in Egypt began in 1882, the urban definition was first introduced in the eighth census in 1960. Basically, the definition is couched in administrative rather than criterion configuration. Specifically, urban areas consist of the four urban governorates (Cairo, Alexandria, Port Said, and Suez), the capitals of nonurban governorates, the capitals of *marakez* (the administration districts to which a governorate is divided) (Department of Statistics and Census, 1963, 3), and cities, towns, and their administrative subdivisions. For more details, see Sayed and Zaky (1985).

REFERENCES

Al-Nasr, A.S., and M. Attiya. 1985. "Urban Inmigration and Outmigration in Egypt, An Analytical Study of Birthplace Data in the 1976 Census." *Population Bulletin of ECWA*, No. 26:9–37.

Central Agency for Public Mobilization and Statistics (CAPMAS). 1987. *The General Census of Population, Housing, and Establishments, 1986, Preliminary Results* (in Arabic). Nasr City, Cairo: CAPMAS Press.

———. 1986. *Statistical Yearbook*. Nasr City, Cairo: CAPMAS.

———. 1980. *1976 Population and Housing Census: Fertility and Internal Migration and Movement of Workers and Students Vol. 11*. Nasr City, Cairo: CAPMAS.

———. 1978. *The General Census of Population and Housing, 1976* (in Arabic). Nasr City, Cairo: CAPMAS.

Department of Statistics and Census. 1963. *1960 Census of Population, Vol. 11, General Tables*. Cairo, S.O.P. Press.

El-Attar, M. 1987. "Internal Migration and Development: Data Sources and Measurement in Developing Countries." *International Journal of Contemporary Sociology* 24:112–25.

———, and J.D. Tarver. 1972. "A Theoretical Model for Predicting Internal Migration in the United States." *1972 Social Statistics Section, Proceedings of the American Statistical Association:* 227–32.

El-Badry, M.A. 1965a. "Internal Migration in the United Arab Republic." *L'Egypte Contemporaine* (in Arabic) 56:31–44.

———. 1965b. "Trends in the Components of Population Growth in the Arab Countries of the Middle East: A Survey of Present Information." *Demography* 2:140–86.

El-Boraey, A.E. 1985. "Internal Migration Differentials in Upper Egypt Economic Regions." *Research Monograph, Series No. 15*, Chapter 13:241–55. Cairo: Cairo Demographic Centre.

Eldridge, H.T., and D.S. Thomas. 1964. *Population Redistribution and Economic Growth, United States 1870–1950, Vol. III, Demographic Analysis and Interpretations*. Philadelphia: American Philosophical Society.

Goldstein, S. 1987. "Forms of Mobility and Their Policy Implications: Thailand and China Compared." *Social Forces* 65:915–42.

Hamilton, C.H. 1959. "Educational Selectivity of Net Migration from the South." *Social Forces* 38:33–42.

Hassan, S.S., and M.A. El-Dayem. 1973. "Characteristics of Recent Migrants and Non-migrants in Cairo." In *Urbanization and Migration in Some Arab and African Countries, Research Monograph Series No. 4*. Cairo: Cairo Demographic Centre.

Ibrahim, M.F.M. 1985. "Volume and Patterns of Internal Migration in Cairo Economic Region." *Research Monograph, Series No. 15*, Chapter 14:257–82. Cairo: Cairo Demographic Centre.

Ibrahim, S.E. 1982. *A Critical Review of Internal Migration in Egypt, Research Monograph V*. Cairo: Population and Family Planning Board.

Nassef, A. 1985. "Some Aspects of Rural/Urban Migration in Egypt." Chapter 6 in Cairo Demographic Centre, *1984 Annual Seminar:*117–45. Cairo: Cairo Demographic Centre.

———. 1973. "Internal Migration and Urbanization in Egypt." *Urbanization and Migration in Some Arab and African Countries, Cairo Demographic Centre Research Monograph Series* No. 4. Cairo: S.O.P. Press.

Sayed, H.A.A., and H.H.M. Zaky. 1985. "Rural-Urban Migration Process in Egypt." Chapter 8 in Cairo Demographic Centre, *1984 Annual Seminar:*165–92. Cairo: Cairo Demographic Centre.

Statistical and Census Department. 1954. *Population Census of Egypt, 1947, General Tables*. Cairo: Government Press.

———. 1942. *Population Census of Egypt, 1937, General Tables*. Cairo: Government Press.

Thomas, D.S. 1938. "Selective Migration." *Milbank Memorial Fund Quarterly* 16:403–7.

Todaro, M.P. 1976. *Internal Migration in Developing Countries: A Review of Theory, Evidence, Methodology, and Research Priorities*. Geneva: International Labour Office.

United Nations. 1987. *The Prospects of World Urbanization, Population Studies No. 101*. New York: United Nations Publication Sales No. E.87.XIII.3.

———. 1976. "National Practices in the Definition, Collection, Compilation and Uses of Internal Migration Statistics." ST/EST/STAT/88 (5 January). New York: United Nations Secretariat.

———. 1970. *Methods of Measuring Internal Migration, Manual VI*. New York: United Nations Publication Sales No. E.82.XIII.4.

Yap, L.Y.L. 1975. "Internal Migration in Less Developed Countries: A Survey of the Literature." *World Bank Staff Working Paper* No. 215. Washington, D.C.: World Bank.

7

FRANCE

Daniel Courgeau

To highlight the features of the French internal migration process it is necessary to link it to the simultaneous demographic transition experienced by this country. Fertility and mortality began to decline substantially at the end of the eighteenth century, more than one century before they did in other European countries. As a result, the country had minimal and occasionally a negative natural increase during the nineteenth and the first half of the twentieth centuries. Its population increased from 29 million at the beginning of the nineteenth century to around 40 million by 1881, where it remained until 1946. To maintain this population, the country had to attract large-scale international migration, while other European countries were sending significant numbers of migrants abroad to prevent excessive growth of their populations.

During the same time, urbanization and industrialization in France occurred at a slower pace than in some other European countries as the population pressure was lower. For example, in England the urban population exceeded the rural by the middle of the nineteenth century, while in France this did not occur until the 1930s. The process of urbanization centered mainly on Paris, while provincial centers had a slower growth rate. In 1982 the Paris metropolitan area had a population of more than 10 million, while the next largest urban area (Lyon) had only 1.5 million.

After World War II, a short-term fertility increase during the 1960s and significant immigration, both of foreigners and of French previously living in Algeria, raised the French population to 55 million in 1982. In this chapter we will show the changes that occurred in the internal migration process, as the country changed from an industrial to a postindustrial economy.

DATA ON MIGRATION

Definitions of Migration

Unlike other demographic events, migration may be defined in terms of space as well as time. We will now review the existing space and time classifications.

A first spatial classification was made at the time of the French Revolution and has remained nearly unchanged ever since. The communes (numbering around 37,000) are local town or village communities. These are grouped into larger administrative units called departments, of which there were originally ninety. In 1968, this figure was adjusted to ninety-five after partitioning the Paris area.

Another spatial classification distinguishes between rural and urban areas. Since 1954 the urban areas (*unites urbaines*) have been defined on the basis of a criterion of uninterrupted urbanization and classified according to their size. The rural areas are defined as nonurban ones, with fewer than 2,000 inhabitants. The final spatial classification consists of metropolitan areas (*Zones de Peuplement Industriel et Urbain*) defined with more functional criteria (such as the proportion of population working in industry or commuting to urban centers). They are classified according to the same size schedules.

The first temporal classification provided data on lifetime migrants; this originated with the 1861 census. One hundred years later the 1962 census contained, for the first time, a question on place of residence at the time of the previous census. These data on migrants are now available for four intercensal periods.

More recently, retrospective surveys have given the entire migration history of individuals, permitting one to follow the migration process in greater detail.

Sources of Data

The main sources of data are censuses and retrospective surveys, since the country has no population register. Up to the 1962 census, data on place of birth were published with various details from one census to another. The most detailed tables are found at the beginning of this century.

Since the 1962 census, data on commune of residence at the time of the previous census have been classified according to sex, age, social class, and marital status. These data are also published for every geographical unit. Since 1975, there has been a complete record of residential mobility which allows international comparisons. However, as the time intervals between censuses have changed (1954–1962–1968–1975–1982), models have to be used to permit temporal comparison (Courgeau, 1983). The annual rates are estimates.

Specific surveys undertaken are more useful to ascertain the entire life history. The last one, undertaken by the Institut National d'Etudes Demographiques (INED) in 1981 provides the family, work, and migration history of 4,602 individuals born between 1911 and 1935. It allows complex analysis of interactions between these different histories.

Quality of Data

We have some information on the quality of these different data sets. The census question on place of birth had a good response rate (99.6 percent) at the 1911 census. The census question on place of residence at the time of the previous census is less accurate: the nonresponse rate increases from one census to the next (2.1 percent in 1962, 2.3 percent in 1969, 2.7 percent in 1975). When comparing the place of residence in 1968 as reported in the 1975 census for a panel of individuals with known place of residence in 1968, 96.1 percent of respondents were correctly located. This attests to the quality of these answers (Courgeau, forthcoming).

To test the quality of the data obtained from the retrospective survey, a presurvey was undertaken in Belgium. Since this country has a population register, the accuracy of the collected data can be checked against the register. The first results show that, even though errors in dating migration are frequent (Duchene, 1985), the logical sequence of events is usually correct (Courgeau, 1985a). Thus, memory seems to be sufficiently reliable for purposes of analysis.

PRINCIPAL POPULATION MOVEMENTS

We can observe these population movements on different spatial scales.

The National Level

Let us first observe the volume of movement over time. Using place of birth data according to age, we are able to give the percentage of those aged 45 living outside their department of birth. Unfortunately, as a change occurred in department definition, we will have two different curves. The first one (ninety departments) consists of generations born from 1816 to 1926 (Tugault, 1973). The second one (ninety-five departments) comprises those born from 1887 to 1947. Nevertheless Figure 7.1 shows that these results are consistent. First, we observe an accelerated increase in this percentage, from 20 percent for cohorts born around 1820 to 25 percent for cohorts born around 1890 (ninety departments). This growth is related to the Industrial Revolution, which began in the middle of the nineteenth century. Afterward an irregular increase appears with some periods of decrease. The first is among the cohorts born from 1895 to 1905 who entered the labor force soon after World War I. Such persons could more easily remain in the agricultural sector as many farms were unoccupied because of war deaths. The second period of decrease concerns the cohorts born from 1920 to 1930, who entered the labor force around the time of World War II. Whatever the nature of these irregularities, we have an increase in the percentage of outmigrants from 38 percent for cohorts born around 1890 to 47 percent for cohorts born around 1940 (ninety-five departments).

We can also observe a reversal in the differences in migration behavior for males compared to females. Until the birth cohort of 1890, males had been more mobile; since then, females have been more mobile. However, the differences are small, and the two curves follow a similar pattern.

When using data from 1962 and later concerning the place of residence at the

Figure 7.1
Percentage of Those Aged 45 Living Outside Their Department of Birth by Sex and Year of Birth

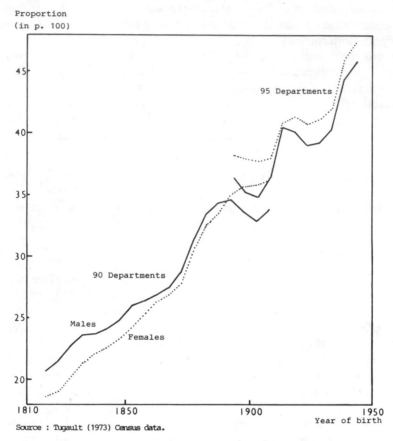

Source : Tugault (1973) Census data.

time of the previous census, we observe growth of annual migration rates, with a reversal occurring in the 1975–82 period (see Table 7.1).

This reduction may also be observed in many other developed countries. It may be linked to the economic crisis beginning in 1974. However, such a reduction appeared in countries with population registers (such as Belgium and Netherlands) or regular population surveys (such as the United States) before the crisis. Thus, reduction may be linked to a more general change in developed countries leading to a postindustrial society.

The age and sex structure of migrants between 1975 and 1982 is given in Figure 7.2.

The age pattern of French migration is very similar to that observed in other countries. Until age 15 the rate of descent of the prelabor force population is similar to the rate of descent of the labor force population aged 25 to 45 (their

Table 7.1
Mean Annual Migration Rates from 1954 to 1982 (persons per thousand)

Changes of	1954-1962	1962-1968	1968-1975	1975-1982
residence	-	-	103.7	101.0
communes	52.3	56.4	64.4	62.5
departments	21.4 *	26.4	30.9	28.3
regions	14.2	15.9	19.0	17.6

*Changes of departments for the period 1954-1962 are not comparable to those for the following periods after partitioning the Paris area.

parents). Between the ages of 15 and 25, there is a significant increase in mobility owing to entry in the labor force and marriage. A retirement peak appears between 60 and 70 years, followed by a new increase in the mobility of the aged, especially women. There are also differences between sexes such as more significant mobility for women aged 20 to 30, explained by earlier marriage, and for women aged 55 to 65, explained by earlier retirement. During the entire life course we have an expectancy of 8.49 moves for men and 8.77 for women. For interregional migration, this expectancy declines to 1.53 moves for men and 1.52 for women.

Interregional Migration

If we observe migration in the interregional context, Table 7.2 shows that important changes have occurred in net annual internal migration flows to these areas during the past two decades.

From 1954 to 1962, only four out of twenty-two regions had a positive net migration. These were the Paris, Rhône-Alpes, Provence-Côte d'Azur, and, to a lesser degree, Alsace regions. This evokes J. F. Gravier's (1947) title *Paris and the French Desert,* which adds Lyon (Rhône-Alpes) and Marseille (Mediterranean) to the capital, leaving behind a depopulating country. From 1975 to 1982 the map is greatly changed. Now fifteen out of twenty-two regions have a positive net migration. Even more interesting is the fact that Paris, the most attractive region in 1954–62, becomes the least so. In contrast, the Languedoc-Roussillon region, one of the less attractive areas in 1962, became the most attractive in 1982. However, this region is not very appealing from a purely economic point of view. Even if it has had an increase in employment, very high rates of unemployment and very low levels of gross domestic product per person persist. Therefore, other noneconomic factors are clearly attracting people to this region. Previously peripheral regions are also becoming very attractive. These include Brittany, Pays de la Loire, Poitou-Charentes, and Limousin among oth-

Figure 7.2
Age and Sex Structure of Movers and Interregional Migrants, 1982 Census

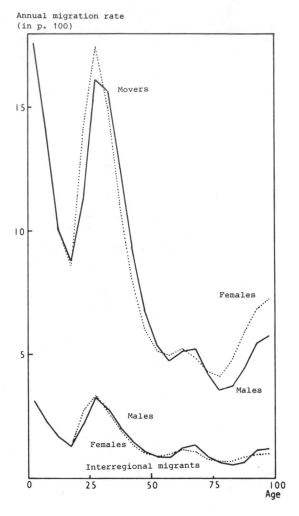

ers. The regions that are least attractive are the old northern industrial regions, which have yet to convert their economic base to tertiary activities.

Migration in the Urban-Rural Context

Figure 7.3 shows that significant changes have occurred in the net migration flows for urban and rural areas.

During the 1954–62 period we observe a general increase of the net internal migration rates proportional to the number of inhabitants, with a slow decrease

Table 7.2
Annual Net Internal Migration Rates for French Regions in 1954–62 and 1975–82 (persons per 10,000)

REGION	1954 - 1962	1975-1982
Région parisienne	52	- 64
Champagne-Ardenne	- 24	- 39
Picardie	- 12	6
Haute-Normandie	- 3	- 2
Centre	- 1	42
Basse-Normandie	- 55	- 7
Bourgogne	- 13	8
Nord-Pas-de-Calais	- 17	- 45
Lorraine	- 4	- 52
Alsace	2	2
Franche-Comté	- 2	- 20
Pays de la Loire	- 29	17
Bretagne	- 49	31
Poitou-Charentes	- 32	13
Aquitaine	- 6	42
Midi-Pyrénées	- 19	32
Limousin	- 30	36
Rhône-Alpes	19	15
Auvergne	- 20	5
Languedoc-Roussillon	- 21	90
Provence-Côte d'Azur	43	73
Corse	-110	82

for areas of 100,000 inhabitants or more. Net migration for the Paris urban area represented around 28 percent of that of all urban areas. At the time it was the most attractive place in France. Rural areas experienced net out-migration.

Twenty years later, the situation was reversed, with rural areas becoming the most attractive and the urban area of Paris the least. Only urban areas of fewer than 20,000 inhabitants continued to attract migrants, on balance, but to a lesser extent than the rural areas.

Let us examine in more detail how age groups are affected by these changes. Figure 7.4 presents changes in age rates for the urban area of Paris, the medium-sized towns (50,000 to 99,999 inhabitants), and rural areas.

In the period from 1954 to 1962 the urban area of Paris had a positive net internal migration rate for all persons less than 50 years old, with the highest levels occurring at ages 20 to 29. At ages 50 and above, the rates became negative, reaching their lowest level around the retirement age. During the more recent periods only those aged 20 to 29 have positive net migration, although the

Figure 7.3
Annual Net Internal Migration Rates for Rural and Urban Areas, 1962 and 1982 Census

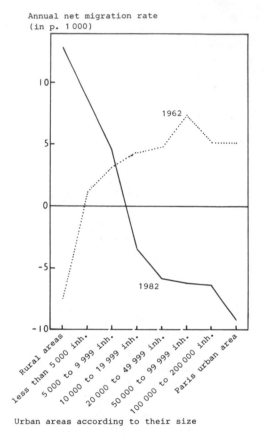

rates are less than those observed previously. The high out-migration of retirement persists, and a secondary minimum appears for those aged 30 to 39, which corresponds to the departure from Paris of parents with young children. It is interesting to note that the main changes result from an increase in out-migration rates rather than from a decrease in in-migration rates.

The rural part of the country experienced the reverse change, with a maximum net migration rate for those aged 30 to 39 and their children since the 1975 census. For the 1975–82 period only those aged 20 to 24 had a negative net migration rate. It is interesting to observe that, even after these rural areas are partitioned according to their connection to a metropolitan area, the two curves are very similar (see Figure 7.4d).

Figure 7.4
Annual Net Internal Migration Rates by Age for the Urban Area of Paris, the Medium-Sized Towns (50,000 to 99,999 inhab.), and the Rural Areas, 1962, 1975, 1982

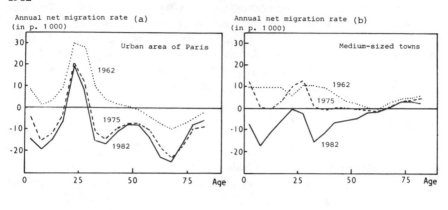

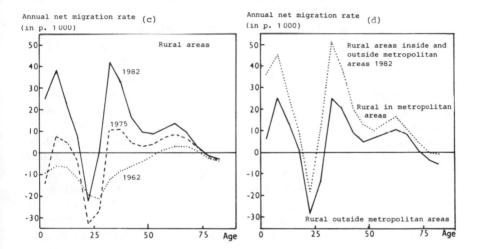

The medium-sized towns show a quite different evolution. During the 1954–62 period, they had positive net in-migration for every age group. However, for those aged 20 to 29, they were still less attractive than Paris. During the period 1968–75, it was primarily those aged 20 to 29 who were still attracted by such towns. This was true to a lesser degree for retired people. For the other age groups, we have essentially zero net migration.

During the last period, net migration becomes negative for those aged 30 to 39 and their children. Only retired people are now attracted by these medium-sized towns.

WHO MOVES

Census data are not the best means of ascertaining the characteristics of migrants. In fact, while these data depict moves between intercensal periods as well as the demographic and socioeconomic characteristics of individuals at the time of census, it is impossible to link these data with precision. Attempting to do so would lead to uninteresting or even incorrect results. For example, census data show a higher mobility for married individuals between 20 and 44 years of age. Such a result corresponds to marriage-related migration occurring before the census, while the mobility of married persons may be highly reduced.

Characteristics of Movers

To provide a better view of who moves, we must use life history data that provide the characteristics of individuals before their moves. Here we are using a model linking the migration rate in a multiplicative way (Courgeau, 1985b) according to the duration of stay, with family, economic, and political characteristics. Here we are considering migration as a change of dwelling or as a change of department.

First, we fitted a model introducing only age at the beginning of the stay and its duration. For age, this model give results very similar to those given by a cross-sectional analysis as in Figure 7.2 The duration effect is also very important, corresponding to a decrease of the mobility rate over time. After a ten-year duration, the rate of change of dwelling place will have been reduced by half and the rate of change of department of residence by two-thirds. When introducing variables corresponding to different characteristics of migrants, the dependence on age disappears or is often greatly reduced. On the other hand, the explanatory power of the model is greatly enhanced by introducing the manner in which such life characteristics may influence spatial mobility.

Let us look at the main results of such an analysis (Courgeau, 1985b). From family origins we are able to pinpoint an important "inheritability" factor: that is, the more mobile a person's parents were during his or her childhood, the more mobile that individual is likely to be. A reduction of mobility occurs after marriage, primarily for changes of dwelling place, showing results that are the opposite of those derived from census data. The same stabilization in changes of dwelling occurs after divorce and widowhood, while increased mobility follows the departure of children. These conclusions tell us that the microeconomic approach generally used to study migration may be extended to include the family life cycle.

Tenure status also plays a major part in the mobility process. As along as individuals live with their parents, their mobility rate will remain low. It they become tenants, their mobility increases. It increases further if they are housed by their employer. However, if they become the owner of a residence, their migration propensity will decrease to one-sixth of the mobility of a tenant for changes of dwelling and to one-fourth for changes of department.

Only for more recent cohorts does the level of educational or vocational training influence mobility. The higher the level of education or training, the higher the mobility rate. An individual with a high academic degree will be more open to employment in an increasingly large field. Similarly, mobility rates differ according to occupational status. The lowest rates occur for farmers. Farm laborers also have low rates but only at the local level. Higher rates are present for those working in a managerial capacity. Again, mobility appears to be related to the spatial extension of the work involved.

Finally, some political factors or events affect mobility rates. First, national service, in the case of men, leads to an increase in the migration rate. World War II provided different results for older and younger cohorts. Those individuals who had already begun work before the war were greatly affected by its outbreak and were influenced by new mobility processes associated with the war (for example, refugees or prisoners of war). Cohorts that began to work during the war exhibited contrasting behavior patterns with longer periods of fixed residence.

Repeat, Return, and Circulatory Moves

To analyze these moves we can return to census data, combining the question on place of birth with that on residence at the time of the previous census. This permits us to calculate primary, return, and secondary migration rates. The last rate will give us some information on circulatory migrants. Figure 7.5 shows these rates at the regional level among the male population by age. The data are from the 1982 census and closely approximate the rates for the female population.

Again, the three curves are very similar to those given in Figure 7.2 for all interregional migration. However, they are situated at very different levels. The lowest level is that of primary migration, and the highest is that of secondary migration. Once any interregional move occurs, a subsequent move to another region has a high probability of occurring. Return migration also occurs at a high rate. If the choice of destination were independent of the region of birth, return migration would be around one-twentieth of the secondary migration rate. In fact, the rate of return migration is approximately 70 percent of the secondary migration rate, showing an important preference for return migration to the region of birth. We also observe a higher proportion of return migration on retirement (80 percent of secondary migration at age 60 to 64), in comparison to other age groups (for example, 57 percent of the secondary migrations at age 45 to 54). Nevertheless, return migration regularly occurs at a high rate throughout the life cycle.

Figure 7.5
Primary, Secondary, and Return Migration Rates for Regional Migration among Males, 1982 Census

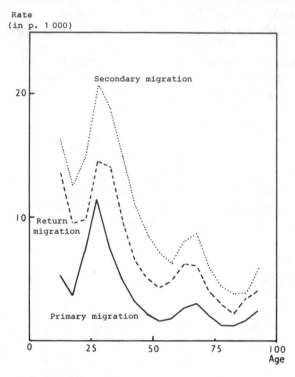

WHY PEOPLE MOVE

It is difficult to ascertain the reasons why people move: The reasons are complex, numerous, and in many cases not easily specified during an interview. Even when using a retrospective survey, it is difficult to know if given reasons are not an a posteriori reconstitution of the interviewee's past.

Economic Reasons

Let us first describe the economic reasons obtained from a retrospective survey (Bastide and Girard, 1974) before trying to ascertain some more social reasons.

Economic reasons are those given first (50 percent) by interviewees to explain a migration from rural to urban areas or between different urban areas. Therefore, they seem to be essential in the migration process. Nevertheless, they represent a great variety of different economic situations. In 37 percent of these cases, migration is linked to a transfer to another working place within the same firm or the same administration. Then for 18 percent of cases, migration is undertaken to pursue education. In only 15 percent of these cases was migration undertaken to find a new job. The remaining 30 percent migrate for other economic reasons such as becoming self-employed, search for better work, and retirement. It seems surprising that wage and income reasons are very rarely given. This may be linked to the fact that when answering such questions the interviewee does not like to give such materialistic reasons.

Social and Environmental Reasons

It is also interesting to notice that these rural-urban or urban-urban migrations are in fact explained by noneconomic reasons in 50 percent of the cases. For the same kind of migrations, family reasons are also important, being given in 22 percent of all cases. Here the principal reason for such moves is marriage, accounting for 60 percent of reported instances. The next most important reason is the desire to be closer to family members (17 percent).

These social and environmental reasons are even more important when migration is observed *within* urban or rural areas. They represent 72 percent of the reasons given for these moves. Of this group housing reasons account for 37 percent, of which "finding a more convenient location" was cited in 57 percent of these moves. Of the remainder, moving to attain home ownership was cited 20 percent of the time.

Family reasons are next in the order of priority, occurring in 35 percent of cases. Marriage is the main family reason (65 percent of them). It is perhaps surprising to observe that the expansion of the family is very rarely given as a reason for migration.

We can use another approach to explore some of the family reasons. First, we can verify that a majority of the interviewees have had a change in residence because of marriage. This was the case for 71 percent of the men and 80 percent of the women studied. Such a change occurred for both partners in 58 percent of the marriages, for the woman alone in 27 percent of them, and for the man alone in 14 percent of them. In only 1 percent of the marriages was there no change of dwelling.

We can also try to study the interdependence between mobility and fertility, controlling for the duration of marriage (Courgeau, 1985b). After the birth of a child, a move may be undertaken to a larger house. But some moves may also be undertaken to provide for forthcoming births. For those married before the age of 22, family size has a clear effect on the cumulative number of moves. For example, women born between 1926 and 1935 had, after five years of marriage, the following cumulative number of moves: 0.61 for women without children, 0.66 for women with one child, and 0.71 for women with two children. This result may be explained by the need to adjust the size of the dwelling to the size of the family. However, the reverse may also be true for other families. For the same cohort and the same duration of marriage, we have a cumulative fertility of 1.49 children for women who remained in the residence they inhabited at marriage, 1.60 for those having undertaken one move since marriage, and 1.64 for those having undertaken two moves. This indicates that some moves are undertaken to provide for forthcoming births.

Among women who married after the age of 22, the second effect disappeared, since no significant differences can be detected between women without children and women with one or two children. These women, mainly wives of executives or management staff, seemed more likely to have a sufficiently large home to accommodate their ultimate family size. On the other hand, the cumulative fertility of these women, according to the number of previous moves, indicates that some of the moves may be undertaken in anticipation of a birth. In these cases we find a local dependence between the two series of events such that if spatial mobility seems to be independent of previous fertility, we found a dependence of fertility on previous spatial mobility.

CONSEQUENCES OF MIGRATION: THE AGGREGATE LEVEL

Let us now examine how migration has redistributed the French population. First, we will observe its main effect at the aggregate level.

Demographic: Population Redistribution

After World War II, we observe that variations in natural increase rates across regions or urban areas were small compared to the corresponding net migration rates in the redistribution of the French population. Migration appears to be an essential factor in the redistribution of the French population. In addition, the age structure of migrants produces a high birthrate and a correspondingly low mortality rate in regions where young migrants are attracted. This inflates the effect of migration, even in areas of low fertility such as the Paris region.

The age and sex structure of regions or urban areas largely reflects the consequences of previous migration. For the urban area of Paris, we observe in 1982 an overrepresentation of young adults between 25 and 44 years of age. When compared to the population of the same age in the whole country, this age group is around 13 percent more numerous than expected. However, the significant reduction of net migration in Paris during recent years also leads to a decreasing overrepresentation (more than 25 percent in 1975 for the ages between 25 and 34, against 15 percent in 1982) and to an extension of the age groups concerned. An underrepresentation of 13 percent among children aged 5 to 19 shows that those in the age group 30 to 44 who remain in the Paris urban area are mainly individuals with few or no children. The elderly form another underrepresented group, with substantial male-female differences. At age 70 this underrepresentation is around 15 percent for women and more than 26 percent for men. This is a consequence of the greater number of widows and divorced females remaining in Paris.

It is also interesting to observe what happens in nonmetropolitan rural areas. All children and adults under the age of 50 are underrepresented by around 15 percent, with some important variations according to age. We can say that the recent reversal of migration flows to rural areas has only reduced this underrepresentation. For example, those aged 25 saw their underrepresentation reduced from 35 to 23 percent in 1982. After age 50, we have an increasing overrepresentation of the aged living outside metropolitan areas. This is more pronounced for men than for women; at age 80 the overrepresentation is around 43 percent for women versus 63 percent for men. We must relate this to the significant number of old men who have remained bachelors in the agricultural sector.

Foreigners living in France enhance these contrasts between Paris, other urban areas, and rural ones. Of the 3.7 million foreigners in 1982, 91 percent were living in urban areas (32.7 percent in Paris), compared to the 72.1 percent of the native population (14.2 percent in Paris). When considering only those immigrating between 1975 and 1982 (0.8 million), the proportion is very similar with 91.6 percent settling in urban areas (37.3 percent in Paris). This indicates that the spatial distribution of foreigners since World War II has been mainly urban.

Social

Since the Industrial Revolution the centralization process has been expressed essentially in the formation of a Parisian monopoly in the industrial, commercial, financial, educational, and intellectual sectors. In 1982, the metropolitan area of Paris accounted for 18.8 percent of the French population. Such a centralization was the consequence of a significant migration inflow from every other region. This migration mixed very different social groups within the same ward or the same block of flats. However, the cutting of ties with the place of origin was seldom complete. Those coming from the same department, and even the same village, located themselves in the same neighborhood, such as the Breton district of Paris in the vicinity of the Montparnasse railway station, and set up regional associations as a means of keeping links with the region of origin.

The urbanization process also led to the concentration of population coming from rural areas around each town. The adaptation problems in this case are less acute than those in Paris. The population remaining in rural areas underwent a different concentration process. The social problems induced by the depopulation of these areas were often solved by regrouping isolated farms or villages into a more populated neighboring town. However, this leads to many social and financial problems linked to the minimal population at which a school or post office may be provided.

More recently, the process of segregation by origin has started to occur on a wider scale. Some social groups are now living in places quite distant from urban areas. For example, executives or management staff may live in rural areas more than 60 km away from the urban center.

Such a segregation process leads to increasing commuting distances. From

1975 to 1982 the mean commuting distance increased from 18.4 km to 19.5 km, and the total number of daily kilometers covered by these commuters increased from 154 million to 197 million. Some of these commuting distances are becoming very long, as is the case for 160,000 individuals where distance covered is more than 200 km.

Economic

If we consider that migration is generated by differential economic development in various regions, it can in turn create problems and difficulties for the regions involved. For example, the important increase in in-migration to the Languedoc-Roussillon region was caused by an increase in employment, though it also led to a simultaneous increase in unemployment. More generally, no link appears between local variation of employment and local variation of unemployment.

In the past, migration within France was related to departure from agriculture and played a significant part in changes within the structure of employment. Now this role is greatly reduced. From 1973 to 1977, the major part of job mobility (87 percent) was of an intraregional nature, with departure from agriculture representing less than 6 percent of male occupation movement (Pohl and Soleilhavoup, 1982).

Political

The centralization process experienced in France led political leaders to adopt a national approach to regional planning. It was developed primarily by DATAR (Delegation a l'Amenagement du Territoire et a l'Action Regionale) after 1963.

The main aims of DATAR were to slow the extreme concentration of population, industry, and administration in Paris and to encourage the development of the remaining parts of France. First, governmental policies were introduced to control the construction of industrial buildings in the Paris region and to encourage industrialization of the rest of France. Later, a series of measures were taken to limit the construction of offices in Paris and to transfer some service activities from Paris. In addition, specific measures were taken concerning the public sector by requiring relocation of some offices from Paris or at least by prohibiting any expansion in metropolitan area. Another political orientation was to promote regional capitals as counterweights to the growth of Paris. Lastly, the transportation network has been greatly improved to break the isolation of certain regions.

Such governmental policies brought about changes in migration flows and in the spatial distribution of economic activity in the period after 1970. Some significant past trends such as the concentration of activities and population in Paris and the depopulation of outlying regions have been reversed during the period in which deconcentration policies have been promoted by DATAR.

A more detailed assessment of the efficiency of some governmental policies leads to a less positive conclusion. In some cases the regional grants appear to sustain development rather than to promote it. For example, J. L. Grelet and C. Thelot (1977) showed that both the four departments of the Pays de la Loire where a development grant was in effect and the noneligible, neighboring Sarthe department had the same increase in the number of jobs created.

CONSEQUENCES OF MIGRATION: THE INDIVIDUAL LEVEL

We present here some results from an analysis of the consequences of migration to or from major metropolitan areas (namely, areas of Paris, Lyon, and Marseille) based on family constitution, using an INED life history survey (Courgeau, 1987).

First, let us indicate how migration affects nuptiality. For women originating either from metropolitan areas or the country, a short delay of their marriage due to migration appears between age 20 and 30. This delay disappears after age 40, leading to the same proportion remaining single at this age. For men, independent of their origin, out-migrants have a nuptiality rate higher than that of nonmigrants. For the nonmetropolitan population, this behavior is related to the behavior of agricultural workers experiencing changes in occupation (Courgeau and Lelievre, 1986). This change in their work life induces an increase in their nuptiality.

Following the family life cycle, we consider how migration to or from major metropolitan areas affects successive births. Figures 7.6 and 7.7 give the cumulative order-specific fertility rates of these women.

The contrast between the two series of graphs is striking. On and after their second birth, women coming from nonmetropolitan areas experience a significant decrease in fertility once they have migrated to metropolitan areas. On the other hand, even for the first birth, women moving to nonmetropolitan areas experience an increase in fertility once they leave metropolitan areas. Convergence to the fertility level at destination, whatever it may be, takes place rather quickly.

However, migrants may not be a random sample of the population in the area of origin. A selectivity hypothesis suggests that migrants have distinct unobserved family size preferences. In this case fertility propensities tend to determine the choice of destination areas, rather than for the area to determine fertility behavior (Hervitz, 1985).

To verify this hypothesis in Figure 7.6 we have also given the cumulative order-specific fertility rates of these prospective migrants. We can see that the behavior of those who will later migrate to major metropolitan areas is consistent with this selectivity hypothesis. Their birth timing is generally very close to that of migrants. However, for those who will later migrate to nonmetropolitan areas,

Figure 7.6
Cumulative Order Specific Fertility Rates for Nonmigrant, Migrant before Migration and after Migration, Women Originating from Metropolitan Areas

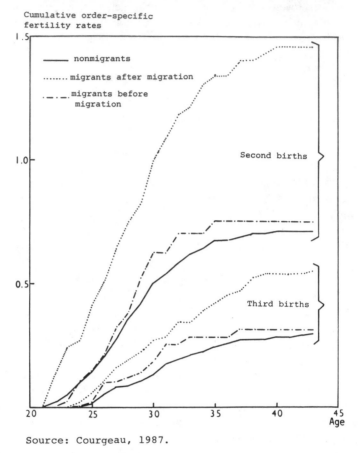

Source: Courgeau, 1987.

such an hypothesis is no longer verifiable. Their birth timing is very close to the one for nonmigrants, without any apparent selection, suggesting that the adaptation hypothesis holds for the out-migrants from urban areas.

With such an analysis we can simultaneously indicate how marriage and successive births modify migration to or from metropolitan areas. The behavior is consistent for both men and women upon marriage. Once married, their mobility rate to metropolitan areas is reduced by half for women and by one-third for men. Marital status appears very discriminative in the migration process; it is primarily single individuals who are drawn to urban areas. The small number of persons migrating from metropolitan areas before marrying precludes drawing any conclusions for these migrants.

The influence of fertility on the migration rates of women from nonmetropoli-

Figure 7.7
Cumulative Order Specific Fertility Rates for Nonmigrant, Migrant before Migration and after Migration, Women Originating from Nonmetropolitan Areas

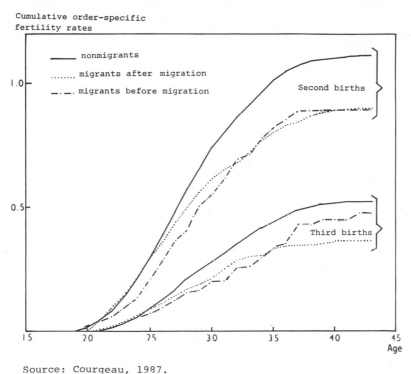

Source: Courgeau, 1987.

tan areas follows that of marriage. According to the number of children already born, migration rates to metropolitan areas are always reduced after a birth, whatever its order. On the other hand, migration rates to nonmetropolitan areas are, to a slight extent, higher after a birth. We can conclude that the inclination to live in nonmetropolitan areas increases with marriage and size of family.

Such analyses may be pursued in different domains (migration and job life history for example); these might lead to the important result that migration must no longer be considered as independent from other relational systems, like the family one. It is not a phenomenon that can be investigated and understood by itself as a dependent variable, but should be viewed as an integral part of a more general process leading to sociocultural change.

REFERENCES

Bastide, H., and A. Girard, 1974. "Mobilite de la population et motivations des personnes: une enquete aupres du public. III.—Les motifs de la mobilite." *Population*, 29:743–69.

Courgeau, D. 1975. "Migrants et migrations." *Population* 28:95–129. (English version: 1979. "Migrants and Migrations." *Selected Papers* 3:1–35).

———. 1980. *Analyse quantitative des migrations humaines.* Paris: Masson.

———. 1983. *Study on the Dynamics, Evolution and Consequences of Migrations—II.— Three Centuries of Spatial Mobility in France.* Paris: UNESCO.

———. 1985a. "Effet de declarations erronees sur une analyse de donnees migratoires." In *Migrations internes: collecte des donnees et methodes d'analyse.* Louvain: Department de demographie.

———. 1985b. "Interaction Between Spatial Mobility, Family and Career Life Cycle: A French Survey." *European Sociological Review* 1:139–62.

———. 1987. "Constitution de la famille et urbanisation." *Population* 42:57–81.

———. Forthcoming. *Methodes de mesure de la mobilite.*

———, and E. Lelievre. 1986. "Nuptialite et agriculture." *Population* 41:303–26.

Duchene, J. 1985. "Un test de fiabilite des enquetes retrospectives biographie familiale, professionnelle et migratoire." In *Migrations internes: collecte des donnees et methodes d'analyse.* Louvain: Departement de demographie.

Gravier, J. F. 1947. *Paris et le desert francais.* Paris: Ed. de Portulans.

Grelet, J. L., and C. Thelot. 1977. "La prime de developpement: role incitatif discutable." *Economie et Statistique* 89:21–37.

Hervitz, H.M. 1985. "Selectivity, Adaptation or Disruption? A Comparison of Alternative Hypotheses on the Effects of Migration on Fertility: The Case of Brazil." *International Migration Review* 19:293–317.

Ledent, J., and D. Courgeau. 1982. *Migration and Settlement: 15. France.* Laxenburg, Austria: IIASA.

Pohl, R., and J. Soleilhavoup. 1982. *Mobilite professionnelle.* Paris: INSEE.

Tugault, Y. 1973. *La mesure de la mobilite.* Paris: INED.

8

FEDERAL REPUBLIC OF GERMANY

Klaus Friedrich

In contrast to highly mobile societies, such as the United States, the Federal Republic of Germany (FRG) has a rather low migration intensity of about 2.5 million internal migrations per year and an average rate of 41.3 migrations per 1,000 inhabitants (1980–85). Hence, in comparison with other European countries, the FRG ranks in the middle (Salt and Clout, 1976). Because the volume of both immigration and emigration is only slightly more than one-third of internal migration and data on natural increase do not indicate much geographic variation, internal migration is an important indicator of the process of regional development.

Among others, three factors predominantly characterize the development and the present structure of the internal migration process in the FRG:

1. A long-term *reduction* of the migration volume with obvious stabilizing tendencies since the mid-seventies.
2. A distinct *selectivity* of migration behavior owing to demographic and socioeconomic characteristics.
3. A dramatic *turnaround* in the direction of the spatial population development with consequences at the national, interregional, and intraregional levels.

DATA ON MIGRATION

The official statistics of the FRG define migration as a permanent change of residence across community borders. Each relocation has to be reported as a consequence of the obligation to register. Movements within corporate limits are not interpreted as migration.

Since 1950 the migration statistics of the FRG have been collected by the statistical offices of the eleven states following standard criteria. Because of the federal structure of the administration, each state is responsible for updating its migration register annually. The Federal Statistical Office in Wiesbaden records these data and publishes information about migration volume, rates, and flows on an aggregated spatial and demographic level. The Federal Institute for Applied Geography and Regional Planning (Bundesforschungsanstalt fuer Landeskunde und Raumordnung—BFLR) disaggregates these data and offers them to users on a microregional scale.

Although the annual availability and the reliability of the continuously updated migration statistics are very useful, some disadvantages should be noted:

1. The absence of disaggregation on a national level as well as the very limited breakdown on the state level with respect to socioeconomic parameters. The register forms don't ask for any personal items about the migrants other than age, sex, marital status, labor force participation, nationality, origin, and destination.
2. The limited comparability between migration before and after the 1970s owing to the changing size of municipalities. Between 1967 and 1978 the number of communities was reduced from 24,357 to 8,518, and the number of counties from 563 to 327 (Fuchs, 1984, 33). Since then, movements within the new (larger) statistical units have no longer been registered as migration. Migration between federal states were not affected by these restrictions as their borders remained unchanged.
3. The problem of reconciling registered migration data to census data. The last published census data are from that carried out in 1970. Considering the length of this period, it is possible that our current estimates of population size are only accurate within a range of +/− 1 million people. The latest census took place in May 1987; the results will be published within the next two years.
4. The impossibility of obtaining information about the motivations for migration directly from available statistics.
5. Finally, the inclusion of only the so-called migration cases instead of the migration units. Consequently, statements about living arrangements, return migration, or repeat migration by the same person cannot be recorded.

PRINCIPAL POPULATION MOVEMENTS

As a result of World War II, a tremendous process of population redistribution throughout Germany has taken place involving about 12.5 million refugees. The immigration from East Germany (nowadays GDR) and from the other former German territories (Silesia, etc.) was clearly directed to the West. These flows were forcibly interrupted by the erection of the Berlin Wall in 1961. By this time the remigration of the evacuees from the rural areas back into their rebuilt cities had come to an end.

Since then, both a downward trend in migration volume and a shift in the direction of migration streams from east-west to north-south could be observed in the FRG. This quantitative reduction of internal migration within the FRG can be studied in Table 8.1. For example, the volume and the intensity of *interstate* migration were almost halved from an annual total of 1,117,560 (18.5 per 1,000) in 1978 to 640,035 (10.5 per 1,000) in 1985. Focusing on the directions of long-

Table 8.1
Internal Migration within the FRG, 1970–85

	Migrations across borders of					
	municipalities		counties		federal states	
	volume	per 1000 inh.	volume	per 1000 inh.	volume	per 1000 inh.
1970 ..	3 661 524	59,8	2 942 036	48,1	1 117 560	18,5
1971 ..	3 733 878	61,2	2 997 785	49,1	1 125 011	18,4
1972 ..	3 697 112	60,1	2 919 595	47,5	1 074 873	17,6
1973 ..	3 675 214	59,5	2 865 346	46,4	1 031 400	16,8
1974 ..	3 432 142	55,3	2 637 751	42,5	929 744	15,0
1975 ..	2 983 631	48,1	2 304 597	37,2	816 324	13,2
1976 ..	2 950 376	47,9	2 276 579	36,9	795 564	12,8
1977 ..	2 995 808	48,8	2 310 142	37,6	817 411	13,3
1978 ..	2 957 072	48,2	2 293 530	37,4	813 716	13,2
1979 ..	2 936 657	47,9	2 259 396	36,8	803 519	13,1
1980 ..	2 023 791	49,2	2 304 300	37,5	819 884	13,4
1981 ..	2 968 950	48,2	2 263 063	36,7	798 430	13,0
1982 ..	2 905 797	47,1	1 193 964	35,6	768 343	12,5
1983 ..	2 732 625	44,4	2 004 829	32,6	674 186	10,9
1984 ..	2 527 675	41,2	1 809 282	29,5	633 556	10,3
1985 ..	2 572 459	42,1	1 850 408	30,3	640 035	10,5

distance migration from 1980 to 1985, the reversed trend favoring the south can be seen in Table 8.2.

A more detailed portrait is given by Figure 8.1, showing the net migration flows between the eleven federal states in 1985. The principal receiving states are Baden-Wuerttemberg and Bavaria, followed by West Berlin (a recent development) and Schleswig-Holstein. Major sending states are the North Rhine-Westphalia, Rhineland-Palatinate, Saarland, Hesse, Lower Saxony as well as the city states of Hamburg and Bremen. A long-term comparison of the interstate flows (Birg et al., 1983) demonstrates that nearly all neighboring states have strong exchanges with each other. But only a few, such as Baden-Wuerttemberg

Table 8.2
Net Migration Rates by Federal Areas, 1980–85

Federal area (excludes West Berlin)   Rates (net migrations across area border
per 1000 inhabit.)

	Rate	Min#	Max#	Stand. Dev#
northern states	2.1	−50.7	67.6	26.1
central states	−7.2	−196.0	51.0	30.4
southern states	9.9	−41.4	91.8	21.9

Source: INFORMATIONEN ZUR RAUMENTWICKLUNG 11/12. 1986, p. 951

#)Difference to aggregate on county level

and Bavaria, are characterized by salient interactions with noncontiguous states. As national patterns often hide important subnational variation, analysis of *interregional* migration really requires a more disaggregated spatial level. Units that match these requirements are the seventy-five areas for regional planning (Raumordnungsregionen or ROR). They were established by the BFLR as a spatial data base for the purpose of planning. Until the end of the 1970s a clear orientation from rural toward urban destinations could be observed between these regions. This polarization lost its importance with the dramatic regional change in economic and social conditions as a consequence of the oil crisis.

Recently, an increasingly diverse pattern of different redistribution tendencies has emerged: the traditional out-migration areas (e.g., Emsland, Oberpfalz, Westpfalz), and the old manufacturing agglomerations such as the Ruhrgebiet, Saarland, and Hannover/Braunschweig suffer significant population losses. Conversely, growing areas are those urban agglomerations with "young" and expanding industries, located mainly in the south. In addition, the areas with growing population and economic concentration (partly owing to new university developments such as in Oldenburg, Paderborn, Kassel, and Regensburg) and rural areas in northern Germany, the Black Forest, and the Forelands of the Alps also belong to the preferred destinations.

Compared with the entire postwar period, we may observe of late a distinctive distance-friction of movements. Approximately 28 percent of all internal migration takes place within county limits and 60 percent within the ROR. Such *intraregional* migration is the numerically dominant type in the FRG. Such moves do not usually require a change of existing functional and sociospatial relationships.

The actual breakdown of the net migration rates by type of county—shown in Table 8.3—reinforces the turnaround between core and fringe. While central cities in general have lost some of their former attractiveness, the result is substantial net in-migration in fringe areas. The surplus of migration emanates

Figure 8.1
Net Migration Flows between the Federal States of the FRG, 1985

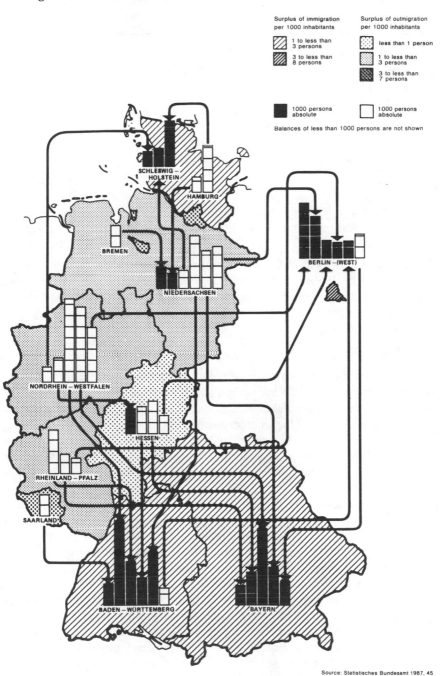

Surplus of immigration per 1000 inhabitants

1 to less than 3 persons

3 to less than 8 persons

Surplus of outmigration per 1000 inhabitants

less than 1 person

1 to less than 3 persons

3 to less than 7 persons

1000 persons absolute

1000 persons absolute

Balances of less than 1000 persons are not shown

SCHLESWIG – HOLSTEIN

HAMBURG

BREMEN

NIEDERSACHSEN

BERLIN –(WEST)

NORDRHEIN – WESTFALEN

HESSEN

RHEINLAND – PFALZ

SAARLAND

BADEN – WÜRTTEMBERG

BAYERN

Source: Statistisches Bundesamt 1987, 45

Table 8.3
Net Migration Rates by Type of Counties, 1980–85

Spatial reference	Balance	Min.	Max.	Stand.Dev.
Metropolitan areas				
- central cities	-19.2	-44.9	35.2	14.2
- densely populated fringes	5.2	-196.0	91.8	42.1
- rural fringes	23.7	-1.1	67.6	18.6
Regions with growing concentration				
- central cities	-10.3	-50.7	34.1	23.6
- rural fringes	8.9	-31.6	48.9	16.5
Rural regions	6.9	-41.0	61.3	17.2

Source: BFLR 1986, 951

from both the central cities and the rural regions. As of now, it is too early to determine whether this development represents a continuation of the suburbanization of the 1960s and 1970s (BFLR, 1984a, 33; Gatzweiler, 1982, 43) or a trend toward the age-selective counterurbanization discussed by T. Kontuly and R. Vogelsang (1986).

WHO MOVES

Knowledge about the characteristics of migrants is a basic need for the assessment of spatial consequences for origin and destination areas. This is due to the situation where large population shifts induced by immigration of foreign workers or natural increase of the German population cannot be expected. As already mentioned, official statistics permit only limited statements about the demographic and socioeconomic components of migrants; data on comigrants, living arrangements, and socioeconomic characteristics are accessible only on a sample basis.

The differentiation of migrants in 1985 by sex and by labor force participation shows only slight variation. However, the differential involvement in the migration process depending on age is quite pronounced. In accordance with the model migration schedule (Rogers and Castro, 1981), it can be observed in the FRG that certain *age groups* (Figure 8.2), representing different stages of the life cycle, relocate more often than others. The disaggregation of internal migration by cohort with similar motivations has led to a classification of four age categories with persistent regularities in migration behavior: education-, labor-, family-, and retirement-migrants. The education- and labor-oriented migrants exhibit the clearest participation peak, in contrast to the decreasing trend in migration frequency with advancing age.

Figure 8.2
Internal Migration Schedule, FRG
Yearly Rates (Per 1,000) in 1985

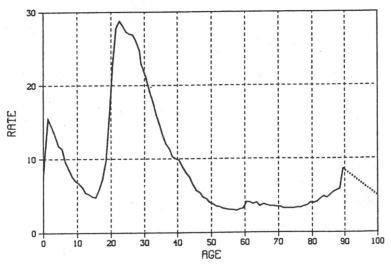

Source: Federal Statistic Office 1986.

Models based on theories of age-specific interregional migration also empha-size the significant selectivity of preferred directions. They argue that younger segments of the population prefer urban locations, whereas the older cohorts tend to migrate to peripheral ones (Gatzweiler, 1975). Although these relocation patterns have remained largely unchanged during the last two decades, they have experienced some remarkable modification.

One obvious result is the actual trend of convergence of regional imbalances (BFLR, 1984, 1160; Gatzweiler, 1982). Now, only those metropolitan agglom-erations with expanding demand for labor are as attractive for younger migrants as they were previously. Those with economic problems experience a similar level of net out-migration as do those in the traditional rural areas. As before, seniors generally migrate from densely populated agglomerations to environmen-tally preferred regions along the coast, some hill areas in the middle part of Germany, the Black Forest, and the Foreland of the Alps.

Within the intraregional context, a strong age-specific component persists. The younger age groups move more often into the central cities, whereas the other population segments are characterized by increasing distance-friction, pre-ferring the suburban and, more recently, peripheral municipalities. This city-hinterland migration started in the 1970s. Many communities tried to control the negative process of suburbanization (Baldermann et al., 1976; Schaffer et al., 1976; Schreiber, 1975) by coordinated measures. This relocation dynamic was disproportionately comprised of skilled workers and families with small children

(Koch and Gatzweiler, 1980). However, during the last few years an increasing remigration to the cities has partially offset this process.

In spite of many peculiarities, the internal migration behavior of *foreign workers* shows certain parallels to that of the younger groups. Their interstate migration rate of 14.9 (per 1,000) is about 50 percent higher than that of the Germans (10.1). Both migration groups prefer the urban centers.

At the beginning of the 1960s, immigration began from Mediterranean regions of Europe via Switzerland to southern Baden-Wuerttemberg, to Stuttgart, and then to Frankfurt and Cologne (see Figure 8.3). With a small delay in time, diffusion via the axis Munich, Nuremburg, Hannover, and Hamburg also took place. Following these successive advances from centers in the south to centers in the north, a second phase of the diffusion set in. Foreign workers increasingly moved to smaller urban centers, where reasonable working and living conditions

Figure 8.3
Spatial Diffusion of Foreign Workers in the FRG, 1960–72

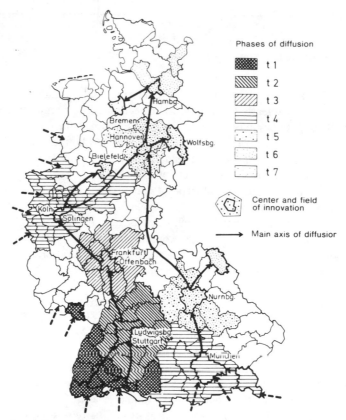

Source: Giese 1978. In: Baehr, J. 1983. Bevoelkerungsgeographie. Stuttgart. p. 331. (with permission of the Ulmer Verlag).

were available (Giese, 1978). Even the limitations on employment for foreign workers (initiated in 1973) and the following restrictions on immigration of their relatives had only slight consequences for their spatial diffusion (Baehr and Gans, 1985, 93).

The socioeconomic status of migrants is best studied by regional surveys. The long-distance migrants with urban destinations are usually wealthier or better qualified and live in smaller households than the population in general (Wagner, 1987). However, the city-hinterland migration includes many households with children, relocating into areas with a less expensive housing market (Mammey, 1977; Schaffer et al., 1976, 137).

CAUSES AND MOTIVATIONS FOR MIGRATION

Within the FRG, the usual way to explore the determinants of migration consist of survey-oriented analyses of individual motivations (microlevel) or aggregate analyses by correlating migration rates with structural or socioeconomic indicators of origin and destination regions (macrolevel). The necessary linkage at both the theoretical and empirical levels as well as the micro- and macroanalytical levels has not yet successfully been accomplished (Vanberg, 1975). This methodological problem and the lack of data dealing with the motivations of migrants are responsible for the absence of a clear insight into the causal structure of the migration process in general and of subgroup-specific migration in particular (Harms, 1975; Marel, 1980).

The few sources that provide empirical information about the *motivation structure* of migrants in the FRG are mainly regional surveys. One exception is the representative 1 percent national housing sample of 1978 covering more than 23,000 households throughout the nation which moved after 1971. In 1982, Gatzweiler published the results of this housing survey, classified into age-specific motivations for internal migration. These can be collapsed into four principal categories (see Table 8.4):

1. Changes in the size of households.
2. Reasons concerning accommodation and living environment.
3. Reasons concerning labor and education.
4. Other reasons.

Significant variation by age in the relative importance of these reasons results from differences in stages of the life cycle. Young and adult family heads generally migrate because of a growing family (marriage, children). Directly associated with this reason is the insufficient size of accommodation. Nearly a quarter of young and middle-aged households state the acquisition of their own home as the reason for migration. Other important motivations for them are employment or education. Quite distinctly, older people relocate to a disproportionate extent because of the reduction of family size (empty nest). In addition,

Table 8.4
Motivations for Internal Migration by Age, 1977–78

Motivation	Percentages of moved households by total of moved households in each age-fraction (mult.responses)				
	total	18-24	25-29	30-49	50-64
Increase of household size	21.1	30.2	29.3	20.4	6.8
Decrease of household size	6.3	3.9	4.3	5.7	11.5
Insufficient size of unit	22.8	24.5	27.0	25.3	12.6
Wanted to own a home	15.8	9.1	14.9	22.1	10.0
Location too peripheral	8.4	12.2	10.6	7.6	4.9
Rent increase/termination	8.3	4.7	6.9	9.1	12.0
Insuff. internal home equipm.	5.3	3.6	4.9	4.4	9.2
Rental costs too expensive	3.8	3.3	3.6	3.7	4.8
Environmental pollution	2.8	-	-	2.4	5.7
Job/education transfer	14.9	14.4	18.6	17.8	6.3
Other reasons	32.1	34.4	28.5	27.3	42.0

Number of answering household-heads: 23,311

Source: Housing sample 1978; in: Gatzweiler 1982, 32

uncomfortable residential environments or increasing rent costs force the elderly to change their location involuntarily.

The necessity of linking life course events with actual changes in residence is a recent but long-neglected perspective in research focusing on the determinants of migration. This analytical approach and a new data source are incorporated in a research project entitled "Life Event Histories and Welfare Dynamics," supported by the German Research Foundation (DFG). Within a representative sample, the residential biographies of more than 2,100 members of three birth cohorts (1929–31; 1939–41; and 1949–51) were collected from 1981 to 1983. These data include the characteristics of some 10,000 relocations. Although the findings cannot be reported here in any detail, they do underline the important influence of earlier lifetime experience of migration behavior (Wagner, 1987). Different experiences of cohort members during the political, economic, social, and regional developments occurring in Germany have led to varying intensities of residential mobility at the same age or stage of the life cycle. For example, the incidence of long-distance migration owing to better employment opportunities varies significantly among the three cohorts.

Macro- and microanalytical approaches aim to discover the causal relationship between migration and characteristics of destinations. Most results suggest that the realization of labor- or education-oriented moves usually involves interregional migration (Gatzweiler and Sommerfeld, 1986). However, relocation in order to obtain better housing conditions is possible within the intraregional scale (Baldermann et al., 1976, 149). Retirement migration occurs within both intraregional and interregional contexts (Kemper and Kuls, 1986).

The influence of a broad range of economic factors is obvious for employment-related migrants. Clear linkages between the long-distance migration and economic cycles are present (Figure 8.4) as the volume of migration increases with the gross national product (Birg et al., 1983). In contrast, there is a close relationship between the supply of new housing and the volume of short-distance migration (Ludaescher, 1986).

For the evaluation of the macroanalytical complex of migrations within the FRG, the stochastic model of Gatzweiler (1975) seems to be the most far-reaching framework. The author's aim is to explain and forecast regional migration patterns not by deterministic parameters, but by the behavior- and decision-making approach. The main argument is that migration as an individual decision tends to equalize regional disparities in living conditions. However, this spatial behavior is conditioned not only by rational arguments such as adequate infrastructures, facilities, and opportunities, but also by attitudes, preferences, and information. This corresponds with the H. Monheim's (1972) comparison of the attractiveness of German communities. He found clear preferences for the cities in southern Germany like Munich, Freiburg, and Stuttgart mainly because of their favorable images. Other recent surveys (Friedrich and Koch, 1988; Friedrich and Wartwig, 1984) underline this perceptual element within the decision-making process. Value-oriented attitudes toward social and spatial environment such as regional identification and attachment dampen the migratory ten-

Figure 8.4
Internal Migration and Economic Cycles, 1960–80

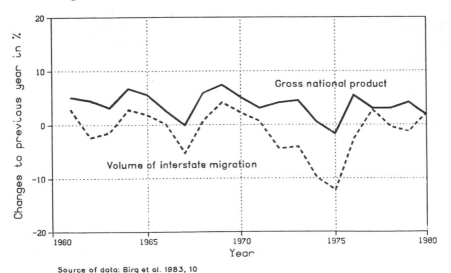

Source of data: Birg et al. 1983, 10

dency especially within the rural population. The social and emotional image of the target region (the so-called mental map), however, is an important predictor of the chosen destination. Ethnic and age-compositional dissimilarities, for example, are indicators of problems of integration which adversely influence the decision of elderly migrants.

MACROANALYTICAL CONSEQUENCES OF MIGRATION

The consequences of internal migration within the FRG are apparent at many levels but have been investigated in only a few. Two of special importance are:

1. Demographic consequences that result from large-scale interstate migration.
2. Socioeconomic consequences that result from the inter- and intraregional migration pattern for the areas of origin and destination.

The geographical impact of population dynamics within the FRG, including the *demographic* consequences of internal migration, have been examined by multiregional population analyses at different points of time (Koch and Gatzweiler, 1980; Friedrich and Koch, 1988). These multiregional life table models are designed to provide an answer to the question: how would the present mortality and migration regime determine the probability of survival of an hypothetical generation in a given region? As expected, senior citizens show a much lower tendency to migrate compared with the younger age groups. On the average only 7 percent of 60 year olds will relocate and cross the border of a federal state in their remaining years. The comparable level for 20 year olds is about 50 percent.

Another indicator of mobility or immobility is the retention level. It describes the proportion of a lifetime that a person may expect to spend in the region of residence. According to the findings of an international comparison between seventeen nations, the largest disparities in retention expectation were observed in the FRG (Rogers, 1984).

This is confirmed by the recent study of Friedrich and Koch (1988). It shows that the probability of a 20 year old remaining in the same federal state is lowest in the city states of Bremen, Hamburg, and Berlin. Such a person would only spend 27 percent of his or her remaining life in Bremen; at the other extreme is Bavaria at 74 percent (Table 8.5). With the exception of Saarland the rank order of 20 and 60 year olds is about the same. The low retention expectations in the city states are based on the fact that there are large amounts of city-hinterland relocations that usually cross the border of a contiguous state; as a consequence, those are registered as interstate migration.

The population projection model that is built on the base of the multiregional life tables ignores the contribution of international migration. Consequently, the population of the FRG in 2003 will be 57.7 million; compared with the 1983 figure this is a decline of about 5.9 percent. On the other hand, the number of

Table 8.5
Regional Retention Expectation (percentage of remaining life time at ages 20 and 60 in region of residence)

federal states	retention expectations			
	20 year-old	rank	60 year-old	rank
Schleswing-Holstein	51.2	7	92.5	7
Hamburg	37.9	10	85.4	10
Lower Saxony	59.9	4	93.6	5
Bremen	27.0	11	85.9	9
North Rhine-Westphalia	70.5	2	94.8	4
Hesse	57.0	5	93.1	6
Rhineland-Palatinate	48.8	8	92.5	7
Baden-Wurttemberg	65.8	3	95.5	2
Bavaria	74.1	1	96.8	1
Saarland	51.3	6	95.3	3
Berlin	43.6	9	85.3	11

persons aged 60 and over will rise to 15.8 million, and their future share will increase from about 20 percent in 1983 to 26 percent in 2003.

The regional implications of these changes can be illustrated with the re-distribution patterns of the elderly. In 1983 the share of the population aged 60 and over was at its highest in West Berlin at 24.8 percent, followed by the other two city states of Hamburg (23.7 percent) and Bremen (22.7 percent). The lowest fraction was found in Baden-Wuerttemberg (18.8 percent). In 2003 the percentage of seniors in West Berlin will remain nearly unchanged (24.9 percent), although their number will decrease by about a fourth. This is a significant distinction between Berlin and the other federal states, where increases of 20 percent and more are expected. The highest shares of the 60 plus population are anticipated in Hamburg (28.3 percent) and Bremen (27.3 percent). However, the percentage in Bavaria will be relatively low (25.2 percent). The peculiar prospective development in West Berlin is mainly a result of its special age structure at the beginning of the projection period: at that time, the size of the population aged 60 or over was above the national average and the immediately younger age groups in this city were much smaller than the preceding ones. Furthermore, the continuous outmigration from West Berlin contributes to the comparatively small number of elderly people who will reside in this city state in 2003. There is no doubt that these expected changes in the regional age structures will result in important implications for the social security system and additional requirements for infrastructure (homes for the aged, social services, etc.) within the several federal states.

The *socioeconomic* consequences of internal migration in Germany for the rural (sending) areas are discussed primarily under the rubric of "social erosion." Among the receiving metropolitan areas, the discussion concentrates on excessive congestion, segregation, and suburbanization.

The planning authorities are in fact aware of the danger of social erosion in the countryside owing to the out-migration of the younger and highly qualified segments of the population (Bundesminister fuer Raumordnung, 1986). Their countermeasures are regional programs of economic support which try to allocate secondary and tertiary activities to these rural areas. Although the depopulation of weakly structured regions has decreased, it is still too early to assert the reversal of the danger of social erosion.

The process of suburbanization within the metropolitan areas suggests an enormous urban sprawl in many of the previously small towns and villages during the 1970s. With the exception of some portions of southern Germany, this process has also slowed down. Besides the observed diffusion of urban values and attitudes following this process of intraregional deconcentration, residential segregation and social differentiation have also been investigated (Schuetz, 1985; Vaskovics et al., 1983).

In a case study of Hamburg, a general tendency toward age segregation in the period from 1961 to 1981 can be observed. Within the inner zone (circuit of 5 km around the city center), the segregation of all age groups shows its highest increase. In the intermediate zone (5 to 10 km) the level of segregation is nonhomogeneous and below average. Within the fastest growing outer zone (10 to 20 km) the segregation shows its lowest level with an increase of 19 percent. Obviously, the age groups are affected by the process of residential change to different extents, mainly induced by parameters of the local housing market. Nevertheless, it could be documented that the segregation levels of Hamburg residents were much less than those observable among foreign workers in Germany and among ethnic groups in U.S. cities.

Recently, the *economic* consequences of the north-south drift of population redistribution into the regions of Munich and Stuttgart have prompted a flurry of interest (BFLR, 1986). The question arises whether this north-south tendency in Germany parallels the "frostbelt-sunbelt" phenomenon in the United States. In both nations, the structure of employment opportunities and income differentials pull migrants into these preferred destinations. The obvious shift of the center of population gravity to the south is another effect of the increasing regional attractiveness of the "new" economic cores, primarily induced by technological innovations.

THE INDIVIDUAL CONSEQUENCES OF MIGRATION

Studies focusing on internal migration often take a fairly restricted view of its implications at the individual level. There do exist several surveys that conducted an ex-post evaluation of the migration decision. In spite of justified reservations against this kind of analysis—assessing decisions for relocation after they were made (Jessen et al., 1979)—the results of the national housing sample of 1978 will be considered again here. In this survey, households that moved evaluated the extent to which certain features of their living conditions had changed in comparison with the previous location (Table 8.6). Responses relating to the

Table 8.6
Comparison of Selected Housing Conditions after Residential Change

Evaluation of households moved between 1972 and 1978

	improved	unchanged	worse now	no answer
Size of appartment	60.2	13.1	20.9	5.7
Internal home equipment	58.9	23.5	11.1	6.5
Housing costs	16.2	13.0	62.5	8.3
Shopping facilities	26.9	48.3	23.8	1.0
Medical service	23.0	59.2	14.0	3.8
Parks	37.9	45.2	14.3	2.6
Access to transportation	30.6	48.9	19.2	1.4
Noise	35.8	42.2	19.6	2.1
Air pollution	32.5	49.1	14.4	4.0
Distance to work*	49.6	25.7	14.9	9.8
Job Security*	29.8	50.3	4.1	15.8
Income*	44.9	33.4	7.5	14.2
Job improvements	29.9	46.9	6.5	16.7

* Answers only from migrants with job orientated motivation

Source: 1 % housing sample 1978

quality of housing and residential environment show that improvements predominate, although housing costs incurred after the move are usually higher. Employment-related migration also improved general living conditions, such as a reduction of travel time to work and increases in income. On the average, only about 20 percent of the answers indicate a change for the worse after migration.

Although these results show conformity with that of other surveys (Prognos, 1977; Schaffer et al., 1976), there is need of more detailed tests of their analytical reliability. Social science demonstrates that the locational decisions of individuals often become justified by ex-post rationalizations, even if the expected goals were not realized (Zapf, 1979). The avoidance of cognitive dissonance, however, reaches its limit if relocation leads to return migration. This phenomenon has not been investigated sufficiently in the FRG. The same is true for the volume and significance of forced migration.

REFERENCES

Baehr, J., and P. Ganns. 1985. "Bevoelkerungsveraenderungen und Migrationsmuster in den Grosstaedten der Bundesrepublik Deutschland seit 1970." In J. Friedrichs (ed.), *Die Staedte in den 80er Jahren*. Opladen: 70–116.

Baldermann, J., G. Hecking, and E. Knauss. 1976. "Wanderungsmotive und Stadtstruktur." *Schriftenreihe 6 des Staedtebaulichen Instituts*, University of Stuttgart.

BFLR (Bundesforschungsanstalt fuer Landeskunde und Raumordnung) (ed.). 1984a. *Informationen zur Raumentwicklung* 12. Bonn.

————. 1984b. *Symposien-Seminare-Arbeitspapiere* 17. Bonn.

————. (ed.). 1986. *Informationen zur Raumentwicklung* 11/12. Bonn.

Birg, H., D. Filip, and K. Hilge. 1983. "Verflechtungsanalyse der Bevoelkerungsmobilitaet zwischen den Bundeslaendern vol 1950 bis 1980." *IBS-Materialien,* University of Bielefeld.

Bundesminister fuer Raumordnung, Bauwesen und Staedtebau (ed.). 1986. *Raumordnungsbericht,* 1986. Bonn.

Friedrich, K., and R. Koch. 1988. "Migration of the Elderly in the Federal Republic of Germany." In A. Rogers and W. Serow (eds.), *Elderly Migration: An International Comparative Study.* Boulder, Colo.: University of Colorado, Institute of Behavioral Science.

————, and H. Wartwig. 1984. "Raeumliche Identifikation. Paradigma eines reginosorientierten Raumordnungskonzeptes." In *Darmstaedter Geographische Studien* 5:73–126. Darmstadt.

Fuchs, G. 1984. *Die Bundesrepublik Deutschland.* Stuttgart.

Gatzweiler, H. P. 1975. "Zur Selektivitaet interregionaler Wanderungen." *Forschungen zur Raumentwicklung* 1. Bonn.

————. 1982. "Neuere binnenwanderungstendenzen im Bundesgebiet." In W. Linke and K. Schwarz (eds.), *Aspekete der raeumlichen bevoelkerungsbewegung in der BRD.* Berlin.

————, and P. Sommerfeld. 1986. "Raumstrukturelle Veraenderungen seit Verabschiedung des Bundesraumordnungsgestzes 1985." *Geographische Rundschau* 38:441–47.

Giese, E. 1978. "Raeumliche Diffusiona auslaendischer Arbeitnehmer in der Bundesrepublik Deutschland 1960–1976." *Die Erde* 109:92–110.

Harms, A. 1975. "Regionale Faktoren und Bestimmungsgruende der Wohnortmobilitaet." In *Forschungs- und Sitzungsberichte der Akademie fuer Raumforschung und Landesplanung* 95:51–68.

Hessisches Statistisches Landesamt (ed.). 1985. "Wandrungsstroeme in Hessen." *Statistische Berichte 1984.* Wiesbaden.

Heuer, H., and R. Schaefer. 1978. *Stadtflucht.* Deutsches Institut fuer Urbanistik (ed.). Berlin.

Jessen, J., B. Meinecke, and U.J. Walther. 1979. "Faktoren innerregionaler Wanderung—Verhalten der Wohnbevoelkerung." In Robert Bosch Stiftung (ed.), *Beitraege zur Stadtforschung* I:10–74. Stuttgart.

Kemper, F., and W. Kuls. 1986. "Wanderungen aelterer Menschen im laendlichen Raum." *Arbeiten zur Rheinischen Landeskunde.* Bonn.

Koch, R. 1976. "Altenwanderung und raeumliche Konzentration alter Menschen." *Forschungen zur Raumentwicklung* 4. Bonn.

————, and H.P. Gatzweiler. 1980. "Migration and Settlement. Federal Republic of Germany." *IIASA research report* 9. Laxenburg, Austria.

Kontuly, T., and R. Vogelsang. 1986. "Counterurbanization and Age Selective Migration in the FRG." *Social Science Research Working Paper.* Salt Lake City.

Kuls, W. 1980. *Bevoelkerungsgeographie.* Stuttgart.

Ludaescher, P. 1986. "Wanderungen und konjunkturelle Entwicklung in der Bundesrepublik Deutschland seit Anfang dersechziger Jahre." *Geographische Zeitschrift* 74:43–61.

Mammey, U. 1977. "Raeumliche Aspekte der sozialen Mobilitaet in der Bundesrepublik Deutschland." *Zeitschrift fuer Bevoelkerungswissenschaft* 3:23–49.

Marel, K. 1980. "Inter- und intraregionaele Mobilitact." *Schriftenreihe des Bundesinstituts fuer Bevoelkerungsforschung* 8. Wiesbaden.

Monheim, H. 1972. "Zur Attraktivitaet deutscher Staedte." *WGI-Bericht zur Regionalforschung* 8. Munich.

Plannungsgemeinschaft Westpfalz (ed.). 1981. *Wanderungsverhalten in der Region Westpfalz.* Kaiserslautern.

Prognos (ed.). 1977. *Kernstadt—Randwanderung: Motive und Tendenzen.* Basel.

Rogers, A. (ed.). 1984. *Multiregional Demography: Four Essays.* Laxenburg: IIASA.

————, and L. Castro. 1981. *Model Migration Schedules.* IIASA Research Report. Laxenburg.

Salt, J., and H. Clout (eds.). 1976. *Migration in Post-War Europe: Geographical Essays.* Oxford.

Schaffer, F., F. Hundhammer, G. Peyke, and W. Posyschwatta. 1976. "Wanderungsmotive und Stadt-Umland Mobilitaet." *Raumforschung und Raunordnung* 34:134–56.

Schnindler, J.W. 1985. "Typisierung der Gemeinden des laendlichen Raumes Baden-Wuerrtembergs nach der Wanderungsbewegung der deutschen Bevoelkerung." *Tubinger Geographische Studien* 91.

Schreiber, K.H. 1975. "Wanderungsursachen und idealtypische Verhaltensmuster mobiler Bevoelkerungsgruppen." *Rhein-Mainische Furschungen.* 79. Frankfurt.

Schuetz. M.W. 1985. "Die Trennung von Jung und Alt in der Stadt." *Beitrage zur Stadtforschung* 9. Hamburg.

Statistiches Bundesamt (ed.). 1981. *Fachserie 5. Wohnungsstichprobe 1978* (1% housing sample). Wiesbaden.

————. 1986. *Statistisches Jahrbuch 1985.* Wiesbaden.

————. 1987. *Fachserie 1. Gebiet und Bevoelkerung 1985.* Wiesbaden.

Vanberg, M. 1975. "Ansaetze zur Wanderungsforschung. Folgerung fuer ein Modell der Wanderungsentscheidungen." In *Forschungs-und Situngsberichte der Akademie fuer Raumforschung und Landesplanung* 95:3–20.

Vaskovics, L., P. Franz, and W. Ueltzen. 1983. "Ursachen der raeumlichen Segregation alter Menschen in bundesdeutschen Staedten." *Forschungsbericht der sozialwissenschaftlichen Forschungsstelle University Bamberg.* 12.

Wagner, M. 1987. "Raeumliche Mobilitaet im Lebenaverlaut." Ph.D. Dissertation, Free University, Berlin.

Weidlich, W., M. Munz, and R. Reiner. 1987. "Ein dynamisches Modell interregionaler Migration." *Spektrum der Wissenschaft* 1:21–24.

Zapf, W. 1979. "Lebensbedingungen und wahrgenommene Lebensqualitaet." *Arbeitspapier 2 des Sonderforschungsbereichs 3.* Frankfurt.

9

GUATEMALA

Michael Micklin

Guatemala is a relatively poor Central American republic, bordered on the north and west by Mexico, on the northeast by Belize, and on the east by El Salvador and Honduras. Its 1988 population was estimated to be 8.7 million, with an annual rate of natural increase of 3.2 percent (Population Reference Bureau, 1988). The per capita GNP is currently around $930. The population is divided into two major ethnic groups: Mayan Indians, who comprise just under half of the total, and non-Indians (or *Ladinos*). The non-Indian group controls social and economic power (Hawkins, 1984, 9–13; Monteforte Toledo, 1959, 251–87; World Bank, 1978).

Internal migration has been a significant feature of Guatemalan society since the middle of the last century when both temporary and permanent labor migration became critical to the development of export agriculture. Moreover, as Guatemala City, the national capital, has grown to be the country's only metropolitan area, it has attracted increasing numbers of migrants from rural areas and small towns and cities.

Recent patterns of migration show that the large majority of the nation's departments (or states) have been net exporters of migrants to those few that offer opportunities for agricultural employment, for land acquisition, or for work in the urban sector of the economy. On the whole, women migrate more frequently than do men, and the non-Indian component of the population is more likely to move than are Indians. During the past two decades a sizeable segment of the population has been displaced from rural communities as a result of civil disruption.

DATA ON MIGRATION

Definitions of Migration

There is no standard definition of migration in official use in Guatemala. Analytic definitions are based on the common-sense notion that a migrant is a person whose residence has changed during a specified period. Prior to 1973, Guatemalan censuses classified a person's residence on a de facto basis, that is, in terms of his or her location on the day of enumeration. Since 1973 the de jure method has been employed, whereby residence is defined according to where a person usually lives. The implications of this shift in the census definition of residence for migration research are discussed below.

The largest unit in terms of which Guatemalan migration is defined is the *departamento* (department or state). The twenty-two departments vary considerably in terms of land area, environmental characteristics, and population (Kluck, 1983; Leonard, 1987; Whetten, 1961, 3–18). To date, nearly all published analyses of internal migration have been focused on interdepartmental migration. Guatemalan departments are divided into *municipios,* similar to the U.S. New England town (Whetten, 1961, 19), of which there were 315 in 1950 and 327 in 1981. The advantage of using the *municipio* as the unit of analysis for studies of internal migration is that it exhibits a degree of sociocultural homogeneity and integration (Tax, 1937), thus allowing more precise identification of the social causes and consequences of population movements. Unfortunately, census data on migration at the *municipio* level are rarely published, and investigators who want to use them must rely on special tabulations (e.g., Early, 1982). It is also possible to examine internal migration according to units defined as "rural" and "urban." However, the definition of urban localities has changed over time (Arias, 1965, 25; Early, 1982, 40–41; Smith, 1978, 591ff.), and the reporting of data on rural and urban migrants is inconsistent from one census to another. Because Guatemala City is the only true metropolitan center in the country, data on movement to that locality provide one indicator of urban migration that can be compared over time.

It is generally agreed that the first reasonably accurate population census using modern techniques was taken in 1950, whereas the most recent one occurred in 1981. Thus, available migration data of one type or another could span a period of about three decades, but, because of changes in reporting formats and census definitions, possibilities for trend analysis are limited. The temporal dimension of internal migration can be measured in three ways on the basis of census data. First, *lifetime migrants* are persons whose place of birth (department, *municipio,* rural/urban locality) differs from the place of residence at some later date. Second, *recent migrants* are those whose current place of residence differs from that five years earlier. Finally, *intermediate migrants* show a difference between place of birth and place of residence five years preceding the census. The first two of these measures are more often available than the last one.

Data on internal migration are available from four national population censuses (1950, 1964, 1973, and 1981) and from several special surveys of varying scope and quality (e.g., Applebaum, 1967; Hoyt, 1955; ICAPF, 1973; Instituto Indigenista Nacional, 1969; Mejia, 1975; Mendez Garcia, 1977; Thomas, 1970, 1971; Roberts, 1973). None of these surveys is based on a national sample, and they are limited to two types of internal movement: migration to Guatemala City and seasonal migration of agricultural workers. Agricultural censuses, taken in 1950, 1964, and 1979, provide additional information that can be useful for understanding patterns of internal migration.

The data available are of highly variable quality, calling for a cautious interpretation of the trends and patterns identified. Census data suffer from several limitations. First, the 1950, 1964, and 1973 counts have been shown to be underenumerated (Camisa, 1969; Chackiel, 1976; Direccion General de Estadistica, 1965; Early, 1974, 1975, 1982). J.D. Early (1982, 30–32) estimates that at the departmental level the 1950 population was underenumerated by 2.8 percent, the 1964 population by 1.2 percent, and the 1973 population by 7.7 percent. Corresponding figures at the *municipio* level are 4.1 percent, 3.1 percent, and 9.5 percent, respectively. Underenumeration of the Indian population is particularly serious, ranging from 7.1 percent at the departmental level in 1950 to around 20 percent at the *municipio* level in 1964 and 1973. The 1981 census has not yet been evaluated for underenumeration, but it is safe to assume that the figures reported are less than the true count. For example, extrapolation of a 1980 estimate of the size of the Indian population provided by Early (1983, 75, Table 1) to 1981 indicates a 12.5 percent undercount. It should be noted, however, that information is nearly complete for the population that was enumerated. For example, place of birth and place of residence five years prior to the census date are available for no less than 97 percent of the population of any department, for both sexes and both ethnic groups. It is also comforting to note that B.J. Arias (1972) finds roughly similar departmental levels of net migration from 1950 to 1964 using three different estimation techniques.

A second problem results from the change in 1973 from a de facto to a de jure definition of residence. Under the de facto definition used in 1950 and 1964, seasonal migrant workers, of whom there are many, were assigned residence in the localities in which they were enumerated. The same was true of travelers away from home on the day of the census. From 1973 onward, these individuals were assigned to their usual community of residence. Comparisons of the number and characteristics of migrants between the earlier and later census periods are therefore imprecise to an unknown degree.

Third, though analysis at the *municipio* level of aggregation would be preferable, the data available are extremely limited, and few such analyses have been attempted (cf. Early, 1982, 80–95). Moreover, the boundaries of several *municipios* are disputed, and twelve new ones have been created since 1950.

Finally, the migration data reported are not consistent from one census to the next. While the sex and ethnicity of migrants can be identified for all four modern censuses for both lifetime and recent movements, their age and education are in some instances not available, in others available only from unpublished special tabulations, and in still others reported for only one type of migration. Comparison of trends and patterns of internal migration is limited accordingly.

The migration surveys that have been conducted differ considerably in terms of the definition of who is a migrant, the questions asked, the geographic area covered, and the sample design.

The analysis that follows is designed to make maximum use of the data available while preserving the integrity of comparisons across time and space. Although some figures will be reported for 1950 and 1964, emphasis will be placed on data from the 1973 and 1981 censuses, particularly the 1981. The unit of analysis employed will be the department and various aggregations of departments. Two types of migration will be examined, lifetime and recent. Migration differentials will be described principally in terms of sex and ethnic status, although age patterns will be mentioned briefly. Finally, the analysis will rely heavily on census data, with information available from special surveys used to complement or elaborate these data or to describe population movements not covered by census materials (e.g., seasonal labor migration).

PRINCIPAL POPULATION MOVEMENTS

The National Level

The number of lifetime internal migrants increased from 326,621 in 1950 to 630,419 in 1964 and 757,068 in 1973 according to official, uncorrected census counts (Arias, 1976, 121, Table 49). These figures correspond to 11.9, 14.9, and 14.8 percent of the total native population, respectively. The 1981 census shows the number of lifetime migrants to be 749,025, or 12.2 percent of the population (Republica de Guatemala, 1985, Table 10).

In 1950 there were 77,778 recent migrants counted (Arias, 1961, Table 3), representing 3.5 percent of the population five years of age or older. By 1973 that number had increased to 232,463, or 5.4 percent of the base population (Arias, 1976, Table 50). The number of recent migrants identified in the 1981 census was 227,711, which is 4.7 percent of the relevant total (calculated from Republica de Guatemala, 1985, Table 8).

In short, the volume of both lifetime and recent migration in Guatemala appears to have increased from 1950 through 1973, and then to have declined to near the 1950 level in the 1973–81 period. Because of the underenumeration problem, it is impossible to know the accuracy of these trends.

Several investigators have observed that the pattern of internal migration varies by age, sex, and ethnic status of the migrant (e.g., Adams, 1970; Arias, 1961, 1976; Whetten, 1961; Zarate, 1967). Migrants tend to be younger than nonmigrants and are more likely to be female and non-Indian (i.e., *Ladino*). This pattern has not changed substantially since 1950 (and probably long before that date as well). A special (unreported) 1981 census tabulation shows that recent migrants have a median age of about 20 years, and that 50 to 55 percent are under 25 years of age. Table 9.1 reports the proportion of the 1981 population in different sex and ethnic categories that has ever moved from the department of birth or has changed department of residence within the preceding five years. Of

Table 9.1
Number and Proportion of Interdepartmental Migrants in Guatemala by Ethnic Group and Sex, 1981

	Resident Native Born, Birthplace Known	Migrant Population	Percent Interdepartmental Migrants
A. Lifetime Migration			
Total Population[a]	5,990,835	729,025	12.2
Males	2,985,925	352,621	11.8
Females	3,004,910	376,404	12.5
NonIndian Population	3,461,424	608,737	17.6
Males	1,715,426	290,559	16.9
Females	1,745,998	318,178	18.2
Indian Population	2,529,411	120,288	4.8
Males	1,270,499	62,062	4.9
Females	1,258,912	58,226	4.6
B. Recent Migration[b]			
Total Population	4,816,581	227,711	4.7
Males	2,449,811	112,668	4.6
Females	2,366,770	115,043	4.9
NonIndian Population	2,769,525	184,488	6.7
Males	1,422,022	89,645	6.3
Females	1,347,503	94,843	7.0
Indian Population	2,047,056	43,223	2.1
Males	1,027,789	23,023	2.2
Females	1,019,267	20,200	2.0

[a] Defined in terms of department of birth.

[b] Defined in terms of department of residence in 1976. Base is population 5 years of age and older in 1981 with known 1976 department of residence.

Source: Republica de Guatemala, Censos Nacionales de 1981, IX Censo de Poblacion. Cifras Definitivas. Tomo I. Guatemala: Instituto Nacional de Estadistica, 1985, Cuadros 8, 10, 38 and 40.

the female population, 12.5 percent are lifetime migrants and 4.9 percent are recent migrants. The figures for the male population are slightly lower. Much larger differences are observed between the Indian and non-Indian categories. While only 4.8 percent of the Indians are lifetime migrants and 2.1 percent are recent migrants, the corresponding figures for non-Indians are 17.6 percent and 6.7 percent, respectively. Within the non-Indian population women are more likely to be migrants than are men, in agreement with the pattern for the general population, but within the Indian population men are slightly more likely to be migrants.

The overall distribution of interdepartmental migrants for 1981 is shown in Table 9.2. Just over four-fifths of both lifetime and recent migrants are non-Indian. Females tend to constitute a slightly higher percentage of the migrant

Table 9.2
Distribution of Interdepartmental Migrants in Guatemala by Type, Ethnic Group, and Sex, 1981

	N		%	
A. Lifetime Migrants[a]				
Total Population	729,025		100.0	
Males		352,621		48.4
Females		376,404		51.1
NonIndian Population	608,737		83.8	
Males		290,559		47.7
Females		318,178		52.3
Indian Population	120,288		16.2	
Males		62,062		51.6
Females		58,226		48.4
B. Recent Migrants[b]				
Total Population	227,711		100.0	
Males		112,668		49.5
Females		115,043		50.5
NonIndian Population	184,488		81.0	
Males		89,645		48.6
Females		94,843		51.4
Indian Population	43,223		19.0	
Males		23,023		53.3
Females		20,200		46.7

a   Defined in terms of department of birth.

b   Defined in terms of department of residence in 1976. Base is population
    5 years of age and older in 1981 with known 1976 department of residence.

Source: Republica de Guatemala; Censos Nacionales de 1981, IX Censo de
          Poblacion. Cifras Definitivas. Tomo I. Guatemala: Instituto
          Nacional de Estadistica, 1985, Cuadros 8, 10, 38 and 40.

population except among Indians where males constitute a slight majority of the migrants. Comparison of the lifetime and recent migration figures suggests that both sex and ethnic differentials are being reduced, although within the Indian population the male-female differential appears to be increasing.

Interregional Migration

Several analytic schemes have been devised for representing Guatemalan regions, based on administrative, geographic, cultural, social, or ecological criteria (Adams, 1970, 155–73, 217–37; Early, 1982, 151–69; Hough et al., 1983, Annex 4; Mendez Dominguez et al., 1988; Smith, 1978, 1984; Whetten, 1961, 8–18). The most useful classifications require data at the *municipio* level and are thus precluded from use here. The analysis that follows defines regions in two ways. First, a simple geographic classification suggested by N.L. Whetten (1961, 16–18) distributes departments into six regions: Central, North, East, South, West, and North Central. A second classification based on the proportion of a department's population defined as Indian and the absolute number of Indians in the department is also used. Indian departments are those that show the highest average rank on these indicators for the period 1950–81. Non-Indian departments are those exhibiting the lowest ranks, and mixed departments show intermediate values. According to this classification, there are eight Indian departments, seven mixed departments, and seven non-Indian departments.

Patterns of interregional migration are examined primarily in terms of measures of net migration. Limitations of space preclude a more detailed analysis of interdepartmental patterns. Prior analyses of net interdepartmental migration (Adams, 1970, 125–37; Arias, 1961, 1976, 121–26; Zarate, 1967), based on the 1950, 1964, or 1973 censuses, show a consistent pattern taking shape. The largest net gain of migrants is seen in the department of Guatemala which contains the only metropolitan center, Guatemala City. Data for 1950 show a net gain of 64,998 lifetime migrants (Arias, 1961, Table 2) for this department, while 1973 data indicate a net gain of 246,000 (Arias, 1976, 121). Other departments showing a net gain of lifetime migrants include Escuintla, which is dominated by large commercial farms that employ both permanent and seasonal migrant workers and also contains a growing urban center, the northern departments of the Peten and Izabal, which have been the site of land colonization movements since the 1960s, and Suchitepequez and Retalhuleu, also located in the commercial farming area of the south coast. All other departments experienced a net loss of lifetime migrants. The pattern for recent migrants is roughly similar, though the number of gains and losses is, of course, lower.

The pattern of net lifetime migration by geographic region and department is detailed in Table 9.3, based on 1981 data. It is clear that the North, Central, and South regions are net gainers of lifetime migrants, while the East, West, and North Central regions are net losers. Although the department of Guatemala continues to dominate the Central region and the country as a whole in terms of

Table 9.3
Net Lifetime[a] Interregional Migration in Guatemala by Ethnic Group and Sex, for Regions and Departments, 1981

Regions and Departments	Total Population			NonIndian Population			Indian Population		
	Both Sexes	Males	Females	Both Sexes	Males	Females	Both Sexes	Males	Females
Central	241,055	101,910	139,145	216,689	91,509	125,180	24,366	10,401	13,965
Guatemala	245,650	104,843	140,807	220,900	94,094	126,806	24,700	10,749	14,001
Sacatepequez	-4,595	-2,933	-1,662	-4,211	-2,585	-1,626	-384	-348	-36
North	105,358	56,444	48,914	82,227	44,096	38,131	23,131	12,348	10,783
Izabal	41,766	22,367	19,399	30,721	16,575	14,146	11,045	5,792	5,253
Peten	63,592	34,077	29,515	51,506	27,521	23,980	12,086	6,556	5,530
East	-223,901	-106,409	-117,492	-213,733	-101,268	-112,465	-10,168	-5,141	-5,027
Chiquimula	-37,481	-18,245	-19,236	-33,887	-16,376	-17,511	-3,594	-1,869	-1,725
El Progreso	-22,226	-10,826	-11,400	-21,329	-10,356	-10,973	-897	-470	-427
Jalapa	-25,237	-12,517	-12,720	-23,526	-11,586	-11,940	-1,711	-931	-780
Jutiapa	-63,391	-29,841	-33,550	-61,964	-29,169	-32,795	-1,427	-672	-755
Santa Rosa	-44,982	-20,590	-24,392	-43,883	-20,111	-23,772	-1,099	-479	-620
Zacapa	-30,584	-14,390	-16,194	-29,144	-13,670	-15,474	-1,440	-720	-720
South	32,883	24,749	8,134	19,461	14,535	4,566	13,782	9,436	4,346
Escuintla	38,638	24,770	13,868	27,266	17,004	10,262	11,372	7,766	3,606
Retalhuleu	3,981	2,856	1,125	2,389	1,930	439	1,592	926	666
Suchitepequez	-9,736	-2,877	-6,859	-10,554	-4,399	-6,155	818	744	74
West	-121,388	-61,299	-60,719	-89,175	-42,861	-46,314	-32,213	-17,660	-14,553
Chimaltenango	-17,635	-8,291	-9,344	-12,731	-6,256	-6,475	-4,904	-2,035	-2,869
Huehuetenango	-19,415	-9,015	-10,400	-12,543	-5,221	-7,322	-6,872	-3,794	-3,078
Quetzaltenango	-21,397	-11,653	-9,744	-19,358	-10,751	-8,607	-2,039	-902	-1,137
Quiche	-16,543	-10,136	-6,407	-11,424	-5,624	-5,800	-5,119	-3,734	-1,385
San Marcos	-32,197	-13,800	-18,397	-27,267	-11,642	-15,625	-4,930	-2,158	-2,772
Solola	-3,439	-1,827	-1,612	-2,156	-1,145	-1,011	-1,283	-682	-601
Totonicapan	-10,762	-6,577	-4,185	-3,696	-2,222	-1,474	-7,066	-4,355	-2,711
North Central	-34,007	-15,395	-18,612	-15,109	-6,011	-9,098	-18,898	-9,384	-9,514
Alta Verapaz	-13,025	-4,500	-8,525	301	1,816	-1,515	-13,326	-6,316	-7,010
Baja Verapaz	-20,982	-10,895	-10,087	-15,410	-7,827	-7,583	-5,572	-3,008	-2,504

a Defined in terms of department of birth.

Source: Republica de Guatemala, Censos Nacionales de 1981, IX Censo de Poblacion. Cifras Definitivas. Tomo L. Guatemala: Instituto Nacional de Estadistica, 1985, Cuadros 10 and 40.

net in-migration, with nearly 246,000 of its 1981 population born in another department, the Peten, Izabal, and Escuintla have shown significant gains over earlier years (cf. Arias, 1961, Table 2; Hough et al., 1983, Annex 1, Table 12; Zarate, 1967, Cuadro 3). Net losses are heaviest in the East, especially the department of Jutiapa, which offers relatively few opportunities for either permanent or temporary agricultural employment. The West region, which is composed largely of highland subsistence-farming communities and whose population is 70 percent Indian, has lost just over half as many out-migrants as the East region and almost four times the number moving from the North Central region.

Sex differences are reflected by the fact that among the departments that have gained lifetime migrants, Guatemala shows an excess net in-migration of nearly 40,000 women, while the agricultural and colonization areas of the South and North, respectively, have attracted considerably more men. The explanation of sex differences among these areas of in-migration is to be found primarily in terms of the types of employment available—domestic and other informal sector jobs in Guatemala City, subsistence farming in the North, and wage-based agricultural labor, seasonal or permanent, in the South (cf. de Janvry, 1981; Grindle, 1986, 1988 regarding relationships between migration and employment in Latin America).

There are also some interesting differences between Indians and non-Indians. The proportion of net in-migrants to the department of Guatemala that is Indian has increased over previous years, as has the proportion moving to the departments of the south coast. Generally, although Indians are still much less likely to be internal migrants than are non-Indians, they appear to be increasingly likely to have left the departments in which they were born. Much of this out-migration is coming from the western and north central highlands, where population densities are relatively high and agricultural land is extremely scarce (see Brockett, 1988; Hough et al., 1983; Smith, 1978, 1984, 1986). This pattern is seen more clearly when departments are grouped according to ethnic composition. For 1981, Indian departments showed a net loss of 21,080 natives and non-Indian departments (largely in the East region), a net loss of 8,212. In contrast, mixed departments recorded a net gain of 29,292 persons, largely women (68 percent) and non-Indians (88 percent). While no Indian department exhibits a net gain of Indian population, two mixed departments (Guatemala and neighboring Sacatepequez) and three non-Indian departments (Escuintla, Peten, and Izabal) do. Net gains of non-Indians are seen in all three types of department: Indian (Alta Verapaz), mixed (Guatemala and Sacatepequez), and non-Indian (Escuintla and the Peten).

The 1981 data for net recent interdepartmental migration are presented in Table 9.4. The regional pattern established for lifetime migration is repeated, with the Central, North, and South regions showing net gains and the others net losses. Only four departments show a net gain of migrants: Guatemala (47,059), the Peten (18,085), Escuintla (7,964), and Alta Verapaz (1,498). All others experienced a net loss, suggesting a continuing concentration of population. However, some important variations on the general motif are evident. First, the department of Izabal, which showed a large net gain of lifetime migrants of both sexes, exhibited a small net loss of total population and females, and a net gain of only 127 males. The explanation probably lies in the fact that during the 1970s Izabal was the site of numerous armed confrontations between rebel forces and government soldiers and, sadly, continuing government reprisals against peasant populations believed to be aiding the rebels (see Handy, 1984; Simon, 1987). It is reasonable to assume that these conflicts stimulated out-migration (discussed below). Note, however, that Izabal showed a small net gain in Indian migrants. In a nation where land is both scarce and unequally distributed, those at the bottom of the social hierarchy may be willing to face hazardous conditions, including political repression and the possible loss of life, in order to gain access to agricultural land.

A second feature distinguishing the interregional movement of recent migrants is seen in the departments of the south coast. Only Escuintla continues to show

Table 9.4
Net Recent[a] Interregional Migration in Guatemala by Ethnic Group and Sex, for Regions and Departments, 1976–81

Regions and Departments	Total Population			NonIndian Population			Indian Population		
	Both Sexes	Males	Females	Both Sexes	Males	Females	Both Sexes	Males	Females
Central	48,275	19,661	28,614	41,213	16,830	24,383	7,062	2,831	4,231
Guatemala	47,059	19,271	27,788	40,089	16,415	23,674	6,970	2,856	4,114
Sacatepequez	1,218	390	826	1,124	415	709	92	-25	117
North	18,027	9,812	8,215	13,974	7,671	6,303	4,053	2,141	1,912
Izabal	-58	127	-185	-830	-253	-577	772	380	392
Peten	18,085	9,685	8,400	14,804	7,924	6,880	3,281	1,761	1,520
East	-44,371	-21,679	-22,692	-41,947	-20,341	-21,606	-2,424	-1,338	-1,086
Chiquimula	-6,118	-3,498	-2,620	-5,566	-3,202	-2,364	-552	-296	-256
El Progreso	-5,198	-1,895	-3,303	-4,995	-1,774	-3,221	-203	-121	-82
Jalapa	-4,050	-2,394	-1,656	-3,366	-2,000	-1,366	-684	-394	-290
Jutiapa	-15,296	-7,422	-7,874	-14,913	-7,221	-7,692	-383	-201	-182
Santa Rosa	-8,186	-3,743	-4,443	-7,954	-3,642	-4,312	-232	-101	-131
Zacapa	-5,523	-2,727	-2,796	-5,153	-2,502	-2,651	-370	-225	-145
South	3,989	4,788	-799	-570	1,122	-1,692	4,559	3,666	893
Escuintla	7,964	6,354	1,610	2,841	2,402	439	5,123	3,952	1,171
Retalhuleu	-932	-284	-648	-626	-123	-503	-306	-161	-145
Suchitepequez	-3,043	-1,282	-1,761	-2,785	-1,157	-1,628	-258	-125	-133
West	-22,488	-11,555	-10,933	-12,917	-6,182	-6,735	-9,571	-5,373	-4,198
Chimaltenango	-2,073	-919	-1,154	-992	-549	-443	-1,081	-370	-711
Huehuetenango	-3,788	-2,001	-1,787	-1,555	-768	-787	-2,233	-1,233	-1,000
Quetzaltenango	-3,706	-1,852	-1,854	-3,112	-1,646	-1,466	-594	-206	-388
Quiche	-3,997	-2,758	-1,239	-1,828	-959	-869	-2,169	-1,799	-370
San Marcos	-6,557	-2,595	-3,962	-4,990	-1,928	-3,620	-1,567	-667	-900
Solola	-147	-98	-49	-9	-33	-24	-138	-65	-73
Totonicapan	-2,220	-1,332	-888	-431	-249	-132	-1,789	-1,033	-756
North Central	-3,432	-1,027	-2,405	247	900	-653	-3,679	-1,927	-1,752
Alta Verapaz	1,498	1,753	-345	3,382	2,621	761	-1,974	-868	-1,106
Baja Verapaz	-4,840	-2,780	-2,060	-3,135	-1,721	-1,414	-1,705	-1,059	-646

a Defined in terms of department of residence in 1976.

Source: Republica de Guatemala, Censos Nacionales de 1981, IX Censo de Poblacion. Cifras Definitivas. Tomo I. Guatemala: Instituto Nacional de Estadistica, 1985, Cuadros 8 and 38.

net in-migration of both sexes and both ethnic groups, while the other two departments in the region show net losses in all categories. The result for the region as a whole is an increased flow of male and Indian in-migrants, most of whom are probably employed on the large commercial farms located in Escuintla. Finally, between 1976 and 1981 the department of Alta Verapaz, located in the North Central region, experienced a net gain of nearly 3,400 non-Indians, over three-quarters of whom were male.

Examination of patterns of recent migration in terms of the ethnic composition of departments shows only minor variations on the patterns evident for lifetime migration, and the results are consistent with those reported for 1973 (Hough et al., 1983, Annex 1, Table 13). In both cases Indian departments are the heaviest losers of both Indian and non-Indian population, and non-Indian departments exhibit a net loss of non-Indians and a net gain of Indians. Mixed departments show a net gain of both ethnic groups, though nearly 90 percent of the increase consists of non-Indians. The recent pattern indicates increased movement of

Indian males into non-Indian departments and Indian females into mixed departments.

Table 9.5 provides an additional perspective on interregional movements, indicating the proportion of 1981 regional and departmental populations made up of migrants in the various ethnic-sex categories. As would be expected from the preceding discussion, the regions with the highest proportion of lifetime migrants in their 1981 populations are the North (41.1 percent), Central (22.1 percent), and South (19.7 percent), while for recent migration the order and magnitudes change slightly: North (13.7 percent), South (7.3 percent), and Central (6.7 percent). Seven departments show at least 10 percent of their 1981 population to consist of lifetime migrants: the Peten (52.4 percent), Izabal (33.3 percent), Escuintla (27.0 percent), Guatemala (23.1 percent), Retalhuleu (16.8 percent), Suchitepequez (11.2 percent), and Sacatepequez (10.2 percent). Considering recent migration, the most important receiving departments are the Peten (22.0 percent), Escuintla (10.0 percent), Izabal (8.4 percent), Guatemala (6.9 percent), and Retalhuleu (5.5 percent). When departments are grouped according to ethnic composition, it is clear that the seven non-Indian departments have the highest proportion of in-migrants (20.4 percent of the 1981 population composed of lifetime migrants and 7.7 percent of recent migrants), followed by the seven departments of mixed composition (16.7 percent and 5.7 percent, respectively). The eight Indian departments show only 3.6 percent of their 1981 population as lifetime migrants and 2.0 percent as recent migrants.

The departments differ, of course, in terms of the conditions that attract migrants. For Guatemala, and to a lesser extent nearby Sacatepequez, it is the social and economic institutions and opportunities of the metropolitan area, while for the others it is largely either opportunities for agricultural employment on the large *fincas* (Escuintla, Retalhuleu, and Suchitepequez) or the promise of land opened up for colonization (the Peten and Izabal).

Non-Indians appear to be attracted to all major receiving departments, whereas Indian migrants tend to be concentrated in those that offer agricultural employment or available land (see Adams, 1965; Peckenham, 1980). Women of both ethnic groups constitute a higher proportion of the population moving to the metropolitan area or its environs, while men are more likely to account for a higher proportion of the migrant population in agricultural areas.

Of particular significance for Guatemala is the tradition of seasonal migration by agricultural laborers from the highlands to the south coast. Beginning in the 1850s, when Guatemala began to produce coffee for the world market, there emerged a demand for a readily available reserve labor force to clear the land and harvest the crops (Lovell, 1988; McCreery, 1983, 1986). Since this labor was required only four to six months per year, powerful landowners and politicians had to devise a system whereby it could be provided cheaply and when needed. Over the years a series of laws were enacted that guaranteed the seasonal migration of highland Indians. In recent years, although the punitive and highly discriminatory laws have been repealed, economic necessity, owing largely to land

Table 9.5

Lifetime and Recent In-Migrants as a Percentage of Guatemalan Population by Ethnic Group and Sex, for Regions and Departments, 1981

Regions and Departments	Lifetime Migrants[a]						Recent Migrants[b]					
	1981 Population[c]	NonIndian Males	NonIndian Females	Indian Males	Indian Females	All In-Migrants	1981 Population[d]	NonIndian Males	NonIndian Females	Indian Males	Indian Females	All In-Migrants
Central	1,403,831	8.6	11.0	1.1	1.4	22.1	1,196,539	2.5	3.3	0.4	0.5	6.7
Guatemala	1,284,152	9.1	11.6	1.1	1.3	23.1	1,096,511	2.6	3.4	0.4	0.5	6.9
Sacatepequez	119,679	3.3	4.2	0.8	1.9	10.2	100,028	1.8	2.1	0.4	0.6	4.9
North	319,473	17.3	15.9	4.2	3.7	41.1	258,406	6.0	5.5	1.2	1.0	13.7
Izabal	190,175	13.6	13.0	3.5	3.2	33.3	155,977	3.6	3.5	0.7	0.6	8.4
Peten	129,298	22.7	20.1	5.2	4.4	52.4	102,429	9.7	8.6	2.0	1.7	22.0
East	937,797	2.6	2.8	0.2	0.2	5.8	773,607	1.5	1.9	0.1	0.1	3.6
Chiquimula	165,937	1.5	1.8	0.1	0.2	3.6	137,177	0.9	1.6	0.1	0.2	2.8
El Progreso	80,907	3.8	4.1	0.1	0.1	8.1	67,094	1.9	2.3	*	*	4.2
Jalapa	135,595	2.1	2.8	0.2	0.2	5.3	110,295	1.3	2.1	0.1	0.1	3.6
Jutiapa	247,511	1.8	1.8	0.2	0.1	3.9	203,988	1.1	1.3	0.2	0.1	2.7
Santa Rosa	193,076	3.7	3.8	0.2	0.2	7.9	159,910	1.8	1.9	0.2	0.1	4.0
Zacapa	114,771	3.7	3.7	0.2	0.2	7.8	95,143	2.2	2.0	0.1	0.1	4.4
South	714,378	8.2	7.7	2.3	1.5	19.7	586,957	2.9	2.6	1.2	0.6	7.3
Escuintla	328,301	11.8	10.9	2.8	1.5	27.0	271,127	4.0	3.5	1.8	0.7	10.0
Retalhuleu	149,952	6.8	6.5	1.8	1.7	16.8	122,572	2.3	2.2	0.5	0.5	5.5
Suchitepequez	236,125	4.0	4.0	1.8	1.4	11.2	193,258	1.7	1.6	0.8	0.6	4.7
West	2,179,927	1.1	1.2	0.6	0.6	3.5	1,767,415	0.6	0.6	0.3	0.3	1.8
Chimaltenango	229,487	1.3	1.6	0.9	0.9	4.7	187,196	0.8	0.9	0.5	0.5	2.7
Huehuetenango	429,376	0.6	0.6	0.2	0.2	1.6	395,840	0.4	0.3	0.1	0.1	0.9
Quetzaltenango	365,395	2.1	3.0	1.0	1.0	7.1	299,324	1.1	1.3	0.4	0.4	3.2
Quiche	327,470	0.9	0.8	1.1	1.0	3.8	265,296	0.5	0.5	0.6	0.5	2.1
San Marcos	470,614	1.2	1.1	0.2	0.2	2.7	378,138	0.7	0.7	0.1	0.1	1.6
Solola	153,630	0.5	0.7	0.7	0.6	2.5	124,877	0.4	0.4	0.5	0.4	1.7
Totonicapan	203,975	0.2	0.3	0.3	0.6	1.4	166,744	0.2	0.2	0.2	0.3	0.9
North Central	434,949	1.8	1.3	0.7	0.5	4.3	348,699	1.3	0.8	0.3	0.2	2.6
Alta Verapaz	319,871	2.0	1.3	0.8	0.6	4.7	254,758	1.5	0.8	0.4	0.3	3.0
Baja Verapaz	115,078	1.1	1.2	0.4	0.4	3.1	93,941	0.8	0.7	0.2	0.1	1.8

a Defined in terms of department of birth.
b Defined in terms of department of residence, 1976.
c Native population with known birthplace.
d Native population 5 years of age or more with known residence in 1976.
* Less than 0.1 percent.

shortages in the home communities, has maintained the pattern of seasonal movement. Although precise data do not exist, estimates of the annual number of seasonal agricultural migrant laborers range from 220,000 to close to 1 million (Handy, 1984, 206; Hough et al., 1983, 23).

Metropolitan Migration

Although migration is an important component of all aspects of the process of urbanization in Guatemala (Arias, 1961, 1965), its consequences in this regard are reflected primarily in the growth of Guatemala City. It has been argued (Smith, 1985, 123) that Guatemala is an example of "extreme primacy," that is, "the 'overdevelopment' of a single city vis-à-vis other cities in the same system." In 1973 Guatemala City had thirteen times the population of the second largest city, Quetzaltenango (Republica de Guatemala, 1975, Cuadro 1), and in 1981 this figure had been reduced only slightly to a ratio of 12 to 1 (Republica de Guatemala, 1985, Cuadro 1). Moreover, if the largely urban *municipios* immediately surrounding Guatemala City are included in the calculation, the evidence of extreme primacy is even stronger (Smith, 1985, 123 n. 6). In short, the vast majority of movement toward truly urban locations is reflected in the growth of Guatemala City. Other writers (e.g., Smith, 1985; Zarate, 1967), have noted that typical of the pattern in high primacy nations, migrants tend to move to Guatemala City directly from their place of origin rather than in a stepwise fashion. R. Hough et al. (1983, 24–25) disagree, however, claiming that step migration is not uncommon. This debate cannot be settled here, because of lack of appropriate data. The analysis that follows is, for these reasons, limited to migration to the national capital.

From Table 9.6 it is evident that there were nearly 198,000 lifetime migrants in Guatemala City on the date of the most recent census, comprising 27 percent of the population (defined here as the *municipio* of Guatemala); the figures for recent migration were 48,884 persons and 7.7 percent. Moderate to large differences are observed by sex and ethnic group. A higher proportion of females than males in both ethnic groups are migrants, and among the Indian population residents of both sexes are more likely to be migrants than are non-Indian residents. This is especially evident for the Indian women, of whom 46.2 percent are lifetime migrants and 18.8 percent are recent migrants.

These differentials are elaborated in Table 9.7. Of the lifetime migrants, nearly 89 percent are non-Indian; for recent migrants this figure drops to 84 percent. The sex differential is approximately equal for both ethnic groups and both types of migrant, ranging from 55.7 to 57.3 percent female. The data suggest an increase in the migration of Indians to Guatemala City in recent years which may be related to a deterioration of living conditions and employment opportunities in rural areas, particularly the western highlands, and growing opportunities for work in the informal sector of the metropolitan economy (see Smith, 1985).

Table 9.6
Number and Proportion of Interdepartmental Migrants Living in *Municipio* of Guatemala by Ethnic Group and Sex, 1981

A. Lifetime Migration[a]	Resident Native Born, Birthplace Known	Migrant Population	Percent Interdepartmental Migrants
Total Population	734,192	197,743	26.9
Males	345,609	85,349	24.7
Females	388,583	112,394	28.9
NonIndian Population	683,656	175,287	25.6
Males	322,130	75,405	23.4
Females	361,526	99,882	27.6
Indian Population	50,536	22,456	44.4
Males	23,479	9,944	42.4
Females	27,057	12,512	46.2
B. Recent Migration[b]			
Total Population	637,582	48,884	7.7
Males	296,861	20,919	7.0
Females	340,721	27,965	8.2
NonIndian Population	593,513	41,046	6.9
Males	276,519	17,534	6.3
Females	316,994	23,512	7.4
Indian Population	44,069	7,838	17.8
Males	20,342	3,385	16.6
Females	23,727	4,453	18.8

[a] Defined in terms of department of birth.

[b] Defined in terms of department of residence in 1976. Base is population 5 years of age and older in 1981 with known 1976 department of residence.

Source: Republica de Guatemala, Census Nacionales de 1981, IX Censo de Poblacion. Cifras Definitivas. Tomo II. Guatemala: Instituto Nacional de Estadistica, 1985, Cuadros 8, 10, 37 and 39.

The regional and departmental patterns of lifetime and recent metropolitan migration for 1981 are shown in Tables 9.8 and 9.9. From Table 9.8 it is clear that the majority of migrants (72 percent) come from the East and West regions, particularly the departments of Santa Rosa and Jutiapa in the East, and Quetzal-

Table 9.7
Distribution of Interdepartmental Migrants to *Municipio* of Guatemala by Type, Ethnic Group, and Sex, 1981

	N	%
A. Lifetime Migrants[a]		
Total Population	197,743	100.0
Males	85,349	43.2
Females	112,394	56.8
NonIndian Population	175,287	88.6
Males	75,405	43.0
Females	99,882	57.0
Indian Population	22,456	11.4
Males	9,944	44.3
Females	12,502	55.7
B. Recent Migrants[b]		
Total Population	48,884	100.0
Males	20,919	42.8
Females	27,965	57.2
NonIndian Population	41,046	84.0
Males	17,534	42.7
Females	23,512	57.3
Indian Population	7,838	16.0
Males	3,385	43.2
Females	4,453	56.8

[a] Defined in terms of department of birth.

[b] Defined in terms of department of residence in 1976. Base is population 5 years of age and older in 1981 with known 1976 department of residence.

Source: Republica de Guatemala. Censos Nacionales de 1981, IX Censo de Poblacion. Cifras Definitivas. Tomo II. Guatemala, Instituto Nacional de Estadistica, 1987, Cuadros 8, 10, 37 and 39.

tenango and San Marcos in the West. There has also been a sizeable influx of people from Escuintla in the South region. For non-Indian lifetime migrants, the regional pattern appears to hold fairly well. For Indians, however, slightly more than 63 percent are from the West region, with a relatively low volume of migration emanating only from the departments of Huehuetenango and Solola. The excess of female over male metropolitan in-migrants is nearly universal, the one exception being observed for the Indian population from the departments of Izabal and Peten in the North.

Table 9.8
Volume of Lifetime Interdepartmental Migration to *Municipio* of Guatemala by Ethnic Group and Sex, for Regions and Departments, 1981[a]

Regions & Departments	Total Population Both Sexes	Males	Females	Non-Indian Population Both Sexes	Males	Females	Indian Population Both Sexes	Males	Females
Total[b]	197,743	85,349	112,394	175,287	75,405	99,882	22,456	9,944	12,512
Central	7,441	3,802	3,939	6,501	3,090	3,411	940	412	528
Sacatepequez	7,441	3,802	3,939	6,501	3,090	3,411	940	412	528
North	7,617	3,356	4,261	7,321	3,203	4,118	296	153	143
Izabal	6,217	2,727	3,490	5,979	2,599	3,380	238	128	110
Peten	1,400	629	771	1,342	604	738	58	25	33
East	73,657	30,376	43,281	71,053	29,090	41,963	2,604	1,286	1,318
Chiquimula	7,586	3,005	4,581	7,292	2,851	4,441	294	154	140
El Progreso	10,363	4,468	5,895	10,075	4,321	5,754	288	147	141
Jalapa	9,347	3,970	5,377	8,877	3,753	5,124	470	217	253
Jutiapa	17,872	7,333	10,539	17,230	7,002	10,228	654	331	311
Santa Rosa	19,248	7,770	11,478	18,555	7,446	11,109	693	324	369
Zacapa	9,241	3,830	5,411	9,024	3,717	5,307	217	113	104
South	29,223	12,558	16,665	27,259	11,708	15,551	1,964	850	1,114
Escuintla	15,013	6,350	8,663	14,417	6,085	8,332	596	265	331
Retalhuleu	4,864	2,114	2,750	4,465	1,936	2,529	399	178	221
Suchitepequez	9,346	4,094	5,252	8,377	3,687	4,690	969	407	562
West	68,522	30,830	37,692	54,315	24,465	29,850	14,207	6,365	7,842
Chimaltenango	11,713	5,123	6,590	8,558	3,882	4,676	3,155	1,241	1,914
Huehuetenango	7,676	3,435	4,241	6,989	3,114	3,875	687	321	366
Quetzaltenango	17,381	7,837	9,544	14,828	6,809	8,019	2,553	1,028	1,525
Quiche	8,479	4,234	4,245	6,018	2,875	3,143	2,461	1,359	1,102
San Marcos	16,055	6,606	9,449	14,213	5,957	8,256	1,842	649	1,193
Solola	2,828	1,349	1,479	1,861	898	963	967	451	516
Totonicapan	4,390	2,246	2,144	1,848	930	918	2,542	1,316	1,226
North Central	11,283	4,727	6,556	8,838	3,849	4,989	2,445	878	1,567
Alta Verapaz	6,227	2,450	3,777	4,481	1,927	2,554	1,746	523	1,223
Baja Verapaz	5,056	2,277	2,779	4,357	1,922	2,435	699	355	344

[a] Excludes migrants from other municipios in Department of Guatemala
[b] Native born, department of birth known and not Guatemala

Source: Republica de Guatemala, Censos Nacionales de 1981, IX Censo de Poblacion. Cifras Definitivas. Tomo II. Guatemala: Instituto Nacional de Estadistica, 1987, Curados 8 and 37.

Table 9.9 reports data on recent migration to Guatemala City. The pattern is very close to that reported for lifetime migration, although the proportion coming from the West region is slightly lower and the proportion from the North region slightly higher.

Earlier studies of Guatemalan internal migration (e.g., Arias, 1961, 1976; Zarate, 1967) showed that Indians are more likely to migrate over shorter distances than non-Indians, that is, they more often move to contiguous departments. Data from the 1981 census indicate that with regard to metropolitan migration the opposite is true. For lifetime migration, approximately 40 percent

Table 9.9

Volume of Recent Interdepartmental Migration to *Municipio* of Guatemala by Ethnic Group and Sex, for Regions and Departments, 1981[a]

Regions & Departments	Total Population Both Sexes	Males	Females	NonIndian Population Both Sexes	Males	Females	Indian Population Both Sexes	Males	Females
Total[b]	48,884	20,919	27,965	41,046	17,534	23,512	7,838	3,385	4,453
Central	1,231	541	690	918	411	507	313	130	183
Sacatepequez	1,231	541	690	918	411	507	313	130	183
North	3,142	1,458	1,684	2,937	1,330	1,607	205	128	77
Izabal	2,307	1,063	1,244	2,145	959	1,186	162	104	58
Peten	835	395	440	792	371	421	43	24	19
East	18,365	7,757	10,608	17,268	7,146	10,122	1,097	611	486
Chiquimula	1,951	795	1,156	1,817	730	1,087	134	65	69
El Progreso	2,160	922	1,236	2,061	870	1,191	99	52	47
Jalapa	2,223	965	1,258	2,005	861	1,144	218	104	114
Jutiapa	5,489	2,422	3,067	5,160	2,208	2,952	329	214	115
Santa Rosa	4,290	1,659	2,631	4,073	1,550	2,523	217	109	108
Zacapa	2,252	994	1,258	2,152	927	1,225	100	67	33
South	7,880	3,419	4,461	6,975	2,479	3,996	905	440	465
Escuintla	4,160	1,800	2,360	3,859	1,636	2,223	301	164	137
Retalhuleu	1,480	648	832	1,267	548	719	213	100	112
Suchitepequez	2,240	971	1,269	1,849	795	1,054	391	176	215
West	15,980	6,666	9,314	11,270	4,859	6,411	4,710	1,809	2,903
Chimaltenango	2,261	869	1,392	1,332	573	759	929	296	633
Huehuetenango	1,629	697	932	1,371	599	772	258	98	160
Quetzaltenango	3,989	1,678	2,311	3,201	1,410	1,791	788	268	520
Quiche	1,923	932	991	1,158	545	613	765	387	378
San Marcos	4,472	1,699	2,773	3,640	1,442	2,198	832	257	575
Solola	622	284	338	276	135	141	346	149	197
Totonicapan	1,084	507	577	292	155	137	792	352	440
North Central	2,286	1,078	1,208	1,678	809	869	608	269	339
Alta Verapaz	1,059	454	615	754	360	394	315	94	221
Baja Verapaz	1,217	624	593	924	449	475	293	175	118

[a] Excludes migrants from other municipios in Department of Guatemala.
[b] Native born, department of birth known and not Guatemala.

Source: Republica de Guatemala, Censos Nacionales de 1981, IX Censo de Poblacion. Cifras Definitivas. Tomo II. Guatemala: Instituto Nacional de Estadistica, 1987, Curados 8 and 37.

of non-Indians and only 30 percent of Indians moved to Guatemala City from the contiguous departments of El Progreso, Sacatepequez, Chimaltenango, Escuintla, Santa Rosa, Baja Verapaz, and Jalapa. With recent migration, the corresponding figures are 37 and 30 percent, respectively. That Indians are now willing (or forced) to move longer distances has surely contributed to their increased presence in the metropolitan area. Another factor may be the hypothesized, but as yet unsubstantiated, tendency for Indians to retain their ethnic identity in spite of migration to non-Indian areas (see Early, 1982, 92–94, 151–69).

WHO MOVES

Characteristics of Movers

The demographic characteristics of interregional migrants have already been discussed. Generally, young non-Indians tend to predominate, although it is clear that Indians and people of all ages are involved to some degree in internal population movements. The sex ratio of migrants varies with the characteristics of places of origin and destination. Overall, women are more likely to migrate than are men. However, among Indians the opposite is true, especially from predominantly Indian communities. The ratio of female to male migrants is highest when the place of origin or destination is a non-Indian department.

Guatemalan migrants, like those in other countries, are most likely to move in search of employment. That fact, in combination with the relatively low educational level of the population and its concentration in agricultural and unskilled occupations, has a determining influence on the socioeconomic characteristics of the migrant population. Male migrants are largely agricultural workers seeking seasonal or permanent employment on the large farms, whereas females are most often looking for work as domestic servants or in the highly variable informal sector of small cities or the national capital.

The characteristics of a not necessarily representative sample of migrants to Guatemala City are provided by B.R. Roberts (1973). Of 112 men who had jobs before arriving in the city, 45 percent worked in agriculture, and the remainder included craftsmen, operatives, construction laborers, shopkeepers, drivers, office workers, and policemen. For the men and women in the sample who were born and educated outside the city, 67 percent had not completed more than five years of schooling.

WHY PEOPLE MOVE

Economic Reasons

Rural poverty is a principal factor underlying internal migration in Guatemala. In a predominantly agricultural population, land is the most valued resource. Land distribution in Guatemala is notoriously unequal (Hough et al., 1983). Data from the 1979 agricultural census showed that 90 percent of farming units had access to only 16 percent of the land, and 2.2 percent of farm units controlled almost 65 percent of arable land (Handy, 1984, 209; also see Hough et al., 1983, 2 9). The proportion of landless or nearly landless agricultural laborers in 1979 has been estimated to be around 90 percent (Kluck, 1983, 57). Hough and his collaborators (1983, Annex 1, Table 7) estimate the number of landless agricultural workers, age 20 or more, to have been 310,119 in 1980. By any of these measures, landlessness is a critical problem for the rural population.

Wages for agricultural workers are extremely low, averaging 50 to 60 cents a day in the 1960s and perhaps $1.00 a day in the 1970s (see Handy, 1984, 207). Urban wages are highly variable but are generally better than those of rural workers (PREALC, 1986, 84–94).

Educational opportunities are limited, especially in rural areas, and school construction is not keeping up with population growth. Roughly 43 percent of the population seven years of age or more is illiterate, and the rates are considerably higher in rural areas and among Indians and women (Republica de Guatemala, 1985, Table 5). Educational attainment data for migrants and nonmigrants have yet to be compared. School attendance is far from universal, with perhaps 65 to 70 percent of school-age children enrolled by 1980 (Kluck, 1983, 76). These economic factors—land distribution, wage levels, unemployment, and educational opportunities—tend to increase out-migration from poor areas and to reinforce movement to the capital and, in some instances, to larger towns.

Social and Environmental Factors

As in many developing countries, Guatemalans tend to move to localities where they have kin and friends. However, the precise role of kinship and friendship ties in migration patterns has yet to be investigated in detail, although B.R. Roberts (1973, 153ff.) suggests they are substantial.

For the past two decades many Guatemalans have migrated involuntarily. One event that uprooted thousands of people, and affected sixteen of the nation's twenty-two departments, was the 1976 earthquake. However, many of them have since returned to rebuild their communities. Of much greater significance, in the long run, has been the social and military conflict related to revolutionary movements (Handy, 1984, 223–54; also see Simon, 1987). S. Jonas (1988, 35) argues that "The war caused massive population migrations and relocations," and claims that "well over 10 percent of Guatemala's population . . . were displaced to other parts of the country or abroad, and over 100,000 children were left orphaned." The United Nations High Commissioner on Refugees (Lamb, 1987) estimates that 1 million Guatemalans have been displaced from their home communities and forced to resettle in other areas of the nation. An additional quarter million have sought refuge in Mexico, Belize, or Honduras.

In 1983, under newly elected President Efrain Rios Montt, the Guatemalan government initiated a new program of forced migration. Under the guise of a joint counterinsurgency/civic action program, 200,000 to 300,000 (some observers argue there were as many as a million) highland Indians were relocated in selected towns and villages (Study Group on United States-Guatemalan Relations, 1985, 7–9). These areas were designated as "poles of development," though the major development activities consisted of road building, by the peasants themselves, to improve the Guatemalan Army's access to remote sites where rebels might be hiding (Fagen, 1987, 91–92). S. Jonas (1988, 35–37) contends that as of late 1987 these "model villages" still contained around 800,000 inhabitants, and that there were plans to expand the program to other areas.

CONSEQUENCES OF MIGRATION: THE AGGREGATE LEVEL

Demographic: Population Redistribution

Migration can influence population distribution directly or indirectly. The direct effect is seen in terms of net migration over some interval of time. The indirect effect is more complex, and operates through the influence of migration on fertility and mortality rates and the variables that influence these demographic parameters.

During the past several decades internal migration has had an obvious direct effect on population distribution at both the regional and departmental levels. As indicated above, the Central, South, and North regions of the country have been net recipients of migrants and the East, West, and North Central regions have been net senders. Moreover, the departments of Guatemala, the Peten, and Escuintla showed a net gain of more than 73,000 migrants between 1976 and 1981, while during the same period Jutiapa, Santa Rosa, San Marcos, Chiquimula, Zacapa, and El Progreso experienced a combined net loss of nearly 47,000 migrants.

With the exception of the department of Guatemala, with an average total fertility rate (TFR) of 4.0 over the period 1973–81 (Republica de Guatemala, 1983, Cuadro 2–66), Guatemalan fertility has remained relatively high. In 1981, only six other departments (Zacapa, Alta Verapaz, Chiquimula, Huehuetenango, Izabal, and Sacatepequez) had TFRs under 6.0, and the lowest of these was 5.3. Nonetheless, between 1973 and 1981 the TFR declined in all departments, ranging from 20.5 percent for Izabal to 1.5 percent for Totonicapan, while their populations were growing. Average annual rates of growth over this period ranged from a low of 0.61 percent (Chiquimula) to a high of 12.71 percent (the Peten). In short, the relative contribution of migration to population growth and redistribution varied among regions and departments but was important in all instances.

Social

There are several ways in which the volume and patterning of internal migration have influenced Guatemala's social structure, but perhaps the most interesting finding from recent research suggests that population change has occurred independently of the evolution of systems of administration and production (Smith, 1978, 1984, 1985). Although a number of regional centers have existed for some time, and new ones are emerging, they do not appear to have attracted migrants in proportion to their regional functions. Referring specifically to the West region, Smith (1985, 159) concludes that:

provincial cities in Guatemala are . . . overlarge in infrastructure and undersize in population. . . . People displaced by the transformations taking place in Guatemala's economy, the petty bourgeoisie as well as the peasantry, pour into the national capital not because it is the only attractive city in the country, but because they are barred from viable employment opportunity in most other places by a mercantile elite attempting to safeguard its own livelihood by keeping out potential competitors.

Thus, the centralization of population in Guatemala City is a result of both pull and push factors. The areas that have experienced significant net in-migration during the past couple of decades are atypical in the employment opportunities they offer.

The pattern of migration is altering the physical density of the population, although in many cases high fertility negates the effects of out-migration and exacerbates the problems of growth associated with heavy in-migration. The departments of the East and West regions, for example, are caught in a vicious circle of events: high unemployment (and underemployment) and land scarcity generate out-migration, but economic pressures are not relieved because of the large birth cohorts entering the population each year, which leads to continued unemployment, out-migration, and so on.

Differential migration is slowly changing the ethnic mix of regions and departments. Indians are moving into non-Indian and mixed departments, although non-Indians do not show a strong tendency to migrate to areas that have traditionally been Indian. In short, there is some evidence of decreased ethnic segregation, at least in a spatial sense.

Environmental

Migration and population concentration pose a serious threat to the environmental quality and the supply of natural resources (Leonard, 1987; Mendez Dominguez et al., 1988). Air and water pollution are readily evident in Guatemala City and the larger towns, while groundwater contamination and soil erosion are problematic in many rural areas. Of particular concern is deforestation, which can be linked to population growth, urban expansion into agricultural hinterlands, and the subsequent need to clear new areas for farm and pasture land (Brockett, 1988, 90–91; Eglin, 1983, 96–100).

The effects of migration on the social environment are nowhere more evident than in the *barrios marginales* that have grown up in and around Guatemala City. Constructed of whatever building materials can be found, these communities often lack even the most basic public services (e.g., electricity, piped water, and sewers). Frequently, these areas are the only housing option available for poor migrant families from the countryside. Once settled, such communities tend to become permanent features of the urban landscape (see Kluck, 1983, 61; Roberts, 1973).

Economic

Internal migration has had several important effects on the Guatemalan economy. First, it has contributed, though not as much as might be expected, to the growth of the urban informal sector of the labor force (PREALC, 1986, 122). While awaiting a job in the formal sector, some migrants generate income through unprotected and unregulated entrepreneurial activities, for example, as street vendors, petty thieves, or prostitutes. How many remain in the informal sector and how many move on to the formal economy is unknown. It was estimated that in 1982 nearly 98,000 persons were employed in the Guatemalan urban informal sector (PREALC, 1986, Cuadro 22).

Seasonal migration plays a critical role in the agricultural economy. As mentioned above, the large commercial farms depend on a supply of cheap temporary labor. Some observers see a symbiotic relationship between land tenure and employment conditions in the western highlands and the system of temporary employment adhered to by the owners of the large *fincas*. This situation has allowed rural wage levels to remain relatively low and legislation providing a minimum wage to go unenforced (Brown, 1983; Eglin, 1983, 100–6).

REFERENCES

Adams, R.N. 1965. *Migraciones Internas en Guatemala. Expansion Agraria de los Indigenas Kekchies hacia El Peten.* Guatemala: Seminario de Integracion Social Guatemalteca.

———. 1970. *Crucifixion by Power: Essays on Guatemalan National Social Structure, 1944–1966.* Austin: University of Texas Press.

Applebaum, R.P. 1967. *San Idelfonso, Ixtahaucan: Un Estudio sobre la Migracion Temporal, sus Causas y Consecuencias.* Cuaderno 17. Guatemala: Seminario de Integracion Social Guatemalteca.

Arias, B.J. 1961. "Internal Migrations in Guatemala." Pp. 395–404 in *Proceedings of the International Conference on Population.* New York: International Union for the Scientific Study of Population.

———. 1965. "La concentracion urbana y las migraciones internas." Pp. 19–45 in *Problemas de la Urbanizacion en Guatemala.* Guatemala: Seminario de Integracion Social Guatemalteca.

———. 1972. "Migraciones internas en Guatemala: una comparacion metodologica." Pp. 509–14 in *Actas Conferencia Regional Latinoamericana de Poblacion,* Vol. 1. Mexico: Union para Estudio Cientifico de la Poblacion.

———. 1976. *La Poblacion de Guatemala.* Guatemala: Impresos Industriales.

Brockett, C.D. 1988. *Land, Power, and Poverty: Agrarian Transformation and Political Conflict in Central America.* Winchester, Mass.: Allen & Unwin.

Brown, A. 1983. "Land of the Few: Rural Land Ownership in Guatemala." Pp. 232–47 in Stanford Central America Action Network (ed.), *Revolution in Central America.* Boulder, Colo.: Westview Press.

Camisa, Z. 1969. *Las Estadisticas Demograficas y la Mortalidad en Guatemala hacia 1950 y 1964.* San Jose: Centro Latinamericano de Demografia.

Chackicl, J. 1976. *Guatemala: Evaluacion del Censo de 1973 y Proyeccion de la Poblacion por Sexo y Edad 1950–2000*. San Jose: Centro Latinoamericano de Demografia. Serie A, No. 1021.

de Janvry, A. 1981. *The Agrarian Question and Reformism in Latin America*. Baltimore: Johns Hopkins University Press.

Early, J.D. 1974. "Revision of Ladino and Maya Census Populations of Guatemala, 1950 and 1964." *Demography* 11:107–17.

———. 1975. "The Changing Proportion of Maya Indian and Ladino in the Population of Guatemala, 1950–1969." *American Ethnologist* 2:261–96.

———. 1982. *The Demographic Structure and Evolution of a Peasant System: The Guatemalan Population*. Boca Raton: University Presses of Florida.

———. 1983. "A Demographic Survey of Contemporary Guatemalan Maya: Some Methodological Implications for Anthropological Research." Pp. 73–91 in C. Kendall, J. Hawkins, and L. Bossen (eds.), *Heritage of Conquest: Thirty Years Later*. Albuquerque: University of New Mexico Press.

Eglin, D.R. 1983. "The Economy." Pp. 83–125 in R. F. Nyrop (ed.), *Guatemala: A Country Study*. Area Handbook Series. Washington, D.C.: U.S. Government Printing Office.

Fagen, R. 1987. *Forging Peace: The Challenge of Central America*. Oxford: Basil Blackwell.

Fox, R.W., and J.W. Huguet. 1977. *Population and Urban Trends in Central America and Panama*. Washington, D.C.: Inter-American Development Bank.

Grindle, M.S. 1986. *State and Countryside: Development Policy and Agrarian Politics in Latin America*. Baltimore: Johns Hopkins University Press.

———. 1988. *Searching for Rural Development: Labor Migration and Employment in Mexico*. Ithaca, N.Y.: Cornell University Press.

Handy, J. 1984. *Gift of the Devil: A History of Guatemala*. Boston: South End Press.

Hawkins, J. 1984. *Inverse Images: The Meaning of Culture, Ethnicity and Family in Postcolonial Guatemala*. Albuquerque: University of New Mexico Press.

Hough, R. et al. 1983. *Land and Labor in Guatemala: An Assessment*. Guatemala: U.S. Agency for International Development and Development Associates.

Hoyt, E. 1955. "The Indian Laborer in Guatemalan Coffee Fincas." *Inter-American Economic Affairs* 9:33–46.

Instituto Centro Americano de Poblacion y Familia (ICAPF). 1973. *Fecundidad en Guatemala*. Guatemala: Impresos Industriales.

Instituto Indigenista Nacional. 1969. "Sintesis del proceso migratorio de braceros del altiplano a la costa sur y sus repercusiones nacionales." *Guatemala Indigena* 4:1–49.

Jonas, S. 1988. "Contradictions of Guatemala's 'Political Opening'." *Latin American Perspectives* 15:26–46.

Kluck, P.A. 1983. "The Society and Its Environment." Pp. 41–81 in R. F. Nyrop (ed.), *Guatemala: A Country Study*. Area Handbook Series. Washington, D.C.: U.S. Government Printing Office.

Lamb, Sidni. 1987. "Guatemalan Exiles and Returnees." *Refugees*, No. 44:30–31.

Leonard, H.J. 1987. *Natural Resources and Economic Development in Central America: A Regional Environmental Profile*. New Brunswick, N.J.: Transaction Books.

Lovell, W.G. 1988. "Surviving Conquest: The Maya of Guatemala in Historical Perspective." *Latin American Research Review* 23:25–57.

McCreery, D. 1983. "Debt Servitude in Rural Guatemala, 1876–1936." *Hispanic American Historical Review* 63:735–59.

———. 1986. "'An Odious Feudalism': *Mandamiento* labor and commercial agriculture in Guatemala, 1858–1920." *Latin American Perspectives* 13:99–117.

Mejia, M.A. 1970. *Migraciones del Area Rural a la Industrial*. Guatemala: Instituto de Investigaciones Economicas y Sociales, Universidad de San Carlos.

Mendez Dominguez, A., M. Micklin, and M. Krieger de Quesada. 1988. "Dondese Fueron los Bosques? Population Growth, Land Scarcity, and Deforestation in Rural Guatemala." Unpublished manuscript.

Mendez Garcia, H. 1977. "La explotacion del trabajador migratorio en Guatemala." Unpublished thesis, Faculty of Juridical and Social Sciences, University of San Carlos, Guatemala.

Monteforte Toledo, M. 1959. *Guatemala: Monografia Sociologica*. Mexico, D.F.: Instituto de Investigaciones Sociales, Universidad Nacional Autonoma de Mexico.

Peckenham, N. 1980. "Land Settlement in the Peten." *Latin American Perspectives* 7:169–76.

Population Reference Bureau. 1988. *World Population Data Sheet*. Washington, D.C.: Population Reference Bureau.

Programa Regional del Empleo para America Latina y el Caribe (PREALC). 1986. *Cambio y Polarizacion Ocupacional en Centroamerica*. Geneva: Organizacion Internacional del Trabajo.

Republica de Guatemala. 1975. *Censos Nacionales de 1973. VIII Censo de Poblacion: Republica. Cifras Definitivas*. Tomo I. Guatemala: Direccion General de Estadistica.

———. 1983. *La Fecundidad en Guatemala, 1950–1981*. Proyecto GUA/79/PO3-OIT/FNUAP. Serie: Resultados No. 3. Guatemala: Departamento de Poblacion y Empleo, Direccion de Planificacion Global.

———. 1985. *Censos Nacionales de 1981. IX Censo de Poblacion: Republica. Cifras Definitivas*. Tomo I. Guatemala: Instituto Nacional de Estadistica.

Roberts, B.R. 1973. *Organizing Strangers: Poor Families in Guatemala City*. Austin: University of Texas Press.

Ruiz, C.H. 1965. "Algunos aspectos de las migraciones interiores en Guatemala." Santiago: Centro Latinamericano de Demografia.

Simon, J-M. 1987. *Guatemala: Eternal Spring—Eternal Tyranny*. New York: W.W. Norton.

Smith, C.A. 1978. "Beyond Dependency Theory: National and Regional Patterns of Underdevelopment in Guatemala." *American Ethnologist* 5:574–617.

———. 1984. "Local History in Global Context: Social and Economic Transitions in Western Guatemala." *Comparative Studies in Society and History* 26:193–228.

———. 1985. "Class Relations and Urbanization in Guatemala: Toward an Alternative Theory of Urban Primacy." Pp. 121–67 in M. Timberlake (ed.), *Urbanization in the World Economy*. New York: Academic Press.

———. 1986. "Survival Strategies Among Rural Smallholders and Petty Commodity Producers: A Case Study of Western Guatemala." *Working Papers*, World Employment Programme Research. Geneva: International Labor Office.

Study Group on United States-Guatemalan Relations. 1985. *Report on Guatemala*. SAIS Papers in International Affairs, No. 7. Boulder, Colo.: Westview Press.

Tax, S. 1937. "The municipios of the Midwestern Highlands of Guatemala." *American Anthropologist* 39:423–44.

Thomas, R.N. 1970. "Internal migration to Guatemala City, Guatemala." Ph.D. Dissertation, Pennsylvania State University.

————. 1971. "The Migration System of Guatemala City: Spatial Inputs." *Estadistica* 29:167–176.

Whetten, N.L. 1961. *Guatemala: The Land and the People*. New Haven, Conn.: Yale University Press.

World Bank. 1978. *Guatemala: Economic and Social Position and Prospects*. Washington, D.C.

Zarate, A.O. 1967. "Principales patrones de migracion interna en Guatemala, 1964." *Estudios Centroamericanos* No. 3. Guatemala: Seminario de Integracion Social Guatemalteca.

10

INDIA

Mahendra K. Premi

In India, information on migrants relating to economic activity at the time of leaving the communities of origin and at the destination has been collected in a number of large-scale and localized ample surveys. Yet the population census has remained the most important source of migration data. Analysis of inter-district and interstate migration streams has been made on the basis of birthplace statistics collected on all people enumerated in all the censuses from 1981 onward (Davis, 1951; George, 1965; Mathur, 1962; Zachariah, 1960, 1964).

It was not until 1961, however, that birthplace was classified as rural or urban and as (1) within the district of enumeration-intradistrict, (2) outside the district but within the state of enumeration-interdistrict, (3) outside the state of enumeration but within India-interstate, or (4) outside India. Information on duration of residence at the place of enumeration was also collected for the first time in the 1961 census. The 1971 census refined these statistics by including a question on "place of last residence," and the 1981 census included yet another question on "reasons for migration." With the availability of these data, researchers undertook several studies during the 1960s and the 1970s to examine the quantum and pattern of migration flow (Bose, 1967, 1980; Gosal and Krishan, 1975; Kumar, 1967; Mitra, 1967; Premi, 1981, 1982, 1984). Characteristics of the migrants in terms of sex, age, marital status, educational attainment, and employment status have also been studied from census data (Mahmood, 1975; Mitra, Mukherji, and Bose, 1980; Premi and Tom, 1985; Zachariah, 1968).

DATA ON MIGRATION

Definitions of Migration

Until 1951, a person was considered a migrant in India only if he or she changed residence from the district of birth to another district or a state. Any permanent or semipermanent change of residence within the district of enumeration did not qualify the person to be counted as a migrant.

Since 1961, data on migration have been collected by considering each revenue village or urban settlement as a separate unit. A person is considered a migrant if birthplace is different from place of enumeration. Furthermore, if a person born at the place of enumeration had shifted subsequently to another village or town for reasons of work or studies and the like, and had come again to the same place, according to the "place of last residence" concept, that person was deemed to have another place of residence prior to enumeration at the present place. Excluded however, were those who were away from their normal residence being on tour or pilgrimage or for temporary business purposes (Census of India 1971, 1975, 19). The normal residence of a person was defined in relation to the period of enumeration.

Those who had been away throughout the enumeration period from what they regarded as their normal residence were not considered eligible for enumeration at that place. Rather, they were enumerated wherever they were actually found during the enumeration period (Census of India 1971, 1975, 16) and became migrants at the place of enumeration. Consequently, in the Indian census, persons become migrants if they are away from their normal place of residence during the entire period of census enumeration—from February 10–28, 1981, or March 10–31, 1971—even though it was a purely temporary move for business or pilgrimage, or for visits with relatives and so on. In contrast, the large-scale sample surveys (particularly those conducted by the National Sample Survey Organisation) have excluded such persons from being counted as migrants. The Census of India overestimates migration to this extent. Such moves, however, are not likely to be very prevalent in any part of India.

Sources of Data

As indicated earlier, a question on place of birth has been included in the Indian census from 1881 onward. Hence, the census has remained the most important and regular source of migration statistics. With the collection of details about the rural and urban nature of the birthplace and duration of residence at the place of enumeration in 1961, and the addition of one question each in the 1971 and 1981 censuses, the migration statistics emanating from the census, giving details by sex, age, marital status, and employment of the migrants, their educational attainment and occupational placement (in case of migrants to cities with populations of 1 million or more persons), have been among the most detailed.

Recognizing the need to study the frequency of periodic movements in relation to economic cycles, the National Sample Survey Organisation of the Government of India began collecting migration data from its ninth round onward. The information was collected in several rounds, but the coverage of population as well as the information on migrants collected in different rounds varied (Visaria and Kothari, 1984, 420).

In addition, a large number of surveys have been conducted by individual researchers from time to time. Recently, John Connell et al. (1976) have examined the process of migration from rural areas by considering the information available in the village studies carried out in different parts of the world, with greater emphasis on studies conducted in India.

Quality of Data

In India most census and survey statistics are supplied by the head of the household who may not be aware of all details about every member of the household. For example, he or she may not know the exact birthplace of each and every person residing in the household on the census night (Zachariah, 1964, 42ff.). But these errors became minimal when data are tabulated at the district level. Furthermore, some special customs make the birthplace of a person a mere accident. In the first place large parts of India follow the custom of village exogamy in marriage. Second, a high percentage of Indian women return to their father's household to bear the first child and often the second and subsequent children as well. The woman returns to her husband's household with the child after a few months (Zachariah, 1964, 43; see also Chatterjee and Bose, 1977; Davis, 1951, 107; Mitra, 1967). Demographically, migration of a child soon after its birth from the birthplace to the place of normal residence, especially if the child has not migrated from that place ever since may be regarded as spurious. This effect, however, does not seem to continue to operate for a long time; otherwise lifetime migration in India would have been much higher than returned in the census.

In the classification of birthplace as rural or urban, we again encounter some difficulties. In the 1961 census, the rural or urban character of the birthplace was determined on the date of census enumeration (Census of India 1961, 1963, 33); in the 1971 census, the rural-urban status of the birthplace was reckoned at the time of the migrant's birth (Census of India 1971, 1975, 18). In the 1981 census, the same thing was determined on the basis of its status on the date of enumeration (Census of India 1981, 1985, 147). As regards rural or urban status of the "place of last residence," it was reckoned in 1971 as it was on the day of leaving that place, but, in 1981, it was as at the time of enumeration (Census of India 1971, 1975, 19; Census of India 1981, 1985, 151). In view of the above, comparability of data is somewhat vitiated.

PRINCIPAL POPULATION MOVEMENTS

The National Level

In the 1961 census, 144.8 million persons (constituting 33 percent of the total population) were enumerated at places other than their birthplaces and, hence, counted as lifetime migrants.[1] In the 1971 census, 166.8 million persons (or 30.4

percent of the population) were counted as migrants by the same criterion. The number of migrants increased further to 204.2 million at the 1981 census[2] and constituted 30.7 percent of the total population. Thus, the proportion of lifetime migrants in the total population declined somewhat at the 1971 census and remained almost at the same level at the 1981 census.

As one would expect, the proportion of lifetime migrants in the rural population in 1981 (28.4 percent) was lower than in the urban population (38.3 percent), but the proportion of male migrants was much less than that of female migrants (Table 10.1). This is true for those living in rural as well as urban areas.

Distribution of Migrants by Migration Streams

Based on place of birth (or last residence) and place of enumeration, internal migrants can be classified into three migration streams which are roughly indicative of distance of migration:

1. *Intradistrict migrants:* persons born (or with last residence) outside the place of enumeration but within the same district
2. *Interdistrict migrants:* persons born (or with last residence) outside the district of enumeration but within the same state
3. *Interstate migrants:* persons born (or with last residence in India but beyond the state of enumeration

Table 10.1
Percentage of Lifetime Migrants in the Total Population by Sex and Type of Residence, India, 1961–81

Type of residence	Year	Both sexes	Males	Females
Total	1961	33.0	20.8	46.0
	1971	30.4	18.9	42.8
	1981	30.7	18.0	44.2
Rural	1961	30.4	15.4	46.0
	1971	28.2	14.1	43.1
	1981	28.4	12.6	44.9
Urban	1961	44.8	43.7	46.1
	1971	39.3	37.5	41.3
	1981	38.3	35.0	42.0

Based on the rural or urban nature of the place of birth or of last residence and the place of enumeration, internal migrants can be further classified into four migration streams: rural-to-rural, rural-to-urban, urban-to-rural, and urban-to-urban. A combination of two types of migration streams gives rise to twelve streams. Table 10.2 depicts these streams separately for male and female lifetime internal migrants for 1961, 1971, and 1981, according to birthplace statistics. There is a substantial decline in the proportion of intradistrict migrants and a corresponding increase in interdistrict and interstate migrants. This seems partly due to an increase in the number of districts in the country from 336 in 1961 to 360 in 1971, and 412 in 1981. This is more clear in the case of Bihar and Haryana, where several new districts were formed breaking the lines of previous districts.

Rural-to-rural migration formed the most dominant stream at the national level, but its importance declined over time for both males and females in all

Table 10.2
Percent Distribution of Lifetime Migrants[1] of Each Sex by Migration Streams Based on Place of Birth and Place of Enumeration, India, 1961, 1971, and 1981

Type of migration streams	1961			1971			1981[2]		
	Males	Females	Sex Ratio[3]	Males	Females	Sex Ratio	Males	Females	Sex Ratio
I Intradistrict									
Rural-to-rural	40.15	65.48	273	38.42	62.01	277	31.90	56.05	237
Rural-to-urban	9.03	4.32	835	9.42	5.19	811	10.51	5.72	769
Urban-to-urban	2.97	1.65	801	2.47	1.47	746	3.51	2.05	715
Urban-to-rural	2.30	1.83	561	3.27	2.92	500	3.35	2.98	470
Subtotal	54.45	73.78	329	53.58	71.59	334	49.33	66.90	308
II Interdistrict									
Rural-to-rural	11.28	12.44	404	10.14	12.23	370	10.04	13.83	304
Rural-to-urban	8.80	3.15	1,245	9.02	3.42	1,178	10.70	4.30	1,042
Urban-to-urban	5.22	2.45	947	6.00	3.04	881	7.62	3.99	799
Urban-to-rural	1.48	0.96	686	2.08	1.51	617	2.38	1.89	528
Subtotal	26.78	19.00	628	27.24	20.20	602	30.84	24.06	536
III Interstate									
Rural-to-rural	5.31	3.38	702	4.97	3.51	633	4.10	3.40	505
Rural-to-urban	7.83	1.76	1,984	7.55	1.91	1,766	8.32	2.35	1,484
Urban-to-urban	4.87	1.72	1,266	5.48	2.17	1,127	6.04	2.54	994
Urban-to-rural	0.76	0.36	946	1.18	0.63	844	1.19	0.71	706
Subtotal	18.77	7.22	1,161	19.18	8.22	1,043	19.83	9.04	917
All Streams									
Rural-to-rural	56.74	81.30	311	53.53	77.75	308	46.04	73.28	263
Rural-to-urban	25.66	9.73	1,175	25.99	10.52	1,104	29.53	12.37	999
Urban-to-urban	13.06	5.82	1,000	13.95	6.69	913	17.17	8.58	836
Urban-to-rural	4.54	3.15	644	6.53	5.05	578	6.92	5.58	519
Total Migrants (million)	41.44	92.97	446	48.35	108.25	447	57.88	138.43	418

Notes: 1. The figures of total migrants in this table exclude immigrants.
2. The 1981 figures of total migrants include those persons also whose birth place as rural or urban could not be ascertained. Hence, the column totals do not add up to exactly 100 percent.
3. Sex ratio has been computed as the number of males per 1,000 females.

three distance categories. The decline was greater in the case of males, which reduced the sex ratio (311 males per 1,000 females in 1961) still further. Whereas the large share of female intradistrict rural-to-rural migration is generally explained in terms of marriage migration, high male rural-to-rural intradistrict migration seems to be due to their migration from regions of low per capita agricultural productivity to sparsely populated areas with new developmental activities, particularly in agriculture, mining, and plantations (Gosal and Krishan, 1975). There seem to be several other similar reasons (Bose, 1967, 22; Connell et al., 1976, 14).

While there has been a substantial increase in the proportion of rural-to-urban migrants over time in all three distance categories, there has also been an increase in the proportion of urban-to-rural migrants (Table 10.2). In fact, the contribution of net rural-to-urban lifetime migration had somewhat declined between 1961 and 1971, but it improved between 1971 and 1981, at which point it was slightly higher than the 1961 level. Intradistrict, interdistrict, and interstate migration streams contributed almost equally in the net rural-to-urban male lifetime migration over the period under consideration. The proportion of net rural-to-urban lifetime migration of females, however, decreased with increasing distance.

The share of urban-to-urban migration of both males and females was comparatively low in the intradistrict stream, but it increased substantially in the interdistrict and interstate streams. As institutions of higher learning, particularly professional and technical institutions, are not available in each district, an urge for higher education motivates urban dwellers as well as some of the rural people to migrate over long distances. This is also partly due to creation of jobs in the modern sector in the major metropolises and big cities.

As migration distance increases, the sex ratio improves sharply in all four migration streams. Among interstate migrants, the sex ratio was favorable to males up to 1971, but in 1981 females outnumbered males. This reflects a greater tendency in recent years toward family migration in long-distance moves and probably a certain amount of independent female migration as well.

Current and Intercensal Migration: 1961–71 and 1971–81

As the migrants are further classified by duration of residence at the place of enumeration, it is easy to estimate the quantum of current migrants (who reached their destination within a year of the census date) and intercensal migrants. Table 10.3 gives the proportion of current and intercensal migrants among total lifetime migrants as well as among intradistrict, interdistrict, and interstate lifetime migrants by sex and by their present place of residence rural or urban. It also gives the current migration rates for the different subpopulations.[3] The proportion of current as well as intercensal migrants declined during the 1971–81 decade, compared to the 1961–71 decade. The proportion of male migrants to

Table 10.3

Percent of Current and Intercensal Migrants to Total Lifetime Migrants, and Current Migration Rates in Different Migration Streams by Sex, and Rural or Urban Place of Enumeration, India, 1971 and 1981

Type of migration stream	Place of enumeration	Year	Duration of migration				Current migration rate	
			Current		Intercensal			
			Male	Female	Male	Female	Male	Female
Total migrant	Rural	1971	12.3	5.6	53.3	35.5	1.72	2.42
		1981	10.3	3.4	50.0	32.4	1.33	1.55
	Urban	1971	8.0	6.0	50.2	45.9	3.05	2.54
		1981	5.9	4.7	48.8	45.4	2.09	1.99
Intra-district	Rural	1971	10.8	5.0	52.2	34.2	0.96	1.65
		1981	8.7	2.9	48.9	31.4	0.73	0.98
	Urban	1971	9.0	5.6	54.9	44.3	0.96	0.88
		1981	7.0	4.6	53.5	45.0	0.77	0.75
Inter-district	Rural	1971	16.9	7.3	60.6	38.9	0.44	0.51
		1981	13.7	4.5	56.5	35.0	0.37	0.39
	Urban	1971	8.4	6.7	54.0	50.1	1.09	0.96
		1981	6.1	4.9	52.1	48.7	0.77	0.75
Interstate	Rural	1971	18.4	9.2	60.7	43.1	0.25	0.20
		1981	17.7	7.2	58.0	40.0	0.21	0.17
	Urban	1971	8.0	6.9	71.1	49.5	0.91	0.64
		1981	5.2	5.2	46.0	46.9	0.51	0.46

Note: The total of the intradistrict, interdistrict, and inter-state current
migration rate does not tally with that of total migrants since the
latter includes immigrants also.

rural areas (rural-to-rural and urban-to-rural) in both current and intercensal streams was comparatively higher than that of female migrants. Similarly, the proportion of male migrants to urban areas (rural-to-urban and urban-to-urban) in both current and intercensal streams was higher than that of female migration, although the difference between the two was comparatively small.

During the two decades of development planning, more rural migrants traveled longer distances than remained in their own district of normal residence. The pattern, however, is reversed for current male migrants to urban areas. It seems that, with the dispersal of industries in the hitherto backward and comparatively less developed regions, the district towns are providing employment opportunities that have restricted their long-distance migration. Proliferation of educational institutions might also have restricted long-distance male out-migration.

In contrast, the increasing proportion of interdistrict and interstate female migration in current streams may imply (1) extension of the marriage market, (2) greater independent female migration for higher education or employment, and

(3) a growing tendency among male migrants to bring their families to the destination as soon as they have settled there. These hunches however, require deeper probes and empirical verification using more detailed data.

When we work out current migration rates for migration to rural and urban areas, respectively, it is observed that these varied between 1.33 percent for males in 1981 to 3.05 percent for females in 1971 (Table 10.3). Furthermore, current migration rates declined over the ten-year period for both sexes.

Interregional Migration

India is divided into thirty-one states and union territories. These states and territories are further divided into 412 districts. Migration data are largely available at the state level, and some are available at the district level. The analysis of interregional migration is, however, presented here at the states/union territories level.

The interstate lifetime migration in India has generally been about 3 to 3.5 percent of the total population of the country (Table 10.4). There was a slight increase in the above proportion for both sexes together between 1961 and 1981, but the proportion has declined by 0.2 percent for males; in contrast, it has increased by 0.7 percent for females. As one would expect, there is greater interstate migration to urban areas as compared to rural areas. An analysis of net migration to the various states of India indicates substantial variations (Table 10.5). Among the major states,[4] Andhra Pradesh, Bihar, Kerala, Rajasthan, Tamil Nadu, and Uttar Pradesh have lost population through net out-migration, whether one considers the lifetime migrants, intercensal migrants, or current migrants. Punjab had net out-migration in all three streams for both sexes in 1971, but in 1981 there was net in-migration of males only in intercensal and

Table 10.4
Lifetime Interstate Migrants as a Percentage of Total Population by Sex, and Rural or Urban Place of Enumeration, India, 1961, 1971, and 1981

Sex	Year	Place of enumeration		
		Total	Rural	Urban
Both sexes	1961	3.3	1.7	10.9
	1971	3.4	1.7	9.9
	1981	3.6	1.7	9.6
Males	1961	3.5	1.4	12.5
	1971	3.4	1.3	11.2
	1981	3.3	1.2	10.0
Females	1961	3.2	2.0	9.1
	1971	3.4	2.1	9.0
	1981	3.9	2.3	9.2

Table 10.5

Statewise Lifetime, Intercensal, and Current Net Migrants as Percentage of Total Population by Sex, 1971 and 1981 (place of last residence statistics)

State/Union territory	Year	Males			Females		
		Lifetime	Inter-censal	Current	Lifetime	Inter-censal	Current
Andhra Pradesh	1971	-0.71	-0.29	-0.01	-0.60	-0.28	+n
	1981	-0.11	-0.23	-0.03	-0.62	-0.24	-0.03
Assam	1971	2.15	1.06	0.18	0.93	0.49	0.07
	1981	Data not available					
Bihar	1971	-3.18	-1.35	-0.15	-1.00	-0.47	-0.06
	1981	-2.60	-1.18	-0.19	-1.10	-0.50	-0.09
Gujarat	1971	-0.31	+0.39	0.21	-0.60	+0.12	+0.14
	1981	+0.18	0.62	0.17	-0.38	+0.21	+0.11
Haryana	1971	0.35	0.67	0.43	0.77	0.63	0.24
	1981	0.36	0.93	0.50	-0.15	0.10	0.23
Himachal Pradesh	1971	-2.38	-0.76	+0.06	-1.71	-0.45	+0.05
	1981	-2.08	-0.40	+-.53	-2.16	-0.61	+0.14
Jammu & Kashmir	1971	-0.73	-0.54	-0.24	-0.26	-0.08	+0.05
	1981	-0.41	-0.14	-0.13	-0.07	+0.13	+0.08
Karnataka	1971	0.43	0.40	0.21	0.30	0.16	0.09
	1981	0.25	0.20	-0.07	0.06	0.01	-0.09
Kerala	1971	-3.23	-1.79	-0.19	-1.74	-1.01	-0.12
	1981	-2.76	-1.27	-0.06	-1.83	-0.88	-0.06
Madhya Pradesh	1971	1.82	0.87	0.25	1.31	0.60	0.12
	1981	1.13	0.28	-0.02	0.79	0.17	-0.05
Maharashtra	1971	4.78	1.88	0.10	2.51	0.98	0.03
	1981	5.38	2.22	0.25	3.34	1.40	0.18
Manipur	1971	0.72	0.38	0.02	0.66	0.16	0.01
	1981	0.58	-0.49	-0.05	0.37	-0.54	-0.03
Meghalaya	1971	3.83	1.71	0.18	1.71	1.23	0.04
	1981	5.10	2.57	0.26	3.54	1.84	0.23
Nagaland	1971	6.45	4.80	0.66	1.52	1.37	0.13
	1981	8.98	5.78	0.84	4.65	3.04	0.41
Orissa	1971	-0.14	0.18	0.04	0.45	0.40	0.10
	1981	+0.37	0.15	0.05	0.78	0.32	0.04
Punjab	1971	-4.74	-1.67	-0.08	-4.10	-3.14	-0.04
	1981	-2.59	+0.20	0.14	-2.57	-0.54	-0.02
Rajasthan	1971	-2.21	-0.94	-0.15	-1.55	-0.52	-0.15
	1981	-1.42	-0.47	-0.01	-0.85	-0.23	-0.01
Sikkim	1971	1.81	1.20	-0.38	-0.66	+0.56	+0.08
	1981	7.43	6.51	1.57	4.12	3.93	0.87

Table 10.5 (cont.)

State/Union territory	Year	Males			Females		
		Lifetime	Inter-censal	Current	Lifetime	Inter-censal	Current
Tamil Nadu	1971	-0.64	-0.31	-0.12	-0.54	-0.23	-0.09
	1981	-1.08	-0.63	-0.11	-0.70	-0.35	-0.05
Tripura	1971	-0.22	+0.17	0.25	-0.54	-0.19	+0.10
	1981	0.73	0.57	0.36	0.74	0.49	0.19
Uttar Pradesh	1971	-3.06	-1.55	-0.24	-1.31	-0.74	-0.11
	1981	-3.53	-1.79	-0.25	-1.80	-0.97	-0.15
West Bengal	1971	4.27	1.22	-0.12	0.92	0.09	-0.12
	1981	3.20	0.73	0.01	1.09	0.19	0.02
Andaman & Nico-bar Islands	1971	31.03	19.38	2.24	23.20	13.69	1.50
	1981	27.13	13.46	1.88	19.71	12.47	1.98
Arunachal Pradesh	1971	9.52	6.94	1.24	4.65	3.11	0.45
	1981	13.00	10.34	3.10	8.21	6.35	1.37
Chandigarh	1971	58.65	39.08	5.53	56.73	37.75	5.38
	1981	54.55	24.99	4.21	49.22	31.42	3.61
Dadra & Nagar Haveli	1971	7.65	5.61	1.76	12.17	7.11	1.20
	1981	13.62	12.39	2.15	13.43	10.03	1.46
Delhi	1971	30.02	15.39	2.14	24.64	12.42	1.65
	1981	31.40	16.87	2.27	25.77	13.39	1.85
Goa, Daman and Diu	1971	-0.46	6.60	2.27	-3.08	+3.70	1.17
	1981	5.44	7.27	0.44	2.23	5.43	1.56
Lakshadweep	1971	5.86	5.72	3.55	2.43	2.50	1.14
	1981	2.88	4.45	2.75	0.75	1.31	0.30
Mizoram	1971*						
	1981	4.11	3.55	0.34	1.29	1.24	0.09
Pondicherry	1971	1.99	2.35	0.53	4.92	3.27	0.54
	1981	-1.78	-0.54	+0.27	-5.18	-2.15	-0.28

Note: n = negligible (less than .005 percent)

* = Mizoram was part of Assam State in 1971. Hence, no separate
data on migration for Mizoram are available for that period.

current migration streams, the lifetime stream still showing a net out-migration.
As regards females, there was net out-migration throughout.

In contrast, Assam,[5] Gujarat, Haryana, Karnataka, Madhya Pradesh, Maharashtra, Orissa, and West Bengal have remained net in-migrating states, except for small variations (Table 10.5). For example, Gujarat lost population through the interstate lifetime migration of both sexes in 1971 and of females in

1981 but gained population on an intercensal or current migration basis. The net lifetime male in-migrants in Maharashtra constituted 5.4 percent of the state's male population in 1981, while female in-migrants accounted for 3.3 percent of the state's female population. West Bengal also experienced substantial in-migration.

Most smaller states and union territories have gained population through net in-migration, the exceptions being Himachal Pradesh, Jammu and Kashmir, and Pondicherry (in 1981). As Chandigarh has been a comparatively new union territory, a little over half its population was of net lifetime migrants. Net migrants in Delhi comprised 28.9 percent of its total population in 1981.

Whereas some states were net out-migrating states on the basis of lifetime migrants, they became net in-migrating states during the 1961–71 or 1971–81 intercensal periods. Examples are Andhra Pradesh (females 1961–71), Gujarat, Himachal Pradesh (on current basis), Jammu and Kashmir (females 1971–81), Punjam (males 1971–81), Tripura (1961–71), and Goa, Daman, and Diu (1961–71). In contrast, among the net in-migrating states, Haryana lost some female population on a lifetime migration basis in 1981, Karnataka and Madhya Pradesh lost some population on a current migration basis during 1980–81, and West Bengal lost during 1970–71, based on current migration.

At the national level (based on place of last residence statistics in 1981), 31.2 percent of the interstate in-migrants moved from rural areas to urban areas of other states, but 7.7 percent moved from urban areas to rural areas. Thus, the net rural-to-urban migration accounted for 23.5 percent of the total interstate migration. In contrast, urban-to-urban interstate lifetime migration constituted 30.9 percent of the total interstate migrants. This indicates the importance of urban-to-urban migration in the interstate migration stream.

WHO MOVES

As observed earlier, females in India migrate more than males because much of the female migration is either marriage or associational migration.[6] It has also been seen that as the migration distance increases from intradistrict to inter-district to interstate, the sex ratio improves substantially in almost all states and union territories. Moreover, the rural-to-rural migration streams have the lowest sex ratio, while rural-to-urban streams generally have the highest sex ratios (occasionally becoming favorable to males but otherwise remaining favorable to females).

The 1981 census data are not amenable to a discussion of the characteristics of the migrants, because they cover only those who indicated employment as a reason for migration. Based on the 1971 census migration data, Mahandra Premi and Judy Tom analyzed the characteristics of migrants to cities with populations of 100,000 and above. An analysis of sex ratios among migrant and nonmigrant populations shows that the ratios were higher among nonmigrants than among migrants. In fact, the sex ratios of the nonmigrants increased with age up to about

40, indicating marriage migration of females from the cities. In contrast, ratios decreased among migrants at ages 20 and above because of in-migration of females in marriage and associational movements with the family breadwinner (Premi and Tom, 1985, 92).

The sex ratio of 138 among lifetime migrants to metropolitan cities indicated male selective in-migration but the ratio was well below 100 in cities with 100,000 to 200,000 population (Premi and Tom, 1985, 92).

More than half of the nonmigrants in the cities were children below the age of 15, whereas their proportion among lifetime migrants was less than one-fifth (17.3 percent). Furthermore, the proportion of children was higher among urban lifetime migrants than rural lifetime migrants (Premi and Tom, 1985, 93).

Migrants to cities had a higher literacy rate than nonmigrants probably because of age-structure variations in the two subpopulations. The proportion of literates and of those with at least a high school education (ten years of schooling) was significantly lower among intradistrict migrants than among interdistrict or interstate inmigrants. A comparison of the educational attainment of migrant and nonmigrant workers showed that proportionately more migrant workers possessed higher educational qualifications (high school and above) than did nonmigrant workers (Premi and Tom, 1985, 93).

As for the occupational placement of migrants and nonmigrants, the authors found that more migrants than nonmigrants were employed in white-collar jobs. Conversely, a greater proportion of nonmigrants were employed in production process occupations, and in sales and related occupations. As a large majority of sales workers in India are in the unorganized sector, the authors conclude that nonmigrants form a greater share of the urban informal sector than the migrants (Premi and Tom, 1985, 93–94).

It would be useful to contrast the characteristics of the migrants to rural areas, noncity urban areas, and city urban areas among themselves and with nonmigrants to understand more clearly the various types of differentials, but this aspect has not been included in this chapter for want of appropriate data and space.

REASONS FOR MIGRATION

In the Indian census, data on reasons for migration were collected for the first time in the 1981 census. The classification used was (1) employment, (2) education, (3) family moved (associational), (4) marriage, and (5) others.[7] The data are available according to the four migration streams—rural-to-rural, rural-to-urban, urban-to-rural, and urban-to-urban—and by intradistrict, interdistrict, and interstate movement from place of last residence. Among male migrants to urban areas—rural-to-urban and urban-to-urban areas—employment was the most important reason (Table 10.6). Almost half of the rural-to-urban male migrants moved for employment purposes. Intensity of employment as a reason for migration increased significantly with increasing distance from intradistrict

Table 10.6

Percentage Distribution of Lifetime Migrants of Each Sex and in Each Migration Stream by Reasons for Migration, India, 1981

Migration stream	Reasons for migration	Males						Females					
		Employ-ment	Educa-tion	Family moved	Mar-riage	Others	Total	Employ-ment	Educa-tion	Family moved	Mar-riage	Others	Total
I Intradistrict													
	Rural-to-rural	15.68	4.54	33.31	6.09	40.37	99.99	0.86	0.41	7.74	82.80	8.19	100.00
	Rural-to-urban	35.59	10.73	27.34	1.75	24.59	100.00	3.59	2.86	24.91	55.84	12.81	100.01
	Urban-to-urban	31.33	4.79	35.25	1.58	27.05	100.00	3.92	1.98	32.89	45.45	15.76	100.00
	Urban-to-rural	22.04	3.17	32.36	2.69	39.74	100.00	2.67	0.83	18.45	61.95	16.10	100.00
II Interdistrict													
	Rural-to-rural	26.02	3.73	35.74	4.28	30.23	100.00	1.70	0.48	10.85	79.56	7.40	99.99
	Rural-to-urban	50.63	8.16	22.97	1.00	17.24	100.00	4.56	2.43	31.78	49.59	11.64	100.00
	Urban-to-urban	40.68	5.91	32.75	0.89	19.77	100.00	4.45	2.17	36.07	44.19	13.13	100.01
	Urban-to-rural	29.71	3.45	32.78	2.06	32.01	100.01	3.73	1.14	23.14	58.23	13.76	100.00
III Interstate													
	Rural-to-rural	37.19	2.16	32.51	2.80	25.34	100.00	3.48	0.49	15.31	72.00	8.72	100.00
	Rural-to-urban	61.45	3.94	18.52	0.51	15.58	100.00	5.30	2.08	37.21	42.69	12.73	100.01
	Urban-to-urban	48.71	4.53	27.20	0.71	18.86	100.01	4.97	2.52	38.44	40.73	13.33	99.99
	Urban-to-rural	34.95	2.61	28.96	1.31	32.17	100.00	5.20	1.33	28.01	51.02	14.44	100.00
IV All streams													
	Rural-to-rural	19.49	4.18	33.74	5.46	37.12	99.99	1.13	0.43	8.64	81.73	8.07	100.00
	Rural-to-urban	47.49	8.07	23.54	1.17	19.73	100.00	4.20	2.58	29.27	51.52	12.42	100.00
	Urban-to-urban	41.12	5.20	31.52	0.99	21.18	100.01	4.46	2.21	35.89	43.56	13.88	100.00
	Urban-to-rural	27.00	3.17	31.89	2.23	35.72	100.01	3.34	1.00	21.23	59.33	15.10	100.00
Total Migrants		30.79	5.15	30.57	3.05	30.44	100.00	1.92	0.88	14.72	72.34	10.14	100.00

Source: Derived from Table D-3; Census of India 1981, 1984: 250-319.

level to interstate level in all four migration streams. In contrast, the proportion of associational migrants and those moving for "other causes" declined with distance. Education accounted for only 5.2 percent of the male migrants.

Among women, marriage accounted for almost three-fourths of the migrants. In fact, in the rural-to-rural migration stream, 81.7 percent of females migrated on account of marriage alone. Among women migrants, employment and education accounted for about 7 percent of the migrants to urban areas and less than 4 percent of those who went to rural areas. With increasing distance, the strength of marriage as a reason for migration declined substantially, leading to an increased proportion of migrants for employment and associational reasons (Table 10.6).

CONSEQUENCES OF MIGRATION

It is well known that migration leads to population redistribution, depending on the extent of total migration in a given geographical area. It has led to greater concentration of population in urban settlements, especially in cities and metropolises. As in any other country, in India this has meant differentials in rural and urban population growth rates, in the sex-age-marital status distributions of these populations, in the occupational and industrial distributions of the workers, and in the overall quality of life of the people living in rural and urban areas, respectively. Furthermore, because of the sex-age selectivity in migration, the phenomenon affects the fertility and mortality rates of both the sending and receiving areas.

Literature on consequences of migration generally relates to rural-to-urban migration with emphasis on growth of slums in communities of destinations and spread of rural poverty (de Souza, 1978, xv). At the microlevel, however, even rural-to-rural and urban-to-urban migration streams can have substantial impacts both on the communities of origin and on destination. For example, in his study of urban out-migration, Premi discusses the loss of the original economic base of certain towns over time and their inability to create new economic viability for themselves, which has ultimately resulted in chronic out-migration of their people to areas of better economic opportunities (Premi, 1980, 151).

From the economic viewpoint, migrants in Bombay were overrepresented in blue-collar and unskilled occupations, while nonmigrants were overrepresented in white-collar occupations because of the difference in their educational attainment (Zachariah, 1968, 284). Mitra, Mukherji, and Bose (1980, 67) have concluded that migrants to the cities had little skill, education, and training, and, as such, most of them were absorbed in either low grade services or in low-grade production process activities and indigenous means of transport. Thus, migrants to the cities are regarded as a sore on the city polity. While comparing migrant workers to cities with nonmigrant workers therein, Premi and Tom have shown that the migrant workers possessed higher levels of education and skills, and were engaged in a much greater proportion of white-collar jobs than the nonmigrants (Premi and Tom, 1985, 69–71). Moreover, the number of migrant workers exceeded nonmigrant workers by four to three, and, in some cities, to a much greater extent. In those cities, migrant workers generally determined their functional specialization (Premi and Tom, 1985, 93).

Migrant workers make systematic remittances to their homes in the places of origin, helping those family members left behind and, in some cases, developing agricultural productivity through purchase of tractors, construction of tubewells, and use of high-yielding varieties of grains.

From a social point of view, the flux of the rural masses in the metropolitan and other cities has led mostly to their unplanned and haphazard growth and some of the worst slums in the country. Rural poverty carried to the cities through rural-urban migration is most visible in slums and squatter settlements along with environmental deterioration, substandard housing, and low levels of health and nutrition (de Souza, 1978, xv).

In the studies relating to consequences of migration, attention has largely been focused on issues relevant to the receiving communities. There is, however, need to pay greater attention to the consequences for the communities of origin. Besides examining economic consequences of different types of migration in different migration streams, it would be useful to consider social and political consequences. As different social groups in the village (or town) have varying propensities to migrate, it is also necessary to analyze separately the impact of migration on each of them. Finally, as the family is the smallest social group, one should also examine the impact of migration on different members of the family—the parents, wife, and children. All these aspects, however, require deeper probes through microlevel studies.

NOTES

1. Lifetime migrants are those who came to the place of enumeration at some point during their lives and have been living there ever since, whether this happened just a week before the census or a few decades ago. When the movement is counted on the basis of last residence, it is the unbroken period of the shift from the previous to the present place.

2. The 1981 figures are based on a 5 percent area sample of enumerators' blocks and, therefore, suffer from a certain amount of sampling fluctuations. Furthermore, these figures exclude Assam where no census could be conducted in 1981. Consequently, the comparability of lifetime migration rates over time is somewhat adversely affected. If Assam figures are excluded from the total population and total migrants, the lifetime migration rate for 1971 becomes 30.3 percent instead of 30.4 percent. A change of similar magnitude is observed in the 1961 figures.

3. Current migration rate for specified area =

$$\frac{\text{number of migrants to a particular area of a particular sex during the preceding year}}{\text{population of that area and of that sex at the end of the period}} \times 100$$

4. The major states are: Andhra Pradesh, Assam, Bihar, Gujarat, Haryana, Karnataka, Kerala, Madhya Pradesh, Maharashtra, Orissa, Punjab, Rajasthan, Tamil Nadu, Uttar Pradesh, and West Bengal.

5. The data for Assam are based on the 1971 census alone.

6. Associational migration is defined as the migration of dependent persons consequent to the migration of the principal breadwinner.

7. This category of "others" largely covers those migrants who arrived at their present destination to meet relatives, to go on pilgrimage, to settle after retirement, to settle after two wars with Pakistan, and, in the case of a number of married women, to deliver the child at their parents' home (a custom that is quite prevalent in India). It may also include those who are in a state of flux at their new destination and are unable to indicate the exact reason for migration. With longer duration of residence, people can indicate more specific reasons according to their present status.

REFERENCES

Bose, Ashish, 1967. "Migration streams in India." *International Union for the Scientific Study of Population, Contributed Papers,* Sydney Conference, Australia, August 21–25.

————. 1980. *India's Urbanisation, 1901–2001.* 2d rev. ed. New Delhi: Tata McGraw-Hill Publishing Co.

Census of India 1961. 1963, Series 1. India. Part II-A, *General Population Tables.* Delhi, Manager of Publications.

Census of India 1971. 1975, Series 1. India, Part II-A (i). *General Population Tables.* Delhi: Controller of Publications.

Census of India 1981. 1985, Series 1. India Part II-A (i). *General Population Tables.* Delhi: Controller of Publications.

Chatterjee, Atreyi, and Ashish Bose. 1977. "Demographic Data on Internal Migration and Urbanisation from Census and NSS—An Appraisal". In Ashish Bose, Devendra B. Gupta, and Gaurisankar Raychaudhuri (eds.), *Population Statistics in India.* New Delhi: Vikas Publishing House Pvt. Ltd.

Connell, John, Biplab Dasgupta, Roy Laishley, and Michael Lipton. 1976. *Migration from Rural Areas: The Evidence from Village Studies.* Delhi: Oxford University Press.

Davis, Kingsley. 1951. *The Population of India and Pakistan.* Princeton, N.J.: Princeton University Press.

De Souza, Alfred (ed.). 1978. *The Indian City.* New Delhi: Manohar Publications.

George, M.V. 1965. "Internal Migration in Assam and Bengal 1901–61." Ph.D. Thesis, Canberra, Department of Demography, Australian National University.

Gosal, G. S., and G. Krishan. 1975. "Patterns of Internal Migration in India." In Leszek A. Kosinski, and R. Mansell Prothero (eds.), *People on the Move.* London: Methuen & Co. Ltd.

Kumar, Joginder. 1967 "The Pattern of Internal Migration in India During 1951–61." *International Union for Scientific Study of Population, Contributed Papers.* Sydney Conference, Australia, August 21–25.

Mahmood, Aslam. 1975. "Patterns of Migration into Indian Cities and Their Socio-Economic Correlates—A Multi-Variate Regional Analysis." M. Phil. Dissertation, New Delhi, Centre for the Study of Regional Development, Jawaharlal Nehru University.

Mathur, P.C. 1962. "Internal Migration in India, 1941–51." Ph.D. Dissertation. Chicago, Department of Sociology, University of Chicago.

Mitra, Asok. 1967. "Internal Migration and Urbanisation, Part I—Text." Papers for the meeting of the ECAFE'S Expert Working Group on Problems of Internal Migration and Urbanisation, Bangkok. New Delhi. Office of the Registrar General, India (mimeographed).

———, Shekhar Mukherji, and Ranendranath Bose. 1980. *Indian Cities: Their Industrial Structure, Inmigration and Capital Investment.* New Delhi: Abhinav Publications.

Premi, Mahendra K. 1980. *Urban Outmigration.* New Delhi: Sterling Publishers.

———. 1981. "Role of Migration in the Urbanisation Process in Third World countries: A Case Study of India." *Social Action* 31. July–September.

———. 1982. *Demographic Situation in India.* Papers of the East-West Population Institute, No. 80, Honolulu, East-West Center.

———. 1984. "Internal Migration in India, 1961–81." *Social Action* 34. July–September.

———, and Judy Ann L. Tom. 1985. *City Characteristics, Migration, and Urban Development Policies in India.* Papers of the East-West Population Institute, No. 92. Honolulu: East-West Center.

Visaria, Pravin, and Devendra Kothari. 1984. *Migration in Gujarat: An Analysis of Census Data.* Ahmedabad: Sardar Patel Institute of Economic and Social Research (mimeographed).

Zachariah, K.C. 1960. *Internal Migration in India, 1941–51.* Bombay: Demographic Training and Research Centre (mimeographed).

———. 1964. *A Historical Study of Internal Migration in the Indian Subcontinent, 1901–1931.* Bombay: Asia Publishing House.

———. 1968. *Migrants in Greater Bombay.* Bombay: Asia Publishing House.

11

INDONESIA

Peter Gardiner and Mayling Oey-Gardiner

Concerns with patterns of population distribution and redistribution in Indonesia currently center around two major themes. The first, defined in part by the archipelagic nature of the country and the concentration of population on the relatively fertile "inner" islands of Java and Bali, deals with levels and trends in population movements between major island regions and, within these regions, between specific provinces. The second deals with a variety of types of permanent and temporary internal migratory movement and, more specifically, with their impact on levels of urbanization and urban population growth—with a particular focus on major regional urban centers and on the capital city of Jakarta.

Given the geographical and cultural complexity of Indonesian society, it is little wonder that patterns of spatial mobility take a myriad of forms and represent a reaction to a variety of social, cultural, political, and economic factors (ESCAP, 1981, 1). This means that there are no simple explanations of patterns of population movement. Rather, to gain an understanding of internal migration in the context of Indonesian demographic, social, and economic change, one must look at a variety of migration processes, including both permanent and temporary forms of population flows.

DATA ON MIGRATION

Definitions of Migration

There is no formal spatial definition of what constitutes an internal migrant in Indonesia. In theory, movement can be defined in terms of any of the four main administrative levels used to divide up the country (Table 11.1). In practice, however, the analytical scope is much more limited because the major national level sources (the 1971 and 1980 population censuses and, to a lesser degree, the

Table 11.1
Indonesian Administrative Divisions

Level	Name	Number	Administrative Head
I	Propinsi (Province)	27	Gubernur (Governor)
IIA	Kabupaten (Regency)	256	Bupati
IIB	Kotayamdya (Municipality)	52	Walikota
III	Kecamatan (District)	3600	Camat
IV	Desa (Village)	68000	Lurah/Kepala Desa

1976 and 1985 intercensal population surveys—SUPAS) deal primarily with migration flows only at the provincial level. This leads to problems in interpreting distance of moves and in making interprovincial comparisons as the provinces vary greatly in shape and size. It also means that intraprovincial migration (between lower level administrative units within provinces) generally cannot be analyzed from these sources.[1]

A similar comment can be made about the temporal dimension of internal migration. In theory, there is recognition of the need to include short-term migration as well as more permanent movements. In practice, temporal coverage is limited by the de jure approach (based on a six-month residency requirement) used by the major censuses and surveys. The tendency here has been to classify persons away from home for less than six months as being resident at their place of origin rather than destination, a situation that has obvious implications for the measurement of short-term migration, particularly that of a circular or seasonal nature.

Sources of Data

The major censuses and national survey sources of data on internal migration have been noted above. Outside of these, the sources of data are limited indeed. Indonesia does have a system of population registration carried out at the village (*desa*) level. Geographic coverage, however, is incomplete, and the quality of the data is such as to make them analytically not very useful.

Limited information on migration is available from some of the National Social and Economic Surveys (SUSENAS) carried out by the Central Bureau of Statistics, as well as from more localized urban labor force surveys carried out in the early to mid-1970s by the Demographic Institute at the University of Indonesia and by the National Social and Economic Research Institute (LEKNAS). More recently, PPT-LIPI (National Research Institute) has carried out a major migration study in three provinces[2] (Bandiyono, 1987) which included the collection of detailed migration histories as a basis for life-cycle analysis of the migration process.

Useful information can also be obtained from village-level socioeconomic studies. While these studies are less likely to be representative, they can help illustrate motives and processes involved in various forms of population mobility that cannot be gleaned from macrolevel sources.

Quality of Data

The major spatial and temporal limitations of the census and survey data have already been noted. To these can be added response problems dealing with specification of province of origin,[3] particularly for data on lifetime migration, and the failure to specify whether the place of origin was urban or rural. Therefore, while it is possible to analyze overall movement to rural or urban areas, it is impossible to specify whether that movement was rural-to-urban, urban-to-urban, rural-to-rural, or urban-to-rural.

A related issue that should also be mentioned involves the major change in the definition of urban areas between the 1971 and 1980 censuses (see Biro Pusat Statistik, 1979). The result of this change nationally was a general overstatement of the true urban growth rate (based on a consistent definition), but the effect varied dramatically among the various provinces with some "outer island" provinces showing less urban growth based on the recorded statistics than actually occurred. Although the revised definition (which is based on a functional as opposed to a purely administrative framework) offers a real improvement in consistent specification of what is urban, it also means that growth rate analysis cannot generally be used as a basis for judging patterns of rural-urban migration flows during the 1970s.

A final limitation is the general lack of published data on characteristics of migrants (not to mention reasons for migration) in the major censuses and surveys. G.J. Hugo obtained a special data set from the 1971 census which he used to create and analyze a number of special tables on migrant characteristics not available elsewhere (ESCAP, 1981). Some unpublished tabulations from the 1980 census were also prepared by the Central Bureau of Statistics and used in a series of summary analyses at the national and provincial levels (Mantra and Kasto, 1984). Other than these, one must rely on indicative information from smaller scale studies which, while more detailed, are limited in their representativeness in terms of overall distributions and trends.

PRINCIPAL POPULATION MOVEMENTS

The National Level

Measured at the regional or provincial level, the overall volume of internal migration is relatively low. The 1971 census reported some 5.7 million lifetime interprovincial migrants, slightly under 5 percent of the total population. Although the census did not include a direct question on period migration, A. Speare (1975) used data on place of previous residence and duration of current residence to derive an estimate of 2.2 million interprovincial migrants over the period 1966–71. The 1980 census, however, clearly points to increased spatial mobility during the 1970s. By 1980, lifetime interprovincial migration had increased to nearly 9.8 million persons, representing nearly 7 percent of the census total. Period migration for 1975–80 stood at some 4.2 million persons[4]— an increase of nearly 90 percent in less than 10 years.

This increase in migration is not entirely unexpected. The 1970s (and particularly from the mid-1970s) was a period of extremely high economic growth stimulated by the rapidly escalating prices of Indonesia's main export commodity, oil. Rising real wages and incomes (particularly in urban areas), major improvements in social and physical infrastructure (roads, schools, health and family planning centers, water supply and irrigation, etc.), and expanded public sector employment opportunities all contributed to a more favorable climate for increased spatial mobility. In this regard, the figures above may even understate the true impact of this change—both because the figures from the 1980 census measured migration only over part of the boom period which lasted until 1982, and because the relatively slow growth in agricultural employment during this period[5] would have likely stimulated even greater rises in more temporary and shorter distance forms of migration that would have remained largely unmeasured under the definitions used by the census.

Interregional Migration

The long-term trend in Indonesia has been for the proportion of the national population resident in "outer Indonesia" (areas outside the central islands of Java and Bali) to increase at the expense of "inner Indonesia" (ESCAP, 1981, 31). The trend has been clearly evident since the first more or less complete census in 1930 and, has, if anything, accelerated in recent years.[6] This shift is partly due to historically lower fertility in Java than in most other parts of the country, but it is also a function of patterns of interregional migration.

In absolute terms, the main interregional flows have been between the islands of Java and Sumatra. The closeness of these islands geographically and the existence of trade and labor-related linkages dating well back into the colonial period have helped reinforce this relationship. Thus, as of 1971, movement from Java to Sumatra represented about 62 percent of the total interregional lifetime migration flow calculated on an island-by-island basis (Table 11.2). By 1980, however, this proportion had declined to about 54 percent, representing not so much a relative decline in Java's contribution to interregional out-migration as an increase in the flows from Java to other islands in the archipelago, most notably to the oil- and timber-rich areas of Eastern Kalimantan.

One factor of increasing importance in out-migration from "inner Indonesia"

Table 11.2
Percentage Distribution of Lifetime Migrants by Island, 1971 and 1980

| Island of Destination | Year | Island of Origin | | | | | | Total Migrants (000) |
		Sumatra	Java	Kalimantan	Sulawesi	Other Isl.	Total	
Sumatra	1971	--	62.6	0.6	3.3	1.0	67.5	1871
	1980	--	54.7	0.4	2.7	0.6	58.4	3102
Java	1971	12.5	--	2.7	3.5	2.3	21.0	583
	1980	13.5	--	2.2	2.6	2.2	20.5	1092
Kali- mantan	1971	0.2	3.2	-	0.8	0.1	4.3	122
	1980	0.5	7.1	-	2.4	0.2	10.2	534
Sulawesi	1971	0.3	2.1	0.2	-	0.6	3.2	87
	1980	0.4	3.2	0.2	-	1.4	5.2	274
Other Islands	1971	0.2	1.9	0.1	1.8	-	4.0	111
	1980	0.4	2.6	0.1	2.6	-	5.7	302
Total	1971	13.2	69.8	3.6	9.4	4.0	100.0	-
	1980	14.8	67.6	2.9	10.3	4.4	100.0	-
Total Migrants (000)	1971	366	1936	100	262	110	--	2774
	1980	787	3585	156	545	231	--	5304

Source: Based on Sunarto 1984. Data do not include migrants born overseas or those with place of birth not stated.

in recent years has been the government-sponsored Transmigration Program which involves the movement of families primarily from rural Java and Bali to established agricultural settlement sites in other parts of the country. A rough analysis (National Urban Development Strategy, 1985a) suggested that trans-migration could have accounted for as much as one-third of out-migration from Java to Bali during the 1970s and about 30 percent of in-migration to Sumatra, 20 to 25 percent to Kalimantan, and over 50 percent of in-migration to Sulawesi during the same period of time. Major increases in the recorded volume of transmigrants during the early 1980s suggest a continuing impact of this pro-gram, particularly on growth rates in provinces in Eastern Indonesia where the population bases are still relatively small.

Metro/Nonmetro and Rural/Urban Migration

Indonesia has long been characterized as one of the least urbanized countries of Southeast Asia. In 1971, some 17.3 percent of the population lived in urban areas. By 1980, this had increased to 22.4 percent, although the pace of ur-banization implied by this change is likely overstated due to the change in urban definition between the two censuses. Independent analysis (World Bank, 1983) suggests an intercensal (1971–80) urban growth rate for Indonesia of about 4 percent per annum, with about 60 percent of this growth a result of urban natural increase and 40 percent a combined result of rural-urban migration and re-classification (consistent with the 1980 definition) of rural areas to urban. A 4 percent urban growth rate implies a relatively low urban-rural growth rate difference of just over 2 percent. Even so, this is almost certainly higher than historical levels in Indonesia, with the possible exception of the immediate postindependence period in the 1950s which, because of a number of factors, was a period of considerable displacement of population to cities and towns (ESCAP, 1981, 60).

Since the census data do not allow differentiation of migrant origin by rural or urban residence, we can only talk about rural or urban migration streams in terms of destination. It is clear, however, that migrants do show a preference for settling in urban areas. Among total migrants in 1971, 50 percent went to urban areas (ESCAP, 1981, 88), and among recent migrants (1966–71), the figure was even higher at 55 percent (Speare, 1975, 79). Similar calculations for the 1975–80 period give a figure of about 52 percent, indicating a modest reduction in urban preference (given the increased percentage urban in 1980). This trend, however, is still consistent with increased migration to urban areas in the 1970s if one considers the even greater increases in flows to rural areas, particularly to areas outside Java opened up under the Transmigration Program.

Regionally, Java has both the largest number of urban in-migrants and the highest percentage of the total migration stream moving to urban areas. In 1975–80, about 71 percent of all interprovincial migrants to Java moved to urban areas. This can be compared to 25 percent for Sumatra, 35 percent for Sulawesi, 47 percent for Kalimantan, and about 53 percent for the remaining islands of the archipelago. The high figure for Java is indicative of the relative attraction of its cities to both intra- and interisland migrants, and to its relatively more mature systems of cities (along with associated ease of access). The lower figures for some of the other islands are due to a generally higher level of rural opportunity, including rural-based raw materials exploitation and agricultural expansion in areas opened up through transmigration or through infrastructure development.

WHO MOVES

Interregional Migration

In the most simplistic terms, an interprovincial migrant in Indonesia is more likely to be a young male adult, to be married, and to be literate and better educated than his fellow nonmigrants at either origin or destination. In 1971, about 54 percent of recent migrants were between ages 15 and 34, with the percentage being somewhat higher for females and for migrants to the largest metropolitan areas.[7] Among nonmigrants only about 30 percent were in this age range. The sex ratio of these migrants was about 117 (113 for lifetime migrants) which can be compared to the overall sex ratio in the census population of 97.[8]

Similar calculations from the 1980 census indicate little change, although use of the five-year period migration data, and including adjustments for measuring age at migration rather than age at the census, suggests a proportion aged 15 to 34 closer to 50 percent nationally. The difference is largely being made up by an increase in the percentage of interprovincial migrants at the youngest ages, particularly 0 to 4. Thus, migration of family units as opposed to individuals may have played a more important role in spatial mobility than had been recognized in some earlier studies (see Hugo, 1975).

Interestingly, even though migrants are more likely to be married,[9] the dependency burden among migrant families is still lower than for nonmigrants. This is both because migrant families tend to be at an earlier stage of the life cycle (not having completed childbearing) and because a substantial proportion of migration, particularly job-related migration to large cities, involves family separation with the wife (or husband) remaining in the area of origin with any dependent children.

Regarding education, there is a clear tendency for migration propensity to increase with the level of schooling (ESCAP, 1981, 125). In general, these differences appear to be more pronounced among recent as opposed to lifetime migrants and, at least as far as literacy is concerned, they are maintained even after controlling for age, sex, and type and size of place of destination (e.g., see Murad, 1980). Literacy is also higher among male migrants than among female migrants, and recent migrants tend to be more literate than those of longer duration, also controlling for age and sex (ESCAP, 1981, 130).

For example, among noninterprovincial migrants aged 25 and over in 1971, 57 percent of males and 28 percent of females had at least some education. Among migrants (ever moved) the figures were 78 percent and 50 percent, and among recent migrants (moved within the last five years) they were 86 percent and 59 percent, respectively (ESCAP, 1981, 201). For 1980, the figures had increased to 84 percent and 61 percent among male and female total migrants and to 70 percent and 44 percent among nonmigrants, indicative of the overall gains made in education during the 1970s. More significantly, this trend seems to be pointing toward a narrowing of the educational gap between migrants and nonmigrants, thus bringing Indonesia more into line with the situation in the relatively more advanced countries in the region. Although this trend will increasingly serve to answer complaints about the low educational levels of migrants, particularly to the major urban centers (e.g., see Suharso et al., 1976), it raises questions about the ability of the still-limited modern sector in most destination areas to absorb relatively more educated migrants as well as an increasingly better educated resident population.

At the higher end of the educational scale there are also significant differences. Thus, while only 3 percent of nonmigrants in 1980 had completed high school, figures were 14 percent among all migrants and nearly 30 percent among those who had moved twice or more.[10]

Education is also correlated with the distance of move. Thus, G.J. Hugo

(1979, 201–2) found that migrants who came to Jakarta from farther away had a higher proportion with at least some schooling. Most of those with little or no education were relatively short-distance migrants from the adjacent province of West Java which, in fact, represents virtually all of Jakarta's rural hinterland.

Given expected relations between education, income, and agricultural employment, it is not surprising that, even after controlling for urban-rural residence, migrants are more likely to be involved in nonagricultural activities. However, at least among recent migrants, this is not complemented by an over-representation of migrants in manufacturing, but rather by a clear propensity for migrants to concentrate in service activities, regardless of type of destination (ESCAP, 1981; Suharso, et al., 1976). Hugo (1978) suggests this may be due in part to a greater ease of access into many more informal service industries than is the case for manufacturing. It may also partly reflect the relatively high mobility of government employees.

The same is true in terms of occupations. Migrants are less likely to be farmers and are more likely to hold white-collar jobs compared to nonmigrants at both origin and destination. Thus, in 1980, only 37 percent of total migrants were classified as farmers compared to 58 percent of nonmigrants, while for white-collar occupations the figures were 15 percent and 6 percent, respectively (Sunarto, 1984). Moreover, the greater the distance of the move, or the greater the number of moves, the more likely migrants are to hold white-collar jobs (Bandiyono and Alihar, 1987; Murad, 1980).

Metro/Nonmetro and Rural/Urban Migration

The special tabulations from the 1971 census (ESCAP, 1981) provide a basis for making a few additional remarks on selectivity of rural and urban migrants by type and size of destination. These tables show that migrant-nonmigrant differences in the proportion of young adults (aged 15 to 24) are most pronounced in Indonesia's largest city, Jakarta, but decline very rapidly as one moves down to the next largest cities of Surabaya and Bundung and become minimal in small towns and rural areas. They also show that females tend to be relatively more dominant in migration streams to the largest cities. This pattern is particularly evident for Jakarta, which actually had a majority of female net in-migrants over the period 1975–80. One reason for this is that, because of the spatial definitions used in the censuses, it is only for Jakarta that short-distance moves are reasonably well measured, and it is these streams that most tend to be dominated by women. It is also arguably related to the relatively high concentration of factory and domestic service jobs in Jakarta, which have a relatively high demand for women.

On the other hand, duration of stay in the major urban centers is positively related to masculinity (ESCAP, 1981; Oey, 1977). This is largely a result of differential return migration between the sexes which tends to favor females who are more likely to come to the city as younger, single migrants and to return to their home villages when they get married.

It might be thought that educational differences would favor the largest metropolitan areas, but apparently this is not the case. In fact, Hugo (ESCAP, 1981, 125) shows that, as a group, migrants to middle-sized cities tend to be better educated than those to Jakarta. The explanation is that Jakarta (and possibly other major cities) attracts migrants at both extremes. Along with the pool of more educated migrants is a relatively large stream of persons with little or no education who perceive their greatest hope of improving their situation as lying in the metropolis.

WHY PEOPLE MOVE

Economic Reasons

Even though more formal economic motives (job-related reasons, education) apparently account for a minority of individual moves, it is still arguable that basically demographic and economic factors underlie much of Indonesia's internal migration. At least as far as major interregional and rural-urban streams are concerned, much of this migration has been, and continues to be, explained in terms of the "push" of rural poverty and the "pull" of perceived opportunity in urban and in relatively less densely populated rural areas. Java, in particular, suffers from extremely high overall population density, with some 60 percent of the national population on just 7 percent of the land. As of 1985, on Java, some 753 persons had to share each square kilometer of land, 11 times the density of Sumatra and over 200 times that in Irian Jaya (Table 11.3). While relatively fertile soils have historically permitted high densities on Java, land pressures have become increasingly severe. Coupled with breakdowns in historical survival strategies which have emphasized agricultural intensification and sharing of limited labor opportunities, such pressure has resulted in recent years in a growing landless and near landless rural population whose only access to local employment is as paid labor on other's land or in nonagricultural activities.

Although data on reasons for migration are almost nonexistent from the national census and survey sources,[11] evidence from a variety of smaller surveys suggests that among migrants over age 10 or 15, about half of the males and a quarter of the females move primarily for formal work or educational motives. Thus, results of the PPT-LIPI migration study in East Java showed that, among those who moved after age 15, 53 percent of males and 22 percent of females gave economic or educational reasons (Nagib and Mujiani, 1987). An earlier study (Suharso et al., 1976) showed that, among rural-urban migrants, 29 percent of males and 12 percent of females gave job-related reasons for their move. However, an additional 51 percent of males and 28 percent of females said they moved "for school" or "to obtain a better life," which obviously includes a

Table 11.3
Population Indicators by Major Islands, Indonesia, 1961–85

	Suma-tra	Java	Kali-mantan	Sula-wesi	Other Islands	Total
Population (000)						
1961	15739	63060	4102	7079	7105	97085
1971	20808	76086	5155	8527	8632	119208
1980	28016	91270	6723	10409	11072	147490
1985	32667	99502	7781	11598	12328	163876
Average Annual Growth Rate (%)						
1961-71	2.86	1.90	2.34	1.90	1.99	2.10
1971-80	3.32	2.02	2.96	2.22	2.19	2.32
1980-85	3.12	1.74	2.97	2.18	2.17	2.13
Area						
Sq. Km.	473606	132187	539460	189216	584974	1919443
%	24.7	6.9	28.1	9.8	30.5	100.0
Density (per sq. km.)						
1961	33	477	8	37	12	51
1971	44	576	10	45	15	62
1980	59	690	12	55	19	77
1985	69	753	14	61	21	85

Source: Oey 1985; Tables 1 and 2; Biro Pusat Statitik 1986.

large proportion of economically motivated migration. Of additional interest here is the fragmentary evidence that the relative importance of educational (versus job-related) reasons has been increasing over time, and that education is a relatively more important motive among migrants originating from urban areas than among those from rural villages (Tirtosudarmo, 1985). Both of these trends are consistent with the rapid expansion of education in recent years and the relative concentration of upper secondary and tertiary educational institutions in urban areas.

A large proportion of "family-related" moves can also be ascribed to economic motives. Among women, the majority, and among men, a significant minority of moves are usually ascribed to "following family." For women and dependent children this reason is usually given as following the husband or father, but patterns of chain migration common to some of the rural-rural and rural-urban migration streams also mean that other siblings or relatives may be included in this category. In such family migration (as is characteristic of transmigration, for example), ascribing an economic motive to the whole family would seem most logical. There is also some question about what the job-related responses actually measure. If this primarily refers to formal-sector job opportunities (wage labor), it undoubtedly understates the more generalized desires on the part of many "push"-oriented migrants for a "better life," even though they may not have specific job-related reasons for moving.

Social and Environmental Reasons

The prevalence of family-related reasons for migration in Indonesia, especially among women and children, is understandable. Thus, while a multitude of lineage systems are represented in Indonesia, all ethnic groups adhere to a patriarchal system of authority, and, in this respect, it is the men who are most likely to make the decision to move. Women and children follow as dependents, even though their real economic contribution to family survival in the destination area is often far from negligible. The 1973 LEKNAS-LIPI survey (Suharso et al., 1976) showed 52 percent of the women giving family-related reasons for their move. In the more recent PPT-LIPI survey in East Java (Nagib and Mujiani, 1987), fully 72 percent of women who migrated at age 15 or over gave such a response.

The family is a factor not only in permanent migration, but also in temporary migration and in not moving at all. The 1973 LEKNAS-LIPI survey identified the following family-related reasons for staying in the village: (1) stay with spouse, (2) stay with parents, (3) stay with relatives, and (40) stay in ancestral home. Among males 45 percent and among females, 77 percent, gave one of the above reasons for staying.

Cultural factors also play an important role in patterns of out-migration from specific regions of the country. Perhaps the most famous and best documented is the movement of Minang-kabau from West Sumatra, primarily to urban centers in Java, but also to other parts of Sumatra and, to a much lesser degree, to other islands (Maude, 1977; Naim, 1974). This involves some permanent migration but emphasizes a process of long-term circular migration in which young men, in this matrilineal society, go on *merantau* (extended journey) to prove their competence before they are accepted into their wife's family. Other ethnic groups that are characterized by high levels of out-migration and interregional dispersal include the Toba Batak of North Sumatra and the Bugis and Banjarese of Southern Sulawesi. The last two groups are particularly noted as seafarers and have historically played a major role in the development of interisland communication and trade.

Other social and environmental factors play a role, and some, such as the forced transmigration of beggars from Jakarta and the displacement of population by major disasters or infrastructure development projects, have received a certain degree of notoriety in the press. Transmigration itself is a vehicle for some forced mobility of local populations in destination areas, as the land selected for development is seldom totally unoccupied. Attempts have been made, however, to incorporate local populations, both physically and socially, within the transmigration schemes, although this has not always met with complete success (Soeratman and Guinness, 1976). On the whole, however, government-sponsored transmigration should not be viewed in a coercive light. By and large, the number of voluntary applicants from the sending areas on Java and Bali have exceeded the capability of the program to move them. Given the uncertainties of life in many of the settlements areas, this reinforces the "push" aspects inherent in the high population densities and rural poverty in "inner Indonesia."[12] It also suggests that travel costs and problems of interregional communication remain issues in levels of interregional mobility, particularly in regard to the eastern islands and provinces that are more physically and culturally removed from Java.

Finally, although it cannot be accurately quantified, social factors probably play a substantial role in return migration.[13] In 1971, return migration constituted nearly one-quarter (23 percent) of total in-migration, but this fell to only 10 percent in 1980 (Sunarto, 1984) as a result of increases in overall mobility during the intercensal period. Not surprisingly, the relative dominance of return migrants in in-migration streams was greatest in those provinces characterized by relatively high levels of net out-migration. In West Sumatra, Central and East Java, North and South Sulawesi, and East Nusa Tenggara, return migration constituted over 20 percent of total in-migration in 1980.

A more temporary form of return migration which is perhaps unique to Indonesia is reflected in the large numbers of urban migrants and other residents who return home at the end of the Islamic fasting month of Ramadan. Over 1 million persons from Jakarta alone are known to take part in this annual process of exodus and to return in the weeks immediately surrounding the Lebaran holiday.

CONSEQUENCES OF MIGRATION

Demographic

On a national basis, the impact of either sponsored migration (transmigration) or more spontaneous interregional migration on broad patterns of population distribution has been limited. At least through the 1970s, differences in rates of natural increase were generally more important than migration in explaining interregional differences in overall population growth. In addition, natural increase continued to be the major component in urban growth in Indonesia, although recent analysis (National Urban Development Strategy, 1985b), as well as results of the 1985 SUPAS, suggests a dominance of the migration factor in the future. Such general comments, however, mask significant local variations. As one moves down the scale of geographic units to provinces, *kabupaten* and even to *kecamatan* and *desa,* migration naturally becomes an increasingly important factor in explaining variations in population growth.

Thus, even though net out-migration from Java during the 1970s represented only 1.3 percent of the 1980 census population and 8 percent of 1971–80 population growth, the impact on growth in several receiving areas (with much lower base populations) was far more substantial. For example, the population growth rate in Lampung (historically a center for transmigration) during the 1970s was 5.5 percent, with about half of this growth (nearly 1 million persons) due to net in-migration. Although absolute numbers were not as large, in percentage terms, East Kalimantan benefited to a similar extent. Other provinces where the contribution of net in-migration to annual population growth averaged over 1 percent included Bengkulu, Jambi, Jakarta, Central Kalimantan, and Central Sulawesi. In virtually all of these (with the obvious exception of Jakarta) transmigration played a substantial role, along with substantial urban growth stimulated by growth in administrative and governmental bureaucracies located mainly in the provincial capitals.[14]

Besides its direct impact on population growth, migration also has an impact on levels of fertility. In general, migrant fertility tends to vary between that of nonmigrants in both origin and destination. Thus, M. Oey (1975) found that migrants from Java to Lampung had higher fertility than nonmigrants on Java and lower fertility than nonmigrants in Lampung. On the basis of the 1971 census, A. Murad (1980) found that migrants from West Sumatra to North Sumatra, Riau, and Jakarta had levels of fertility similar to those of nonmigrant women in these provinces. Given existing fertility differentials, this meant that women moving to Jakarta had lower fertility than those remaining in West Sumatra. On the other hand, West Sumatran women moving to North Sumatra and Riau had higher levels of fertility than those staying in their province of origin.

Social

In broad terms, interregional migration has tended to reduce centralization, concentration, and segregation. Reductions in the share of population on Java, the more or less balanced growth of urban areas throughout the country, and the geographic spread of various ethnic groups have tended to support national development goals related to balance and equity. However, a number of social concerns, which are at least in part a function of migration processes, still demand a degree of attention.

Thus, while transmigration and labor market forces have stimulated movement of ethnic Javanese and Sudanese from Java, questions have been raised about the effect of this movement on ethnic groups in areas of destination. Based on a 1980 census question on language spoken at home, it was found that nearly 80 percent of the population of Lampung spoke Javanese or Sudanese. Native Lampungese (who were classified under an ''other language'' category) made up a maximum of only 16 percent. Even where such migrants remain a minority, integration is the exception rather than the rule. Intermarriage among ethnic groups is still relatively rare, and cultural identity is relatively strong even where it results in social conflict between migrant and local populations. This has happened, for example, where Javanese sedentary agricultural practices have come into conflict with the swidden agricultural systems practiced in many of the ''outer island'' areas. In rural areas, land rights (and rights to forest and other products on communal land) are frequently a problem.[15]

On the urban side, while Indonesia has not shown dramatic trends toward an urban primacy characteristic of some other countries, there is increasing concern about the sheer size of some of the major metropolitan centers. The capital city of

Jakarta had nearly 7 million population in 1980 and is projected to reach 12 or 13 million by 2000. If one includes the satellite cities within 50 or 60 kilometers of Jakarta, the projection is increased to over 20 million. Levels of urban congestion implied by such figures impinge not only on the living conditions of the people, but also on the costs of providing required urban infrastructure (water supply, housing, sanitation, roads, etc.) to meet basic needs.

Concerns related to availability of infrastructure and, perhaps more importantly, to ease of access to bureaucratic channels, have and continue to force a Jakarta-centric and, more generally, a Java-centric pattern of industrial location (National Urban Development Strategy, 1985b). The only notable exceptions are for sectors where industrial location is determined largely by natural resource availability or where marketing systems demand a dispersed locational strategy.

Migration and urban growth have also affected residential patterns within cities. During the colonial period there was a tendency toward mixed residential areas, with the poor, largely indigenous, population concentrated in *kampung* (slum) areas behind the luxurious houses of the colonial elite. These were, in effect, urban villages, which were largely ethnically homogeneous and which differed little in terms of cultural organization from their rural counterparts.[16] Downtown areas, or central business districts, tended to be dominated by ethnic Chinese.

Largely through the mechanism of bureaucratic and commercial expansion and fueled by escalating land prices, the development policies and programs of the last two decades have forced a change in this pattern. For example, while the Kampung Improvement Program of the 1970s increased the accessibility of inner city *kampung* to vehicular traffic and improved local infrastructure, it also forced out many of the very poor as a result of rising land values. Displacement can also be traced to large-scale government and commercial development, particularly in prime central city areas. The same problems have also made it increasingly difficult for many in the near poor and lower middle classes (e.g., lower level government employees) to obtain land or housing in inner city areas or close to their place of employment.

The end result, noticeable particularly in the largest metropolitan centers of Jakarta and Surabaya, has been for the poor to be pushed to the periphery where they remain residentially segregated, but now more in terms of economic class than of ethnic group or culture. This class segregation is perhaps most evident where new residential areas (public housing, real estates) have been constructed.

Another factor worth mentioning, which is likely both a cause and an effect of mobility, is the overall improvement in communication over the past 15 to 20 years. Improvements in road networks, particularly in Java, have facilitated an extremely rapid growth of relatively cheap public transport, typified by the ubiquitous Japanese "Colt" minibus (which has, in turn, lent its name to this so-called Colt Revolution). This has undoubtedly been a major factor in promoting circular migration on Java (see Hugo, 1978) as well as facilitating the generally higher levels of interregional mobility observed during the late 1970s.

Environmental

Internal migration has contributed to environmental degradation in both rural and urban areas, although it is equally clear that damage to the environment must be tied in with the effects of overall population growth and with changing patterns of production and consumption dictated by national and international economic forces. For example, overall population growth, coupled with internal and international demand for wood and wood products, has led to increasing deforestation and, more specifically, to environmentally unsound logging or land-clearing practices that leave areas open to erosion and/or infestation of *alang-alang* (*Imperata Cyclindrica*) (bugs). Migrants, notably transmigrants, have reportedly played a role in this process.[17]

Environmental and health problems in crowded urban *kampung* and squatter settlements along canals, railroad rights-of-way, and the like, are also of obvious concern. Even with disproportionately greater availability of health facilities, urban mortality rates in the larger cities remain distressingly high, particularly among infants and young children. Evidence from censuses and surveys indicates higher survival ratios in many rural areas compared to the major metropolitan centers.

Urban congestion also affects the cost of providing basic services related to water supply, human and solid waste control, drainage, roads, and housing. The problem here is that at higher densities, requirements for more expensive technologies more than offset the potential savings of shorter per capita service networks. This, in turn, creates a quandary for the government: Should it use limited resources to meet the real needs of the larger metropolitan areas, or should it emphasize per capita equity and spread resources more evenly among various regions and size classes of cities? Per capita equity considerations have tended to dominate in the past, and while there is evidence of some shift in this philosophy toward a more needs-based investment strategy, the issue has by no means been fully resolved.

On the social side, mobility results in anonymity which, in turn, reduces the effectiveness of social control in smaller residential areas. Rising crime rates are one result, although, in the face of such threats, new types of allegiances are being formed.

Economic

Interregionally, there are few labor market differentials because, similar to many other less developed countries, the labor market in Indonesia has a relatively narrow base. Differences are more noticeable between rural and urban areas, with the rural dominated by agriculture and the urban by service occupations, particularly in the so-called informal sector. Migration has undoubtedly contributed to the growth of the urban informal sector, characterized by petty traders, and transport and construction workers. On the other hand, the informal sector itself remains a force in overall development, maintaining relatively cheap provision of goods and services to the local population.

Of critical importance to the argument here, however, is that relatively few people in either urban or rural areas can afford to be openly unemployed. According to various censuses and surveys, open unemployment has continually been as low as 2 to 3 percent of the labor force, although underemployment in terms of time and income is considerably more widespread. Open unemployment is more pronounced in urban than in rural areas and among those with upper secondary education than those with less or more education.

This makes it extremely difficult to judge to what degree migration affects employment chances either regionally or between rural and urban areas. Even so, microstudies suggest that informal sector jobs still result in higher incomes for the poor and temporary migrants compared to what they could have found in their villages of origin.

NOTES

1. Of these sources only the 1985 SUPAS collected data on migrant origin at the *kabupaten* level and published summary tables on intra- as well as interprovincial migration.

2. East Java, Bali, and South Sulawesi.

3. This was largely due to the creation of several new provinces in the 1960s.

4. Including an estimate for migrants aged 0 to 4 for whom period migration data were not directly collected.

5. Agricultural employment grew at about 1.4 percent annually compared to nearly 3 percent for the total labor force (Oey, 1985).

6. The average rate of decline in the percentage of the national population on Java was about 0.12 percentage points annually between 1930 and 1971. Between 1971 and 1980 it was about 0.27.

7. Based on data (ESCAP, 1981, 177) on place of previous residence for the period 0 to 4 years before the census.

8. The sex ratio equals the number of males per 100 females.

9. In 1980, about 64 percent of total migrants were married compared to 55 percent of nonmigrants. The difference was almost entirely made up by a lower proportion of single people among migrants (Sunarto, 1984).

10. Defined as persons whose place of birth, place of previous residence, and place of current residence were all in different provinces.

11. Only the 1985 SUPAS contained a question on reasons for migration. Three "economic" responses were allowed (transmigration, education, and work), which accounted for 45 percent of male and 22 percent of female migrants. The remainder were classified in a residual "other reasons" category.

12. The major "pull" factor in transmigration is undoubtedly the assurance of land-ownership in the settlement area.

13. Measured in the censuses in terms of persons whose place of birth and place of current residence were the same, but which were different from place of previous residence or place of residence five years ago.

14. Three of these provinces, Bengkulu, Central Kalimantan, and Central Sulawesi, were only created during the 1960s.

15. Particularly for land, the legal system has long given preference to the *adat,* or culturally based judicial-legal system within specific ethnic communities, as opposed to national laws regulating landownership and transfers.

16. *Kampung* names frequently incorporated ethnic identities. For example, *Kampung Ambon* would refer to an area dominated by people from Ambon, capital of Maluku Province.

17. Although transmigrants, in theory, are supposed to survive on the basis of agricultural or other activities within the settlement area, in practice, resources are seldom sufficient and a considerable proportion of household income is derived from off-site activities.

REFERENCES

Bandiyono, S. (ed.). 1987. *Migrasi Permanen Penduduk Jawa Timur* [Permanent Migration in East Java]. Jakarta: PPT-LIPI.

————, and F. Alihar. 1987. "Pola Migrasi Permanen" [Types of Permanent Migration]. In S. Bandiyono (ed.), *Migrasi Permanen.*

Biro Pusat Statistik. 1979. *Definisi Desa Dalam Sensus Penduduk 1980* [Village Definition in the 1980 Census]. Jakarta.

ESCAP (Economic and Social Commission for Asia and the Pacific). 1981. *Migration, Urbanization and Development in Indonesia,* Vol. 3. Comparative Study on Migration, Urbanization, and Development in the ESCAP Region. New York. United Nations.

Hugo, G.J. 1975. "Population Mobility in West Java, Indonesia." Ph.D. Dissertation, Australian National University.

————. 1978. *Population Mobility in West Java.* Yogyakara: Gadjah Mada University Press.

————. 1979. "Migration to and from Jakarta." In R. J. Pryor (ed.), *Migration and Development in Southeast Asia.* Kuala Lumpur: Oxford University Press, pp. 192–203.

Mantra, I.B., and Kasto (eds.). 1984. *Analisa Migrasi Berdasarkan Data Sensus Penduduk Tahun 1971 dan 1980* [Analysis of Migration in Indonesia Based on the 1971 and 1980 Census Data]. Jakarta: Biro Pusat Statistik.

Maude, A. 1977. *Inter-village Differences in Out-migration in West Sumatra.* Adelaide: School of Social Science, Flinders University.

Murad, A. 1980. *Out-migration in a Matrilineal Society of West Sumatra.* Canberra: Department of Demography, Australian National University.

Nagib, L., and Mujiani. 1987. "Proses Migrasi" [The Migration Process]. In S. Bandiyono (ed.), *Migrasi Permanen.*

Naim, M. 1979. "Merantau: Minangkabau" [Voluntary Migration]. Ph.D. diss., University of Singapore.

National Urban Development Strategy. 1985a. *Provincial Population Projections: Requirements, Methodology, Results.* Report T1.4/C3. Jakarta.

————. 1985b. *Final Report.* Jakarta.

Oey, M. 1975. "Migration and Fertility in Indonesia." In W.F. Ilchman, H.D. Lasswell,

J.D. Montgomery, and M. Weiner (eds.), *Policy Sciences and Population*. Lexington, Mass.: Lexington Books.

———. 1977. "Jakarta dibangun oleh kaum pendatang" [Jakarta is developed by migrants]. *Prisma* 5:63–70.

———. 1985. "Poverty, Economic Change and Migration in Indonesia." In P.M. Hauser, D.B. Suits, and N. Ogawa (eds.), *Urbanization and Migration in ASEAN Development*. Tokyo: Nira.

Soeratman and P. Guinness. 1976. Transmigration in South Kalimantan and South Sulawesi." Yogyakarta: Universitas. Gadjah Mada, Lembaga Kependudukan, Working Paper No. 1.

Speare, A. 1975. "Interpreting Migration Data from the 1971 Census." *Majalah Demografi Indonesia* 2 (3):66–85.

Suharso, A. Speare, Jr., H.R. Redmana, and I. Husin. 1976. *Rural Urban Migration in Indonesia*. Jakarta: LEKNAS-LIPI.

Sunarto, H.S. 1984. "Analisa migrasi Indonesia berdasarkan data Sensus Penduduk tahun 1971 dan 1980" [Analysis of migration in Indonesia based on the 1971 and 1980 census data]. In Mantra and Kasto (eds.), *Analis: Migrasi Berdasarkan*.

Tirtosudarmo, R. 1985. *Migration Decision Making: The Case of East Java*. Jakarta: LEKNAS-LIPI.

World Bank, 1983. *Indonesia: Selected Aspects of Spatial Development, Annex 2, Demographic Patterns and Population Projections*. Washington, D.C.

12

ISRAEL

Dov Friedlander and Eliahu Ben-Moshe

During the first years of its existence, the state of Israel witnessed dramatic changes that were critical for demographic processes in general and internal migrations in particular. Founded in 1948, when the Jewish population was about 650,000 and the Arab population 160,000, Israel received within a period of 30 months nearly 700,000 immigrants.[1] The ethnic division of this "mass migration"—half from European and half from Middle Eastern countries—was strongly associated with socioeconomic status. Consequently, in mid-1951 Israel's Jewish society was transformed from a population with modern European demographic characteristics, as it was in 1948, to a heterogeneous society with about one-third originating from Asian and African countries. Hence, the wave of mass immigration with its particular socioeconomic profile in the early years had a very dominant impact on nuptiality, fertility, longevity, and, not least, on internal migration patterns (e.g., Friedlander and Goldscheider, 1979, 1984). This impact of mass immigration on internal migration is intertwined throughout this chapter.

Israel is a small country, located in Southwest Asia on the eastern wing of the Mediterranean. Its total land area is 21,502 square kilometers or about the size of the state of New Jersey. The country's length from the northern border to the Gulf of Aqaba at its southernmost tip is 555 kilometers, and it has a 266 kilometer Mediterranean coastline. Its width is in places not more than 26 kilometers. The densely populated coastal Mediterranean plain contains two of the country's three largest cities: Haifa and Tel Aviv-Yafo, which are separated by only 95 kilometers. The population residing in the metropolitan areas of these cities, along with those living in Jerusalem—the capital (about 63 kilometers from Tel Aviv-Yafo), make up almost half of the nation's total population. Hence, the short and dramatic demographic history, the smallness of the country, and the fact that over half of its population is concentrated in a relatively small area, have obvious implications for the overall rate of internal migration and its more specific patterns.

DATA ON MIGRATION

In Israel address changes must be registered, by law, at the National Registration Office. In practice, only about 80 percent of all migration events are registered within one year of their occurrence. Hence, the use of migration data from this source requires caution, but it is the major source for internal migration information in Israel.

Another source for internal migration data is the general census. Censuses have been taken in 1961, 1972, and 1983. They contained the standard questions concerning place of residence at the time of the census and five years earlier, in addition to duration of present residence. Thus, various types of migration estimates can be obtained from these in addition to the implied net migration estimates that can be derived from consecutive censuses. However, because immigration was so heavy in some periods, and new immigrants have a high intensity of "settlement migration" after arrival, our estimates for each intercensal period exclude movements by immigrants arriving during that period. Since Israel's first census was taken in 1961 and migration events have been registered only since 1955, there are virtually no data on internal migration prior to 1955.

There are several possible areal unit classifications for the measurement of internal migration. These include residential addresses, local authority areas (1,091 in 1983), statistical areas (nearly 2,000), subdistricts (14 in 1983), and districts (6 in 1983). The choice among these for analytic purposes obviously depends on the particular research aim.

The Overall Dimensions of Internal Migration

Table 12.1 presents various migration rates for the period 1955–80. Migration estimates for the entire period are available only for moves within and between local authority areas. As seen in column 6 migration was very high through 1957, declined after this year, but was relatively high through the mid-1960s, and declined since then to about half its initial level. A comparison of columns 4 and 5 in Table 12.1 shows that it was the migration rates *between* local authority areas which declined most sharply after 1957, which was six to eight years after the mass migration wave. The decline of migration rates *within* local authority areas was relatively less severe. E. Ben-Moshe (1988) has demonstrated that these exceptionally high migration rates were tightly interrelated through the particular mechanisms of immigration absorption. Immigration to Israel was "assisted migration." Not only was transportation provided by the state, but also the initial needs in Israel and the means necessary for permanent settlement were provided. However, considering the very high relative immigration volume and Israel's severe economic difficulties in the 1950s, the means that were provided

Table 12.1

Overall Migration According to Different Migration Definitions, Absolute Numbers (in thousands) and Rates (per 1,000), Israel, 1955–80

Year	Number Migrants Between Local Authority Areas	Number Migrants Within Local Authority Areas	Migration Rate Between Local Authority Areas	Migration Rate Within Local Authority Areas	Migration Rate Within And Between Local Authority Areas	Migration Rate Between Counties	Migration Rate Between Districts
(1)	(2)	(3)	(4)	(5)	(6)	(7)	(8)
1955	122.9	93.2	79.0	59.9	138.9	—	—
1956	19.2	91.7	79.4	56.4	135.8	—	—
1957	130.7	94.9	76.0	55.1	131.1	—	—
1958	116.0	78.3	65.0	43.9	108.9	—	—
1959	103.5	121.6	56.4	66.2	122.6	—	—
1960	97.4	112.6	51.7	59.8	111.5	—	—
1961	99.9	97.5	51.4	50.1	101.5	—	—
1962	129.4	99.8	63.7	49.2	112.9	—	—
1963	138.0	82.7	65.4	39.2	104.6	—	—
1964	133.4	87.5	60.7	39.8	100.5	—	—
1965	128.8	108.3	56.8	47.7	104.5	37.5	41.5
1966	94.0	97.4	40.5	41.9	82.4	24.3	26.7
1967	78.1	65.1	33.1	27.6	60.7	18.8	21.8
1968	87.5	78.2	36.3	32.4	68.7	21.3	23.4
1969	113.9	128.6	46.2	52.1	98.3	26.9	32.2
1970	99.9	97.0	39.5	38.4	77.9	22.7	25.1
1971	103.4	100.5	39.8	38.7	78.5	24.2	26.6
1972	98.1	—	36.5	—	—	22.8	25.3
1973	99.5	88.5	35.6	31.7	67.3	—	—
1974	117.1	104.7	40.7	36.4	77.1	—	—
1975	107.2	95.7	36.6	32.7	69.3	22.6	25.0
1976	120.6	115.4	40.3	38.6	78.9	23.6	26.6
1977	128.2	149.9	42.1	49.2	91.3	24.2	27.1
1978	112.0	140.8	36.0	45.3	81.3	20.4	28.6
1979	110.1	122.7	34.6	38.6	73.2	20.1	22.5
1980	113.7	131.3	35.0	40.4	75.4	21.8	24.1

Source: Central Bureau of Statistics publications based on population register data.

for migrant settlement were necessarily limited and modest. Nevertheless, almost all migrants were settled with aid provided by the state (Friedlander and Goldscheider, 1979).

It is out of the scope of this chapter to discuss in detail the mechanisms and criteria used to allocate immigrants among Israel's cities, towns, and villages. It is important to remember, however, that the residential distribution in a "normal" society depends, apart from past fertility and mortality patterns, on a continuous process of residential mobility and internal migration, all of which are strongly associated with the socioeconomic characteristics of people and places. In Israel this was not the case, as about half of its population in the early 1950s was placed by the administrative mechanisms of absorption and settlement, and not necessarily in association with the socioeconomic characteristics of migrants or places. Hence, an exceptionally high proportion of Israel's population in the early 1950s was under strong strains originating from the discrepancy between the satisfaction expected from place of residence and its actual satisfaction. These strains formed motivations among a high proportion of the population to respond (i.e., to migrate).

These strains and responses were not evenly distributed among major ethnic groups. Indeed, both ethnicity and socioeconomic status influenced migration subsequent to immigration. One would expect that the rates of internal migration for immigrants of European origin would be higher than the rates for persons of Asian and African origin. However, the opposite was the case. Partial evidence indicates that this was so because immigrants from Asian and North African countries, who on average came later, were settled in less desirable places. This, in turn, stimulated a stronger overall migration response (Ben-Moshe, 1988). This is the major explanation for the very high level of internal migration and its ethnic differences through the 1950s. Subsequently, after a period of high-intensity internal migration, rates declined by about 25 percent. A further decline of 40 to 50 percent occurred after the mid-1960s.

The general pattern of age-specific migration rates in Israel is fairly typical of those commonly observed in other countries (see Table 12.2), and the levels of these rates reflect the patterns already discussed. The age-specific migration rates increase considerably from the 0 to 14 age group to a maximum rate for ages 15 to 29, with relatively high rates for the 30 to 44 age group, declining gradually afterward. There are no sex differences in age-specific migration rates.

Interdistrict Migration

Israel is divided into six districts. In-migration, out-migration and net-migration balances for 1956–61 and for 1978–83 are shown in Table 12.3 for each district. Migration levels were generally higher in the earlier period (1956–61). Although in both periods net migration was a rather small proportion of the sum of the gross migration rates, in the earlier period (1956–61) these proportions were generally higher than in the later. This is again connected with the wave of mass immigration and its absorption. Indeed, while high overall rates of migration do not necessarily imply high *net* migration rates, in this case the migration rates were exceptionally high in several districts during the early years of statehood. Thus, these patterns suggest that substantial adjustments were also necessary to the size distribution among geographic units—as reflected in the high net migration rates—and not only at the individual level—as reflected in the high overall migration rates. The process of absorption and geographic distribution of the immigrants formed strong strains that required an exceptionally high level of migration responses.

A comparison of the six districts suggests that the migration rates of the Central and Tel Aviv districts have been dominant over time. (The high rates for the Southern District are partly due to a very small initial population.) This

Table 12.2
Age- and Sex-Specific Migration Rates for Interlocality Migrants, 1956–80

Period	Sex	All Ages	0-14	15-29	30-44	45-64[**]	65+[**]
			Censuses based five year rates				
1956-61	Both Sexes	178.0	166.0	258.0	188.0	109.0	137.0
	Males	178.0	172.0	245.0	204.0	110.0	121.0
	Females	178.0	160.0	280.0	173.0	107.0	152.0
1978-83[*]	Both Sexes	83.8	70.9	159.1	67.2	25.4	28.2
	Males	80.7	70.9	138.4	77.2	25.4	26.7
	Females	86.8	70.9	181.1	57.7	25.5	29.7
			Registration based annual rates				
1965		56.7	39.0	95.7	58.1	41.1	43.9
1970		39.5	27.6	69.4	41.2	20.6	26.4
1975		36.2	25.0	65.4	38.9	17.3	21.0
1980		35.0	21.9	63.8	44.2	15.7	17.2

[*]For 1978-83 the rates are based on inter district migrations.

[**]For 1978-83 the age groups are 45-59 and 60+ respectively.

Table 12.3
In-Migration, Out-Migration, and Net Migration Rates (x 1,000) by District, 1956–61 and 1978–83

District	1956-1961			1978-1983		
	In Migration	Out Migration	Net Migration	In Migration	Out Migration	Net Migration
Total	102.1	102.1	----	74.6	74.6	----
Jerusalem	85.2	113.7	-28.5	66.1	79.0	-12.9
Northern	77.8	184.1	-106.4	92.5	89.1	+3.4
Haifa	83.0	93.6	-10.6	55.5	70.5	-15.0
Central	84.7	146.6	-61.9	102.7	68.2	+34.5
Tel Aviv	117.9	43.6	+74.3	50.8	67.6	-16.8
Southern	195.0	143.7	+51.3	67.6	80.7	-13.1

Source: 1961 and 1983 census data.

dominance is, no doubt, connected with their central position as the major metropolitan area. (It should be noted that Tel Aviv District does not coincide with Tel Aviv City. It also contains several other towns located near Tel Aviv City.) Hence, the Central and Tel Aviv districts occupied a relatively important place in the internal migration system during both 1956–61 and 1978–83. Table 12.4, which provides rates for migration streams between all pairs of districts for both periods, shows that the highest rates among all migration streams are between these two districts. However, while net migration from Central to Tel

Table 12.4
Gross and Net Interdistrict Migration Rates,[1] 1956–61 and 1978–83

To	Jerusalem	Northern	Haifa	Central	Tel Aviv	Southern
From						
			Gross Rates	1956–61		
Jerusalem	---	9.8	10.2	18.2	26.6	19.1
Northern	14.5	---	44.5	25.4	28.8	31.7
Haifa	14.3	21.2	---	15.5	27.5	15.9
Central	14.9	12.3	14.3	---	75.8	33.1
Tel Aviv	11.8	7.7	11.3	22.4	---	17.7
Southern	10.9	12.2	13.9	21.7	21.4	---
			Gross Rates	1978–83		
Jerusalem	---	8.3	5.6	10.7	10.7	9.7
Northern	7.8	---	25.0	12.7	10.6	9.2
Haifa	8.0	28.7	---	10.2	12.7	8.4
Central	10.4	11.3	8.8	---	24.3	16.1
Tel Aviv	9.1	10.2	7.3	50.8	---	10.7
Southern	11.8	10.5	8.5	21.1	14.4	---
			Net Rates	1956–61		
Jerusalem	---	-4.7	-4.1	3.3	14.8	8.2
Northern	---	---	23.3	13.0	21.1	19.5
Haifa	---	---	---	1.2	16.2	2.0
Central	---	---	---	---	53.4	11.4
Tel Aviv	---	---	---	---	---	-3.8
Southern	---	---	---	---	---	---
			Net Rates	1978–83		
Jerusalem	---	0.5	-2.4	0.4	1.4	-2.0
Northern	---	---	-3.7	1.4	0.4	-1.3
Haifa	---	---	---	1.5	5.4	-0.1
Central	---	---	---	---	-26.5	-5.0
Tel Aviv	---	---	---	---	---	-3.7
Southern	---	---	---	---	---	---

[1]A gross rate from district i to ji is defined as $(M_{1j}/JP_1P_j)1000 = m_{ij}$. The net rate from i to j equals $m_{ij} - m_{ji}$.

Source: 1961 and 1983 census data.

Aviv District in 1956–61 was large and positive, the high rate between these districts in the later period was in the opposite direction. Therefore, like many metropolitan areas in the world, Tel Aviv District was undergoing a transformation in terms of migration streams associated with concentration and dispersal of population.

The net rates in Table 12.4 show that in 1956–61 there were just two other high rates not associated with the Central and/or Tel Aviv districts. One was between Northern and Haifa districts, which was connected with the metropolitan development of Tel Aviv and the other was from the Northern to Southern district which was experiencing large investments for industrial development. By 1978–83, there were no high interdistrict migration rates apart from those involving either the Tel Aviv or the Central District. In conclusion, the distribution of interdistrict migration streams highlights the important role of the Central urban area of Israel, in particular the Tel Aviv and Central districts.

Migration between Places Classified by Size/Type

Similar to other developed societies, Israel's is an urban society. With only 15 percent of its population living in rural areas at the time of the establishment of the state of Israel, the nation has continued to urbanize to the point where less than 10 percent of its population now resides in rural areas. This minor weight of the rural sector implies that no massive rural-to-urban migration can be expected in the future. At the other end of the rural-urban scale the three largest cities have ceased to grow through migration. Hence, migrations tend to be directed to the medium and small-size urban places, as well as toward rural places (see Tables

Table 12.5

In-Migration, Out-Migration, and Net Migration Rates (per 1,000) by Type (Size) of Places, 1956–61 and 1978–83

Population Size of Category	Type of Place	1956–1961			1978–1983		
		In Migration	Out Migration	Net Migration	In Migration	Out Migration	Net Migration
Large Cities:							
Pop. of 150,000 or over	Jerusalem	88.7	97.4	-8.7	71.1	90.3	-19.2
	Tel Aviv	120.3	138.8	-18.4	94.2	147.6	-53.4
	Haifa	141.2	110.9	30.3	79.1	121.0	-41.9
10,000 to 150,000	Other cit. or towns	214.4	88.9	125.6	67.1	58.4	8.7
2,000 to 10,000	Urban Settlements	121.7	204.8	-83.1	150.7	116.9	33.8
Under 2,000	Rural	82.0	212.3	-130.3	138.7	122.3	16.4

Source: 1961 and 1983 census data.

12.5 and 12.6). The tables suggest that in the earlier period (1956–61) one of the largest cities (Haifa) was still gaining from the smaller urban places; this stream had reversed by the later period. In addition, other cities and towns (sized 10,000 to 150,000) were the most attractive places to migrants in the earlier period, while the smaller urban settlements became the most important migration destinations in 1978–83. Thus, it can be concluded that the decentralizing pattern of migration that has characterized many developed societies is also evident in Israel.

Table 12.6
Gross and Net Migration Rates[1] between Types of Localities, 1956–61 and 1978–83

From \ To	Jerusalem	Tel Aviv	Haifa	Other Cities	Settlements	Villages
			Gross Rates 1956-61			
Jerusalem	---	16.3	7.3	22.5	10.2	10.8
Tel Aviv	9.2	---	7.6	95.0	9.5	12.0
Haifa	11.9	11.3	---	18.6	27.1	10.6
Other towns and cities	14.3	45.4	16.5	---	21.1	22.2
Urban settlements	9.4	33.7	48.1	70.7	---	23.4
Villages	18.3	25.0	23.4	75.8	53.3	---
			Gross Rates 1978-83			
Jerusalem	---	6.7	4.9	13.0	7.4	24.7
Tel Aviv	6.7	---	3.9	50.8	17.5	8.3
Haifa	6.8	6.9	---	25.4	15.6	12.7
Other towns and cities	12.5	28.5	16.9	---	43.5	30.8
Urban settlements	11.2	11.2	9.4	37.1	---	17.5
Villages	1.2	8.4	8.9	27.0	23.8	---
			Net Rates 1956-61			
Jerusalem	---	7.0	-4.5	8.2	-1.6	-7.5
Tel Aviv	---	---	-3.7	9.6	-24.3	-13.0
Haifa	---	---	---	2.1	-21.0	-12.7
Other towns and cities	---	---	---	---	-49.6	-53.6
Urban settlements	---	---	---	---	---	-29.9
Villages	---	---	---	---	---	---
			Net Rates 1978-83			
Jerusalem	---	0.04	-1.9	0.4	6.2	12.7
Tel Aviv	---	---	-3.1	22.4	6.3	-0.15
Haifa	---	---	---	8.5	6.1	3.8
Other towns and cities	---	---	---	---	6.4	3.8
Urban settlements	---	---	---	---	---	-6.3
Villages	---	---	---	---	---	---

[1]A gross rate from district i to ji is defined as $(M_{1j}/JP_1P_j)1000 = m_{ij}$. The net rate from i to j equals $m_{ij} - m_{ji}$.

Metropolitan Migration

The major metropolitan area in Israel is located around the city of Tel Aviv. This Central Area is made up of Tel Aviv and all localities in Tel Aviv *District* plus most of the localities in the Central District. Its total population in 1983 was 1 million. The core of this metropolitan area (Tel Aviv City) was founded in the early years of this century and reached its largest size (385,000) in 1965. Since then its population has been declining. The city's population decline was a consequence of both low rates of natural increase and net losses from internal migration which have become more salient in recent years.

Specifically, in terms of internal migration, Tel Aviv had a negative balance after the mid-1950s (see Table 12.5); however, as in other large cities, a major part of its losses resulted from out-migration to its suburban areas within the metropolitan area. Consequently, while Tel Aviv City had a history of negative migration balances, the whole of the Central Area (including Tel Aviv) had a positive migration balance. Table 12.7 shows a comparison of natural increase, international migration, internal migration, and population growth in the whole Central Area and in the remainder of Israel.

Evidently, although the internal migration balance in the Central Area was positive and fairly high until the beginning of the 1970s, population growth was always lower in this area compared to the remainder of Israel. The explanation of this "contradiction" is to be found in the low rates of both immigration and natural increase of the Central Area when compared to the rest of Israel. The data in Table 12.7 also point out that internal migration was not made a dominant contribution to the growth of the Central Area. Nevertheless, the place of the Central Metropolitan Area in Israel's internal migration system is undoubtedly

Table 12.7
Annual Rates (x 1,000) of Population Change by Components, 1953–83

Period	Area	Internal Migration	International Migration	Natural Increases	Total Growth Rate
1953	Central	6.7	7.0	16.2	29.9
	Remainder	−7.3	19.3	22.5	34.5
−1961					
	Difference	+14.0	−12.3	−6.3	−4.6
1962	Central	2.9	9.1	14.1	26.1
	Remainder	−3.0	17.6	19.1	33.6
−1972					
	Difference	+5.9	−8.5	−5.0	−7.5
1973	Central	0.3	3.0	14.4	17.6
	Remainder	−0.3	6.2	17.9	23.8
−1983					
	Difference	+0.6	−3.2	−3.5	−6.2

Source: Migration rates are "implied" and based on C.B.S. population estimates

important. One indication of its significance is that the proportion of interdistrict movements *into* the Central and Tel Aviv districts is around 75 percent of all interdistrict movements in the country.

Factors Associated with Migratory Movements and Characteristics of Movers

In addition to being associated with age and ethnicity, internal migration is also associated with socioeconomic status. For example, Table 12.8 shows the association between migration and educational attainment controlling for ethnicity. These data show the strong positive effect of education, and we may note that similar results are obtained with other socioeconomic status variables such as occupation or income. These interrelationships reflect the selectivity among higher status groups, as they respond to perceived opportunities. Not unrelated to migration and status is the association between the intensity of internal migration and change in place of work. Table 12.9 demonstrates a very strong association between migration and change in workplace when educational attainment and ethnicity are controlled. Considering the availability of modern efficient transportation facilities, this relationship is somewhat surprising.

Another factor influencing migration and its age pattern is marriage. Since all marriages for which partners come from different places of residence, and a high proportion of other marriages, involve a migratory movement (and often more than one), the effect of this variable is not surprising. Indeed, some calculations suggest that the rate of "marriage movements" is so high that it may account for as much as 20 percent of all internal movements.

Table 12.8
Five-Year Migration Rates (x 1,000) by Educational Attainment and Ethnicity, Males Aged 18 to 34, 1978–83

	Ethnicity		
Years of Study	Europe or America	Asia or Africa	Total
0 - 8	90.8	57.6	62.7
9 - 12	141.5	94.9	110.2
13+	253.4	210.6	238.9
Total	187.2	105.0	137.2

Source: 1983 census data.

Table 12.9

Five-Year Migration Rates (x 1,000) by Educational Attainment, Ethnicity, and Change in Place of Work during the Five-Year Period, 1978–83

	Ethnic Origin			
Years of Study	Europe and America		Asia and Africa	
	Change Work	Same Work	Change Work	Same Work
0 - 8	69.6	21.4	74.5	20.4
9 - 12	162.5	45.2	142.2	49.8
13 +	232.9	65.5	218.3	72.5

Source: 1983 census data.

Table 12.10

Growth Rates (x 100) of the Population in the Districts by Components, 1956–83

	Jerusalem	North	Haifa	Central	Tel Aviv	South	Total
Total Growth Rate	119	92	72	123	75	423	111
Growth Rate Due To:							
Natural Growth	77	70	35	60	39	102	69
International Migration	46	54	41	48	20	309	42
Internal Migration	-4	-32	-4	+15	+16	+12	---
The Components Relative Contribution (in percentages)							
Total	100.0	100.0	100.0	100.0	100.0	100.0	100.0
Net Growth	64.7	76.1	48.6	48.8	52.0	24.1	62.2
International Migration	38.7	58.7	56.9	39.0	26.7	73.1	37.8
Internal Migration	-3.4	-34.8	-5.5	12.2	21.3	2.8	---

Source: Migration rates are "implied" and based on C.B.S. population estimates

Internal Migration and Population Redistribution

In relative terms we have already shown that population growth in the Central Metropolitan Area was not significantly affected by internal migration. Table 12.10 enables us to make a similar evaluation for *all* the districts of Israel. Total growth for each district is divided into the three components: natural increase, international migration, and internal migration. It can be seen that for no district is internal migration a dominant component. Moreover, we have constructed estimates showing the population distribution in districts in 1956 and in 1983 (see Table 12.11). We ask what would have been that distribution if there was no international migration, if natural increase was equal among districts, and if there was no internal migration. These three hypothetical distributions may then be compared with the actual for 1983. It can be seen that the "without internal migration" hypothetical distribution for 1983 is very similar to the 1983 actual distribution, which suggests that internal migration has had a small impact on population distribution. This observation, however, requires qualification. First, it has been shown that internal migration rates in the second half of the 1950s were very high indeed and had, no doubt, a significant effect on the distribution at that time. Second, although lack of data prevented us from assessing the effect of internal migration on population distribution up to 1955, it may well be—and is even likely—that our conclusion about the minor importance of internal migration is incorrect for the pre-1956 period for the same reasons as it was incorrect for the 1956–61 period. Third, the residual method used in this section underestimates internal migration rates because it excludes the internal move-

Table 12.11
Relative Distribution of the Population by Districts and the Effects of International Migration, Internal Growth, and Internal Migration during 1956–83

District	1956 (CBS estimation)	1983 without international migration	1983 without natural growth	1983 without internal migration	1983 (Census)
Total	100.0	100.0	100.0	100.0	100.0
Jerusalem	10.0	10.9	9.1	10.9	10.4
North	10.7	9.4	8.4	11.8	9.8
Haifa	17.0	14.1	14.9	14.6	14.0
Central	21.6	23.0	22.5	22.0	23.0
Tel Aviv	35.5	34.7	31.0	27.6	29.8
South	5.2	7.1	14.1	13.1	13.0

Source: Migration rates are "implied" and based on C.B.S. population estimates

ments of the immigrants. The inclusion of these movements may also affect our conclusions about the impact of internal migration on population redistribution.

NOTE

1. The work for this chapter was supported by a grant from the Jerusalem Institute for Israel Studies. This chapter deals with internal migrations of the Jewish population. No satisfactory data exist for the Arab population.

REFERENCES

Ben-Moshe, E. 1988. "Internal Migration Processes in Israel: Demographic, Ethnic and Social Aspects." Ph.D. thesis, Hebrew University of Jerusalem, 1988 (in Hebrew).

Friedlander, D., and C. Goldscheider. 1979. *The Population of Israel*. New York: Columbia University Press.

Goldscheider, C., and D. Friedlander. 1984. "Reproduction Norms in Israel." In *Studies in the Population of Israel*. Jerusalem: Hebrew University.

13

ITALY

Alberto Bonaguidi

Since the Second World War, industrialization combined with very low level of natural increase has been a potent triggering factor for massive migration from depressed regions of Italy. During the 1950s, the regions of the so-called industrial triangle (North-West) and Lazio (Rome) were the only regions with net in-migration; heavy migratory losses were observable not only in the south, but also in many of the northeastern regions. Over time this pattern has changed. During the 1960s the migration balance of the northeast improved because of the socioeconomic development, while that in the south worsened. This situation can be ascribed to a lack of growth experienced by this depressed part of the country during the years, characterized by intensive economic development in the rest of Italy.

Studies of the phenomenon made at the time led to the conclusion that there was no hope that things for the South could change, at least in the short term (Golini, 1974). Nevertheless, during the 1970s, the evolution of the internal migration pattern showed some remarkable changes. The migratory balance of the southern regions, which had traditionally been an area of heavy net out-migration, now began to improve significantly. Moreover, the attractiveness of the northeastern and central regions began to increase at the expense of the northwestern regions. Some argue that these new trends do not necessarily reflect better economic conditions in the south. Indeed, the southern economy seems to be still largely dependent on the rest of the country, so that once the economy of the northern and central areas enters a new phase of expansion, it is likely to revert to the old pattern (Bonaguidi, 1985). However, a recent study has demonstrated that the recent evolution of migration in Italy is something more than a simple transitory, cyclical phenomenon (Termote, Golini, and Cantalini, 1985).

The purpose of this chapter is to discuss the main characteristics of internal migration in Italy, the importance of more recent changes, and the meaning and social-economic implications of the new trends. More precisely, after some critical remarks on the data sources available for the study of migration in Italy and on the quality of migration statistics utilized in this study, we will illustrate the long-term evolution of internal mobility, both over a short distance (intra-regional) and over a long distance (interregional). Then, we analyze some important aspects of migration, such as its level and demographic and socioeconomic selectivity. This is followed by an analysis of the interregional migration pattern (recent changes, demographic and socioeconomic impact, regional scale of preferences). In a concluding section we will summarize the results and assess their main implications.

DATA ON MIGRATION

The mobility of the Italian population can be studied using two kinds of data: migration statistics obtained from population registers and those derived from the population census. The population register is kept in the smallest administrative unit, the municipality. Any changes of residence have to be declared to the authorities of the municipality of destination. The declaration includes the municipality (or foreign country) of origin and some personal attributes of the migrant (age, sex, marital status, profession). This change of residence will then be recorded in the population register of the municipality of out-migration. The system of declaring at the place of destination seems to be preferable to the system of declaring at the place of origin because, while a nonnegligible number of migrants may not declare their departure it is more difficult to avoid declaring one's arrival. This does not mean, of course, that there are no problems of underregistration for these data, but, as we will see, the quality of the migration data derived from the population register in Italy is to be considered as quite acceptable, especially in the more recent period. All individual declarations are then collected and classified by the Central Institute of Statistics (ISTAT). Migration is defined as any change of municipality of residence. Thus, register data in Italy refer to moves between the more than 8,000 municipalities that make up the national territory.

The population census is another way of obtaining information on migration in Italy. In the last census (1981), fixed-period migration data were collected through a question on the place (municipality) of residence five years before the census date. According to this source, migrants are those persons whose municipality of residence on the census day differs from the municipality of residence some years earlier (five years in the case of the 1981 census). As is well known, the figures on migration provided by the census are smaller than those obtained from population registers, because the population register records the act of migration. Therefore, the data refer to the number of moves and not to the number of the migrants as derived from the census. The number of migrations is larger than the number of migrants since the same person may make more than one migration during a given period. Of course, as the period lengthens, the greater will be the difference between these two kinds of data.

In this chapter we will use the migration data derived from the population register and published by the Central Institute of Statistics. Moreover, we have subjected the data on individual migration for the 1980–82 period to a special processing in order to study the correlation between the migration propensity and some demographic and socioeconomic characteristics of the migrants. Migration over this three-year period has been crossclassified by age, sex, marital status, and origin and destination. The differences in the migration behavior of distinct demographic and socioeconomic groups may indirectly provide responses to questions concerning the determinants of migration. Before starting our analysis, a brief critical discussion on the quality of the data used seems in order.

Quality of Data

Even if the registration of a new residence is required by law in Italy, this does not mean that the data provided by ISTAT are without problems. Indeed, a certain number of migrants do not care to declare their arrival or departure to municipal authorities, with the result that these data most probably underestimate the volume of migration. The problem of underregistration of migrants in Italy should, however, not be overevaluated. One way to check the quality of migration data is to compare the so-called calculated population with the population enumerated at the census (see Termote, Golini, and Cantalini, 1985). If births and deaths are correctly registered and if there is no underenumeration of the census population, then any difference between the calculated population and the census population may be attributed to errors in the registration of migration. By adding to the population calculated on January 1, 1981, the number of births and immigrants (internal and international) registered between January 1 and October 24, 1981 (census date), and subtracting the number of deaths and emigrants registered over the same period, we obtain the calculated population at the census date. The difference between the calculated population and the population enumerated on the census day was 1.3 percent at the national level, with a range of 0.5 to 3.0 percent across the twenty regions.

LONG-TERM EVOLUTION OF INTERNAL MIGRATION

As a first step, let us now consider the long-term evolution of internal migration in Italy. In our analysis of this long-term evolution, we must consider that the trend may be affected by some characteristics of the data. For example, the periodic postcensus adjustments as well as a decrease over time in the underregistration rate are factors to be taken into account in correctly interpreting the long-term trend of the phenomenon.

Because factors stimulating migration tend to be different in short-distance and in long-distance moves, it is useful to examine the evolution of intraregional and interregional migration. Table 13.1 depicts the annual evolution between 1956 and 1983 of the rates of interregional migration as well as the rates of intraregional migration and total (interregional plus intraregional) migration in Italy. A pronounced trend of a lower propensity to migrate between and within regions is clearly observable.

On the whole, at the beginning of the 1980s, slightly more than 2 percent of Italy's population changed their municipality of residence every year, down from nearly 3 percent through the 1960s. The decline of the total migration rate was particularly pronounced during the 1970s. The temporary increase in the early 1960s was due to postcensus adjustments made in those years. A temporary increase in the rate as a result of postcensus adjustments is also observable in the years immediately after the 1971 census and 1981 census, but for these censuses the adjustments were much less important than for the 1961 census, which

Table 13.1
Evolution of Internal Migration in Italy, 1956–83 (rate per 1,000 persons)

Year	Intraregional	Interregional	Total
1956	19. 0	8. 0	27. 0
1957	19. 0	8. 0	27. 0
1958	19. 5	8. 5	28. 0
1959	19. 0	9. 0	28. 0
1960	19. 5	9. 5	29. 0
1961	21. 0	12. 0	33. 0
1962	28. 0	14. 5	42. 5
1963	24. 0	13. 0	37. 0
1964	19. 0	10. 0	29. 0
1965	18. 0	8. 5	26. 5
1966	17. 5	8. 0	25. 5
1967	17. 5	9. 0	26. 5
1968	17. 5	10. 0	27. 5
1969	17. 5	10. 5	28. 0
1970	17. 0	11. 0	28. 0
1971	17. 0	10. 0	27. 0
1972	18. 5	10. 5	29. 0
1973	17. 0	8. 5	25. 5
1974	15. 0	8. 0	23. 0
1975	13. 5	7. 0	20. 5
1976	13. 5	7. 0	20. 5
1977	13. 0	7. 0	20. 0
1978	13. 0	6. 5	19. 5
1979	13. 5	6. 5	20. 0
1980	15. 0	6. 0	21. 0
1981	17. 0	6. 0	23. 0
1982	18. 0	6. 0	24. 0
1983	16. 0	6. 0	22. 0

note: rates are rounded to nearest one half of one percent

Source: ISTAT, Annuario di Statistiche Demografiche, various years

revealed a larger shortfall with respect to the registration of migration. The fact that in the past the migration data underestimated the real extent of migration much more than they do now reinforces some of the above-mentioned characteristics of the evolution. The real decline of the migration rate over the period has probably been higher than the published data would lead one to suppose.

If the long-term evolution of intraregional and interregional migration appears rather parallel, one should note that over the entire period the decline in long-distance migration seems to be less pronounced than that in short-distance migration. However, if we only consider the recent evolution of both types of migration, then it is clear that during the past decade, interregional migration has declined more rapidly. These different trends may be related to economic factors. If the recent decline in the propensity to migrate is a function of the economic depression experienced during the 1970s, then it is not surprising that the long-distance migration, which is much more related to economic factors than short-distance migration, has been affected more severely.

Even if the figures for the most recent years are affected by a nonnegligible number of postcensus adjustments, there is still an underlying upward trend in the migration propensity. This holds true, however, only for short-distance migration and not for long-distance migration, which continues to decrease slowly. The recent trend of internal migration in Italy seems to reinforce the process of substitution of short distance for long-distance migration, which had started in the 1970s. Not only do Italians move less now than in the past, but also they increasingly prefer to move over shorter distances.

Gross Migraproduction Rate

Tables 13.2 and 13.3 show the age-specific rates by sex and marital status for both intraregional and interregional migration in the 1980–82 period. These rates have been obtained by relating the yearly average of the migration over this three-year period, crossclassified by age, sex, and marital status, to the corresponding population at the 1981 census (Bonaguidi, 1987). By taking three-year averages, we eliminate possibly erratic components in the data and we reduce to some extent the impact of postcensal adjustments. In any case, only the migration level would be affected since the influence on differences in migration propensity between various population groups will be rather negligible.

Nevertheless, taking the average of the 1980–82 period, we have the advantage that the middle of this period is sufficiently close to the census date (October 1981), and only the census can provide the population data with sufficient detail and reliability to be used as denominator of the rates. Summing the age-specific rates over all ages, and multiplying this sum by five (the span of the age groups), we can obtain a measure of the "true" level of intensity of migration that is not affected (as in the case of the "crude" rate) by the age structure of the population. This measure, called GMR (gross migraproduction rate) is analogous to the GRR (gross reproduction rate) and can be interpreted as the total number of

Table 13.2
Age-Specific Rates by Sex and Marital Status for Intraregional Migrations, 1980–82

Age	M A L E S				F E M A L E S			
	N. MARRIED	MARRIED	W S D	TOTAL	N. MARRIED	MARRIED	W S D	TOTAL
0-4	24. 93	0. 0	0. 0	24. 93	24. 80	0. 0	0. 0	24. 80
5-9	16. 31	0. 0	0. 0	16. 31	16. 30	0. 0	0. 0	16. 30
10-14	11. 52	0. 0	0. 0	11. 52	11. 53	0. 0	0. 0	11. 53
15-19	9. 72	67. 96	12. 46	10. 08	10. 25	150. 16	27. 16	16. 60
20-24	15. 36	94. 61	35. 02	25. 11	14. 65	77. 59	37. 08	40. 31
25-29	19. 76	50. 07	21. 11	35. 95	21. 93	37. 67	25. 47	33. 76
30-34	19. 19	28. 36	24. 06	25. 55	22. 34	22. 08	19. 90	22. 05
35-39	16. 42	19. 12	20. 87	18. 84	19. 91	14. 93	15. 96	15. 43
40-44	13. 06	13. 17	17. 90	13. 27	16. 75	10. 30	11. 39	10. 91
45-49	11. 26	9. 44	13. 84	9. 72	14. 49	8. 23	9. 41	8. 89
50-54	9. 93	7. 57	11. 61	7. 89	12. 43	7. 52	8. 65	8. 14
55-59	10. 56	7. 48	10. 57	7. 84	12. 15	7. 44	8. 47	8. 14
60-64	11. 66	7. 51	10. 14	7. 96	12. 10	6. 78	8. 04	7. 72
65-69	10. 93	6. 38	9. 67	6. 99	11. 25	5. 90	7. 65	7. 17
70-74	11. 06	5. 65	9. 51	6. 56	10. 73	5. 66	7. 51	7. 19
75-79	12. 69	5. 49	9. 58	6. 89	10. 68	6. 00	8. 12	7. 90
80-84	14. 65	6. 01	10. 23	8. 03	12. 91	7. 77	9. 29	9. 54
85 +	18. 95	6. 77	10. 76	9. 55	14. 57	11. 36	10. 47	11. 07
Total	15. 23	16. 62	12. 08	15. 83	15. 21	18. 65	9. 08	16. 11

Sources: ISTAT, Annuario di Statistiche Demografiche, 1980-1982
         Census of Italy, 1981

migrations expected to be made by an individual over his or her lifetime, if that individual were exposed to the observed migration rates and not exposed to death before reaching the last age group.

For intraregional and interregional migration and for the two sexes separately, the values of GMR are the following:

Type of migration	Males	Females
Intraregional	1.270	1.337
Interregional	0.539	0.507
Total	1.809	1.844

Table 13.3
Age-Specific Rates by Sex and Marital Status for Interregional Migrations, 1980–82

Age	M A L E S				F E M A L E S			
	N. MARRIED	MARRIED	W S D	TOTAL	N. MARRIED	MARRIED	W S D	TOTAL
0-4	9. 25	0. 0	0. 0	9. 25	9. 24	0. 0	0. 0	9. 24
5-9	6. 03	0. 0	0. 0	6. 03	6. 08	0. 0	0. 0	6. 08
10-14	4. 39	0. 0	0. 0	4. 39	4. 40	0. 0	0. 0	4. 40
15-19	7. 19	13. 63	0. 83	7. 22	5. 34	43. 83	1. 06	7. 08
20-24	17. 25	24. 44	4. 05	18. 11	8. 74	22. 86	8. 14	14. 46
25-29	15. 90	15. 07	6. 11	15. 38	13. 37	12. 51	7. 29	12. 61
30-34	12. 71	9. 65	5. 92	10. 17	12. 26	7. 92	5. 72	8. 37
35-39	8. 45	6. 81	5. 96	6. 98	10. 17	5. 49	4. 61	5. 89
40-44	5. 64	4. 86	5. 15	4. 94	9. 52	3. 87	3. 37	4. 33
45-49	4. 31	3. 41	4. 21	3. 51	7. 56	3. 17	3. 01	3. 56
50-54	3. 50	2. 87	3. 20	2. 94	6. 49	3. 13	2. 73	3. 43
55-59	3. 57	3. 14	3. 11	3. 17	6. 65	3. 39	2. 97	3. 67
60-64	3. 98	5. 57	3. 56	3. 60	6. 63	3. 14	3. 08	3. 52
65-69	3. 13	2. 74	3. 22	2. 81	5. 86	2. 62	2. 95	3. 12
70-74	2. 42	2. 28	3. 03	2. 39	4. 24	2. 33	2. 91	2. 85
75-79	1. 98	2. 18	3. 14	2. 39	3. 29	2. 35	2. 88	2. 80
80-84	1. 64	2. 17	3. 02	2. 45	3. 03	2. 43	3. 15	3. 02
85 +	1. 28	1. 77	2. 37	2. 06	2. 54	2. 10	3. 03	2. 91
Total	8. 76	5. 69	3. 53	7. 05	6. 81	6. 46	3. 12	6. 19

Sources: ISTAT, Annuario di Statistiche Demografiche, 1980-1982
         Census of Italy, 1981

The overall level of migration in Italy can be synthetically expressed as slightly less than two movements between municipalities per person over a lifetime. Even if the total level of migration is approximately equal for the two sexes, females have a higher propensity for shorter distance mobility, while males tend to be more mobile over longer distances. More specifically, the figures produced above indicate that, according to the migratory behavior observed in the 1980–82 period, a birth cohort of 100 males (females) would "generate" over their lifetime 127 (134) migrations within the same region and 54 (51) migrations between regions (if, of course, all of them reached the last age group).

Age and Sex Selectivity

As is well known, the selectivity of migration is particularly pronounced with respect to age. The curve of the age-specific migration rates shows a characteristic profile, which exhibits remarkably persistent regularities across time and space (Rogers and Castro, 1981). After a fairly high level following birth, the propensity to migrate drops until age 15. Between the age of 15 and about 25, migration intensity sharply increases and then it once again declines. In old age the migration curve can show three different profiles: a retirement peak, that is, a temporary increase around the normal age of retirement; an upward slope in the older age; or a profile without any specific component for the elderly, that is, continuous decline with advancing age.

Even if the empirical schedules appear to be remarkably similar, the age profile nevertheless exhibits differences in some components of the curve to be related to factors underlying migration. Thus, we can have "young" and "old" profiles, "labor-dominant" or "child-dependent" profiles, profiles with or without the "retirement peak," and so on. Analysis of the age selectivity of migration then represents one of the fundamental approaches to the study of migration.

Let us now compare the age profile of the two categories of internal migration. We can thus study the influence of distance of migration on the age selectivity, and, as we will consider male and female schedules separately, we will be able to assess the impact of sex on this age selectivity. Because of the large differences in the level of intraregional and interregional migration, it is very difficult to visually assess the difference in their age profile. For this reason, we must standardize the area under the migration curve by rescaling the rates to a GMR of unity (GMR=1). The standardized age profiles, that is, those not affected by difference in migration level, are produced in Table 13.4.

The age profile of interregional migration, with a large "jump" from the "low point" to the "high peak," a relatively lower propensity to migrate among infants and adolescents, and an anticipated high peak age, appears to be a more labor-dominant profile than that of intraregional migration. This seems true only for males, however. The female curve appears to be approximately the same in intraregional and interregional migration, except at the older ages.

As far as age selectivity of migration in the older ages is concerned, important differences emerge according to distance moved. In the case of intraregional migration the propensity to migrate, after a very slight decline beyond the age of retirement, tends to increase in the oldest ages. For the case of interregional migration, the curve of the elderly is characterized by a marked surge around retirement age, followed by a gradual decline with the advance of age. The upward slope observed in shorter distance mobility is more pronounced among females, while the retirement peak observed in longer distance mobility is more pronounced among males (Bonaguidi, 1986).

Table 13.4
Standardized Age Profiles of Intraregional and Interregional Migration by Gender, 1980–82

	Male		Female	
	Intra-	Inter-	Intra-	Inter-
Age	regional	regional	regional	regional
0	.115	.100	.110	.110
5	.080	.075	.075	.075
10	.055	.045	.050	.050
15	.035	.040	.040	.050
20	.060	.090	.090	.090
25	.125	.170	.155	.145
30	.130	.120	.110	.110
35	.090	.080	.070	.070
40	.070	.055	.050	.050
45	.045	.040	.040	.040
50	.035	.030	.030	.035
55	.030	.025	.030	.035
60	.030	.030	.030	.040
65	.030	.030	.030	.035
70	.025	.020	.030	.030
75	.025	.020	.030	.030
80	.030	.020	.035	.030
85	.040	.020	.040	.035

Sources: ISTAT, Annuario di Statistiche Demografiche, 1980–1982
         Census of Italy, 1981

THE INFLUENCE OF MARITAL STATUS

Migration is a selective process in relation not only to age and sex, but also to other characteristics, such as marital status. The variation of the propensity to migrate by age is certainly related to changes in marital status which characterize the different stages of the life cycle. In order to study the impact of marital status on the migration age profile, we have produced age specificities for three distinct categories of marital status: never married, married, and WSD (widowed, separated and divorced). These three curves are shown for intraregional (Table 13.2) and interregional migration (Table 13.3) and for both sexes.

A first general conclusion that may be derived from this variety of age profiles is that migratory behavior is markedly affected by marital status. More specifically, among young adults married people have much greater mobility than the never married and those widowed, separated, or divorced, while after the age of about 30, married people become less mobile than others. This is true for males as well as for females and for short-distance migration as well as for long-distance migration, but the influence of marital status on the migration age curve seems to be stronger among males than among females and for short-distance rather than long-distance migration. One can note that among males who make an interregional move the curve for the never married is relatively close to that of the married. In other words, the impact of marital status on migratory behavior tends to be minor in the more economically induced migrations (males over longer distances).

CHANGES IN INTERREGIONAL MIGRATION PATTERNS

The migration behavior of the Italian population has particularly changed in the last decade. Not only has there been a marked drop in the interregional migration propensity, but also there has been a profound reversal in the pattern of the interregional redistribution of the population. Table 13.5 presents, for each of the twenty regions of Italy, the rate of interregional in- and out-migration as well as the rate of net interregional migration for the 1970–72 and 1980–82 periods. During 1970–72 there were eleven regions with a negative migration balance, eight of which were located in the south of the country (including the Islands), two in the center (Marche and Umbria), and one in the northeast (Trentino-Alto Adige). The southern regions experienced the highest negative values of net migration rates. In two of these (Basilicata and Calabria) the migration losses were particularly heavy. (The net migration rate was −14 and −12 per 1,000, respectively). Among the regions with a positive migration balance, the most attractive were

Table 13.5
Interregional In-Migration, Out-Migration, and Net Migration Rates for Each Region, 1970–72 and 1980–82

	1970–1972			1980–1982		
Regions	IN	OUT	NET	IN	OUT	NET
1 – Piedmont	19. 07	12. 16	6. 91	8. 20	9. 24	−1. 03
2 – Valle d' Aosta	20. 30	15. 03	5. 27	11. 59	10. 64	0. 95
3 – Lombardy	13. 96	7. 90	6. 06	6. 79	6. 26	0. 53
4 – Trentino A. A.	7. 54	8. 74	−1. 20	4. 76	5. 06	−0. 30
5 – Veneto	7. 41	6. 73	0. 69	4. 73	3. 77	0. 96
6 – Friuli V. G.	10. 96	9. 20	1. 75	7. 51	5. 75	1. 76
7 – Liguria	16. 07	12. 21	3. 87	9. 93	9. 50	0. 43
8 – Emilia-Rom.	9. 21	6. 99	2. 22	7. 36	4. 67	2. 69
9 – Tuscany	10. 03	6. 68	3. 35	7. 07	4. 68	2. 39
10 – Umbria	8. 80	11. 77	−2. 98	8. 33	6. 06	2. 27
11 – Marche	8. 07	9. 63	−1. 56	6. 60	5. 04	1. 56
12 – Lazio	12. 40	8. 78	3. 61	8. 13	6. 77	1. 37
13 – Abruzzi	9. 54	12. 48	−2. 94	8. 49	7. 55	0. 93
14 – Molise	11. 83	17. 19	−5. 36	9. 97	11. 74	−1. 75
15 – Campania	6. 30	12. 35	−6. 05	4. 81	7. 61	−2. 79
16 – Puglia	7. 90	13. 76	−5. 86	6. 27	7. 36	−1. 09
17 – Basilicata	11. 39	25. 33	−13. 94	8. 67	13. 60	−4. 93
18 – Calabria	8. 02	19. 73	−11. 71	7. 49	10. 96	−3. 48
19 – Sicily	6. 41	13. 17	−6. 76	5. 44	6. 84	−1. 40
20 – Sardinia	8. 53	12. 91	−4. 38	6. 20	6. 94	−0. 74
I T A L Y	10. 53	10. 53	0. 00	6. 77	6. 77	0. 00

Sources: ISTAT, Annuario di Statistiche Demografiche, 1970–72 and 1980–1982
    Census of Italy, 1971 and 1981

those located in the northwest (Piedmont, Lombardy, Liguria), but Tuscany and Lazio also experienced relatively high levels of net in-migration.

Between 1970–72 and 1980–82 all the southern regions considerably improved their migration balance, even if they continued to experience the highest migration losses. The most attractive regions in the first period (1970–72) experienced a particularly pronounced decline in terms of attractiveness. The central regions of Umbria and Marche also improved their migration balance, now showing a positive net migration rate. Currently, three regions located in the northeast and center (Emilia-Romagna, Tuscany, and Umbria) are experiencing the highest net migration rates. The migratory gains of these regions are much lower, however, than those observed in the most attractive regions (northwestern) ten years before.

Looking at the evolution of net migration, we may conclude that in Italy there is a clear trend toward a spatially more balanced migration pattern, with gainers and losers of the earlier period tending toward zero net migration in the later.

As long as we limit our analysis to the evolution of net migration, we will not know much about the changes in the interregional migration pattern. It is indeed very important to know whether a region's decline (or rise) in migration attractiveness, measured by the net migration rate, is due to an increase (or decrease) in the propensity to leave or to a decrease (or increase) in the capacity to attract.

If we look at the two components of migration, we find that the improvement of the migration balance observed in all regions of the south and in some regions of the center is due mainly to a more rapid decline in out-migration rather than to increased in-migration. The decline of the net migration rate observed in the regions that were the most attractive in 1970–72 generally results from a more rapid decline in the in-migration component. In other words, the improving regions (mostly in the south) are less undesirable rather than more attractive, whereas the declining regions are simply less attractive rather than more undesirable. Since fewer out-migrants imply fewer in-migrants, these results are simply two sides of the same coin.

AGE AND REGIONAL MIGRATION PATTERNS

In the previous section we discussed the characteristics of the new migration pattern in Italy. However, as long as we consider the aggregate flows without considering the age of the migrants, we do not know much about the more recent features of Italian internal migration. Indeed, the demographic and socioeconomic impact of migration on the population of origin and destination depends largely on the age composition of the flows.

To demonstrate the usefulness of introducing age into the study of the internal migration system, let us consider migration by age between the four Italian macroregions (northwest, northeast, center, and south).[1] In Table 13.6 we have reproduced the age-specific rates of in-migration and out-migration as well as net migration for each macroregion. The rates refer to the male population only.

Table 13.6

Age-Specific Rates (per 1,000) for In-Migration (I), Out-Migration (O), and Net Migration (I-O) in Italian Macroregions, Males, 1980–82

AGE	NORTH-WEST			NORTH-EAST			CENTRE			SOUTH		
	I	O	I - O	I	O	I - O	I	O	I - O	I	O	I - O
0–4	9.53	10.76	−1.23	14.05	5.33	8.73	12.51	5.97	6.54	4.66	6.74	2.08
5–9	5.23	6.98	−1.75	7.61	3.27	4.35	7.18	3.90	3.28	2.97	4.31	−1.34
10–14	3.70	4.67	−0.96	5.35	2.31	3.04	5.22	2.94	2.28	2.24	3.28	−1.04
15–19	9.25	5.32	3.92	13.24	2.68	10.56	12.98	3.99	8.99	5.83	9.14	−3.31
20–24	21.47	12.87	8.60	30.51	7.55	22.98	29.98	12.46	17.51	14.38	22.31	−7.93
25–29	15.10	12.24	2.86	22.30	7.42	14.88	21.85	10.71	11.14	11.35	16.28	−4.93
30–34	8.28	9.39	−1.10	12.55	5.14	7.40	12.33	6.46	5.88	6.86	9.29	−2.43
35–39	4.80	6.94	−2.14	7.09	3.66	3.44	7.24	4.52	2.72	4.33	5.41	−1.09
40–44	3.04	4.56	−1.51	4.75	2.66	2.09	4.69	3.26	1.43	3.03	3.84	−0.82
45–49	2.34	3.17	−0.93	3.53	1.95	1.58	3.36	2.40	0.96	2.10	2.68	−0.58
50–54	1.85	2.72	−0.87	2.83	1.63	1.20	2.64	1.88	0.76	1.69	2.18	0.49
55–59	1.70	3.37	−1.67	2.37	1.45	0.92	2.23	2.06	0.18*	1.49	2.02	−0.52
60–64	1.78	4.70	−2.92	2.40	1.36	1.05	2.22	2.07	0.15	1.51	1.92	−0.41
65–69	1.68	2.83	−1.14	2.29	1.14	1.15	2.23	1.73	0.49	1.45	1.78	−0.33
70–74	1.71	2.04	−0.33	2.35	0.99	1.35	2.28	1.49	0.79	1.48	1.73	−0.26
75–79	2.00	1.70	0.30	2.85	1.05	1.80	2.67	1.47	1.20	1.70	1.92	−0.22
80–84	2.31	1.72	0.59	3.26	1.27	1.99	3.00	1.27	1.73	1.87	1.99	−0.12
85 +	1.53	1.50	0.03	2.15	0.92	1.23	1.91	1.28	0.64	1.21	1.23	−0.02
TOTAL	6.38	6.24	0.14	9.33	3.33	6.00	8.99	4.50	4.49	4.78	6.88	−2.10

Sources: ISTAT, Annuario di Statistiche Demografiche, 1980–1982
Census of Italy, 1981

These data clearly document the existence of three interesting territorial migration patterns.

The northwest experiences migratory gains in the ages of initial entry into the labor force (15 to 30) and migratory losses at all other ages. These losses are more pronounced at the beginning of postlabor ages because of the existence of a marked retirement peak in the out-migration curve. The overall level of mobility is almost exactly the same for in-migration as for out-migration. In this macroregion, therefore, the age distribution of gains and losses is due exclusively to the difference in the age profile of the two migration components.

The migration pattern of the northeast and center appears to be quite similar. The curve of in-migration is higher at all ages than that of out-migration, so that these two macroregions gain population at all ages, with the largest surplus in the younger labor force ages (15 to 34).

The migration pattern of the south is the complete opposite of those just discussed. In this case the curve of out-migration is above the curve of in-migration, so that this area experiences migratory losses at all ages, with the heaviest losses in the younger labor force ages (15 to 34).

These results shed some light on the current pattern of internal migration in Italy. The northwestern area of the country, even with diminished net migration, has maintained a capacity to attract and retain the demographically and economically most important segments of population. Thus, the general decline in migration to the northwest in recent years has been confined mostly to individuals in the mid- to late labor force ages and, in particular, in postlabor force ages. The southern area, even if it has experienced a general improvement in its migration balance, continues to send large shares of its "best" population to the other areas, demonstrating that this area is still largely dependent economically on the rest of the country. If we considered only the migration exchanges of the economically and demographically most significant groups of the population, the migration pattern in Italy would not have changed much compared to the past.

INTERREGIONAL ORIGIN-DESTINATION FLOWS

If we do not consider the migration flows by origin and destination, we, of course, neglect a fundamental aspect of the internal migration pattern. In this section, we will briefly discuss the changes in the matrix of interregional origin-destination flows over the last decade.

The region-to-region matrix for the 1970–72 and 1980–82 periods are shown in Table 13.7. We will limit our analysis to the distribution by destination of out-migrants from each macroregion. The distribution of interregional flows by destination has changed considerably during the period considered. There has been a marked decline in the share of migration from the southern regions toward the traditional destinations of the northwest (Piedmont, Lombardy, Liguria), while there has been an increase in the importance of migration originating in southern regions destined for the northeast and central regions.

If there has been a marked decrease in the importance of the northwest as a destination for migration from the south, there has been, on the contrary, a marked increase in the importance of the south as a destination for migration originating in the northwest. A rise in the share of southern destinations is also observable for migration from the northern and central regions. The previously noted improving and declining migration conditions, in the south and northwest, respectively, are associated with marked changes in the structure of migration exchanges between these two regions which have characterized the recent history of internal migration in Italy.

Table 13.7
Interregional Migration in Italy, 1970–72 and 1980–82

1970 to 1972
number of persons:
destination

origin	Northwest	Northeast	Central	South	Total
Northwest	0	27611	20728	58565	106904
Northeast	28896	0	12816	12703	54415
Central	21214	13566	0	28840	63620
South	147928	20880	53955	0	222763
Total	198038	62057	87499	100108	447702

percent:
destination

origin	Northwest	Northeast	Central	South	Total
Northwest	0.0%	6.2%	4.6%	13.1%	23.9%
Northeast	6.5%	0.0%	2.9%	2.8%	12.2%
Central	4.7%	3.0%	0.0%	6.4%	14.2%
South	33.0%	4.7%	12.1%	0.0%	49.8%
Total	44.2%	13.9%	19.5%	22.4%	100.0%

1980 to 1982
number of persons:
destination

origin	Northwest	Northeast	Central	South	Total
Northwest	0	18837	16723	53582	89142
Northeast	12988	0	8755	12770	34513
Central	12252	8914	0	24640	45806
South	64898	23506	39745	0	128149
Total	90138	51257	65223	90992	297610

percent:
destination

origin	Northwest	Northeast	Central	South	Total
Northwest	0.0%	6.3%	5.6%	18.0%	30.0%
Northeast	4.4%	0.0%	2.9%	4.3%	11.6%
Central	4.1%	3.0%	0.0%	8.3%	15.4%
South	21.8%	7.9%	13.4%	0.0%	43.1%
Total	30.3%	17.2%	21.9%	30.6%	100.0%

Sources: ISTAT, Annuario di Statistiche Demografiche, 1970–72 and 1980–1982
        Census of Italy, 1971 and 1981

AGE AND SCALE OF REGIONAL PREFERENCE

One way to obtain a measure of the spatial orientation of interregional flows is to calculate a ''preference index'' for each possible region of destination. To compute this preference index for a given region, say *k*, we may use the following formula (Wunsch and Termote, 1978):

$$I_k = \frac{\sum_h (M_{hk} - \bar{M}_{hk})}{\sum_i \sum_j M_{ij} - \sum_j M_{kj} - \sum_i M_{ik}}$$

(for all h's such that $M_{hk} > \bar{M}_{hk}$

According to this formula, the observed volume of migration from region h to region k (M_{hk}) is compared with the "expected" (based on regional population and total migration) level of migration ($\bar{M}_{hk}$) from h to k. The larger the difference between these two figures, the more out-migrants from h prefer to migrate to k. By relating the sum over all regions of origin of these positive differences between observed and expected migration ($M_{hk} > \bar{M}_{hk}$) to the total volume of interregional migration (excluding out-migration from k and in-migration to k), we obtain what may be considered a measure of general preference for region k. By computing this preference index for all possible regions of destination and considering migration for distinct age groups, we have a measure of the influence of age on regional migration preferences.

We have adopted four broad age groups, which are relevant from a socioeconomic point of view: the prelabor force age group (0 to 14); the initial labor force age group (15 to 34); the mid- and late labor force age group (35 to 59); and the post-labor force age group (60 and over). Table 13.8 shows the

Table 13.8
Migration Preference Indices by Region and Age, 1980–82

Regions	0-14	15-34	35-59	60+	Total
1 - Piedmont	.024	.029	.023	.039	.028
2 - Valle d' Aosta	.001	.001	.001	.001	.001
3 - Lombardy	.034	.040	.026	.036	.036
4 - Trentino A. A.	.003	.002	.003	.004	.003
5 - Veneto	.013	.010	.018	.020	.013
6 - Friuli V. G.	.005	.006	.007	.007	.006
7 - Liguria	.007	.008	.015	.038	.010
8 - Emilia-Rom.	.010	.011	.012	.017	.011
9 - Tuscany	.013	.013	.013	.016	.014
10 - Umbria	.006	.006	.010	.014	.007
11 - Marche	.007	.006	.009	.014	.007
12 - Lazio	.028	.028	.037	.046	.030
13 - Abruzzi	.008	.007	.011	.014	.009
14 - Molise	.003	.003	.003	.004	.003
15 - Campania	.017	.019	.013	.013	.015
16 - Puglia	.016	.015	.011	.013	.013
17 - Basilicata	.004	.003	.004	.003	.004
18 - Calabria	.010	.010	.007	.005	.009
19 - Sicily	.022	.021	.014	.012	.018
20 - Sardinia	.008	.008	.006	.003	.007

Sources: ISTAT, Annuario di Statistiche Demografiche, 1980-1982
Census of Italy, 1981

preference index for each region and for each age group. From these data we may derive some interesting conclusions. There is a considerable increase in the preference for Liguria for people in their preretirement age and, particularly, in retirement age. In fact, this region experiences an impressive upward shift in the regional hierarchy when the 60 and over group is considered. This confirms the important role that Liguria plays in elderly interregional migration in Italy. Lombardy, Piedmont, and Lazio have large indices in all age groups; for Lombardy the highest share of national in-migration not expected but received is observable at the initial ages of the labor force, and for Piedmont and Lazio this occurs in older ages.

In general, the southern regions experience a decline in the scale of preference from younger to older ages, whereas preference for the northern and central regions tends to increase with age.

CONCLUSIONS

Our analysis has illustrated the salient characteristics of Italy's internal migration and its temporal evolution. As far as the recent changes in migration behavior are concerned, there has been, first of all, a marked decline in the general propensity to migrate, especially over long distances. Second, the impact of migration on the spatial redistribution of population has also changed considerably. Indeed, during the last decade, together with a decline in the interregional migration rate, we have observed a decline in the "efficiency" of migration in terms of population redistribution. In other words interregional migration tends to be a much more balanced phenomenon at present, relative to ten years ago. Third, in this new picture we can observe a shift in the most attractive areas toward the northeastern and central part of the country from the regions (northwest) that had been the favored destinations in the relatively recent past. A remarkable improvement of the migration conditions of the southern area is another characteristic of Italy's current internal migration pattern. But, as results from the analysis of the age-specific migration suggests, the northwestern area is still relatively dominant in attracting the economically and demographically more important population. A large share of this population still leaves the south toward the north and center. Finally, the territorial pattern of interregional migration tends, as expected, to be influenced by age and other characteristics of migrants.

All these results present interesting implications. The substitution process of long-distance migration by short-distance migration leads to the conclusion that, on the whole, the influence of economic factors as determinants of internal migration is declining, because short-distance moves appear to be less economically induced than those over a long distance. The existence of a more balanced migration pattern does not necessarily mean a reduction in the traditional spatial disparities within the country, because the heavy net losses of the young labor force still experienced by the south once more demonstrates that the southern economy is still rather weak and dependent on the rest of Italy. In the future, given the current trends of natural increase, the demographic weight of the country will shift toward the South. Our results introduce important implications for north-south dualism, which continues to be one of the crucial issues in the country.

Because of the high variability of migration with the demographic and socioeconomic characteristics, the evolution of the migratory phenomenon also reflects the influence of changes in the demographic and socioeconomic structure of the population. For example, the aging process itself leads to a decline in the overall mobility level and an increasing share of migration made by older persons. This latter fact in turn affects the entire migration picture because elderly migration presents different characteristics and is induced by different factors than is migration of younger people.

In conclusion, the internal migration pattern in Italy shows significant structural changes to be related to the evolution of the socioeconomic conditions experienced by the various areas of the country, but it retains many of its traditional features. The most important of these aspects is that migration is still an expression of the inherent imbalance between north and south which has characterized the migration history of the country over the centuries.

NOTE

1. The composition of these macroregions is as follows:

Northwest: Liguria, Lombardy, Piedmont, Valle D'Aosta

Northeast: Emilia-Romagna, Friuli-Venezia Giulia, Trentino-Alto Adige, Veneto

Center: Lazio, Marche, Tuscany, Umbria

South: Abruzzi, Basilicata, Calabria, Campania, Molise, Puglia, Sardinia, Sicily

REFERENCES

Bonaguidi, A. (ed.). 1985. *Migrazioni e Demografia regionale in Italia*. Milano: Franco Angeli.

———. 1987. *Alcuni aspetti meno noti delle migrazioni in Italia*. Report 7, Dipartimento di Statistica e Matematica Applicata all'Economia, Universita di Pisa.

———. 1988. "Migration of the Elderly in Italy." In A. Rogers and W. Serow, eds., *Migration of the Elderly: An International Comparative Study*. Boulder, Colo.: University of Colorado, Institute of Behavioral Science.

Golini, A. 1974. *Distribuzione della popolazione, migrazioni interne e urbanizzazione in Italia*. Istituto di Demografia, Universita di Roma.

Rogers, A., and L. Castro. 1981. *Model Migration Schedules*. RR 81-30. Laxenburg, Austria: International Institute for Applied System Analysis.

Termote, M., A. Golini, and B. Cantalini. 1985. *Interprovincial Migration in Italy During the Seventies*. Roma: Istituto di Ricerche sulla Popolazione.

Wunsch, G.J., and H. Termote. 1978. *Introduction to Demographic Analysis: Principles and Methods*. New York: Plenum Press.

14

JAPAN

Atsushi Otomo

Internal migration of population in Japan has exhibited different patterns not only of migratory flows, but also of spatial mobility over time since 1950. Keeping pace with the changes in fertility and mortality of the Japanese population, the structures of regional population also have been changed in recent decades. Furthermore, there exist significant differences in the structures of regional population owing to differences in selectivity of migration. In this chapter, various aspects of internal migration of population for the periods chiefly after 1955 are described briefly.

DATA ON MIGRATION

In Japan internal migration data are derived from two kinds of data sources: Resident registers and national population censuses. Resident registers refer to movement on an intercommunal basis, or between minor administrative areas, or Shi, Ku, Machi, and Mura, and have been collected and published monthly and annually by the Statistics Bureau, Management and Coordination Agency, Government of Japan since 1954. The data present the number of migrants who changed their residence across the boundary of a minor administrative area, by sex and by prefecture. Data on age and other attributes of the migrants are not available.

On the other hand, migration data derived from the question on "place of usual residence one-year before" in the 1960 population census, as well as the questions on "time of last move" and "place of previous residence" in the 1970 and 1980 censuses, show movement on a residential basis, or all spatial movements in terms of residential change during the one-year period before each census. The data present the number of migrants by sex, age, marital status, educational attainment, labor force status, industry, occupation, employment status, and household status, and by various types of administrative divisions and other statistical areas such as major metropolitan areas and densely inhabited districts. Above all, for the 1980 census which provides migration data for a five-year period as well as for a one-year period, the number of both migrant population and of migrant households is available. All data derived from the national population censuses are published by the Statistics Bureau, Management and Coordination Agency. In addition, the censuses of 1920, 1930, and 1950 provide migration data based on place of birth.

Besides the migration data mentioned above, a certain kind of migration data derived from national housing surveys and national employment status surveys, which have been conducted quinquennially by the Statistics Bureau, are available periodically. Particularly, the 1983 Housing Survey furnished data on reasons for migration of household heads on a residential basis. Data from the employment surveys present the number of employed persons who migrated between regions during the one-year period before the survey. In addition, migration data can be obtained through the number of students newly enrolled and of graduates tabulated in the basic statistical survey on school enrollment conducted annually by the Ministry of Education. Furthermore, the ad hoc survey on reasons for migration undertaken by the National Land Agency, Government of Japan, as of 1982, supplies data on reasons for migration of people who changed their residence across the boundary of minor administrative areas.

PRINCIPAL POPULATION MOVEMENTS

The National Level

According to the 1980 census, 11,178,483 persons (10,963,742 persons aged 1 year and over) changed their residence during the one-year period from October 1, 1979, to September 30, 1980. For the period 1969 to 1970 a total of 12,534,721 persons (12,348,194 persons aged 1 year and over) shifted their residence. The comparable number of migrants between 1959 and 1960 was 7,268,900 persons. The rate of overall migrants over the age of 1 was recorded as 7.9 percent for 1960, 12.0 percent for 1970, and 9.5 percent for 1980. Therefore, not only the volume but also the intensity of overall migration increased remarkably until 1970 but declined thereafter.

The trends mentioned above can be observed not only for intercommunal migration (the moves within prefecture), but also for interprefectural migration (the moves between prefectures) during the period 1959–60 to 1979–80 (Table 14.1).

Table 14.2 shows the number and rate of migration between minor administrative areas, or Shi, Ku, Machi, and Mura, derived from the resident register. The number and rate of intercommunal migration had shown increasing trends since 1956, but they decreased after the mid-1970s when a peak was reached. The same table indicated similar trends for inteprefectural migration.

For the periods prior to 1954, the proportions of lifetime migrants derived

Table 14.1
Number and Proportion of Migrants by Different Spatial Units, 1959–60 to 1979–80

| | Population aged 1 yr. and over | Overall migrants | Migrants aged one year and over | Inter-communal migrants | | |
			Intra-communal migrants (With-in Shi, Ku, and Mura)	Total	Within a pref-ecture	Between prefec-tures [1]
			Number (1,000 persons)			
1959–60[2]	91,759	7,269	2,059	2,611	2,582	17
1969–70	102,767	12,348	4,832	3,712	3,775	29
1979–80	115,403	10,964	4,411	3,471	3,025	50
			Proportion			
1959–60[2]	100.0	7.9	2.2	2.8	2.8	0.0
1969–70	100.0	12.0	4.8	3.6	3.7	0.0
1979–80	100.0	9.5	3.8	3.0	2.6	0.0

1) : Inter-prefectural migrants.
2) : Excludes for Okinawa prefecture.

Source: Statistics Bureau. 1982. 1980 Population Census of Japan, Vol. 2
        Statistics Bureau. 1972. 1970 Population Census of Japan, Vol. 2
        Statistics Bureau. 1968. Summary of the Results of 1960 Population
        Census of Japan.

Table 14.2
Number and Rate of Migration between Shi, Ku, Machi, and Mura (intercommunal migration), 1954–85

Year	Number (1,000 persons)			Rate of migration		
	Total	Within a prefecture	Between prefectures	Total	Within a prefecture	Between prefectures
1954	5,498	3,145	2,352	6.27	3.59	2.68
1955	5,141	2,914	2,227	5.80	3.29	2.51
1956	4,860	2,738	2,122	5.43	3.06	2.37
1957	5,268	2,888	2,380	5.83	3.20	2.64
1958	5,294	2,914	2,381	5.81	3.20	2.61
1959	5,358	2,915	2,443	5.82	3.17	2.65
1960	5,653	2,973	2,680	6.09	3.20	2.89
1961	6,012	3,060	2,952	6.42	3.27	3.15
1962	6,580	3,277	3,303	6.95	3.46	3.49
1963	6,937	3,464	3,472	7.26	3.62	3.63
1964	7,257	3,622	3,634	7.51	3.75	3.76
1965	7,381	3,688	3,692	7.56	3.78	3.78
1966	7,432	3,747	3,684	7.55	3.81	3.74
1967	7,479	3,718	3,761	7.51	3.73	3.78
1968	7,775	3,838	3,937	7.72	3.81	3.91
1969	8,126	4,010	4,116	7.97	3.93	4.04
1970	8,273	4,038	4,235	8.02	3.92	4.11
1971	8,360	4,103	4,257	8.00	3.92	4.07
1972	8,350	4,193	4,157	7.88	3.96	3.92
1973	8,539	4,304	4,234	7.87	3.97	3.90
1974	8,027	4,094	3,932	7.30	3.72	3.58
1975	7,544	3,846	3,698	6.78	3.46	3.32
1976	7,392	3,827	3,568	6.57	3.40	3.17
1977	7,395	3,828	3,568	6.51	3.37	3.14
1978	7,292	3,804	3,487	6.37	3.32	3.04
1979	7,295	3,826	3,469	6.32	3.31	3.00
1980	7,067	3,711	3,356	6.07	3.19	2.88
1981	6,902	3,584	3,318	5.89	3.06	2.83
1982	6,852	3,564	3,288	5.81	3.02	2.79
1983	6,674	3,478	3,196	5.62	2.93	2.69
1984	6,589	3,422	3,137	5.49	2.86	2.62
1985	6,482	3,365	3,117	5.39	2.80	2.59

Note: The figures for 1954 to 1972 excludes for Okinawa prefecture.

Source: Statistics Bureau. 1975-1986. Annual Reports on the Internal
        Migration in Japan, derived from the Basic Resident Registers,
        1974-1985.

from place-of-birth data in the previous population censuses indicate that inter-communal mobility increased for the period from 1920 to 1930 but declined from 1930 to 1950, although the mobility within a prefecture continued to decrease through the two periods (Table 14.3).

As period-migration data are unavailable for periods prior to 1954, net migration rates, which were calculated on the basis of prefectural populations derived from quinquennial population censuses and vital statistics since 1920, indicate time-series trends of mobility of population throughout the quinquennial periods

Table 14.3
Number and Proportion of Lifetime Migrants by Different Spatial Units, 1920, 1930, and 1950

Year	Population 1)	Total	Between Shi, Ku, Machi & Mura within a prefecture	Between prefectures	Abroad
		Number	(1,000 persons)		
1920	55,391	20,338	11,899	8,275	164
1930	63,872	24,364	13,292	10,431	641
1950	71,998	29,641	14,946	12,964	1,731
		Proportion			
1920	100.0	36.7	21.5	14.9	0.3
1930	100.0	38.1	20.8	16.3	1.0
1950	100.0	35.7	18.0	15.6	2.1

1) : Excludes for Okinawa prefecture.

Source: Statistics Bureau, 1955. 1950 Population Census of Japan, Vol. 8.

since 1920 (Table 14.4). Current mobilities, measured by positive net balance in interprefectural migrations since 1970, show lower levels than those in the 1920s and 1930s.

Among overall migrants men exceed women in number, although among total population the reverse is true. The sex ratio of overall migrants was 112.2 for

Table 14.4
Number and Rate of Interprefectural Net Migration, 1920–80

Period	Net-migrants	Population	Rate
1920 - 1925	2,373	57,850	4.1
1925 - 1930	2,381	62,093	3.8
1930 - 1935	3,088	66,852	4.6
1947 - 1950	5,694	80,651	7.1
	(3,416)		(4.2)
1950 - 1955	4,962	87,096	5.7
1955 - 1960	5,613	92,189	6.1
1960 - 1965	6,300	96,755	6.5
1965 - 1970	5,194	101,937	5.1
1970 - 1975	3,414	108,302	3.2
1975 - 1980	2,428	114,500	2.1

Note: The figures in parentheses are those estimated for 5 years on the basis of the figures for 1947-1950.

Source: Okazaki, Y., "Jinkoido," 1980 Population Census Monograph
          Series No. 2.

Table 14.5
Sex Ratios of Migrants by Different Spatial Units, 1959–60 to 1979–80

Period	Population aged 1 year and over	Overall migrants	Intra-communal migrants (Within Shi, Ku, Machi & Mura)	Inter-communal migrants		
				Total	Within a prefecture	Between prefectures 1)
1959–602)	96.4	112.2	99.3	117.9	107.0	130.5
1969–70	96.3	110.1	100.3	117.0	105.3	128.8
1979–80	96.7	107.7	98.4	114.9	103.0	129.3

1) : Inter-prefectural migrants.
2) : Excludes for Okinawa prefecture.
Source: See Table 14.1.

1959–60; however, it declined to 110.1 for 1969–70 and to 107.7 for 1979–80. Such a trend in the sex ratio can be observed for intercommunal migrants which is higher than that for overall migrants. On the contrary, the sex ratio of interprefectural migrants, which is much higher than intercommunal migrants, did not show as much change over time (Table 14.5).

Table 14.6
Age Composition of Nonmigrants and Overall Migrants, 1959–60 to 1979–80 (percent)

Age	Non-migrants			Overall migrants		
	1959–601	1969–70	1979–80	1959–60	1969–70	1979–80
Both sexes2)	100.0	100.0	100.0	100.0	100.0	100.0
1 – 14	29.9	46.5	45.7	16.1	17.7	20.6
15 – 19	9.4	13.7	11.1	18.1	12.1	9.3
20 – 24	8.0	10.2	7.8	20.6	20.6	14.3
25 – 29	8.2	4.2	5.6	17.3	17.1	15.8
30 – 39	14.7	7.0	7.4	14.7	16.9	20.5
40 – 49	11.1	6.7	6.8	6.2	7.8	8.9
50 – 59	9.0	4.6	6.8	3.9	4.1	5.2
60 +	9.6	7.0	8.8	3.0	3.8	5.4

1) : Excludes for Okinawa prefecture.
2) : Excludes for population under 1 year old.
Source: See Table 14.1.

When we compare age compositions between nonmigrants and overall migrants as of 1959–60, we see that the proportions of young-adult age groups are remarkably large for overall migrants, while that of children is distinguishably large for nonmigrants. However, the proportions of young-adult age groups decreased and those of older adult age groups increased over time (Table 14.6).

Interregional Migration in Metropolitan-Nonmetropolitan Context

Interregional migration in Japan focuses on migration between metropolitan and nonmetropolitan regions. According to Table 14.7, showing migratory flows between metropolitan regions and each nonmetropolitan region for one-year

Table 14.7
Migratory Flows to and from Metropolitan Regions for Each Nonmetropolitan Region, 1960, 1970, and 1980

Origin or destination	To metropolitan regions			From metropolitan regions		
	1960	1970	1980	1960	1970	1980
Number						
Hokkaido	39,842	105,270	49,851	19,031	45,945	45,508
Kita-tohoku	55,727	93,640	54,553	18,019	46,973	43,561
Minami-tohoku	104,276	106,458	66,300	34,604	68,116	60,950
Kita-kanto	110,546	109,135	83,882	52,105	112,795	108,305
Hokuriku	87,863	99,365	65,221	38,864	65,031	58,892
Tosan	109,206	120,875	96,808	59,794	102,069	92,154
Higashi-kinki	60,115	75,805	61,662	37,968	88,282	88,379
Sanin	30,573	33,301	17,089	11,362	21,938	17,014
Sanyo	80,028	100,237	71,730	35,717	82,413	67,619
Shikoku	87,239	90,363	50,531	30,481	63,205	47,605
Kita-kyushu	125,112	177,796	87,101	35,415	97,911	83,739
Minami-kyushu	282,105	150,347	63,138	15,117	74,840	64,956
Okinawa	*	*	21,247	*	*	18,144
Percentage of total						
Hokkaido	55.4	70.7	62.0	35.7	61.7	60.6
Kita-tohoku	55.7	68.9	60.3	52.8	66.1	64.5
Minami-tohoku	72.2	72.2	64.1	58.5	52.5	51.5
Kita-kanto	86.1	81.5	75.3	74.7	75.6	78.0
Hokuriku	80.1	77.9	72.2	73.8	74.7	72.4
Tosan	83.8	77.9	75.7	72.0	71.9	76.5
Higashi-kinki	83.8	76.1	74.6	75.7	75.5	81.7
Sanin	64.3	64.5	55.7	49.2	61.4	56.1
Sanyo	59.9	62.3	55.8	43.6	51.0	54.9
Shikoku	70.2	74.0	66.8	59.6	69.3	67.8
Kita-kyushu	44.7	66.2	54.5	30.4	56.9	53.8
Minami-kyushu	51.5	70.3	56.9	36.9	61.3	57.9
Okinawa	*	*	70.6	*	*	66.2

Source: See Table 14.2.

periods as of 1960, 1970, and 1980, more than 50 percent of the outmigrants from each nonmetropolitan region, except for Kita-kyushu, moved to metropolitan regions in 1960. On the other hand, more than 30 percent of the in-migrants to each nonmetropolitan region came from metropolitan regions during the year prior to 1960.

In 1970, the number of migrants from and to metropolitan regions increased distinctly in each nonmetropolitan region, except for the in-migrants to Minami-kyushu. On the contrary, the proportion of out-migrants to metropolitan regions decreased in the above-mentioned nonmetropolitan regions while it increased in the other nonmetropolitan regions. In addition, the proportion of in-migrants from metropolitan regions expanded in each nonmetropolitan region, except for Minami-tohoku and Tosan where it decreased slightly. The increase in the proportion was remarkable in remote nonmetropolitan regions such as Hokkaido, Kita-kyushu, and Minami-kyushu.

In 1980, however, the number of migrants from and to metropolitan regions decreased in each nonmetropolitan area, excluding Higashi-kinki where the number of in-migrants increased slightly. The proportion of migrants from and to metropolitan regions among all migrants also decreased in each nonmetropolitan region, except for Kita-kanto, Tosan, and Higashi-kinki where the proportion of the in-migrants from metropolitan regions increased.

INTERPREFECTURAL MIGRATION IN THE METROPOLITAN-NONMETROPOLITAN CONTEXT

According to Table 14.8, which shows the number of interprefectural migrants between metropolitan regions and nonmetropolitan regions over time, the number of migrants from nonmetropolitan regions and that from metropolitan to nonmetropolitan increased until the early 1970s, but they have decreased thereafter. Moreover, the number of migrants from nonmetropolitan to metropolitan regions exceeded that from metropolitan to nonmetropolitan until the early 1970s. However, during the late 1970s, the excess in metropolitan regions decreased significantly. In the 1980s, the increase in metropolitan regions began to resume, although both numbers of migrants from nonmetropolitan to metropolitan areas and of those from metropolitan to nonmetropolitan areas continued to decrease.

WHO MOVES

Demographic Characteristics

Selectivity in intercommunal migration between sexes has shown male dominance since 1955 (Table 14.9). In addition, male dominance in the migratory flows is greater in the interprefectural migration or long-distance migration than in the intercommunal migration within a prefecture or short-distance migration.

Table 14.8
Number of Interprefectural Migrants between Metropolitan and Nonmetropolitan Areas, 1954-85 (1,000 persons)

Year	Total	Metro to Non-metro	Non-metro to Metro	Metro to Metro	Non-metro to Non-metro	Excess in Metro
1954	2,352	403	788	588	573	385
1955	2,226	385	738	563	540	353
1956	2,123	342	743	539	499	401
1957	2,380	359	866	593	562	507
1958	2,382	393	815	618	556	422
1959	2,442	389	880	649	524	491
1960	2,679	406	999	706	568	593
1961	2,953	449	1,104	794	606	655
1962	3,303	536	1,184	919	664	648
1963	3,472	589	1,209	995	679	620
1964	3,633	639	1,217	1,089	688	578
1965	3,692	705	1,186	1,116	685	481
1966	3,684	732	1,138	1,144	670	406
1967	3,761	750	1,154	1,180	677	404
1968	3,937	784	1,202	1,241	710	418
1969	4,115	827	1,252	1,301	735	425
1970	4,236	870	1,263	1,346	757	393
1971	4,255	926	1,214	1,351	764	288
1972	4,157	921	1,127	1,361	748	206
1973	4,235	985	1,099	1,378	773	114
1974	3,933	949	987	1,259	738	38
1975	3,698	901	912	1,174	711	11
1976	3,565	873	850	1,150	692	- 23
1977	3,567	867	858	1,136	706	- 9
1978	3,488	829	837	1,123	699	8
1979	3,469	827	812	1,129	701	- 15
1980	3,360	795	789	1,084	692	- 6
1981	3,318	768	799	1,050	701	31
1982	3,290	751	806	1,032	701	55
1983	3,256	711	794	1,006	685	83
1984	3,137	692	782	986	678	90
1985	3,117	679	782	983	673	103

Note: The figures for 1954 to 1972 exclude for Okinawa prefecture.
Source: See Table 14.2.

Table 14.9
Rate of Migration by Sex, Japan, 1960 to 1980 (percent)

Year	Total		Within prefecture		Between prefectures	
	Male	Female	Male	Female	Male	Female
1960	6.5	5.6	3.3	3.1	3.3	2.5
1965	8.2	6.9	3.9	3.6	4.3	3.2
1970	8.7	7.3	4.0	3.8	4.7	3.5
1975	7.2	6.3	3.5	3.4	3.7	2.9
1980	6.5	5.6	3.3	3.1	3.3	2.5

Note: Migration refers to residential movement between minor administrative
        areas, or shi, ku, machi and mura, which excludes the movement within
        a minor administrative area, for each year.

Source: Statistics Bureau, Prime Minister's Office, Japan, Annual Report on
        the Internal Migration in Japan, derived from the Basic Resident
        Registers, 1980.

When we observe migration rates by age groups, we find that the rate of intercommunal migration is highest at ages 20 to 24, second highest at ages 25 to 29, and third highest at ages 15 to 19. The rate declines sharply at older ages. On the other hand, the interprefectural migration rate is second highest at ages 15 to 19 and the third at 25 to 29, with the highest rate at 20 to 24. Between 1959–60 and 1969–70, migration rates increased at each age group, but between 1969–70 and 1979–80 they decreased at each age group (Table 14.10).

Comparison of the age pattern of the overall migration rate between sexes reveals that the rate is higher for males than females at each age group, excepting the ages of 20 to 24 and 65 and over (Table 14.11).

Socioeconomic Characteristics

The never-married and the divorced are overrepresented in overall migration, particularly in interprefectural migration. More than 60 percent of in-migrants to a metropolitan prefecture and more than 50 percent of out-migrants from a remote prefecture were never married in 1979–80 (Table 14.12).

Educational attainment of movers is higher than that of nonmovers. Among movers the interprefectural migrants or long-distance movers show the highest attainment in education. In addition, it should be noted that in-migrants to the Tokyo metropolitan prefecture include a large proportion of students (Table 14.13). This means that the Tokyo metropolis attracts not only persons entering employment, but also persons going into universities.

Table 14.10
Rates of Overall and Intercommunal Migration by Age, 1959–60 to 1979–80

Age	Overall migration rate			Inter-communal migration rate			Inter-prefectural migration rate		
	1959-60[1]	1969-70	1979-80	1959-60[1]	1969-70	1979-80	1959-60[1]	1969-70	1979-80
Both sexes	8.0	12.0	9.5	5.8	7.1	9.0	2.8	3.7	2.6
1 - 14	4.5	9.4	8.7	2.9	5.0	4.6	1.2	2.4	2.1
15 - 19	14.5	16.4	12.5	12.2	12.5	9.4	7.5	7.7	5.5
20 - 24	18.1	23.7	20.1	13.9	15.9	13.7	7.2	8.5	6.7
25 - 29	15.5	23.1	19.0	10.7	13.9	11.9	4.7	6.5	5.1
30 - 39	8.2	12.5	11.3	5.5	7.1	6.5	2.4	3.4	2.9
40 - 49	4.6	7.2	6.0	3.1	4.0	3.2	1.4	1.9	1.4
50 - 59	3.6	5.4	4.4	2.3	2.9	2.4	1.0	1.3	1.0
60 +	2.7	4.2	3.9	1.7	2.1	1.9	0.7	0.9	0.7

1) : Excludes for Okinawa prefecture.

Source: See Table 14.1.

Table 14.11
Rates of Overall Migration by Sex and Age, Japan, 1970 and 1980 (percent)

Age	Male		Female	
	1970	1980	1970	1980
15–19	17	13	15	11
20–24	23	20	24	20
25–29	25	20	22	19
30–34	20	15	15	13
35–44	10	9	8	7
45–54	7	6	6	5
55–64	5	5	5	5
65+	5	5	5	5

Source: 1970 and 1980 Censuses of Japan

Among people 15 and over, labor force participation was slightly higher for movers than for nonmovers. However, the reverse was found for females (Table 14.14). Among movers, the proportion in the labor force was larger for intra-communal migrants than for intercommunal migrants for each sex. On the other hand, the proportion of unemployed persons was larger for intercommunal migrants than for intracommunal migrants or for nonmigrants for each sex. The largest rate of unemployment was for interprefectural migrant males.

WHY PEOPLE MOVE

According to the results of a survey on reasons for migration conducted by the National Land Agency in 1981 (Table 14.15), the most important reason for intercommunal migration in Japan for 1986–77 was "employment." Additional evidence that the primary reason for migration is economic can be shown by the fact that fluctuation of the annual rate of increase in intercommunal migration for 1956–1982 has a distinct association with that of annual economic growth rate for the same period (Okazaki, 1984).

Other significant reasons for migration were those relevant to noneconomic factors such as "family's reason," "marriage," "housing," and "schooling." The proportion of economic reasons (38.9 percent) was less than that of non-economic reasons (61.1 percent) for both sexes (Otomo, 1983). However, the reasons for movement differed between male and females. The "employment" reason accounted for 44.0 percent of male movers, but for 33.5 percent of female movers. On the contrary, the "family's reason" including "marriage" showed 21.6 percent for males but 32.3 percent for females.

The reasons for migration varied between types of migratory flows and be-tween different spatial units of migration. In the cases of migration within a metropolitan core area, of movement within a metropolitan fringe, and of move-ment from the core to the fringe within one of the three major metropolitan areas, the most important reason for migration was "housing" for each sex. On the

Table 14.12
Marital Status of Migrants Aged 15 and Over by Different Spatial Units, 1979–80

	Total	Never Married	Married	Widowed	Divorced
Male	100.0	30.2	66.2	2.4	1.2
Non-migrants	100.0	26.3	69.9	2.6	1.1
Overall migrants	100.0	40.4	56.0	1.5	2.1
Intra-communal migrants	100.0	29.0	66.7	1.9	2.3
Inter-communal migrants	100.0	47.0	49.9	1.2	1.9
Within prefecture	100.0	39.2	57.0	1.6	2.2
Between prefectures[1]	100.0	54.8	42.7	0.9	1.6
To Tokyo[2]	100.0	67.6	30.4	0.6	1.4
From Tokyo[2]	100.0	44.6	52.9	0.9	1.6
To Saitama[3]	100.0	46.8	50.7	1.0	1.5
From Saitama[3]	100.0	45.2	52.3	0.8	1.7
To Akita[4]	100.0	32.3	64.7	0.8	1.2
From Akita[4]	100.0	58.8	39.2	0.8	1.2
Female	100.0	20.9	64.2	12.4	2.5
Non-migrants	100.0	20.4	64.4	12.9	2.3
Overall migrants	100.0	25.9	62.8	7.2	4.1
Intra-communal migrants	100.0	20.5	65.4	9.0	5.1
Inter-communal migrants	100.0	29.7	61.0	6.0	3.4
Within prefecture	100.0	26.4	63.4	6.5	3.7
Between prefectures[1]	100.0	33.9	57.9	5.2	3.0
To Tokyo[2]	100.0	51.1	42.4	4.0	2.5
From Tokyo[2]	100.0	23.2	68.1	5.7	3.0
To Saitama[3]	100.0	23.9	67.6	6.0	2.4
From Saitama[3]	100.0	23.5	68.1	4.8	3.6
To Akita[4]	100.0	28.3	62.4	5.1	4.2
From Akita[4]	100.0	54.0	39.1	4.6	2.3

1) Inter-prefectural migrants

2) Example of metropolis

3) Example of metropolitan fringe

4) Example of non-metropolitan or remote area

Source: Statistics Bureau, 1980 Population Census of Japan, Vol.6, Part 1.

Table 14.13
Educational Attainment of Migrants Aged 15 and Over by Different Spatial Units, 1979–80

	Total[5]	Primary	Second-ary	Higher	Students
Both sexes	100.0	35.8	40.9	13.7	9.3
Non-migrants	100.0	37.1	40.5	12.9	9.1
Overall migrants	100.0	23.5	44.2	21.2	10.9
Intra-communal migrants	100.0	31.1	44.9	15.8	7.9
Inter-communal migrants	100.0	18.6	43.7	24.6	12.8
Within prefecture	100.0	21.3	46.2	22.4	9.8
Between prefectures[1]	100.0	15.6	41.0	27.2	16.1
To Tokyo[2]	100.0	9.5	36.6	27.0	26.9
From Tokyo[2]	100.0	14.6	41.1	38.1	6.1
To Saitama[3]	100.0	17.1	44.3	26.7	11.8
From Saitama[3]	100.0	15.3	44.1	30.3	10.3
To Akita[4]	100.0	40.6	34.5	18.5	6.2
From Akita[4]	100.0	27.9	38.9	12.9	20.3

Primary: Persons completed primary education only.
Secondary: Persons completed secondary education only.
Higher: Persons completed higher education.
1) Inter-prefectural migrants
2) Example of metropolis
3) Example of metropolitan fringe
4) Example of non-metropolitan or remote area
5) Includes "persons never attended school".
Source: Statistics Bureau, 1980 Population Census of Japan, Vol.6,
        Part 1.

other hand, it was "employment," excluding "other reasons," in the cases of other migratory flows. Particularly in the cases of interprefectural flows, excluding the moves relating to the three major metropolitan areas and of inflow for each sex, and in the cases of outflow and of local flow for males and of inter-metropolitan flows for females, more than half of the migrants moved for the reason of "employment." The second main reason for migration was "family"; this is especially distinguishable in the outflow from the three major metropolitan areas. It was also significantly observed in the flow of return migration from

Table 14.14
Labor Force Status of Migrants Aged 15 and Over by Different Spatial Units, 1979–80

	Total	Labour force			Non-labour force
		Total	Employed	Unemployed	
Both sexes	100.0	64.1	62.5	1.6	35.9
Non-migrants	100.0	64.0	62.5	1.5	36.0
Overall migrants	100.0	64.3	61.9	2.4	35.7
Intra-communal migrants	100.0	67.0	64.7	2.3	33.0
Inter-communal migrants	100.0	62.1	59.7	2.4	37.9
Within prefecture	100.0	62.6	60.7	2.0	37.4
Between prefectures[1]	100.0	61.6	58.8	2.9	38.4
Male	100.0	82.2	79.8	2.3	17.8
Non-migrants	100.0	82.1	79.8	2.3	17.9
Overall migrants	100.0	82.7	80.0	2.7	17.3
Intra-communal migrants	100.0	85.0	82.8	2.2	15.0
Inter-communal migrants	100.0	80.7	78.1	2.6	19.3
Within prefecture	100.0	82.3	80.2	2.1	17.7
Between prefectures[1]	100.0	79.5	76.5	3.0	20.5
Female	100.0	47.0	46.1	0.9	53.0
Non-migrants	100.0	47.3	46.4	0.8	52.7
Overall migrants	100.0	44.3	42.3	2.0	55.7
Intra-communal migrants	100.0	49.1	47.3	1.8	50.9
Inter-communal migrants	100.0	40.0	37.7	2.3	60.0
Within prefecture	100.0	42.5	40.7	1.8	57.5
Between prefectures[1]	100.0	37.4	34.7	2.7	62.6

1) Inter-prefectural migrants
Source: Statistics Bureau, 1980 Population Census of Japan, Vol.6, Part 1.

Table 14.15
Main Reasons for Migration of the Population Aged 15 and Over by Sex, Japan, 1981 (percent)

Type of flow	Employment	Family	Marriage	Housing	Schooling	Environ-mental	Others
Female							
Total flows	33.5	14.5	17.0	9.6	2.9	4.6	17.9
Within core[1]	14.7	13.7	14.1	23.9	2.4	9.8	21.4
Within fringe[2]	12.1	12.1	17.4	21.9	0.5	8.2	27.8
Core to fringe[3]	11.5	14.6	16.4	19.5	2.7	9.7	25.6
Fringe to core[4]	24.4	17.2	15.4	8.9	4.1	11.9	18.7
Intermetropolitan[5]	69.1	14.8	8.6	0.0	3.7	0.0	3.8
Outflow[6]	44.1	26.8	10.6	3.6	2.6	1.6	10.7
Inflow[7]	57.2	5.9	19.5	0.8	8.9	0.4	7.3
Interprefectural[8]	60.9	10.2	14.5	0.4	3.0	1.3	9.7
Local flow[9]	36.1	13.6	24.2	4.9	2.1	5.3	13.8
Male							
Total flows	44.0	12.2	7.4	8.4	4.9	7.1	16.0
Within core[1]	15.7	13.8	15.7	19.0	1.5	11.2	23.1
Within fringe[2]	18.8	11.7	12.7	19.1	1.2	11.8	24.7
Core to fringe[3]	16.5	10.9	3.4	19.9	0.4	12.1	26.8
Fringe to core[4]	31.2	10.4	7.8	5.2	7.8	17.4	20.2
Intermetropolitan[5]	32.7	3.8	0.8	0.8	6.8	0.0	5.1
Outflow[6]	57.2	22.4	1.8	1.6	2.9	3.0	11.1
Inflow[7]	66.1	5.3	1.1	0.0	18.6	2.7	6.2
Interprefectural[8]	69.0	9.8	2.9	0.8	8.2	1.6	7.7
Local flow[9]	52.1	12.6	7.9	4.5	3.6	5.6	13.7

1) The inter-communal migration within the core area or the central cities in each of the three major metropolitan areas.
2) The inter-communal migration within the fringe area in each of the three major metropolitan areas.
3) The migration from the core area to the fringe area in each of the three major metropolitan areas.
4) The migration from the fringe to the core area in each of the three major metropolitan areas.
5) The migration between the three major metropolitan areas.
6) The outmigration from the three major metropolitan areas to other areas.
7) The inmigration to the three major metropolitan areas from other areas.
8) The inter-prefectural migration excluding the migrations mentioned in 1) to 7).
9) The inter-communal migration excluding the migrations mentioned avove.
Source: National Land Agency, "Report on the Survey on Reasons for Migration", 1982.

those metropolitan areas, which accounted for 7.4 percent of total intercommunal migrants. In that flow, family reasons accounted for 33.4 percent as opposed to 43.5 percent for "employment" reasons (Otomo, 1983).

CONSEQUENCES OF MIGRATION

Population Redistribution

Interregional or interprefectural migration affects the pattern of regional or prefectural distribution of the national population. Recently, the fertility and mortality of the Japanese population have been low. Regional and prefectural differences have also been decreasing. Therefore, it can be said that, in Japan, recent regional and prefectural distributions of population have been determined chiefly by migration. The change in the proportion of regional population since 1950 illustrates that only in Minami-kanto (the Tokyo metropolitan region) was the share of regional population increased over time owing to excess in-migration from other regions for 1950 to 1985. On the contrary, the regions that had a declining trend in the share because of excess in-migration after 1950 were Tohoku, Hokuriku-Tosan, Chugoku, Shikoku, Kyushu, and Okinawa. Meanwhile, the share continued to increase in Nishi-kinki (Hanshin metropolitan region) and in Tokai (Chukyo metropolitan region) from 1950 to 1975. Thereafter, it has declined in Nishi-kinki and remained unchanged in Tokai. In 1985, the proportion of population living in Minami-kanto was 25.0 percent of the national population, and that of populations in the three metropolitan regions exceeded half of the national population (Statistics Bureau, 1986).

Intercommunal migration after 1950 within a metropolitan region, in particular outflow from a metropolitan center to its suburban zones, brought a significant change in the distribution of population within a metropolitan region. With the passage of time, after 1950 deceleration of population growth, or its decrease, has occurred in the metropolitan center, while expansion of zones has undergone rapid increase in population in its metropolitan fringe, accompanying the accumulation of population in the metropolitan region itself (Otomo, 1986).

Change in Population Structure of Region

Selectivity of migration in Japan, as described in previous sections, caused changes in the structure of regional population in this country. In particular, age selectivity of migration induced change in the age structure of regional populations and regional variations in aging. Furthermore, in remote nonmetropolitan regions, where fertility has been at a low level, fertility decline accelerated further because of the heavy out-migration of young adults to metropolitan regions. As a consequence, regional variations in population aging have been significant (Sagaza, 1984).

REFERENCES

Okazaki, Y. 1984. *Jinko Ido* [Population Migration]. 1980 Population Census Series No. 2. Tokyo: Statistics Bureau, Prime Minister's Office. (In Japanese.)

Otomo, A. 1983. "Nihon-niokeru Kokunai Jinkoido-no Ketteiin" [Determinants of Internal Migration in Japan]. Jinkogaku Kenkyu (The Journal of Population Studies, No. 6, Tokyo: The Population Association of Japan. (In Japanese with English Summary.)

————. 1986. "Changes in Geographical Distribution of Japanese Population." In T. Kuroda (ed.), *Urbanization and Development in Japan*. Tokyo: Asian Population and Development Association (Foundation).

Sagaza, H. 1984. *Konenrei Jinko* [Population Aging]. 1980 Population Census Monograph Series No. 8. Tokyo: Statistics Bureau, Management and Coordination Agency. (In Japanese).

Statistics Bureau. 1986. *Wagakuni Jinko-no Gaikan* [Outlook of Japanese Population]. 1985 Population Census Abridged Report Series No. 1. Tokyo: Statistics Bureau, Management and Coordination Agency. (In Japanese.)

15

KENYA

John O. Oucho

In a pioneering work on Kenya, S.H. Ominde (1968) examined four types of internal migration, namely, rural-rural, rural-urban, urban-urban, and urban-rural. Although three of these types are self-explanatory, the rural-rural type is a composite of nomadic pastoralism and of movements to and from the agricultural wage sector. The type of data used determines the extent to which any of the four types of internal migration can be analyzed. Rural-rural and rural-urban migration have attracted greater attention than the other two because of their significance in Kenya's total migration picture.

Using lifetime migration data from the 1969 census, D.F. Sly and J.M. Wrigley (1986) have established that rural-rural migration accounted for about two-fifths of all the movements, rural-urban one-third, urban-rural about one-quarter, and urban-urban for about 4 percent of all movements (World Bank, 1980, 32). The contemporary forms of internal migration in Kenya are consistent with the country's level of socioeconomic development and its phase of the demographic transition (Zelinsky, 1971).

DATA ON MIGRATION

In Kenya the *districts* are generally the geopolitical unit that defines migration, but *provinces* (which are made up of districts) are also used. Kenya's eight provinces are divided into forty-one districts, including the Nairobi Extra-Provincial District.

The first three Kenyan censuses (1948, 1962, and 1969) provided data on lifetime migration. The 1979 census did the same but also contained data on migration during the year prior to the census.

In addition to census data, several special surveys have yielded information that is particularly useful for analyzing migration at the microlevel. H. Rempel, J. Harris, and M. Todaro (1970), in their study of rural-urban migration to

Kenya's eight major towns (Nairobi, Mombasa, Kisumu, Nakura, Eldoret, Thika, Nanyuki, and Nyeri) interviewed 1,091 men aged 15 or more years on a diverse array of demographic and socioeconomic issues. Special surveys have also been carried out for university theses and dissertations on rural-rural migration (Matingu, 1974; Migot-Adholla, 1977; Nakitare, 1974; Ogungo, 1971; Oucho, 1981) and rural-urban migration (Nyaoke Owuor, 1974; Oucho, 1974), with some attention to reverse urban-rural migration.

A survey of the extent to which youth transform their migration expectations into reality was made by Sly in 1980–81 and yielded useful data on the various types of migration in Kenya (Khasiani, 1982; Sly and Wrigley, 1986). Another major survey investigated the impact of rural-urban migration on rural development at both household and community levels (Oucho and Mukras, 1983).

The data collected on migration in Kenya surely differ in quality and coverage, but to date there has been no systematic effort to evaluate their relative coverage and representativeness.

PRINCIPAL POPULATION MOVEMENTS

The National Level

The national perspective of migration is best explained by net migration. Table 15.1 shows migration in Kenya at both the national and provincial levels. In both 1969 and 1979, the districts are almost equally divided between out-migration and in-migration areas. The situation is complicated by the Rift Valley in which nine out of a total of thirteen districts are net in-migration areas. Another peculiarity is noted in Nyanza Province made up of four districts, all of which lost population to the rest of Kenya. This is different from the situation in 1969 when the four districts were equally represented in net in- and out-migration. North Eastern and Western provinces also experienced some changes over the two periods.

Lifetime migration estimated from the 1979 census can be used to describe the primary, secondary, and tertiary destinations of migrants from each district. Three main types of destinations emerge.

The significance of rural-urban migration is explained by the importance of Nairobi and Mombasa as the primary destinations of migrants from rural districts. For example, Nairobi receives population from Kirinyaga, Muranga, and Nyeri (three of the five districts) in Central Province; all the districts in Eastern Province; Kisumu, Siaya, and South Nyanza (three of the four districts) in Nyanza Province; Nakuru, Narok, Trans Nzoia, and Uasin Gishu (four of the thirteen districts) in Rift Valley Province; and Busia and Kakamega (two of the three districts) in Western Province. Mombasa is a primary destination for migrants originating from Coast Province; and Mombasa itself loses population to Nairobi (the only interurban migration).

One primary destination for rural-rural migration is Laikipia which receives

Table 15.1

Net In- and Out-Migration in Districts and Lifetime Migration in Kenya by Province, 1969 and 1979

1969	Number of Districts			Life time migrants		
	Total	Net Out	Net In	Inmigrants	Net migration	
Nairobi	1	0	1	330403	303580	26823
Central	5	3	2	151421	332555	-181134
Coast	6	2	4	155210	26331	128879
Eastern	6	5	1	33454	161871	-128417
North Eastern	3	2	1	8919	10280	- 1361
Nyanza	4	2	2	169329	186069	- 16740
Rift Valley	13	4	9	403020	88823	314197
Western	3	2	1	58699	200946	-142247
Kenya	41	20	21	-	-	-
1979						
Nairobi	1	0	1	615942	91570	524373
Central	5	3	2	191102	465253	-274151
Coast	6	2	4	222229	47983	174246
Eastern	6	4	2	89966	263957	-173991
North Eastern	3	1	2	14998	30347	- 15349
Nyanza	4	4	0	109130	375596	-266466
Rift Valley	13	4	9	625594	146385	479209
Western	3	3	0	103181	390808	-287627
Kenya	41	20	21	-	-	-

Notes: In-migrants = enumerated in province, born outside;

Out-migrants = born in province, enumerated outside.

Source: Calculated from the 1969 and 1979 Kenya Population Census tables.

migrants from the neighboring Nyandarua district in Central Province; and from Samburu District in Rift Valley Province. Another important destination is Uasin Gishu, which gains population from the arid Elgeyo-Marakwet and Nandi in the neighborhood. Trans Nzoia is the primary destination for migrants from Turkana, another arid district, and from Bungoma District which borders it. Kericho District receives migrants from Kisii and West Pokot districts, which are farther away from this primary destination. The most important destination of rural-rural migration is Nakuru, which receives migrants from Kiambu in Central Province, and Baringo and Kericho both in Rift Valley Province. Primary destinations with migrants from only one district are Tana River (from Garissa), Wajir (from Mandera), and Garissa (from Wajir).

The two principal cities, Nairobi and Mombasa, dominate as secondary destinations. Six districts—Kilifi, Kwale, and Taita-Taveta in Coast Province, Kisii in Nyanza Province, Laikipia in Rift Valley Province, and Bungoma in Western Province—contribute to the rural-urban migration streams terminating in Nairobi. These streams signify long-distance migration to the capital city. Mombasa also receives long-distance migrants from Kitui. Nairobi and Mombasa together are secondary destinations of rural-urban migration streams from twelve districts.

The most important secondary destination of rural-rural migrants is Laikipia District, which receives migrants from Meru, Nakuru, Trans Nzoia, and Uasin Gishu districts. All four origins are among the richest agricultural districts in Kenya; it is not immediately clear why they lose population to Laikipia. In the same vein, it is not immediately clear why Nakuru receives migrants from Muranga and Nyandarua, but here the colonization of agricultural land is a plausible reason. Migration from West Pokot and Kakamega districts to Nandi District is attributable to aridity and population pressure on the land, respectively.

The third-level destinations are dominated by rural-rural migration streams. Nakuru District is by far the most important, receiving migrants from ten districts from all the provinces except Coast and North Eastern. Half of the origins include five far-removed districts—Kirinyaga, Kwale, Embu, Meru, and Turkana. The second major destination is Laikipia, whose in-migrants at the tertiary level originate from West Pokot, Bungoma, and Busia districts. This is an important agricultural district that attracts migrants from Kiambu and Muranga primarily for the purpose of land settlement.

Rural-urban migration at the tertiary level terminates only at Mombasa. Long-distance migration is experienced at this stage, the only short-distance migration being from Machakos district.

WHO MOVES

While census enumerations provide data on age, sex, and education, surveys may generate more data on characteristics such as marital status, family background, and possession of property. This section therefore draws from these two data sources to describe the characteristics of migrants by types of move.

At the Interregional Level

Interregional migration is best estimated from census data; those data relating to the last two censuses are used here to illustrate migrant characteristics. In 1969, 70 percent of the male population in the Nairobi metropolitan province were lifetime migrants compared with 59 percent of females (Table 15.2). All other provinces, except Nyanza and Western, experienced the same general pattern. In all the provinces except Nairobi, male out-migration constituted a higher proportion of provincial population than female out-migration. This suggests higher out-migration rates for males than females, which is a typical feature in African countries. Net migration figures depict the situation even more vividly, being much higher for male net migrants in each province (except North Eastern).

Survey data provide useful insights into the demographic and socioeconomic characteristics of migrants, of which age and education, respectively, are the most salient.

Table 15.3 reports some of the findings from five surveys with respect to age. In both the national rural-urban migration survey of eight major towns (Rempel

Table 15.2
In- and Out-Migration as a Percent of Total and Native Populations and Net Migration in Kenya by Sex, 1969

Province	In-migration as a percent of total population		Out-migration as a percent of population born in Province		Net internal migration	
	M	F	M	F		
Nairobi	70.0	58.6	62.2	64.7	-61,815	-34,992
Central	20.1	18.6	30.0	24.8	-109,193	-71,941
Coasta	29.0	21.8	15.7	11.5	74,469	53,075
Eastern	4.0	3.1	12.4	6.9	-87,771	-40,646
N. Eastern	6.0	4.2	5.9	5.5	95	-1,456
Nyanza	10.7	11.5	13.1	10.5	-28,398	11,658
R. Valley	28.1	24.3	14.4	13.1	179,582	135,390
Western	5.2	6.0	16.9	12.6	-90,599	-51,648

Source: H. Rempel (1977):   7-8

Table 15.3
Age Distribution of Migrants Reported in Five Kenyan Migration Surveys, 1970–85

Age group (in years)	Percent of migrants by migration type/author				
	Rural-urban migration		Rural-rural migration		
	Rempel et al (1970)	Oucho (1974)	Oucho (1981)	Odallo (1985)	Oucho (1986)
15–19	25.2	8.3	15.2	–	–
20–24	43.0	20.0	28.1	5.4	19.4
25–29	18.2	29.3	24.5	30.2	35.2
30–34	8.4	21.0	17.3	24.5	17.2
35–39				19.1	9.9
40–44	4.6	14.5	10.8	7.9	5.9
45–49				7.9	4.4
50+	5.5	6.9	4.1	5.0	11.6
TOTAL	100.0	100.0			100.0
(N)	(1018)	(509)	(825)	(278)	(273)

Sources: Authors cited above appear in References

et al., 1970) and a rural-rural migration survey of the dominant tea plantation area in western Kenya (Oucho, 1981), migration peaked at 20 to 24 years. In the three other surveys the peak ages are 25 to 29 years. This suggests that the age bracket 20 to 29 years is a crucial one in the two dominant types of internal migration. From age 30 the percentage of migrants drops, suggesting that population mobility occurs steadily up to the 40s.

In all five surveys migrants who attained a primary education predominate. They make up 53.0 percent of the migrants in Kisumu town (Oucho, 1974), 46.6 percent in the Kericho tea plantations (Oucho, 1981), 46.8 percent in the Nzoia-Mumias sugar plantation (Odallo, 1985), and 42.1 percent in the SONY sugar plantation (Oucho, 1986a). However with the expansion of secondary education since Kenya's independence in 1963, more and more secondary school graduates have been attracted to the rural agricultural wage sector.

Interurban, Urban-Rural, and Return Migrants

Rempel et al. (1970) found that only 12 percent of their respondents made an interurban move (Rempel, 1981, 155). Among the eight urban centers surveyed, the highest magnitude of interurban movement involved Nairobi and accounted for 33 percent of the interurban movements to seven other urban centers— Nakuru for 22 percent, Mombasa for 14 percent, Thika for 11 percent, Nyeri for 8 percent, Kisumu for 5 percent, Eldoret for 4 percent, and Nanyuki for 3 percent (Rempel, 1981, 156). The urban destinations of the out-migrants from each urban center show strong links between Nairobi and all other centers, and between Kisumu and Mombasa, largely attributed to road and rail links (Rempel, 1981, 157). Analysis of the future mobility preferences of the migrants surveyed in Kisumu indicates that 22.0 percent of them expected to move to another town (Oucho, 1974, 315). These results suggest that, although interurban movement is still in its infancy in Kenya, it is expected to increase as the rate of urbanization rises and as the size of urban centers increases.

Given the rural orientation of Kenyans at the present stage of the country's development, urban-rural migration is inevitable. Almost all surveys carried out in Kenya provide evidence showing that urban migrants, at the end of their sojourns, do expect eventually to return to their rural origins.

This observation relating to return migration is predicated on a number of indicators of urban-rural links: periodic visits; exchange of visits between urban migrants and their rural kith and kin; criss-crossing of transfers of money and goods; and identification of one's rural home (original or adopted) as the place for retirement. Over the last decade, a number of studies (Johnson and Whitelaw, 1974; Knowles and Anker, 1981; Moock, 1978; Oucho and Mukras, 1983; Rempel and Lobdell, 1978) have analyzed these urban-rural links.

Also influencing urban-rural migration are the recently emergent agroindustrial economic islands, for example, the sugar belts of western Kenya. Evidence from recent studies (Oucho, 1986a) indicates that semiskilled and skilled personnel prefer the newly emergent destinations to the urban areas where the cost of living is becoming increasingly unbearable.

These three forms of movement involve mainly males who are older than males among rural-urban or rural-rural migrants. In urban areas where the textile industry has emerged, females tend to dominate interurban movement, as can be seen in Thika, Nakuru, and Eldoret, for instance. Kenya's current demographic situation suggests that repeat, return, and circulatory movers will be on the scene until the urban-rural divide narrows.

WHY PEOPLE MOVE

Studies in Kenya show that people move for economic, social, and environmental reasons. Census data used with other secondary data (e.g., economic statistics) can tell us something about the areas of origin and destination of migrants. Survey data have an advantage over census data because the reasons for moving have been directly asked of migrants. Determinants of migration can, therefore, be considered at both the macro- and microlevels.

Reasons Given by Migrants

The reasons stated by migrants for leaving their home areas for specific destinations differ considerably, and this is particularly so of economic considerations. In one rural-urban migration survey, 78 percent of the out-migrants moved because they could not find work (Rempel, 1981, 70). Yet, in another survey only about 40 percent reported unemployment as the primary reason (Oucho, 1974). In a rural-rural migration survey, 26 percent moved because of the availability of job opportunities and 22 percent because of better income potential at the destination (Oucho, 1981). In another such survey, 51 percent moved because they had temporary jobs and 19 percent because of low salaries at the origin (Nyagero, 1985). These data suggest that many people who move do so for economic reasons, but they do not tell us why so many people who are in similar circumstances do not move.

Nevertheless, no other reason for moving given by migrants appears to rival economic reasons. For example, education was mentioned by only 5 percent of the migrants (Oucho, 1974), and landlessness by 2.7 percent (Oucho, 1974) and 4 percent (Rempel, 1981, 70). Reasons attributed to the "bright lights" theory of migration, such as the availability of amenities, do not seem to be important in Kenya as they account for 1 percent or less of all the reasons (Oucho, 1974; Rempel, 1981, 70).

In these surveys, "other reasons" ranks second to economic reasons. This suggests that other noneconomic reasons may in fact be more important than education, amenities, and landlessness.

Social and environmental reasons for migration have not been systematically investigated in the many studies to provide a clear picture of the role of the family (Sly and Wrigley, 1986), the extent of retirement, and the nature of involuntary moves. We expect (1) that the desire of migrants to maintain links with and give assistance to their families sustains chain migration; (2) that retirement, which is likely to increase with the reduction of retirement age in Kenya will become a major reason for return migration from urban as well as rural destinations; and (3) that involuntary moves caused by environmental hazards (floods, drought, and famine) continue to affect the arid and semiarid lands of Kenya.

Determinants of Migration Based on Regression Analysis

A number of different variables have been included in regression models examining different types of migration (Anker and Knowles, 1983; Rempel, 1981; Bilsborrow et al., 1986; Sly and Wrigley, 1986) No matter the type of migration analyzed or the level of analysis, these models clearly demonstrate the large number of factors influencing migration and the complexity of the process. Indeed, taken together and in the context of some other similar studies (Bilsborrow et al., 1986; Oucho, 1981), the data suggest that the multiplicity of factors influencing migration range from economic factors such as income and employment opportunities, to social organization as well as from geographic and environmental factors such as distance, land quality, and resource base, to psychological and social psychological factors such as intergenerational attitudes and orientation to self.

Although a large number of factors influencing migration have been identified, there is still little understanding of how these factors are interrelated and how their influence varies from one type of migration to the next. A particularly salient void in the migration literature on Kenya has been a lack of studies examining how individual level factors vary under different contextual conditions. As studies of this type are undertaken, it may lead to better predictive and explanatory models.

CONSEQUENCES OF MIGRATION

The consequences, like the causes, of migration, appear to vary depending on the type of migration and whether we are looking at individuals, households/families, or the communities of origin and destination. The consequences of migration, however, have not been studied in nearly the detail that "causes" have. It is important to realize that in many instances it is difficult in a country growing as rapidly as Kenya to separate the consequences of migration from those that are a product of growth and for the interaction of migration and growth.

Rural-urban migration has contributed to the rapid growth of many urban centers, but the rural population of the country has continued to grow and at a rate not substantially lower than that found in the urban population. Thus, although rural-urban migration is helping to alleviate the population pressure in rural areas, it is also contributing to economic pressures and demands in urban centers. There is also some evidence to suggest that rural areas are losing a portion of their younger and better educated population as a result of migration. Some researchers have argued that this type of selectivity has a substantial negative consequence on rural areas. While this argument appears to have face validity, it is again important to note that the point needs to be substantiated. In this sense, we need to know much more than merely that migration is selective. It is possible, for instance, that if these people remained in rural areas they would be largely economically inactive. If the migrants are successful in urban places, it is possible that they might contribute to rural development directly through remittances and assistance to those left behind and indirectly through their contributions to national development in the urban economy.

As opportunities in rural areas improve, this situation may change. For example, with the current emphasis on district planning, opportunities are being created for both rural- and urban-based employment. This could discourage long-distance migration to the current main employment centers. Employment grew at the rate of 4.7 percent in the urban informal sector, 3.6 percent in the rural nonfarm sector, and 3.5 percent in the modern (formal) sector during the late seventies (Kenya, 1983, 7). Urban wages remain higher than rural wages, although the cost of living in urban areas depresses actual earnings in these regions. This phenomenon is partly responsible for the urban-rural migration that has recently been taking place to the rural economic islands.

The Household and Individual Levels

Considerably fewer studies have focused on the consequences of migration at the household and individual level, and these frequently come to contradictory conclusions. For example, some researchers have argued that there is a flow of personnel and capital from rural areas to the towns (Byerlee, 1972, 14) in the form of migrants' educational costs and other material support (Essang and Mabawonku, 1974, 26). Others have countered that this loss is balanced by the reverse flow of money and goods for "conspicuous investment" in rural areas (Adepoju, 1983; Mukras, Oucho and Bamberger, 1985; Oucho and Mukras, 1983). Similarly, some have noted that out-migration tends to have adverse effects on family labor in rural farms. The absence of the able-bodied out-migrants, they argue, partly accounts for the stagnation of the rural economy, which is heavily dependent on agriculture. Yet, it is quite possible that the out-migration of some rural workers opens up job opportunities for others. Given cultural traditions, some researchers have suggested that the imbalanced sex ratios found in some rural areas curtail household decision making and other aspects of existence in which males are given dominant roles because of their absence. The extent to which this is so has not been thoroughly studied, and it is possible that the absence of males may even be a modernizing force in transforming gender roles.

REFERENCES

Adepoju, A. 1983. *Selected Studies on the Dynamics, Patterns and Consequences of Migration, IV; Medium-sized Towns in Nigeria: Research and Policy Prospects.* Reports and Papers in the Social Sciences, No. 53. Paris: Unesco.

Anker, R., and Knowles, J.C. 1983. *Population Growth, Employment and Economic-Demographic Interactions in Kenya: Bachue-Kenya.* New York: Gower and St. Martin's Press.

Beskok, O. 1981. "Data on Migration from the 1979 Population Census." University of Nairobi, Population Studies and Research Institute (mimeo).

Bilsborrow, R.A., Oucho, J.O., and Molyneaux, J. 1986. "Economic and Ethnic Factors in Kenyan Migration Movements." *Eastern Africa Economic Review* (New Series) 2:31–50.

Byerlee, D. 1972. *Research on Migration in Africa: Past, Present and Future.* African Rural Employment Paper No. 2. East Lansing: Michigan State University.

Essang, S.M., and Mabawonku, A.F. 1974. *Determinants and Impact of Rural-Urban Migration: Case Study of Selected Communities in Western Nigeria.* African Rural Employment Paper No. 10. East Lansing: Michigan State University.

International Union for the Scientific Study of Population. 1982. *Multilingual Demographic Dictionary: English Section.* Liege: Ordina Editions.

Johnson, G.E., and Whitelaw, W.E. 1974. "Urban-Rural Transfers in Kenya: An Estimated Remittance Function." *Economic Development and Cultural Change* 22:473–79.

Kenya, Republic of 1983. *Development Plan 1984–1988.* Nairobi: Government Printer.

Khasiani, Shanyisa A. 1982. "Social and Psychological Factors Influencing Migration Dispositions in Kenya." Ph.D. dissertation, Florida State University.

Knowles, J.C., and Anker, R. 1981. "An Analysis of Income Transfer in a Developing Country: The Case of Kenya." *Journal of Development Economics* 8:205–26.

Matingu, Mary N. 1974. "Rural Migration and Employment: A Case Study in a Selected Area in Kenya." M.A. thesis, University of Nairobi.

Migot-Adhola, S. 1977. "Migration and Rural Differentiation in Kenya." Ph.D. dissertation, University of California, Los Angeles.

Moock, Joyce L. 1978. "The Content and Maintenance of Social Ties Between Urban Migrants and Their Home-based Support Groups: The Maragoli Case." *African Urban Studies* 3:15–31.

Muckras, M.S., Oucho, J.O., and Bamberger, M. 1985. "Resource Mobilization and the Household Economy in Kenya." *Canadian Journal of African Studies* 19:409–21.

Nakitare, P.E. 1974. "Socio-economic Consequences of Intra-Rural Migration." M.A. thesis, University of Nairobi.

Nyagero, O. 1985. "Causes of Migration in Rural Kenya." M.A. thesis, University of Nairobi.

Nyaoke Owuor, S. 1974. "Primacy of Determinants of Rural-Urban and Reverse Urban-Rural Migration in Kenya." M.A. thesis, University of Nairobi.

Odallo, S. 1985. "Migration in the Nzoia-Mumias Sugar Plantation Region." M.A. thesis, University of Nairobi.

Ogungo, B.P. 1971. "Migrant Labour in Miwani Sugar Estate and Its Effects on Neighbouring Locations." B.A. dissertation, University of Nairobi.

Ominde, S.H. 1968. *Land and Population Movements in Kenya.* London: Heinemann.

Oucho, J.O. 1974. "Migration Survey in Kisumu Town." M.A. thesis, University of Nairobi.

———. 1981. "Rural-Rural Migration and Population Change: A Study of the Kericho Tea Estates Complex." Ph.D. thesis, University of Nairobi.

———. 1983. "Lifetime and Recent Migration in Kenya Based on the 1979 Population Census." University of Nairobi, Population Studies and Research Institute (mimeo).

———. 1986a. "Migration of Labour Force into the Sugar Industry in Kenya: The Sony Case." Paper presented at the Kenya Sugar Industry Development and Man Power Utilization Seminar, Kisumu, Kenya, May 11–17.

———. 1986b. "Rural Orientation, Return Migration and Future Movements of Urban Migrants: A Study of Kisumu Town, Kenya." *African Urban Quarterly* 1:207–18.

———, and Mukras, M.S. 1983. "Migration, Transfers and Rural Development: A Case Study of Kenya." Research Report prepared for the International Development Research Centre. Nairobi: University of Nairobi (mimeo).

Preston, S.H., and Coale, A.J. 1982. "Age Structure, Growth, Attrition, and Accession: A New Synthesis." *Population Studies* 48:217–59.

Prothero, R.M. 1968. "Migration in Tropical Africa." In J.C. Caldwell and C. Okonjo (eds.), *The Population of Tropical Africa*. London: Longmans, 250–63.

Rempel, H. 1977. "An Analysis of the Information on the Inter-District Migration Provided in the 1969 Kenya Census." Discussion Paper No. 224. University of Nairobi, Institute for Development Studies.

———. 1981. *Rural-Urban Labor Migration and Urban Unemployment in Kenya*. Laxenburg, Austria: International Institute for Applied Systems Analysis.

———, and Lobdell, R.A. 1978. "The Role of Urban-to-Rural Remittances in Rural Development." *Journal of Development Studies* 14:324–41.

———, Todaro, M., and Harris, J. 1970. "Rural-to-Urban Labour Migration: A Tabulation of Responses to the Questionnaire Used in the Migration Survey." Discussion Paper No. 92. Institute for Development Studies, University of Nairobi.

Sly, D.F., and Wrigley, J.M. 1986. "Migration and Decision Making and Migration Behavior in Rural Kenya." In J.F. Fawcett (ed.), *Migration Intentions and Behavior: Third World Perspectives. Population and Environment* 8 (1-2), Spring-Summer, 78–97.

United Nations. 1958. *Multilingual Demographic Dictionary*. New York: United Nations.

Wakajuma, J.O. 1986. "Intercensal Net Migration in Kenya: District Level Analysis." M.A. thesis, University of Nairobi.

Waller, P.P. et al. 1986. *Basic Features of Regional Planning in the Region of Kisumu, Kenya*. Berlin: Deutsches Institute for Entwicklungspolitik.

World Bank. 1980. *Kenya: Population and Development*. Washington, D.C.: Development Economics Department, East Africa Country Programs Department, The World Bank.

Zelinsky, W. 1971. "The Hypothesis of Mobility Transition." *Geographical Review* 61:219–49.

16

THE NETHERLANDS

Dick Vergoossen

Remarkable developments in internal migration in the Netherlands can be explained by the rapidly changing economic processes during the postwar period. Both the intensity of migration and its spatial distribution are indicative of these developments. During the first postwar years, mobility was generally low compared with the levels of the 1930s. Mobility rates fluctuated around 4 percent in the 1950s. This pattern of low mobility is a direct reflection of the housing shortage at that time. Between 1950 and 1960 mobility rates seemed stabilized, before an abrupt increase to 5.3 percent took place in 1973. Favorable economic perspectives and an increasing rate of car ownership offered, to a large extent, the possibility of living outside the city. After 1973 a remarkable decline was apparent, until the year 1979 when migration numbers seemed to stabilize at the level found in the 1950s. This decline was to a large extent the result of growing unemployment, stabilized income levels, rising housing costs, and a collapse of the housing market.

Along with the changing intensity of migration, the spatial pattern changed in the period 1950–84 (Figure 16.1). The withdrawal of the labor force from the agricultural sector, together with the growing importance of industrial employment, especially in the western parts of the country, caused a migration flow in the 1950s from the northern and southwestern regions to those in the west.

After 1960, however, the direction of net migration flows changed. The eastern part of the country, the province of Gelderland, and the southern section, in the province of North-Brabant, became the predominate destination of migrants. This trend coincided with the end of the rural exodus toward the cities, at which point the suburbanization trend took over. According to H. ter Heide and C. Leo Eichperger (1974), this spatial reversal can to a large extent be seen to result from the fact that economic considerations were overruled by those directly related to residential contexts. As such, increased mobility allows for greater freedom in the decision-making process with regard to place of residence, while

Figure 16.1
Net Internal Migration by Direction

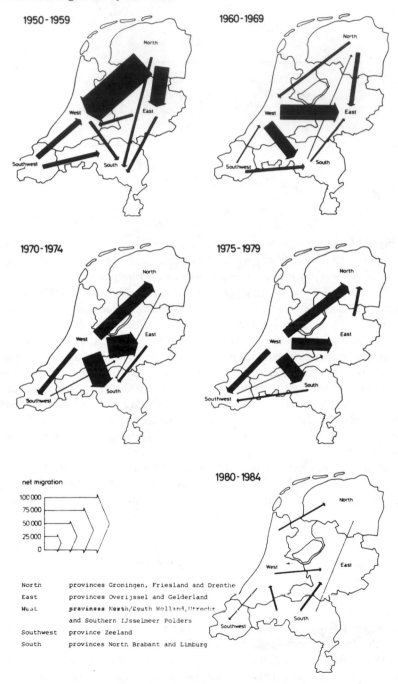

Source: Netherlands Bureau of Statistics.

still making it possible to work in urban areas. This suburban flow reached its highest level in the 1970s.

Although the intensity of migration diminished sharply in the years after 1973, the direction of migration flows remained constant, with one exception (the period 1980–84), when there was again a positive net migration balance in the western part of the country as compared with the southern section. The strong reduction in out-migration rates is characteristic of the western part, where subsidized housing projects in and around the cities (growth centers) are now being realized on a large scale. This phenomenon has been termed a clustered form of suburbanization (J.A. Van Ginkel, 1977), by combining a decline of out-migration with in-migration to specific locations within the rural areas of the west.

DATA ON MIGRATION

The principal sources of data on internal migration in the Netherlands are the population registration system and different national surveys. In contrast to many other countries, the population census is not a source of information on migration. Not only has there been no census since 1971, but also there have been very few suitable questions on migration in the census. The text of this section is a compilation of the studies of J.C. van den Brekel (1977), R.F. van den Erf (1984) and Nico Keilman (1986).

The Population Register

The main source of internal migration data in the Netherlands is the population register. A population register is defined as a system of continuous recording and/or coordinated linkage of selected information pertaining to each resident of the country. This system of registration was introduced in 1850 in accordance with a Royal Decree of 1849.

In principle, all persons living in the Netherlands are registered in the population register of the municipality where they normally reside. Persons without a fixed address are entered in the Central Population Register. Individuals temporarily in the country are excluded from registration.

The register consists of a set of personal cards with entry to the system upon birth or immigration. All changes in one's personal situation such as a marriage, divorce, and change of address are entered on this card. In case of migration to another municipality in the Netherlands, the personal card is forwarded to the municipality of new residence. In case of emigration, the card is removed from the register and sent to the Central Government Inspection in the Hague.

After administration use, removal cards are forwarded to the Central Bureau of Statistics (CBS) for statistical processing. Originally, the information mentioned on the card was very limited. Gradually, the format was extended and now contains many characteristics of migrants, such as points of origin and destination, sex, age, marital status, nationality, and occupation.

Because migration statistics are based on information from the removal cards, a migration is defined as the change of municipality of residence during a fixed period of time. Changes of address within a municipality are excluded.

Survey on Intramunicipal Migration

As already mentioned, migration statistics give no real picture of total mobility in the Netherlands, since intramunicipal moves are excluded. This means, for instance, that a move from the center of a large municipality to its fringe is considered intramunicipal, as opposed to a move to an adjoining suburb in a neighboring municipality. In large municipalities, intramunicipal moves will often cover greater distances than migration between adjoining smaller municipalities. Therefore, it becomes clear that complementary information about intramunicipal migration is needed. In cases of intramunicipal migration, no removal card is completed, since a change of address only results in a modification of the personal card. Since 1977, the CBS has also sent out a questionnaire to all municipalities to get complementary information about intramunicipal migration by sex and family context. These additional data enable CBS to produce information annually for total mobility (i.e., both intermunicipal as well as intramunicipal).

Labor Force Survey

The Labor Force Survey (LFS) has assembled statistical data biannually, since 1973, on the supply of labor. For our purposes, the most important questions are those concerning removal as used as sociodemographic and socioeconomic characteristics. The LFS records transitions, classifying individuals according to their present municipality and municipality of residence one year ago. Information is available by sex, age, position in the household, marital status, education, type of main activity, occupation, social status, and place of work.

Housing Survey

The Housing Survey (HS) primarily collects statistical information on the housing situation. Such studies were organized in 1964, 1967, 1970, 1977, 1981, and 1985. Mobility data consist of two parts: past and intended removals. Motives are recorded for removals made within three years prior to the interview. Important background variables include those on household characteristics. Questions about mobility intentions are an important part of this survey. Extensive tabulations on mobility have been published for all housing surveys up to 1981.

PRINCIPAL POPULATION MOVEMENTS

The National Level

Although migration rates increased gradually until about 1960, the overall level remained rather low in comparison with the 1920s and 1930s. The importance of intraprovincial migration in total internal migration became more important, representing about 50 percent. This was especially the case during the prewar period, when the proportion fluctuated between 60 and 70 percent. Ter Heide (1965) has examined the possible interrelationship between inter- and intraprovincial migration and the movements of the economic cycle. During the period 1924–38, both migration patterns displayed a strong negative relationship ($r = -0.90$) with unemployment rates. After 1950, this relationship seemed to have disappeared completely, at least regarding intraprovincial migration. Increasingly, this type of migration, consisting mainly of short-distance migration flows, became subject to residential preferences. When compared with the prewar period, this rather low level can be explained by the effects of the urbanization process, which tended to increase the commuting distance.

Mobility rates increased strongly after 1964. As shown in Figure 16.2, this increase was essentially due to intraprovincial migration, the proportion of which

Figure 16.2
Internal and Intraprovincial Migration

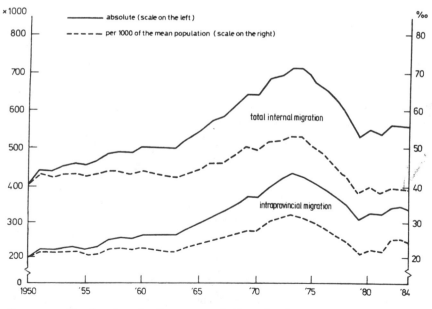

Source: Netherlands Bureau of Statistics.

in total mobility exceeded 60 percent. This may be explained by the current process of suburbanization and increased income, together with a growing degree of car ownership, changing attitudes toward leisure and an apparent preference for small communities with an informal social network.

After 1973, mobility rates showed a strong decline, reaching 3.8 percent in 1979, the lowest level since World War II. The decline after 1973 is, to a large extent, related to the regressive trends of suburbanization, just as the suburbanization process had influenced short-distance migration patterns in the 1960s.

Several interpretations can be given for this process of regression. Limiting suburbanization has been a major objective of spatial planning policies. On the national level, the authorities tried to curb the urban exodus and at the same time establish balanced migration between the western provinces on the one hand and Gelderland and North Brabant on the other hand. At the provincial level, the main emphasis has been placed on a pattern of residential concentrations in a limited number or rural settlements. Besides this, demographic and economic trends have also exerted a considerable influence. Demographic processes can, to a large extent, explain the reduction of urban overspill, especially from the larger agglomerations, in favor of indicated growth centers (van Gestel, 1981). The demographic processes referred to are changing population composition, marriage trends, household size, and a lessened tendency to live in rural areas.

Some economic processes have also been relevant to the decline of migration. A. Ogilvy (1979) pointed at the relationship between reduced levels of migration and increasing unemployment levels (after 1973), reduced income levels, and increased building costs. At the individual level, this means a growing insecurity regarding income.

Interregional Migration

Net interprovincial migration is shown in Figure 16.3. The results reflect migration trends in the north and southwest, where a migration deficit in the 1950s turned into a migration surplus during the second half of the 1960s and into the 1970s. From 1980 onward, net migration rates hovered around zero. The loss during the 1950s is accounted for primarily by the withdrawal of the labor force from the agricultural sector. The migration surplus after 1964 was to a large extent caused by the regional industrialization policy of the national government, where induced industrial decentralization resulted in growing employment rates. Furthermore, in the provinces of Drenthe and, to a lesser extent, Friesland, their attractiveness as a residential area explains the additional migration flow from the west.

Net migration in the provinces of Overijssel and Limburg has shown minimal change, usually fluctuating around zero. These provinces are largely removed from the migration flows from the west. The regional economic situation, traditionally dominated by the textile industry and by mining, developed most unfavorably. These provinces entered into strong "competition" for migrants with

Figure 16.3
Net Internal Migration per Province

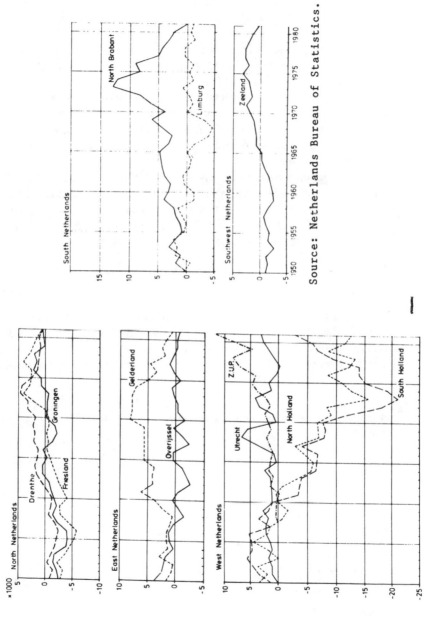

Source: Netherlands Bureau of Statistics.

Gelderland and North Brabant, the provinces that displayed a net migration surplus during the whole period. Industrial decentralization, especially in North Brabant, and the attractive residential environment account for the strong increase in the migration surplus during the 1960s, but, as was the case at the national level, the period after 1973 shows a decline of net migration to about zero.

As far as the provinces in the west are concerned, the net migration surplus during the 1950s may be explained by an economic revival after the war on the one hand and the withdrawal of the agricultural labor force in the north and southwest on the other. The reversal of migration flows, resulting in an important migration deficit, is mainly a result of increasing relocation to the province of Utrecht. Unlike the situation in the province of North Holland, differences between in-migration and out-migration in the province of South Holland considerably diminished after 1973.

The net migration deficit in the province of North Holland at the end of the 1970s can almost entirely be explained by the special situation regarding the Southern Ijsselmeer Polders. In this 12th Province (established on January 1, 1986, under the name "Flevoland"), two growth centers have been earmarked as overspill areas for the agglomeration of Amsterdam. This was an intentional issue of spatial planning policy.

Rural-Urban Migration

Table 16.1 gives an impression of migration trends in the rural and urban municipalities. The net out-migration from the rural municipalities in 1957 reflects the observed loss of employment opportunities in the agricultural sector. From the largest cities there was already net out-migration accompanied by net

Table 16.1
Net Internal Migration by Municipality Type, Netherlands, 1957–83 (rates per 1,000 persons)

	1957	1960	1973	1983
Rural municipalities	-5. 6	2. 0	16. 9	2. 9
Industrial rural municipalities	8. 6	6. 2	13. 4	0. 7
Commuter suburbs	17. 1	18. 7	10. 9	5. 0
Country and small towns	11. 5	7. 6	13. 7	6. 0
Medium-sized towns	2. 2	- 0. 5	-11. 1	- 0. 6
Large towns	- 3. 3	-12. 2	-25. 8	- 7. 3

Source: Central Bureau of Statistics, Continuous Population Register of the Netherlands

high in-migration into specifically residential municipalities. A decade later, as the suburbanization process gained momentum, medium as well as large cities suffered losses. In the rural municipalities, net out-migration turned into in-migration. In 1973, when mobility reached its peak, the in-migration surplus was highest in the rural municipalities, followed by country towns and industrial rural municipalities, while commuter suburbs trailed. These trends are indicative of a strongly dispersed and hardly systematic pattern of residential migration. Despite numerous memoranda on physical planning, the Dutch government did not at that time have any control over migration processes. However, that situation changed drastically in 1983. On the basis of the internal migration rates for the different groups of municipalities (Table 16.1), we can observe a leveling of migration flows.

Table 16.2 shows out-migration rates, per 1,000 of the population, for each

Table 16.2
Internal Migration between Municipalities by Type of Municipality, Netherlands, 1958–83 (rates per 1,000)

Destination

Origin		I	II	III	IV	V	VI
I. Rural	1958	17. 2	7. 2	2. 2	5. 5	5. 7	6. 9
municipalities	1968	15. 7	6. 9	2. 8	6. 6	5. 5	6. 1
	1973	16. 4	7. 7	2. 8	7. 1	5. 3	6. 1
	1983	7. 9	7. 6	3. 5	6. 5	5. 8	5. 4
II. Industrial rural	1958	9. 2	9. 8	2. 4	4. 2	7. 2	9. 4
municipalities	1968	8. 4	9. 5	3. 2	5. 7	6. 7	7. 8
	1973	10. 3	11. 3	2. 9	5. 9	6. 7	7. 5
	1983	3. 7	9. 3	3. 5	4. 3	5. 9	6. 3
III. Commuter	1958	9. 0	7. 3	11. 2	4. 3	11. 4	24. 9
suburbs	1968	10. 4	7. 8	12. 4	4. 8	10. 4	19. 8
	1973	14. 0	9. 6	12. 6	5. 6	8. 8	17. 6
	1983	3. 2	6. 0	11. 0	4. 2	7. 3	14. 9
IV. Country and	1958	12. 8	8. 5	3. 0	6. 6	8. 6	11. 8
small towns	1968	13. 8	10. 6	3. 8	8. 3	8. 7	10. 5
	1973	17. 2	10. 4	3. 3	7. 5	7. 0	8. 1
	1983	6. 3	8. 5	4. 9	5. 5	6. 0	7. 6
V. Medium-sized	1958	7. 9	7. 9	4. 7	4. 0	7. 6	13. 9
towns	1968	9. 8	9. 4	6. 3	5. 7	9. 0	11. 5
	1973	15. 7	13. 4	6. 3	7. 0	8. 5	10. 8
	1983	4. 1	7. 9	7. 9	3. 9	6. 0	8. 5
VI. Large towns	1958	5. 2	5. 7	6. 5	3. 0	7. 0	8. 4
	1968	8. 9	7. 6	10. 4	5. 1	7. 6	7. 4
	1973	12. 9	10. 8	11. 7	6. 9	7. 4	6. 4
	1983	4. 1	6. 9	11. 9	5. 3	5. 5	6. 2

Source: Central Bureau of Statistics, Continuous Population Register of
the Netherlands

group of municipalities, subdivided by the degree of urbanization of place of origin. Total out-migration between 1958 and 1973 was fairly constant, with the exception of medium and large cities. In both cases, out-migration increased sharply. In 1983, departure rates declined abruptly in each group of municipalities, although the decline was stronger in commuter suburbs and in the cities than nationally.

In 1958 the largest outflows from each group of municipalities were directed to large cities. In 1973, on the other hand, the direction of the major outflows changed considerably. In-migration was greatest among rural municipalities. Then there followed a period of suburbanization, which made it all the more surprising that out-migration to commuter suburbs lagged behind out-migration to the rural municipalities. Thus, spatial planning policy lacked the necessary instruments to be able to achieve the aim of a clustered form of deconcentration which was desired at that time. Within a period of ten years, this situation had changed. It is not possible, however, to state objectively whether this came about because of or despite government policy. However, it is a fact that the flows toward rural municipalities have slowed down considerably, whereas commuter suburbs, including a number of growth centers, have become more important.

WHO MOVES

With the exception of the forced migration of entire populations, migrants do not usually constitute a cross-section of society. The selectivity found in migration is generally most apparent with regard to age, though factors such as sex, marital status, and occupation also play a role in the selectivity of migration. We will now examine the extent to which these variables influence migration frequency at the national level. We have opted for a comparison between the year 1973, when mobility was highest, and 1983. No attention is given to migration in the 1960s because no information is available about the age of migrants before 1972.

Characteristics of Movers at the National Level

Table 16.3 gives the absolute and relative number of migrants, according to three demographic characteristics—gender, age, and marital status. Social differences between males and females are not reflected in mobility differences, although the decline in mobility was steeper among males. Moreover, the generalization that, on average, single women migrate over shorter distances than single men cannot be substantiated. However, the share of single women who migrate is smaller than that of single men.

Migration rates are quite different among age groups. People in their 20s tend to migrate a great deal, mainly because it is at this age that most people marry and embark on a career. The lowest migration rates are found at ages 50 to 64, with increases in mobility at older ages. This was particularly apparent in 1973

Table 16.3

Internal Migration by Gender, Age, and Marital Status, Netherlands, 1973 and 1983

	1973		1983		
	number	rate per 1,000	number	rate per 1,000	Index (1973=100)
Gender:					
Male	360,690	53.8	275,704	38.7	76
Female	355,790	52.8	279,721	38.5	79
Age:					
0–14	154,300	44.2	89,826	30.7	58
15–19	76,010	66.8	55,877	45.2	74
20–24	156,190	138.2	132,499	105.4	85
25–29	119,350	105.9	90,580	76.4	76
30–39	94,780	57.4	88,841	38.7	94
40–49	42,820	28.2	33,579	20.2	78
50–64	38,430	20.0	34,423	16.2	90
65+	34,590	24.5	29,800	17.4	86
Marital Status:					
Married	336,500	51.7	197,082	28.6	59
Single	349,180	57.1	312,111	49.8	90
widowed and divorced	30,810	37.5	46,232	37.0	150
Total	716,480	53.3	555,425	38.7	78

Source: Central Bureau of Statistics, Continuous Population Register of the Netherlands

and may be attributed in part to retirement migration, found especially among 65-year-old men (Vergoossen, 1983). By 1983, this retirement peak had more or less disappeared, partly as a result of societal trends such as the widespread introduction of early retirement schemes. The high migration rate among the elderly may also be attributed to the migration of the very old, especially women, who move to old people's homes and service flats.

As for the selectivity of migration by marital status, it is primarily the changes between 1973 and 1983 that deserve mention, rather than the differences between the three categories. The mobility of married persons has dropped much more sharply than that of the total population. This is also reflected in the reduction in mobility among persons under 15 years of age, who would migrate with their parents. This may be attributed to declining suburbanization, which often includes families with young children. Moreover, the decline in the number of married migrants has also undoubtedly been caused by the rising number of cohabitants, who do not possess the "married" status, but often involve a move when the couple decide to live together. This trend has also contributed to the limited decline in mobility among the unmarried.

The overall lack of change among "ever-married" is the result of divergent behavior by its component members. If we subdivide this group into the divorced and the widowed, we see that migration among the divorced increased by no less than 251 percent! Migration among the widowed, on the other hand, declined by 13 percent. The only socioeconomic characteristic that can be derived from official "removal cards" is the migrant's profession. This piece of information is available only for heads-of-family and for persons who migrate individually. The professional data given on the card are not, however, very useful. Some groups of professions given on the card are fairly heterogeneous since the classification used lacks detail. For example, the category listed as "no professions" also includes students. In addition, the listing of a profession does not necessarily mean that the person actually works. This is particularly pertinent since unemployment has risen sharply in the past ten to fifteen years and has influenced the pattern of migration. The extent to which this trend influences migration cannot, however, be measured by the available data. For this reason, we have not categorized migration by profession.

Interregional Migration by Family Context

The differences observed between married and nonmarried migrants warrant further analysis of the question of whether the general mobility decline and the concomitant changes in spatial migration patterns (Figure 16.1) also apply to specific groups. The data provided by the Netherlands Central Bureau of Statistics on spatial migration patterns can be subdivided only by sex and family formation patterns. The latter aspect will be looked at in more detail here because of its relationship to the suburbanization process.

In 1950, 40 percent of all migrants moved as part of a family. Because of suburbanization, this percentage rose to 57.3 percent in 1973, after which it again dropped sharply to 46.8 percent. This decline was caused by both socioeconomic and demographic factors, namely, declining nuptiality and an increasing number of divorces. The decline in "family migration" is most apparent in intraprovincial migration and may be interpreted as a slowing down in the process of suburbanization. Compared with the decline in family migration, the declining proportion of individual migrants is minimal: 26.7 percent as opposed to 30.5 percent, respectively, in the period 1973 to 1983.

Table 16.4 shows the different spatial migration patterns for both groups of migrants. For "family migrants" net migration surpluses or deficits for each region declined, with the exception of the Southern Ijsselmeer Polders, where a net migration surplus has risen sharply. As has been mentioned before, this is due in part to the overspill function of a number of growth centers, particularly the urban agglomeration of Amsterdam.

As for individual migrants, net migration surpluses in the north, east, and southwest become deficits; the deficit of the west became a large surplus, while the deficit of the south and the surplus of the southern Ijsselmeer Polders grew. Factors that have influenced these movements are employment and educational opportunities, as well as a varied urban living environment.

Table 16.4
Net Migration to Regions by Family Status, Netherlands, 1973 and 1983

	Persons in Families		Individuals	
	1973	1983	1973	1983
North	6,329	1,140	1,071	- 513
East	11,445	2,094	496	- 2,073
West	-32,133	-16,155	- 340	3,498
Southwest	1,311	790	165	- 145
South	11,143	2,278	- 1,709	- 3,255
Southern Ijsselmeer Polders	1,905	9,853	317	2,488

Source: Central Bureau of Statistics, Continuous Population Register of the Netherlands

Both categories of migrants have contributed to the leveling off of regional migration, as a result of (1) the decrease in net migration of family migrants from the west and (2) the net migration surpluses of individual migrants.

Urban-Rural Migration By Family Situation

Table 16.5 provides a deeper insight into the changes in net migration levels by family situation for municipalities according to their degree of urbanization.

Table 16.5
Net Internal Migration by Family Status and Municipality Type, Netherlands, 1973 and 1983

	1973		1983	
	in families	indi-viduals	in families	indi-viduals
Rural municipalities	54,710	- 3,571	8,327	- 3,463
Industrial rural municipalities	31,864	456	9,091	-6,920
Commuter suburbs	10,356	1,624	13,925	-3,527
Country and small towns	12,159	6,035	6,574	2,924
Medium sized towns	-22,087	415	- 4,108	2,627
Large towns	-87,002	- 4,959	-33,817	8,250

Source: Central Bureau of Statistics, Continuous Population Register of the Netherlands

Once again, net migration is seen to level off. Note, however, that the decline in net migration is restricted solely to the category of those who migrated as a family. This applies for all groups of municipalities, except for commuter suburbs, especially for rural municipalities and large cities.

Net migration levels for individual migrants, however, do not follow this general trend. With the exception of the group of rural municipalities and medium-sized towns, net migration levels have risen. In addition, for the group of industrial rural municipalities and of commuter suburbs, the net migration surplus has changed into an even greater net migration deficit.

An important part of this migration deficit may be attributed to the fact that the children of those who moved to the suburbs ten to fifteen years ago had to leave these municipalities to seek work or educational opportunities. This assumption is supported by the negative net migration figures found for both groups of municipalities in the 15 to 19 and 20 to 24 age groups. The 50 percent decline in positive net migration levels in the countryside and small towns is also undoubtedly related to (the lack of) educational and employment facilities. In a typology by degree of urbanization of internal migration, the presence of losers means, by definition, that there must also be winners. In our case, the winners are medium-sized and large towns. The development of the large towns is particularly remarkable: a significant net migration deficit has changed into an even more significant net migration surplus. Since 1983, the migration surplus in the large towns has been comprised exclusively of people in the age groups 15 to 19 and 20 to 24. It is hardly surprising that the individual migrants are those young adults who, as mentioned above, have migrated from other places.

WHY PEOPLE MOVE

Analysis of the motives for migration requires specific surveys, since removal cards do not include such information. The best source for this is the housing survey, which includes questions on motives for past moves. Here we will use data derived from the 1981 survey. National data on an individual basis are not available for the period preceding 1960.

The data in Table 16.6 refer to moves in the three years preceding the survey (1978 and later). In addition, the moves have been divided into those within a municipality, within a housing market area, and between housing market areas.

The significance of various motives, and changes therein, are in some cases clearly related to the distance between the old and new residence. For example, the importance of the factor "employment" increases as the distance migrated increases. The opposite is true for the factor "unattractive housing." The motive "unattractive living environment," on the other hand, is hardly sensitive to the influence of distance. The factor "health" is most important in intramunicipal migration; this would include the movement of elderly to less independent living arrangements such as old-people's homes and nursing homes. The most impor-

Table 16.6

Most Important Reasons for Moving by Type of Move, Netherlands, 1978–81 (percent distribution)

Reasons	Within a Municipality	Within a Housing Market Area	Between Housing Market Area	Total
Marriage/Divorce	21. 6	27. 2	17. 7	21. 7
Education	0. 9	2. 7	8. 9	2. 9
Wish to live alone	9. 1	6. 8	4. 2	7. 6
Work	2. 5	10. 5	31. 7	10. 1
Housing	23. 0	15. 3	8. 4	18. 5
Environment	7. 5	7. 6	6. 0	7. 2
Health	8. 3	4. 2	4. 1	6. 6
Involuntary	4. 3	1. 0	0. 5	2. 9
Other	21. 7	16. 1	15. 6	19. 5
No response	1. 1	8. 6	2. 9	2. 8

Source: Central Bureau of Statistics, 1981 Housing Survey

tant migration motive is the transition to the next life-cycle phase following marriage, such as the beginning of nonmarital cohabitation or divorce.

If we compare the major migration motives by age group, interesting differences are revealed. Among those under 25 years of age, personal reasons, such as marriage, cohabitation, further education, or the desire to live independently, predominate. Together they form 57.5 percent of the migrants' major motives. As one grows older, the factor "unattractive housing" becomes more important. In the 35 to 44 age group, this is the most important migration motive (27.5 percent). Among the elderly, health reasons predominate, accounting for more than 50 percent of migration in the 75 and over age group.

POPULATION REDISTRIBUTION POLICY AT THE MACRO- AND MICROLEVEL

Although regional differences in births and deaths have, until a few decades ago, been responsible for an unbalanced distribution of the population across various regions of the Netherlands and across the provinces, this imbalance may now be attributed primarily to age-specific migration. Regions that are sparsely populated as a result of net out-migration are usually economically deprived and predominantly rural. On the other hand, the living environment in such regions can be very attractive. For example, there is a greater supply of reasonably priced housing, especially for single family houses.

At the municipal level, migration has resulted in an unbalanced urban population structure and the decline of the inner cities, a loss of open space, and most probably also the disappearance of typical urban facilities. In view of these developments, in the postwar period the government of the Netherlands (like most European countries) has followed a policy aimed at effecting a more even distribution of the population across the country, with special emphasis on controlling suburbanization. In the Netherlands, population redistribution policy forms part of the overall spatial policy.

Two important reports in this respect, which also deal with population redistribution issues, were the First Memorandum (1960) and Second Memorandum (1966) on Physical Planning. The main goals laid down in these reports were the stimulation of population growth in the north of the country through migration from the west and a clustered form of decentralization. The major motives for this policy were the desire to curb congestion in the west, to stimulate the development of the deprived regions, and to end further destruction and dispersion of open spaces.

In the 1970s, however, a number of trends triggered changes in the population (redistribution) policy. We mention but a few of these trends:

1. A sharp decline in forecast population growth. It is now expected that in the not far distant future, the Netherlands will have a stationary—or even a declining—population.

2. Growing consciousness and interest in environmental problems as witnessed, among other things, by growing concern regarding per capita land use—not only in the urban areas, but also in rural areas.

3. Large-scale migration from the west to the south and east, which had not yet reached its peak. In fact, it was feared that problems related to population pressure and congestion would move from the west to the provinces of North Brabant and Gelderland.

4. Long-distance commuting, and concomitant unsolvable traffic problems which increased dramatically because of migration.

5. The beginnings of an economic slump, giving rise—for the first time since the war—to growing unemployment rates.

As a result, the Urbanization Report of 1976 no longer mentioned the need for population redistribution, and stimulation of population growth in the north was no longer felt to be necessary. Moreover, migration from the Randstad (Rotterdam to Amsterdam) conurbation to North Brabant and Gelderland had to be curbed. All in all, the aim was to arrive at a balanced net migration. At the microlevel, this meant that one wanted to stimulate the clustered form of decentralization by directing the suburbanization flows into growth centers.

In the 1984 Structural Outline Plan for Urban Areas, policy goals at the macrolevel were adapted. In view of the economic slump, the former goal of decentralizing employment was rejected even in regional economic policy. Regional economic development should not so much be stimulated from the outside, but should rather emerge from the intrinsic economic possibilities of the region itself. As such, spatial policy, which in the past was directed at reducing differences in population and employment, is now concerned with the growth potential of the individual regions. In this respect, emphasis is placed on the west as the region with greatest employment opportunities.

At the microlevel, the 1984 Structural Outline Plan also envisages changes with respect to urban overspill. The philosophy of the "compact city" is introduced here, chiefly with respect to the big cities. Much more so than was thought possible in the past, housing should be developed in the inner cities to prevent the population from leaving. Employment should also be concentrated in the cities. As a result, large-scale construction activities in the growth centers will have to be terminated. This will not, of course, happen immediately. The disruption to the growth centers, which will now no longer be able to carry out their plans, will be spread over several years. Judging by the migration trends after 1973, one would say that spatial policy (and particularly the population redistribution policy) which has been mapped out in the most recent government reports has been a success. Interregional net migration has, for example, leveled off. However, a number of studies point out that the changes in net migration have had little effect on the spatial pattern of internal migration (Bargeman, 1986; Gores and Vergoossen, 1986). Autonomous processes seem to be responsible for declining migration rates and for the reduction of net migration deficits in the west and in the big cities. Although some of these processes, especially the demographic trends (e.g., slow population growth and an increasing number of single and two-person households who prefer to live in urban areas) are expected to continue in the coming years, the direction that some other trends will take still remains unclear. For example, if the economy continues to recover and the market for owner-occupied housing grows, migration to the suburbs may be stimulated once again.

REFERENCES

Bargeman, C.A. 1986. *Migratie in Nederland: enn analyse van de migrate ontwikkelingen in stedelijke agglomeraties, periurbane gebieden en extra urbane gebieden in de periode 1970–1983 [Migration in the Netherlands: an analysis of the migration developments in large agglomerations, peri-urban areas and extra-urban areas in the period 1970–1983]*. The Hague: National Physical Planning Agency.

Brekel, J.C. van den. 1977. *The Population Register: The Example of the Netherlands System*. Chapel Hill, N.C. Scientific Report Series, No. 31.

Erf, R.F. van. 1984. Internal Migration in the Netherlands: Measurement and Main

Characteristics. Pp. 47–68 in Henk ter Heide and Frans J. Willekens (eds.), *Demographic Research and Spatial Policy*. London: Academic Press.

Gestel, P. van. 1981. *Overloopperspektieven in de Noord-vleu-gel van de Randstad tot 1990 in het licht van de demograpfishe ontwikkelingen [Overspill perspectives in the Northern Wing of the Randstad until 1990 in the light of demographic developments]*. Amsterdam: Vrije Universiteit, Geografisch en Planologisch Instituut.

Ginkel, J.A. van. 1977. *Suburbanisatie en recente woonmilieu's, deel I en II [Suburbanisation and recent residential areas, vols. I and II]*. Utrecht: Utrechtse Geografische Studies: No. 16.

Gores, H., and Th.W.M. Vergoossen. 1986. *Country Report: Elderly Migration in the Netherlands*. Workshop Elderly Migration. Nijmegen.

Heide, H. ter. 1965. *Binnelandse migratie in Nederland [Internal migration in the Netherlands]*. Den Haag: Staatsuitgeverij.

———, and C. Leo Eichperger. 1974. "De interne migratie" [The internal migration]. Pp. 222–43 in H.J. Heeren and P.K. van Praag, *Van nu tot nul: bevolkingsgroei en bevolkingspolitiek in Nederland [From now to zero: population growth and population policy in the Netherlands]*. Utrecht: Het Spectrum.

———, and C. Leo Eichperger. 1978. *Dynamic Interrelations Between Population Redistribution Policy and Demographic Developments*. The Hague: National Physical Planning Agency.

Keilman, Nico. 1986. *Data and Sources on Mobility in the Netherlands*. The Hague: NIDI.

Ogilvy, A. 1979. "Migration: The Influence of Economic Change." *Futures*. 12:383–94.

Vergoossen, Th.W.M. 1983. *Pensioenmigratie in Nederland* [Retirement migration in the Netherlands]. Nijmegen: Geografisch Instituut.

17

POLAND

Piotr Korcelli

Both the nature and intensity of internal migration in Poland have evolved over the last forty years or so. This process began shortly after the Second World War when large-scale, interregional population movements resulted from shifts in national boundaries. The postwar resettlement lasted until around 1948 and was followed by another stage of high spatial mobility of the population during the 1950s owing to reconstruction and extensive industrialization.

Since then, large-scale rural-to-urban flows, as well as net population relocations from small- to middle-sized and large urban places, have remained among the salient features of internal migrations in Poland. The evolution of the age composition of the population, together with changes in spatial development policies, have contributed to fluctuations in the overall migration volume which decreased notably during the late 1960s, expanded again during the 1970s, and fell sharply in the 1980s.

DATA ON MIGRATION

Definitions of Migration

According to the Central Statistical Office (1986), internal migration is defined as a change of permanent residence which involves crossing the boundary of one of the smallest administrative units (i.e., towns and rural townships), which numbered 812 and 2,121, respectively, in 1985. Throughout this chapter, they will also be referred to as urban and rural places. Interregional migration represents a move between any pair of the forty-nine voivodships (i.e., administrative units of the upper level), whereas a move within a voivodship is an intraregional migration.

In the population register, migration is recorded at the point of destination at the time of the move. Data are reported for periods of one year without adjustment for multiple transitions. In comparison, in the population census, information is entered about the previous place of de facto residence, the year in which the move took place, and the place of birth.

Sources of Data

The 1978 census of population included a migration survey that covered 10 percent of all households. In addition to an array of demographic and socioeconomic characteristics of migrants, census materials provided rather detailed information concerning reasons for migration. The current population register, along with some geographical detail, offers a disaggregation of migrants by sex, age, family status, level of education, source of income, industry, and occupation. The census and the population register represent largely alternative rather than complementary sources of migration data, and attempts to make the two sets compatible often result in serious estimation problems (see Kupiszewski, 1986).

A number of special migration surveys have also been conducted over the last fifteen years. Among these are nationwide studies on the socioeconomic mobility of the population and the causes of internal migration, carried out by the Central Statistical Office in 1972 and 1974. There have also been several regional surveys focusing on the socioeconomic status of migrants. More recently, the results of a survey on the consequences of internal migration were discussed by A. Ochocki (1986). Furthermore, K. Stolarczyk (1985) has conducted similar questionnaire-based research on elderly migration. Finally, J. Witkowski (1985) has used results of a special survey on living conditions to analyze the spatial and social mobility of the Polish population.

Quality of Data

Two specific problems deserve a brief treatment under this heading. These concern the distinction between "permanent" and "temporary" migration, and the effects of boundary changes on migration time series. In the population register, moves are enumerated which are accompanied by changes of the place of permanent residence. Hence, a shift of residence without a physical move is recorded as migration while a move without a change of status is not. Disparities between these two processes were particularly noticeable in large urban regions during periods of migration control. This was the case in the city of Warsaw where such measures were in force between 1954 and 1983.

For any macrolevel analysis, the quality of migration data depends largely on the stability of the system of spatial reporting units. In the case of Poland, the current system was introduced during 1972–75. Hence, data comparability is restricted to the last fifteen years. Some estimates of the pattern of in- and out-migration within present administrative divisions exist for earlier years such as 1970.

PRINCIPAL POPULATION MOVEMENTS

The National Level

According to the 1978 census of population, 46.4 percent of the total population lived in locations other than the place of birth at the time of the census. This figure, of course, is an aggregate that conceals substantial variations in spatial mobility levels among individual population cohorts and among time periods. In the early 1960s, after the postwar resettlement and subsequent large-scale population movements resulting from extensive industrialization came to an end, the crude internal migration rate (i.e., the number of moves per 1,000 population) became stabilized at twenty-six to thirty. A decrease in this rate to around twenty-four during 1973–74 represented a statistical artifact as a consequence of an increase in the size of the smallest administrative units.

Spatial mobility rates increased again in the late 1970s when the pull of industrial labor markets was very strong. However, since that time there has been a pronounced, continuous decline (see Figure 17.1). In 1978, every thirty-sixth Pole changed his or her town or township of residence, but only one out of fifty-five did so in 1985.

It is estimated that around one-third of the recent decline in the internal migration rate is attributable to changes in population age composition, particularly the smaller proportion of those aged 20 to 29 who have the highest migration propensity. The other two-thirds of this decline are thought to be caused by economic and social factors such as a breakdown of housing construction programs in major urban areas and a better outlook for private farming.

The age structure of migrants reveals a very pronounced peak in the young adult ages, a descending gradient for those aged 0 to 14 years, and an ascending gradient at ages 55 and older (see Figure 17.2). This pattern is close to the model migration schedule described by A. Rogers and L. Castro (1981). However, unlike the model schedule, which shows a retirement peak, migration propensities among the elderly increase with age. In fact, migration of the elderly is related mainly to such factors as health and family reasons rather than to retirement (see Korcelli and Potrykowska, 1986).

Differences between the age schedules of male and female migrants are typical of many industrial countries; age-specific rates for females are generally higher among young adults. In the case of female migrants, the labor force peak corresponds to those aged 20 to 24. In the case of male migrants, this shifts to those aged 25 to 29. As Figure 17.2 also shows, both the age and sex composition of migrants is rather stable over time, despite considerable variations in the volume of movement between 1978 and 1985.

Figure 17.1
Number of Internal Migrations and Internal Migration Rates, 1970–85

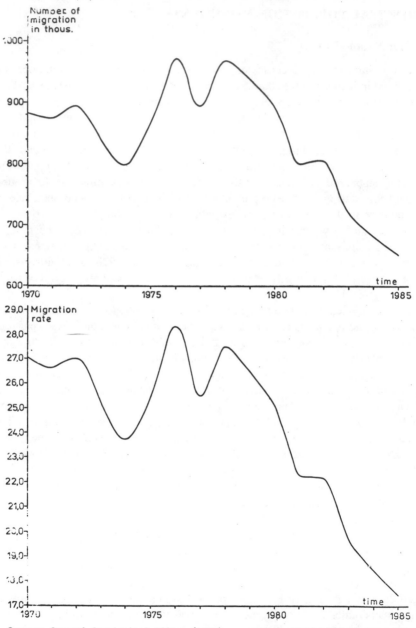

Source: Central Statistical Office (1986), current Population Register
        of Poland.

Interregional Migration

Many authors have noticed that most of the internal migration in Poland involves moves over relatively short distances (see, for example, Gawryszewski, 1974). Actually, intraregional movement accounted for 61.3 percent of all migration in 1985, in comparison with 59.7 percent in 1983. The recent contraction of spatial population mobility seems to disproportionately affect long-distance migration.

Out of the 251,566 interregional moves in 1985, about one-third (86,527) were between individual urban places. At the intraregional level, only about one-fifth were between urban places. These proportions were consistent with the findings of Ochocki (1986), who found that moves originating in urban areas typically involve longer distances than moves originating in rural areas.

The age pattern of interregional migration is characterized by a considerable degree of regularity and stability through time. Such results were obtained by A. Potrykowska (1986) who fitted the Rogers-Castro model to 1978 and 1981 data for several major regions of Poland. At a more disaggregated level, different types of regions, such as large-city or rural regions may be found to display specific age distributions of both in-migrants and out-migrants. For example, the outflow schedule for the capital region tends to be less labor-force dominant than the corresponding inflow schedule (Korcelli, 1982). At the same time, however, specific differences may be found between the central city and the metropolitan ring. For example, the share of migration to the city of Warsaw, in terms of the total inflow to urban regions, is higher for older individuals and lower for younger age categories.

The peak in the labor-force age groups is poorly articulated. This is in contrast with the schedules provided by W. Frey (1984) for six major cities in the United States. However, both Frey's profiles and those for Warsaw have ascending values in the age categories starting at 35. (For a more detailed discussion, see Korcelli, 1987a.)

Migration in the Urban-Rural Context

The concept of mobility transition (Zelinsky, 1971) allows one to place some aggregate characteristics of migratory flows within a general temporal framework. Let us consider the evolving intensity and directions of internal migration in Poland against this standard. In the development process it is assumed that parallel to the vital revolution, countries undergo a transition from low to high and then again to low mobility. Along with this change the dominant direction of migratory flows shifts from rural-rural to rural-urban to urban-urban and, finally, to an urban-rural orientation.

Data in Table 17.1 offer some support to the above interpretation. As mentioned earlier, the postwar peak of labor migration occurred in the mid-fifties, followed by a secondary peak in the late seventies. Since then, internal migration

Figure 17.2
Migration by Age Schedules. A - 1978, B - 1985, 1 - total, 2 - males, 3 - females

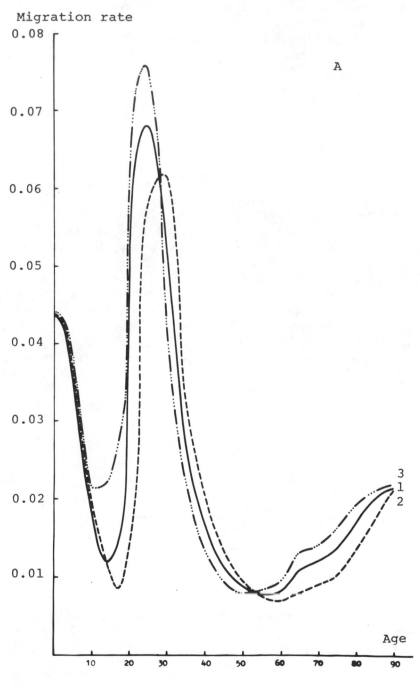

Figure 17.2 *(Continued)*

Migration rate

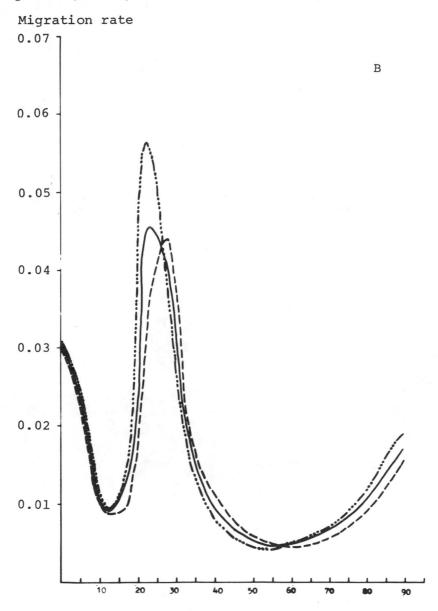

Source: Central Statistical Office (1986), current Population Register
of Poland.

Table 17.1
Internal Migration in Poland by Urban and Rural Status

Number (in 1,000) and percentage of moves: mean annual figures

Time periods	Total Number	%	urban–urban Number	%	rural–urban Number	%	urban–rural Number	%	rural–rural Number	%
1952–1955	1408.5	100.0	392.7	27.8	363.2	25.7	263.4	18.7	389.2	27.6
1956–1960	1343.5	100.0	311.6	23.2	322.1	24.0	238.1	17.7	471.7	35.1
1961–1965	1006.2	100.0	225.7	22.4	260.8	25.9	160.2	15.9	359.5	35.7
1966–1970	864.8	100.0	189.4	21.9	253.1	29.3	113.5	13.1	308.8	35.7
1971–1975	854.2	100.0	201.9	23.6	291.1	34.1	103.5	12.1	257.7	30.2
1976–1980	932.5	100.0	262.7	28.2	336.5	36.1	123.0	13.2	210.3	22.5
1981–1985	732.2	100.0	201.2	27.4	252.8	34.5	115.6	15.8	162.6	22.2

Source: Central Statistical Office (1986)

rates have declined precipitously. The initial dominance of rural-rural migration was replaced around 1970 by the preponderance of rural-to-urban moves. The share of migration which is interurban has increased markedly since the early 1970s, although it remains below the corresponding rural-to-urban share. Regardless of changing overall mobility levels, the rural areas generate a persistently high proportion of the total number of moves. Whereas the percentage of the rural population decreased from 51.7 to 39.8 between 1960 and 1985 (and from 15.4 to 14.9 million in absolute terms), the share of moves from rural origins changed insignificantly throughout that period (from 59.1 percent during 1956–60 to 56.7 percent during 1984–85).

Differences in the relative size of the four migration categories reflect different propensities to move, the relative size of the rural and urban populations, and the nature of areal units for which data on migration are reported. In particular, consolidation of some 4.3 thousand communes into some 2.2 thousand townships in the early 1970s produced a reduction in the number of reported rural-to-rural moves by about one-third. Urban-to-urban flows, on the other hand, fail to account for the bulk of intraurban residential mobility, since only moves between major districts of the five largest cities, along with interurban moves are included in the statistics.

While taking these data limitations into account, it appears that the change in the structure of migration between urban and rural areas has been rather slow when compared to the evolution of overall spatial mobility. This suggests the recent mobility decline to be a transitional, rather than persistent, phenomenon. In fact, spatial mobility rates may be expected to increase again during the early 1990s. At the time, the relatively large cohort born between 1975 and 1983 will be entering the labor market or enrolling in institutions of higher education, which are concentrated in the major cities. It seems, however, that the main phase of rural-urban migration in Poland drew to an end around 1980 and that any future increase in spatial mobility is likely to involve urban populations.

Urban-to-urban migration in Poland has consistently conformed to a hierarchical pattern, in which urban places in a given size category are net gainers in their interaction with places in each of the smaller size categories and net losers with respect to each of the larger size groups.

The above regularity may be found in the matrix of interurban migration for 1985 (Table 17.2). Of the fifteen possible pairs of size categories, fourteen conform to the hierarchical migration concept. The only exception to the rule is the slightly larger volume of movement from cities of over 100,000 population to those within the 50,000 to 100,000 population category relative to the size of the reverse flow. The same holds true for the pattern of destination-specific net migration rates, an example of which is shown in Figure 17.3. In this process, each of the size categories of urban places from below 5,000 to those of 20,000 to 50,000 inhabitants suffered losses, while places of 50,000 inhabitants and above gained more migrants than they lost. However, when rural-to-urban and

Table 17.2
Interurban Migrations in Poland, 1985

From Urban Places of:	To Urban Place of:						
	total	below 5000	5000– 9000	10000– 19000	20000– 49000	50000– 99000	100000– and above
below 5000	10.3	0.5	0.8	1.6	2.4	1.7	3.3
5090–9000	14.7	0.5	1.1	1.8	3.0	2.4	6.0
10000–19000	22.4	1.1	1.5	2.7	4.5	3.1	9.5
20000–49000	32.6	1.3	2.7	3.7	5.7	4.2	15.0
5000–99000	21.8	0.9	1.5	2.1	3.5	2.5	11.5
100000 and above	66.2	2.3	4.6	8.2	12.8	11.6	26.8
total	168.1	6.7	12.1	20.1	31.9	25.5	71.8

Source: Central Statistical Office (1986)

Figure 17.3
Destination-Specific Migration Rates, Urban Places of 10,000 to 19,000 Inhabitants
A - In-Migration, B - Out-Migration

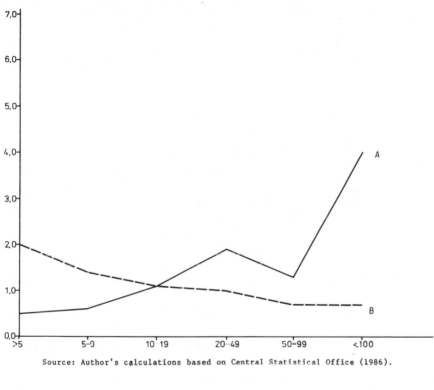

Source: Author's calculations based on Central Statistical Office (1986).

A--In-Migration   B--Out-Migration

urban-to-rural flows were accounted for, all places except those of the smallest size (i.e., below 5,000 inhabitants) had a positive migration balance.

A more comprehensive approach to the study of interurban migration would require the identification of an urban hierarchy, with reference to functions and spatial distributions of urban places, rather than simply in terms of population size. Such an attempt was made by Z. Rykiel and A. Zurkowa (1981) who used a complete matrix of urban-to-urban movements for 1974. Their findings corroborate the rule of hierarchical migration with dominant flows occurring from urban places of lower order to those of higher order. For a typical urban place, the largest number of out-migrants moved directly to one of the eleven regional centers, which were in turn subordinated to the national capital.

To summarize this section, one may conclude that the recent decline of spatial mobility in Poland cannot be readily interpreted within Zelinsky's mobility transition framework. The numerical dominance of rural-to-urban flows, along with the prevailing hierarchical pattern of interurban migration, are both features of an intermediate rather than a late stage of mobility transition.

The transition concept cannot account for policies that have the effect of accelerating, or slowing down, this transition. The slowing effect has been dominant in the case of Poland. In particular, urban growth limitation policies, carried out during the 1960s, contributed to a decrease of spatial population mobility during that decade.

WHO MOVES

Characteristics of Movers

Aside from the age and sex structure of population movement which has been discussed earlier in this chapter, current population statistics allow a look into the composition of migrants relative to the total population including characteristics such as martial status and education. Regarding marital status, 75.5 percent of all male and 69.1 percent of all female migrants were married, while, among the total population, the levels were 68.9 and 63.7 percent, respectively. Widowers, widows, and the never married were underrepresented among migrants. Finally, there were more divorced men among migrants (2.9 percent) than among the population as a whole (1.7 percent); the reverse was true in the case of divorcees (2.3 and 2.9 percent, respectively).

With regard to educational status, migrants are characterized by a much higher level of attainment when compared with the total population. Among migrants, 8.9 percent had higher (i.e., university) education in 1985 (against 5.8 percent of the nation as a whole); 31.1 percent were persons who had completed a secondary school (while nationally the level was 23.3 percent); and 32.6 percent were graduates of secondary vocational schools (though only 20.2 percent did so nationally).

Some of the difference between the migrant population and the total population are counterintuitive, while others are not. A striking feature of the data referred to is the low share of never married men among migrants. This stems from the fact that a large share among young male migrants move on a "temporary" basis and are not covered by current migration statistics. Results of the comparison between migrants and the total population in terms of educational levels may also be partly misleading owing to considerable variation among the individual population age categories. In particular, the predominance of younger age groups among migrants causes the higher educational attainment of migrants when compared to the total population. This suggests that a more disaggregate approach is needed to deal with these questions in a systematic way (see Korcelli and Potrykowska, 1986).

An alternative set of data on migrants' socioeconomic characteristics has recently been developed by Ochocki (1986), whose questionnaire-based study included 2,096 migrants aged 15 and over and covered the period from 1970 to 1983. In this study, younger migrants, particularly those of labor market-entry age (from 18 to 29 years of age), tended to move over shorter distances than did older migrants. In addition, in the case of migrants moving from urban areas, a positive statistical association was found between the population size at the origin and the distance of migration.

The level of education among the migrants at the time of their move was also positively correlated with the population size of the place of origin. For example, 26.1 percent among those who moved out of cities with at least half a million inhabitants were college and university graduates. The corresponding shares for rural areas and small towns were 3.0 and 9.4 percent, respectively. The relevant in-migration shares showed smaller amounts of variation (2.5 percent for rural areas, 7.9 percent for small towns, and 9.9 percent for the largest urban center).

WHY PEOPLE MOVE

Economic Reasons

At the macrolevel, the magnitude and direction of internal migration in Poland have been influenced primarily by industrialization and urbanization (see Latuch, 1970). In fact, industrial expansion represented the main driving force of urban growth, particularly during the 1950s. Out of 241 urban centers with 10,000 inhabitants or more in 1960, 140 had at least 50 percent of their total employment in industry and construction (Dziewonski et al., 1977). As a result, large and middle-sized centers expanded at the expense of small towns where the economic base had been affected by the socialization of private trade and small industry during the late 1940s. Interdependence of industrial change and migration also persisted during the 1960s and the 1970s. For example, during 1966–70, administrative districts with net in-migration accounted for 64 percent of industrial employment growth and 88 percent of all new investment outlays in industry (Stpiczynski, 1972).

Spatial policies generally followed industrial location policies until the late 1970s. This held true with respect to the allocation of housing, transportation improvements, and public services. In the case of skilled and professional migrants, the pull of industrial jobs and higher industrial wages gradually became overshadowed by such factors as availability of alternative employment opportunities and educational facilities.

In order to meet the expanding demand for labor in both the established (in particular, Upper Silesia) and new (for example, the copper district of Legnica-Glogow) industrial regions, an active recruitment policy was implemented, especially in the 1970s. Incentives to the prospective migrant, including transfer subsidies and installation payments, were offered by enterprises in various industrial sectors (see Dziewonski and Korcelli, 1981). Following the decline of industrial output and a contraction of industrial employment, the level of statistical association between the size and share of employment in industry and net migration gain by individual voivodships fell substantially during the early 1980s. Nevertheless, the major industrial regions have retained a positive balance in internal migration.

Social and Environmental Reasons

At the microlevel, the most important causes of migration appear to be those related to family and housing rather than to jobs and wage levels. This divergence between the macro- and the microperspective stems from at least three factors. First, the macroperspective typically focuses on migration by persons in the labor force, while the micro involves both family heads and their dependents as well as the elderly population. Second, for a substantial percentage of migrants (about 30 percent), a move is preceded by a period of commuting to a job in the town or township of future residence. Finally, the importance of housing factors in the process of migration is related to the availability of jobs and the scarcity of housing, which has been experienced in Poland over the last four decades.

Two migration surveys that have been concluded may help to illustrate these points. W. Mirowski (1986) presents the results of a study that covered about a thousand persons who received permanent resident status in the city of Warsaw during 1983. Their migration decisions were interpreted following the push-pull concept. Among the push factors (those that pertain to the former place of residence), inadequate housing conditions were listed as the major cause by 25 percent of all respondents, with family-related reasons cited by 12 percent. Job-related reasons (including the necessity to commute to work) were identified by 16 percent, and other factors were reported by 10 percent of the sample. As many as 32 percent of all respondents could not identify any single push factor, while the remaining 5 percent gave no answer to the question. Pull factors, related to the place of destination, included the availability of a dwelling (44 percent), job-related (20 percent), and family-related reasons (18 percent).

A similar framework was chosen by A. Rodzewicz (1986) who used materials from a family budget study. Among 2,063 migrants in the sample, 44 percent could not identify any "push" factor in their decision to move, and 35 percent gave "unsatisfactory living conditions" as the reason to migrate; residual factors were related to family (6 percent), health (4 percent), employment (3 percent), and lack of infrastructure (8 percent). With respect to factors that prompted the move to the particular place of destination, 50 percent of migrants pointed out the availability of a dwelling, 19 percent cited a better job, 18 percent listed marriage, and 13 percent indicated other reasons. A higher percentage of females than of males identified housing-related factors; the reverse was true in the case of job-related reasons.

CONSEQUENCES OF MIGRATION: THE AGGREGATE LEVEL

Demographic: Population Redistribution

Owing to internal migration, the population of Poland has become increasingly concentrated (see Dziewonski et al., 1977, for a detailed analysis). Changes in population distribution, however, have been rather slow because of the moderating effects of fertility differentials. Areas with net in-migration have generally been characterized by relatively low levels of natural increase, with the reverse being true in the case of out-migration areas.

A balanced urban hierarchy and a relatively uniform distribution of urban places have also had a major impact on the range of internal migration by causing a large proportion of moves to be contained within individual regions. The highest rates of spatial population mobility appear to have occurred in the northern and western regions where younger age groups account for large proportions of the total population.

The early 1980s have witnessed a discontinuity in the trend of population concentration on a macroregional scale. The reduced volume of internal migration has failed to offset interregional differentials in birthrates since about 1983. The continuation of current demographic patterns through the end of the present century suggests minimal changes in population distribution. According to a recent multiregional projection (Korcelli, 1987b), the share of Poland's population residing in the five largest urban agglomerations (Warsaw, Lodz, Katowice, Krakow, and Gdansk) will decline from 27.0 (1985) to 26.7 percent. Modest increases are projected for both the more rural eastern portion of the nation (34.5 to 34.7 percent) and the more urban, western portion (38.3 to 38.6 percent).

Social and Economic Consequences

During the 1970s, rural areas lost some 2 million migrants aged 18 to 29. Rural out-migration could not be explained by the substitution of capital for labor in agriculture, since the farm size structure changed little and a shortage of farm labor was observed in many of the demographically declining areas. P. Eberhardt (1988) noted that population outflow was particularly strong in the case of small communities that were remote from major cities. Deficiencies in the social and technical infrastructures of such rural areas were identified as major causes of this large-scale out-migration which, in turn, resulted in distortions of age and sex structure of the rural population. Although the secular decline in the rural population has been arrested owing to decreased mobility rates during the early 1980s, depopulation of rural areas still continues on a local scale, making this a policy issue for both the present and coming decades.

At the other end of the spatial scale, the recent contraction of internal migration has contributed to disparities between the demand for and the supply of labor within large urban agglomerations. Commuting to work, which involves some 3 million persons in the country, seems to have reached its maximum size given the present level of transportation services. Housing construction seems to be moving to smaller urban places owing to costs and land availability. Hence, a short- and midterm solution to the labor shortage in the large urban areas is believed to be increased labor productivity. In the longer run (i.e., from the mid-1990s), the volume of in-migration may be anticipated to increase because of the age composition effect and structural change in agriculture.

CONSEQUENCES OF MIGRATION: THE INDIVIDUAL LEVEL

Decisions to move are typically associated with "possibilities of improvement in the economic and social position of migrants, the desire for better living conditions, and the expectation of an improved social and physical environment" (Dziewonski and Korcelli, 1981, 29). Recent studies on internal migration in Poland offer some answers to the question of how these expectations are matched by reality. J. Witkowski (1985) has found that migration stimulates the occupational mobility of the population. For example, migrants tend to move more freely from one occupational group to another, while the careers of non-migrants are more often determined by the first job held. Witkowski also found that migrants were overrepresented in the high-ranking categories, including managerial and professional groups. Nevertheless, the higher vertical mobility of migrants is expressed in their greater chances of moving both up and down the socio-occupational scale.

For a rural, or a small-town dweller, a move to a middle-sized town is associated with a greater probability of career advancement than migration to a large city (having 200,000 or more inhabitants). Interestingly female migrants, once they migrate to urban areas, find employment predominantly in white-collar occupations, regardless of the city size (Ochocki, 1986). This suggests that migrants may be selective in terms of their socio-occupational mobility potential.

Many of the rules and generalizations concerning internal migration do not apply to elderly migrants (Korcelli and Potrykowska, 1986; Stolarczk, 1985). This is largely the case of the consequences of migration. A majority of the elderly perceive migration as an inevitable rather than an opportune event. Although migration frequently results in an improvement of well-being on a daily basis, it often implies movement from a state of self-reliance to one of dependence.

REFERENCES

Central Statistical Office. 1986. *Demographic Yearbook of Poland, 1986*. Warszawa: Central Statistical Office (in Polish.)

Dziewonski, K. et al. 1977. *Population Distribution, Migrations and the Settlement System of Poland.* Prace Geograficzne 117. Wroclaw: Ossolineum (in Polish).
————, and P. Korcelli. 1981. *Migration and Settlement: 11. Poland.* RR-81-20. Laxenburg, Austria: IIASA.
Eberhardt, P. 1988. *Depopulation Regions in Poland.* Prace Geograficzne 152. Wroclaw: Ossolineum (in Polish; in print).
Frey, W. 1984. "Lifecourse Migration of Metropolitan Whites and Blacks and the Structure of Demographic Change in Large Central Cities." *American Sociological Review* 49:808–27.
Gawryszewski, A. 1974. *Spatial Interdependence of Migration and Commuting to Work and Factors of Population Movement.* Prace Geograficzne 109. Warszawa: IG-PAN (in Polish).
Korcelli, P. 1982. "Migration and Urban Change." *International Regional Science Review* 7:193–216.
————. 1987a. "Migration and Residential Mobility in the Region of Warsaw." Paper presented at Dutch-Polish Seminar on Housing and Residential Mobility. Utrecht.
————. 1987b. "Interregional Patterns of Population Change in Poland." Paper presented at the Symposium of the Commission on Population Geography, International Geographical Union. Greifswald, German Democratic Republic.
————, and A. Potrykowska. 1986. "Elderly Migration in Poland: Trends, Prospects and Issues." Paper presented at the International Conference on Elderly Migration. Boulder, Colo.
Kupiszewski, M. 1986. "Two Types of Migration Data as Inputs to Multi-regional Demographic Model." *Przeglad Geograficzny* 58:735–64 (in Polish).
Latuch, M. 1970. *Internal Migrations in Poland Against the Background of Industrialization.* Warszawa: PWE (in Polish).
Mirowski, W. 1986. Social Factors of Migration Decisions and Adaptation of Migrants in the New Communities." Pp. 72–88 in *Sociodemographic and Economic Aspects of Contemporary Migrations in Poland.* Mongrafie i Opracowania 212. Warszawa: SGPIS (in Polish).
Ochocki, A. 1986. *The Impact of Migration upon the Distribution of Labor Resources in Poland Between 1970 and 1983.* Monografie i Opracowania 221. Warszawa: SGPIS (in Polish).
Potrykowska, A. 1986. "Modelling Inter-regional Migrations in Poland, 1977–81." *Papers of the Regional Science Association* 60:29–40.
Rodzewicz, A. 1986. "Factors of Migration Decisions as Seen in Survey-Based Studies." Pp. 185–203 in *Socio-demographic and Economic Aspects of Contemporary Migrations in Poland.* Monografie i Opracowania 212. Warszawa: SGPIS (in Polish).
Rogers, A., and L. Castro. 1981. *Model Migration Schedules.* RR-81-30. Laxenburg, Austria: IIASA.
Rykiel, Z., and A. Zurkowa. 1981. "Inter-urban Migrations in Poland: National and Regional Systems." Pp. 138–88 in K. Dziewonski and P. Korcelli (eds.), *Studies on Migrations and Settlement System of Poland.* Prace Geograficzne 140. Wroclaw: Ossolineum (in Polish).
Stolarczyk, K. 1985. *Socio-economic Factors of Elderly Migration in Poland.* Monografie i Opracowania 188. Warszawa: SGPIS (in Polish).
Stpiczynski, T. 1972. "Spatial Structure and Factors in Internal Migration During 1951–

1971." In Central Statistical Office, *Ludnosc*. Warszawa: Central Statistical Office (in Polish).

Witkowski, J. 1985. *Migrations and Social Mobility in Poland*. Monografie i Opracowania 196. Warszawa: SGPIS (in Polish).

Zelinsky, W. 1971. "The Hypothesis of the Mobility Transition." *Geographical Review* 61:219–49.

18

THE SOVIET UNION

Richard H. Rowland

A considerable stability has characterized migration processes in the territory now occupied by the USSR over the past few centuries. After being driven by the Mongols into the forests of Northern European Russia, the Russian population based on a Moscow-centered state began to move southward and eastward, first to agricultural frontiers and later to areas of urban-industrial development. Around the turn of the present century the eastern migration to Siberia accelerated and continued through the mid-twentieth century. At the same time, there was an appreciable colonial-style Russian migration into the lesser developed, predominantly Turkic-Moslem areas of the south.

In recent years, however, these two major eastward and southward streams have been reversed. Although substantial in-migration continues to occur to Siberia, it has been exceeded by out-migration since the late 1950s. In addition, since the late 1970s, a clear south-to-north migratory shift has occurred, one that is now chiefly dominated by Russians but may eventually become more Turkic-Moslem in character.

The Soviet Union has also experienced a very high level of rural-to-urban migration. Indeed, economic policies have emphasized industrialization, leading to a very rapid urbanization process.

Given possible misconceptions, it is important to emphasize that migration processes in the USSR as elsewhere in the world have also been largely age selective, voluntary, and dominated by such economic motives as availability of jobs and higher wages. Although an internal passport system and a certain amount of forced labor migration do exist, these should not obfuscate the basic similarities between the Soviet migration experience and the experience of migration in other areas of the world. In short, the USSR generally conforms to the "Laws" of Migration put forth by Ravenstein and Lee (Grandstaff, 1980; Lewis and Rowland, 1979).

DATA ON MIGRATION

Definitions of Migration

Data on migration for the USSR have been inconsistent, both spatially and temporally (Rowland, 1986c). When available, migration data have been presented in inconsistent sets of spatial units. It might be useful to describe briefly the political administrative unit structure of the USSR (Lydolph, 1979, Chapter 2). The USSR is subdivided into fifteen union republics (Soviet Socialist Republics or SSRs), which are based on and named after fifteen of the most important nationalities in the USSR. The largest by far is the RSFSR or Russian Republic. The larger of the fifteen republics are subdivided into oblasts or "equivalent" units (krays or Autonomous Soviet Socialist Republics—ASSRs). The USSR also makes use of a system of economic regions, which may consist of individual union republics, combinations of union republics, or combinations of oblasts or equivalent units within a republic. Economic regions for more recent years, which will also be used in this chapter, differ only slightly from those of 1961. Although available migration data are always presented for the union republic level, data for the subrepublic units and many economic regions are frequently unavailable. In addition, unlike the United States, political unit boundaries in the USSR occasionally change, thus making comparisons over time difficult.

Sources of Data

Migration data have been available only on an irregular basis over time. Indeed, migration data in censuses have varied in terms of definition and even availability in that some censuses have had no migration data at all.

The chief sources of population data in Russia and the USSR have been the national censuses taken in 1897, 1926, 1939, 1959, 1970, and 1979 (Russian Empire, 1899–1905; USSR, 1929, 1962–63, 1972–74, 1984). Migration data for 1897, the only census of the Russian Empire, and for 1926, the first and arguably the best census of the USSR, were based on the place-of-birth concept. The 1926 census is superior in terms of detail on migration characteristics. The political units of 1926 were also radically different and completely incomparable to those of 1897 with the political administrative unit changes brought about by the Bolshevik Revolution. The censuses of 1939 and 1959, on the other hand, contain *no* migration data.

Thus, it was not until 1970 or nearly a half century after 1926 that migration data were again present in a Soviet census. The 1970 census, however, incorporated a relatively unique definition of a migrant: one who resided in the place of enumeration for less than two years preceding the census.

The recent census of 1979 marked a return to the place-of-birth concept. In this census, migrants were defined as "those who have resided uninterruptedly at their permanent place of residence *not* from birth." Unfortunately, data for 1979 were published only at the union republic level, whereas those for 1897, 1926, and 1970 were also published for subdivisions of union republics. Some 1979 census migration data have occasionally "leaked out" in noncensus sources (for example, *Naseleniye SSSR*, 1983). The 1979 migration definition will also apparently be employed in the census planned for 1989 (*Vestnik statistiki*, 1986, No. 3, 19).

The Soviets have also published migration data based on the registration of arrivals and departures in association with the internal passport system. Such data have not been published since 1974 and pertain only to the urban population (*Vestnik statistiki*, 1975, 77–92).

Although no regular surveys are undertaken, a special survey or "microcensus" was conducted in January 1985 (*Vestnik statistiki*, 1984, No. 6, 34–39; 1984, No. 12, 41–45; 1986, No. 6, 53–55; 1986, No. 8, 75–80). The migration definition employed was similar to that for 1979 and that planned for 1989. However, unlike 1970 and 1979 migration data, which were based on a 25 percent sample, 1985 data were based on only a 5 percent sample of the population. In addition, the sampling process of the 1985 microcensus had a different regional structure than that of 1970 and 1979. Whereas the 1970 and 1979 censuses sampled one out of every four households throughout the entire country, the 1985 microcensus sampled 5 percent of Supreme Soviet electoral districts and then asked questions to everyone who lived permanently within each of these selected districts. In addition, the microcensus of January 1985 did not cover the entire country, as the Far North and several other regions were excluded because communication with these areas (*Vestnik statistiki*, 1986, No. 6, 34–35; *Zdravookhraneniye Rossiyskoy Federatsii*, 1984, No. 36, 4). Thus, when results from the 1985 microcensus are compared to those for the 1970 and 1979 censuses, it should be understood that there is always an implicit qualification that they are not strictly comparable owing to these different sampling procedures. Fortunately, however, migration data from the census planned for 1989, like those of 1970 and 1979, will be based on a 25 percent sample (*Vestnik statistiki*, 1986, No. 3, 19). It is hoped that any questions about the validity of the 1970–79 to 1985 migration trends discussed throughout this chapter will be reconciled by the 1989 census. Furthermore, only limited data have been published from the 1985 microcensus, and the lack of specific regional migration rates is an especially notable deficiency.

Fortunately, despite the relative lack of migration data per se for the USSR, it is possible to estimate net migration based on the vital statistics or residual technique. In particular, for the 1959–87 period, net migration by union republic can be assessed using annual union republic total population estimates and crude birth and death rates in the *Naradnoye khozyaystvo SSSR* statistical series.

Quality of Data

Although it is difficult to make a precise statement about the quality of migration data in the USSR, those available appear to be of acceptable quality. This conclusion is based on the general correspondence between migration patterns that emerge from the above data and known migration patterns. (For example, in recent years, the existence of net out-migration from Siberia was clearly indicated by data from the 1970 census (Lewis and Rowland, 1979.) On the other hand, net migration data based on the vital statistics or residual technique may be partly tainted by inadequacies in the recording of births and deaths (Grandstaff, 1980, 10–12, 17). Nonetheless, Grandstaff (1980, 65–84) has checked the accuracy of residual estimates by comparing them to census-survival estimates and found a very high correlation between the two. In addition, registration data available through the mid-1970s had some deficiencies, especially incomplete registration of out-migrants and in rural areas (Grandstaff, 1980, 14; Lewis and Rowland, 1979, 111–15). However, the overriding problem of Soviet migration data seems to be not so much their quality, but rather their availability and the inconsistency of their definitions and spatial units of presentation. These problems are especially unfortunate when it is remembered that the Soviet Union is by far the world's largest nation and alone accounts for one-sixth of the land area of the world.

PRINCIPAL POPULATION MOVEMENTS

The National Level

The volume and rate of migration have, as might be expected, apparently increased over time, although it is difficult to make a firm estimate, given the data problems discussed above and universal problems of defining and measuring "migration." Rough comparisons can be made between data for 1926, 1970, 1979, and 1985, because the 1926, 1979, and 1985 migrant populations are subdivided into duration-of-residence categories, and the existence of a less-than-two-year residence category in each thus affords some comparability with the 1970 definition. It should also be pointed out that the national territory of 1926 was slightly smaller than that of the post-World War II period. Based on this less-than-two-year criterion, in 1926, 4.9 million people or 3.4 percent of the total population of the country were migrants. By 1970, the number of such migrants had more than doubled to 13.9 million or 5.7 percent of the total population and by 1979, had increased further to 20.1 million or 7.7 percent.

The 1985 microcensus suggests a regression, however. According to the microcensus, 43 percent of the total population were migrants. An estimated 13.5 million people were less-than-two-year residents, which, in turn, accounted for only 4.9 percent of the total population (USSR, 1985, 8; *Vestnik statistiki*, 1986, No. 6, 55). Both figures were not only less than those of 1979, but also 1970.

If we view the total number of migrants based on place-of-birth data for 1926, 1979, and 1985, the same overall increase in migration through 1979 and subsequent regression is apparent. In 1926, the total number of migrants was 34.7 million or 23.6 percent of the total population. By 1979, the absolute number of migrants had more than tripled to 123.5 million, and the migration rate had virtually doubled to 47.1 percent. However, corresponding figures for 1985 (118.8 million and 43 percent) indicate a recent reduction.

Few data are available in recent years on the age-sex structure of migrants. No age data for the migrant population are published in the 1979 census. However, the 1970 census subdivides the migrant population into three broad categories: (1) able-bodied or "working ages" (males 16 to 59; females 16 to 54); (2) younger than able-bodied (0 to 15); an (3) older than able-bodied (males 60 and over, females 55 and over). According to these data, the working ages, not unexpectedly, accounted for the vast majority (72.5 percent) of all migrants, a proportion that was much higher than their corresponding share of the total population (54.0 percent). In addition, the 1985 microcensus indicates that the able-bodied population still accounted for the vast majority (69 percent) of all migrants (*Vestnik statistiki*, 1986, No. 3, 55). These data, as well as other sources, thus suggest that, as elsewhere in the world, migration in the USSR is age selective, with the working-age population being more mobile and constituting a relatively high share of the migrant population (Grandstaff, 1980, 59–61).

Data on sex composition are available for 1970 and 1979 but not for 1985. Given the relatively low and imbalanced sex ratio of the USSR caused by the large male population losses in World War II and low fertility, it is not surprising that females sometimes comprise the majority of the migrant population. In 1970, females accounted for 50.2 percent of the migrants. However, this share was lower than the corresponding share for the total population (53.9 percent). As a result, the female migration rate was lower than that of males: 5.4 percent of the females and 6.2 percent of the males were migrants.

Although no migration data by sex were published in the 1979 census, some "leaked out" in another source (*Naseleniye SSSR*, 1983, 49). According to this source, females were now more mobile, with 49.4 percent being migrants as opposed to 44.5 percent among males. When applied to the total male and female populations of the USSR in 1979, this means that a decided majority (56.1 percent) of migrants in 1979 were females.

Since the migration definitions in the 1970 and 1979 census were not similar, some comparability can be made by focusing on 1979 population data which indicate that the migrants resided in their place of residence less than two years. Based on "leaked" data according to the 1979 census, 8.3 percent of the total male population were migrants who lived at their permanent place of residence less than two years, while the corresponding share for females was 7.2 percent (*Naseleniye SSSR*, 1983, 49). When applied to the 1979 total male and female populations of the USSR, each constituted one-half of the less-than-two-year migrants. Consequently, this less-than-two-year comparison ultimately suggests little change from 1970 to 1979 in that males were somewhat more migratory than females, and the share of the migrants who were males and females was virtually identical in both years.

Interregional Migration

As noted above, the chief overall interregional migration streams have been from the western USSR to the east and south, although each stream has been reversed in very recent years. In particular, during the twentieth century there has been a predominantly Russian migration from European Russia eastward into Siberia, Kazakhstan, and Central Asia. In the quarter century prior to World War I it is estimated that more than 4 million people migrated to Asiatic Russia, while according to place-of-birth data from the 1926 census, there was a net in-migration of nearly 3 million people to the Urals, Siberia per se, and the Far East, and nearly 1 million to Kazakhstan and Central Asia (Lorimer, 1946, 26, 49). Although there was a considerable lack of regional migration data until the 1960s and 1970s, the eastward and southward movements evidently continued through the 1930s, 1940s, and 1950s (Lewis and Rowland, 1979, 42–151).

The most striking interregional migration trend in recent years has been a *reversal* of the eastward and southward migrations. A reversal of the Siberian or eastward migration became apparent during the 1960s, whereas a reversal of the southward migration has become very evident only since the late 1970s.

Interregional migration based on economic regions and oblast or equivalent units can be investigated through the 1979 census. Net migration patterns by economic region for 1959–70 and 1970–79 have been presented elsewhere (Rowland, 1982, 558–64). The existence of net out-migration from the Russian East or the Siberian regions combined (the Urals, West Siberia, East Siberia, and Far East) is clearly evident. Net out-migration from these four regions combined totaled −1,700,000 million between 1959 and 1970, and roughly −800,000 between 1970 and 1979. The Urals and West Siberia accounted for most this net out-migration, whereas net in-migration existed for the Far East in both periods and for East Siberia during 1970–79 (Lewis and Rowland, 1979, 116; Rowland, 1982, 562).

Net out-migration from Siberia was also clearly evident from migration data in the 1970 census. Although Siberian regions continued to have relatively high in-migration rates, they also had relatively high out-migration rates. As a result, net out-migration occurred from the two most populous subregions of the region, the Urals and West Siberia, although East Siberia and the Far East continued to have net in migration (Lewis and Rowland, 1979, 119).

It appears, however, that a high level of net out-migration from Siberia was confined to the 1960s and much of the 1970s, and that it began to decrease in the 1970s (Baldwin, 1979, 33–36; Rowland, 1982, 558–64). Indeed, since 1979, and unlike 1959–70 and 1970–79, the total population of Siberia has again begun to grow somewhat more rapidly than that of the USSR as a whole, which probably reflects an improving migration situation (Rowland, 1986b). In short, one of the major reversals in Soviet interregional migration trends may, in turn, be in the process of being reversed.

A preoccupation with Siberian migration trends may itself be in the process of taking a backseat to what may be developing into the more dominant interregional migration trend and issue in the USSR, namely, a south to north migration.

Since the late 1970s a south to north migration shift has clearly occurred in the USSR, which is a sharp contrast to preceding periods, especially 1959–70 and earlier. Between 1979 and 1987, only the more northern republics (the RSFSR, Latvia, Lithuania, and Estonia) had net in-migration, while each of the remaining eleven and more southern republics had net out-migration (Table 18.1). Indeed, between 1979 and 1987 the northern USSR had a net in-migration of roughly 1.5 million, while the southern USSR had a net out-migration of roughly −1.4 million, figures that are almost completely reversed from those of 1959–70 (Table 18.1). At this stage, this major migration reversal probably involves changes in ethnic Russian migration patterns. However, given the labor surpluses among the indigenous Turkic-Moslem peoples in the southern USSR, it is also possible to foresee their eventual migration northward (Lewis and Rowland, 1979, 408–24). This topic will be discussed in more detail later in this chapter.

In retrospect, the south to north migration shift was becoming apparent based on earlier data. Between 1970 and 1979, a turn toward the north was in the process of occurring (Table 18.1), and the 1970 census, which assessed migration from 1968 to 1970, was already indicating a south to north shift (Grandstaff, 1980, 159).

The only systematic census or microcensus age-sex data for the interregional total migrant population in the post–World War II period are from the 1970 census. Age data are presented only for the in-migrant population and the three categories noted earlier, while sex data are presented for both in-migrants and out-migrants.

Data from the 1970 census by economic region indicate no appreciable regional differences in the age composition of the in-migrants. For all regions the vast majority of the in-migrants were in able-bodied or "working ages." In particular, the range in percentages comprised by the able-bodied ages were roughly from two-thirds (67.6) to three-fourths (77.5), while the national average was 72.5 percent.

Data from the 1970 census indicate that, despite the fact that the majority of the total Soviet population and virtually one-half of the migrants were females, the majority (53.5 percent) of *interregional* and thus longer distance in-migrants were, not unexpectedly, males. This conclusion is based on the economic regions of the USSR as of 1970 and excludes intraregional and thus shorter distance migrants. It should also be noted that interregional age-sex data from the 1970 census have been discussed by Grandstaff (1980, 58–63).

Table 18.1
Net Migration by Union Republic, 1959–87

Republic	Total Period			Average Annual			Average Annual Net Migration as Percent of:		
	1959–70	1970–79	1979–87	1959–70	1970–79	1979–87	1959–70 July 1964 Population	1970–79 July 1974 Population	1979–87 Jan. 1983 Population
RSFSR	-1,700,000	200,000	1,442,772	-154,545	22,222	180,347	-0.1	+0.0	0.1
Ukrainian	500,000	300,000	-28,436	45,455	33,333	-3,555	0.1	0.1	-0.0
Belorussian	-287,000	-89,000	-3,166	-26,091	-9,889	-396	-0.3	-0.1	-0.0
Uzbek	514,000	135,000	-246,365	46,727	15,000	-30,796	0.5	0.1	-0.2
Kazakh	795,000	-464,000	-504,572	72,273	-51,556	-63,072	0.6	-0.4	-0.4
Georgian	-92,000	-136,000	-144,070	-8,364	-15,111	-18,009	-0.2	-0.3	-0.4
Azerbaydzhan	-58,000	-62,000	-207,892	-5,273	-6,889	-25,987	-0.1	-0.1	-0.4
Lithuanian	51,000	66,000	92,165	4,636	7,333	11,521	0.2	0.2	0.3

Moldavian	63,000	-23,000	-112,044	5,727	-2,556	-14,006	0.2	-0.1	-0.3
Latvian	158,000	104,000	78,415	14,364	11,556	9,802	0.6	0.5	0.4
Kirgiz	161,000	-79,000	-96,918	14,636	-8,778	-12,115	0.6	-0.3	-0.3
Tadzhik	69,000	41,000	-70,228	6,273	4,556	-8,779	0.3	0.1	-0.2
Armenian	146,000	111,000	-79,567	13,273	12,333	-9,946	0.6	0.4	-0.3
Turkmen	13,000	-13,000	-57,813	1,182	-1,444	-7,227	0.1	-0.1	-0.2
Estonian	92,500	60,000	50,578	8,409	6,667	6,322	0.7	0.5	0.4
Central Asia	757,000	84,000	-471,324	68,818	9,333	-58,916	0.4	+0.0	-0.2
Transcaucasus	-4,000	-87,000	-431,529	-364	-9,667	-53,942	-0.0	-0.1	-0.4
West (Baltic)	301,500	230,000	221,158	27,409	25,556	27,645	0.4	0.4	0.4
Northern USSR	-1,122,500	618,000	1,520,284	-102,045	68,666	190,035	-0.1	+0.0	0.1
Southern USSR	1,548,000	-467,0400	-1,407,425	140,727	-51,889	-175,928	0.4	-0.1	-0.3

Urban-Rural Migration

Appreciable data are available on migration to urban areas. However, no migration data are available on broader metropolitan/nonmetropolitan areas, because the Soviet Union does not have an official metropolitan definition. The author and others have tried to estimate overall metropolitan populations (for example, see Lewis and Rowland, 1979, 322–52; Rowland, 1983, 1986a). The lack of an official metropolitan definition partly reflects the fact that, although the USSR contains numerous individual large cities (nearly 300 of 100,000 and over and nearly two dozen of 1 million and over in 1987), metropolitan development and urban sprawl is relatively meager, chiefly because of the relative absence of the automobile and single-family housing in the USSR (Lewis and Rowland, 1979, 279–355; Rowland, 1983, 1986a; USSR, 1987, 395–400). Furthermore, even an assessment of basic urban trends over time is difficult to make owing to changing urban definitions (Lewis and Rowland, 1979, 162–65).

In the very broadest terms, few if any countries have ever likely experienced a more significant rural-to-urban migration than has the USSR during the last half century. Between 1926 and 1970 it is estimated that there was a net rural-to-urban migration of nearly 60 million people, which accounted for more than half (56.5 percent) of the growth of the urban population during this period. Net rural-to-urban migration, however, declined in relative importance during this period both as a percentage of urban growth and the urban population (Lewis and Rowland, 1979, 189). Strictly comparable data for 1970–79 are not available, although data do exist apparently for 1971–80 (Korel', 1985, 104). They indicate that net rural-to-urban migration amounted to 13.4 million people. This accounted for slightly less than a majority (48.9 percent) of the urban growth during this period (USSR, 1980, 7). Net rural-to-urban migration as a percentage of the urban population during 1971–80 was also lower than in preceding periods in that the average annual absolute amount of migration was only 1.0 percent of the mid-period urban population (average of the 1971 and 1980 urban populations), as compared to 1.3 percent for 1959–70 and 1.7 percent for the entire 1926–70 period (Lewis and Rowland, 1979, 189). A declining relative importance of rural-to-urban migration is, of course, inevitable with modernization and urbanization.

Recent urban-rural migration trends can also be assessed based on the 1970 and 1979 censuses and the 1985 microcensuses. Not unexpectedly, the urban population had a higher rate of in-migration than the rural population in 1970, 1979, and 1985. In 1970, in-migrants comprised 7.1 percent of the urban population, but only 4.0 percent of the rural population. If only those residing in their permanent place of residence less than two years in 1979 are considered, to provide comparability with 1970, the corresponding percentages were higher than those for 1970 (8.7 and 6.0). Based on *eleven* migrants, corresponding percentages were 56.5 and 31.8.

According to published figures from the 1985 microcensus, 74.1 percent of all migrants went to urban centers, whereas 25.4 went to rural areas. (The author is aware that these published percentages total only 99.5 percent; *Vestnik statistiki,* 1986, no. 8, 80.) When applied to the above estimated total migrant population of 118.8 million for 195, this means that some 88.0 million migrants went to urban centers, while 30.2 million went to rural areas. When these figures are, in turn, applied to the urban and rural populations of the USSR in January 1985, it can be estimated that in-migrants comprised 48.9 percent of the urban population, but only 31.4 percent of the rural population (USSR, 1985, 8–9). Once again, when only those migrants residing less than two years are considered, the urban rate is higher, although there is very little difference between the urban and rural rates of in-migration (5.0 and 4.7 percent, respectively). Both rates were also lower than those for 1978.

Data from the 1970 and 1979 censuses and 1985 microcensus can also be used to assess the share of all migrants who went to urban centers. Based on the two-year categories for 1970, 1979, and 1985, a predominant but ultimately declining share of all migrants went to urban centers: 1970 (69.5); 1979 (70.2); and 1985 (66.3). This is generally consistent with data for *all* migrants for 1979 and 1985 (that is, all years of residence as opposed to less than two years of residence). In 1979, 74.3 percent of the migrants went to urban centers, and in 1985, the corresponding percentage just noted (74.1) was virtually the same. In addition, net migration data for twenty-one of the largest cities of the USSR suggest a lower net urban in-migration rate for 1979–85 as compared to 1970–79 (Rowland, 1986a, 654–56). These patterns may be a further reflection of a lessening rural-to-urban migration and urbanization process (Rowland, 1986a, 1986b).

The 1970 census and 1985 microcensus allow for a more detailed investigation of urban and rural migration both by origin and destination. However, unlike the situation for the urban and rural migrant populations as a whole, it is not possible to distinguish the more comparable "less-than-two-year" category for each of the *four* possible categories in 1985. Nonetheless, both sources suggest that the two major types of migrations have been either rural-to-urban (31.4 percent of all "migrants" in 1970 and 40.4 percent of all "migrants" in 1985) or urban-to-urban (38.1 and 33.7 percent, respectively). Rural-to-rural migration ranked third of the four possibilities (17.8 and 18.5 percent, respectively), while only a small share went from urban to rural areas (12.7 percent in 1970 and 6.9 percent in 1985). These urban-rural origin and destination data further suggest the existence of *net* rural-to-urban migration in the USSR.

WHO MOVES

Few data are available on the composition of migrants in the USSR. Age-sex composition and urban-rural destination patterns has been discussed earlier: the working-age population comprises the greatest share of migrants; the male-female ratio has been roughly equal; and the majority of migrants have gone to urban centers.

Data for 1970 and 1985 also allow some comments on the urban- or rural-*origin* composition of the migrants for 1970 and 1985. While the 1970 census indicated that a slight majority (50.8 percent) of the migrants were *urban*-origin, the 1985 microcensus conversely indicated that a decided majority (58.9 percent) were *rural*-origin. However, these percentages are not based on a comparable less-than-two-year definition for 1985, because such specific data cannot be derived from the 1985 microcensus (*Vestnik statistiki,* 1986, No. 8, 80).

Origin data for 1970 and 1985 also suggest that the urban population was less mobile than the rural. Urban-origin migrants comprised 5.2 percent of the urban population in 1970, while rural-origin migrants comprised 6.5 percent of the rural population. Moreover, in 1985 the corresponding urban rate was *much* lower than the rural rate (26.8 versus 72.8 percent), although the different migration definitions should again be kept in mind (*Vestnik statistiki,* 1986, No. 8, 80). The base urban and rural populations are, of course, not the actual migrant-source populations.

Especially relevant to the Soviet internal migration experience is the ethnic composition of the migrant population. The USSR is the most multinational state in the world with over 100 different nationalities being recognized, chiefly on the basis of the language criterion. Russians are the most numerous individual nationality, but comprise only a very slight majority of the total population (53.4 percent in 1970 and 52.4 percent in 1979).

The dominant Russians comprise the largest share of the migrants. According to the 1970 census, they comprised 62.6 percent of all migrants, a proportion that was roughly ten percentage points higher than their share of the total population. Their migration rate was also the highest of the fifteen union republic nationalities, the only nationalities for which migration data were published (6.7 percent of the Russians were migrants versus the national average of 5.7 percent and 6.0 percent for the next highest ranking nationality).

Conversely, the rapidly growing and increasingly important Turkic-Moslem nationalities of Soviet Central Asia experienced relatively low migration rates. Most notably, the Uzbeks, the largest Turkic-Moslem nationality and the third largest nationality in the USSR, had a migration rate of only 1.4 percent. As a result, they comprised only 0.9 of the migrant population of the USSR, as compared to 3.8 of the total population.

Although interregional migration data by nationality are not presented in the 1970 census, urban-rural nationality migration data are. They indicate that the Russians were especially highly represented among *urban*-origin migrants (69.8 percent of urban-to-urban migrants and 66.6 percent of urban-to-rural migrants). In contrast, they comprised smaller shares of rural-origin migrants (57.1 percent of rural-to-urban migrants and 53.9 percent of rural-to-rural migrants). These differences reflect the fact that the Russian population is relatively highly urbanized (68.0 versus the national average of 56.3 percent in 1970).

Nationality-migration data for 1979 have "leaked out" in a noncensus publication. Migration rates by union republic nationality based on the less-than-two-year residence criterion are available, although no urban-rural breakdown is provided (*Naseleniye SSSR,* 1983, 39). These data indicate appreciable increases in the migration rates for all fifteen nationalities between 1970 and 1979, some even doubling or tripling. Russians continued to have a relatively high migration rate (8.4 percent). However, their share of the migrant population, though still higher than their share of total population (57.3 versus 52.4 percent in 1979), was not superior as in 1970. In addition, two other nationalities now had higher migration rates than Russians: Lithuanians (9.6 percent) and Kazakhs (9.5). Although the Kasakhs are a Turkic-Moslem nationality, such nationalities in general were still characterized by relatively low migration rates. The Uzbeks, in fact, along with the Moslem Tadzhiks, had the lowest migration rates of any of the fifteen nationalities (3.8 percent each). As a result, Uzbeks who comprised 4.8 percent of the total population, comprised only 2.4 percent of the migrant population.

Little information is available on relatively nonpermanent migrations in the USSR. Nonetheless, such movements are known to exist. For example, commuting to and from cities occurs, and some city dwellers go to their country homes or *dachas* (Bater, 1982, 111–17). In addition, there has been an appreciable return migration from Siberia, which can be regarded as part of the universal phenomenon of migration stream and counterstream (Grandstaff, 1980, 54–56).

WHY PEOPLE MOVE

The most fundamental point to be made about the reasons for migration in the USSR is that, as elsewhere in the world, economic factors predominate and people generally move voluntarily. The fact that the USSR is a totalitarian state with migration policies, an internal passport and registration system, and some forced migration should not distract one from the basic similarities to universal migration factors.

Although migration policies in the USSR had a relatively minor impact on migration patterns, a few comments should be made on such policies (Grandstaff, 1980, 18–45; Lewis and Rowland, 1979, 14–27). The chief interregional migration policy has probably been to stimulate migration to Siberia, for example, by paying a higher wage for a comparable job in Siberia than in the western regions of the country. Although people migrate to Siberia partly because of the higher nominal wages of the region, they also leave Siberia because of its higher cost of living and thus relatively low real wages (Grandstaff, 1980, 18–22, 57–58; Lewis and Rowland, 1979). In addition, the Soviets have had a policy to limit the growth of large cities, chiefly by attempting to restrict migration to such cities and shifting investment to smaller cities. But, to repeat, the high out-migration from Siberia and the virtually universal and continued substantial growth of large cities in the USSR are major testimonies to the ineffectiveness of these policies (Lewis and Rowland, 1979; Rowland, 1983, 1986a).

A certain segment may also migrate for educational opportunities. However, the major destinations would be the largest cities, especially Moscow and Leningrad, because unlike the United States, there are very few small "college towns" (Rowland, 1983, 272). In addition, given the standardized educational system throughout the country, probably little migration is associated with moving to a specific area because it has a superior educational system.

There is also apparently little migration for retirement purposes in the USSR. Given the generally severe climate, there are very few resort-retirement areas. To the contrary, given the relatively great attraction of and difficulty of migrating to large cities such as Moscow, once people are able to surmount these migration restrictions they tend to want to remain (Lewis and Rowland, 1979, 303).

To repeat and emphasize, involuntary moves are of relatively minor importance in the USSR. In addition to some forced labor camp migration and the assignment of military draftees, the state can assign graduates of secondary specialized and higher educational institutions to any area of the country for three years, although, not unexpectedly, many graduates may be able to dodge this "obligation" (Lewis and Rowland, 1979, 20–21). In addition, persons convicted of serious crimes in large cities may be forced to move out (Bater, 1980, 147–49). Such movements account for only a very small share of the total number of migrants in the USSR.

CONSEQUENCES OF MIGRATION

Demographic Consequences

As elsewhere in the world, interregional and rural-to-urban migration trends have had a major effect on population redistribution in the USSR. Since the turn of the century, the chief overall population shift has been from the western areas to the eastern and southern areas of the country. Although substantial war losses in the west and high fertility in the south have contributed to this overall shift, the migration from western regions to the east or Siberia and partly to the south has also been very influential. Moreover, the recent shift away from Siberia has been due chiefly to substantial out-migration (Lewis and Rowland, 1979, 42–151)

In very recent years, however, the tie between overall redistribution and the migration component has become somewhat *unshackled*. As discussed above, since the late 1970s a clearcut south-to-north migration shift has occurred in the USSR. Despite this migration away from the south, the total population of the USSR is actually shifting to the south, especially Central Asia. Indeed, even though Central Asia now has relatively high net out-migration, it is by far the most rapidly growing region of the country; in the mid-1980s it actually became the most populous region of the country. Moreover, Central Asia now has more than 10 percent of the total Soviet population, and the magnitude of the shift to this region in recent years has been unprecedented since the turn of the century (Rowland, 1986a; Rowland and Lewis, 1982). This apparent contradiction is, of course, easily reconciled by the fact that relatively high net out-migration from

Central Asia has been more than offset by its relatively high fertility and natural increase.

Massive rural-to-urban migration has contributed to perhaps the most rapid urbanization process ever experienced by any major country (Lewis and Rowland, 1979, 158–96). In the early twentieth century only about one-tenth of the total population resided in cities, but as a result of rapid industrialization and migration to cities the Soviet Union has been transformed into an urbanized country. By 1987, nearly two-thirds (66.0 percent) of the total population resided in urban centers (USSR, 1987, 389).

Age selectivity apparently has the same significant implications as it does elsewhere in the world. Areas of in-migration have a relatively large working-age or young adult population. For example, in 1970, the Far East, which had the highest rate of net in-migration among the nineteen economic regions during the prior two years (Lewis and Rowland, 1979, 119), had the highest share of the 20 to 39 age group (35.6 percent). Conversely, the Central Chernozem region, which had the highest rate of net out-migration (tied with West Siberia), had the second lowest share of the 20 to 39 group (25.9 percent).

The impact of net rural-to-urban migration on the age structure is also evident. In 1970, those aged 20 to 39 comprised a much higher share of the urban population (32.3 percent) than of the rural population (25.0 percent). Not only do regions of high urban in-migration typically have a high urban 20 to 39 share (for example, 36.8 percent for the Far East in 1970), but also, elsewhere, regions of prolonged rural out-migration have correspondingly low rural 20 to 39 shares. For example, in 1970, two such regions, the Central Chernozem and Volgo-Vyatsk, had two of the three lowest rural 20 to 39 shares in the USSR (22.9 and 23.6 percent, respectively). Unfortunately, as noted above, no basic age data are available in the 1979 census or 1985 microcensus. However, urban-rural age data from the 1979 census have emerged in another source (Feshbach, 1985, 178–79). Although such data may be questioned since the source from which they were "acquired" is not documented, it is not surprising that they further indicate a much higher share of persons aged 20 to 39 in urban than in rural areas (32.4 versus 22.9 percent, respectively). This basic differential is further confirmed by estimates of the age composition for 1987, which show that the urban 20 to 39 share was much higher than that for the rural population (34.7 versus 25.3 percent, respectively) (Vestnik statistiki, 1987, 44).

The somewhat greater mobility of males as compared to females is also manifested by regional and urban-rural populations. For example, based on economic regions of 1970, the Far East had a relatively high sex ratio (101.9 males per 100 females) versus the national average of only 85.5, whereas the Central Chernozem had a very low ratio (79.6) (Baldwin, 1979, 91, 96, 102). In addition, in 1970, males comprised a higher share of the urban population as compared to the rural population (respective sex ratios were 86.4 and 84.3).

A higher urban sex ratio was not observed in the 1979 census as the urban and rural ratios were virtually identical (Feshbach, 1985, 179; Shabad, 1979, 444).

This may reflect the fact that, as mentioned above, according to the 1979 census migration definition, females were more mobile than males, although based on less than two-year residence categories, males were somewhat more mobile in both 1970 and 1979. It may also be due in part to relatively high urban male mortality (Shabad, 1979, 443–45; *Vestnik statistiki,* 1987, 33). However, estimates for 1987 suggest that the urban male sex ratio was again higher that the rural one (88.8 versus 87.7) (*Vestnik statistiki,* 1987, 44).

Given the multinational nature of the USSR, migration trends have had a major impact on the changing ethnic composition of various regions of the country. Most important, perhaps, has been the significant migration of ethnic Russians into non-Russian areas. Between 1926 and 1970, the Russian share of the total population of republics outside the RSFSR consistently increased up to 19.0 percent in 1970. The Russian migration to non-Russian areas has been oriented toward urban areas; consequently, they comprised an even higher share of the urban population (31.4 percent) outside the RSFSR in 1970. Especially high Russian shares were registered in the less developed regions of Central Asia and Kazakhstan, as well as the more advanced republics of the Baltic Region (Lewis, Rowland, and Clem, 1976, 149–50). Needless to say, this increasing Russian presence has often been resented by the indigenous peoples, for example, the peoples of the Baltic States (Lewis, Rowland, and Clem, 1976, 352).

The Russian migration retreat from the southern non-Russian areas was becoming apparent by the 1979 census. In contrast to the consistent increase prior to 1970, Russians maintained the identical share of the total population outside the RSFSR in 1979 (19.1 percent). Following increases up to 1970, their share of the total population *decreased* between 1970 and 1979 in Central Asia (15.1 to 13.0 percent) and Kazakhstan (42.4 to 40.8 percent) (Lewis, Rowland, and Clem, 1976, 149–50).

Somewhat comparable 1979 urban-rural data "leaked out" in a noncensus source and further suggest this retreat. When combined with relevant 1979 census data, it seems that outside the RSFSR the Russian share of the urban population had declined to 29.1 percent (*Sotsial'no . . . ,* 1986, 38; USSR, 1984). Unfortunately, it is not possible to derive the Russian share of the urban population for each non-Russian republic and, thus, Central Asia and Kazakhstan in 1979.

Social Consequences

A combination of centralization and concentration versus decentralization and deconcentration has occurred in the USSR. Interregional migration has led to an overall deconcentration of the population from west to south and east, although some reversals have, as discussed earlier, occurred in very recent years (Lewis and Rowland, 1979; Rowland, 1986b; Rowland and Lewis, 1982).

On the other hand, with substantial rural-to-urban migration the population of the USSR has been increasingly concentrated in large cities and "metropolitan

areas.'' Within such cities and areas, little deconcentration or sprawl has occurred, however (Lewis and Rowland, 1979, 279–355; Rowland, 1983, 1986a).

An additional facet of Soviet migration is that relatively little segregation
occurs in cities (French, 1979, 97–102). Given the relative equalization of
incomes and, as of yet, little non-Russian representation in largely ethnic Russian cities, there is a general absence of low-income, ethnic minority-dominated
inner areas coupled with high-income, ethnic majority-dominated outer areas.

Journey-to-work generally occurs over a short distance via public transportation, given the relative absence of the automobile and urban sprawl. On the other
hand, restrictions on migration to large cities contribute to longer distance commuting, because some people, who are denied residence in the central city,
simply reside in the suburbs and then commute in (Bater, 1980, 111–17, 148).

Environmental Consequences

Migration also has an influence on the environment, although with some
variations as compared to elsewhere. One of the chief reasons for the migration
to Siberia has been to exploit the vast mineral resource base of the region, which
has certainly created environmental concerns about the region (Pryde, 1987,
107–26).

On the other hand, even though there has been a perhaps unprecedented rural-
to-urban migration and increased concentration in large cities, in certain respects
relatively few environmental problems have occurred. Despite high urban densities, relatively little automobile-created air pollution occurs due to the relative
lack of automobiles. However, in heavy industrial areas such as the Donetsk-
Dnepr relatively high industrially related air and water pollution does occur. In
addition, despite high urban densities, there is relatively little crime, although
housing shortages and high divorce rates are present (Bater, 1982, 145–53).

Economic Consequences

It is difficult to assess the relationship between migration and employment
levels in the USSR. Not only are there problems with migration data, but also
there is essentially an absence of unemployment or underemployment data.
However, economic consequences apparently do follow expected patterns, with,
nonetheless, some deviations. One interesting deviation was that between 1959
and 1970 migration went from labor-deficit to labor-surplus areas. Net migration
from labor-deficit Siberia was also an unexpected pattern. Furthermore, rural-to-
urban migration has occurred despite labor shortages in rural areas, owing in part
to the lesser mechanization of Soviet agriculture. As P.J. Grandstaff (1980, 118)
states, ''workers left labor-deficit areas for labor-surplus ones. As a consequence, underemployment and unemployment or employment problems existed
in surplus areas while labor shortages persisted in areas where the state sought to
develop production at above-average rates.''

More recent trends suggest some changes. As discussed above, it appears that net migration from Siberia is being reduced and that the rural out-migration and the urbanization processes have apparently slowed. In recent Five-Year Plans the Soviets have, in fact, had a major program to improve rural life in the Non-Chernozem Zone of Northern European RSFSR, an area of chronic rural depopulation, and it appears that rural out-migration and population decline have slowed here (Makarova, 1985, 32; Makarova, Morozova, and Tarasova, 1986, 69–70; Rowland, 1987, 2–4).

The decided south-to-north net migration since the late 1970s has been associated with a northern labor deficit and a southern labor surplus differential. Nonetheless, as suggested above, little migration has occurred from the chief source area of the labor surplus in Central Asia, namely, the rural Moslem-dominated population. On the other hand, the apparent Russian retreat northward is probably related to some real labor shortages in the north and a decrease in demand for Russian labor in the south with increased educational levels among the indigenous peoples there (Rywkin, 1984, 88–91).

A further problem associated with the Siberian migration in particular is the existence of high labor turnover in the region, which is a further reflection of high in-migration and even higher out-migration rates. This leads to the all too-frequent necessity to train new workers (Grandstaff, 1980, 112–117). Substantial out-migration from Siberia during the 1960s may have induced an expansion of wage incentives in this area, which may, in turn, have contributed to the apparent recent slowing of out-migration from Siberia (Lewis and Rowland, 1979, 150–51).

Political Consequences

Internal migration in the USSR has also been partly politically motivated, and probably the chief political consequence has been an extension of the political presence of Russians outside the RSFSR. For example, Russians comprised 21.5 percent of the Uzbek Communist party in 1967 as compared to only 12.5 percent of the total population of the Uzbek Republic in 1970, although their share of this party was declining (Carlisle, 1975, 289, 291). In addition, by the 1970s, there was a political overrepresentation of indigenous nationalities among republic elites both in Central Asia and most other republics, although this trend may have been short-lived (Jones and Grupp, 1984, 172–75).

CONCLUDING REMARK

If one of the main purposes of this book is to highlight unexpected patterns, then perhaps the most *unexpected* pattern that should be stressed here is that the migration experience of the USSR generally follows *expected* patterns. Namely, any conception that the totalitarian Soviet state has controlled and thus created migration experiences decidedly different from the standards of general scientific laws or theories is *not* supported by the Soviet migration experience. In short, perhaps the most *unexpected* conclusion about internal migration in the USSR may be that it generally follows *expected* patterns and thus generally supports the tenets of migration theory.

Thus, it should not be *unexpected* if the now clear south-to-north migratory shift probably of ethnic Russians eventually changes into an expected northward migration of indigenous peoples from a relatively underdeveloped region living under labor-surplus conditions, here, most notably, the Turkic-Moslems of Central Asia, to a relatively developed, labor-deficit region, most notably, the Russian Republic. Such a migration and its potential for ethnic interaction and tensions would generally parallel recent migration experiences which have been directed toward the United States and Western Europe from such areas as Latin America, the Far East, the Mediterranean Basin, and the Indian Subcontinent (Rowland, 1987). It is hoped that migration and nationality data from the impending 1989 Soviet census will provide a more detailed assessment of the status of such an expectation.

Sources, Procedures, and Regional Definitions

Net migration and natural increase data for 1959–70 and 1970–79 derive from various union republic newspapers as presented in T. Shabad (1979, 445–56). For 1979–87, annual republic natural increase rates are available, and they were multiplied by estimates of annual midyear (July) populations in order to derive absolute natural increase, which, in combination with the total populations of January 1979 and 1987, resulted in an estimate of absolute net migration. Absolute net migration totals for each period were divided by the number of years (11, 9, and 8, respectively) to obtain average annual totals. July 1964, July 1974, and January 1983 are the midpoints for each period. For 1959–79 each population was calculated by averaging the adjacent available populations for January from various issues of *Narodnoye khozyaystvo SSSR v g.* January 1964—*1963 g.*, 12; January 1965—*1964 g.*, 12; January 1974—*1973 g.*, 9; January 1975—*1974 g.*, 9. For 1979–87, the midyear (July) population was estimated on the basis of adjacent January populations. Annual January populations for 1979–86 come from *Narodnoye khozyaystvo SSSR v g.*: January 1979 and 1980—*1979 g.*, 10–11; January 1981—*1980 g.*, 10–11; January 1982, *1922–82*, 12–13; January 1983—*1982 g.*, 8–9; January 1984—*1983 g.*, 8–9; January 1985—*1984 g.*, 8–9; January 1986—*1985 g.*, 8–9. The January 1987 population comes from *Narodnoye khozyaystvo SSSR za 70 let*, 374–75. Natural increase rates for 1979–85 come from *Narodnoye khozyaystvo SSSR v g.* 1979—*1979 g.*, 38–39; 1980—*1980 g.*, 32–33; 1981—*1922–1982*, 28–29; 1982—*1982 g.*, 32–33; 1983—*1983 g.*, 32–33; 1984—*1984 g.*, 34–35; 1985—*1985 g.*, 32–33. The natural increase rate for 1986 comes from *Narodnoye khozyaystvo SSSR za 70 let*, 406–7.

Larger regional combinations are defined as follows: Central Asia (Uzbek,

Kirgiz, Tadzhik, and Turkmen); Transcaucasus (Georgian, Azerbaydzhan, and Armenian); West or Baltic (Lithuanian, Latvian, and Estonian); Northern USSR (RSFSR, Ukrainian, Belorussian, Lithuanian, Moldavian, Latvian, and Estonian); and Southern USSR (Uzbek, Kazakh, Georgian, Azerbaydzhan, Kirgiz, Tadzhik, Armenian, and Turkmen).

REFERENCES

Baldwin, G.S. 1979. *Population Projections by Age and Sex: for the Republics and Major Economic Regions of the USSR 1970 to 2000,* Series P–91, No. 26, U.S. Bureau of the Census. Washington, D.C.: U.S. Government Printing Office.

Bater, J.H. 1982. *The Soviet City.* Beverly Hills, Calif.: Sage Publications.

Carlisle, D.S. 1975. "Uzbekistan and the Uzbeks." Pp. 283–314 in Z. Katz, R. Rogers, and F. Harned (eds.), *Handbook of Major Soviet Nationalities.* New York: Free Press.

Feshbach, M. 1985. "The Age Structure of Soviet Population: Preliminary Analysis of Unpublished Data." *Soviet Economy* 1:177–93.

French, R.A. 1979. "The Individuality of the Soviet City." Pp. 73–104 in R.A. French and F.E. Ian Hamilton (eds.), *The Socialist City: Spatial Structure and Urban Policy.* New York: John Wiley and Sons.

Grandstaff, P.J. 1980. *Interregional Migration in the U.S.S.R.: Economic Aspects, 1959–1970.* Durham, N.C.: Duke University Press.

Jones, E., and F.W. Grupp. 1984. "Modernization and Ethnic Equalisation in the USSR." *Soviet Studies* 36:159–84.

Korel', L.V. 1985. "Osnovnyye etapy razvitiya migratsionnogo obmena mezhdu gorodom i selom." Pp. 101–8 in *Sovremennyye problemy migratsii.* Moscow: Mysl'.

Lee, E.S. 1966. "A Theory of Migration." *Demography* 3:47–57.

Lewis, R.A., and R.H. Rowland. 1979. *Population Redistribution in the USSR: Its Impact on Society, 1897–1977.* New York: Praeger Publishers.

———, R.H. Rowland, and R.S. Clem. 1976. *Nationality and Population Change in Russia and the USSR: An Evaluation of Census Data, 1897–1970.* New York: Praeger Publishers.

Lorimer, F. 1946. *The Population of the Soviet Union: History and Prospects.* Geneva: League of Nations.

Lydolph, P. 1979. *Geography of the USSR: Topical Analysis.* Elkhart Lake, Wis.: Misty Valley Publishing.

Makarova, L.V. 1985. "Problema stabilizatsii sel'skogo naseleniya i arealy yeye pasprostraneniya." Pp. 29–46 in *Sovremennyye problemy migratsii.* Moscow: Mysl'.

———, G.F. Morozova, and N.V. Tarasova. 1986. *Regional'nyye osobennosti migratsionnykh protsessov v SSSR.* Moscow: Nauka.

Naseleniye SSSR. 1983. Moscow: Izdatel'stvo politicheskoy literatury.

Pryde, P.R. 1987. "Siberian Development and the Formulation of Environmental Impact Studies." Pp. 107–26 in L. Holzner and J.M. Knapp (eds.), *Soviet Geography Studies in Our Time: A Festschrift for Paul E. Lydolph.* Milwaukee: University of Wisconsin-Milwaukee.

Ravenstein, E.G. 1885. "The Laws of Migration." *Journal of the Royal Statistical Society* 48:167–227.

Rowland, R.H. 1982. "Regional Migration and Ethnic Russian Population Change in the USSR (159–79)." *Soviet Geography: Review and Translation* 23:557–83.

———. 1983. "The Growth of Large Cities in the USSR: Policies and Trends, 1959–1979." *Urban Geography* 4:258–79.

———. 1986a. "Changes in the Metropolitan and Large City Populations of the USSR: 1979–85." *Soviet Geography* 27:638–58.

———. 1986b. "Regional Population Redistribution in the USSR: 1979–84." *Soviet Geography* 27: 158–81.

———. 1986c. "Urbanization and Migration Data in Russian and Soviet Censuses." Pp. 113–30 in R.S. Clem (ed.), *Research Guide to the Russian and Soviet Censuses.* Ithaca, N.Y.: Cornell University Press.

———. 1987. "Regional Migration and Development in the USSR: 1979–86." Paper presented at the European Population Conference, Jyvaskyla, Finland, June 11–16.

———, and R.A. Lewis. 1982. "Regional Population Growth and Redistribution in the USSR, 1970–79." *Canadian Studies in Population* 9:71–93.

Russian Empire, Tsentral'nyy statisticheskiy komitet ministerstva vnutrennikh del. 1899–1905. *Pervaya vseobshchaya perepis' naseleniya Rossiyskoy Imperii, 1987 g.* St. Petersburg.

Rywkin, M. 1984. "The Impact of Socio-economic Change and Demographic Growth on National Identity and Socialisation." *Central Asian Survey* 3:79–98.

Schwartz, L. 1986. "A History of Russian and Soviet Censuses." Pp. 48–69 in R.S. Clem (ed.), *Research Guide to the Russian and Soviet Censuses.* Ithaca, N.Y.: Cornell University Press.

Shabad, T. 1979. "News Notes." *Soviet Geography: Review and Translation* 20:440–56.

Sotsial'no-kulturnyy oblik sovetskikh natsiy. 1986. Moscow: Nauka.

USSR, Gosudarstvennyy komitet SSSR po statistike. 1987. *Narodnoye khozyaystvo SSSR za 70 let.* Moscow: Finansy i statistika.

USSR, Tsentral'noye statisticheskoye upravleniye SSSR. 1929. *Vsesoyuznaya perepis' naseleniya 1926 goda.* Moscow.

———. 1962–63. *Itogi vsesoyuznoy perepisi naseleniya 1959 goda.* Moscow: Gosstatizdat.

———. 1972–74. *Itogi vsesoyuznoy perepisi naseleniya 1970 goda.* Moscow: Statistika.

———. 1980. *Narodnoye khozyaystvo SSSR v 1979 g.* Moscow: Statistika.

———. 1984. *Chislennosti' i sostav naseleniya SSSR: po dannym vsesoyuznoy perpisi naseleniya 1979 goda.* Moscow: Finansy i statistika.

———. 1985. *Narodnoye khozyaystvo SSSR v 1984 g.* Moscow: Finansy i statistika.

Vestnik statistiki. 1975. g.

———. 1984. 6 and 12.

———. 1986. 3, 6, and 8.

———. 1987. 12.

Zdravookhraneniye Rossiyskoy Federatsii. 1984. 10.

19

THAILAND

Theodore D. Fuller

Internal migration in Thailand has contributed greatly to the growth of Bangkok and thus to the country's overall level of urbanization. Internal migration has had relatively little impact, however, on regional population redistribution or levels of urbanization outside Bangkok. Although it might be anticipated that the overall rate of migration increased as Thailand underwent social and economic development, such is not the case. Instead, the five-year migration rate was lower in the second half of the 1970s than it was in the second half of the 1960s. Closer examination shows that, while the rate of rural-rural migration declined, there were increases in the rate of rural-urban, urban-rural, and urban-urban migration.

DATA ON MIGRATION

Sources of Data

There are a number of sources of data on migration patterns in Thailand. First, the national censuses of population and housing conducted in 1960, 1970, and 1980 provide data on national trends in migration. Following the censuses of 1970 and 1980, special subject reports on migration were prepared by the National Statistical Office (Arnold and Boonpratuang, 1976; Pejaranonda et al., 1984). Analyses of migration patterns based on the 1960 and 1970 censuses have also been published by the World Bank (1980) and the United Nations (1982). Second, there has been a series of special surveys of migration to Bangkok, such as that for 1977 (National Statistical Office, 1978). A special followup study of the 1977 survey of migrants to Bangkok was conducted by A. Chamratrithirong et al. (1979). Third, the several waves of the nationally representative Longitudinal Study of Social, Economic and Demographic Change provide data on migration patterns. (Rural waves were conducted in 1969 and 1972, while urban waves were conducted in 1970 and 1973.) Some results of the Longitudinal Study are presented in Visid Prachuabmoh and Penporn Tirasawat (1974), S. Goldstein et al. (1974), and Goldstein et al. (1977). Finally, a number of special studies of migration and population mobility have been conducted in specific locations in Thailand (e.g., Lauro, 1979; Singhanetra-Renard, 1981; Fuller et al., 1983, 1987; Steinstein, 1971, 1986). These studies shed light on specific aspects of migration.

Definitions of Migration

Each person enumerated in the 1960, 1970, and 1980 censuses was counted as an inhabitant of his or her usual place of residence, that is, the place where the person lived and slept most of the time. All three censuses obtained data that permit classification of individuals by lifetime migration status and five-year migration status. The specific definition of migration, however, varies to some extent depending on the specific census.

As is customary, lifetime migration status was determined by asking the province or country of birth for those born outside Thailand. The basic unit for measuring lifetime migration is the province (*changwat*). By assigning provinces to one of four regions (Central, North, Northeast, or South) or Bangkok, it is possible to analyze interregional migration in addition to interprovincial migration.

Five-year migration status was determined by ascertaining the length of residence at the current place of residence. For those reporting movement within the five years prior to the census, information on the last previous place of residence was obtained, including the province (or country). Thus, the "five-year migration status" actually refers to migration during a variable period of time.[1]

The procedure for determining five-year migration status in 1960 differed in two important respects from the procedure used in 1970 and 1980. First, in 1960 the basic unit for measurement of five-year migration status was the province. Thus, as with lifetime migration, it is possible to analyze both provincial five-year migration and interregional five-year migration. In 1970 and 1980, however, the basic unit for measurement of five-year migration was the community (village or municipality). While a change in residence within a community was not regarded as migration, a change in residence from one community to another within five years prior to the 1970 or 1980 census qualified as five-year migration. Hence, for 1970 and 1980 migration, it is possible to analyze intraprovincial five-year migration as well as interprovincial and interregional migration. Second, the rural or urban nature of the previous residence was ascertained only in 1970 and 1980, not in 1960.

Clearly, the data on five-year migration status for 1960 are not completely comparable with the data for 1970 and 1980. Furthermore, as Goldstein and Goldstein point out (1986, 11), "both the lifetime and five-year migration data for Thailand have all the defects inherent in these types of migration statistics." Perhaps the most serious limitation of such data is the tendency to underestimate the extent of migration. For example, any person who lived in his or her birth province on the census date is commonly classified as a "lifetime nonmigrant," regardless of the number of times that person may have actually moved. While a person who returned to a birth province within the five years before a census could be regarded as a "return migrant," such census data provide no way to make a distinction between (1) a person who migrated but returned to a birth province more than five years prior to a census and (2) a person who never moved from his or her birth province. More generally, such census data can record at most two moves during the lifetime of an individual regardless of the number of moves a person has made. Similarly, the census is equipped to record only one move in the most recent five-year period, regardless of the number of moves a person might have made during that period.

There is, of course, no way to determine precisely how many moves may be missed by the three censuses, or how this may distort the analysis of migration patterns. As shown below, however, the overall level of migration appears to be relatively low. This finding permits the cautious conclusion that repeat migration during any given five-year period may represent a relatively small proportion of all migration. This conclusion must be modified, however, with respect to short-term circular mobility (see below).

PRINCIPAL POPULATION MOVEMENTS

The National Level

The overall volume of migration in Thailand is relatively low. By 1960, some 10.8 percent were lifetime interprovincial migrants (Table 19.1). This level of lifetime migration increased to 13.1 percent by 1970 and 14.1 percent by 1980. In 1970, 5.8 percent of the total population (or 43.9 percent of all native-born lifetime migrants) were living outside their region of birth.

In 1960, 3.6 percent of Thais were five-year migrants. By 1970, this figure had increased sharply to 11.6 percent. However, part of this increase is illusory, that is, due to the more inclusive definition of five-year migration. In 1980, when the definition of five-year migration first used in 1970 was again applied, 7.5 percent were classified as five-year migrants. Thus, the volume of five-year migration appeared to rise between 1960 and 1970, and then fell between 1970 and 1980. During 1955–60, 3.6 percent of Thais were interprovincial migrants, as opposed to 5.9 percent in 1965–70 and 4.1 percent in 1975–80. Most of the increase in five-year migration recorded between 1960 and 1970 therefore reflected the inclusion of intraprovincial migration, as opposed to interprovincial migration. The drop in five-year migration between 1970 and 1980 applies to both interprovincial and intraprovincial migration.[2] Not only the percentage migrating, but also the absolute number of Thais migrating declined between 1965–70 and 1975–80. Altogether, 2.9 million Thais migrated during the five years prior to the 1980 census, compared to 3.3 million in 1965–70. This decline

Table 19.1
Lifetime and Five-Year Migration: 1960, 1970, 1980 (numbers in thousands)

	1960		1970		1980	
	Number	Percent	Number	Percent	Number	Percent
Lifetime interprovincial migrants	2761	10.8	4491	13.1	6238	14.1
Lifetime interregional migrants	NA	NA	1970	5.8	3482	7.9
Five-year migrants						
Total	789	3.6	3331	11.6	2948	7.5
Interprovincial[1] [2]	789	3.6	1675	5.9	1613	4.1
Interregional	335	1.5	770	2.7	858	2.2
Rural-rural	NA	NA	2087	62.6	1533	52.0
Rural-urban	NA	NA	348	10.5	421	14.3
Urban-rural	NA	NA	180	5.4	278	9.4
Urban-urban	NA	NA	297	8.9	506	17.2
Stream unknown	NA	NA	419	12.6	210	7.1
Total	NA	NA	3331	100.0	2948	100.0

Source: Goldstein and Goldstein (1986), Tables 2, 3, 10.

NA = Not Available

[1]Excludes migrants whose province of origin is unknown

[2]Movement between the provinces of Phra Nakhon and Thonburi was not considered interprovincial migration; by 1975-80 the two provinces had been merged to form the Bangkok Metropolitan Area.

in migration is perhaps surprising; many observers anticipated an increase in internal migration (e.g., Cochrane, 1979, 33).

Examination of the four migration streams among rural and urban areas (Table 19.1) shows that there was a decline in the rural-rural stream (from 2.1 million migrants in 1965–70 to 1.5 million in 1975–80), but an increase in each of the other three streams. Specifically, there was a 21 percent increase in the number in the rural-urban migration stream, a 54 percent increase in the urban-rural migration stream, and a 70 percent increase in the urban-urban migration stream. The increases in these three migration streams are consistent with the thesis that the level of migration increases as a developing country proceeds along the course of social and economic development. Although the rural-rural migration stream remains by far the largest migration stream in Thailand, the reduction in the size of this stream may be a function of (1) less rural land available for settlement, (2) rural development efforts in the 1970s, or (3) the increased importance of international labor migration from Thailand to the Middle East (Goldstein and Goldstein, 1986, 40; Piampiti, 1985, 9).

The Age and Sex Structure of National Population Movements

As in most other areas of the world, internal migration in Thailand primarily involves young adults. For both 1965–70 and 1975–80, the migration rate for Thais 20 to 24 and 25 to 29 years of age was higher than for any other age group; this was true for both males and females (Table 19.2). The concentration of migrants in these two age groups can be shown by comparing the percentage of migrants versus nonmigrants age 20 to 29. In 1970, among the population aged five years or older, only 15.8 percent of the nonmigrants were 20 to 29 years of age, while fully 27.3 percent of the migrants were in this age group. In 1980, among the population aged five years or older, 18.9 percent of the nonmigrants were 20 to 29, while 36.8 percent of the migrants were 20 to 29. Similar percentages are found for males and females separately.

Table 19.2
Percentage of Population Who Are Five-Year Migrants by Age, Sex, and Time Period

Age Group	1965-70			1975-80		
	Whole Kingdom	Male	Female	Whole Kingdom	Male	Female
Total	11.6	12.7	10.6	7.6	8.0	7.1
5-9	10.0	10.1	9.8	5.4	5.5	5.3
10-14	9.4	9.8	9.0	5.2	5.2	5.1
15-19	12.7	12.5	12.8	8.7	7.7	9.7
20-24	19.2	22.2	16.2	14.3	14.8	13.8
25-29	17.6	21.2	14.2	13.1	15.5	10.9
30-34	13.4	15.6	11.3	9.1	10.5	7.7
35-39	10.5	12.0	9.1	7.1	8.1	6.0
40-44	9.6	10.9	8.2	5.7	6.6	4.8
45-49	8.3	9.6	7.0	4.6	5.2	3.9
50-54	7.8	8.2	7.4	3.7	4.4	3.1
55-59	6.9	7.3	6.6	3.6	3.8	3.4
60-64	6.7	7.0	6.4	3.5	3.8	3.1
65 and Over	7.0	7.7	6.4	2.7	2.9	2.6
Percent age 20-29:						
Five-year migrants	27.3	29.2	25.1	36.8	37.5	36.0
Five-year nonmigrants	15.8	15.2	16.4	18.9	18.3	19.5

Source: 1965-70 data from Arnold and Boonpratuang (1976); 1975-80 data from Pejaranonda, Goldstein, and Goldstein (1984).

In general, males are somewhat more likely to migrate than females. In 1970, 12.7 percent of males were five-year migrants, versus 10.6 percent of females (Table 19.2). In 1980, 8.0 percent of males were five-year migrants, versus 7.1 percent of females. Males are more likely than females to be five-year migrants for every age group except those 15 to 19.

Interregional Migration

For statistical purposes, Thailand is usually subdivided into four regions—the North, Northeast, South, and Central regions. The Northeast is the most populous region but the least urbanized—only 4.0 percent of the 13.5 million people in the Northeast in 1980 lived in urban areas. The Central region and the North were just about equal in population size in 1980—just over 9 million each—but the Central region was slightly more urbanized than the North (9.9 percent versus 7.5 percent). In the South, which had only 12.6 percent of the national population, 12.6 percent of the population lived in urban areas in 1980.

Bangkok is located within the Central region but, because of its size and importance, statistics for Bangkok are often reported separately from those of the Central region. Bangkok, with a population of 4.6 million in 1980, is central to the interregional migration system. One aspect of Bangkok's centrality is that, during each of the three five-year migration periods, Bangkok received a net gain in population as a result of migration from every other region in the country (calculated from Table 19.3). Furthermore, in 1955–60, 1965–70, and 1975–80, more interregional out-migrants from the Central region, the Northeast, and the South went to Bangkok than to any other region (Table 19.3). Migrants from the North, however, were more likely to go to the Central region than to Bangkok. Altogether, in each time period, Bangkok received nearly 40 percent of all interregional migrants (calculated from Tables 19.1 and 19.3).

The centrality of Bangkok in the national migration system is further demonstrated by examining the preference indexes for interregional migration. These preference indexes, shown in Table 19.4 for 1955–60, 1965–70, and 1975–80, are defined as "the ratio (times a constant) of the actual to the expected number of migrants in a stream when the expected number is directly proportionate to both the population at origin and the population at destination" (Shryock, Siegel, and Associates, 1976, 394). This index can vary from 0 to infinity; the higher the index, the more the actual migration between the two regions exceeds the expected level of migration; a value of 100 means that the actual number of migrants from one region to another equals the number that would be expected, taking into account only the size of the population of each region and ignoring issues such as the distance between the two regions and the strength or nature of their economic systems.

Another indicator of Bangkok's centrality in the national migration system is that the preference index for total in-migrants to Bangkok is over 300 for each time period. That is, Bangkok received more than three times as many in-

Table 19.3

Interprovincial Recent Migration Streams by Region, 1955–60, 1965–70, 1975–80

Current residence	Total interprovincial migrants	Region of previous residence				
		Bangkok	Central	North	Northeast	South
1955-60						
Bangkok	131,370	--	81,214	13,947	26,745	9,464
Central	210,211	40,006	123,762	15,560	25,860	5,023
North	156,721	8,900	30,270	90,702	26,002	847
Northeast	206,149	8,890	10,758	4,896	180,353	1,252
South	84,555	6,529	10,850	1,482	6,998	58,696
1965-70						
Bangkok	298,791	--	166,181	36,555	66,813	29,242
Central	456,081	82,823	248,103	47,231	62,936	14,988
North	315,734	14,646	58,035	195,703	43,920	3,430
Northeast	430,668	23,592	45,646	26,130	330,486	4,814
South	173,730	8,867	18,486	3,775	11,519	131,083
1975-80						
Bangkok	340,792	--	144,397	43,178	119,661	33,556
Central	502,869	115,355	218,084	53,727	95,890	19,813
North	269,827	20,945	38,746	165,972[1]	40,558	3,606
Northeast	314,910	20,059	32,142	17,438	241,034[1]	4,237
South	183,642	14,033	20,046	7,225	12,582	129,756

Source: Goldstein and Goldstein (1986), Table 6, page 29.

[1]Adjusted for movement between provinces split into two provinces during the period 1970-80. Such movement was not considered interprovincial migration.

migrants from all other regions combined than would be expected on the basis of the size of Bangkok's population. For only one other region—the Central region—did the preference index exceed 100. For each of the other regions, the preference index for in-migration was less than 100 in each time period.

Although Bangkok is clearly a preferred destination for Thai migrants, this picture is tempered by recognizing that the rate of net migration actually declined substantially, from 62.7 in 1965–70 to 40.1 in 1975–80. This decline in net migration resulted from a large drop in migration to Bangkok (from 110.9 to 80.2) and a small decline in migration from Bangkok (from 48.2 to 40.1). However, while the rate of net migration declined, the absolute of net migration increased slightly, from 168,863 to 170,400.

The reduction in in-migration and net migration to Bangkok should not be construed as heralding any reduction in the primacy of Bangkok. The primacy index, that is, the ratio of the population of Bangkok to that of the second most populous city, has increased steadily during this century, especially during the past several decades. The primacy index is estimated to have risen from approximately 11 in 1900, to 23 in 1950, 25 in 1960, 33 in 1970, and 51 in 1980 (Steinstein, 1984, 67). It seems likely that Bangkok's primacy will continue to increase.

The attractiveness of Bangkok as a destination is further demonstrated by the

Table 19.4
Preference Indexes for Interregional Migration, 1955–60, 1965–70, 1975–80

Current Residence	Total in-migrants	Region of previous residence				
		Bangkok	Central	North	North-east	South
1955-60						
Total						
out-migrants	--	234	169	50	75	39
Bangkok	384	--	960	184	188	239
Central	107	568	--	72	63	44
North	86	137	136	--	69	8
Northeast	28	87	31	16	--	8
South	51	173	84	13	32	--
1965-70						
Total						
out-migrants	--	180	169	67	71	55
Bangkok	338	--	810	179	180	286
Central	117	470	--	98	72	62
North	68	83	120	--	50	14
Northeast	47	87	61	35	--	13
South	38	90	68	14	23	--
1975-80						
Total						
out-migrants	--	184	125	69	91	58
Bangkok	306	--	556	180	248	256
Central	145	508	--	110	98	75
North	55	98	78	--	44	14
Northeast	31	56	39	23	--	10
South	43	109	67	26	23	--

Source: Calculated from Goldstein and Goldstein (1986), Tables 3 and 6, pages 20 and 29.

fact that the preference ratio is greater than 175 for migration from each region to Bangkok during each of the three five-year time periods. The Central region, on the other hand, is an attractive destination primarily for migrants from Bangkok; for each time period, the preference index exceeds 110 only for migration from Bangkok.[3] The only other migration stream for which the preference index was greater than 100 involved migration from the Central region to the North. This migration stream was of declining importance over the twenty-five years, falling from 136 in 1955–60 to 120 in 1965–70, and finally to 78 in 1975–80.

As suggested above, by far the largest population interchange occurred between Bangkok and the Central region. The preference indexes for migration from Bangkok to the Central region were 568, 470, and 508 for 1955–60, 1965–70, and 1975–80, respectively. In other words, there were approximately five times as many migrants from Bangkok to the Central region as one would expect on the basis of the size of these two regions. Not surprisingly, the preference indexes for migration from the Central region to Bangkok are even larger: 960, 810, and 556 for the three time periods. These high indexes result in part, of course, from the close proximity of the two regions and their economic integration.

Examination of the preference indexes for out-migration shows that for each time period the largest such preference index pertains to Bangkok. This means that Bangkok not only receives more than the expected number of in-migrants, but it also sends more than the expected number of out-migrants. The preference index for in-migration to Bangkok, of course, exceeds that for out-migration by a considerable margin. Nevertheless, the high index for out-migration means that Bangkok not only represents a magnet attracting migrants from other regions; it also contributes disproportionately to migration to other regions.

The preference index for out-migration from the Central region is also over 100 for each time period, although it declined from 169 in 1955–60 and 1965–70 to 125 1975–80. Each of the other regions supplied fewer than the expected number of out-migrants in each time period.

The South had the lowest preference index for out-migration in each time period. Indeed, the lowest interregional preference indexes involved migration from the South to the North and Northeast. For 1955–60, only 8 percent as many people as expected on the basis of population size alone migrated from the South to either the North or Northeast. These preference indexes remained extremely low during the two more recent periods, reaching 14 and 13 in 1965–70 and 14 and 10 in 1975–80. Migration from the South to the Central region was also less than expected in each time period but was growing over the twenty-five-year period. The low level of migration from the South to the North and Northeast can no doubt be explained in part by the fact that the South is not adjacent to either of those regions.

Just as the South sends relatively few migrants to the North and Northeast, the North and Northeast send relatively few migrants to the South. The preference index for migration from the North to the South increased from 13 in 1955–60 to 26 in 1975–80, but even so remained at a rather low level. The preference index for migration from the Northeast to the South declined from only 32 in 1955–60 to 23 in 1975–80.

One other pair of migration streams involved relatively low preference indexes, namely, migration from both the North and the Central region to the Northeast. These preference indexes were 16 and 31 in 1955–60 for the North and Central regions, respectively, roughly doubled to 35 and 61 for 1965–70, and then declined to a level somewhat higher than that found for 1955–60.

Migration between Rural and Urban Areas

In Thailand, the term *urban* is usually applied only to communities legally regarded as "municipalities." The boundaries of specific municipalities are occasionally revised to reflect population growth in adjacent areas. The number of municipal areas, however, has changed little in recent decades (e.g., 116 municipal areas in 1947 versus 119 municipal areas in 1960, 1970, and 1980). It might reasonably be argued that certain other communities should be counted as "urban" (e.g., Goldstein and Goldstein, 1978). Most statistical treatments of migration in Thailand, however, continue to rely on the "municipal-non-municipal" distinction. In this chapter, we therefore equate the urban population with the population living in municipal areas.

As is true in most other developing countries, most of the internal migration in Thailand involves migration between two rural areas (Table 19.1). Note that these figures refer to all five-year migrants, not just five-year interprovincial migrants. A large portion of all five-year migrants were intraprovincial migrants—45.3 percent in 1975–80). It may well be that many, if not most, of the intraprovincial migrants were rural-rural migrants; it may even be that many of the rural-rural migrants were intraprovincial migrants. Unfortunately, the tabulations that would enable us to address these questions are not available.

Rural-to-urban migration comprises a relatively small portion of all five-year migration. Specifically, 10.5 percent of migrants in 1965–70 were rural-urban migrants; this increased to 14.3 percent in 1965–80 (Table 19.1). If, as suggested above, many of the rural-rural migrants are intraprovincial migrants, it may well be that rural-urban migrants comprise a larger proportion of five-year interprovincial migrants than is indicated in Table 19.1.

In spite of the relatively low level of rural-urban migration, the level of urbanization has increased in recent decades, although the level of urbanization in Thailand still lags behind that found in most Southeast Asian countries. Natural increase, net migration, and area annexation contributed 49.9 percent, 43.6 percent, and 6.5 percent, respectively, to urban population growth in the 1960s (United Nations, 1982, 29). Area annexation became a more important component of urban population growth in the 1970s contributing 29.4 percent, whereas the net migration component fell to 29.8 percent and natural increase contributed 40.8 percent (United Nations, 1982, 29). While natural increase made substantial contributions to urban population increase during this period, the rate of natural increase in urban areas was less than that found in rural areas. As a result of migration and annexation of land adjacent to municipal areas, the level of urbanization increased from 12.5 in 1960 to 13.5 in 1970 and 17.0 in 1980.

As seen in Table 19.3, during 1955–60 Bangkok received over 131,000 migrants from other regions of the country; during 1965–70, the number of migrants to Bangkok increased to nearly 300,000; and during 1975–80, the number exceeded 340,000. During these same periods of time, migrants left Bangkok for other regions. However, during each time period the number of migrants entering Bangkok was at least double the number of migrants leaving Bangkok. The net gain for Bangkok was 67,045 for 1955–60, 168,863 for 1965–70, and 170,400 for 1975–80 (calculated from Table 19.3). Partially as a result of this migration stream, Bangkok's level of urban primacy has increased in recent decades. In 1960, 51.9 percent of the Thai urban population lived in Bangkok; by 1970, the percentage had increased to 54.8; an by 1980 it rose to 61.1 percent (Goldstein and Goldstein, 1986, 37).

In addition to the rural-urban migration stream, there is a significant amount of migration between urban areas. In 1965–70, the urban-urban migration stream was nearly as large as the rural-urban migrant stream (297,000 migrants versus 348,000 migrants; Table 19.1). In 1975–80, the size of the urban-urban migration stream exceeded that of the rural-urban migration stream (506,000 migrants versus 421,000 migrants). It is not known how many of these urban-urban migrants were going to Bangkok, how many were leaving Bangkok, or how many were moving between two cities other than Bangkok. It is clear, however, that while Bangkok remains a major destination of migrants to urban areas, other urban areas are attracting a larger share of migrants to urban areas than they did previously. If we regard both rural-urban and urban-urban migrants as "city-ward" migrants, then the migrants to Bangkok comprised 46 percent of the 645,000 cityward migrants in 1965–70, compared to 37 percent of the 927,000 cityward migrants in 1975–80.

Migration from urban to rural areas is the smallest of the four migration streams among rural and urban areas. Still, about 180,000 Thais moved from an urban to a rural area during 1965–70 and nearly 280,000 Thais made an urban-rural move during 1975–80. A large part of this stream was probably return migration (Goldstein et al., 1976, 131–35). Another part of the urban-rural migration stream is no doubt comprised of government officials who have been assigned to work in nonmunicipal areas.

Age and Sex Structure of Migration between Rural and Urban Areas

As noted above, young adults are disproportionately likely to migrate, and the highest rate of five-year migration for both males and females was for ages 20 to 29. With one exception, this generalization holds in 1965–70 and 1975–80 for both males and females and for each of the four migration streams distinguished by rural and urban origin and destination (Table 19.5). The surge in the rate of migration for men and women aged 20 to 29 is particularly noticeable for rural-urban migration. The only exception to the overall pattern is that the rural-urban migration of females peaks during ages 15 to 24 and remains high during ages 25 to 29.

As noted above, by far the most common migration stream—in both 1970 and 1980—is rural-rural migration. The smallest migration stream is urban-rural. The rural-urban and urban-urban streams are similar in magnitude, with the rural-urban stream somewhat stronger in 1965–70 and the urban-urban stream somewhat stronger in 1975–80. These generalizations hold for both males and females in the two time periods.

When we examine the patterns by age groups, we note that for both males and females in both time periods, the rural-rural migration stream is by far the largest for each age group. Otherwise, however, patterns for specific age groups some-times differ from the overall patterns. In 1965–70, for example, while the rate of rural-urban migration was especially high for the young adult age groups, it

Table 19.5
Percentage of Population Who Are Five-Year Migrants by Age, Sex, Time Period, and Rural-Urban Origin and Destination

	1965–70								1975–80							
	Male				Female				Male				Female			
Age Group	RR	RU	UR	UU	RR	RU	UR	UU	RR	RU	UR	UU	RR	RU	UR	UU
Total	80.2	13.2	7.1	10.5	65.2	11.0	5.4	10.2	43.5	10.1	7.9	12.7	35.3	11.5	6.4	13.3
5–9	67.3	5.3	6.2	6.4	63.6	5.2	5.3	6.2	31.6	4.2	6.2	8.3	31.1	4.1	5.9	7.1
10–14	62.4	8.5	5.3	7.4	57.8	8.9	5.1	7.9	30.8	5.1	4.2	7.7	28.2	7.0	4.6	7.5
15–19	71.0	21.3	5.2	14.0	73.3	22.4	5.0	15.1	37.1	15.4	5.4	13.5	41.7	25.3	5.9	17.5
20–24	128.1	40.3	11.3	17.9	96.1	23.9	6.9	19.5	79.0	23.3	14.5	21.4	64.5	27.4	10.8	25.8
25–29	142.8	20.5	11.8	17.4	86.3	15.7	7.4	16.0	86.8	19.0	15.1	22.2	52.1	15.1	10.9	23.6
30–34	101.0	13.7	10.0	14.8	73.6	10.1	5.7	11.4	54.7	13.5	10.1	19.5	37.3	10.7	7.9	16.1
35–39	80.0	9.5	7.3	10.4	57.4	7.0	7.5	8.9	43.0	8.5	10.6	14.2	29.5	6.5	7.8	12.2
40–44	73.2	7.5	8.7	8.7	50.6	5.7	5.6	6.5	34.4	5.6	9.1	12.1	24.3	4.8	5.3	9.3
45–49	63.3	6.2	5.7	7.3	47.0	4.4	4.0	6.4	29.7	4.5	5.3	9.4	22.3	2.8	3.3	9.8
50–54	54.0	4.7	5.7	8.0	46.3	4.5	4.7	7.1	24.4	3.6	5.3	8.2	17.6	2.8	2.8	6.0
55–59	51.2	3.6	3.6	6.2	38.1	4.7	4.5	6.2	22.9	2.7	4.6	6.8	17.6	2.7	5.3	6.6
60–64	42.6	4.0	6.0	5.3	35.2	4.6	1.9	5.2	23.6	2.1	3.5	5.2	13.5	4.8	2.5	7.6
65 or over	45.3	3.9	4.7	4.1	34.6	4.2	1.9	4.8	17.5	2.6	2.5	3.3	13.6	2.1	2.3	5.3

Source: Calculated from Arnold and Boonpratuang (1976); Table 4 and from Pejaranonda, et al. (1984); Table 5.

KEY: RR = Rural-rural; RU = Rural-urban; UR = Urban-rural; UU = Urban-urban

dropped off for the older age groups. Hence, there is a reversal such that, for both males and females, the rate of rural-urban migration was lower than the rate for urban-urban migration for all five-year age groups 30 to 34 and older. Similarly, in 1975–80 rural-urban migration peaked in the young adult years and then tapered off. In this case, rural-urban migration was greater than urban-urban migration only for males and females 15 to 19 and 20 to 24.

Among the population of Thais five years and older, females outnumber males. This is true in urban (metropolitan) areas as well as in rural areas. The sex ratio was approximately 98 in both 1970 and 1980 (Table 19.6). This was not true for migrants, however. For most migration streams, males outnumbered females in both 1970 and 1980. The sex ratio for all five-year migrants was 118 in 1970 and 109 in 1980. Similarly, the sex ratio was 115 and 106 for inter-

Table 19.6

Sex Ratio of Population Aged 5 Years and Over by Migration Status and Residence, 1970 and 1980

Migration Status	1970	1980
Five-year nonmigrants	96	97
All five-year migrants	118	109
Five-year interprovincial migrants	115	106
Five-year in-migrants to:		
Bangkok	99	89
Central	117	105
North	117	111
Northeast	122	134
South	134	108
Rural-rural	121	121
Rural-urban	118	86
Urban-rural	130	120
Urban-urban	101	94
Urban residents	97	94
Rural residents	99	99

Source: 1970 data from Arnold and Boonpratuang (1976); 1980 data from Pejaranonda, Goldstein, and Goldstein (1984).

regional migration in 1970 and 1980, respectively. Examination of sex ratios by regional destination shows that the sex ratio was over 100 for every region except one, namely, Bangkok. During 1965–70, Bangkok attracted nearly equal numbers of males and females. During 1975–80, Bangkok attracted only 89 males per 100 females. Each of the other regions attracted more males than females. Migration to the Northeast during 1965–70 involved substantially more males than females, and the sex ratio of this migration stream became even more lopsided during 1975–80. During 1965–70, the sex ratio was particularly lopsided for migration to the South. However, during 1975–80 the numbers of males and females migrating to the South were much more equal. The relative increase in the migration of women to the South is no doubt due in part to a growth of tourism in the South, for example, Phuket (see Piampiti, 1985, Chapter 2).

Sex ratios for migration between the rural and urban sectors are also shown in Table 19.6. Migration to rural areas involves more males than females: The sex ratios for rural-rural migration and for urban-rural migration were at least 120 for both 1965–70 and 1975–80. Migration among urban areas involved nearly equal numbers of males and females during 1965–70 but involved more females than males during 1975–80 when the sex ratio dropped to 94. A dramatic shift occurred with respect to rural-urban migration. During 1965–70, the sex ratio was 118, but during 1975–80 the sex ratio dropped to 86. Thus, while male rural-urban migrants substantially outnumbered females during the last half of the 1960s the opposite was true a decade later. The shift in the sex ratio of rural-urban migrants may be due to improved economic opportunities for women in urban areas, particularly in the service sector, where the largest number of female rural-urban migrants work (see Piampiti, 1985, 34).

WHO MOVES

As in the case in many other countries, five-year migration in Thailand involves positive educational selectivities. Published data permit consideration of four levels of education: no education, primary education, secondary education, and university education. The patterns, presented in detail in Table 19.7, can be summarized fairly easily: Individuals with higher levels of education are more likely to be five-year migrants. This is true as we move from each educational level to the next; it is true for males as well as females, for 1965–70 as well as 1975–80, and for interprovincial migration as well as total five-year migration. Note that education was ascertained after the move, not before. It is conceivable that some migrants increased their education after their move. Indeed, some Thais migrate in order to improve their education. It is plausible to argue, however, that the education selectivities reflect not only moves to pursue an education, but also the different opportunities available to individuals with higher levels of education and their need to be mobile in order to capitalize on these opportunities.

In 1970, going beyond a primary education seemed to represent a watershed. Those who had either a secondary or a university education were substantially more likely to migrate than those with either a primary education or no education. In terms of the potential for migration, however, it did not seem to make a great deal of difference whether one had a secondary education or a university education. In 1980, the chance of being a five-year migrant was substantially higher for those with a university education rather than a secondary education.

Similar educational selectivities are found when controlling for age. When we examine each of six age groups for persons age 15 or older, we note that Thais with a secondary or university education were more likely to migrate than those with a primary education or no education. This is true for males and females, for 1965–70 as well as 1975–80, and for interprovincial migration as well as total five-year migration. (The data are not presented here because of space considerations.)

As noted before, males are somewhat more likely to be five-year migrants than are females. In 1970, this difference is found even when controlling for educational level, especially for those with a secondary or university education. For example, 26.1 percent of the males with a university education but only 21.8 percent of the females with a university education were five-year migrants. In 1980, however, the difference between males and females almost disappears after controlling for education. For example, 19.4 percent of males with a university education versus 19.1 percent of the females with a university education were five-year migrants.

Table 19.7

Percentage of the Population 6 Years of Age and Over Who Are Five-Year Migrants by Educational Attainment and Sex

Educational Attainment	1970				1980			
	Male		Female		Male		Female	
	All 5-year migrants	5-year inter-provincial migrants[1]	All 5-year migrants	5-year inter-provincial migrants[1]	All 5-year migrants	5-year inter-provincial migrants[2]	All 5-year migrants	5-year inter-provincial migrants[2]
No Education	10.6	4.2	9.3	4.0	5.4	3.1	5.1	3.0
Primary Level	12.0	5.5	10.4	5.0	7.3	4.3	6.8	4.1
Secondary Level	22.6	15.0	18.5	12.7	12.9	8.2	12.6	7.7
University Level	26.1	18.0	21.8	15.8	19.4	13.4	19.1	13.2
Other Education	35.9	14.1	5.8	4.3	15.8	8.1	13.7	3.9

[1]Includes migrants from abroad.

[2]Includes migrants from abroad and migrants whose previous province and place of residence are unknown.

Sources: 1970 data from Arnold and Boonpratuang (1976), Table 11; 1980 data from Pejaranonda, Goldstein, and Goldstein (1984), Table 10.

Just as there are educational selectivities in Thai internal migration, so there are occupational selectivities. Agriculture is the principal occupation for the vast majority of Thai men and women (70 percent for men, 76 percent for women). Those involved in agriculture have the lowest rates of five-year migration of all occupational categories: 5.8 percent and 4.4 percent for men and women, respectively (Table 19.8). In fact, the five-year migration rate is at least twice as high for all other occupational categories. Most occupational categories consist of a relatively small percentage of the workforce. Besides agriculture, only two occupational categories have as much as 5 percent of the workforce: sales and craftsmen. For both males and females, sales workers have the second lowest rate of five-year migration. Women in the craftsman category (which includes production workers and laborers) have the third lowest rate of five-year migration.

The highest rates of five-year migration are for men involved in administrative or service work and women involved in service or transportation. Relatively few men and women are involved in these occupations, however. Only 2.1 percent and 2.8 percent of the men are involved in administrative or service jobs, respectively; only 3.1 percent and 0.1 percent of the women are involved in service or transportation jobs, respectively. Note also that occupation is ascertained after the move rather than before. It is quite conceivable that some of these migrants were not administrative, service, or transportation workers prior to the move, but entered these occupations after their move.

Examination of specific migration streams shows that, with few exceptions, agricultural and sales workers have the lowest rates of migration, or nearly the lowest, for each stream. This is true for both males and females. For most occupational categories—not just for agricultural workers and miners—the rural-rural migration stream is the largest of the four streams. Thus, even male professional and technical workers, transport workers, craftsmen, and service workers are more likely to be involved in rural-rural movement than any of the other three migration streams. Male administrative and clerical workers, however, are most likely to be urban-urban migrants. Similarly, females in most occupational categories are involved primarily in rural-rural migration. However, female clerical and transportation workers are most likely to be involved in urban-urban migration, and female service workers are most likely to be involved in rural-urban migration.

Repeat, Return, and Circulatory Movers

Judging from published analyses of census data, the extent of repeat and return migration is low. Goldstein and Goldstein (1980) utilize a 2 percent sample of the 1970 census to analyze patterns of repeat and return migration. In this context, return migrants are those who moved back to their province of birth between 1965 and 1970, while repeat migrants are those who resided in three different provinces in 1965, 1970, and at birth.

Repeat migrants are much more numerous than return migrants, but Goldstein and Goldstein (1980) report that in 1970 repeat and return migrants together accounted for less than 2 percent of all adults (age 15 and over). The volume of repeat and return migration appears larger if viewed as a proportion of migration. For example, repeat and return migrants made up approximately 10 percent of all migrants, and repeat and return migrants comprised nearly 30 percent of all recent (i.e., five-year) migrants. Furthermore, a relatively large proportion of total and recent migrants to urban places other than Bangkok were repeat or return migrants. On the other hand, according to these census statistics, repeat and return migrants made up less than 5 percent of the total migrants to Bangkok and less than 15 percent of the recent migrants to Bangkok.

A somewhat different picture emerges from analyses of the Longitudinal Study. Goldstein and Goldstein report that "almost half of all migrants resident in Bangkok and smaller urban places had histories of residence in three or more provinces and over one-fourth had lived in at least three different urban locations" (1980, 37). The contrast between these figures and those from the census underscores the conclusion reached by others that census statistics, as valuable as they are, often conceal a large part of total population mobility. As a result, migration rates determined from census statistics may convey the inaccurate impression that the Thai population is highly stable in terms of residence.

Although repeat and return migration may be underestimated by the census, until recently circular mobility has been a relatively neglected topic in Thai population studies. In the past ten years, however, several studies have focused on circular mobility. Studies of circular mobility are based on the recognition that a great deal of population mobility may not be captured by standard questions about migration, and that such mobility has important social and economic consequences (Goldstein, 1978).

Perhaps the first study of circular mobility in Thailand was Robert B. Textor's (1956) classic study of pedicab drivers in Bangkok. His evidence showed that the movement of pedicab drivers from the Northeast to Bangkok involved substantial back-and-forth mobility, rather than permanent migration to Bangkok by train. Textor also showed that very few of these migrants intended to stay in Bangkok permanently.

More recently, there have been several village-based studies of circular mobility from the Central region (Lauro, 1979), the North (Singhanetra-Renard, 1981), and the Northeast (Fuller et al., 1983; Lightfoot et al., 1983). These studies document the fact that there is a high level of circular mobility in rural Thailand. Lauro's study in Central Thailand, for example, showed that 35 percent of adult villagers had been seasonal migrants at some time. Inasmuch as the rate of seasonal mobility had increased since the early 1960s, 46 percent of adult villagers less than 30 years of age had been seasonal migrants. Singhanetra-Renard's work in Northern Thailand classifies mobility according to the amount of time the villager is outside the village, with the lowest threshold for mobility being a six-hour absence from the village. Casting such a broad net, she finds

Table 19.8

Percentage of Economically Active Population 11 Years of Age and Over Who Are Five-Year Migrants by Principal Occupation, 1980

Principal Occupation	Male						Female					
	All 5-year migrants	5-Year inter-provincial migrants[1]	5-Year rural-rural migrants	5-Year rural-urban migrants	5-Year urban-rural migrants	5-Year urban-urban migrants	All 5-Year migrants	5-Year inter-provincial migrants[1]	5-Year rural-rural migrants	5-Year rural-urban migrants	5-Year urban-rural migrants	5-Year urban-urban migrants
Professional Technical and Related Workers	16.9	9.7	6.9	1.3	3.2	3.9	17.6	10.8	5.6	2.0	4.0	5.1
Administrative, Executive, Managerial Workers and Government Officials	23.9	17.2	6.8	2.0	4.4	9.0	15.6	10.2	2.9	1.6	2.4	0.8
Clerical and Related Workers	16.0	10.6	3.6	2.6	2.8	5.6	16.1	9.1	2.5	3.6	2.5	5.7
Sales Workers	12.9	7.4	3.9	2.4	1.9	3.8	10.5	6.0	3.7	2.0	1.1	2.8
Agricultural, Animal Husbandry and Forest Workers, Fishermen and Hunters	5.8	3.1	5.0	0.1	0.3	0.1	4.4	2.3	3.8	0.1	0.2	0.0

Miners, Quarrymen, Well Drillers, and Related Workers	13.5	11.4	8.7	0.3	2.4	1.4	17.3	11.0	15.0	0.8	0.8	0.8
Transport Equipment Operators and Related Workers	15.9	9.1	5.8	3.5	2.2	3.5	20.5	12.3	4.1	4.1	2.7	6.8
Craftsmen, Production Workers and Laborers	17.3	12.3	6.6	4.9	1.6	3.3	13.7	9.4	5.4	3.5	1.2	2.7
Service Workers	20.1	13.7	6.0	4.8	2.9	4.7	26.7	20.1	3.6	13.2	1.0	6.8
Workers not Classifiable by Occupation or Unknown	13.2	7.5	0.9	5.7	0.9	1.9	23.2	17.9	3.6	8.9	1.8	3.6

[1]Includes migrants whose province and place of previous residence are unknown.

Source: Calculated from Pejaranonda, Goldstein, and Goldstein (1984), Table 13A.

that 64 percent of the 1,039 de jure resident population was involved in moves during the four-month period of her mobility study. Working in Northeast Thailand, Fuller and Lightfoot focused on mobility which involved an absence of overnight or longer from the village. In fact, most of these moves involved an absence of more than one month from the village. In the study area, 23 percent of the villagers aged 10 or over had made a move to a town at some time during a three-year period. Expressed differently, movement had occurred from 77 percent of all households. Fuller and Lightfoot also demonstrate that much of the circular mobility in Northeast Thailand is not strictly seasonal in nature. Actually, only one-third of those involved in circular mobility during the three-year reference period moved only during nonfarming seasons; the other two-thirds were at least sometimes absent during farming seasons.

WHY PEOPLE MOVE

Beginning in 1980, the Thai census included a question to ascertain from all five-year migrants the reason for their move. Analyses of these data reveal a number of interesting differences between men and women in the reasons they report for making different kinds of moves defined according to the rural or urban nature of the origin and destination. Economic reasons (e.g., looking for work or job transfer) constitute one major category of reasons for both men and women involved in each of the four migration streams. Family reasons (e.g., a change in marital status, or a move to accompany a person in the household) are a second major category of reasons for the moves of both men and women. Data on reasons for migration are not presented here for reasons of space. They are, however, published in C. Pejaranonda et al. (1984) and in Goldstein and Goldstein (1986); major results are summarized below.

Although family reasons are important for both men and women, in all four migration streams such reasons are more important for women than for men. For men and women alike, family-related reasons are mentioned more often than are economic reasons for migrants involved in three out of the four streams; however, for two migration streams, men mention economic reasons nearly as often as family-related reasons. Economic reasons are the most important category of reasons for males and females involved in rural-urban migration. In the case of rural-urban migration, however, while a clear majority of men report economic reasons for their move, only a plurality of women—not a majority—report economic reasons, and nearly as many women report family-related reasons. Thus, it is clear that family-related reasons are in general more frequently involved in the migration decision making of women, while economic reasons are more often cited in the decision making of men.

As noted above, there are two main types of economic reasons: looking for work is by far the most common economic reason for migrating. Job transfers are most often involved in moves *from* urban areas, whether those moves are to rural areas or other urban areas; moves from rural areas rarely involve job transfers, especially for women. Moves to accompany a person in the household are by far the most common type of family-related reason. Inasmuch as newlyweds usually live with one or the other set of parents for several years after getting married, change in marital status is often given as a reason for moves from one rural area to another. In rural Thailand, the bridegroom customarily lives with his wife's family for a period of time after marriage. This no doubt accounts for the finding that male rural-rural migrants more often mention a change in martial status as the reason for their move than do female rural-rural migrants.

Education is another reason sometimes given for migration. Not surprisingly, education is more often given as the reason for a move to an urban area than for a move to a rural area. Education is mentioned as a reason for about 10 percent of the moves men make to urban areas. Women are slightly more likely to move for educational reasons. Naturally, young people are much more likely to move for educational reasons than are older individuals. Specifically, 68 percent of those moving for educational reasons were less than 20 years old at the time of the census, and 95 percent were less than 25 years old.

One other reason for migration, one not revealed in the census data, is the search for excitement. Young villagers often find that life in urban places, especially Bangkok, offers a welcome change from the village routine. They therefore enjoy the opportunity to work temporarily in the city, even if they accumulate little or no cash in the process (Lauro, 1979, 260). As Juree Vichit-Vadakan (1983, 90) writes, "The magic, mystery, light and sound, modernity, and conveniences of Bangkok form an irrepressible desire in the young villager to go and see Bangkok. The relatively calm, uneventful and monotonous village life pales in the face of an exciting, complex and everchanging Bangkok filled with all possibilities and adventures." Excitement may more often form the basis for circular mobility than for the permanent mobility captured by the census.

CONSEQUENCES OF MIGRATION

Internal migration in Thailand has contributed greatly to the growth of Bangkok and thus to the country's overall level of urbanization. The population of Bangkok more than doubled in twenty years, increasing from 1.8 million in 1960 to 4.2 million in 1980. Largely as a result of the growth of Bangkok, the level of urbanization increased from 12.5 percent in 1960 to 17.0 percent in 1980.

Internal migration had relatively little impact, however, on regional population redistribution and levels of urbanization outside Bangkok. The percentage of the total national population found in Bangkok increased from 8.2 percent to 10.8 percent. The percentage of the population in each of the other four regions changed by less than 2 percent over the twenty-year period. Moreover, while the level of urbanization increased in each region, the amount of increase was small. For example, the South, which had the highest level of urbanization in 1960, 1970, and 1980, increased its level of urbanization from 10.1 percent to 12.6

percent. The Northeast, which had the lowest urbanization level at each census date, increased its level from 3.5 percent to 4.0 percent. Thus, the pace of urbanization was exceedingly slow outside Bangkok.

One of the most obvious social consequences of internal migration in Thailand has been in terms of the ability of Bangkok to provide customary urban social services to its rapidly growing population. Although social services are clearly more readily available in urban areas than in rural areas, adequate housing, medical facilities, and schools have been in short supply in Bangkok. The shortages in urban infrastructure as well as concerns about employment prompted the government to identify population redistribution as an important policy issue in the fourth national social and economic development plan (1977–81). The goals of the Decentralized Urbanization Strategy explicitly included a reduction of migration to Bangkok and an increase in migration from Bangkok. While only modest progress, at best, has been made toward the goal of reducing Bangkok's population growth, the government has reiterated its commitment to this basic goal in the fifth and sixth five-year plans.

Studies of migrant adjustment suggest that, at least in economic terms, rural-to-urban migrants adapt rather well to the urban environment and often achieve a reasonable level of success in a relatively short period of time. One study of recent migrants in Bangkok, for example, reports that a majority of both male and female migrants felt that they were better off in Bangkok than they were in their origin community in terms of income, living conditions, work environment, and housing environment (Chamratrithirong et al., 1979). A study of recent migrants in Northeast Thai towns yielded similar results (Fuller, 1980, 1981b).

Even though rural-to-urban migrants in both Bangkok and Northeast towns are rather content with their circumstances, those in Northeast towns tend to be more successful in terms of socioeconomic achievement than do those in Bangkok (Fuller, 1981a). Less information exists concerning the adjustment of rural-rural, urban-urban, or urban-rural migrants, but the literature does suggest that among migrants to Bangkok, the rate and extent of economic adjustment is a function of place of origin, with migrants from urban areas achieving more rapid economic adjustment than migrants from rural areas (Tirasawat, 1978).

NOTES

Acknowledgments: I am grateful to Anchalee Singhanetra-Renard, Chintana Pejaranonda, Penporn Tirasawat, and Samroeng Chantrasuwan for their comments on an earlier draft of this chapter.

1. There has been confusion in the literature as to the definition of five-year migration utilized in the 1960 census. In a number of publications, both Thai and non-Thai scholars have stated that in 1960 the definition of five-year migration referred to residence exactly five years prior to the census date. In fact, however, as stated in the 1960 census publications themselves, five-year migration in 1960 referred to previous residence for those who migrated within the five years prior to the census. Thus, in this respect the 1960 definition is identical to the 1970 and 1980 definitions of five-year migration. I am

indebted to Chintana Pcjaranonda and Penporn Tirasawat for bringing this to my attention.

2. In each census, the origin is unknown for some proportion of five-year migrants. As shown in Tirasawat (1986), in 1965–70 a particularly large proportion of five-year migrants had unknown origin. There is evidence that many of these "migrants" of unknown origin were not migrants at all. It might be suggested, therefore, that the decline in migration between 1965–70 and 1975–80 was due to an artificially high level of migration in 1965–70. This suggestion can be ruled out, however, for two reasons. First, the decline in five-year migration is observed whether the "unknown origin" migrants are included or excluded. Second, as shown below, the decline in migration applies only to rural-rural migration and not to the other three migration streams.

3. Much of the migration from Bangkok to the Central region involves migration to provinces adjacent to or near Bangkok. This pattern has been documented for the 1950s, 1960s, and 1970s (Piampiti, 1985; Steinstein, 1971; Vichit-Vadakan and Nakata, 1976).

REFERENCES

Arnold, F., and S. Boonpratuang. 1976. *Migration*. Subject Report No. 2. Bangkok: National Statistical Office.

Chamratrithirong, A., K. Archavanitkal, and U. Kanungsukkasem. 1979. *Recent Migrants in Bangkok Metropolis: A Follow-up Study of Migrants' Adjustment, Assimilation and Integration*. Bangkok: Institute for Population and Social Research, Mahidol University.

Cochrane, S.H. 1979. *The Population of Thailand: Its Growth and Welfare*. Staff Working Paper No. 337. Washington, D.C.: World Bank.

Fuller, Theodore D. 1980. "Satisfaction with Urban Life: The Judgment of Villagers Transplanted to Small Urban Centers in Thailand." *Rural Sociology* 45:723–30.

———. 1981a. "Migrant-Native Socioeconomic Differentials in Thailand." *Demography* 18:55–66.

———. 1981b. "Migrant Evaluations of the Quality of Urban Life in Northeast Thailand." *Journal of Developing Areas* 16:87–104.

———, Peerasit Kamnuansilpa, Paul Lightfoot, and Sawaeng Rathanamongkolmas. 1983. *Migration and Development in Modern Thailand*. Bangkok: Social Science Association of Thailand.

———, Paul Lightfoot, Peerasit Kamnuansilpa, Sukaesinee Subhadira, and Samroeng Chantrasuwan. 1987. "Altering Patterns of Rural-Urban Mobility: Design and Evaluation of an Information Program." In Harry K. Schwarzweller (ed.), *Research in Rural Sociology and Development: A Research Annual*, Vol. 3. Greenwich, Conn.: JAI Press.

Goldstein, Sidney. 1978. *Circulation in the Context of Total Mobility in Southeast Asia*. Papers of the East-West Population Institute, No. 53. Honolulu: East-West Center.

———, and Alice Goldstein. 1978. "Thailand's Urban Population Reconsidered." *Demography* 15:239–58.

———, and Alice Goldstein. 1980. *Differentials in Repeat and Return Migration in Thailand, 1965–1970*. Paper No. 35. Bangkok: Institute of Population Studies, Chulalongkorn University.

————, and A. Goldstein. 1986. *Migration in Thailand: A Twenty-Five Year Review.* Paper No. 100. Honolulu: East-West Population Institute.

————, Pinchit Pitaktepsombati, and A. Goldstein. 1976. "Migration and Urban Growth in Thailand: An Exploration of Interrelations Among Origin, Recency, and Frequency of Moves." In A.H. Richmond and D. Kubat (eds.), *Internal Migration, the New World and the Third World.* Beverly Hills, Calif.: Sage Publications.

————, Pichit Pitaktepsombati, and Alice Goldstein. 1977. *Migration to Urban Places in Thailand: Interrelations Among Origin, Recency, Frequency, and Motivations.* Paper No. 21. Bangkok: Institute of Population Studies, Chulalongkorn University.

————, Visid Prachuabmoh, and Alice Goldstein. 1974. *Urban-Rural Migration Differentials in Thailand.* Research Report No. 12. Bangkok: Institute of Population Studies, Chulalongkorn University.

Lauro, Donald J. 1979. "The Demography of a Thai Village." Ph.D. Dissertation, Australian National University, Canberra.

Lightfoot, Paul, Theodore Fuller, and Peerasit Kamnuansilpa. 1983. *Circulation and Interpersonal Networks Linking Rural and Urban Areas: The Case of Roi-et, Northeastern Thailand.* Papers of the East-West Population Institute, No. 84. Honolulu: East-West Center.

Meinkoth, Marian Richards. 1962. "Migration in Thailand with Particular Reference to the Northeast." *Economics and Business Bulletin* 14:2–45.

National Statistical Office. 1978. *The Survey of Migration in Bangkok Metropolis 1977.* Bangkok: National Statistical Office.

Pejaranonda, C., S. Goldstein, and A. Goldstein. 1984. *Migration.* Subject Report No. 2. Bangkok: National Statistical Office.

Piampiti, Suwanlee. 1985. *Internal Migration in Thailand, 1970–80.* Bangkok: National Institute of Development Administration.

Prachuabmoh, Visid, and Penporn Tirasawat. 1974. *Internal Migration in Thailand.* Paper No. 7. Bangkok: Institute of Population Studies, Chulalongkorn University.

Shryock, H.S., J.S. Siegel, and Associates. 1976. *The Methods and Materials of Demography.* New York: Academic Press.

Singhanetra-Renard, Anchalee. 1981. "Mobility in North Thailand: A View from Within." In G.W. Jones and H.V. Richter (eds.), *Population Mobility and Development: Southeast Asia and the Pacific.* Canberra: Australian National University.

Steinstein, Larry. 1971. *Greater Bangkok Metropolitan Area: Population Growth and Movement, 1956–60.* Research Report No. 3. Bangkok: Institute of Population Studies, Chulalongkorn University.

————. 1982. *Portrait of Bangkok.* Bangkok: Bangkok Metropolitan Administration.

————. 1984. "The Growth of the Population of the World's Pre-eminent 'Primate City': Bangkok at Its Bicentenary." *Journal of Southeast Asian Studies* 15:43–68.

————. 1986. *Spatial Aspects of Migrant Preference for Krung Thep Maha Nakhon (Bangkok).* Bangkok: Institute of Population Studies, Chulalongkorn University.

Textor, Robert B. 1956. "The Northeast Samlor Driver in Bangkok." In *The Social Implications of Industrialization and Urbanization.* Calcutta: Unesco.

Tirasawat, Penporn. 1978. "Economic and Housing Adjustment in Greater Bangkok." *International Migration Review* 12:93–103.

————. 1986. "Interregional Migration Assumptions." Pp. 81–134 in *Studies in As-*

sumptions for Population Projections and Results of the Population Projection for Thailand, 1980–2015. Bangkok: Division of Human Resources, National Economic and Social Development Board.

United Nations. 1982. *Migration, Urbanization, and Development in Thailand*. New York: United Nations.

Vichit-Vadakan, Juree. 1983. "Small Towns and Regional Urban Centers: Reflections on Diverting Bangkok-Bound Migration." *Thai Journal of Development Administration* 23:79–99.

Vichit-Vadakan, Vicharat, and Thinapan Nakata. 1976. *Urbanization in the Bangkok Central Region*. Bangkok: Thai Universities Research Associates, Social Science Association of Thailand.

World Bank. 1980. *Economic Motivation Versus City Lights: Testing Hypotheses about Interchangwat Migration in Thailand*. World Bank Staff Working Paper No. 416.

20

THE UNITED KINGDOM

Philip Rees and John Stillwell

The population of the United Kingdom has experienced very low rates of growth, averaging 1 per 1,000 per annum over the past decade and a half. Despite the close approach to zero population growth, redistribution of the population has been substantial. One region (East Anglia) gained 18 percent in population over the 1971–86 period, while another (Greater London) lost 10 percent. In some instances fertility differences, mortality differences, or the pattern of external migration have had an important influence on population change, but most of the redistribution has been effected by internal migration. This chapter examines the principal population movements that have changed and continue to change the demographic map of the country. Comments on the characteristics and motivations of migrants, and on the consequences of migration are of necessity brief.

DATA ON MIGRATION

Definitions of Migration

There is broad agreement that a migration constitutes a change in a person's place of usual residence. No definitional restrictions are placed on the time interval or spatial distance over which migration may be measured. Moves from one apartment to another in a block or moves from Cornwall to Shetlands are equally regarded as migration. This eclecticism is forced on British researchers because no ideal source of migration statistics exists. However, for present purposes, attention is confined to migration with both origin and destination within the United Kingdom of Great Britain and Northern Ireland.

Operational definitions of migration constrain the general definition in various ways. Fixed period questions in a census or survey measure a person's migration as the shift in location between two set points in time, with intermediate moves being ignored. We refer to these data as "transition," and the United Kingdom has employed such questions in the last four censuses. An alternative procedure is to focus on the move rather than the person involved in migration. Extensive use is now made of the Central Register of the National Health Service (NHSCR) patients to count "moves" between places.

Sources of Data: Censuses

April censuses in 1961, 1966, 1971, and 1981 contained questions about migration in the preceding twelve months, and for 1970–71 and 1980–81, tabulations of migrants into an area are available at all spatial scales employed in the census: countries, regions, counties, districts, wards, and enumeration districts. Interaction data in which both origin and destination are identified are available in full for districts and larger units, although our later analyses focus on migrations among a set of twelve broad regions or twenty county amalgams. The quality of census data is generally high, but migration data are probably the least reliable because most of those missed in the census are likely to have been migrants and because of mis- or nonreporting of origin by the recorded migrants. The Post-Enumeration Survey held after the 1981 census suggests that up to 14 percent should be added to the fully reported figures for migrants (Devis and Mills, 1986, 18–19) to allow for these shortcomings.

Sources of Data: Population Registers

The NHSCR keeps a record of all patient re-registrations which involve transfers of patient records from one Family Practitioner Committee Area (FPCA) to another. Records of inter-FPCA re-registrations are provided for each quarter. Because of the marked seasonal pattern of migration, quarterly figures are aggregated to annual counts for either calendar years or for years between midyear dates, applying a lag of three months to reflect the average delay between migration and re-registration. Some population groups such as families with children, women in general, and the elderly re-register soon after migration; young men do so less diligently. Therefore, there may be some bias in the statistics toward those groups making the most current use of the NHS. The NHSCR records an average 1.245 moves for each transition recorded in the census.

The reasons for this result are explained by differences in population at risk covered in the two sources, underenumeration, and the recording of multiple, return, infant, and nonsurvivor moves in the NHSCR but not the census. Despite the marked difference in how the census and NHSCR collected statistics on migration, the two sources agree closely as to migration pattern (Boden, Stillwell, and Rees, 1987; Devis and Mills, 1986), and we can confidently use NHSCR re-registration data to update the picture of internal migration provided by the 1981 census to 1985–86.

Sources of Data: Surveys

Two national surveys administered by the Office of Population Censuses and Survey (OPCS) provide information on migration: the annual General Household (GHS) and the biennial Labour Force Survey (LFS). They provide valuable data on the household and socioeconomic context of migration but cannot be regarded as providing any reliable spatial detail or even, because of biases in the sampling frames, any reliable account of how the level of migration activity is changing over time.

PRINCIPAL POPULATION MOVEMENTS

The National Level: The Volume of Movement over Time

At what rate do British people engage in internal migration activity? Table 20.1 attempts to synthesize the results of the one-year migration question in the last four censuses and the annual rate of inter-FPCA re-registrations over the last decade. The broad picture is that between 8.4 and 10.5 percent of the U.K. population migrates each year. This is well below migration rates in other Anglophone countries (the United States, Canada, Australia) but above rates in France,

Table 20.1
The Level of Migration Activity in the United Kingdom, 1960–61 to 1985–86

Year	Migration within England, Wales & Scotland	Migration within Great Britain				Migration in England & Wales	Synthetic index (1960-61 = 100)
	Total Internal	Total inter-district	Total inter-county	Total inter-region	Total inter-FPCA	
	a	b				c	d
1960-61	9.58						100
1965-66	9.70						101
1970-71	10.45	10.88	4.61	2.86	1.55		109
1975-76						3.62	109
1980-81	8.40	8.98	3.46	2.25	1.16	2.93	88
1985-86						3.23	97

Sources: a & b Stillwell and Boden. 1986, Tables 1 & 2: original OPCS sourced cited
                      in paper;
              c   NHSCR re-registration computer summaries supplied by OPCS;
              d   Computed by authors

the Netherlands, or Japan (quoted in Long and Boertlein, 1976). From 1960–61 to 1973–74 (most probably), migration activity increased by about 10 percent. It then fell to 1981–82 in tandem with the shrinkage of new vacancies in the job and housing markets. The level of migration activity has revived since the early 1980s, although it has not yet regained the peak levels of the early 1970s.

A more refined measure of migration which avoids any of the age structure bias involved in the crude migration rate is the sum of the age-specific migration rates, commonly called the gross migraproduction rate (GMR). This can be interpreted as the total number of migrations people would make over their lifetime if they were exposed to the current, observed schedule of age-specific migration rates. In 1970–71 Britons migrated at the rate of nearly 8 transitions per lifetime: 4½ of these transitions occurred within local government districts; 1¼ between districts within counties or Scottish Regions; just under 1 between counties within regions; and just over 1 between regions. Women were slightly less migratory than men. By 1980–81 the GMR had decreased to just under 6½ transitions per lifetime. The decrease was least at the most local scale and greatest at the interdistrict, intracountry scale.

The National Level: The Age and Sex Structure of Movement over Time

The propensity of a person to migrate varies by almost five times over a lifetime. At some stages in a life cycle the probability of migration is low, and at others it is high. The form of the migration rate schedule with its life cycle-related peaks and troughs is now a thoroughly familiar one. Figure 20.1 shows the observed schedules at six different spatial scales for male and female one-year migrants within Great Britain recorded in the censuses of 1971 and 1981. The age scale refers to single years of age at the time of the census.

The first part of each observed rate schedule is that for child dependents which parallels the descending adult part of the schedule, separated from it by "rough-ly" the average age of parents of children at given ages. The rate of descent of the child-dependent portions of the curves is always slightly less than the corresponding adult portion. This implies that migration rates in the parental ages are higher, reflecting the higher migration propensity of nonfamily adults in this age range. The child-dependent curve ends slightly later in 1980–81 than in 1970–71, and the labor force component's mean age is slightly greater. This probably results from the shift in the age at which compulsory schooling ends from 15 to 16 in the 1970s.

The next section of the migration age schedule is referred to as the labor force curve. Entry into the labor force necessitates many migrations before comfortable niches are found in middle age. However, our interpretation should be broader since the curve characterizes spatial scales in which the predominant motives for migration are related to the housing and not the job market. The steeply rising migration curve between ages 15 (1970–71) or 16 (1980–81) and

21–22 (females) or 22–24 (males) signals the creation of new households by young adults.

One idiosyncratic feature of the labor force peaks is the interruption of the rising limb for longer distance migrants (interregion or intercountry migrants). This is most pronounced for males in 1980–81, but it is present in subdued form in 1970–71 and in the female schedules. It is most probably an artifact of the rules governing the treatment of students. The census instructions required that students be recorded as resident at their parental homes rather than at their term-time addresses. In many cases the term-time address constitutes the student's true usual residence rather than the parental home, and this instruction is not followed. The date of the 1981 census (April 5) fell in the vacation period of most institutions of higher education, whereas in 1971 it did not (April 25). This perhaps explains why the "bite" out of the schedule was more pronounced in 1980–81. The impact on female schedules was less pronounced because a smaller proportion are students in higher education.

The final feature of note on the migration schedules are the small peaks at retirement age (65) for males and slight rises at age 60 (retirement age) for women, with peaks more pronounced for longer distance migration. The peak at retirement is not a universal feature of all migration streams but is found to characterize migration from metropolitan cores to favored retirement areas. It is largely absent in short-distance migration, where it is replaced by an upturn in the rate of migration for the very old (75+), reflecting migration precipitated by the death of a spouse or by ill health (see Rees and Warnes, 1986, for more detail).

Interregional Migration: The Volume of Net Movement over Time

The United Kingdom can be divided into twelve major geographical regions, which can be grouped into four broad regional divisions. Table 20.2 assembles net migration statistics on this basis over the past two decades and reveals clear patterns of net internal movement. The regions of the Periphery were net losers over the two decades, but these losses were less marked in the last decade, with one region, Wales, recording net inflows. The regions of the Industrial Heartland were consistent net losers in both 1966–76 and 1976–86, and these losses probably increased in the second decade. The Southern regions outside of London were consistent net gainers through the four quinquennia, but these gains decreased in the 1980s compared with the 1970s or 1960s. Finally, the Capital region was a consistent loser of net migrants, at least 1.5 million over 1966–86, although the volume of loss has been considerably reduced. In summary, the net migration statistics suggest a broad regional pattern of losses in the North and gains in the South, interacting with a pronounced pattern of loss from regions containing the nation's largest cities and gains or lesser losses in other "non-metropolitan" regions.

Figure 20.1.
Migration Rate Schedules, Great Britain, 1970–71 and 1980–81

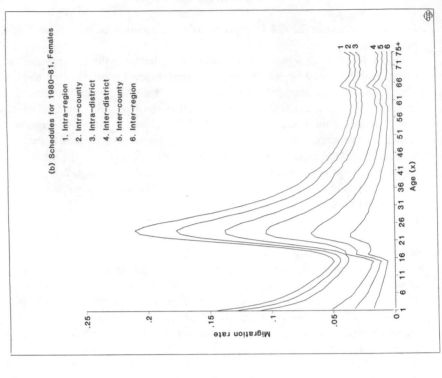

(a) Schedules for 1970–71, Females

1. Intra–region
2. Intra–county
3. Intra–district
4. Inter–district
5. Inter–county
6. Inter–region

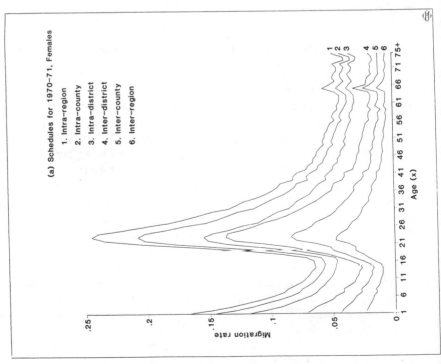

(b) Schedules for 1980–81, Females

1. Intra–region
2. Intra–county
3. Intra–district
4. Inter–district
5. Inter–county
6. Inter–region

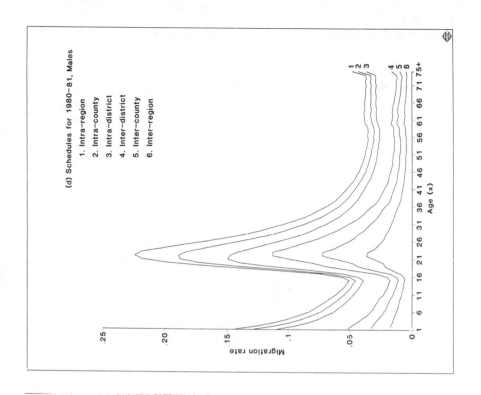

(d) Schedules for 1980–81, Males

1. Intra–region
2. Intra–county
3. Intra–district
4. Inter–district
5. Inter–county
6. Inter–region

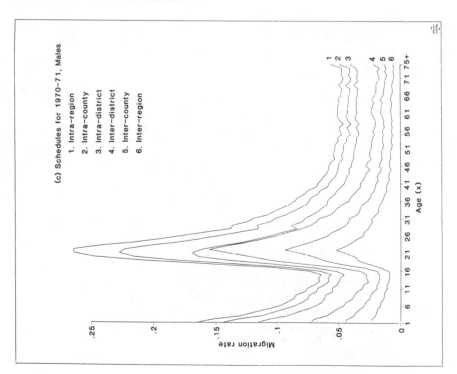

(c) Schedules for 1970–71, Males

1. Intra–region
2. Intra–county
3. Intra–district
4. Inter–district
5. Inter–county
6. Inter–region

Table 20.2
The Pattern of Net Migration for U.K. Regions and Broad Regional Divisions, 1966–86

Broad regional division[a] and region	Net migration (1000's)			
	Internal 1966–71	Total[b] 1971–76	Internal 1976–81	1981–86
NORTH				
Periphery				
Northern Ireland	–10	–55.5	–18.1	–15.1
Scotland	–41	–59.3	–34.8	–37.4
Northern	–36	–27.7	–31.3	–32.2
Wales	7	35.1	22.5	14.3
Sub-total	–80	–107.4	–61.7	–70.4
Industrial Heartland				
North West	–38	–84.7	–89.3	–104.6
Yorks & Humb	–37	–11.7	–17.6	–35.7
West Midlands	–38	–42.1	–55.6	–62.4
Sub-total	–113	–138.5	–162.5	–202.7
North, sub-total	–193	–245.9	–224.2	–273.1
SOUTH				
Rest of the South				
East Midlands	45	48.1	41.2	30.3
East Anglia	74	95.4	81.7	75.4
South West	133	164.6	137.7	163.8
Rest of the East	414	214.5	255.2	196.0
Sub-total	666	522.6	515.8	465.5
Capital				
Greater London	–473	–461.4	–291.3	–192.2
Sub-total	–473	–461.4	–291.3	–192.2
South, sub-total	193	61.2	224.5	273.3
United Kingdom	0	–184.7	0.0	0.0

Notes
a. The broad regional divisions are those adopted in Champion et al, 1986, Figure 1.4
b. Estimates for 1971–76 include external flows. Figures for all regions bar the capital (which was a net gainer of external migrants) should be adjusted upwards for comparison with 1966–71 and 1976–86 figures

Sources: 1966–71: Rees and Stillwell (1984), Table 3 from the 1971 Census migration statistics
1971–76: Rees (1979) from OPCS population estimates & vital statistics
1976–86: NHSCR re-registrations from OPCS computer tabulations and OPCS MN Monitors

Interregional Migration: The Rates of Movement over Time

Employing information from the NHSCR, Figure 20.2 displays the trends in interregional migration over the 1975–86 period. The U.K. graph shows that interregional migration declined, with fluctuations, to 84 percent of the 1975–76 level in 1981–82 and then rose, more smoothly, to 96 percent of the 1975–76 level in 1985–86. The pattern of out-migration followed the national trend in all regions, more or less, except in Northern Ireland and Greater London. Not too much notice should be taken of the fluctuations in the time series for Northern Ireland for 1982–83 onward as the estimates are rather rough, but the reduction in outflows from Greater London reflects the slowing down of urban de-centralization through urban redevelopment and the development of the financial and services economy of London. The rate of net out-migration in the post–1981 period has been half that of the later 1970s.

The trends in in-migration are more varied. The Peripheral regions all show greater decreases and smaller recoveries in in-migration than the United Kingdom. The Industrial Heartland regions follow roughly the national trends in in-migration. The rest of the South and the Capital regions follow the national trend to 1981–82 but experience above-average increases in in-migration since then. All Northern regions have experienced less decline in out-migration than in-migration over the period to 1981–82, and better recovery since 1981–82, while the reverse pattern applies in Southern regions.

To account for these trends in internal migration, it is necessary to relate them to the performance of the regional economies over the period since 1975. It is interesting to observe that the share of in-migrants attracted to all Northern regions has fallen well below their share of the population, whereas the reverse is true for Southern regions. Unemployment rates have been above average in Northern regions and below average in Southern. However, the national trends in neither employment nor unemployment mirror those we have found in migration. The number of persons employed continued to rise from 1975 to 1979 while migration rates fell, although a rise in the number of employees paralleled the rise in migration levels. If the migration series followed unemployment rates closely, we would expect greater decline in the 1979–82 period and no recovery from 1982–83 in migration activity.

Other components of labor market change have been important: the natural rate of growth of the labor force, the change in female activity rates, and the role of net emigration. The natural increase in the labor force over the 1975–86 period has been strong as the large birth cohorts of 1960–71 have entered working ages. At the same time, there have been significant transfers of women from economic inactivity into part-time jobs in the service sector of the economy. Migration was therefore not needed to fill such job vacancies as were occurring. In addition, over the 1979–82 period severe job losses occurred in all regions: migration does not occur between mutually depressed areas. In this period of severe recession in the United Kingdom but much better economic

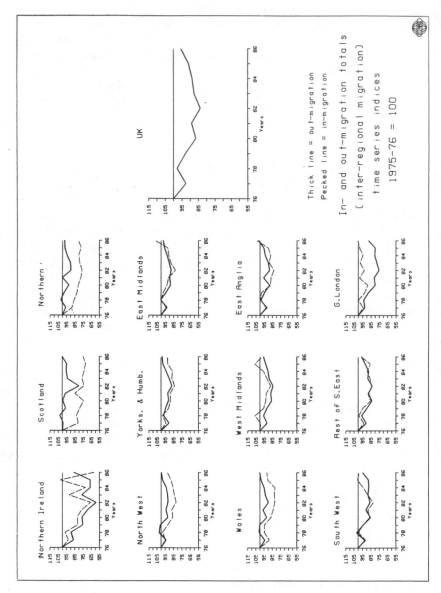

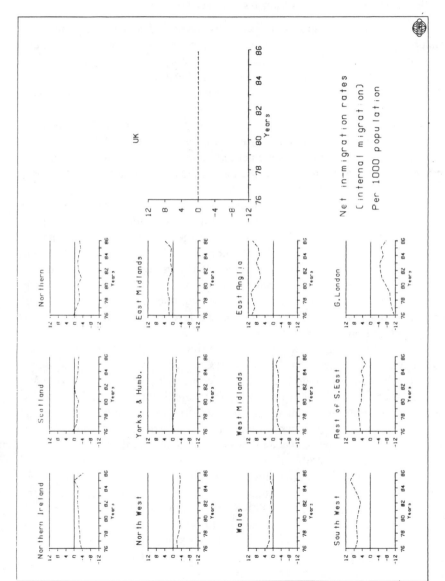

Net in-migration rates
(internal migration)
Per 1000 population

Source: OPCS

conditions in other developed countries, migrants went abroad: In the four years 1979 to 1982 there was a net emigration of 325,000.

Migration in the Metropolitan-Nonmetropolitan Context

The broad regional trends in migration discussed to date mask very important changes occurring between and within Local Labour Market Areas. Considerable work at this fine spatial scale has been carried out by British geographers and is summarized in the volumes by N. Spence et al. (1982) and A.G. Champion et al. (1987), but virtually all recent work is confined to examining intercensal change in population. We can be fairly confident in assuming that population change is predominantly a function of migration for most places, although there are some exceptions such as the continued growth due to high rates of fertility of the Northern Ireland population despite net migration losses, and the importance of interarea differences in mortality at the older ages in explaining shifts in elderly population (Rees, 1986b).

Champion et al. (1987) classify small areas in the country on the basis of their journey to work connections into some 228 functional regions (FRs). Functional regions are classed as dominant if they are the largest functional region contained within the twenty largest metropolitan regions of Great Britain and subdominant if they are one of the smaller FRs within metropolitan regions. Freestanding FRs lie outside the metropolitan regions and cover the rest of the country. Within each functional region small areas are assigned to one of four concentric zones: core, ring, outer, and rural, depending on the level of commuting to principal workplaces and population density.

Figure 20.3 reproduces population change figures for the decade between the 1971 and 1981 censuses from Table 2.2 in Champion et al. (1987). The dominant theme is one of decentralization in the urban system: from core to ring and beyond in each functional region type; from dominant functional regions to subdominant within metropolitan regions; and from metropolitan regions to the rest of the country. These trends characterize all regions within the country, though they are more pronounced in the South than the North (Champion et al., 1987, Figures 2.5 and 2.6).

Some idea of the migration flows that underlie the decentralization from metropolitan regions to the rest of the country can be obtained by aggregating the inter-FPCA migration matrix for 1980–81 into North and South and metropolitan and nonmetropolitan categories. Of the 1,717,500 moves that took place in that year between FPCAs, 187,200 gross moves and 65,300 net moves were recorded into nonmetropolitan areas in the South from metropolitan areas in the South, and 130,500 gross moves and 35,700 net moves were recorded into nonmetropolitan areas in the North from metropolitan counties in the North. When migration between broad regions is examined, each Southern zone gains from each Northern zone, so that there is a net gain from nonmetropolitan areas in the North by metropolitan cores in zones in the South of 9,100. To summarize, there

Figure 20.3
Population Change by Type of Functional Region and Zone, 1971–81

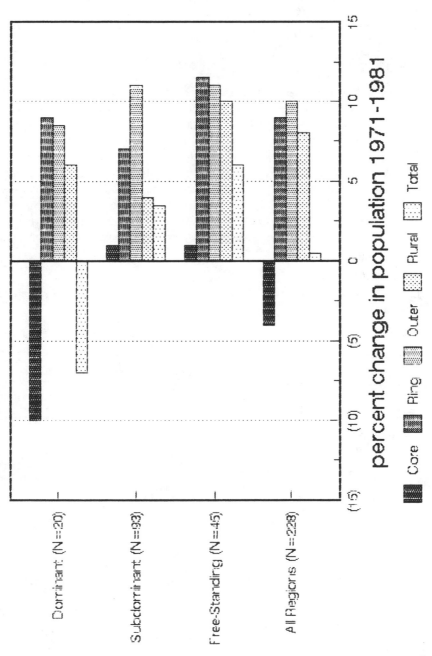

percent change in population 1971-1981

Core Ring Outer Rural Total

Source: British censuses of 1971 and 1981

was a net gain of 50,700 migration from the North to the South but a net gain of 107,400 migration from metropolitan into nonmetropolitan zones. The metropolitan/nonmetropolitan dimension of migration shifts was thus twice as important numerically as the North/South shift.

WHO MOVES

Enough has already been said about the role of age and life course characteristics in influencing the rate at which Britons migrate. Here we concentrate on selected socioeconomic attributes of migrants.

Almost three quarters of male migrants aged 16 and over who moved in the year prior to the 1981 census were working (Table 20.3). About one in eight were seeking work (unemployed), about one in fifteen were retired, and one in twenty were students. Just under half of female migrants aged 16 and over were working at the time of the census, one in sixteen were seeking work, one in seventeen were retired, and one in twenty-six were students. Just over one-third were other economically inactive persons, primarily housewives. The unem-

Table 20.3
Composition of Migrants Aged 16 and Over Resident in Great Britain by Economic Position, 1980–81

Economic position	Males		Females	
	Percent of total	Migration rate (%)	Percent of total	Migration rate (%)
Economically active				
Working	72.7	10.5	47.3	10.5
Seeking work	12.1	15.1	6.2	19.6
Temporarily sick	0.8	9.8	0.6	12.8
Economically inactive				
Permanently sick	1.7	3.2	1.4	8.1
Retired	6.7	4.5	5.7	6.4
Student	4.9	10.9	3.8	9.0
Other inactive	1.0	20.3	35.0	8.1
All migrants	100.0	9.9	100.0	9.3

Source: OPCS (1983)

ployed had the highest rates of migration (apart from a small male "other inactive" group). Even in the depths of the worst postwar recession the United Kingdom has experienced, the unemployed were prepared to get "on their bikes" (to borrow Norman Tebbitt's infamous phrase). Those working had a migration rate just above average, as did male students. The other inactive groups had below-average rates.

A high level of interregional migration among university students (Rees, 1986a) launches them on work careers characterized by much higher long-distance migration than those in manual occupation (Figure 20.4). The highest

Figure 20.4
Interregional Migration Rates of Different Occupational Groups, 1970–71 and 1980–81

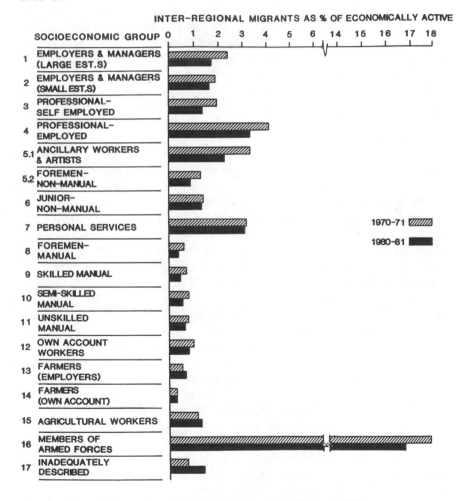

Source: Salt and Flowerdew (1986), Table 3 from the 1971 and 1981 censuses.

migration rates are experienced by armed forces personnel, whose careers are characterized by a progression of planned repostings. Within white-collar occupations, planned career moves within the large firm or government organization probably account for a large proportion of moves, as the public or private corporation seeks to match labor supply and demand from within its ranks. The specialized skills in many of these occupations necessitate interregional movement because job opportunities are widely but thinly spread across the country. Conversely, manual skills are more universal in their occurrence and tend to be filled first from the local labor market, and interregional migration occurs only when labor shortages appear.

WHY PEOPLE MOVE

In this chapter the temporal and spatial trends and patterns in nonlocal migration have been described and interpreted. The interpretations have constituted an informal answer to the question "why do people move?" There is insufficient space to give this vast topic detailed treatment here, but some general observations will put the preceding material in context.

Migrants can be divided into perhaps three groups classified on the basis of their stage in the life course. Each group has different motivations for migration and responds to different push and pull factors. The three groups are (1) members of the labor force without family responsibilities; (2) families with children with one or more parent in the labor force; and (3) retired persons. For the first group, migration results from the need to find a job or an educational place; the person's status (educational level, skills seniority, maturity) is changing rapidly, and frequent moves result. Members of the second group will also be motivated by labor market opportunities, but since their status is not changing as rapidly and since family responsibilities usually mean more permanent investment in a home or location of children's education, moves become less frequent. In the final group, ties to the job market are broken, and migration can be motivated by residential, environmental, or social factors: The distribution of career opportunities no longer matters.

In making the decision to move, the potential migrant has to select from among competing opportunities. Here the role of information and geographical proximity becomes important. British internal migrants are heavily constrained by distance between origin and destination. Frictions caused by distance are highest for migrants originating in the Industrial Heartland regions, least in the two Peripheral regions of Scotland and Northern Ireland, and at intermediate levels elsewhere (Stillwell and Boden, 1986, Figures 15 and 16). Distance frictions appear to be inversely related to the mean distance of migration both over time (Stillwell and Boden, 1986, Figure 14) and over the age range from early working ages (15 to 19) (Rees and Warnes, 1986, Figure 10). The latter relationship parallels the falling rate of mobility, but also means that the longer distance moves tend to diminish as age increases.

CONSEQUENCES OF MIGRATION

It is clear from the population trends identified that internal migration is having a profound and ongoing impact on the distribution of population. Here we report just one consequence: the likely future population distribution for 20 metropolitan counties and nonmetropolitan areas in 2031. The projections are

Table 20.4
Population Projections for Metropolitan Counties and Nonmetropolitan Areas, 1976–2031

Regions	Populations (1000's)		Ratio of 2031/1981 population	% of UK population		Change in %
	1981	2031		1981	2031	
NORTH						-
Metro Counties						
Central Clydeside	1,705	1,045	61	3.04	1.97	-1.07
Tyne and Wear	1,144	850	74	2.04	1.60	-0.44
Merseyside	1,516	1,109	73	2.71	2.09	-0.62
Greater Manchester	2,619	2,111	81	4.68	3.98	-0.70
West Yorkshire	2,043	1,776	87	3.65	3.35	-0.30
South Yorkshire	1,310	1,161	89	2.34	2.19	-0.15
Region remainders						
Scotland Rem	3,425	3,210	94	6.12	6.06	-0.06
North Rem	1,924	1,671	87	3.44	3.15	-0.29
North West Rem	2,310	2,200	95	4.12	4.15	0.03
Yorks & Humb Rem	1,516	1,486	98	2.71	2.80	0.09
West Midlands Rem	2,508	2,665	106	4.48	5.03	0.55
Other regions						
Northern Ireland	1,562	1,800	115	2.79	3.40	0.61
Wales	2,769	2,623	95	4.94	4.95	0.01
REST OF SOUTH						
East Midlands	3,780	3,783	100	6.75	7.14	0.39
East Anglia	1,878	2,126	113	3.35	4.01	0.66
South East	4,349	4,670	107	7.77	8.81	1.04
Outer South East	4,830	5,763	119	8.63	10.87	2.24
CAPITAL						
Outer Metro Area	5,344	5,192	97	9.54	9.79	0.25
Greater London	6,808	5,730	84	12.16	10.81	-1.35
United Kingdom	55,998	53,015	95	100.0	100.0	0.00

Source: projections carried out using a multiregional forecasting model and rates of migration, mortality and fertility observed in 1976–81. See Rees and Warnes (1986) for further details.

produced using a multiregional accounts-based forecasting model with rates of internal migration, emigration, mortality, and fertility set at their observed 1976–81 levels and with immigration set at constant numbers. The projections thus enable us to examine the consequences of current redistribution patterns. However, they must be regarded as underestimates of the absolute size of future regional populations because mortality rates have continued to improve, fertility rates have recovered marginally, and external migration is closer to a zero balance than in 1976–81.

Table 20.4 presents the projected populations, associated shares of the U.K. total, and changes in shares between 1981 and 2031. The South moves to a majority position with 51.4 percent of the national population by 2031, with 30.8 percent in the Rest of the South outside the Capital (up from 26.5 percent) and 20.6 percent in the Capital region (down from 21.7 percent). Metropolitan counties in the North lose very heavily, having less than one in five of the nation's population in 2031 (19.0 percent) compared with just under one in four in 1981 (23.2 percent). Region remainders in the North lose population (they did not do so between 1971 and 1981) but not share of the national total (which increases from 20.9 to 21.2 percent). Wales shares these trends, but Northern Ireland continues on a path of increasing population growth, driven by high fertility rates.

Our earlier analyses of trends in regional migration reveal that the redistribution implied by the migration pattern of 1981–86 would be less than that projected using 1976–81 rates. Although the changes in the population of individual places may be very large (Central Clydeside loses 39 percent of its population, for example), the process of redistribution in the United Kingdom is a fairly measured one by international standards. The British response to major events continues to be Herbert Asquith's "Wait and see" rather than Winston Churchill's "Action this day."

REFERENCES

Bates, J., and I. Bracken. 1987. "Migration Age Profiles for Local Authority Areas in England, 1971–81." *Environment and Planning A* 19:521–35.

Boden, P., J.C.H. Stillwell, and P.H. Rees. 1987. "Migration Data from the National Health Service Central Register and the 1981 Census: Further Comparative Analysis." *Working Paper 495*. Leeds: School of Geography, University of Leeds.

Champion, A.G., A.E. Green, D.W. Owen, D.J. Ellin, and M.G. Coombes. 1987. *Changing Places: Britain's Demographic, Economic and Social Complexion.* London: Edward Arnold.

Devis, T., and I. Mills. 1986. *A Comparison of Migration Data from the National Health Service Central Register and the 1981 Census.* Occasional Paper 35. London: Office of Population Censuses and Surveys.

Long, L.H., and C. Boertlein. 1976. *The Geographic Mobility of Americans: An International Comparison.* Current Population Reports, Special Series, Series P-23, No. 64. Washington, D.C.: U.S. Department of Commerce, Bureau of the Census.

Office of Population Censuses and Surveys, (OPCS). 1983. *Census 1981 National Migration, Great Britain. Part 1 (100% Tables)*. CEN 81 NM(1). London: Her Majesty's Stationery Office.

Rees, P.H. 1979. *Migration and Settlement: 1 United Kingdom*. Research Report RR-79-3. Laxenburg, Austria: International Institute for Applied Systems Analysis.

———. 1986a. "A Geographical Forecast of the Demand for Student Places." *Transactions of the Institute of British Geographers* NS 11:5–26.

———. 1986b. "Components of Elderly Population Change." Paper presented at the Colorado International Conference on Elderly Migration, October 1–4, 1986. Aspen Lodge, Colo.

———, and J.C.H. Stillwell. 1984. "A Framework for Modelling Population Change and Migration in the UK." In A.J. Boyce (ed.), *Migration and Mobility: Biosocial Aspects of Human Movement*. London: Taylor and Francis.

———, and A.M. Warnes. 1986. "Migration of the Elderly in the United Kingdom." Working Paper 473. Leeds: School of Geography, University of Leeds.

Salt, J., and R. Flowerdew. 1986. "Occupational Selectivity in Labour Migration." Paper presented at the Conference on Comparative Population Geography of the United Kingdom and the Netherlands, Oxford, September 17–19.

Spence, N., A. Gillespie, J. Goddard, S. Kennett, S. Pinch, and A. Williams. 1982. *British Cities: Analysis of Urban Change*. Oxford: Pergamon.

Stillwell, J.C.H., and P. Boden. 1986. "Internal Migration in the UK: Characteristics and Trends." Working Paper 470. Leeds: School of Geography, University of Leeds.

———, P. Boden, and P.H. Rees. 1987. "Migration Schedule Construction Using MODEL and GIMMS." *Computer Manual* 29. Leeds: School of Geography, University of Leeds.

21

THE UNITED STATES

Daniel T. Lichter and Gordon F. De Jong

Migration is an increasingly important demographic component of change in the size, distribution, and composition of the U.S. population. The demographic significance of migration has grown over recent decades as natural increase has slowed and spatial differences in the vital rates have narrowed (Goldstein, 1976). Moreover, U.S. migration patterns since midcentury have undergone several major and sometimes unexpected changes. The historic pattern of population movement to urban and industrial cities has been replaced by an oscillating pattern of net migration to and from rural areas. There is also a continuing realignment of interregional migration flows. The movement of population to the South has persisted into the 1980s, but other regions, such as parts of New England, are experiencing new growth from in-migration. On the other hand, the West has become a less significant destination of population flows, yet continues in the 1980s to be a net importer of population from both the Midwest and Northeast (U.S. Bureau of the Census, 1987).

In this chapter, we highlight recent patterns of internal migration in the United States. Specifically, we examine: (1) issues of data availability and quality; (2) the volume and character of U.S. migration flows; (3) migration selectivity; (4) reasons for moving; and (5) the effect of migration on individual lives. Given the transitory nature of recent trends, it seems increasingly difficult to anticipate emerging shifts in the character of U.S. migration patterns, or their potential social and economic consequences for people and places. Nevertheless, the 1980s have produced a considerably more balanced pattern of migration in the United States, as some of the dominant migration flows and differentials of the past have waned in importance or have been replaced by newly emerging patterns.

DATA ON MIGRATION

There are four principal sources of U.S. migration data: (1) decennial censuses, (2) periodic administrative surveys; (3) multipurpose panel surveys; and (4) net migration estimates.

Beginning in 1940 (but only on a sample basis since 1950), the U.S. decennial census schedule has included a question asking individuals to report place of residence five years earlier (U.S. Bureau of the Census, 1984). The classification of individual mobility status is then based on the comparison of current and previous residence. These data are available in several forms. Printed reports, such as *Population Characteristics,* provide basic information on the volume of mobility, including movement within and between counties, states, and regions, and on the general demographic and economic characteristics of movers. For more detailed tabulations for specific geographic units, data are also available on microfiche and on computer tapes in the form of Summary Tape Files (STFs). For more specialized uses, the Public Use Microdata Sample (PUMS) provides individual or household records on computer tape for generating tabulations or analysis of migration not available in printed form (see Dahmann, 1986, for discussion). In addition, the recent release of the 1940 and 1950 PUMS files, along with files from 1960, 1970, and 1980, provides an opportunity to give recent U.S. migration trends some historical context (Wilson, 1986, 1987).

There are also a number of specialized administrative surveys providing information on migration status. The most widely used is the March annual demographic supplement of the Current Population Survey (CPS), which provides information on changing residence patterns for varying time intervals. During the 1970s, the retrospective migration question varied in length between one and five years. In the 1980s, the one-year migration interval was used exclusively for the 1981 to 1984 period, while both one- and five-year migration intervals were used in 1985. These data are in published reports (e.g., *Geographic Mobility: March 1983 to March 1984*) and are available on computer tape, which provides timely information on current migration trends during the interim between censuses. Other administrative sources of data, such as the *American* (formerly *Annual*) *Housing Survey* (Brown, 1981; Plane and Isserman, 1983; Wardwell and Gilchrist, 1980), the *National Health Interview Survey* (Tucker and Urton, 1987), and the Internal Revenue Service migration flow data (Rogerson and Plane, 1985), also provide migration information. In addition, the *Survey of Income and Program Participation* (SIPP) provides a promising new source with the capability of tracking migrants over an extended period (Dahmann and McArthur, 1987).

Although less useful in evaluating current trends in the volume or flow of migration, several continuing multipurpose panel surveys provide useful information on the causes and consequences of migration (Dahmann, 1987). *The Panel Survey of Income Dynamics* (PSID) (see Morrison and DeVanzo, 1986), the *National Longitudinal Surveys* (Bartel, 1979; Spitze, 1984), and the *Quality of Employment Survey* (Martin and Lichter, 1983), monitor changes in residence directly, without recourse to retrospective questions. They provide information on *changes* in factors associated with the migration experience, such as income or employment changes and nondemographic information (e.g., attitudes) related to geographic mobility.

Finally, the Federal-State Cooperative Program annually provides estimates of net migration and population change (U.S. Bureau of the Census, P-26 series). Whereas the sources described above measure migration at the individual level, estimates of net migration are available for areal units, including counties and states. Calculated on the basis of various administrative records, these estimates are an integral component of government efforts to monitor population change through net migration. These estimates, however, are not disaggregated by origin and destination, and rarely provide age, sex, or race detail.

Quality of Data

The retrospective residence question used in the decennial census and the CPS is an excellent source on the volume and character of recent migration. These data are limited, however, in several respects: (1) multiple moves cannot be determined; (2) return migration cannot be ascertained; (3) migrant and non-migrant characteristics are measured at the end-of-period, which limits analyses and inferences regarding the "causes" of migration; (4) information on migration of young children (less than 1 or 5 years of age) is unavailable; (5) migration is measured and tabulated at the individual level, which creates serious difficulties in modeling family or household migration; and (6) we cannot discern the motivational basis of geographical mobility.

Panel survey data, such as the PSID or SIPP, have several advantages over standard census-type measures of migration, including the ability to track changes in the sociodemographic characteristics of migrants and nonmigrants over some time interval (Dahmann, 1987). Yet, panel data are not without limitations. First, the small sample sizes characteristic of most panel surveys often preclude detailed analyses of the volume or characteristics of specific migration streams. Second, panel surveys suffer from sample attrition. Unfortunately, migrants are disproportionately represented among sample nonrespondents, which raises obvious questions about sample bias (Speare and Kobrin, 1980).

County and state net or gross migration estimates, based on the retrospective migration question, are available in the decennial census STFs. However, because of small sample sizes at the county level, these data have some problems of unreliability (Kennedy et al., 1986). As a result, intercensal county net migration estimates have typically been calculated using a census or life table survival technique, or a vital rates approach based on the demographic accounting equation (see Bowles et al., 1975; White et al., 1987).

PRINCIPAL POPULATION MOVEMENTS

Population Mobility in the United States

The United States is a highly mobile society. Between 1984 and 1985, the Census Bureau estimated that about 46.5 million people, or 19.6 percent of the U.S. population, changed places of residence. Not surprisingly, the extent of mobility was even greater for the five-year period between 1980 and 1985 when 39.9 percent of all Americans changed residences (U.S. Bureau of the Census, 1987). Such numbers are particularly impressive if we consider that they are conservative estimates of the true volume of migration because repeat and return migrants are not counted.

As shown below, much of the U.S. mobility during 1984–85 involved short distances.

Type of Move	% Moving
1. Total intercounty migration	6.3
Different county, same state	3.1
Different county, different state	3.2
Different county, different region	1.6
2. Local movement	13.1
3. Total geographical mobility (1 + 2)	19.6

Local movers constitute about two-thirds of all U.S. moves; over one in eight residents move locally each year. In contrast, about 6 percent, or about one in every fifteen Americans, move between counties each year. The majority of these migrants continue to reside within the same state.

Despite substantial geographic mobility, including a continuing increase in the overall volume of migration, rates of mobility declined modestly throughout much of the 1970s and early 1980s (U.S. Bureau of the Census, 1986). The rate declined from 18.7 percent for 1970–71 to 17.7 for 1975–76, to 17.2 for 1980–81, and finally to 16.6 for 1982–83. Intercounty migration rates reveal much the same pattern of decline. There has been widespread speculation but little empirical evidence to suggest that this trend has been influenced by (1) the rise in female labor force participation, which anchors households to particular locales; (2) the rise in the cost of home mortgages; (3) government assistance programs (e.g., unemployment compensation) which reduces the fluidity of labor mobility; (4) spatial convergence in standards of living which reduces incentives to move; and (5) the aging of the population.

Whether recently released evidence of a slight upturn in migration rates for 1984–85 (U.S. Bureau of the Census, 1987) is due to changes in any or all of these factors is unclear. Nor is it clear whether this upturn is a temporary adjustment brought on by the low mobility during the recession of the early 1980s, or represents a permanent return to the higher mobility characteristic of the past.

Regional Migration Patterns

During much of this century, population not only shifted westward away from the industrial Northeast and Midwest, but also emptied out the rural agricultural heartland. This pattern continued during the 1970s. Indeed, during the 1970–75 period, the Northeast was a net exporter to each of the other major census regions of the country. The South, on the other hand, gained population on balance from every other region, importing nearly 2 million more people than it exported (Kasarda, 1980). Not only did the South attract unprecedented numbers of new residents, but it also lost fewer people to out-migration (Kennedy, 1986). The rise of the "Sunbelt" and the decline of the "Frostbelt" captured the public imagination, as efforts were made to explain the accelerated regional realignment of population growth and migration in the United States (Berry and Dahmann, 1977; Sternlieb and Hughes, 1975).

In some ways, the South appears to be strengthening its position as the leading destination of interregional migrants. For the 1980–85 period, 1.9 million more people entered the South than left, while the West, the only other region to experience in-migration during this period, gained about 650,000 net migrants (U.S. Bureau of the Census, 1987). In fact, during the 1983–84 period the West experienced an unprecedented reversal to net out-migration of over 50,000 residents. By way of contrast, the exchange of migrants favored the South by 201,000 residents during 1975–76, while net in-migration in the West was substantially higher at 367,000 (U.S. Bureau of the Census, 1986). Net out-migration from the Northeast, on the other hand, slowed substantially during the past decade. After losing 213,000 residents through out-migration during 1975–76, the Northeast exported only 91,000 more than it gained during 1983–84. Indeed, for the 1980–85 period, the Northeast was a net exporter of about 1 million people to other regions (Kasarda et al., 1986). This is a substantial reduction over that of the 1975–80 period, when the Northeast lost over 1.6 million to net migration. In the early 1980s, Massachusetts, Vermont, and New Hampshire experienced population gains well above the national rate of growth (Engels, 1986).

This demographic portrait of the South should be tempered with the understanding that the South remains a demographically and economically heterogeneous region. Nevertheless, when considered as a whole, several factors underlie the new pattern of overall Southern growth and immigration. Included are: (1) the increased salience of environmental and recreational amenities in attracting migrants; (2) the growth of jobs; (3) convergence in standards of living with the rest of the nation; (4) an improving racial climate; and (5) and the attractiveness of the South, particularly Florida, as a destination for elderly immigrants (Kasarda, 1980; Kasarda et al., 1986).

Elderly Migrants to the Sunbelt

The mobility rates of the elderly—those over age 65—are substantially lower than those of the total U.S. population. Only 6.0 percent of the population aged

65 or older changed residences between 1984 and 1985, and a miniscule 2.2 percent moved between counties (U.S. Bureau of the Census, 1987). Despite low overall mobility, elderly migration continues to draw the attention of demographers and other social scientists for several reasons (Frey, 1986; Heaton, 1983; McCarthy, 1983).

First, unlike the population as a whole, the elderly are an increasingly mobile segment of the U.S. population (Flynn et al., 1985). Second, a disproportionate share of elderly migrants are represented in the interregional flows to the South (Biggar et al., 1984). Third, elderly immigrants to the Sunbelt are concentrated in a few states such as Florida (Longino, 1984). This state has maintained its position as the leading importer of migrants for the past three decades. California, on the other hand, although still the second leading net importer of elderly persons, has seen its attractiveness as a destination decline significantly over recent decades. Fourth, the exchange of elderly persons to and from the South not only has quantitative implications but also qualitative consequences. New evidence suggests that a disproportionate share of elderly migrants who return North are older, poorer, and less likely to be living independently than North-to-South elderly migrants (Longino, 1984). Traditional economic models of labor mobility seem less appropriate in explaining their behavior (see Heaton et al., 1981; McLeod et al., 1984; Serow, 1987), and this has led to a reevaluation of traditional assumptions about migration motivations and redirected attention to noneconomic factors underlying migration.

Black Interregional Flows

Displaced by the social and technological reorganization of Southern agriculture, blacks left the rural South in unprecedented numbers during the 1910–60 period (Fligstein, 1983; Sly, 1972). This massive redistribution of the black population was eased by the industrial expansion of large Northern cities, which provided opportunities for employment generally unavailable in the South (Johnson and Campbell, 1982; Sly, 1981).

The so-called Great Migration of blacks was finally halted during the 1970s, (McHugh, 1987). Blacks continued to migrate to the South during the 1980s, albeit at a slower pace than the late 1970s. For the 1980–85 period, 324,000 moved out of the South, while 411,000 moved in (Robinson, 1986). For the one-year period 1983–84 alone, 152,000 blacks relocated to the South, while 136,000 left the South for other regions (U.S. Bureau of the Census, 1986). The South was a net importer of black people from both the Northeast (+34,000) and the Midwest (+17,000). But, unlike the total population the South lost blacks in its exchange with the West. This was due largely to the fact that the West has a small black population at risk of out-migration. In fact, our calculations suggest a rate of black West-to-South out-migration of 11.64 per 1,000, compared to a rate of black South-to-West out-migration of 4.53 per 1,000 (U.S. Bureau of Census, 1986; calculations based on Table 2).

Urban-to-Rural and Rural-to-Urban Migration

The history of U.S. internal migration during this century has been one of population concentration in and around metropolitan and urban areas (Beale and Fuguitt, 1978; Johnson and Purdy, 1980). Since 1970, however, two largely unanticipated shifts in migration flows between metro and nonmetro areas occurred. First, the metro-nonmetro "turnaround" in net immigration rates during the 1970s rivals the demographic significance of the Southern population revival (see review by Fuguitt, 1985). During 1970–73, 4.7 million people moved from metro to nonmetro areas, while only 3.7 million moved from nonmetro to metro areas (U.S. Bureau of the Census, 1974).

A second significant shift has occurred since 1980, which has caused demographers to reevaluate theoretical assumptions about the "turnaround." That is, population growth and net migration in nonmetropolitan areas have slowed once again (Forstall and Engels, 1984; Richter, 1985). During 1983–84, nonmetropolitan areas experienced net out-migration, losing on balance over 350,000 residents (Beale and Fuguitt, 1986). Whether this recent reversal will continue is difficult to predict, but it reinforces the need to monitor the metropolitanization process (Frey, 1987; Fuguitt et al., 1988; Wilson, 1988).

There are a number of facets to recent trends in the exchange of migrants between metropolitan and nonmetropolitan areas. (1) The post-1970 nonmetropolitan net immigration was due to increases in metropolitan out-migration and decreases in nonmetropolitan out-migration (Tucker, 1976). (2) Nonmetropolitan growth and net migration did not simply represent expanded urban concentration (Beale and Fuguitt, 1978; McCarthy and Morrison, 1977). (3) Metro-to-metro migration became the dominant stream (U.S. Bureau of the Census, 1984), and, like the shift to nonmetro areas, metro-to-metro migration contributed to the spatial diffusion of population. Large central cities experienced population decline through out-migration and suburbanization, and less populated metropolitan areas experienced the most rapid population growth (Fuguitt et al., 1988; Long, 1981). (4) The significance of economic factors in the new nonmetropolitan in-migration declined as noneconomic forces, including rural residential preferences and amenity-motivated movement, played a larger role in internal migration (Heaton et al., 1981; Murdock et al., 1984; Voss and Fuguitt, 1979; Williams, 1981). (5) Overall, net in-migration to nonmetropolitan areas was not pervasive across population subgroups, as nonmetro areas continued to lose the youngest and best educated to metro areas during the 1970s (e.g., Lichter et al., 1979; Zuiches and Brown, 1979).

The pattern of net in-migration to nonmetro areas generated theoretical discussion about its causes. This has become more controversial as net migration rates again favored metro areas in the early 1980s (e.g., Frey, 1987; Kephart, 1988; Wilson, 1987, 1988). J.M. Wardwell (1977) suggested that U.S. migration flows between metro and nonmetro areas might be in a state of equilibrium, with net migration between metro and nonmetro areas oscillating around zero. Regardless of future migration flows, it seems clear that the improved accessibility fostered by technological advances in transportation and communication, and the continuing process of spatial convergence in living standards, are likely to feed the deconcentrative migration tendencies observed over recent decades.

Elderly Nonmetro Migration to Nonmetro Areas

Whereas metro-nonmetro migration rates reversed unexpectedly in the 1970s, the elderly population experienced a metro-nonmetro migration "turnaround" during the 1960s (Fuguitt and Tordella, 1980). For the 1960–70 period, non-metropolitan areas experienced net in-migration of 159,000 elderly migrants (aged 65 and over), compared to a net loss of nearly 3 million persons aged less than 65. This elderly migration turnaround intensified in the early 1970s, and it became clear that it was not simply an artifact of elderly interregional shifts, such as the movement to Southern nonmetropolitan destinations (Longino, 1982).

What explains the continuing attractiveness of nonmetropolitan destinations for elderly migrants? Part of the reason is that the elderly are less subject than younger migrants to national and subnational shifts in the economy and employment opportunities (Serow, 1987). Recent declines in employment growth in rural areas, coupled with the crisis in the farm economy, have not greatly affected the elderly with their portable pension and social security incomes. The spatial integration of the rural and urban sectors also means that finding health care and other services for the elderly is less problematic than in the past regardless of residence. Finally, it is important to note that elderly migrant flows are dominated by some clearly nonmetropolitan identifiable locations, such as the Ozarks, the upper Great Lakes region, and rural parts of New England (Ploch, 1978; Voss and Fuguitt, 1979), which provide highly attractive retirement settings.

Black Migration to Nonmetro Areas

Blacks have not shared greatly in the revitalization of rural and nonmetropolitan America during the past two decades (Cheong et al., 1986; Lichter et al., 1985). Indeed, metropolitan central cities experienced substantial black population increases from in-migration, while experiencing white depopulation. This contributed to a black population increase of 32.5 percent in central cities between 1970 and 1980, compared to a white decline of 1.1 percent (Long and DeAre, 1981). Although black rates of suburbanization exceeded white rates, this was due in part to declining white suburbanization (Edmonston and Guterbock, 1984; Frey, 1985), as whites increasingly bypassed the suburban fringe for nonmetropolitan areas.

The continuing centripetal drift of U.S. blacks to urban areas is also reflected in data from the 1980s. During 1983–84, 144,000 blacks migrated from non-metro-to-metro areas, compared to 98,000 moving from metro-to-nonmetro areas (U.S. Bureau of the Census, 1986, Table 1). Consistent with the continuing spatial concentration of blacks, nearly 75 percent of metro destination in-migrants relocated in central cities (U.S. Bureau of the Census, 1986, Table 1).

To date, there has been little comparative research on factors underlying these apparent racial differences in population movements between metropolitan and nonmetropolitan areas (Lichter et al., 1986). The literature on residential prefer-ences suggests that blacks are considerably less likely than whites to prefer to live in smaller communities and rural areas (Zuiches, 1981). At the same time, some suggest that current governmental assistance programs (e.g., public hous-ing) may actually create disincentives to migration by anchoring blacks in eco-nomically declining central cities (Kasarda, 1983). Finally, black-white dif-ferences undoubtedly reflect continuing racial inequalities in economic opportun-ity, as well as the persistence of overt racial hostilities and discrimination in rural areas (Johnson and Campbell, 1982).

MIGRATION SELECTIVITY

In this section we cannot provide an exhaustive review (for reviews, see Greenwood, 1975; Ritchey, 1976; Shaw, 1975) of selectivity for interregional and metropolitan-nonmetropolitan streams. Our emphasis is on the social and economic characteristics of individual migrants, but we also discuss factors related to family and household migration.

The CPS, for example, reveals that migration rates vary by sex and race (see also Concord, 1982; Frey, 1985; Sandefur, 1985). Between 1983 and 1984 males had higher overall mobility rates, and they were more likely to move longer distances than females. On the other hand, overall mobility rates among blacks and whites were very similar (U.S. Bureau of the Census, 1986). Whites, however, tended to move longer distances than blacks, as indicated by rates of intercounty movement exceeding blacks. In contrast, between 1975 and 1980, one-third of blacks compared to one-fourth of whites moved within the same county (U.S. Bureau of the Census, 1981).

The CPS also reveals substantial age selectivity in migration. Over one-third of all 20-to 24-year olds changed residence during 1983–84, but less than 5 percent of persons over age 65 did (U.S. Bureau of the Census, 1986). Young adulthood is a period of transitions (e.g., leaving the parental home, entering the labor force, finishing school, getting married, and having children), and each transition is typically associated with a move (Sandefur and Scott, 1981; Speare and Goldsheider, 1987). Moreover, age patterns of migration are consistent with human capital models; adult migration rates decline with age as the period over which to reap "returns" declines and as the costs increase with the accumulation of location-specific capital.

Mobility in the United States also varies by education and employment charac-teristics (Long, 1974). College graduates are considerably more likely to move than high school-educated persons who, in turn, move more frequently than persons with an elementary school education. For 1983–84, over 18 percent of college graduates moved compared to about 10 percent of persons with an elementary education (U.S. Bureau of the Census, 1986). Given education differences by occupation, it is not surprising then that professional workers have a higher mobility rate than blue-collar farm workers (Kleiner, 1982; U.S. Bureau of the Census, 1986).

Household utility models of migration are gradually replacing traditional concerns based on an individual cost-benefit calculus (DaVanzo, 1976; Mincer, 1978). This shift in orientation is overdue because nearly one-half of all moves involve married persons (U.S. Bureau of the Census, 1986). Recent studies have shown that geographic mobility is affected by the age and number of children (Long, 1972), by marital status changes (Speare and Goldscheider, 1987), and by the employment of the wife (Long, 1974; Polachek and Horvath, 1977; but also see Bartel, 1979). Although labor force participation of the wife appears to anchor family households to particular locales, there is little evidence that her specific employment characteristics (i.e., occupation, relative earnings) are related systematically to the likelihood of family migration (Lichter, 1982).

Characteristics of Interregional and Metro-Nonmetro Migrants

Table 21.1 presents selected characteristics of interregional and metro-nonmetro migrants for 1983–84 (U.S. Bureau of the Census, 1986). The data show considerable similarity in the age distribution of migrants, with young adult-age categories accounting for a disproportionate share of all migrants to each of the regions. (Compare columns 2–5 with the age distribution for the overall United States provided in column 1.) The West received a higher proportion of persons 45 years and over, including retirees, but a lower proportion of young people aged 15 to 24. The nonmetro-to-metro migration stream contained a disproportionate share of high school and college-age youth, while the metropolitan-to-nonmetropolitan stream had a higher proportion of persons 45 years and over. This provides additional evidence that nonmetro areas continue to lose some of their "best and brightest" to urban areas (Lichter et al., 1979; Zuiches and Brown, 1978).

There is little evidence of racial selectivity in in-migration to the various regions, although in-migrants to the Midwest are somewhat overrepresentative of whites (see Table 21.1). The metro-to-nonmetro and nonmetro-to-metro streams were strongly overrepresentative of whites compared to the migration streams of regions. This suggests that black migration is less likely than white migration to be associated with major changes in *type* of residence (e.g., urban and rural) and that metro to metro streams are disproportionately black in racial composition (U.S. Bureau of the Census, 1986).

Comparisons of the socioeconomic characteristics of interregional migrants reveal considerable migration selectivity. For example, the most positively selected migrants with regard to education were to the Northeast where 55.7

Table 21.1

Selected Characteristics of Interregional and Metropolitan–Nonmetropolitan Migrants, 1983–84

Characteristics	U.S. Population	Interregional Migrants to:				Intermetropolitan Migrants:	
		Northeast	Midwest	South	West	Nonmet-to-Met	Met-to-Nonmet
Age:							
Under 15	21.0%	20.9%	23.1%	22.4%	23.8%	21.7%	23.9%
15–24	17.3	28.5	26.5	24.7	31.5	30.3	24.8
25–34	17.6	26.1	25.6	26.2	25.5	25.5	24.7
35–44	13.2	12.3	12.4	12.2	10.0	11.7	10.9
45 +	30.9	12.2	12.4	14.5	9.2	10.8	15.7
Race							
% White	85.4	83.8	90.9	86.8	85.4	92.7	95.4
Education: 25 yrs. old and over College:							
1–3 years	15.8	24.8	20.4	20.2	25.3	19.6	17.4
4 or more years	19.1	30.9	25.5	30.7	25.0	27.5	23.4
Employment Status: 16 yrs. & over							
% Unemployed: Males	8.6	9.2	18.1	10.9	12.0	11.0	14.6
% Unemployed: Females	7.8	22.7	22.9	17.5	15.3	12.1	16.7
Occupational Status (Males):							
% Executive, Adm. & Managerial	13.2	18.8	10.4	17.5	13.6	14.4	10.9
% Professional & Technical	14.9	23.2	11.8	24.2	14.5	17.8	15.9
Occupational Status (Women):							
% Executive, Adm. & Managerial	8.6	15.3	6.3	3.8	6.5	7.5	4.9
% Professional & Technical	18.2	23.5	23.4	19.1	15.9	21.8	26.0
Relative Income, 1983:							
% Family Householder Above Property Level	87.7	85.4	75.6	83.8	83.6	82.6	83.5

Source: U.S. Bureau of the Census, Geographical Mobility, March 1983 to March 1984: Current Population Reports, P-20, No. 407, Tables 4, 8, 22, 28, 36 and 40.

percent had at least some college education, with nearly 31 percent having earned a college degree. During this time period the percentage of unemployed male migrants was lowest in the Northeast (9.2 percent) and highest for migrants to the Midwest (18.1 percent). The percentage of unemployed female migrants was higher than that for males. Unemployment for female migrants was lowest for nonmetro migrants (12.1 percent) and migrants to the West (15.3 percent). The highest unemployment was for female migrants to the Northeast (22.7 percent) and to the Midwest (22.9 percent).

With regard to occupational and relative income characteristics of inter-regional and metro-nonmetro migrants, the data in Table 21.1 indicate that both male and female migrants to the Northeast were positively selected for executive and professional occupations. Male migrants to the South and female migrants to the Midwest and to nonmetro areas were also positively selected for professional occupations. Proportionately fewer executive and professional male migrants moved to the Midwest and from metro-to-nonmetro areas. Consistent with these selectivity patterns, the percentage of migrant households above the poverty level in 1983 was lowest in the Midwest (75.6 percent) but was quite similar for all other migration streams.

These data show that there is considerable interregional and metro-nonmetro selectivity in the socioeconomic characteristics of migrants. The resulting gains or losses in human capital through migration clearly affect the social and economic development potential of areas (Greenwood and Hunt, 1984; Morrison and Wheeler, 1976). At the same time, we should not lose sight of the fact that migrants to all regions are above average in their educational and occupational skills.

WHY PEOPLE MOVE

The appraisal of population redistribution streams within the United States inevitably leads to the question: Why do people move? Researchers have examined the motivations for migration by (1) inferring motives based on the analysis of objective structural determinants (e.g., characteristics of areas of origin or destination); (2) accepting the migrant's own statement of motives (reasons for moving); or (3) a combination of the two approaches (Taylor, 1969). While the last is preferable, it has seldom been pursued rigorously in migration surveys (Goldstein and Goldstein, 1981).

The analysis of motives, nevertheless, remains a key element in theories linking migration explanations to economic and social change (Zelinsky, 1971). In response largely to the need to better understand the new metro-to-nonmetro migration patterns of the 1970s, studies of reasons for moving have proliferated during the past decade. This interest also reflects the assessment that migration patterns in the United States involve a complex set of causal factors not easily captured by theories based largely on economic factors.

Local versus Long-Distance Moves

Reasons for moving vary by distance moved. It is therefore important to differentiate between local movers (within county or within metropolitan area labor markets) and more distant migrants (across county boundaries or outside of metropolitan labor markets). L.H. Long and Diane DeAre (1980) show that (1) approximately 50 percent of all local movers gave housing and neighborhood reasons for moving; (2) another 25 to 30 percent of local movers reported family or relational reasons; and (3) less than 10 percent of the respondents cited employment and job-related reasons.

These results were decidedly different from those of longer distance migrants, of whom about 45 percent reported economic factors as the most important reason for moving. Housing and neighborhood reasons were given by only about 15 percent of these movers, while family and relational reasons were cited by approximately 18 percent. Entering or leaving the armed forces, attending school, and retiring constituted most of the balance. As these results suggest, economic and employment factors are considerably more important in long-distance than local movement.

Metro versus Nonmetro Migration

Most community and regional studies (see Steahr and Luloff, 1985; Voss and Fuguitt, 1979; Williams and Sofranko, 1979) have provided results generally consistent with the patterns reported by Long and DeAre (1980) from national data. Economic (or employment) reasons constitute almost half (48.5 percent) of the responses given by household heads moving to metro areas compared to 41 percent of those moving to nonmetro areas. Noneconomic reasons emphasized by metro-destination migrant household heads include attending school, entering or leaving the armed forces, and changing marital status. Noneconomic reasons emphasized by nonmetro-destination migrant household heads include neighborhood satisfaction, retirement, housing size and lower costs, and closer proximity to relatives.

It is important to identify not only reasons for moving, but also reasons for choosing particular destinations. In a study of in-migration to the upper Great Lakes region, C.C. Roseman and J.D. Williams (1980) identified reasons both for moving out of metro areas and for selecting particular nonmetro destinations. They found that, while employment considerations were important for leaving metro areas, choosing a particular nonmetro destination was greatly influenced by previous ties to the area (e.g., family or relatives, vacation home). Such results reinforce popular notions that noneconomic incentives played a major role in the rural population revival of the 1970s.

Finally, evidence on how reasons for moving have changed over time or how they vary across age, race, class, and other demographic subgroups in the population is not well known and represents a frontier area for research on why people move. As indicated above, while migrants both to metro and to nonmetro areas report that employment considerations constitute the major reasons for longer distance moves, a distinctly higher proportion of nonmetro destination movers cite noneconomic reasons. Clearly, explanations of both metro and nonmetro destination migration must include noneconomic as well as economic factors.

Involuntary Moves

Not all migration is voluntary or subject to a high degree of choice. The issue of involuntary as opposed to voluntary migration has important implications for the adequacy of traditional explanations about why people move. Indeed, involuntary migration raises serious questions about the appropriateness of most micro decision-making models of migration, especially for certain segments of the U.S. population such as military personnel and children (Long, 1983).

To study the incidence of involuntary migration, R.R. Sell (1983) utilized reason-for-moving data from the *Annual Housing Surveys* of 1973–77. He reported that about 1 percent of the migration was described by respondents as forced (i.e., owing to natural disaster, displacement from housing). For local residential mobility that did not result in the formation of a new household, the figure was somewhat higher—6.3 percent.

Imposed migration, on the other hand, was a characteristic of about 38 percent of migration across major political boundaries but 17 percent of local residential mobility (Sell, 1983). This definition includes employment-related reasons as job transfers, moves to enter or leave the armed forces, moves to attend college, family-related reasons such as marriage, separation, divorce, and the death of a spouse. While it appears that the majority of both local and more distant moves are voluntary and preference-dominated, a substantial minority of moves—perhaps as much as 25 percent of local and 40 percent of more distant moves—have at least some nonvolitional characteristics.

Evaluation of Reasons for Moving Data

There are several specific criticisms of reasons-for-moving data (Goldstein and Goldstein, 1981; Hugo, 1981), which center around five broad issues. First, study designs are seldom longitudinal, and this inhibits an assessment of motives prior to migration behavior and an evaluation of how effective people are in acting on the basis of their migration motives. (For exceptions, see De Jong, 1977; McHugh, 1985.) Indeed, in a rare longitudinal study, K.E. McHugh (1985) discovered, first, that only about 40 percent of movers gave the same reasons for moving before and after their move. Second, reasons given for moving are an oversimplification of the complex factors that are actually considered in migration decisions. Respondents in a survey are likely to mention only one salient or dominant reason, and this may actually be a proxy for the desire for wealth, status, comfort, stimulation, or affiliation which De Jong and Fawcett (1981) have identified as some of the major motivations for moving.

Third, some people may not know why they migrate, so reasons given may be meaningless or systematically biased toward culturally acceptable responses. Fourth, reasons for moving implicitly suggest an individual decision process that may be inappropriate (e.g., some household members may be "secondary" migrants with little decision-making power). Fifth, missing from most analyses are reasons for *not* moving. A comparison of motivational factors for movers and nonmovers, matched on sociodemographic dimensions, would address a central question in migration decision making: Why do most people *not* move in the face of economic and social disparities among places? Regardless of the criticisms, questions on reasons for moving are still viewed as a simple and direct method for assessing "motivational factors" underlying human migration.

CONSEQUENCES OF MIGRATION

Compared to the extensive literature on the determinants of migration, substantially less research has focused on the consequences of internal migration. A large share of this literature has concentrated on the socioeconomic and demographic implications of changing patterns of internal migration (e.g., Frey, 1980; Greenwood and Hunt, 1984; Sternlieb and Hughes, 1975). In this section, we review the consequences for individuals and families, focusing on employment status and earnings, residential satisfaction, health, and social interaction and participation.

Consequences for Employment and Earnings

A dominant paradigm underlying much of the work on migration is the human capital model. Migration is viewed as an investment that is expected to "pay off" in the form of increased earnings or other kinds of pecuniary and nonpecuniary "returns" (Bowles, 1970; Sjaastad, 1962). Before panel surveys became widely available, much of the evidence supporting this framework was indirect and based on aggregate analyses (Cebula, 1979; Kau and Sirmans, 1976; White, 1977). The volume and direction of migration flows were greatly influenced by differentials in the economic character between areas of origin and destination (see an excellent review by Greenwood, 1975). More recently developed models have incorporated noneconomic variables, such as climate or other "quality-of-life" factors, in order to assess the relative significance of potential economic and noneconomic returns (Fields, 1979; Graves, 1980; Heaton et al., 1981).

These aggregate studies typically made inferences about individual motivations on the basis of ecological correlations (see the discussion by Navratil and Doyle, 1977). Like the earlier aggregative studies, recent analyses of individual migration and associated changes in employment circumstances have provided substantial support for the economic model of migration. (DaVanzo, 1976; Mincer, 1978; Polachek and Horvath, 1977). There is evidence that migration is positively related to earnings changes (Bartel, 1979; Milne, 1980; Nakosteen and Zimmer, 1980; Polachek and Horvath, 1977), reduced unemployment (DaVanzo, 1978), and occupational mobility (Wilson, 1985), despite well-known problems of potential sample selection bias in the analysis (DaVanzo and Hosek, 1981). Such results reinforce the significance of economic and employment changes as dominant factors in labor mobility.

Although micromodels provide general support for cost-benefit or human capital models, they nevertheless seem ill suited for the study of female migrants. Among married women, for example, migration promotes increased unemployment, labor force nonparticipation, and relative earnings losses (Lichter, 1983; Long, 1974; Spitze, 1984). On the other hand, the family as a whole receives a positive return from migration because the earnings gains of the husband more than offset the relative losses of his spouse (Polachek and Horvath, 1977). Indeed, J. Mincer (1978) suggests that women are often "tied movers"; they frequently move despite expectations of negative individual earnings returns to migration. Such studies have redirected attention toward family models of migration.

Another agenda for research has been to identify how returns vary by the different social/economic characteristics of movers. For example, earnings returns have been shown to vary by the pre-move employment status of the mover. Data from the *National Longitudinal Survey of Young Men* and the Coleman-Rossi sample show that returns depend on whether migrants quit their jobs, are laid off, or are transferred (Bartel, 1979). Returns have also been found to vary by type of move, such a primary, repeat, or return migration (DaVanzo, 1981; Kiker and Traynham, 1977; Lieberson, 1978).

Consequences for Residential Satisfaction

Wardwell and Gilchrist (1980) have argued that metro-to-nonmetro migrants are particularly interested in improving their residential environments and may be willing to forego greater earnings to achieve this goal. This argument was supported by G.F. De Jong and Kenneth G. Keppel (1979), who found that both metro-to-nonmetro and nonmetro-to-metro migrants in Pennsylvania were able to increase housing and neighborhood satisfaction. In general, this conclusion has been supported by Paul R. Voss and Glenn V. Fuguitt (1979) for in-migrants to the Upper Great Lakes region, and by J.B. Stevens (1980) in a study of migrants to nonmetropolitan areas in Oregon. Moreover, support for this conclusion was provided by A. Speare's (1983) analysis based on longitudinal data on residential satisfaction.

Whether these satisfactions promote greater life satisfaction or whether movers are happier with their new jobs is another matter, however. For example,

J.K. Martin and D.T. Lichter (1983) demonstrated that intercounty geographic mobility is largely unrelated to increases in global measures of life and job satisfaction. Apparently, pecuniary returns to migration are not easily translated into greater satisfaction.

Consequences for Health Status

Another potentially important consequence of migration is its effect on health status (Campbell, 1981; also see Fall 1987 issue of the *International Migration Review*). Although evidence is mixed, some research indicates that migration can have negative consequences for migrants, especially older migrants, and there are strong age differences in the nature of the interrelationship between migration and health status. For example, elderly migrants often report more days ill in bed and less ability to accomplish self-care tasks, such as grocery shopping (Ferraro, 1982). Yet other studies have been unable to show a postmigration deterioration in health status, even among the elderly who are initially in poor health (Borup et al., 1979).

The migration-health relationship may depend, in part, on the type of migration and the amount of change or stress associated with the move (McKinlay, 1975). Positively selected migrants on such characteristics as education, income, and marital status seem less likely to experience postmigration deterioration (Rosenfield, 1983), while migration involving major geographic changes are most likely to show a negative impact on health.

Consequences for Social Interaction

Longer distance migration often has the effect of severing community attachments, including ties to family and friends (Glasgow and Sofranko, 1980; Rank and Voss, 1982). On the other hand, family and community relations are frequently cited as reasons for migrating. How well then do in-migrants form new social interactions in their new residential settings?

In a regional analysis using cross-sectional data, L.A. Ploch (1985) compared the social interaction of migrants in four metro/nonmetro origin and destination streams. The results indicate that metro-to-nonmetro migrants were significantly less likely to interact with family than were migrants in the other streams. However, M.R. Rank and P.R. Voss (1982) found that metro origin migrants were more involved (e.g., belonging to clubs) in their destination communities than nonmetro-origin migrants. As importantly, both metro and nonmetro origin in-migrants to the Upper Great Lakes region adjusted quickly to their communities.

Speare's (1983) analysis, based on longitudinal data, included the premove location of the respondent's parents, spouse's parents, and the respondent's children at the time of the first as well as the followup survey. The data showed that migrants had fewer close relatives living within the same state compared to nonmigrants. The increase in distance to relatives, which most migrants experience, results in a substantial reduction in the number of interactions per year with those relatives. The frequency of getting together with friends and relatives also showed that migrants suffered from a decrease in social interaction, although the loss of interaction was greatest for the most recent migrants. After about five years, however, the difference between migrants and nonmigrants was no longer significant, a finding which parallels that of Rank and Voss (1982).

CONCLUSION

As Goldstein (1976, 432) lamented more than a decade ago, "improvement in the quantity and quality of our information on population movement has not kept pace with the increasing significance of movement itself as a component of demographic change." This sentiment probably rings less true today. The past decade has seen substantial progress in both the production and quality of migration data (e.g., in the form of multipurpose panel surveys and in the promise of the SIPP). Still the United States has no population register from which to monitor, model, and forecast interregional migration flows and evaluate spatial policy issues (ter Heide and Willekens, 1984).

The migration analysis tools at our disposal, however, have improved with the development of techniques for analyzing self-selection in migration data (DaVanzo and Hozek, 1982), event-history modeling (Sandefur and Scott, 1981), and multiregional migration models (Long and Frey, 1982; Rogers, 1988). But perhaps as significant, scholarly attention has increasingly shifted from the "what" to the "so what" question, with greater emphasis now placed on the consequences of migration for the society and individual life chances. As a result, demographers have found a receptive audience among elected officials, public policy makers in government, and various segments of the business community.

In many respects, the United States is now at a crossroads with regard to internal migration dynamics. Migration patterns seem increasingly transient, shifting back and forth without clear direction. Mobility rates have alternately decreased and increased during the past decade, and large metro central cities lost population to out-migration in the 1970s but appeared to be growing again in the early 1980s as downtown and neighborhood revitalization became more widespread. Conversely, over the 1970–85 period nonmetropolitan areas gained and then lost net migrants in their exchange with metropolitan areas. Yet, many rural parts of nonmetropolitan America have continued to grow more rapidly than urban areas in the 1980s, which seems to discount claims that population is again becoming concentrated (Fuguitt et al., 1987). The dynamic character of recent U.S. migration flows makes it difficult to anticipate future demographic change, even in the short term.

Despite the changing nature of recent trends, one fact seems clear. The past decade has produced a more balanced pattern of net migration and population redistribution in the United States. Differentials in net migration between metro and nonmetro areas have narrowed. The rapid suburbanization of the recent past has slowed substantially. Population movements to the West and to parts of the South are less prominent, and some states in the industrial North are experiencing population and economic revitalization. U.S. migration selectivity patterns have continued but are less pronounced than in the past (e.g., shifts of blacks to the South; the exodus of the young and highly educated from rural areas).

Taken together, such trends may portend an equilibrium in U.S. migration patterns, as spatially based incentives to move decline with the increasing interdependence of the U.S. economy and spatial convergence in standards of living. Whether this will take the United States "back to the future," as J. Herbers (1986) argues, by blending economic development with nature in low-density exurban environments outside of city-suburban conglomerates is difficult to tell. It is certain, however, that the deconcentration forces evident during the recent past will occupy the attention of migration scholars as they begin to chart the uncertain course of future U.S. migration trends.

REFERENCES

Bartel, A.P. 1979. "The Migration Decision: What Role Does Job Mobility Play?" *American Economic Review* 69:775–86.

Beale, C.L. 1975. *The Revival of Population Growth in Nonmetropolitan America.* Washington, D.C.: U.S. Department of Agriculture, Economic Research Service.

————, and G.V. Fuguitt. 1978. "The New Pattern of Nonmetropolitan Population Change." Pp. 157–77 in K.E. Taeuber, L.L. Bumpass, and J.A. Sweet (eds.), *Social Demography.* New York: Academic Press.

————, and G.V. Fuguitt. 1986. "Metropolitan and Nonmetropolitan Growth Differentials in the United States Since 1980." Pp. 46–62 in Joint Economic Committee of Congress (ed.), *New Dimensions in Rural Policy.* Washington, D.C.: U.S. Government Printing Office.

Berry, B.J.L., and D.C. Dahmann. 1977. "Population Redistribution in the United States in the 1970s." *Population and Development Review* 3:441–71.

Biggar, J.C., C.B. Flynn, C.F. Longino, Jr., and R.F. Wiseman. 1984. "Sunbelt Update: Older Americans Head South." *American Demographics* 6 (December):22–25, 27.

Bogue, Donald J., Kenneth Hinze, and Michael White. 1982. *Techniques of Estimating Net Migration.* Chicago: University of Chicago, Community and Family Study Center.

Borup, J.H., D.T. Gallego, and P.G. Hefferman. 1979. "Relocation and Its Effect on Mortality." *The Gerontologist* 19:135–42.

Bowles, G.K., C.L. Beale, and E.S. Lee. 1975. *Net Migration of the Population, 1960–1970 by Age, Sex, and Color.* Washington, D.C.: Economic Research Service, U.S. Department of Agriculture.

————, and J.D. Tarver. 1965. *Net Migration of the Population, 1950–60 by Age, Sex, and Color.* Washington, D.C.: Economic Research Service, U.S. Department of Agriculture.

Bowles, S. 1970. "Migration as Investment: Empirical Tests of the Human Investment Approach to Geographic Mobility." *Review of Economics and Statistics* 52:356–62.

Brown, D.L. 1981. "Spatial Aspects of post-1970 Work Force Migration in the United States." *Growth and Change* 12:9–20.

———, and John M. Wardwell. 1980. *New Direction in Urban-Rural Migration*. New York: Academic Press.

Campbell, D.E. 1981. "Microenvironments of the Elderly." Pp. 419–46 in F.J. Berghorn and D. Schafer (eds.), *Dynamics of Aging*. Boulder, Colo.: Westview Press.

Cebula, Richard J. 1979. *The Determinants of Human Migration*. Lexington, Mass.: Lexington Books.

Cheong, K., M.B. Toney, and W.F. Stinner. 1986. "Racial Differences Among Young Men in the Selection of Metropolitan and Nonmetropolitan Destinations." *Rural Sociology* 51:222–28.

Concord, C.M.S. 1982. "Sex Differentials in Recent U.S. Migration Rates." *Urban Geography* 3:142–65.

Dahmann, D.C. 1986. "Population and Migration Trends—Data Sources." *Urban Geography* 7:81–92.

———. 1987. "Geographic Mobility with Panel Data." *Growth and Change* 17:35–48.

———, and E.K. McArthur. 1987. "The Analysis of Geographical Mobility and Life Events with the Survey of Income and Program Participation." Proceedings of the Social Statistics Section of the American Statistical Association, pp. 203–8.

DaVanzo, J. 1976. *Why Families Move: A Model of the Geographical Mobility of Married Couples*. R-1972. Santa Monica, Calif.: Rand Corporation.

———. 1978. "Does Unemployment Affect Migration? Evidence from Micro-data." *Review of Economics and Statistics* 60:504–14.

———. 1981. "Repeat Migration, Information Costs, and Location-Specific Capital." *Population and Environment* 4:45–73.

———, and J.R. Mosek. 1981. *Does Migration Increase Wage Rates? An Analysis of Alternative Techniques for Measuring Wage Gains to Migration*. Rand Note N-1582-NICHD. Santa Monica, Calif.: Rand Corporation.

De Jong, G.F. 1977. "Residential Preferences and Migration." *Demography* 14:169–178.

———, and J.T. Fawcett. 1981. "Motivations for Migration: An Assessment and Value-Expectancy Research Model." Pp. 13–57 in G.F. De Jong and R.W. Gardner (eds.), *Migration Decision Making*. New York: Pergamon.

———, and Kenneth G. Keppel. 1979. *Urban Migrants to the Countryside*. Pennsylvania State University, Agricultural Experiment Station Bulletin No. 825.

Edmonston, B., and T.M. Guterbock. 1984. "Is Suburbanization Slowing Down? Recent Trends in Population in Deconcentration in U.S. Metropolitan Areas." *Social Forces* 62:905–25.

Engels, R.A. 1986. "The Metropolitan/Nonmetropolitan Population at Mid-decade." Paper presented at the annual meetings of the Population Association of America, San Francisco.

Ferraro, K.F. 1982. "The Health Consequences of Relocation Among the Aged in the Community." *Journal of Gerontology* 38:90–96.

Fields, G.S. 1979. "Place-to-Place Migration: Some New Evidence." *Review of Economics and Statistics* 61:21–32.

Fligstein, N. 1983. "The Transformation of Southern Agriculture and the Migration of Blacks and Whites, 1930–40." *International Migration Review* 17:268–90.

Flynn, C.B., C.F. Longino, Jr., R.F. Wiseman, and J.C. Biggar. 1985. "The Redistribution of America's Older Population: Major National Migration Patterns for Three [*sic*] census decades, 1960–1980." *The Gerontologist* 25:292–96.

Forstall, Richard L., and Richard A. Engels. 1984. *Growth in Nonmetropolitan Areas Slows*. Washington, D.C.: U.S. Bureau of the Census.

Frey, W.H. 1980. "Black In-migration, White Flight and the Changing Economic Base of the Central City." *American Journal of Sociology* 85:1396–417.

———. 1985. "Mover Destination Selectivity and the Changing Suburbanization of Metropolitan Whites and Blacks." *Demography* 22:223–43.

———. 1986. "Lifecourse Migration and Redistribution of the Elderly Across U.S. Regions and Metropolitan Areas." *Economic Outlook*, Second quarter 1986:10–16.

———. 1987. "Migration and Depopulation of the Metropolis: Regional Restructuring or Rural Renaissance? *American Sociological Review* 52:240–57.

Fuguitt, G.V. 1985. "The Nonmetropolitan Population Turnaround." *Annual Review of Sociology* 11:259–80.

———, T.B. Heaton, and D.T. Lichter. 1989. "Monitoring the Metropolitanization Process." *Demography* 25:115–28.

———, D.T. Lichter, M.J. Pfeffer, and R.M. Jenkins. 1987. "Nonmetropolitan population deconcentration in the 1980s." Paper presented at the annual meetings of the Rural Sociological Society, Madison, Wis.

———, and S.J. Tordella. 1980. "Elderly Net Migration: The New Trend of Nonmetropolitan Population Change." *Research on Aging* 2:191–204.

Glasgow, N., and A.J. Sofranko. 1980. Pp. 87–108 in A.J. Sofranko and J.D. Williams (eds.), *Rebirth of Rural America*. Ames, Iowa: North Central Regional Center for Rural Development.

Goldstein, S. 1976. "Facets of Redistribution: Research Challenges and Opportunities." *Demography* 13:423–34.

———, and Alice Goldstein. 1981. *Surveys of Migration in Developing Countries: A Methodological Review*. Honolulu: East-West Population Institute, Paper No. 71.

Goss, E.P., and N.C. Schoening. 1984. "Search Time, Unemployment, and the Migration Decision." *Journal of Human Resources* 19:570–79.

Graves, P.E. 1980. "Migration and Climate." *Journal of Regional Science* 20:227–37.

Greenwood, M.J. 1975. "Research on Internal Migration in the United States: A Survey." *Journal of Economic Literature* 13:397–433.

———. 1981. *Migration and Economic Growth in the United States: National, Regional, and Metropolitan Perspectives*. New York: Academic Press.

———, and G.L. Hunt. 1984. "Migration and Interregional Employment Redistribution in the United States." *American Economic Review* 74:957–69.

Heaton, T.B. 1983. "Recent Trends in the Geographical Distribution of the Elderly Population." Pp. 95–113 in M.K.W. Riley, B.B. Hess, and K. Bond (eds.), *Aging in Society*. Hillsdale, N.J.: Lawrence Erlbaum Associates.

———, W.B. Clifford, and G.V. Fuguitt. 1981. "Temporal Shifts in the Determinants of Young and Elderly Migration in Non-metropolitan Areas." *Social Forces* 60:41–60.

Herbers, J. 1986. *The New Heartland*. New York: Times Books.

Hugo, G.J. 1981. "Village-Community Ties, Village Norms, and Ethnic and Social Networks." Pp. 186–224 in G.F. De Jong and R.W. Gardner (eds.), *Migration Decision Making*. New York: Pergamon.

Johnson, Daniel T., and Rex Campbell. 1982. *Black Migration in America*. Durham, N.C.: Duke University Press.

Johnson, K.M., and R.L. Purdy. 1980. "Recent Nonmetropolitan Population Change in Fifty Year Perspective." *Demography* 17:57–70.

Kasarda, J.D. 1980. "The Implications of Contemporary Redistribution Trends for Natural Urban Policy. *Social Science Quarterly* 61:373–400.

————. 1983. "Entry-level Jobs, Mobility, and Urban Minority Unemployment." *Urban Affairs Quarterly* 19:21–40.

————, M.D. Irwin, and H.L. Hughes. 1986. "The South Is Still Rising." *American Demographics* 8 (June):32–39, 70.

Kau, J.B., and C.F. Sirmans. 1976. "New, Repeat, and Return Migration: A Study of Migrant Types." *Southern Economic Review* 43:1144–48.

Kennedy, John M. 1986. "Changes in the Selectivity of Interregional Migrants, 1970–1983." Ph.D. dissertation, Pennsylvania State University.

————, G.F. De Jong, and D.T. Lichter. 1986. "Updating Local Area Population Projections with Current Migration Estimates." *Journal of Economic and Social Measurement* 14:107–20.

Kephart, G. 1988. "Heterogeneity and the Implied Dynamics of Regional Growth Rates: Was the Nonmetropolitan Turnaround an Artifact of Aggregation?" *Demography* 25:99–113.

Kiker, B.F., and E.C. Traynham. 1977. "Earnings Differentials Among Nonmigrants, Return Migrants, and Nonreturn Migrants." *Growth and Change* 8:1–7.

Kirk, D. 1960. "Some Reflections on American Demography in the Nineteen Sixties." *Population Index* 26:305–10.

Kleiner, M.M. 1982. "The Migration of Dual-Worker Families: Does the Wife's Job Matter?" *Social Science Quarterly* 63:48–57.

Lichter, D.T. 1982. "Some New Comparisons: Evidence on Occupational Migration." *Growth and Change* 13:43–48.

————. 1983. "Socioeconomic Returns to Migration Among Married Women." *Social Forces* 62:487–503.

————, G.V. Fuguitt, and T.B. Heaton. 1985. "Racial Differences in Nonmetropolitan Population Deconcentration." *Social Forces* 64:487–98.

————, T.B. Heaton, and G.V. Fuguitt. 1979. "Trends in the Selectivity of Migration Between Metropolitan and Nonmetropolitan Areas, 1955–1975." *Rural Sociology* 44:645–66.

————, T.B. Heaton, and G.V. Fuguitt. 1986. "Convergence in Black and White Population Redistribution in the United States." *Social Science Quarterly* 6:21–38.

Lieberson, S. 1978. "A Reconsideration of the Income Differences Found Between Migrants and Northern-Born Blacks." *American Journal of Sociology* 83:940–66.

Linneman, P., and P.E. Graves. 1983. "Migration and Job Change: A Multinomial Logit Approach." *Journal of Urban Economics* 14:263–79.

Long, John F. 1981. *Population Deconcentration in the United States.* Special Demographic Analysis CDS-81-5. Washington, D.C.: U.S. Government Printing Office.

————. 1983. "The Effects of College and Military Populations in Models of Interstate Migration." *Socio-economic Planning Sciences* 17:281–90.

Long, L.H. 1982. "The Influences of Number and Ages of Children on Mobility." *Demography* 9:371–82

————. 1973. "Migration Differentials by Education and Occupation: Trends and Variation." *Demography* 10:243–58.

————. 1974. "Women's Labor Force Participation and the Residential Mobility of Families." *Social Forces* 52:342–48.

————, and Diane DeAre. 1980. *Migration to Nonmetropolitan Areas: Appraising the Trend and Reasons for Moving.* Washington, D.C.: U.S. Bureau of the Census, Special Demographic Analyses, CDS-80-2.

————, and Diane DeAre. 1981. " The Suburbanization of Blacks." *American Demographics* 3:16–21, 44.

————, and W.H. Frey. 1982. *Migration and Settlement: 14. United States.* Laxenburg, Austria: International Institute for Applied Systems Analysis.

————, and K.H. Hansen. 1975. "Trends in Return Migration to the South." *Demography* 12:601–14.

————, and K.H. Hansen. 1977. "Selectivity of Black Return Migration to the South." *Rural Sociology* 42:317–31.

Longino, C.F. 1982. "Changing Aged Nonmetropolitan Migration Patterns, 1955 to 1960 and 1965 to 1970." *Journal of Gerontology* 37:228–34.

————. 1984. "Migration Winners and Losers." *American Demographics* 6 (December):27–29, 45.

————, R.F. Wiseman, J. Biggar, and C.B. Flynn. 1984. "Aged Metropolitan-Nonmetropolitan Migration Streams over Three Census Decades." *Journal of Gerontology* 39:721–29.

Martin, J.K., and D.T. Lichter. 1983. "Geographic Mobility and Satisfaction with Life and Work." *Social Science Quarterly* 64:524–35.

Massey, D.S., and B.P. Mullan. 1984. "Processes of Hispanic and Black Spatial Assimilation." *American Journal of Sociology* 89:836–73.

McCarthy, K.F. 1983. *The Elderly Population's Changing Spatial Distribution: Patterns of Change Since 1960.* R-2916-NIA. Santa Monica, Calif.: Rand Corporation.

————, and P.A. Morrison. 1977. "The Changing Demographic and Economic Structure of Nonmetropolitan Areas in the United States." *International Regional Science Review* 2:123–42.

McHugh, K.E. 1985. "Reasons for Migrating or Not." *Sociology and Social Research* 69:586–89.

————. 1987. "Black Migration Reversal in the United States." *Geographic Review* 77:171–82.

McKinlay, J.B. 1975. "Some Issues Associated with Migration, Health Status, and the Use of Health Services." *Journal of Chronic Disease* 28:579–92.

McLeod, K.D., J.R. Parker, W.J. Serow, and N.W. Rives. 1984. "Determinants of State-to-State Flows of Elderly Migrants." *Research on Aging* 6:372–83.

Milne, D. 1980. "Migration and Income Opportunities for Blacks in the South." *Southern Economic Journal* 40:913–17.

Mincer, J. 1978. "Family Migration Decisions." *Journal of Political Economy* 86:749–73.

Morrison, P.A., and J. DaVanzo. 1986. "The Prism of Migration: Dissimilarities Between Return and Onward Movers." *Social Science Quarterly* 3:504–16.

———, and J.P. Wheeler. 1976. "Rural Renaissance in America? The Revival of Population Growth in Remote Areas." *Population Bulletin,* Vol. 31, No. 3. Washington, D.C.: Population Reference Bureau, Inc.

Murdock, S.H., F.L. Leistritz, R.R. Hamm, S. Hwang, and B. Parpia. 1984. "An Assessment of the Accuracy of a Regional Economic-Demographic Projection Model." *Demography* 21:383–404.

Nakosteen, R.A., and M. Zimmer. 1980. "Migration and Income: The Question of Self-Selection." *Southern Economic Journal* 46:309–18.

Navratil, F.J., and J.J. Doyle. 1977. "The Socioeconomic Determinants of Migration and the Level of Aggregation." *Southern Economic Journal* 46:840–51.

Plane, D.A., and A.M. Isserman. 1983. "U.S. Interstate Labor Force Migration: An Analysis of Trends, Net Exchange, and Migration Subsystems." *Socio-Economic Planning Sciences* 17:251–66.

Ploch, L.A. 1978. "The Reversal in Migration Patterns—Some Rural Development Consequences." *Rural Sociology* 43:293–303.

———. 1985. "Migration Origin/Destination and Participation/Interaction." Pp. 91–109 in T.E. Steahr and A.E. Luloff (eds.), *The Structure and Impact of Population Redistribution in New England.* University Park, PA.: Northeast Regional Development Center.

Polachek, S.W., and F.W. Horvath. 1977. " A Life Cycle Approach to Migration: Analysis of the Perspicacious Peregrinator." *Research in Labor Economics* 1:103–49.

Rank, M.R., and P.R. Voss. 1982. "Patterns of Rural Community Involvement: A Comparison of Residents and Recent Immigrants." *Rural Sociology* 47:197–219.

Richter, K. 1985. "Nonmetropolitan Growth in the Late 1970s: The End of the Turnaround?" *Demography* 22:245–62.

Ritchey, P.N. 1976. "Explanations of Migration." *Annual Review of Sociology* 2:363–404.

Robinson, I. 1986. "Blacks Move Back to the South." *American Demographics* 8 (June):40–43.

Rogers, A. 1988. "Age Patterns of Elderly Migration: An International Comparison." *Demography* 25:355–70.

Rogerson, P.A., and D.A. Plane. 1985. "Monitoring Migration Trends." *American Demographics* 7 (February):27–29, 47.

Roseman, C.C., and J.D. Williams. 1980. "Metropolitan to Nonmetropolitan Migration: A Decision-Making Perspective." *Urban Geography* 1:283–94.

Rosenfield, Patricia L. 1983. "Population Movements and Health: Global Research Needs." Discussion Paper for the 22nd Meeting of the PAHO Advisory Committee on Medical Research, Mexico City, July 7–9. UNDP/WHO/World Bank Special program for Research and Training in Tropical Diseases.

Sandefur, G.D. 1985. "Variations in the Interstate Migration of Men Across the Early Stages of the Life Cycle." *Demography* 22:353–66.

———, and W.J. Scott. 1981. "A Dynamic Analysis of Migration: An Assessment of the Effects of Age, Family and Career Variables." *Demography* 18:355–68.

Sell, R.R. 1983. "Analyzing Migration Decisions: The First Step—Whose Decisions?" *Demography* 20:299–311.

Serow, W.J. 1987. "Determinants of Interstate Migration: Differences Between Elderly and Nonelderly Movers." *Journal of Gerontology* 42:95–100.

Shaw, R. Paul. 1975. *Migration Theory and Fact*. Philadelphia: Regional Science Research Institute.

Sjaastad, L. 1962. "The Costs and Returns to Migration." *Journal of Political Economy* 70:80–93.

Sly, D.F. 1972. "Migration and the Ecological Complex." *American Sociological Review* 37:615–28.

———. 1981. "Migration." Pp. 109–36 in D.L. Poston and R.H. Weller (eds.), *The Population of the South*. Austin: University of Texas Press.

Speare, A., Jr. 1983. *Consequences of Migration*. Brown University Population Studies and Training Center Working Paper 83-04.

———, and F.K. Goldscheider. 1987. "Effects of Marital Status Changes on Residential Mobility." *Journal of Marriage and the Family* 49:455–64.

———, and F.K. Kobrin. 1980. "Biases in Panel Studies of Migration." Pp. 366–71 in *Proceedings of the Social Statistics Section of the American Statistical Association*. Washington, D.C.: American Statistical Association.

———, F. Korbin, and W. Kingkade. 1982. "The Influence of Socioeconomic Bonds and Satisfaction on Interstate Migration." *Social Forces* 61.

Spitze, G. 1984. "The Effect of Family Migration on Wives' Employment: How Long Does It Last?" *Social Science Quarterly* 65:21–36.

Steahr, Thomas E., and A.E. Luloff. 1985. *The Structure and Impact of Population Redistribution in New England*. University Park, Pa.: Northeast Regional Center for Rural Development.

Sternlieb, George, and James W. Hughes. 1975. *Post-industrial America: Metropolitan Decline and Inter-regional Job Shifts*. New Brunswick, N.J.: Rutgers University, Center for Urban Policy Research.

Stevens, J.B. 1980. "The Demand for Public Goods as a Factor in the Nonmetropolitan Migration Turnaround." Pp. 115–36 in D.L. Brown and J.M. Wardwell (eds.), *New Direction in the Urban-Rural Migration*. New York: Academic Press.

Stolnitz, G.J. 1983. "Three to Five Main Challenges to Demographic Research." *Demography* 20:415–32.

Taylor, R.C. 1969. "Migration and Motivation: A Study of Determinants and Types." Pp. 99–133 in J.A. Jackson (ed.), *Migration*. Cambridge: Cambridge University Press.

ter Heide, H., and F.J. Willekens. 1984. *Demographic Research and Spatial Policy: The Dutch Experience*. New York: Academic Press.

Tucker, C.J. 1976. "Changing Pattern of Migration Between Metropolitan and Nonmetropolitan Areas in the United States: Recent Evidence." *Demography* 13:435–43.

———, and W.L. Urton. 1987. "Frequency of Geographic Mobility: Findings from the National Health Interview Survey." *Demography* 24:265–70.

U.S. Bureau of the Census. 1974. *Mobility of the Population of the United States: March 1970 to March 1973*. Current Population Reports, Series P-20, No. 262. Washington, D.C.: U.S. Government Printing Office.

———. 1977. *Geographical Mobility: March 1975 to March 1976*. Current Population

Reports, Series P-20, No. 305. Washington, D.C.: U.S. Government Printing Office.

―――. 1981. *Geographical Mobility: March 1975 to March 1980*. Current Population Reports, Series P-20, No. 368. Washington, D.C.: U.S. Government Printing Office.

―――. 1984. *Geographical Mobility for Metropolitan Areas*. 1980 Census of Population. Vol. 2, Subject Reports. Washington, D.C.: U.S. Government Printing Office.

―――. 1986. *Geographical Mobility: March 1983 to March 1984*. Current Population Reports, Series P-20, No. 407. Washington, D.C.: U.S. Government Printing Office.

―――. 1987. *Geographical Mobility: 1985*. Current Population Reports, Series P-20, No. 420. Washington, D.C.: U.S. Government Printing Office.

Voss, Paul R., and Glenn V. Fuguitt. 1979. *Turnaround Migration in the Upper Great Lakes Region*. Population Series 70-12. Madison, Wis. Applied Population Laboratory, Department of Rural Sociology, University of Wisconsin-Madison.

Wardwell, J.M. 1977. "Equilibrium and Change in Nonmetropolitan Growth." *Rural Sociology* 42:156–79.

―――, and C.J. Gilchrist. 1980. "Employment Deconcentration in the Nonmetropolitan Turnaround." *Demography* 17:145–58.

White, M.J. 1977. "Three Models of Net Metropolitan Migration." *Review of Regional Studies* 7:20–44.

―――, P. Mueser, and J.P. Tierney. 1987. "Net Migration of the Population of the United States: 1970–80, by Age, Race, and Sex." Unpublished manuscript. (Machine readable data file available from ICPSR, University of Michigan.)

Williams, J.D. 1981. "The Nonchanging Determinants of Nonmetropolitan Migration." *Rural Sociology* 46:183–202.

―――, and A.J. Sofranko. 1979. "Motivations for the Immigration Component of Population Turnaround in Nonmetropolitan Areas." *Demography* 16:239–55.

Wilson, F.D. 1985. "Migration and Occupational Mobility: A Research Note." *International Migration Review* 19:278–92.

―――. 1986. "Temporal and Subnational Variations in the Reversal of Migration Flows Between Metropolitan and Nonmetropolitan Areas, 1935–80." *Social Forces* 65:501–24.

―――. 1987. "Metropolitan and Nonmetropolitan Migration Streams: 1935–1980." *Demography* 24:211–28.

―――. 1988. "Aspects of Migration in an Advanced Industrial Society." *American Sociological Review* 53:113–26.

World Health Organization. 1984. "Migration and Health. Population Distribution, Migration and Development." Proceedings of the Expert Group on Population Distribution, Migration and Development, United Nations International Conference on Population, Tunisia, March 1983.

Yeats, D.E., J.C. Biggar, and C.F. Longino, Jr. 1987. "Distance Versus Destination: Stream Selectivity of Elderly Interstate Migrants." *Journal of Gerontology* 42:288–94.

Zelinsky, W. 1971. "The Hypothesis of the Mobility Transition." *Geographical Review* 61:219–49.

Zuiches, J.J. 1981. "Residential Preferences in the United States. Pp. 72–115 in A.H.

Hawley and S.M. Mazie (eds.), *Nonmetropolitan America in Transition*. Chapel Hill: University of North Carolina.

————, and D.L. Brown. 1978. "The Changing Character of the Nonmetropolitan Population, 1950–75." Pp. 55–72 in T.R. Ford (ed.), *Rural U.S.A.: Persistence and Change*. Ames: Iowa State University Press.

SELECTED GENERAL
BIBLIOGRAPHY

Amin, S. 1974. *Modern Migrations in West Africa*. London: Oxford University Press.

Boyce, J. (ed.). 1984. *Migration and Mobility: Biosocial Aspects of Human Movement*. London: Taylor and Francis.

Brown, A.A., and E. Neuberger (eds.). 1977. *Internal Migration*. New York: Academic Press.

Brown, D.L., and J.M. Wardwell (eds.). 1980. *New Directions in Urban-Rural Migration*. New York: Academic Press.

Cebula, R.J. 1979. *The Determinants of Human Migration*. Lexington, Mass.: Lexington Books.

Clark, W. 1986. *Human Migration*. Beverly Hills, Calif.: Sage Publications.

DaVanzo, Julie. 1976. *Why Families Move: A Model of the Geographic Mobility of Married Couples*. Santa Monica, Calif.: Rand Corporation.

De Jong, G.F., and R.W. Gardner (eds.). 1981. *Migration Decision Making*. New York: Pergamon Press.

Du Toit, B.M., and H. Safa (eds.). 1975. *Migration and Urbanization*. The Hague: Mouton.

Fawcett, J.F. (ed.). 1986. "Migration Intentions and Behavior: Third World Perspectives." *Population and Environment* 8 (1–2):passim.

Goldstein, S. 1958. *Patterns of Mobility*. Philadelphia: University of Pennsylvania Press.

———. 1976. "Facets of Redistribution: Research Challenges and Opportunities." *Demography* 13:423–34.

———, and A. Goldstein, 1981. *Surveys of Migration in Developing Countries: A Methodological Review*. Honolulu: East-West Population Institute.

Gosling, L.A.P., and L.Y.C. Kim (eds.). 1979. *Population Redistribution: Patterns, Policies and Prospects*. New York: United Nations Fund for Population Activities.

Greenwood, M.J. 1975. "Research on Internal Migration in the United States: A Survey." *Journal of Economic Literature* 8:397–433.

Harris, J.R., and M.P. Todaro. 1970. "Migration, Unemployment and Development: A Two-Sector Analysis." *American Economic Review* 60:126–42.

Jackson, J.A. (ed.). 1969. *Migration*. Cambridge: Cambridge University Press.

Jansen, C.J. (ed.). 1970. *Readings in the Sociology of Migration*. London: Pergamon Press.

Kosinski, L.A., and R.M. Prothero (eds.). 1975. *People on the Move*. London: Methuen.

Kuznets, S., and D.S. Thomas (eds.). 1960. *Population Redistribution and Economic Growth—United States, 1870–1950*. Philadelphia: American Philosophical Society.

Lansing, J.B., and E. Mueller. 1967. *The Geographic Mobility of Labor*. Ann Arbor: University of Michigan, Survey Research Center.

Lee, E.S. 1966. "A Theory of Migration." *Demography* 3:47–57.

Long, L.H., and C.G. Boertlein. 1976. *The Geographic Mobility of Americans: An International Comparison*. Washington, D.C.: U.S. Bureau of the Census.

McNeill, W.H. (ed.). 1978. *Human Migration*. Bloomington: Indiana University Press.

Mincer, J. 1978. "Family Migration Decisions." *Journal of Political Economy* 86:749–73.

Petersen, W. 1958. "A General Typology of Migration." *American Sociological Review* 23:256–66.

Portes, A. 1978. "Migration and Underdevelopment." *Politics and Society* 8:1–48.

Price, D.O., and M.M. Sikes. 1975. *Rural-Urban Migration Research in the United States*. Bethesda, Md.: National Institute of Child Health and Human Development.

Pryor, R.J. (ed.) 1975. *The Motivation for Migration*. Canberra: Australian National University.

———. (ed.). 1979. *Migration and Development in Southeast Asia*. Oxford: Oxford University Press.

Ravenstein, E.G. 1885. "The Laws of Migration: I." *Journal of the Royal Statistical Society* 48:167–235.

———. 1889. "The Laws of Migration: II." *Journal of the Royal Statistical Society* 52:242–305.

Richmond, A.H., and D. Kubat (eds.). 1976. *Internal Migration: The New World and the Third World*. Beverly Hills, Calif.: Sage Publications.

Ritchey, P.N. 1976. "Explanations of Migration." *Annual Review of Sociology* 2:363–404.

Rogers, A. 1984. *Migration, Urbanization and Spatial Population Dynamics*. Boulder, Colo.: Westview Press.

———, and W. Serow (eds.) 1988. *Elderly Migration: An International Comparative Study*. Boulder: University of Colorado Institute of Behavioral Science.

———, and F. Willekens (eds.). 1986. *Migration and Settlement: A Multiregional Comparative Study*. Dordrecht: Reidel.

Roseman, C.C. 1971. "Migration as a Spatial and Temporal Process." *Annals of the Association of American Geographers* 61:589–98.

Rossi, P.H. 1955. *Why Families Move*. Glencoe, Ill." Free Press.

Salt, J., and H. Clout (eds.). 1976. *Migration in Post-War Europe: Geographical Essays*. Oxford: Oxford University Press.

Shaw, R.P. 1975. *Migration Theory and Fact*. Philadelphia: Regional Science Research Institute.

Sjaastad, L.A. 1962. "The Costs and Returns of Human Migration." *Journal of Political Economy* 70:80–93.

Sly, D.F. 1972. "Migration and the Ecological Complex." *American Sociological Review* 42:615–28.

Speare, A., S. Goldstein, and W.H. Frey. 1975. *Residential Mobility, Migration and Metropolitan Change.* Cambridge: Ballinger.

Stouffer, S.A. 1940. "Intervening Opportunities: A Theory Relating Mobility and Distance." *American Sociological Review* 5:845–67.

Thomas, D.S. 1938. "Selective Migration." *Milbank Memorial Fund Quarterly* 16:403–7.

Todaro, M.P. 1969. "A Model of Labor Migration and Urban Development in Less-Developed Countries." *American Economic Review* 59:138–48.

———. 1976. *Internal Migration in Developing Countries: A Review of Theory, Evidence, Methodology, and Research Priorities.* Geneva: International Labour Office.

Uhlenberg, P. 1973. "Non-economic Determinants of Non-migration: Sociological Considerations for Migration Theory." *Rural Sociology* 38: 297–311.

United Nations. 1984. *Population Distribution, Migration and Development.* New York: United Nations.

Vining, D.R., and T. Kontuly. 1978. "Population Dispersal from Major Metropolitan Regions: An International Comparison." *International Regional Science Review* 3:49–73.

Yap, L. 1975. *Internal Migration in Less-Developed Countries: A Survey of the Literature.* Washington, D.C.: World Bank Staff Working Paper.

Zachariah, K.C., and J. Conde. 1981. *Migration in West Africa: Demographic Aspects.* New York: Oxford University Press.

Zelinsky, W. 1971. "The Hypothesis of the Mobility Transition." *Geographical Review* 61:219–49.

Zipf, G.K. 1946. "The P_1P_2/D Hypothesis on the Intercity Movement of Persons." *American Sociological Review* 11:677–86.

INDEX

ABOUT THE EDITORS
AND CONTRIBUTORS

CHARLES B. NAM is Professor of Sociology and Research Associate, Center for the Study of Population, Florida State University, Tallahassee. His expertise is the result of almost forty years in the field, including work with the U.S. Bureau of the Census in 1950 and 1960.

WILLIAM J. SEROW is Professor of Economics and Associate Director of the Center for the Study of Population, Florida State University, Tallahassee. He is the author of three previous books and numerous articles.

DAVID F. SLY is Professor of Sociology and Director of the Center for the Study of Population, Florida State University, Tallahassee. In addition to his work in the United States, he has lived and worked in Kenya, Holland, Belgium, and Indonesia. He has written three previous books on population and migration.

ELIAHU BEN-MOSHE was a Ph.D. student at the Hebrew University of Jerusalem and is currently a postdoctoral fellow at the Center for Demography and Ecology, University of Wisconsin-Madison. His doctoral dissertation was on internal migration processes in Israel. He has coauthored articles on this and other topics in journals such as *Demography* and *Population Studies*.

ALBERTO BONAGUIDI is Professor of Demography in the Department of Statistical Science, University of Pisa, Italy. He has published widely in the fields of spatial population distribution and migration and is the editor of *Migrazioni e Demografia Regionale in Italia* (1985).

JAMES COBBE is Professor of Economics and Associate Dean, Social Sciences, at Florida State University, Tallahassee. He is the author of *Governments and Mining Companies in Developing Countries* (1979) and coauthor of *Lesotho: Dilemmas of Dependence in Southern Africa* (1985). He has published articles in such journals as *World Development, Journal of Economic Development, Journal of Developing Areas, International Migration Review, Journal of Modern African Studies, African Affairs,* and *International Organization.*

DANIEL COURGEAU is Director of Research at the Institut National d'Etudes Demographiques, Paris, France. He has authored numerous articles on internal migration and life history analysis in such professional journals as *European Sociological Review, L'espace Geographique,* and *Population.* He has also published several books including *Methodes de mesure de la Mobilite Spatiale* (1988) and *Analyse Demographique des Biographies* (1989, with E. Lelievre).

GORDON F. DE JONG is Professor of Sociology, Research Associate of the Population Issues Research Center, and Director of the Graduate Program in Demography at Penn State University. He is the current editor of the journal *Demography.* His books include *Migration Decision Making, Social Demography,* and *Appalachian Fertility Decline.* He has published numerous articles on migration, immigration, fertility, and social demography in *Demography, Social Science Quarterly, Social Forces, Population Studies,* and other professional journals.

MOHAMED EL-ATTAR is Professor of Sociology at Mississippi State University. He has served twice with the United Nations as a senior migration expert. He has published numerous articles concerned with internal migration, fertility, family planning, and occupational studies in such professional journals as *Social Biology, Journal of Biosocial Science, Growth and Change, The Gerontologist, Demography-India, The Egyptian Population and Family Planning Review, L'Egypte Contemporaine, The Arab Journal of Social Sciences,* and *International Journal of Contemporary Sociology.*

DOV FRIEDLANDER is Professor of Demography at the Hebrew University of Jerusalem. He has published on a range of population processes, mostly in the leading demographic journals. He has coauthored *The Population of Israel* with Calvin Goldscheider.

KLAUS FRIEDRICH is Akademischer Oberrat at the Geographic Institute, Technical University of Darmstadt, Darmstadt, West Germany. His work has dealt with spatial identification of individuals and the living arrangements and geographic mobility of the elderly. Among his numerous publications are articles in *Darmstaedter Geographische Studien* and *Zeitschrift fuer Wirtschaftsgeographie.*

THEODORE D. FULLER is Associate Professor of Sociology at Virginia Polytechnic Institute and State University. He has conducted research in Thailand since 1974 and was a senior Fulbright Scholar to Thailand in 1982–83. He has published articles on Thai migration in professional journals such as *Demography, Social Forces, Rural Sociology, Journal of Developing Areas, Economic Development and Cultural Change,* and *Sociological Quarterly.* His coauthored monograph *Migration and Development in Modern Thailand* was published in 1983.

PETER GARDINER is currently a United Nations consultant working with the National Urban Development Strategy Project in the Ministry of Public Works, Jakarta, Indonesia. His research interests include trends in population size and the spatial distribution of population. His articles have appeared in a wide variety of journals including most recently the *Indonesian Journal of Demography.*

ALICE GOLDSTEIN is Senior Researcher at the Population Studies and Training Center at Brown University. Her work focuses on population mobility as related to development, especially in Thailand and the People's Republic of China. She has authored many articles on these topics in journals such as *Demography, Social Science History, Studies in Comparative International Development,* and *American Asian Review.*

SIDNEY GOLDSTEIN is George Hazard Crooker University Professor and Professor of Sociology and the Director of the Population Studies and Training Center at Brown University. An internationally recognized expert on migration and urbanization, he has published widely on these topics, particularly as they relate to Thailand and the People's Republic of China. His work has appeared as monographs, several of which have been published by the East-West Center, and in professional journals, including *Demography, Social Forces, Studies in Comparative International Development,* and *Population Studies.*

PIOTR KORCELLI is Professor of Geography at the Institute of Geography and Spatial Organization of the Polish Academy of Sciences in Warsaw. During 1979–83 he was research scholar at the International Institute for Applied Systems Analysis in Laxenburg, Austria. He has published and edited several volumes as well as a number of articles on urban spatial structure, urban policies, migration, and population projections.

JACQUES LEDENT is Professor-Researcher at INRS-Urbanisation, a Montreal-based unit of the Institut National de la Recherche Scientifique (a research institute of the University of Quebec). He has authored numerous articles on internal migration, which he has studied using quantitative methods and models. His articles have appeared in the leading journals of various disciplines such as *Demography; Economic Development and Cultural Change; Environment and Planning, A Geographical Analysis;* and *International Regional Science Review.*

DANIEL T. LICHTER is Associate Professor of Sociology and Research Associate of the Population Issues Research Center at Penn State University. His research has focused on patterns of rural population redistribution and change, family models of migration, and the spatial distribution of underemployment. Recent articles have appeared in such journals as *Demography, American Journal of Sociology, American Sociological Review, Rural Sociology,* and *The Monthly Labor Review.*

GEORGE MARTINE is presently coordinator of a UNDP/ILO technical assistance project to the Ministry of Planning in Brasilia, Brazil, and Visiting Professor at the Federal University of Minas Gerais in Belo Horizonte. He has published numerous articles and books on internal migration, urbanization, population policy, rural development, colonization, and social policy, particularly with regard to Brazil. His articles have appeared in the *Journal of Developing Areas, Demography, International Migration Review, Revista Brasileira de Estudos de Populacao* and other professional journals as well as in various international readers.

MICHAEL MICKLIN is Professor of Urban and Regional Planning and Research Associate, Center for the Study of Population, the Florida State University in Tallahassee. He has authored articles on various aspects of Latin American demography and socioeconomic development that have appeared in *The American Journal of Sociology, The Journal of Developing Areas, The Journal of Health and Social Behavior, Social Forces,* and other professional journals.

MAYLING OEY-GARDINER is affiliated with the Centre for Policy and Implementation Studies in Jakarta, Indonesia. Her research interests focus on migration, demographic characteristics, and population policies and programs, with particular reference to Indonesia. Examples of her work are to be found in several professional journals and collected volumes, including *Urbanization and Migration in ASEAN Development.*

ATSUSHI OTOMO is Professor of Geography at Utsunomiya University in Japan. He has published numerous books and articles on population distribution, internal migration of population, and urbanization in developing countries as well as in Japan. His articles have appeared in a number of Japanese professional journals such as *The Journal of Population Studies, Annals of the Tohoku Geographical Association,* and others.

JOHN O. OUCHO is Associate Professor of Demography at the Population Studies and Research Institute, University of Nairobi, Kenya. He is also the Secretary General of the Union for African Population Studies based in Dakar, Senegal. He has published numerous articles on Kenya's population with particular emphasis on migration and rural development. His book *Population and*

Economy in Kenya is widely circulated. His articles have appeared in *Genus, East African Economic Review, Canadian Journal of African Studies, Geografiska Annaler,* and *Development Policy Administration Review.*

DIEGO PALACIOS is currently the Country Representative of the United Nations Fund for Population Activities in Quito, Ecuador. His principal areas of interest include internal migration and policy matters pertaining to population and economic development.

MAHENDRA K. PREMI is Professor at the Centre for the Study of Regional Development at Jawaharal Nehru University, New Delhi, India. He is the author of many works on migration and population developments in India, including books such as *Urban Outmigration* and *The Demographic Situation in India* and articles in journals such as *Social Action* and *Demography India.*

PHILIP REES is a Reader in Population Geography in the School of Geography, University of Leeds. His main field of research has been in the study of regional populations using multistate methods, applied in particular to the problem of population projection. His publications include (with Alan Wilson) *Spatial Population Analysis, Migration and Settlement: 1 UK,* and (with Bob Woods) an edited collection, *Population Structures and Models,* in addition to many articles published in major geographical journals. He recently presented a paper that incorporated the effect of AIDS on the projected population of the U.K. at a United Nations Conference in Japan and is acting as consultant in subnational population projections to the United Nations Population Division.

RICHARD H. ROWLAND is Professor and Chair of Geography at California State University, San Bernardino. He has coauthored two books, *Nationality and Population Change in Russia and the USSR* and *Population Redistribution in the USSR,* and has contributed chapters to edited books. He has also published numerous articles on the population geography of Russia and the USSR, especially on migration, urbanization, and nationalities. His articles have appeared in *Soviet Geography, Annals of the Association of American Geographers, International Migration Review, Urban Geography, Canadian Studies in Population, Jewish Social Studies,* and other professional journals.

JOHN STILLWELL is a Lecturer in Regional Development and Planning at the School of Geography, University of Leeds. His research interests have been largely focused on the empirical and model-based analysis of internal migration. He has recently cosupervised an ESRC-funded project in collaboration with the Office of Population Censuses and Surveys, which has examined the relationship between migration data from the two primary sources in the United Kingdom. He has written numerous papers on migration and is coauthor of *Contemporary Research in Population Geography: A Comparison of the United Kingdom and the Netherlands*. Currently he is developing a microcomputer-based geographical information system for European Community regions.

DICK VERGOOSSEN is Associate Professor of Population Geography, Department of Geography, Faculty of Policy Sciences, University of Nijmegen, the Netherlands. He has published several articles on migration, with particular attention to retirement migration. Recent articles have appeared in *Regional Studies, Journal of Economic and Social Geography, Bevolking en Gezin,* as well as in many edited volumes.